are languishing in misery or on their bunks, fortified slightly by Eric's pills. They had all forgotten to buy any. I haven't even thought of taking one.

But, after all, They are very nice, except for the old girl in the fur coat. The girl from Uplands is ~~~~~~ son - she was a ~~~~~~ to me. Pam i ~~~~~~ girl - & rather ~~~~~~ we both went on deck last night after dinner & discussed our respective love lives while the other 3 went to bed. The remaining girl, & I'm not sure what her name is yet, is the nicest of the lot I think. She has the bunk below mine & each time my dressing gown a sheet starts falling between my bunk & the wall she pulls it down. However, I can retaliate

AFRICA
IN MY BLOOD

Also by Jane Goodall

REASON FOR HOPE (with Phillip Berman)

VISIONS OF CALIBAN (with Dale Peterson)

THROUGH A WINDOW

THE CHIMPANZEES OF GOMBE

GRUB THE BUSH BABY (with Hugo van Lawick)

INNOCENT KILLERS (with Hugo van Lawick)

IN THE SHADOW OF MAN

MY FRIENDS THE WILD CHIMPANZEES

Also by Dale Peterson

STORYVILLE, USA

DEMONIC MALES (with Richard Wrangham)

CHIMPANZEE TRAVELS

VISIONS OF CALIBAN (with Jane Goodall)

THE DELUGE AND THE ARK

COCO LOGO (with Don Inman and Ramon Zamora)

INTELLIGENT SCHOOLHOUSE

GENESIS II

BIG THINGS FROM LITTLE COMPUTERS

A MAD PEOPLE'S HISTORY OF MADNESS

JANE GOODALL

AFRICA
IN MY BLOOD

AN AUTOBIOGRAPHY
IN LETTERS

THE EARLY YEARS

Edited by Dale Peterson

HOUGHTON MIFFLIN COMPANY

BOSTON • NEW YORK

Copyright © 2000 by Jane Goodall
Introductions and notes © 2000 by Dale Peterson
All rights reserved

For information about permission to reproduce selections
from this book, write to Permissions, Houghton Mifflin Company,
215 Park Avenue South, New York, New York 10003.

Library of Congress Cataloging-in-Publication Data
Goodall, Jane, date.
Africa in my blood : an autobiography in letters : the early years /
Goodall ; edited by Dale Peterson
p.   cm.
Includes index.
ISBN 0-395-85404-0
1. Goodall, Jane, 1934 — Correspondence. 2. Primatologists —
Correspondence. 3. Women primatologists — Correspondence.
I. Peterson, Dale. II. Title.
QL31.G58 A3   2000a
590'.92 — dc21 [B] 99-086680

Printed in the United States of America

Book design by Robert Overholtzer

QUM 10 9 8 7 6 5 4 3 2

CONTENTS

LIST OF CORRESPONDENTS

Family
Mummy or Mum: mother, Margaret Myfanwe (Vanne) Morris-
Goodall
Jif or Jiff: sister, Judith Daphne Morris-Goodall (Waters)
Danny: maternal grandmother, Elizabeth Hornmby Legarde Joseph
Olly: maternal aunt, Elizabeth Olwen Joseph
Audrey or Audey: maternal aunt, Mary Audrey Gwyneth Joseph
Uncle Eric or Eric or Rix or Rixy: maternal uncle, William Eric Joseph

Friends
Bernard: Bernard Verdcourt, botanist at the Coryndon Museum and
Kew Gardens
Desmond: Desmond Morris, author and zoologist
FFF (Fairy Foster Father): Louis S. B. Leakey
Sally, Puffin, Beloved Peach Blossom, Specimen of an Old Friend, Kins:
Sally Cary
Sue: Susan Cary

Professional Contacts at the National Geographic Society
Andrew: Andrew Brown, senior staff member
Bob: Robert E. Gilka, assistant illustrations editor and director of
photography
Dr. Carmichael: Leonard Carmichael, chairman of the Committee for
Research and Exploration and secretary of the Smithsonian
Institution
Mary Griswold: assistant illustrations editor

Dr. Bell Grosvenor: Melville Bell Grosvenor, president of society, editor of the magazine

Mr. Payne or Dr. Payne: Melvin M. Payne, executive vice president and secretary

Mr. Roberts: Joseph B. Roberts, assistant director of photography

Mr. Vosburgh: Frederick G. Vosburgh, vice president and associate editor

Other Professional Contacts

Paul Brooks: editor at Houghton Mifflin Company, Boston

Dr. Wolff: Nigel O'C. Wolff, director of the Maryland Academy of Sciences

Acquaintances, Associates, and Others

Douglas: Aunt Olwen's friend

Lyn: a visiting friend of the family

Pets

Kip: mongoose

Pickles: cat

Figaro or Figs: cat

AFRICA
IN MY BLOOD

INTRODUCTION

I really do simply adore Kenya. It is so wild, uncultivated, primitive, mad, exciting, unpredictable. It is also slightly degrading in its effect on some rather weak characters, but on the whole I am living in the Africa I have always longed for, always felt stirring in my blood.

— Jane Goodall, first (extant) letter home, April 1957

A ROMANTIC and very young Englishwoman arrived in British colonial Africa in early April 1957 and soon, quite possibly in her first letter home, wrote the astonishingly dramatic, precocious, and prophetic words "I am living in the Africa I have always longed for, always felt stirring in my blood."

Prophetic because she was to spend most of the rest of her life in Africa and because in so many ways — as a citizen, journalist, scientist, activist, and environmentalist — she came to be associated with that continent. Her name was Jane Goodall.

Jane Goodall's fame was initiated by the machinery of the National Geographic Society, which from 1963 on produced a series of glossy articles and television documentaries on her chimpanzee research. That early fame has since been reinforced by her own writing for a popular audience, including award-winning children's books and the 1971 bestseller *In the Shadow of Man,* which has been translated into forty-seven languages and is still in print three decades after publication. With the possible exception of Marie Curie, Jane Goodall must be the most widely celebrated woman scientist of our century.

And yet the very gloss of that celebrity may, paradoxically, have dulled the luster of her actual accomplishment. Hundreds of articles, features, interviews, reviews, and books have told or touched on her life story; but they are limited in scope and too often verge on the sentimental or the iconic. She has been presented as the little girl who thought she could; the sweet Ophelia who dreamed of animals; the feisty feminist in a man's world; the ironic traditionalist in a woman's world; the inspired nurturer; Mother Teresa of the apes; Tarzan's better half; and so on. While each of these images may arise from an appropriate truth, altogether they contribute to a larger untruth, an inappropriate devaluation of what she has actually done.

Based on several criteria — the number of scholarly references in her field directly and indirectly attributable to her research, the number of former students and associates who have reached influential positions in the biological sciences, the volume of data amassed in her forty-year-long study — Jane Goodall ought to be considered a uniquely distinguished pioneer in the science of ethology and the world's preeminent field zoologist. Yet her achievement can be stated more simply and directly: she opened the door to our understanding of the social and emotional lives of chimpanzees.

Wild chimpanzees are dangerous, though before Goodall began her work the dangers were misunderstood and exaggerated. Prior to Goodall's early discoveries, no one knew that chimpanzees ate meat. We had no idea that they or, indeed, any large mammals other than ourselves fashioned and used tools. If we thought that these apes were closely linked to humans in evolutionary history, as Darwin speculated, we nevertheless had no sense how close that link was. More important, we did not recognize what that kinship might mean for our own self-understanding. We did not realize that chimpanzees share with humans a similar repertoire of emotions or that their social systems are startlingly similar to ours. We would not have believed that chimpanzee communities across Africa possess various distinctive cultural traditions. And we could not have imagined that *Pan troglodytes* holds in common with *Homo sapiens* a dark side that includes cannibalism, intercommunity raiding promoted by adolescent and adult male gangs, and persistent male battering of females.

Goodall's scholarly tome, *The Chimpanzees of Gombe: Patterns of Behavior* (1986), ranks as the single most authoritative work in primatology, the first encyclopedia for chimpanzee research. Her long-term and ongoing field study of wild apes along the shores of Lake Tanganyika has turned out to be, in the words of biologist Stephen Jay Gould, "one of the Western world's great scientific achievements." Jane Goodall helped create a revolution in the way we study animals, and because the animals she studied are humankind's closest relatives, she helped alter the way humans think about themselves.

Valerie Jane Morris-Goodall was born to Margaret Myfanwe ("Vanne") Joseph and Mortimer ("Mort") Herbert Morris-Goodall in London on April 3, 1934, between wars; and the great European wars marked her upbringing and character. Her father, who worked as a telephone cable testing engineer in London during the early 1930s, discovered a passion for fast, beautifully engineered sports cars. He became a race car driver, a well-liked and highly valued member of Britain's Aston Martin team, competing on the tracks and courses of Europe against various French, Italian, and German automotive teams for excitement and national glory. By the time he finished his racing career in the 1950s, Mort was the only British driver in history to have competed ten times in the grueling Le Mans race.

Her father's world of noise, speed, and centrifugal daring — the machine world — seems barely to have touched the young Valerie Jane. "He sometimes took me for a ride in the car, but I don't remember much about that."* While her father skillfully and courageously drove in circles and made a name for himself in that glamorous milieu, the child was raised by her mother, Vanne, and a loving and steady nanny, Nancy Sowden, both of whom introduced her to a second possible world, that of gardens.

---

* *My Life with the Chimpanzees* (1988), p. 8.

Gardens. Sunlight. Then flowers, birds. Then a pet tortoise and a dog, a dragonfly, earthworms, snails, a pony, a horse, chickens. Most children, possibly all, experience a special identification with small animals and tame nature, a gently atavistic fascination that they usually soon outgrow and forget, or dimly remember in the way one does a dream. But in this instance the public gardens of central London and, after the fall of 1936, a backyard garden in suburban Weybridge, and soon a series of small animals and pets, seem to have impinged fundamentally on the personality of this special child. Valerie Jane combined her father's constitution (focus of intent, surprising endurance, iron stomach, minimal appetite, excellent eyesight) with her mother's sensibility (sociability, effective habits of observation, and literary bent). But who could have imagined how successfully she would gather those gifts in pursuit of her life's goal?

There were a few early indicators of the person she would become. By far the clearest one from her early childhood occurred in the fall of 1939, when she was five years old. Germany had invaded Poland; England had declared war on Germany. The Morris-Goodalls (including now a younger child, Judy), having moved to France earlier in the year to be near the great European automotive racing courses, precipitously returned to England, living temporarily with Mortimer's family. One autumn day, a "golden afternoon" as her mother remembers it, Valerie Jane disappeared. The police were called and began the search. Neighbors and all available family members joined in. Soldiers billeted nearby volunteered to help. After an increasingly frantic search, as dusk moved to dark, the child suddenly reappeared, alone, with fragments of straw in her hair and clothes. "Wherever have you been?" her mother asked. Valerie Jane explained that she had wondered where a hen had an opening big enough for an egg to drop through. To find out, she crawled inside the henhouse, concealed herself in the straw, and lay perfectly still for five hours until the hen raised herself up, wiggled, and provided an answer.

Near the end of that year, Mortimer joined the Royal Engineers. He served his country in Europe and the Far East, and in the process, unhappily, disappeared from his daughter's life. The children's nanny, in ill health, left the family in the late spring of 1940 and eventually married. Vanne, Jane, and Judy then moved to Bournemouth, a seaside resort town in Dorset, where they settled into the brick Victorian house owned by Jane's maternal grandmother, Elizabeth Hornmby Legarde Joseph. The house was called the Birches, and from 1940 on, it was the Morris-Goodall family residence: an entirely female household consisting of Valerie Jane, Judy, their grandmother ("Danny"), mother ("Mum"), and two aunts (Olwen or "Olly" and Audrey or "Audey"). Uncle Eric ("Rix"), Jane's mother's brother, a consulting surgeon at a suburban Hampshire hospital, often visited.

That Jane Goodall was interested in animals from a very early age is well known and must be obvious. Less so is the fact that from childhood on she loved language, both the getting and the giving: reading and writing. Language use may be the single skill that most immediately distinguishes humans from chimpanzees, and it is at least mildly ironic that the one person who has spent her entire adult life understanding a group of often quiet and always wordless animals should be unusually attuned to the expressive possibilities of the human voice.

In any case, she read. She read many of the usual English childhood classics, but, perhaps starting with *The Story of Dr. Dolittle,* a Christmas gift in 1942, her imagination was profoundly engaged by nature and adventure novels — soon including all the Dr. Dolittle books and the Tarzan series. These books and others thoroughly expressed her own ecstatic feelings about the natural world and, over time, enabled her to develop and articulate "the dream": to study wild animals in Africa. How she might study these animals, how she might actually manage to insert herself into the African wilderness, remained among the vaguer aspects of that dream. She may have guessed that her writing would help. She wrote stories, poems, plays, journals, a nature newsletter to her friends — and letters.

Of course, letter writing today is a dead art. Easier to pick up the phone and visit by electromagnetically transmuted sound. Cheaper to log on and visit by electronically stimulated phosphorescence.

Paper-based correspondence today sometimes seems an almost Victorian habit, bordered by lace and dust, and one can easily imagine that very soon we will see no more collections of consequential letters by famous people, since famous people no longer write consequential letters.

Still, letters have dimension and permanence. They have weight. You can hold them, feel them, save them. You can possess them. You can write them in meditative solitude rather than on noisy demand, and you can read them in the same circumstances. A good letter you can read more than once. A serious letter you will read again and again. A great letter you may save in a box or folder. A love letter you might even press up to your face and smell, hoping to pull away any molecules still lingering from the hands and body of your lover on the other side. And, fortunately for us, when Jane Goodall first went to Africa in 1957, there were no easy or cheap alternatives to written correspondence. Telegraph and telephone were more expensive and less reliable than they are now and, of course, nonexistent out in the forest. Writing letters was a sensible, a natural and normal, thing to do, and Jane Goodall wrote home regularly, every week at first. Many of her letters from Africa, especially the early ones, were very long and sometimes quite rambling. Particularly the letters home to her "Darling Family" — to Mum and Danny, Jif and Olly and Audrey, sometimes Uncle Eric — were frank and open, full of detail and feeling. They were communications from a quite young woman who was, if not homesick, at least strongly and wistfully attached to her family and home in England. Clearly, writing home was far more pleasure than chore. At the same time, Jane Goodall's early letters were and remain simply letters as opposed to self-conscious documents or crafted products. They are candid. The imagined audience is small, intimate, and eternally sympathetic.

When in 1957 the letters from Africa first began appearing at the front door of the Birches — crisp and efficient blue aerogrammes, thick and heavy yellow envelopes, or lighter white ones decorated with exotic stamps and crumpled after a lengthy journey — perhaps none of the family imagined that their Jane would be famous or that these messages would have historical value. It is easy to believe that the family developed a habit of saving Jane's letters from Africa simply because they were delightful, so full of guileless enthusiasm and compelling observation. It would have seemed a crime to discard them. At home they were read aloud again and again. The letters were, as mother, aunt, and grandmother variously declared in their own return correspondence, "devoured," "gobbled up," fallen upon by the family "like a pack of hungry wolves."

"Sometimes now I feel you are utterly lost," Vanne wrote to her daughter in the fall of 1957. "That great gorgeous primitive continent has swallowed you whole — you are engulfed in huge clouds of heat — stolen by a thousand alien voices — utterly remote from this tiny grey island where cold winds take the warmth from the sun." But when the postman drops that mail through the slot, she continued, "an electric thrill rushes round the house."

Jane's letters from Africa accumulated in the Goodall household in England for nearly four decades, preserved in drawers and folders and boxes. Then, one day in March of 1996, Vanne, with amazing trust and generosity, pressed the whole collection into my hands. Many other letters, including a long correspondence between Jane and her second husband, the Honorable Derek Bryceson, M.P., were stored at the home they shared in Dar es Salaam between their marriage in 1975 and his death in 1980. Those were also passed my way, as were additional collections from her voluminous business and research files, both in Africa and England. More turned up one day inside a tin trunk on the floor of a cabin in Gombe Stream National Park. Additionally, as I gradually discovered, further collections of Jane Goodall's correspondence have been preserved in institutional archives, including most obviously those of the National Geographic Society and the Jane Goodall Archives at the University of Minnesota, as well as the Green Library of Stanford University, the Houghton Library of Harvard University, the L. S. B. Leakey Foundation, and the National Museums of Kenya. From the vaults of those institutions some splendid treasures appeared. And even more have come from several of Jane's good and loyal friends: Neva Folk, Professor

Robert Hinde, Paul Kase, Mary Lewis, Dr. Franklin Loew, Dilys MacKinnon, Dr. Desmond Morris, Jean Nitzsche, Sally Cary Pugh, Professor Anne Pusey, Emilie Riss, Joan Travis, and Vivian Wheeler.

All told, I was able to assemble more than 1,800 letters written by Jane Goodall, the bulk of them originals and often torn, fading, and fragile. Typically the letters home were undated, with envelopes and therefore postmarks missing. Postmarks that were available, on aerogrammes, for example, were often smeared and illegible or, sometimes, dated by day and month but not year. I had all the letters typed so that I could examine the contents carefully, frequently if necessary, without damaging the originals. Then, with the substantial help of an assistant, Dr. Valerie Rohy, I sorted them chronologically. Finally, from a total of roughly 1.2 to 1.6 million words I selected the most revealing and representative letters for publication.

An editor's first job is to be kind to the author by keeping out of the way. And with that principle in mind, I have reproduced the selected letters as accurately as possible, being careful to retain habitual spelling idiosyncrasies; useful, significant, or habitual punctuation and capitalization idiosyncrasies; and significant or referred-to typing errors. Since an editor's second job is to be kind to the reader, I have also added commentary at the beginning of each chapter and in occasional notes; regularized the format of the letters; and identified the dates or probable dates when the letters were written or posted. I have cut portions that seemed distracting because they were too long, too slow, or irrelevant. And I have eliminated those occasional passages that might offend someone or violate a living person's sense of privacy. Since Goodall virtually never uses standard ellipses spaced in the standard fashion (. . .) in her writing, I found it convenient to use them as my own indicator for editorial cuts.

Those are the details. The grand concept has always been to preserve the quality and feel of the letters while making them accessible and presenting them together in a way that will create a functional narrative, an epistolary autobiography. Both the personal and the professional correspondence, each in different ways, provide a level of detail, immediacy, and personal drama that all biographies and most autobiographies cannot possibly achieve. Biographies, even very sympathetic ones, are by definition written by people who must remain cool strangers to their subjects' deepest inner lives. And most autobiographies are written well after the facts narrated, with the author standing bravely in the present and squinting weakly into the past, or clawing desperately into the amnesiac maze. Everyone forgets. The best memory retains a shadow of what was. The tenor of the moment, the telling detail, the enveloping mood, feelings and conversations and events, all are always and inevitably fading. Letters therefore remain precious caches of utterance, the closest thing we have to perfect memory, and these particular letters collectively amount to Jane Goodall's only fully realized memoir. They are her autobiography in letters.

1

꙰ ꙰ ꙰

CHILDHOOD
1942–1952

> I had been fascinated by live animals from the time
> when I first learned to crawl.
>> — *In the Shadow of Man*

ANE GOODALL'S CHILDHOOD letters take us from early 1942,
when she was seven years old, to the end of her school years in
the summer of 1952, when she was eighteen. Her family usually
called her Valerie Jane during this time, while her friends often referred to her as "V.J." The stretch from 1942 to 1952 is long
enough, and critical enough, that we can easily watch a transforma-
tion in writing style — including the development of that ironic,
mock-literary voice first appearing in letters to her friend Sally in
1951. But in spite of the metamorphosis taking place during those
years, as the writer moves from young child to young adult, it is
striking how persistently her love of and fascination with animals
remains a central theme — replaced to some degree only in the last
two letters by the love of and fascination with a man, Trevor.

The earliest letter, written in a pencil-in-fist cursive to "Darling
Mummy," addressed from "The Manor House" and dated February 16 with no year, was probably, but not certainly, done on February 16 of 1942. Valerie Jane did not start formal schooling until
later in 1940, and it is likely she did not learn to write in cursive until 1941 or 1942. The location and some of the details of this letter
might seem to suggest an earlier year. During the fall and winter of
1939–40, when Mortimer first enlisted in the army, Valerie Jane

and her mother and sister were regularly staying with Mortimer's mother ("Danny Nutt") and stepfather, who lived at the Manor House, a grand sixteenth-century brick and stone edifice rising out of the shambles of the fourteenth-century Westenhanger Castle in Kent.* Other regular visitors to the Manor House at that time included Mortimer's sister Joan and her fiancé, Michael Spens; but they would not have been "Mr and Misis Spens" until their marriage in 1941. Still, the mention of that "big dog called Jacky who is going to live here untill Uncle Micel come back" reminds us both of the young writer's eager excitement about the animals all around her and of the background drama: the men were going to war.

Beyond the visible carnage of the war during those years (including the 1942 death of Mortimer's younger brother, Rex, in an RAF plane crash) lay the vast if invisible damage of broken lives and families. By the time Valerie Jane's father reentered civilian life, in 1951, the marriage was over. So "Daddy" was nearly always a remote presence, the source of occasional letters and long-distance phone calls and the rare visit on leave. The note in the middle of this chapter, written to "Mummy," possibly in late 1946, describes with only good cheer ("it was jolly good fun") the experience of "seeing Daddy off" on the *Eastern Prince,* bound apparently for Bombay. Mortimer was shipping out to his first posting in the Far East.

Valerie Jane entered the Uplands Girls School in 1945 and began her riding lessons around the same time. On Saturdays she would take a local bus out of Bournemouth to the small village of Longham, where Miss Selina Bush (often called "Bushel") lived in a rambling Queen Anne brick house with field and stables out back. Miss Bush's place was called Longham House, and her assistant, Sheila MacNaughton, was known as "Poosh." Some of the letters beginning with the one of September 1945 refer to the delightful Saturdays at Longham House with Bushel and Poosh.

The bulk of letters from Jane Goodall's childhood have been preserved by her friend Sally Cary Pugh, the daughter of the Honorable

---

* The stepfather was the manager of a nearby racecourse, which included on its property the Manor House; he and his family were allowed to live in the historic mansion rent free.

Byron and Daphne Cary, a couple who had long been good friends of the Morris-Goodalls. Mortimer had gone to school with Byron, and they had been roommates in a London boarding house when, in the early 1930s, Mortimer met Vanne. Sally was born a year after Valerie Jane; Sally's younger sister, Sue, was only two months older than V.J.'s sister, Judy. The girls made a natural foursome, in other words, particularly after the mid-1940s, when Sally and Sue regularly stayed at the Birches in Bournemouth during school holidays. Starting probably during their summer holidays of 1946, Valerie Jane invented for everyone's entertainment a nature club, the Alligator Society, which involved projects, games, rituals, and even — when the girls were apart during school sessions — nature quizzes by mail and an *Alligator Society Magazine,* to which everyone was expected to contribute articles. The girls had an Alligator Camp, in the garden. They walked into town in the Alligator style: single file with V.J. at the head and the other three girls bringing up the tail, strictly according to the order of their ages. They all took on Alligator code names: Valerie Jane, the oldest and therefore leader, was "Red Admiral," in reference to a dramatic-looking butterfly. Sally was "Puffin." Sue became "Ladybird." And Judy, the youngest, was "Trout." Unhappily, there seem to be no surviving copies of the *Alligator Society Magazine,* and we are left with only the few tantalizing references to it in some of these letters.

Holiday sessions of the Alligator Society were enlivened during the later 1940s and early 1950s by all-day visits from Rusty, the black spaniel cross owned by the managers of a hotel around the corner (first mentioned in the letter of March 7, 1951). Rusty was an unusually intelligent dog who found an unusually attentive human partner. He loved to do tricks, including the ordinary (shake hands, play dead, jump the hoop) and the less so (climb a tall stepladder, close the door). Unlike most dogs, Rusty adored being dressed up in clothes and so would sometimes find himself wearing pajamas and being pushed down the street in a pram. But as the girls learned, he had a real personality. If anyone laughed at him while he was dressed up, for example, Rusty "hated that and would walk off at once, trailing clothes behind him." He acted apologetic whenever he did something he had been taught was wrong, but he would sulk bitterly when unfairly accused. "Rusty was the only dog I have ever known who seemed to have a sense of justice," Jane was later to comment.*

The family, deeply religious if cheerfully unorthodox, attended the First Congregational Church in Bournemouth, known, because of its location, as the Richmond Hill church. (Vanne's father, William Joseph, had been a Congregational minister, though never at Richmond Hill.) And Valerie Jane, a passionate and idealistic girl, was increasingly attracted to the grandeur of the church, its gargoyle-lined bell tower, the grand arched bank of stained glass windows, and (as we can gather from the letters of June and August 1952) the new minister, a charismatic Welshman named Trevor Davies. This was an utterly idealized and platonic infatuation of late adolescence. The Reverend Trevor Davies, B.A., M.A., Ph.D., cast his light on the Richmond Hill congregation between 1951 and 1971 and across the end of Valerie Jane's "childhood": the summer of 1952, when she finished school, passed her Higher Examinations, and prepared to enter the world of work and practicality.

*   *   *   *

The Manor House
Westen hanger
Hythe. Feb 16 [probably 1942]
Darling Mummy
the day befor yestoday Mr and Misis Spens broght a big dog called Jacky who is going to live here untill Uncle Micel come back. I dont know how to spell that word. Yestoday Danny Nutt gave me two china dogs and I call them Trouble and Terry. Jublee has got a new dress.† I have got a birds nest and a catepiler in a box of calaig leaves. Now I will drow a pictuer of him.

---

* *My Life with the Chimpanzees* (1988), pp. 22, 23.
† Jubilee was Valerie Jane's toy stuffed chimpanzee, a present from her father for her first birthday.

Today I found a ded rook he died of cold. I hop you can read this letter. I had a bold egg for my tea, new bread and real butter. When I went to tea Gremlin came with me and he stad all night till Gras* came with the tea. Mouse sends you her love and a lik. Kincin is giving you his best bone. Jacky and Trouble send you a lik and the Hen's send you a cluck. Eevry body sends you there love.

with lots and lots of love from

valerie jane

[Possibly November 1945]

Dear Sally

I'm sorry I've not written before but what with school and things I've been rather busy. You must, must, must, must, must, must, must, must, must, must, <u>MUST</u>, come and stay with us this hols. My Ma has written to your Ma to ask if you can, so do write and tell me that you can. I have got quite a lot of caterpillars one is a Lime Hawk Moth looking like this,

and if you come you will be able to see his skin. Another is a green looper (or stick catepillar) who feeds on mountain ash and he has made a cocoon, another is an ordinary cabbige white, who has made a cocoon, and another is a black hairy tortishell who feeds on nettle. If you come you will be able to see them all. Oh! I have another little yellowy, orang looper who feeds on lime, and a green caterpillar who feeds on cabbage, and has turned brown.

Chase, my Blue Roan Spaniel is sweet. Also he is very mischives and bites anything that comes in his way. He comes when he is called and also I play a cirtain game with him. I run my fastest away from him and soon he gets tired and sits down. Then I lie down flat, and the minute he see's me lying down he runs straight for me at full speed, with which I hurridly rise to my feet, for if I did not, all the hair of my head would be stuffed down Chase's throaght. He is very greedy, and gobbles down his food at a great rate. I have

---

* Grace was a cook at the Manor House.

learned quite a few good poems this term: The Spanish Armardar
by Sir Walter Scott. How They brought the good news by Robert
Browning. John Gilpin by William Cowper. The Leap of Roushan
Beg by Longfellow. It would be nice if you could learn some of them
and then we might be able to have a play with people reciting together.

I must end now!

> Lots of Love from
> Valerie Jane

not to be read aloud
P.S. In this one code sighns A=R S=E I=K O=V U=W

[Possibly spring 1946]

Dear Sally

I am very sorry I have not written before but with this new school
of mine I am kept rather busy. We have lovely gym there, bars,
horses, ropes and every thing else. Some of the girls are quite nice,
others very nice, and others simply stinking (excuse my word
please). This week I was really top of my form, although, I REALLY
think that — , well anyhow I was. Pauline was top of her form too.
She is in one higher form than me. We are supposed to have a lot of
games, but one day when it was too wet for games and we went for
a walk, some of us were naughty, so for a punishment we have been
going regualy for walks, instead of games. How are you getting on
in your school? By the way, the Prefects and seniors of my school
are jolly decent. What form are you in? The work in my form is
soppy and so far I have only had three things under 8. 6 1/2. 7.
7 1/2. Yesterday we had a horrible thing to do for english prep: —
explain how to do up and adress a letter. What do you think of it.
Last Saturday I had a great thrill, for when we went riding, we had
our first jumping lesson.* Not Judy and Liza, (Liza was in bed) but
Pauline, Jill and me. As there is not a Guide company at this school I
am becoming a Lone Guide. I don't really know how to explain that

---

* At her Saturday riding lessons with Miss Bush at the Longham stables.

to you, but maybe you can find someone who can tell you what it means. Anyhow it means a lot of writting and filling up forms. Do you have a lot of prep. I have three preps a day except Wednesday, and on that day I have two. I expect you are getting bored with this lengthy letter, so now I will end.

Lot of love

V.J.

P.S. I shall have to write again soon, as I have not told you <u>HALF</u> the things I have to say.

P.P.S. give my love to every one in the house.

P.P.P.S. Chase got ill but he is better now.

[Around July 28, 1946]

Dear Sally,

I'm counting the days till you come. Don't forget to bring you bathing-dress with you. We are all very sad, because Chase has been killed. He was in the middle of the road, and a lorry was backing out of a gate (and so could not see him) and he was run over. A man saw him and took him to the vet, but he was dead. It's an awful shame, poor Chase.* How have you done in your exams. Ours were terribly easy, but we wern't helped. Excuse writing, but I'm in rather a hurry. Another of my fishes: —

He's got a nice little dinner. Ha! Ha! We break up this week, me on Monday, 29th and Judy on Wednesday, 31st. On Thursday we're going to the baths, Friday is a pony-club. Thursday you're coming. Friday another pony club. What full days. Don't forget to learn First Class, because you must all pass when you come to stay. If Susie is not sure of no. 2, I will tell here some things. You have to be

---

* Jane deliberately underplayed the importance of Chase's death here; in reality, as she recently recalled, "I cried and cried and cried."

able to recognize 10 birds, 10 dogs, 10 trees and 5 butterflys or moths:

(10 birds) (1) robbin, (2) blackbird (3) thrush (4) blue tit (5) wren (6) house sparrow (7) gull (8) hawk (9) starling (10) wood-pigeon.

(10 dogs) (1) cocker spaniel, (2) terrier (smooth and wire) (3) collie (4) alsation (5) bull-dog (6) bull-terrier, (7) pekenese (8) old english sheep-dog, (9) dalmatian, (10) airdale.

(10 trees) (1) oak (2) birch (3) fir (4) pine (5) sycamore (6) mountain-ash (7) plain (8) lime (9) Ash, (10) Horse-chestnut.

(5 butterflies or moths) (1) Red Admiral (2) Six Spot Burnet Moth (3) Purplple Emperor (4) Painted Lady (5) Privit Hawk Moth. These are only some of the many things. I did not bother to put in ten wild flowers, because here are such a lot that almost everybody knows 7 × 10. I can think of masses to tell you, it would take a book to write it down, and as its Mummy's writing paper, I can't afford to use much. Must stop now.

Lots of love from
V.J. V.J.M.G.

[Postmarked October 18, 1946]

Dear Sally,

This is a very short messy pencil letter. I'm terribly sorry, but I shant have time to get the Aligator Society Magazine together. I come home at 6.0 and do prep till about 7, and on Saterday mornings I do prep and then ride, on Sunday I do prep on and off all day. You see I have 8 preps in the weekends, and about 6 of them are usualy writing ones. I usualy have three preps every night, and I do one of them at school, and bring the others home. So you see, I don't have much time. Don't lets talk about school any more. I've started making Christmas Cards, and I've drawn two. One is a perky horse, pulling an old fasioned handsome cab and a street lamp shining brightly. The other is a tiny picture of Joseph, Mary & Jesus (as a baby) in the middle, and two angels one on either side, kneeling praying. Peter has completely moulted, & is hopping around without a tail, looking very unhappy. I found a little mole out riding, and it bit me hard. Mummy found a hedgehog in the middle of the road.

[Possibly fall of 1946]

Dear Sally

The new Aligator thing will arive soon. I was able to get it ready quickly because I was tossed and got a slight conncussien, so the beastly Doc made me take a short holiday in bed. However I'm getting up this afternoon, thank goodness for that. I am so glad you are going to learn riding. You will be able to ride here when you next come. I have said in A.S. (Aligator Society) that you need not make a badge but if you want to make one each ready for when you come to stay, you can. You must not wear them untill you have passed 1st class. To make them: find a fairly small aligator and trace it out and pin it onto some green material. Cut round the edge of the paper, so that you have a green cloth Aligator. Then get an oblong piece of card board about the size of the Aligator. Cover the cardboard with white cloth and stitch the aligator onto it. Put a safety pin in the back. As all the badges must be the same send me a tracing of the Aligator you use and also a piece of the paper the sieze of the card board. If you have not any green stuff get some green die. Try to use quite thick material. You must make Susie's for her. As I am the leader I will give my Aligator an eye and you must not.

Lots of love

VJ

[On outside of envelope:]

P.S. I meant to send this but [torn] wast of a stamp.

P.P.S. If you wread the inside of this letter you will see about the badge. The aligator of the cover we will use. Make the card-board just smaller than round the aligator.

[Possibly late 1946]

Dear Mummy,

I do hope that you are having a lovely holiday, and wish I was with you. I have just come back from seeing "Hamlet" and it was simply georgeous. We went on the way back from seeing Daddy off. It was jolly good fun. We arrived at Southampton and went to the wrong docks, & met a policeman with dermithitis or some such disease on his face. We at last arrived on the quay side & there was the "Eastern Prince". Daddy was up on the 2nd deck looking very smart in his hat. He said he would come & see us but had to go to his cabin & we were too late. Olly marched up the gangplank with his parcels & was stopped by a member of the millitary police. Olly asked if the parcels could be given to Major Morris-Goodall, on which piece of information he looked uterly flabbergasted until that person, very vexed, & having lost his hat, appeared, leaping over his fellow soldiers, grabbing said parcels, and calling, "comming in 10 mins". He did not reappear until the band began to play and then Dad appeared on lower deck. The noise was deafening — from the men, and below Dad's rank & dignity so he disappeared, & reappeared on the Poop — or some such place. The noise was deafening as all the men cheered. Then the Millitary Police got ashore, and were promptly booed & booed by the men. Then the gangway was hauled up by the crane & the "Eastern Prince" slowly sailed out of port. Daddy waved until we could no longer see him & the band played.

The Birches,
10, Durley Chine Rd.
[February, probably 1947]

Dear Sally,

I have written to you so much that there isn't really anything to tell you. I am doing a lot of things this year to do with nature — and it is jolly interesting. I have vowed to keep them up for the whole year, but I don't know if I shall. I will tell you what they are. If you are not interested, of course you need not read them, but the sad thing is, that at the moment, I can think of nothing else to say.

Well: —

I am going to keep up my nature log book, in the front, interesting events, such as watching the nest of the Willow wren, and in the back are my nature walks. I have determined to go for one each month of the year. If it is an interesting month with nests, I might go for two.

I am going to keep buds of diferent trees in water, and draw them as they open.

I am going to keep seeds and nuts and grow them behind blotting paper — you know, you line a jar with bloting paper (on the inside) then fill the hollow with earth, and press the seeds down between the bloting and the glass. You watch them grow, and draw them at various intervals. In March I am going to get some frog spawn, and if possible some toad spawn. The book says you can find it in the south. I think that is all.

I went for a nature walk the other day, and I found some jolly good things. Almost everything that Enid Blyton had in the diary.* I found a wren, blackbird, song thrush, mistle thrush, blue tit, coal tit, primrose, grounsel, a lovely red beetle, wood lice, a spider, a tiny flie & a funny little insect under an old log. The chestnut buds were geting sticky and the lime's red. I also found 5 Feb. things: — a crocus, a snowdrop & ivy berries. Now I must go and feed the guinea pigs, the time being 7.40 am.

I will end now, and if I think of anything else to say, I will add it as a P.S. or P.P.S. or P.P.P.S etc. Buck up and send your drawing comps. With lots of love to, Daphne, Uncle Byron, Susie, Robert, Rooky, Mandy, Tammy and Tuppy (Oh! is Mandy getting fat yet) and to yourself 🐦 from 🦋

Red Admiral, Jane, Spindle or V.J.
(I refuse to put V<u>aa</u>lerie)

---

* Enid Blyton (1897–1968) wrote many books for children.

Tel. W'stbourn 63723
May 23rd or — 23.4.47

Dear Sally,

Thanks very much for your letter. Sorry I haven't answered the one before, yet, but I've been busy. Please excuse writing because I've left my pen at school. What did you write to Francis Pitt about? I've now got — oh dear, I shall have to count them all, so hold on. — 67, if my arithmetics right. Oh! Sh! The Robin came right into my room just then, so I must dash down to get some bread in case he comes again. His babies are all over the garden, five of them. The thrush (mistle) has three which she proudly brings into the garden, and to day there were some hedge sparrow babbies. The chafinches have got a nest somewhere behind the hut, but we can't find it. The blackbird is still sitting on her new nest. Yesterday we saw a pair of BULL finches in the garden. I will collect dogs names, and I am going to do it like this: —

KIND OF Dog.	NAME.	KIND OF OWNER.
e.g) Scottie.	Jock	Nice lady. Rather fussy.

Lets say we can't put down a dogs name if we haven't seen its owner, or the person thats with it, but we can count it if we hear it being called. I am at home to day as I have a cold, and I am practising drawing birds from real life. I am determined to get good at drawing them. Yesterday I drew a picture of a forest on fire, and all the creatures running away. It went wrong, but I'll show it you one day if you like. That bird we thought was a lady chaffinch, definatly is a lady chaffinch, as she is always with the male. By the way, the Francis Pitt's, seem to come every other Sunday, don't they. That means there's one this Sunday. I have been to the baths twice. I am glad your going to jump in. Hope Susies quite recovered by now. The baby birds in the garden make such a din you can hardly hear your self think. I am reading all the penguin books, with green covers, that is, all the murders. I must end. Now. Give my love to Daphne, Byron, Susie and your kitten when it comes. R.Ad.

 (poor effort)

P.S. Do you like the envelope?

The Birches
10 Durley Chine Rd
Bournemouth.
Tel: Westbourne 63723.
23.11.48

Dear Sally

Thank you very much for your letter. It was a jolly quick reply. I am very interested in your mice and you are jolly lucky to be able to keep them without losing them, especially as they do such adventurous things.

About the Jumping Competition. We had a wizzard time. I showed Bonus, and we got a 4th, but it was feeble as there were only 6 people altogether. If somebody else had showed her she would have got first. (I was not jumping her). Miss Forestier Walker asked Sheila if I could ride Quince* in the Inter Branch Jumping team, for the Portman pony club. She already had one team, but she thought that she would like another. There were only three teams, with four people in each, 2 from the Portman hunt, and 1 from some other Pony Club. We were 2nd. My prize was a nose bag (as it was for all others in the team). Jolly feeble! Then there was the branch team jumping. I was on Urchin, with Hopper on Wellington, Leza on Blitz, and Pauline (notice I put her last) on Daniel. We were not to bad, but you should have seen some of the teams. They were absolutly wizzard. Sheila's team was second, so that meant that Quince had to red rossets. Then came the open jumping, and Hop was in that on Wel, and good old Wel was actually second. Everyone was awfully surprised, as he had refused 3 times, and we were so sure that he had got nothing, that Hopper had actually taken off his saddle, and when they called her no. out, she had to go in bareback.

Then came the bareback jumping in pairs. Me & Hop went in on Dan, and Wel. They were jolly good old men (together their ages add up to 48) and didn't make a single fault, but evidently they were judged entirely on pairs, for the pairs who were 3rd & 4th had rapped many jumps, while we had a clear round.

---

* Sheila MacNaughton's horse.

Then came me on Urch in the under 14.2.

Have you ever had the feeling that on thinking something over, you think how silly you were, and you know that if you had another chance you would do it again. I expect you have! Well, that's how I feel.

Me & Urch. got on fine, and then at the last jump Urch ran slightly crooked, and once you let Urch go crooked at a jump in the Show Ring, you've had it. He is unstopable. He ran right out into the collecting ring before I got him back. Anyhow we had a clear round beyond that, and if they had judged it in the ordinary way, we might have got something but they had 3 faults for a refusal & 1/2 for knoking of with some legs or other, but I've forgotten. Anyhow, I know I could do it right now.

The Birches,

10, Durley Chine Road,

Bournemouth.

7th March 1951

My dear little Puffin,

I am quite positive that it is your turn to write to me, in fact I'm quite certain of the fact, but I will forgive you because I expect you are working for Mock (if you ever do work) or don't you have a Mock. We did, and it was far worse than School Cert, we all thought. I hear that you might do your Maths if you had 2 days instead of 2 hours (or was it 2 weeks, months, or even years). Well, cheer up, it was exactly the same with me.

Life is very boring, and, as I tell everyone I meet, but for the thought of next hols, I would stick my head in a gas oven — except that that would be a crime & I might be hung. It would be odd to hang a dead body, wouldn't it. Especially mine! I don't know why it would be especially odd to hang my dead body, at least, odder than anyone elses, only my alive body, is odd, so my dead one would be even odder.

(I hope you have skipped that last bit, only I got in one heck of a muddle. I nearly said H*LL etc)

Well my dear, and how are you? Still the same old 'Lally I suppose! What do you think of these miserable curs who are trying to overule our "blesséd England". Are not they a scurvey crowd of ostentatious thugs? Also, what about "Brittania Rules the waves."?? I have decided to start a civil war, and I shall lead the poor misled, ill-treated, squashed, and long-suffering middle class to a triumphant victory over the pompous upper class (composed of glorified char-women and road-workers). I do hope you will join my noble army. Of course, it will be a well paid job, hours of work 10 am–3.30 pm, Wednesday afternoon off, and of <u>course</u> I shan't expect my army to work more than 4 days a week. Any little squabbles will go before a specially appointed Trade Union of the British Middle Class Defence League. (That by the way is my idea of a Socialistically run Civil War!) I hope you agree with me.

By the way, to cease from penning such utter and complete drivel, do you ever listen to a program called "Any Questions" which is on Friday at 8.0–8.45 pm on the Light Program. If you have tell me and I will tell you my idea for an afternoon's fun next hols, when you (I hope) will be coming to pay this filthy town of mine a visite. If you havn't and you have any odd time over, I should, 'cos it's jolly good fun. It was a hoot last week!

I am going to have a super time next hols (I hope) Hunter Trialing Quince. I say "I hope" because Poosh is quite sure I shall break my neck. Have you been riding since I last saw you, and if so, who did you ride?

Jacob, the turtle in case you'd forgotten, has woken up from his hibernation, and I took walk in the garden on Sunday, as it was so warm and sunny (sorry for the change of ink). Mrs Churcher is moving out to the country in about a fortnight, so there will be no Buds to take for walks anymore, which will be rather sad.* Rusty is still the same as ever, but I think his fighting is getting even worse than it has been before. Hamlette,† that wicked little orange demon, has been awfully wicked. I can't remember if I told you this, but if I did, you must forgive me. Well, we left her in Our Room whilst we

---

* Budleigh was a collie owned by Mrs. Churcher, who ran a candy store.
† A golden hamster.

solomly masticated our supper, and, when we got back we found that the naughty little critter had gnawed clean through the Telephone wire as it went under the door. Was Ma in a bait!!!! It was when Danny was so ill, and we were expecting a call from Uncle Eric etc etc. At least half of the British population decided to give us a tinkle that night, and it was infuriating as we could hear it ringing almost incessantly and were unable to lift a fingur to stop it. As a matter of fact its a wonder the <u>dear</u> little animal didn't electrocute her stupid little yellow body.

At the moment I am frightfully busy typing our form magazine for the second time. I have written hundreds more poems — about 6 to be precise, and one is about the Grand National and is miles long — 144 lines to be exact. That is going in the magazine so I hope everyone enjoys it.

About a fortnight ago I went to a lecture with Audy at the Richmond Hill lecture hall. It was on Reptiles Ancient and Modern and it was absolutely <u>wizzard</u>. I did wish you could have been there, as there were live specimins afterwards. He had a gecko lizzard — the sort that run on the ceiling, an adder, 2 grass snakes, a python skull, and a pickled smooth snake. There was also a "healing serpent" at least so called in Greek Literature — ancient Greek I mean, — but I never caught its proper name. I had it, and a grass snake round my neck, and it was wizzard. Audy & I stayed right to the end talking to him — he was wizzard. I wonder if he has been to your school, as he said he goes to a lot of schools. His name is something like Leucher.

Danny has now gone off to Whipps X for a kind of rest cure, and she is being spoilt most terribly.* All the doctors and nurses pop in all day long and she is never alone for more than 10 minutes. She really is having a wizzard time, and she writes us billions of letters. She has been gone a week, and in that time the family has had two, Judy has had one, I have had one, and Audy has had two, & I think another family one came this morning. All her "boy-friends" as she calls them cluster round her, and would do anything for her, and she has found 2 or 3 which she thinks suitable for Olly. They bring her

---

* Uncle Eric was a surgeon at Whipps Cross Hospital.

flowers, fruit, nuts, books and in fact, she has only to name an object & it will be brought her, even if it means scouring London at mid-night. Hey — ho!

I think it's a swizz that we have to go to school on Easter Monday! Do you have to? I don't expect so. Last Saturday I had to go early to the stables as it was a) Hopper 21st Birthday and she had gone up to London, and — b) Poosh was at Brockenhurst at a dressage affair. The South Dorset Dressage Group were having a sort of schooling by the marvellouse man who teaches Mrs. Beckett, so naturally Poosh and Quince went. Apparently Quince was quite good, but went most terribly badly on the last day, which was rather disapointing.

Anyhow, that left Bushel and I to cope with the school — 7 small, pretty hopeless childeren. Two of them nearly got run away with. My two (on the leading rein) both nearly fell off, one 'cos the saddle slipped round, & the other 'cos the leather came off. On top of that Sally kept trying to run away. There was <u>masses</u> of tack to do, & on top of everything (sorry, I've used that expression twice) Bushel's brother was coming for the night and had to be met by her in the car. On the whole, it was a busy day and I cleaned tack so hard in order that Bushel could finish early and "enjoy" her brother (if I may use such a word) that my arms still ache. Then, after all that, Ruin went and got collic so that Bushel was up half the night. Such is life, but I must not grumble.

And now my dear (sorry to begin with "and") I really must end this nonsensical epistle, and cart my aching limbs up the stairs, unclothe them, and lay them, in all their beauty, between the white sheets. Of course, I hope to lay the rest of myself between the sheets as well, all but my head in fact. I must also submerge all but my brain case beneath the clear water (which will soon become delightfully cloudy owing to the formation of a scum, & will efectively conceal my maidenly figure).

Much love & hope to see you soon.

Give my love etc to all.

Jane (Red Admiral)

[Possibly summer of 1951]

Dear Sally,

Thank you very much for your letter. I hardly dare write to you, and I hardly dare think or talk about you, without feeling the bitterest remorse, as I havent written to you for so long. I am truly most terribly sorry. My remorse is of the very greatest imaginable. Do not however think illy of your freind, for, as the sun sets and rises, and the moon travels around the world, I think of you greatly and truly. I was going to the hospital, to have a truly beloved piece of myself, cut out with a pair of cruel scissors, but I did not, I could have wept for gladness, as a mighty joy swept me from end to end. Please forgive my truly beloved pencil, as although I have a wondrous pen, I have no pure cool ink, with which to make my marks, which are christened writing.

I'm sorry I wrote all that nonsense. Translation I'm honestly and truly terribly sorry I havent written befor, but I was going to have my tonsils out and I didn't because of infitile peralisis.* Excuse pencil, but I don't know where the ink is as I am staying with Auntie Joan, by my self. I am longing to see you all again. How are you all. I got a 4th prize at a gymkana, in a fancy dress race, a little while ago. There are two dogs here, Juno, a black cocker, and Domino a golden dashound. There is also a cat, Smoke, and a shetland pony, Jimpy. There are as well, 6 ponies which Auntie Joan is exercising for a man. Please excuse writing, but it is horiball pencil. I came from London to here by myself. It is very hot here, out in the garden, as I am in the sun, and I am just going to go in, as I have sat here long enough, and Auntie Joan is calling me, so I will finish this lettre in bed tonight and post it tommorrow sometime. There wasn't time yesterday at bed time so I am writing in the morning this — oh! I've forgotten what I was going to say. Never mind. Last night some queer things went past my window last night. I went to look to see what they were, and I found they were one thing. It was very big, and I thought it might be a bat, but it made a whirring noise, and I

---

* A tonsillectomy was postponed for fear that the operation might make her more vulnerable to polio infection.

thought it must be a moth. It came very near the window, but it flew so fast, and fluttered so, that I could not see its shape. I rode the little pony last night, and he bucked a lot, making Auntie Joan screech with laughter. David, her yongest son, is sprawled beside me on the bed, talking away, as he looks at a horse book of mine, and making me forget what I was going to say. I must end now, as this letter must be posted. I hope Daphne is better,

Love to all including Rook.

VJ

The Birches,

10, Durley Chine Road,

Bournemouth.

[Around December 1951]

Dearest Sally,

I am afraid that I have been rather a long time in replying to your last letter, and your reply will have to follow rather speedily if you don't want a nice cold swim. Or do you? I am sorry if I have underated your capacity for enjoying a cold bath. However, enough of this nonsensical monologue — or is it a dialogue? I don't know.

I have just emerged triumphant from my first attempt at sonnet writing. By that I don't mean that I have writen a wonderful sonnet, I mearely mean to impart unto my dear friend — none other than thine own dear self (you see I have been reading a Jeffrey Farnol)* — that I have actually written a sonnet (don't get alarmed, I am not going to send it for your perusal). We have been doing the sonnet in English, and the wretched woman made us write them for prep.

It is a real hoot! Canford School for boys has asked us to a dance,

---

* Jeffrey Farnol (1878–1952) wrote several popular works of fiction, including the best-selling *The Broad Highway* (1911).

and all the seniors and Pre's are going (I don't know if I told you that I was made a Pre?). Anyhow, I have got to spend the night at school. It really is going to be a hoot! Canford School is well renowned for having awful boys — George Elis comes from there, and if he is an example of a Canford boy, they must be pretty ghastly. I am dreading it, but I had to go (I hope I am not boring you).

As I am writing this letter at school, I have not got your letter here, and so I cannot answer any questions you may have asked as I cannot remember them — I hope they were not vital. We are making wizard plans for next holidays, but I don't yet know whether they will work, or whether I am meant to tell you, so please do not get worked up, or dismal or anything which might be your reaction if it did work or really was happening. (I don't think that that makes sense, but you will have to try & see if it does). Well, Ma is endeavouring to take me to see Winter's Tale up in London next hols, as I am doing it for Higher, and she is trying to get them on the 7th, 8th or 9th of Jan, 1952 (not 1 or 3 but 2). We shall then stay the night (probably at Whipps X), and then our plan was for you to come up, and we could either go to the Museum again — as it is all open now I believe, or else we could spend hours wandering round the Zoo. I don't quite know what happens to Sue — she might go on the through train to Bournemouth if she was allowed to go by herself, or come with you, or something. It depends on everything — I don't know. Ma & I havn't even got as far as talking about that. The trouble is that it seems expensive for Jif & I to trail up to London — in fact I'm sure Judy won't be able too, and it seems unfair for her to be left out — I dunno. Anyhow, I don't even know yet just exactly if you can come — so don't imagine this is all arranged. It is NOT. Later I am now very unsure — in fact positively unsure of this arrangement, because we had seats for Sat (next Sat) which Ma was trying to change when I began this letter. Now we know they cannot be changed, so I don't know what will happen. So let me start a fresh subject.

It is now Sunday evening, and I can tell you all about Saturday. Everything went off wizardly except that it was carried out in a howling gale. Oh bother! I have just read through this letter, and observed that you must be quite at sea as I have not mentioned what was happening on Saturday. I am so sorry. Well, I will now proceed to explain! On Sat, the School at Longham got up a Christmas Bazar, and they had a Father Christmas. They asked Bushel to lend Polly & the Wagon. Well, the Wagon was beautifully draped in green velvet curtains with a chair draped in the middle, and beautiful furs down the back and notices about the bazar down the side. Polly's mane & tail were bedecked with gay red and yellow ribbon. We had two choir boys behind the chair in red and black to blow bugles, and Poosh and I were out riders. Bushel was dressed up as a coachman, and you could honestly hardly recognize her — lots of people didn't. She had a top hat, side whiskers, & a big black coachman's coat. Father Christmas sat beside her, and sang occasionally. His hood came halfway down his face. Poosh rode side-saddle in a habit with an <u>18 inch</u> waiste, and a top hat with a veil, and a frilly lace thing as a sort of crevat affair, on Quince. I rode Summer Time, and was her squire. I had Admiral Bush's tail coat, a blue spotted crevat, side whiskers — my own hair stuck down the side of my face — trousers stitched down the side to look like those riding trousers which the very posh show riders still wear, with my riding boots underneath, and I carried my hunting whip. We had great difficulty in a) getting Poosh into her 18″ waiste, and b) getting my hair up under the top hat, so that it was presentable when I took it off to Father Christmas. Mrs McDonald — a person who lives at Longham House now — was jolly useful, and rushed madly around at the last minute. You can't image what a mad rush there was at the last min. There was such a gale that the notices began to blow off, so Mrs McDonald stitched them on, and we were late as we got back late from taking the school out. We had to trot all the time and Poosh got so sore. I was pretty sore as I had to sit all the time as otherwise I sat on my tails. It was super fun. I stayed that night with Poosh which was also jolly dee.

I can't think specially of any more news — certainly not enough to fill another of these large sheets, & so I had better stop. I suppose I told you about the rats killing all the [guinea] pig babies — I can't remember. Don't forget to write me today or tomorrow at the latest — by today I mean Monday when I fondly hope you will get this letter. We have got an extra 6 days of hols because of the fuel shortage.

Tons of love

<u>V.J.</u> Jane: Red Admiral.

The Birches,
10, Durley Chine Rd,
<u>Bournemouth</u>.
[Around June 24, 1952]

Dear Sally,

I am very offended with you. Do you realize that you have up-set your old friend beyond words. I would have you know that the Rev. J. Trevor Davies is not yet <u>50</u>. I would also have you know that Richmond Hill broadcast the other evening and everyone who heard it said it was the best service they'd heard for ages. I would also have you know that I do not <u>ALLOW</u> people to say nasty things about him. Now do you understand. I was going to write a very short note, saying that I should never see you again unless you applogized. Now I have finished Higher I am so happy that I feel forgiving, and also that it would be a waste of a stamp — BUT! Un-less you write and tender your very sincere appologies for so hurting me, I shall <u>not</u> write to you again!!

Now that I have got that off my chest, I will proceed to relate some news to you — not that there is any. My dear, I am being so teased that I don't know where to look for shame! On Saturday I went out to the stables and was not going to ride, and then Poosh said there was some one to ride with, and there wouldn't be next week, so would I rather then. I said yes if it was a nice person. You may guess who it was. Clive! come for a weekend from Aldershot (he is in the army now). Well of course, I'd absolutely had it then. I said I would go if Poosh sent me, so she sent me. As a matter of fact we had a jolly nice ride — I am absolutely <u>sick</u> of riding with either myself or a lot of stupid kids. We both got run away with all the time on Summer & Sol. The worste is yet to come! On Sunday I was peacefully shelling broad beans when Olly appeared to say I was wanted on the phone. You can guesse the next. This time I did not have you as an excuse and I had to go. We went to the Rufus Stone in the new forest, and had tea in a little place where the ponies came and put their heads in at the windows. It was a hoot!

There is worse still! (and this is the most dreadful part of the whole story). Someone from school in my form — saw me!!!!! It really is terrible. She suddenly said before prayers when everyone was there, "Who was that young man you were out with on Sunday?" Of course I went puce, and everyone was in fits. Somehow or other she knew his name (she is going to tell me how soon) and now everyone calls me Clive. But worse was to come! Whilst I was still hiding my face, Wendy (a day girl I come to school with & who I had told about George) said "Is that the one I know about?" And like a fool I said no. My dear, you can just imagine what it was like, can't you.

Oh, I am so happy. Higher is over. 3 weeks with no work, and then I've left — ! Oh! It's so super you can't imagine. I am looking foreward very much to the end of the term as I have arranged a midnight feast for all the Pre's and Senior's in our house. We are having it on the last but one night of term, and we are going down the fire escape and down to the bottom tennis court through the woods. There are about 12 of us and it should be smashing fun. The difficultest (sorry for the coined word) part is getting me smuggled in, but we have worked it out, and I am going into a little 2 room with 2 pre's in it, and no one ever seems to go in there. I shall either sleep on Liza B's bed, under it, or just on the floor. It really will be super, although we are sure to be caught.

Our exams have been foul, I promis you. We had one English exam, "Passages for Comprehension and Interpretation" in which was a poem all about Public Lavatories (at least, very nearly, but there were a few other things in it as well.) I simply popped. I will show it to you when (or rather if) you come to stay. (You can't come unless you take back the words you wrote). That reminds me, there was a picture of him in the Echo the other day. Oh! I do love him.

He knows me now, and next Sunday I'm going to see him, all by myself, to ask him if I can become a Member of Richmond Hill. You can't imagine how I'm longing for it.

~~(but one night of term, and somehow I have got to be smuggled up to the bedroom. I am)~~

[N.B. I started the letter again after a pause & thought I had ended on page 3. Hence the false start.]

Now I will begin again, although why I have started a new page I can't imagine as I have nothing to say. We (3 of us) finished Higher on Monday morning, and Pongo said we could go down to "Bournemouth" after much persuasion. We decided we wanted to go to Shell bay, and as Hillary had no bike she had to come to our house, & we bagged the 2 bikes (one is unsafe & we are not allowed to use it!) and met Jill and really had a smashing time. We got a picnic lunch from home & Jill had some oranges & apples, so we got on fine. Then Hilly and I nearly got lost coming home, which was also rather funny!

My dear, you really should see poor Mrs Jimmy. She is so fat that I'm sure she'll burst if she gets any fatter, and she won't produce. Each morning I go down expecting to find at least 8 pigs instead of 2 — but no go. She can hardly get through the door as it is.

Mummy is away at the moment, staying with Deb (I can't remember whether you knew or have met her, but anyhow, her daughter is Jo — you may have heard of her). Did you hear "Morris Mortimer Goodall" being shrieked over the wireless during Le Mans.* It made me hoot with laughter. Apparently everyone in the motor racing world calls him Morris or something.

I shall really have to buck up now, and fill the remainder of the page with rappid rubbish as it is nearly time to set off for school. It is wiz now as we have no work to do at all so I read all day. I have read my first two novels for about 3 months since higher ended — "The Talisman Ring" and "The Great Roxhythe" both by G. Heyer, and am in the middle of "Royal Escape" also by her. Have you read any of them.

---

* Mortimer raced in that year's LeMans.

You must come and stay in the hols — sometime before August 18th as I am going to Germany then (I'm not looking foreward to it one bit I can assure you). You must forgive writing but the pen is a) full of sand, b) crossed, and c) running out (or not running as the case may be). Must stop, and will post this just as soon as I can find some stamps.

Much love

Jane

P.S. Mind you write & send your deepest appologies.

The Birches,

10, Durley Chine Road,

Bournemouth.

[Early August 1952]

Dear Sally,

Thanks tons for your last epistle (or is it episel — still wrong but you knew what I mean) which I very nearly fell over backwards to receive. I certainly never expected one for weeks and weeks! I'm so glad you are having a nice time, but the G.G's sound quite balmy. Bad luck about your back and shirt — have you managed to mend your jhods yet?

Now! About the great day! It was SMASHING!! Everything worked and went off wizardly! It was wonderful! Glorious! Splendid! Delightful.

Michael didn't come in the end as he went to the Circus — they had the tickets muddled up — at least that was the excuse. Kitty (the little dog) came and she was sweet. Rusty sulked and lay down by the door all the time. Even during cake time at tea he never moved a muscle.

I sat in a little arm chair beside HIM. Danny and Mrs. sat on the couch, and Ma sat behind the tea table on her little setee affair. I wore my white dress — <u>AND</u> <u>he</u>!! said how nice it looked — him <u>not</u> her! We talked about everything under the sun — and oh! he was so wizard. I put a feather and a piece of cotton for him to sit on — I still have them, also his cigarette but, his matchstick and his tea-leaves. I went to bed on the couch that night with his cushion for my pillow. When he first came my chair was quite far back, and while I was handing food round he got up and pulled it closer up!

I have never seen such a lively little man. He couldn't keep still for a second, and he couldn't bear a conversation to be carried on without him. He <u>hated</u> his wife to tell a story, and always managed to get his word — or rather word<u>S</u> in. He had a beautiful long nose and he adores dogs. Of course when they got out of the front door Kitty disappeared and do you know! if I hadn't noticed they would have gone off without her! They must have enjoyed themselves. They'd even started the car. Then Trevor & I looked for her, & Audy found her by the pigs. "Oh hurry Trevor" says Mrs. Davies & he came pounding after me doing exagerated running — you know — knees up & hands up & head back. It was a hoot. The naughty dog made a hole in the wire netting. We did nothing but laugh all afternoon, and do you know! They stayed from 3.45 till 6.30.

Another wizard thing! They may be coming down to our beach hut and I am going with them to show them where it is. We have planned that I shall take the dingy and Trevor & I are going to drift out to sea — just us two. Won't it be smashing! Judy & Susie have sealed my future — & Michael's. They kept making me laugh in church by saying "There's your husband". Apparently he's going to do Journalism too.

My dear. Something else! I've got Higher & although I only scraped through in Bilge* I got 70% in English which is a distinction only they don't give them now. Unfortunately! Hilary failed hers — Bilge only so that was all she did. Poor thing!

My dear. Do you remember Isabel Abbay? Well, she came here to go to Quo Vadis with me — I never rang her that time I promised, so when she rang again I <u>had</u> to do something. Well, she arrived & we had had trestles made for the ping pong table & were playing. The first back-putting-up thing she said was she wouldn't deign to

---

* Biology.

play with us because we wern't good enough, then that the table wasn't proper, & then that Queen's College (where I hope to go for my Secretarial) was inferior to her place. Ma squashed her wizardly though, & made her go quite pink. My dear! Quo Vadis was simply wonderful — the best film I've seen for years. Trevor told us he'd seen it when he came so of course I <u>HAD</u> to go — though I was going anyhow. We all wept buckets and it was jolly well worth the 5/9 d. Trevor & Alice (his wife) said they have made it do for 2 films so the next one they want to see they won't be able to. Poor man!

I did an awfully silly thing before he came — apart from polishing all the brass till it was so bright it hurt you to look at; polishing all the drawing room furniture; cleaning the drawing room window; scrubbing the entire conservatory floor & washing all the white woodwork, cleaning the window by the door; and repainting all the windows & doors that look into the yard — the one's that were peeling & had things scratched all over them!!! Now, where was I? Oh! yes. The other silly thing. I made a vow that if he didn't take sugar in his tea, I never would. I felt sure he would, & blow me, the man didn't. I have now given sugar up and I <u>HATE</u> it!!!!!!!!!!

We all 3 went to the B'mouth Aquarist's Exhibition yesterday & spent all morning looking at fish. There were some jolly good ones, and some most beautiful aquariums. Also some iguanas and other water loving reptiles.

Every evening now I go to the General Post Office, so everyone loves me because they have till 1/4-9 to write their letters instead of 8.0 which is our last post at Westhill P.O. <u>Reason</u>? Because my trip takes me past the Manse.* It's wizard as there's usually a light, the only blow being I can't see in.

I also gave Rusty a bath on Saturday and he still looks beautiful. I think Kitty must have given him fleas again though, after all my careful de-fleaing.

Jill's Budgerygar (can't spell) is here for a time while they are in France & the poor thing is in awful condition — all its neck is raw & featherless before & its feathers are frayed & its always scratching. Poor Kim.

---

* The Victorian rectory of Richmond Hill church.

Mr. Parry is coming tomorrow & so is Jo so we have to tidy up the house once again. It's shocking.

You should see me my marrow [squash] now. It's simply <u>gigantic</u>! I've seldom seen such an enormous affair. We are going to eat it on Sunday & Mr. Parry will be able to have some.

Do write again soon & tell me some more about your place,

Tons of love,

Jane

2

◆ ◆ ◆

TRANSITIONS
1952–1957

And then, quite suddenly, my school days were over. What would
I do next? I only wanted to watch and write about animals. How
could I get started? How could I make a living doing that?

— *My Life with the Chimpanzees*

SO JANE GOODALL has described the quandary of her life following the end of school in the summer of 1952. If she had previously indulged in childhood fantasies about being close to
nature, going to Africa, becoming a Dr. Dolittle or a Tarzan, living
in the "jungle" at peace with wild beasts, becoming a naturalist or a
journalist writing about natural history, now was the time to put
away childish things, to move from the dream into reality. And reality in postwar Britain, living in a middle-class family with much
love but little money, may have seemed constraining.

Jane had done well enough on her examinations to apply for admission to a university. But the family could hardly afford university tuition, and Vanne urged her daughter to develop practical
skills. From September to mid-December of 1952, Jane lived with a
family in Germany, intent on learning German but not very successful at it. She returned in time for Christmas at the Birches and then,
on May 4, 1953, she began to polish her typing, shorthand, and
bookkeeping skills at Queen's Secretarial College in South Kensington. During this period she rented a room in the London home of
Mrs. Hillier, the mother of her mother's friend Deb Seabrook, who
had married a prosperous apple farmer and lived at a farm known

as the Chantry in Kent. Many of Jane's weekends were spent gloriously in the country, riding horses with Jo, the Seabrooks' daughter. The first letter in this chapter, written three weeks after Jane began the London secretarial course, refers to "super times at the Chantry" with Jo.

By Easter 1954, Jane had finished her secretarial training and was back at the Birches, cleaning out her old bedroom, sorting, rearranging, tidying up. She reported, in the second letter of this sequence (April 26, 1954), being delighted to visit once again the Longham stables, finding Miss Bush's assistant, Poosh, to be "suddenly . . . grown up." Her infatuation with the Reverend Trevor Davies continued, though now she described her feelings in tones that seem increasingly ironic and self-deprecatory. As for her earlier ambition to write about animals, to be a journalist of nature and natural history, that too appeared less immediately certain: "I havn't given up the journalism idea by the way, but I have decided that to write anything worth anyone reading I must have lived a few more years and acquired a little experience of life, as they say."

She hoped to find a secretarial job in Oxford, but while waiting for something to transpire, Jane began, probably in May of 1954, assisting her aunt Olly with clerical work. Olwen was a skilled physiotherapist who ran a clinic for children and adults in need of physical therapy. The "dullness of the actual work," Jane wrote to Sally in the letter of June 26, "finds recompense in my interest at being up at the clinic & seeing all the cases."

By early August she had begun typing letters and documents for the Oxford University Registry. It was an uninteresting job, but among its few perks was the opportunity to work in Clarendon House, a superb neoclassical edifice with a grand double entrance, great Doric columns, a dramatic frieze at the central portico, and some serious temple statuary on the roof. Constructed in the early eighteenth century, during the mid-twentieth it housed the registry's various administrators, clerks, and typists. Jane and two coworkers explored the pleasurably "dark & cob-webby" attic (July 27 letter). Her ultimate boss was "the Reg"; her immediate supervisor was Miss Shearer (or "M.S."), who was kind enough to allow

Jane to bring her pet hamster, Hamlette, to work (noted in November 1954). But by February of 1955 Jane would confess in a letter home that "I have been miserable these last few weeks because of the boredom of this foul job."

Imperfectly counterbalancing the boredom of her job was the excitement of being in Oxford and the pleasure of living in a boarding house (at 225 Woodstock Road) with an agreeable landlady, Miss Kersey. Her fellow boarders included Anne (who departed for Italy and New Zealand in the summer of 1954), Rosie Coates-White, and Mr. Davies (disappeared in a huff in November), as well as three others who became during the year her good friends: Stuart Ramsden, John Butler, and Eileen. In the letter of November 1954, Jane relates most delightfully the experience of "jumping with fog-fever" in Oxford. The letter written in early May 1955 describes a timeless spring day (and Oxford's official May Day) spent punting and picnicking with her friends.

Jane left Oxford early in June 1955, and in late July or early August, she returned to London, where she had found a job choosing music to accompany documentary films produced by Stanley Schofield of Schofield Productions, at 6, 7, 8 Old Bond Street. The job had its pleasures, and London certainly did. With what seems a typically high level of energy, Jane squeezed the most she could out of her time in the city, taking classes in philosophy, going to concerts ("I seem to spend my life in the Festival Hall"), and dealing with eager young men — including David and then Brian (first mentioned in the letter of August 7, 1955). Brian had become "B." by May 1956 and was by August or September replaced briefly by a "chap I have met called Douglas." Other young suitors mentioned in the letters include Horst and Hans from Germany and Keith, who was temporarily replaced, on the ship to Kenya, by "not a bad chap" also named Keith.

The position at Schofield Productions lasted until May of 1956, when she received a letter from Africa. It was an invitation from Marie Claude ("Clo") Mange, one of Jane's best friends from her Uplands School days, inviting her old chum "V.J." to come visit her in Kenya, where her father had recently acquired a large farm. Jane instantly accepted Clo's invitation, gave notice at the film studio, and returned to the Birches, where she could live rent- and board-free and walk a short distance each day to her job as a waitress in a large hotel, the Hawthorns. She worked herself "absolutely to the bone," as she declared in a letter to Sally written in August or September 1956. But she was able to save almost everything she earned; every weekend she brought home her wages and tips and hid them under a carpet, saving her pounds, shillings, and pence until the day when she had accumulated enough to buy a ticket to Africa. The last letter in this sequence, written on stationery provided by the S.S. *Kenya Castle,* is her first letter home at the start of a three-week voyage to Kenya Colony, East Africa.

The theme of this chapter is Jane Goodall saying good-bye, in a gradual and unconscious way, to the people and pets and places of her childhood; it is fascinating and satisfying indeed to observe how the central fantasy of that childhood turns out to be the guiding reality of her adult life. The motion of this chapter is a slow drift from place to place and job to job, things begun with wild eagerness and ending in mild disappointment — leading to a final sweep of movement: the invitation from Clo, the waitressing job, the boat trip to Africa: the focus of attention, the direction of a dream, the start of a life's great adventure.

*   *   *   *

c/o Mrs Hilliard,
8, Beaufort House,
Beaufort Street,
Chelsea.
[Postmarked May 27, 1953]

Dear Sally,

I'm dreadfully sorry I havn't written before — at least I don't think I answered your last letter before did I? How are you old thing!

I'm very nearly dead. This shorthand is terribly hard work, and also rather monotonous as it only requires learning, learning, learning. The typing is not too bad, but that again, is a little bit automatic.

I have simply super times at the Chantry at the weekends —

when I don't (or rather can't) go home to Trevor & the Birches as Jo has two ponies and we ride nearly all the time. You can't imagine how super it is to be able to do just what you want on a horse, instead of always having to behave yourself. The weekend before last when I went down we had one quite mad ride when we both nearly fell off from laughing. We had just come back from a dog show, and wanted to take the dogs out. We got onto the horses just as we were, & as I had to take my stockings off, I took my shoes off too. Jo followed suite of course, & so we were sockless, shoeless, johdless, hatless, & saddleless. We went through the orchards (which incidentally were glorious with apple blossom) and Joker kept bucking. That made me laugh, & so I nearly fell off, and then I saw Jo quite helpless with laughter. On enquiring the reason, I discovered that when my skirt blew up (as it frequently did) she could see my suspenders wildly flopping up and down under my knickers. That set me off, and honestly, I've never laughed as much in my life. And as you know it's most queer laughing when cantering. In the end we both had to collapse on the ground, quite helpless & weak. It took about two days to recover from.

On Saturday I went to a horse show, and although it wasn't particularly hot, it was sunny & windy, & for the first time in its life, my face really caught the sun. It is still as red as a beetroot (remember the 'darling' beetroot!) and I only hope that it's not going to peel.

I expect Daphne* told you that she came to Oedipus with me. Oh! It was absolutely <u>smashing</u> and never have I seen a better play. I think your Ma enjoyed it too. I went twice, and I've also been to the Twelfth Night which was also jolly good.

I have heaps more I could say, but also lots of work awaiting me, which must be done. Drop me a line sometime soon old pal, and until then I'll wish you

'Adieu'

love

<u>Jane</u>

---

* Sally's mother.

The Birches,
10, Durley Chine Road,
Bournemouth.
[Postmarked April 26, 1954]

My darling and much beloved peach blossom,*

(So Miss Mary Audey Gwyneth Joseph has told me to salute you.) I'm so terribly sorry that I havn't answered your letter before, but I've been having the most ghastly time imaginable with my room. You know my large white article of furniture with the drawers and the glass cupboard on top? You know the rubbish and piles and mounds of old papers that had conglomerated within? Well, we decided to get rid of it as I was to have a new piece of furniture — brown and much nicer. I was also to have a different dressing table, and move the wardrobe to the other side of the room. Well, you should just have seen me executing said re-arrangements and re-movals. Gosh, it was a sight you would never have forgotten. For one thing, while the spirit so moved me I decided to untidy everything all at once, so that even if the spirit left me, necessity would force me to continue the good work. So, imagine your little friend one glorious sunny afternoon sitting in a room where every inch of floor is littered with piles of newspaper cuttings, old magazines, file paper, notebooks, old school books, and bits and pieces of every sort and description. Closely piled along the walls are rows and rows of books, while the empty bookcases stare out with hollow empty shelves. Piled onto the bed are dresses, jumpers, vests, knickers, blouses, laddered stockings, socks with undarned holes leering blankly up at the ceiling — etc. etc. etc.! Just imagine it, and spare the poor sweating toiling creature on the floor, begrimed and becobwebbed, a moment of pity in your tender heart.

And I have only just finished it, rehung the pictures, filled my crests with flowers, arranged the ornaments, and got all to my liking. And now, apparently, everything has got to come out for the blasted room to be painted. The thought is driving me slowly but surely insane!

---

* Sally Cary.

But enough of such dismal thoughts, for the sun is shining, and my heart is full of the joys of spring — and fond thoughts of my Beloved. Oh Sally my sweet, I have had such a wonderful Easter, that the memory must surely sweeten my thoughts for all the rest of my life. I think this time of year is the very best of all, and I would rather have an Easter than hundreds of Christmases, because everything is so green and new and beautiful with the promise of new life and sunshine. I' troth, I find myself waxing poetic in praise of the season.

This year I was specially asked for to help with the decorating of the Church, and I was given the most fiddly and laborious job of tying jam jars along the altar rail, hiding them with fronds of foliage, and then filing (sorry 'll') them with water, primroses and wood-anemones. It did look super when it was finished though, and I think it was worth the trouble. I had an old fat dear from the choir to assist me, so while she sat stolidly on her bottom, I had to wriggle backwards and forwards under the rail and between the vases of tulips and daffodils tying knots which invariably slipped and had to be tied again, a process involving more wriggling and crawling. And matters were complicated by Rusty (who was there of course) because every time I squirmed under the rail, he had to lumber through after me, and he had very little respect for the floral decoration, I am sorry to say. However, it was accomplished in the end with no accidents whatsoever.

I must say the Church looked super when we had finished. The window sills were thick with flowers of all kinds, the altar rail blossomed out in green, yellow and white, and on the table in the center was the most heavenly bowl of arum lilies — one of my softest spots is for arum lilies, and, oh joy, after the services were over on Sunday, and I had stayed behind to help clear the church, I was allowed to take two of the beautiful gracious, slender, exotic creatures home with me, together with a basket full of primroses, and a glorious bunch of daffodils and tulips. Truly I felt like an Easter queen.

And you just should have seen the congregation on Easter Sunday morning. We got there an hour before the service began, and even so

it was at least half full, and we only just got our front seat. Mummy, of course, was late, and though we just managed to squash her into our pew, it was such an uncomfortably tight fit that I sat on the stairs for the sermon, and was much more comfortable. By about 10.45 every available inch of the church was packed, with rows and rows of chairs down all the gangways and in every nook and cranny possible. And there were about 80 people sitting upstairs in the lecture hall, where Prickles* had laid on a loud speaker the day before, and which we had also decorated. It was quite wonderful, and we had 75 members of the Welsh National Opera Company crammed into that round place in between the choir because they were singing the anthem. They have been singing at the Pav.† all this week.
Later.

I was interrupted from this wonderful epistle for the funniest reason. You have heard from Susie, I am sure, of Mummy's Colonel?‡ Well, he is really a sweet old boy. As I was writing this letter the day before yesterday, Mummy was in London, and the Colonel rang up to ask if I would go round and talk to him because he was so lonely. It was about 8.0 but I had to go, and it was a great pity because it spoilt my nice little plan which was to take this letter to the post and then wait for Olly who was at choir practise — and you know why I wanted to do that, don't you? However, I had a very nice little evening, and he gave me the most super volume of Shakespeare. It looks like an ordinary book, only when you open it, inside are four little tiny volumes with tiny print, real India paper, and the most super pictures imaginable.

On Saturday I went out to the stables for the first time in years, and then went with Poosh to the Portman Hunt Point-to-Point afterwards. Poosh has changed considerably — for the better. Quite suddenly she seems to have grown up, and is no longer so silly and giggly and jealous as she used to be. You remember what she said at first when I told her that Pelletier§ was still writing to me — "What

---

* A nickname for Aunt Olwen's boyfriend, Mr. Hollis.
† The Bournemouth Pavilion.
‡ Susie was Sally Cary's younger sister. The Colonel was a close friend of Vanne's.
§ An admirer.

a conscientious young man he must be" — and how horrified I was that she could make such a foul remark? Well, when I told her that he had rung up for my birthday, she was very amused and not beastly about it at all. I told her to test her out in a way.

Did you ever hear that poor old Rack had to be put down? He got some internal stoppage and after being ill for weeks they had to give up hope as he couldn't eat anything at all. Poor Poosh is still very upset about it, especially as her family say she can't have another big dog because it's too expensive to feed. She is riding Quince's foal, Quick, now, and already doing dressage with her. It seems very early to start, but Chasm did the same, and it suited her very well.

Did Susie tell you that I am really off to Oxford to try and get a job? or was I that far when Daphne came here. Anyway, I am going to stay with these people at the beginning of May definitely, and it should be rather fun, as they live outside Oxford in the country, and have lots of ponies and there is a farm next door to them which is almost a part of the family.

And there is another super thing about this Oxford business. Trevor is great friends with one of the Principals of one of the colleges — a certain Dr. Marsh who was at college with T. He is going to write him a letter of introduction — or should I say, he is going to write one for me. Which means I can go down to the Manse to fetch it and tell him particulars. I havn't given up the journalism idea by the way, but I have decided that to write anything worth anyone reading I must have lived a few more years and acquired a little experience of life, as they say.

I enclose this very private poem for your interest and perusal. You can read it to anyone of your family that you consider suitable. I made it up the day before I wrote this letter first, and two of the juiciest lines were composed, of all places, outside the Manse on my way back from taking the mail to the post! Olly and Mummy of course, adore it, and even Danny rather reveled in it!

I am typing this end part of the letter out in the garden. It is very hot when the sun is shining, but every time a cloud comes along it goes suddenly freezing, and the shock makes me type a mistake generally — that's a nice excuse for the shocking typing, but I think the real reason is that I havn't done any for such a long time that I've forgotten how to use the wretched machine. . . .

And now, my dear, I must cease. I hope you will have a nice term, and that you will write again soon and let me hear of your doings and progress etc., etc. I also hope that you have had a smashing holiday as I have, and that we shall meet again soon.

Tons of love, old spud.

Your ever faithful,

Jane

The Birches.

26th June, 1954

My foul & revolting specimen of an old friend,

How I loathe you Madam! You owe me a letter — I hope you have no objection to be reminded of that highly disagreeable fact. Anyway, if I was anyone but Trevor's little lamb, & if I wasn't feeling heartbroken at his departure, I should most decidedly treat you to an infuriated piece of my mind, and a very severe blowing up! None the less, considering that I <u>AM</u> T's little lamb, & all that he would desire me to be, I will forgive you from the heart of my spleen, & turn the other cheek — i.e. write another letter in readiness of not being answered.

How goes the old career, best beloved? All the little children getting on well with their A.B.C.'s eh?

I don't know whether you have heard any recent news from your "little one" but I will assume for the moment that you are in ignorance of your Red Admiral's flutterings, & proceed to elucidate you forthwith.

For one thing I am working for Olly up at the Clinic — I dare say you do know that. I proffer my services for a mere kick-in-the-pants — 2/6 per hour; but even that is better than nothing, & is given for a good cause. Poor little Olly lost her assistant physio & was left single handed. She was so over-worked & over-worried, that she very nearly had a nervous breakdown — she actually gave herself shingles! The clinic was shut for about 4 days while she recovered.

Anyway, I nobly stepped into the breach & am doing all her clerical work — which incidentally is a heck of a lot, & rather boring. But the dullness of the actual work finds recompense in my interest at being up at the clinic & seeing all the cases. Actually one gets a peculiar complex from being amongst crippled children all the time. It makes one realize how damnably lucky one is to have one's body the same as any other ordinary person's. Some of the cases are so pathetic that my heart aches for them, & yet one and all are happy and bright, & they never complain. I have come to the conclusion that it must be a special gift from God to compensate for the loss of activity, or horrible deformity. One poor little girl is paralysed from the waist down & will never be able to walk. She had polio at 8 yrs old, & as she was such an athletic little thing it got her very badly. But I have never yet seen her with a disagreeable face or a cross voice. It certainly teaches one a lesson!

But I think the worst, the very worst thing of all is this dreadful creeping paralysis. It strikes a child at the age of about 7. Until then they are quite normal — they wake suddenly one day & cannot use an arm or leg. There is absolutely <u>no</u> cure, and it just gets worse & worse until they cannot move at all. Luckily they generally die at about 14 of some other complaint as they have no resistance at all — but just think of it!

One boy came up to the Surgeon's clinic on Wednesday with this dreadful complaint. He was 16, and <u>enormously</u> fat. He could just move his hands & head — nothing else. He was incontinent, & how his poor wretched mother managed to look after him I hate to think. Oh dear, life does seem unfair when looked at from some angles!

There is one man who goes once a week (Olly treats 4 adults, who have been to Alton) and he is quite smashing. His determination to get about has enabled him to walk (with calipres & a stick) although the actual power in his muscles is almost nothing. But for sheer determination he would still be lying in bed, or hobbling about on crutches. He is so nice, & terribly handsom. At the moment he is as pleased as punch as his wife has just had their second baby, & he adores children.

I told you about Pelletier ringing me up on my birthday? Well, now he has the nerve to write & ask me to exchange with him. He wants to come here this autumn, & then I am to go over to his house next spring! I ask you! But he sounds very determined to <u>come</u> to England somehow, & my heart is trembling. I shall positively <u>DIE</u> if I ever see him again!

Have you been to "Beneath the 12-mile Reef"? I went last night, & in spite of catching a flea from someone, & a mosquito biting my legs non stop, I enjoyed it so much that I stayed round twice. The first time I was so perturbed as to what was going to happen, that I could not enjoy the marvelous under-water photography. Gosh, how dangerous, exciting, & beautiful it must be to go down under the water. How I should love & dread it at the same time. As they said "You don't know how scared you can be till you go down for the first time into deep water".

I am becoming very musical my dear. By which I don't mean that I am becoming adept at any instrument (though I should absolutely adore to play the harp) but I have taken to going to concerts, & love them very much. Now that my darling is miles away over the ocean waves, music must be my consolation.* In case it interests you, he left last Wednesday from Southhampton, and the passage takes about a week, so he will still be tossing as you read these words. I do hope the sea is not too rough, as Alice anyway, is a bad sailor.

I really wrote to say that if you had any spare time one weekend, it would be super if you could pop down & see me. Of course, money is the greatest problem I know, but it would be lovely if you could manage a visit.

I had a simply lovely time at Oxford, as the people I stayed with are nice & horsey. Next door to them is a farm, & the man breeds horses & has lots of smashing hunters & a few point-to-pointers. His daughter, though only 15, was very nice, & we went for some heavenly rides. I didn't manage to get a job at the time, but I got a letter from the University Registrar yesterday offering me one in her

---

* Trevor Davies and his wife had gone to the United States, probably on a ministerial exchange.

office. It starts in August, & I am taking it as then I shall be on the spot to seize anything decent which is going. Anyway, it will be experience, & I don't feel capable really of applying for a really good job without a little experience — especially as it is such a long time since I left College.

Well peach blossom, I think I've wasted quite enough ink, time, energy, brains & paper in penning this illiterate scrawl. I hope it doesn't seriously impare your respite for weeks to come. But please drop me a line sometime.

Much love,

Jane

Tuesday, 6.35 p.m.

[Probably July 27, 1954]

My darling Family!

How charming & adorable you all are! Thanks simply masses for the Diary, beans, & your letter Mummy. The diary is super, being the larger size, and jolly well worth the extra money which I will give you, Danny, when I come back. I assure you that Butler & Ramsden* won't be jealous of the bean smell — they do themselves proud! By the way, I hope Jif is also charming & adorable — i.e., that she has de-flead Rusty by now!!! Because if he is not done by Friday — Just wait for it, oh sister mine!!!

I have just been composing a very lengthy letter to Sally as today has been slack in the extreme. Sheila, Pamela & I had such fun this afternoon. Sheila was showing us the way up to the roof of the Clarendon Buildings — & gosh, it's simply gorgeous up there, & one feels on top of the world. Then we started to explore the roof — the 'atticy' part, not outside. It was all dark & cob-webby, and there were great long spaces with crumbling boards beneath. Sheila & I were very venturesome, & got all mixed up in a place where some queer soft stuff lay on the ground between two planks. We couldn't think what it was, & took a handful out to the light with us — but

---

* Stuart Ramsden and John Butler also rented rooms in the boarding house.

were no wiser. It was white & looked rather like flour that has become clogged up with weevils — or whatever those bugs are that used to be in Danny's store of war-time flour & appeared baked in her bread on numerous occasions! It felt like dust.

I'm not sure that I shall be able to start on Monday morning — though I hope so. Can't tell till M.S. gets back from her holiday.

Can't stop to write any more now or I shall miss the post — not that you will get it tomorrow anyway, though I don't know why the post here is so bad.

Anyway tons of love, & thanks tons for the parcel. I love getting parcels & letters you know.

See you soon —

Jane

UNIVERSITY REGISTRY
OXFORD
18 August, 1954

Dearest All,

Today is just about the slackest one I have met so far, and already, at 11:30 I have run out of all work. Miss Shearer has been sending me over to the Indian Institute to find out where various people were for future reference — that's how little there is to do. Do look out for a little Johna (Jonah?) to put in her whale Mummy. He can be bigger than I thought — in fact I think my little professor would do, but I don't want to part with him. Will you send him to me if you find him — I'm sure he would feel very much at home in these academic surroundings.

Thanks for your letter Mummy, and will you thank Olly for her super P.C. when she comes back. I'm glad they are having a nice time, but do tell me what she said when she discovered she had to sleep miles away through a wilderness of gorse and bracken. Also I want to know the result of Jif's Scholl Cert. — if you can make out the meaning of 'Scholl'.

When I next come home I have got an <u>Adventure</u> to relate. Now I have tantalised you havn't I? But it is much too long to write decently in a letter that wasn't a miniature novelette, and even though we are slack, I still havn't got time for a work of that sort. At any moment I feel sure I shall receive a great pile of letters to be re-done from the Reg. And Miss Shearer too no doubt because I did all hers on his note paper by a mistake. Not that she will mind really, but she's not in a very wonderful mood this morning.

Last night when it was time to go, it was absolutely pouring with rain — a real deluge. A lot of people, me included, had brightly set out in the morning — a lovely sunny one — in cotton dresses and cardigans. Anyway, Miss Shearer said she would lend me the old mac which she uses to clean the car in. Of course, by the time I had found the car, struggled vainly with a most awkward lock, and retrieved the mac, I was drenched to the skin. It was frightfully funny. But some people had to bike back with no mac at all, so I was better off than they. The really silly part about it was that by the time I had got the mac, returned the key, and tidyed up all my belongings, the rain had practically ceased.

One of the girls here who was on holiday when I started came back on Monday, and I think she is one of the nicest here. I had lunch with her yesterday, and we went round Christ church afterwards. N.B. I am now having lunch once more — an early lunch which means I leave at 12.30 & have to be back by 2.0 in case the Reg. wants to dictate after he gets back. I had to stop typing because, as I said, the Reg rang for me. He gave me a beaming smile when I went in, & actually said "You're getting on rather well you know. I like the stuff you are serving me with". So there. What a clever daughter, grandaughter, niece, niece & sister you have respectively.

There is pandemonium at 225 at the moment. Anne is leaving today — going off for a fortnight's holiday in Italy before leaving for New Zealand, lucky child. All her baggage is strewn around, & she has been bequeathing all the things she can't take to Rosie (Coates White) & me. She has also given me her wireless to house & use for the fortnight. Then, Miss Kersey is busy doing up the kitchen, so all the pots & pans are in long rows up either side of the stove, & the kitten keeps playfully rolling things down so that they are lost amongst Anne's trunks. It's rather a hoot.

I suppose Byron will have gone now — though I shouldn't be at all surprised if not. Give him my love in the later case. Also give love to Colonel, & I'm very sorry I didn't see him. Please thank Madam from me for being so decent if you hear her again (on the phone) & say I am writing to the Loms (doesn't that sound funny) to thank them for having me that evening.

Do take good care of my poor darling little Black Fellow,* won't you? And Judy is to go on taking him out when she gets back. Swartz should have given her great zeal by then. Give my very best love to Deb — & the others, & say I am dying for her to come up to Oxford to see her old school. But it would really have to be a Sunday, & anyway PTO. Since they are off to Scotland she will probably have forgotten when she gets back. None the less! And also (for your ears alone Meine Mutter) what about the B? How is wee Hughie! I shall send Olly the name of that specialist she is to ask Wilson about if you have really lost my long & beautiful letter — which is disgusting in the extreme. I must now go & buy some sugar.

Danny, my frying pan works very well, but the bacon I got is so smashingly lean it makes less fat — so I have to use Magic!!

Tons of love
Your distant <u>Jane</u>

[Probably November 1954]

Darling Mummy,

Didn't we have a smashing weekend? Thanks tons for doing my hair. It's jolly nice now, and I hope it will be so on Saturday.

I have got my lift! From Mr. Butler, (only it's John now!) I went to help him drain his car of water the other night because we thought it was going to freeze. It was Monday night — did you have a foggy journey Mummy? Because here it was the thickest fog I've ever been in, from 6.00 onwards. I had a gorgeous time in it — I just couldn't face the thought of German, so I went into the Library and looked up Unicorns — I can't get the material I want from any of the books

---

* Her dog, Rusty.

in the Ref. Library, so I don't know what I'll do. Anyway, after doing that the fog had not got into my blood and I feebly got a bus. That however set me jumping with fog-fever, as it crept along at about 2 m.p.h. and kept mounting the curb with alarming lurches. The cars in front were making equally heavy weather of it. When I got back I seized a hunk of bread and a biscuit and had a chat with Miss Kersey who said that she adored wandering about in the fog too. Then I sallied forth, and in a few moments was caught up by Ramsden (only I have to call him Stuart now to make it fair). He was walking into Oxford to do some work at the lab. So I went part of the way with him, and then did some smashing wandering on my own. It was really chronic for the poor wretched motorists, and a wall and a pillar box were knocked flat — only I didn't see them unfortunately. At last I meandered home, having made myself useful to the extent of guiding three cars to a turning on the other side of the road, and helped a man whose car battery had given out to point out the curb to people. Just there the road was very very wide you see, and so having left the curb, their only guide, by the time they had crossed over to the opposite curb they couldn't see it at all. And when one stood on one side, though shouts and calls came looming through the fog from the other side, one just could not see a thing.

Anyway, I got back, & John was in a perfect state as he had no anti-freeze in the car and he felt he ought to go & drain it. I said I'd help him — I thought the car was in the drive but to my horror I found it was in a garage miles away. Actually I did not mind much as the fog was still smashing. We walked about 1/2 a mile — there and back — all the way up to the roundabout, (only you won't know how far that is). And when we got there we found there was a fire in the kitchen the other side of the wall, & the temp. was <u>very</u> warm in the garage. So he didn't drain it after all.

However, I then went up & had coffee with them, & he offered to take me on Saturday. So it was well worth my foggy tramp! I rang Mrs. Lom who said she could have got me a lift so it would have been OK anyhow — but it's nice to be independent.

Will you send a little bag, or I suppose I <u>could</u> take your black one? And don't you think I need something on my wrist — or I shall feel awful naked.

Miss Shearer says I <u>can</u> have a hamster. Won't it be fun. The shoes are fine now, & I like them as much as ever.

Mr. Davies is going. Miss Kersey wrote him a noble little note, & he, in a very childish way, left it lying there all day & wrote her a note saying he thought he would look for somewhere else as it was 'too regimentated' here — he must have guessed what would be in her note. Last night he left all his things lying round in the kitchen. We had not room at all, and Butler got cross & banged the whole lot in <u>Adcroft's</u>* cupboard. I heard bangs and crashes, & went to investigate. I met a spoon flying downstairs — she threw them <u>all</u> out of the kitchen door — in this case I don't blame her!!!

[Probably February 1955]

Darling Mummy and Danny,

I've decided only to write to you two because you're the only ones who ever write to me, so I will miss the others out — oh, Olly does occasionally of course, but only once in a blue moon! Anyway, that's neither here nor there. Thanks tons for your lovely long letter Dan.

Now the thing I want to write about is this vile job. Do you not think it is time I got something else? I have given the matter serious consideration, and have decided I should honestly like another medical job, and wondered if dear Mr. Wilson could pull any strings to get me into the Wingfield Morris, or even Uncle Eric. . . . I have been miserable these last few weeks because of the boredom of this foul job, but now the thought of future jobs perks me up no end. And if I stay here until July, say, and then had a nice holiday at home, wouldn't it be fun?

The next thing I want to talk about is the party at 225. The numbers are increasing alarmingly — thank heavens one is only 21 once, or one would live in a permanent state of bankruptcy. Anyway, can you suggest where I should turn for a cake? I shall probably find somewhere to do one in Oxford, but perhaps you have some advice on the subject. Everyone is adament that I must have

---

* Another boarder at 225 Woodstock Road.

one, with 21 candles. 14 or 15 if Sue comes, will be the number —
crikey. Also I am told that I shall have to make a speech as I shall be
formally toasted at dinner — now, dear Mummy, come to my rescue and tell me what I should say? Please. I rely on you entirely.
Also, I am to be an elegant hostess while the others do all the work
— once the guests arrive that is — and they all insist on my getting my red dress for the occasion. What do you think of that plan?
It would be rather nice, and a wonderful excuse to get out of all
the dashing up and down to the kitchen — which is fun actually,
but still.

It is going to be on 26 January — sorry, March, and I really think
it should be rather fun, don't you. Have you any bright suggestions
as to what we should do at it? Apart from Stuart's repertoire on the
piano, and an act which Sandy is to be persuaded to put on, together with an odd game or two such as charades, we cannot think
of anything. And Eileen and Stuart have been tucked away with the
most lousy colds so that we have not had a really communal conversation and discussion as yet. And that brings me to the fact that such
things are happening at 225. It is mainly between Eileen and Stu,
and it is all such a muddle that I can't explain it all in a letter, but
they want to stop seeing each other for a long time, and Eileen's in a
flat spin because her John doesn't come back from Canada until
May, and she's getting fonder and fonder of Stuart, and doesn't
know what to do. Oh dear oh dear. We were discussing it for hours
last night. The sooner they <u>both</u> get out the better it will be. I only
hope that in all the confusion of hearts I get a party at all. The only
immune heart, so far as I can see, is mine!

Now, I shall really have to stop — for the moment anyway, and
get on with a little work. It is M.S's half day, and the Reg is in London, so I am having a peaceful time, but unfortunately I have one or
two odds and ends to tidy up to-day. However, I dare say I shall be
able to continue this letter at a later time, so farewell till then.

It is now later, and this is no time to write any more as it is 5.55,
and, therefore, time to go — and I hate staying here a moment longer than I need. I am expecting a letter from you tomorrow about
various matters, so I daresay this will cross with yours. I hope so —

I mean, I hope a letter comes. Have you got my toothbrushes? I can't afford another one. Honestly. D'you know, I havn't done any work all afternoon, and everyone has come in here to chat. The Vienna Boys' choir last night was marvellous, though they did not seem quite as perfect as the ones I heard in Germany.

Tons of love,

Jane

[Early May 1955]

Darling anyone who thinks herself entitled to a letter!

Thank you for your letters Mummy and Danny — or have I written since then? I really don't know. The hamster box should be on its way by now, but if they take as long in delivering it as they did my trunk, I don't suppose you'll get it until about Friday or Saturday. Anyway, I hope she survives until then.*

I had a simply gorgeous time on May morning. We got up at 3.45 and took a smashing breakfast with us. We got to the punt at 4.30, where we met Eileen's friend, Moira, who, poor thing, had had to rise at 3.00 to get there. It took us the hour and a half to get down to Magdalen Bridge — as we got the punt from Tim's at Bardwell Road. It wasn't at all cold, and John and Stu. punted very well. We got a very good place — oddly enough very near the people I met at the Beagle Ball. They looked funny in the cold and sober light of 5.45. We could see the top of the tower, but not the choir boys. It really was beautiful sitting there in the punt and listening to the pagan hymn floating out across the water. All the babble that had been going on stopped suddenly as the clock chimed the hour — all except one stupid fool who chose that moment to leap into the water and swim — in bathing trunks. It was really mean of him — he could easily have waited until the singing was over, but some people must draw all the attention to themselves if they can. As a matter of fact, he didn't, and everyone completely ignored him, so soon he stopped his splashing. We were fairly near the front of the queue for getting

---

* Hamlette was being delivered back home to the Birches.

out, and so dashed away upstream to find a good place for breakfast. We didn't go very far as we were mighty peckish by this time, and stopped at the edge of an enormous meadow round which the river curved on three sides. It was a popular place — but then so was most of the bank as there were a large number of people all looking for breakfast sites. We tied the punt to a tree, and having got the primus going, I supervised the cooking of the breakfast with Moira, and the others built a fire.

The primus really worked supremely, which was just as well as I had to cook: — sausages, bacon, tomatoes and fried bread. At one time John was to have brought three cousins with him, but at the last moment they decided not to come, and so we had all their rations as well. It was scrummy — and cooked to a T. It was most plutocratic having a fire as well, and kept us nice and warm. John and Stu. made toast over the fire — which for camp toast was really very good, though it took rather a long time.

The undergrads. next to us were really quite clueless. They took hours getting their fire going, and then it was so feeble that the sausages they were cooking on sticks were all half raw. And I thought their kettle would never boil, so offered them our primus. But though it started off all right, it soon conked out, and they brought it back. The kettle was still only warm. So I examined the primus, and found it had run out of petrol. So we filled it up for them, and once more they borrowed it — with success. It was a whistling kettle, and when the whistle went off, what cheers there were. They made the tea by pouring the leaves down the spout! At which we went into fits of mirth. Someone fell in just by us. It was very funny, but we didn't laugh for long as we thought how cold it must be. Several other canoes went by containing people with sodden trousers. Near us a large party of people had a gramophone and were doing country dancing, and the other side of the meadow a large crowd first sang, and then a long and energetic game of rounders. It was great fun sitting and watching everything, and thinking that nowhere else in the world could one see anything quite like it. Good old Oxford. I hate the idea of going now, and yet I daresay it is all for the good. Still, I wish I could have seen the summer out.

After we had been sitting there for about 1 1/2 hours we decided to make a move — Eileen was dying to show off her punting. So we set off. She managed very well until we got to a tricky bend, when she first lost the pole behind a sticking out branch of a tree, and then, put off her stride, went round and round in circles, bumping into everything that came along. We nearly died of laughing.

Then they persuaded me to try. We sort of drifted idly from mid-stream to the bank, and from the bank to mid-stream, and then the pole got caught in a tree. Like a clot, I leant out to try and free it, and the punt rapidly departed outwards. If I hadn't jumped I should have gone flat onto my face. So I jumped!!

Oh it was funny. Really funny. They just sat in the punt and roared and roared with laughter. And I stood in the water — up to my chest — and roared and roared with laughter. And we were so weak with laughing that I had no strength to crawl out of the water, and they had no strength to paddle back and fetch me. Gosh it was funny. And the odd part about it was that it wasn't cold. Not at all cold. Queer. At last they managed to stop laughing for long enough to fish me out, and we set off again. And still it wasn't cold. Curiouser and curiouser.

But that was by no means the end of the comedies of the morning. Really it would have made a dashed good film. I insisted on being allowed to punt again, and was doing fine until we got to a tricky bend. Here the river received a little tributary, in the middle of the entrance to which sailed a large male swan — his wife was on the nest on the bank. Well, you know how dangerous swans can be. I swear it was entirely the fault of the punt, but anyway it began to head for the swan. Straight at the wretched bird. Stu. who was sitting out on the front bit bravely grasped his paddle more firmly and said he'd try and keep it off. All very well, but I knew better. It began to hiss, the punt pole was being unwieldy, and John was foolishly saying that it wasn't at all dangerous. He really thought it, but the rest of us knew better — at least, Stu and I did. Luckily I managed to control the pole hastily, and rapidly backed us away with all possible speed. Danger averted. Then, as the corner was very tricky, and my steering was negligible, the boys said they'd paddle us round — John's paddle being the frying pan. Well, they paddled straight for a low overhanging branch. I was by then in Stu's place in the front, and there was absolutely no room for me to go under — so I did what seemed to me the sensible thing to do — I jumped onto the branch, and the punt actually slid underneath. The others were all sitting actually inside, so it was fine for them. How we laughed again. And some other people in punts nearly split themselves as well.

Then the final joke occurred after they had come back to fetch me off the tree. I was once again punting. It was a straight bit of river, and I was doing fine — really getting the hang of the thing. Stu and John had their backs to me, Eileen was facing me. Suddenly the pole stuck in the mud, and Eileen looked up to see me tugging frantically and nearly overboard. "Drop it! drop it!" says she in a stern voice. John, who was idly paddling with the frying pan dropped it — just like that, and it sank straight to the bottom. I shouted grimly 'I'm not going to' and hung on until the wretched thing came out. That was almost the funniest of all. After that Eileen had another go, and then Moira was going to try but it began to pour with rain so Stu thought we'd better get back quickly and took over himself.

By the time we got back to the car I must admit that I was beginning to be a trifle chilly, but we soon got back. I showed myself to Miss Kersey who was rather worried about me as my cold had only just gone. She took away my skirt and has since ironed and washed it — the other way round of course — as it was all over green stains from the tree. Also the hem was down, and she has hemmed it all for me. She did it last night when I sat and talked to her. Isn't she decent. She also brought me a cup of hot coffee to the bathroom. Eileen had run a bath while I took my sodden garments off, and I sat in front of her fire till it was ready. Spoilt girl, arn't it?

After my bath we all had coffee, and then John's cousins came round, and Stu and Eileen began the lunch — roast beef and Yorkshire Pudding — but nothing like your Yorkshire pud. Danny. I have vaguely asked Stu and Eileen to come for a weekend in the summer — either during my holiday, or perhaps afterwards — they could drive up to London, collect me, and we could all arrive together perhaps. But if that comes off, we simply must have Yorkshire pudding!

I have got to meet wretched old Bob this evening, but seeing I am going to get a lot of going on the river out of him, I don't mind.

Since finishing the last paragraph I have had a terrific row with Miss Shearer over writing letters* — which is quite ridiculous as I have nothing — absolutely nothing — else to do. So I told her this, and we have hardly spoken since. Now there has been a muddle over M.A. taking the Reg. and V.C. to the Radcliffe in her car for a meeting. The Reg thought she had not turned up and actually she had been waiting all the time. So, as you can imagine, MS is now in an even worse mood. Hey-ho. I rather enjoy these rows now that I am definitely leaving.

It is raining at the moment, and cold into the bargain. I had really better stop now I think. I nearly rang you up on Sunday night, but thought it would be rather a waste of money. Give my love to the Colonel. How is Piggy?†

Masses of love,
Janey

6, 7, 8 Old Bond Street.
W.1.
[Postmarked August 7, 1955]

Best beloved family — Hail!

How is my darling black man? and has Hamlette been cleaned — is she being fed? Did Kenneth bring some decent corn for her?

I am really having rather a nice time you know. Dinner & theater with Pop on Thursday — <u>marvellous</u> play. Daddy has seen it twice now & it's most original. Only 4 of the cast speak English. The rest are Japanese. It is terribly amusing & there's a lot in it as well.

On Friday, as I told you, Daddy & I had dinner with a Solex‡ chap & his girl friend. We also took a very, very nice . . . Australian man with us. We saw Eric & Judy during the evening — they really <u>are</u> an extremely nice couple.§

---

* That is, writing personal letters during working hours.
† Rusty.
‡ Solex, a manufacturer of carburetors, was Mortimer's employer then.
§ Eric and Judy were friends of Mortimer's.

Yesterday morning Daddy took me to his Bank Manager and I now have my first cheque book! It is a very nice feeling. He also says that he may pay in a small amount monthly — which wouldn't half help to make ends meet. I hope he does.

I met David at 2.0. He had arranged nothing definite so we wandered round & decided to see 'The Private Life of Major Benson'. It was a most enjoyable film with a gorgeous little boy in it. Gosh he was sweet. Then we had something to eat & went to see Terence Rattigan's play 'Separate Tables' at St. James's. It was excellent. I'm afraid poor David's as smitten as the rest. I've had an invitation from Dora's Brian as well. And Mummy, I've fixed up with Mrs. Hindley* for Tuesday & Wed. next week — or rather, <u>this</u> week.

Tons of love all,

Jane

P.S. Our iron has bust so I'm just off to Pop's flat, + dresses, to use his. Doesn't that seem funny!
Poor David spent all last weekend looking through files of Sheres & Tatlers hoping to find a photo of me when I was presented!!†
Daddy is by now firmly convinced that Judy could do nothing better than learn the Clar-o?-i?-net. Most impressed with the Distinction — I do my best.
P.P.S. Please give my love to Byron & say I'm hoping to see him next week-end. Can you please book a trim with Jean for the Saturday. My hair's nearly to my waist!!

[Postmarked September 16, 1955]

Darling family,

It is a long time since I have owed every single one of you a letter at the same time — in fact I'm pretty sure it is the first time on record. Thank you ALL very much for your letters, etc. (The etc. being a very nice postcard from Audrey — thanks tons old cockolorum — a bundle of postcards from Horst from Olly, and the book

---

* The mother of Jane's godmother.
† Jane was presented as a debutante to Queen Elizabeth at Buckingham Palace; her uncle by marriage, Michael Spens (son of Sir Patrick Spens, lord chief justice of India), arranged the debut.

from Jif. Raymond thought it was wonderful and he chuckled all the way home in the train last night. Also thank you for getting me that bread knife which works wonderfully and I am now able to eat respectable looking sandwiches for my lunch. And the 5/- which you left and which you shouldn't have done because you couldn't possibly have eaten that amount of money value in 2 days even if you'd eaten anything at all which I doubt.)

I'm very sorry that I havn't written before to let you all know that I'm still in the land of the living, but what with one thing and another life has been pretty hectic. I hope that all the invalids have recovered, or are recovering. And talking of such things, I am just developing a lovely cold.

I went to the proms on Tuesday and Wednesday — and was going to go on Monday as well but I had to work late showing some people nice films of cows! Really, I have seen so many films of shorthorns lately that I almost began to dream about them.* On Tuesday it was the planets, Delius' piano concerto, Dvorak's 4th and the Wasps (to put everything in the wrong order). The pianist was Moiseivitsch (I expect that I spelt that wrong!). Well, I didn't realize what a popular concert it was going to be, and arrived at the usual time only to find that the gallery entrance had a notice up saying "Full House" and the arena door had a long queue outside. Just as I had joined the end of this queue a little man came out and said he was sorry, but all the seats were sold. A few people still hung around, me among them. A girl went up to him and I could hear her saying she'd come for miles and couldn't he possibly squeeze one more in, but he only shook his head and told her to try the box office. So a few more people drifted off. I don't know what made me stay, but just after she'd gone this little man opened the door a crack and beckoned to me. He then whispered that if I could slip him 2/6 without anyone in the queue seeing he would get me in somehow, although it was strictly illegal.

As luck would have it I had only a 10/- note on me, but even this did not put him off as might have been expected. He couldn't change it as the top door man was hovering around and my chap

---

* As part of her job at Schofield Productions.

would have got the sack. But he gave me a ticket and told me to go and change the note, and when I returned I was to say I'd had to go and make a telephone call. So off I went and changed the note with a programme seller (after having tried a taxi driver in vain, though he must surely have had some change really) and marched back. There were about 4 officials who clustered round me as I opened the door, and they all told me it was strictly illegal and they shouldn't allow me in at all. It was rather difficult to smuggle the money to my little man without any of the others seeing. Gosh, the concert was worth it though. I don't think there has been one prom which I enjoyed better. I got a very good place, and was able to see Moiseivitsch beautifully. I stood up for all the things except the Dvorak, and within a radius of 5 yards around me no less than <u>three</u> people fainted. So how many there must have been in the whole hall I hate to think. None of them were taken out. Their friends were so enthralled with the music that they just shoved them on the floor, bunged their heads between their knees for a bit, and then left them to recover as best they could. The Brahms 2 which I heard on Wednesday was simply superb — maybe you heard it on the wireless. Mrs. Hindley did and she said it didn't come over very well. But in the Albert Hall it was really terrific — and I really and truly think that apart from my darling Mendhelsohn (that looks a bit odd!) violin concerto I enjoyed it more than any other symphony. It was most probably because I was in a specially receptive mood that evening. Although I thoroughly disliked the woman singing the Mozart aria earlier on. She was vile. The orchestra didn't like her at all either. The sub-leader who was incidentally rather handsom absolutely refused to clap when she had finished — and as half her notes were distinctly wuzzy I was quite in agreement with him.

The Japanese dancing last night was very great fun, and really beautiful. Somehow it was more static than I had expected, but so lovely that I could have watched it all night. The Spider dance was terrific, and the man looked really horrible. Dear Mr. Wilsden lent us some opera glasses so we were able to see very well. We went for some coffee in the first interval because we both had sore throats and it really was funny. We went along winding stone passages, in and out and round about, and by the time we got there the interval was nearly over. So after gulping down the coffee we simply dashed back. We tore for miles along passages that seemed even longer and more winding than they had before, and at last got to a door which we thought led to the gallery slips. We flung it open — only to find ourselves back in the buffet! There was the same woman finishing off her coffee, and the same man smoking his cigarette. It really was most terribly funny, and when we finally got back we laughed and laughed.

There really isn't very much news. I met Daddy for lunch yesterday — he came along to the Overseas Club with me to try and get some addresses — we got a lot, but they were mostly too expensive. Then we went to the Sports Car Club, and there I met Daddy's boss — a really charming man, who insisted that as he'd never met me before he be allowed to give us lunch. So we had an excellent meal — and I was about 2 hours late back!

I've just had a postcard from Brian H. He is having a lovely time in South France — lying around in the sun all day and getting fat he said.

And now really there is nothing more to say, and since I want you to get this letter before the week-end I must go and find an envelope and get John to post it. Also it is very nearly the end of my lunch hour — and I don't want to have a lot of extra time today after yesterday.

Thank you all again, and I'm longing for next week-end — I must collect some warm cloths when I come home. At the moment I am shivering in cotton dresses while everyone else prances round in thick winter wool. Most unfair, but there is nothing I can do about it. We havn't heard about Ray's scripts yet. He was simply thrilled with the Sammy stuff, and is firmly convinced that that is the best script. It is really a mixture of Sammy's and mine, because I wrote out all the dope for him, and he has used a lot of it practically word for word.

Incidentally, Mummy, I never found that 3d piece. I and an old porter searched around for ages, and in the end had to give it up. Perhaps someone picked it up while I was waving to you.

Now do give my love to all the other people I have not mentioned — is Uncle Eric still there? And Rusty, Hamlette, etc. Also to Trevor please if you see him. I keep dreaming about him which makes life very much pleasanter.

Tons and tons of love,

Jane

6, Courtfield Gardens,

London, S.W.5.

27th March, 1956.

My dear Sue,

This is very naughty of me as I have a great deal of work to do, but I was so upset when I had a letter from Eileen saying that you had rung Miss Kersey after all. I still don't quite understand how it all went wrong — except to start with I didn't get there on Friday evening after all and so was unable to prepare 225 for your call.* But when I rang them on Saturday they said no one had rung, and so I presumed that either you were away, or else had been unable to make it. I really do apologize for all the muddle — when I come to think of it perhaps it was rather a stupid arrangement, but it was all I could think of at the time. It was a great shame that I couldn't see you — I havn't for simply ages.

The next I'm going to Oxford is the last week-end in April, so you must write and let me know in good time whether I might be able to see you then. As you may have noticed, I have now changed my digs, and my present room is a hundred percent nicer than the old one. I don't know if you heard about the vile dark little place I was forced to live in for so many months, but when the spring weather started coming I decided I simply could not endure waking up and wondering whether it was the middle of the night any more. Luckily Olly happened to glance through her physiotherapy journal quite by chance one day — usually it gets thrust away and never opened.

---

* On a visit to Oxford, Jane intended to meet Susan Cary, who was to call and leave a message at Jane's old boarding house at 225 Woodstock Road.

And she saw that a physio was advertising a room for £2 2s. at the above address. I went along and saw her, and there I am. Of course, I can't really afford the extra 7s a week — but my goodness, it really is worth more than that when I wake up in the morning and see lovely sky. Added to that the room looks out over the garden in the middle of the square, and there are trees, and even an odd black-bird sometimes sings — not to mention sparrows and pigeons of course! It is only very small, and right up at the top of the house. It is a huge place, and so far, having been there only two weeks, I have hardly seen any of the inhabitants, but so far as I can gather they are mostly medical students or physios. Up on my landing there are four medical students! Mummy came up to London last week-end to inspect my new abode, and she roared with laughter — fancy landing up next to four young men — she thought it was quite typi-cal. One of them has the most beautiful skull — it cost him £8 12s 6d. Apparently it would have been even more had it had its own teeth. But the poor fellow must have lost his, and had someone else's stuck in with glue. This particular chap is also madly keen on motor racing, so we have quite a bit to talk about.

I have just been watching a film called "The British Midwife". It is most interesting — it shows you everything about the birth of a baby — well, not quite everything because it doesn't start early enough!! Margaret, the girl who works here with me, can't bear watching it, but I quite like it because I think it might come in useful — you never know when you might be the only person to hand in an emergency, and to know what is supposed to happen, what is normal, would be very useful. Does midwifery come into your training at any time? I suppose it must do.

I had better tell you the sad news — unless you have heard it already from Jif. Poor old Rusty got run over two weeks ago. It was apparently instantaneous death. I was so upset when I got Mummy's letter, that I didn't think I would ever be able to go home again — well, you know how I loved him. It was a pretty grim weekend really. There would be long pauses when we all knew what we were all thinking, but nobody said a word about him. When a dog barked, or anything occurred which might remind me of Rusty everyone tried to think of something, anything, to say. Really it made it much worse. Danny burst into floods of tears when I set off back to London, but luckily not before. It is so sad, but I suppose it is just one of those things which has to happen sometime — it was better I suppose than if he had got old and blind — but that was such a long way off.

Dear Alvar Lidell* took me all round the B.B.C. the other day, and it really was most interesting. He had been round here doing a commentary for us, and afterwards, as it was about lunch time, he just took me off to lunch. I felt very grand being whisked away by him, leaving everyone else just standing — they all worship him here you see, and Stanley's secretary was mad with jealousy when I got back. He is such a very nice man. We had lunch at the canteen, and then he took me on a conducted tour of all the studios. The drama ones were most fascinating. They have all sorts of doors with locks of different kinds, latches, chains, squeaking hinges — everything. And windows of different sorts, and stairs — leading to nowhere — which are concrete down one side and wood the other — to produce the different effects you see. He showed me the room where the commentator was sitting (I forget his name) when the bomb exploded in the B.B.C. during the war. It is quite a famous story. He was reading the 9 o'clock news, and suddenly he heard a terrific bang followed by a tremendous scuffling and commotion. Clouds and clouds of muck came pouring down the ventilation holes and covered his script with a thick layer of black muck. But he saw that the red light was still glowing — i.e. that he might, with any luck, still be on the air, and so he calmly brushed the dirt off his paper, and continued to read as though absolutely nothing had happened. Alvar said that all the other commentators were green with envy — and quite sure that had they been in his place when a bomb had exploded they would never have had the presence of mind to just carry on so coolly. It was pretty good, wasn't it.

Honestly, I am getting as bad as Judy as far as music is concerned

---

* Lidell, well known as one of the great BBC "voices" during the war, was a friend of the family. He helped Jane get the job with Schofield Productions.

— though not so mad — at the moment she is trying to make a flute out of a bamboo chair leg!! Rosemary is to take her flute round, and they are going to measure up the various distances between the different holes! But I seem to spend my life in the Festival Hall — well, as much of my life as I can afford. I really do love music now, and of course, London is the ideal place to be so far as that is concerned. I have been booking tickets for months ahead, and now have about 8 — I shall probably forget when they are for. But the thing is, if you book early enough, you get very good seats very chaply — that word is supposed to be 'cheaply' — whereas if you leave it until nearer the time you are faced with paying about three times the amount for a seat which may not even be so good — some people may like being right up in the front, but I don't. It gives me great pleasure to set off by myself to the Festival Hall. I am quite in love with the place I think.

The other thing which is great fun at the moment is my philosophy class. I go to lectures once a week, and perhaps the most interesting part is the people one meets there — people of all descriptions who have all gone along for various different reasons, and have all got caught up in the swing of the course. I must admit that it is not the type of philosophy I was expecting — there is no studying the great philosophies of Plato, Spinoza, Hegel, etc. If we study any recognized philosophy at all, it is the ancient wisdom of the east — she is always quoting passages from the Upanishads and Buddha. But in the main it is a philosophy distilled from all the ancient philosophy which might help the school to grasp what it is trying to teach — the New Testament is also often quoted. I'm not at all sure that I shall go with them very far along the path they are trying to lead us. It has tremendous possibilities, but you have to really march forward with no looking back, and I'm not so sure that it is a good thing. To go so far, with one's eyes wide open — yes. But after that, I think enough is as good as a feast. But we really do have fun after the lectures. About 10 of us or more go round to one of the little coffee houses, and get down to a good old discussion about all sorts of different things, and it is most entertaining. There is one very nice man — we nicknamed him Mr. Immaculate before getting to know him, because of the way in which he dresses. He assumes a very earnest manner, and wears a beard, but there is the most delicious twinkle in his eye. He asked me round to a little party at his house the other day, but unfortunately I couldn't go.

It is now a little later on in the afternoon — which, incidentally, seems to be never ending. I simply had to go and view some prints that came in as all sorts of people had been screaming out for them all day. As a matter of fact it is quite strange having so little to do. For the past three weeks we have been working so hard that we all nearly collapsed from exhaustion at the end. I had to come in for two solid week-ends, Saturday and Sunday, and we were here almost every day for that time until 9 or 10 o'clock at night. But I don't suppose this sounds particularly impressive to you. I know how hard nurses have to work. Most people, when I tell them the odd hours we have to work, say "Well never mind, just think of all the extra overtime you are getting". To which statement the answer is easy — we don't get a penny. Then they say we are silly to do the work for nothing, but in a job like this one can't just lay down tools — there is a certain pride in the work, and we don't like to see a film go out that isn't as good as we can get it in the time.

I have decided to get another little water turtle like Jacob and install the vivarium in my new room. Later on, when I have got to know the landlady a bit better — and the woman who cleans — I may try to keep a hamster, but I couldn't have one in the room because they do make such an infernal noise with their chewing at night. Did you hear that poor little Ham died as well? And I'm sure that Pickles won't last much longer. Actually, my great desire is to have a budge,* but unless Stanley is amenable to my keeping it here during the day — or during most days — it will be out of the question — because I should never see the poor little thing otherwise.

One other thing I must tell you before I close. Uncle Eric has got a Bentley! Did you know that it was his overwhelming desire to possess one of these cars? The thought has haunted him for years, but I don't think any of us ever thought he would satisfy it. But a Harley Street specialist upon whose wife he operated had to give his up,

---

* A budgerigar.

and as he wanted it to go to a good owner, and was not particularly bothered about the price received, he let Uncle Eric have it for £4001. That, incidentally is supposed to be four hundred, and not four thousand and one! It is a 3 1/2 litre 1937 model in simply superb condition. It has really been looked after marvellously, and shines and glistens like new. Every time Eric approaches it a terrific beam spreads all over his face — he has only been the proud possessor for about 3 weeks. Apparently he rang up Daddy and asked him to drive it out to the hospital as he wasn't insured — and a very puzzled Daddy rang me to know if I knew a thing about it — he just turned up at the Birches in it the weekend before last, and kept it as a surprise. I have not yet been in it, but he collected Mummy and took her home on Sunday, the start of his holiday.

I really must stop now, because although I have attended to all the pressing work, there are one or two matters that I must clear up while I have the chance. It is very peaceful up here. Margaret is having two days of her holiday, and poor old Ted has gone to the dentist. So I am in sole charge of the upper cutting room.

Do write if you ever have a moment and let me know how you are getting on — and whether there might be anything doing at the last weekend in April.

With lots of love,
Jane

[Probably May 1956]

Darling Mummy,

I have <u>had</u> to give in my notice under force of circumstances. I have also had a letter from Clo & it really is O.K. to go out there next year — though not <u>quite</u> so early as I had hoped. However, things are nicely arranged in my mind & I <u>had</u> to leave here. Stanley has behaved very badly over the whole thing — by which I don't mean he is on bad terms with me at all — but I will explain all at the week-end. Is it really O.K. for B. to bring me down? I shall give you the £1 I should otherwise have spent on the coach — otherwise I shall not come. Don't do anything extra for B. I have decided, even more firmly than when I spoke to you on the phone, that he is no husband for me. He knows how I feel too, so he is just coming down as a kind of repayment of hospitality which I feel is due. Heaven alone knows what we shall do. I hope the Healey will be mended by then & perhaps I can have a driving lesson. I could take him onto the Swanage downs — make him climb!! Any suggestions welcomed.

If you want to know any reasons for my never marrying him I can let you have a string — e.g's television, too settled, too fond of creature comforts, doesn't like books etc., doesn't stand up straight, too fat, not handsom — I could go on for ever, but it boils down to the fact that I just don't love him one bit, so that's that — AND he knows it.

Will it be O.K. if Margaret* & I come on the 15th — or 16th June or something? We are as excited as kids over the idea of sleeping in the hut — but don't <u>DARE</u> to tidy it till we come — that is half the fun. I'm so looking forward to living at home again, especially in the summer. Can you get jobs for us or not? Because soon they will all be booked up. I don't mind how hard I work. But if you <u>can't</u> you see, we <u>MUST</u> get something arranged. They are advertising for living in waitresses all over the place at the moment, but soon we shall have no chance at all. I am very sorry to thrust this on you — I can pop along for interviews this week-end if you hear of anywhere — I will give you a commission!! Must do some work. All news later.

Tons of love,

Jane

10, Durley Chine Road,

Bournemouth.

[August or September, 1956]

My dear Sally,

Thanks for the post card, & I'm glad you had such a lovely time on your holiday. I am working myself absolutely to the bone. It really is dreadful during the peak of the season. We only get one day off a fortnight, two afternoon teas & one late night per week. I hon-

---

* Margaret Arthur worked as a receptionist at Schofield Productions.

estly can't remember whether I last wrote to you before or after I got my job at the Hawthorns — I feel it was after. However, I am still there, with a huge station of my own now, and apart from the ghastly rush of some meals — more especially lunch when we are all up the wall — it is quite entertaining. I have met some really delightful people — one television producer who is a darling — unfortunately engaged. His engagement to this girl — who joined him during his second week — is a really romantic and wonderful story which I must tell you when you come & see us — I presume you <u>are</u> coming in the fairly near future? There was also a very nice man from Halifax who unfortunately fell for me & insisted on coming down for another week. I had a nice time with him but it is a bit exhausting being proposed to every few minutes. At the moment I have two delightful families — one husband writes children's books, the other one act plays. No 1 has a son of 17 or so who will be incredibly handsom when about 25. No 2 has a daughter of about the same age — very pretty. No 1 has a girl of about 8: No 2 has a son of about 10. Both wives are charming — No 2's has long chats with me about Kenya. Last week I had a party of 7 to look after — 4 children. That really was exhausting & I had them for a fortnight. But they were very charming. Pop was a doctor. They gave me £3.

Brian came to stay with Dora a few week ends ago & it was rather awkward as we both knew it was all over between us. However, we had a dinner party & invited another chap I have met called Douglas, & it all passed off fairly well. B took me out to tea both days, & of all places he suggested Wimborne — I told you Hans was staying there for 2 weeks, didn't I? My heart was leaping around all over the place — I thought I should literally pass out or something equally daft if I should see him. Brian kept asking what was the matter. However, all was well.

Since writing the last word I have fallen sound asleep. I was lying in the garden in the first hot sun we've had for about a fortnight. Add this to the fact that I've been to bed at about 1.30 for the last week & you will realize the reason for my slumbering. I should still be asleep but Audrey arrived with a nice little tea on a tray.

Last week end dear Horst arrived for a night from Oxford — he leaves for Germany on Tuesday & will not be returning — anyway for 8 years. He left here very sadly. All the family seem to think he is quite devastating — even Danny thinks so when she isn't frantically asserting that he's a German. But he simply doesn't appeal to me in the slightest.

One very sad thing has happened. The gales blew down the silver birch — the one between this garden & the bottom. Uncle Eric actually saw it snap off. It went right across the lawn and was like a living tent of green. Poor tree. I almost cried over it. . . .

Do come soon — absolutely any time will do. I won't write any more just at present because I must write to Brian & return the cheque for £40 which arrived this morning towards my passage!!!

Lots of love to you and all your family,

Jane

10, Durley Chine Road,
Bournemouth.
[October or November 1956]

My dear Sally,

Thanks for the letter — do come here at half-term. I am now not sailing until after Christmas because the family were so woebegone at the idea of my going just before. I finished at the Hawthorns on Friday and am having a well-earned holiday — so far I havn't even looked for a new job. My goodness, I don't think I've ever had such a physically strenuous summer as this. It really was hard work round there from the start to the finish, and during August & September it was most sheer unadulterated slave labour. But I have now safely got my outward & return fare with a certain amount over & above — most of which latter I have almost decided to spend on a winter coat. I have it in the room on appro. at the moment.

I certainly seem to have chosen the best time of the year for my holiday. The last few days have been really delicious and I have been having a good 'go' at the garden. You never saw such a mess as it is at the moment — though it is a little better since I started on it.

In spite of the hard work I have managed to get a good deal of fun out of my strange job, and a very great amount of amusement.

The trouble is that I just can't remember when I last wrote to you. Did I mention Douglas? The boy I met at the Marine beach party? Well, whether I did or not, I have been seeing him quite often during the last two months and he is great fun — the first man of my own age I have ever liked and not got bored with. During my last week at the Hawthorns I had 8 people on a conference — at least the 4 men were — the wives were with them merely. They said one morning — "Would you like us to try and get 2 tickets for you for the reception & dance at the Pavillion tonight?" I thought it might be rather fun so I roped old Douglas in & got him into a dinner jacket so that I could wear evening dress which was optional. And it really was fun. We were late but the people had kept two places at their table and when the refreshments came round they said ha, now it was their turn to wait on me. They were very charming. . . .

Little Poosh came over to supper the other day. She has just got back from Malaya where she was staying with her brother & his wife — & my goodness it has improved her enormously. She has quite matured now, and is a normal person to speak to. She enjoyed herself tremendously & would love to go back — but she is now caught up in the old Longham regeme (however you spell it) all over again. She wants me to go out & ride her horses sometime & now that my slaving has stopped I hope to do just that.

Gosh, I am so tired just at the moment that I can hardly focus the paper. Well no, not tired — sleepy. I used to be tired after a day at the Hawthorns. After a day of sweeping, chopping and bonfires I am that other much nicer thing — sleepy. This is further induced by my sitting right in front of a glorious fire on the floor — oh dear, it's me on the floor, not the fire of course. I've got on a funny little thing that was sent from America — it's shorts (very short!) and blouse all in one, doing up down the front. Green. The rest of the family are in winter clothes and it is rather amusing.

Later. (Next day). This morning I dashed out with great zeal to creosote the hut. Pot of creosote in one hand & brush in the other I leapt, sylph-like, onto the table. But oh, most unsylphlike was my descent when the table overbalanced. And I was covered in the horrid black stuff. Dripping and slightly hysterical I went & dripped in the yard. Mummy & Danny with exclamations of horror dashed out, stripped me, & frantically rubbed me down with bits of cloth. Just then Audrey arrived and was at first horrified to find a completely naked niece, & then furious because I fled to a bath and didn't have it on to show Olly when she came back for lunch! I laughed for some time — but my clothes, I fear, have had it.

We have now embarked on clearing the entire air raid into the out house so that it can be decorated.* As the out house floor has collapsed this is likely to become highly entertaining. I can just see Mummy staggering out with armfulls of bottling jars & hammers & disappearing through the floor. Also I am moving back to my room which was let all through the summer & everything taken out — including all bookcases etc. Think of it. I rather fear I shall not even be able to get into bed tonight. Also the scullery floor has to be painted. For all this we have despatched Danny off to Swanage for a few days. At the present rate I fear she will be back too soon.

Olly & her Douglas have been on Shell Bay in the rain all afternoon. They leap around in the sand dunes and play red Indians amongst the grasses!!

Must stop as Judy is just being driven out to the post. Luckily my hair is wet — as I washed it. Much love, & please let me know when you can come.

Love,

Jane

[March 14, 1957]

Darling Family,

It is now 4 p.m. on Thursday and I still find it difficult to believe that I am on my way to Africa. That is the thing — AFRICA. It is easy to imagine I am going for a long sea voyage, but not that names

---

* During the war, the family's standard steel air-raid shelter had been kept in a small, closetlike room. That room was ever after known as "the air raid."

like Mombasa, Nairobi, South Kinangop, Nakuru, etc., are going to become reality.

We are just going into the Bay of Biscay — and out of 365 passengers over 200 are sea sick. And that is not counting the stewards etc, a good many of whom are invisible today. The rest of my cabin are languishing in misery on their bunks, fortified slightly by Eric's pills. They had all forgotten to buy any. I havn't even thought of taking one.

But, after all, they are very nice, except for the old girl in the fur coat. The girl from Uplands is Helen Paterson — she was a form or two below me. Pam is a very pretty girl — & rather mad like me. We both went on deck last night after dinner & discussed our respective love lives while the other 3 went to bed. The remaining girl, & I'm not sure what her name is yet, is the nicest of the lot I think. She has the bunk below mine & each time my dressing gown or sheet starts falling between my bunk & the wall she pulls it down. However, I can retaliate by tickling her face with my belt, or even better, turning her air blower on & directing it into her face. So I really have the upper hand! Poor Pam succumbed in the middle of breakfast. It suddenly got very much more 'swelly' and the dining room emptied rapidly. The other two just got through lunch.

I had to move my table. It was simply ghastly last night at dinner. There was the old fur coat misery, and the other two were both foreign. One, I believe, is travelling as a sort of companion or governess to two children. No one spoke more than 4 words the whole dinner. The funny part was that the fur coat woman had made a mistake. She should have been at another table. But the man who was there at lunch time, having been temporarily put at a single table, asked at once if he could stay there. So the Head Waiter came over to W & said she could stay. All girls together he said. What great fun. I spoke to this man afterwards — he thought it was I who had made the mistake as I had not been there at lunch time. Had he known it was Fur Coat, he said, he might have elected to return to the table! However, I am now sitting with Helen & the nice girl. They are a larger table with a very charming older couple, a dear old foreign lady, and a ghastly young man with a mustache. We all took our hats off to him, however, for coming down to lunch at all. He was simply pea green. And he sat looking at his dish of fruit salad for fully 10 minutes before making a rather rapid exit. It is now so rolling about that I keep sliding off the chair which doesn't make writing any too easy.

When I really started looking round in the cabin I suddenly noticed that there were two large vases of flowers for me. One from Poosh & one from Keith. The other 3 young ones also had a rose each so it is absolute heaven in there now. I put Keith's into two — the smaller ones looked much better in a glass — & they are now on the shelf over my bed. I only hope they havn't slid off onto my bunk in this swell. Then today there was a native saying that a parcel had arrived — well, it arrived yesterday but they weren't sorted out till this morning. Some sun glasses from Keith. And I was just going to buy some, too. They are smashing ones — light as a feather, rimless, & tested in Paris by the Institute d'Optique. They really are beauties.

There is only one handsom young man so far, and I think he is married. So Pie* quite safe so far!! I have been out on deck all afternoon. I have found a favourite spot as far forward as one can get. There one gets more movement than anywhere else. Sitting there watching the waves is simply heavenly. One is right in the teeth of the wind and no one else goes there at all because it is so cold. Just under the ship the sea is dark inky blue, then it rises up a clear transparent blue green, and then it breaks in white and sky blue foam. But best of all, some of this foam is forced back under the wave from which it broke, and this spreads out under the surface like the palest blue milk, all soft and hazy at the edge. Here I had a long chat with a very handsom young waiter who told me that soon I would be able to watch the porpoises gamboling around scraping their sides against the ship. And at night all the water glows with brilliant phosphorescence and phosphorescent fish swim below the surface.

Unfortunately we stop at Las Palmas during the night so we shan't see a thing. A shame. All my letters are taken by a homeward

---

* A nickname for Keith.

bound castle vessel and posted in England. So it will be some time before you get this letter I suppose.

I feel quite absolutely helpless about thanking you all for everything. You did far, far, far too much, and spent 100% too much money. All I can say is — just wait till I come home. Thank you Jif very much for your birthday presents. The ear rings are simply sweet, and the nail things just what I need.

I must finish off this letter now as we are nearing Las Palmas and everything has to be packed by 6 o'clock. We are going ashore despite the midnight arrival. I am going with this fellow from Uganda — I don't think I've mentioned him yet. He's not a bad chap does Engineering, 26, good fun. But what is quite horrible is his name — Keith. I just couldn't believe it at first. Still, I suppose one can get used to anything.

It is a whole lot calmer now, & we have begun playing deck games — tomorrow I think there will be water in the pool.

We had a dance last night which was quite fun. There are two foul Germans aboard — I have told Dora about them at length so she can tell you. I have also told her that you will tell her any other news from this letter.

I discovered that THE sea sick pills, which really revived Pam from the dead, are the ones Charles gave me. Marzine.

I am down in the cabin just now, as up on deck or in the lounge it is impossible to get any peace. The High Commissioner of Malapin is going to give me & a boy friend a wacking great night out if I'm not married this time next year — in Malapin.

I will write a longer letter from Cape Town, but there is really no more news just now. So far, & I don't think there are any other sufferers confined to their cabins at present, this Ugandan is the only presentable young spark aboard. He's certainly full of life. The chap Helen has fixed for is tall & good looking & has knocked round the world — but he can't speak the King's English. The two chaps we saw the first day, Ginger Top & friend, are quite good fun of their type. Ginger Top made advances, but was gently laid aside, the second day. Mossy Face, the sickly young man on the table, is going out to a leper colony for 3 years.

You will be nice to poor Keith, won't you? And find the books of mine on the list to lend him. I'm sure he will like the Durrell books. I am sending him the penicillin — disguised as pen & pencil! I hope it gets through.

Honestly, the food is wonderful, & what with that, sleep, & fresh sea air, I was taken for 19 last night. So you can cease worrying. Our waiter, Mick (and a real darling — big & handsom) says it is the best ship for fruit he has ever been on. We live on it.

I miss you all a lot if I let my mind dwell on it too much, but in these circumstances it is best not to.

Thank you again, 10,000 thousand times for <u>everything.</u>

Tons & tons of love,

Jane

<u>P.S.</u> After spending hours wrapping up that <u>blasted</u> penicillin for Keith, and wondering what on earth to say it was for customs, one can't post it. The only way is to try to do it from beyond the dock area in Las Palmas — unlikely to work at 3 in the morning even if we <u>do</u> go ashore — or else from Cape Town. If you could get some more it would save a lot of bother — it seems a little silly to spend pounds doing it from the Cape. But I should be very pleased if you could tell Keith I have sealed his letter up, telling him I was sending it disguised as pen & pencil.

I have just saved the cabin from a flood as the gale turned into a squall & it is absolutely pelting.

Romantic music is being played over the speakers, rain is falling into a rough grey sea from a leaden grey sky and people are now talking or frantically writing last minute letters. I must end, so again good bye, God Bless, many thanks, and I'll post to you again from the Cape. By then there will be porpoises & tropical sunsets to describe I hope.

Tons & tons & tons of love,

Jane.

<u>Sunday.</u> P.S. The girls are going to put on the zip!! It is now blowing up a gale again, & the sea far from calm. I went to the service this morning.

3

༺ ༺ ༺

KENYA COLONY
1957–1958

I think that during those weeks at Olduvai Dr. Leakey realized
that my interest in animals was not merely a passing one.
— *My Friends the Wild Chimpanzees*

THE *KENYA CASTLE* docked in the port of Mombasa at dawn
on April 2, 1957. The young Englishwoman cleared customs
by noon and soon was rolling upcountry on the train to Nairobi station, arriving on April 3 — her twenty-third birthday — to
be met by Clo Mange, Clo's father Roland ("Papa"), and a friend,
Tony. They drove north out of Nairobi, climbing higher and higher
on a rough dirt road into the Kinangop (also known as the White
Highlands), turning onto the South Kinangop Road and stopping at
last, not far from the tiny trading center of Naivasha, at Greystones,
the Mange family farm.

So began Miss Jane Goodall's African life. From her arrival in
April 1957 to her departure on December 1, 1958, her stay lasted
some twenty months, primarily though not entirely within the bor-
ders of Kenya Colony. Those months were exciting but chaotic. She
lived in more than a half dozen places: the Mange family farm, a
hostel on Kirk Road in Nairobi, the flat of an acquaintance (Gillian
Garret) in the Kinangop, the Leakey camp at Olduvai Gorge in
Tanganyika, a room in the women's halls of Nairobi Technical Institute in Nairobi, the Leakey home in the Langata area outside of
Nairobi, the house of a friend (Jean Hyde) in Langata, and finally,
starting in April 1958, her own apartment in staff housing (the Mu-

seum Flats) behind the Coryndon Museum in Nairobi. The latter residence she shared with her friend Sally Cary, who came out for an extended visit in late April of 1958, and then also with her mother, who arrived in September of that year.

Jane was socially active as well. She flirted regularly, was courted frequently, pestered often, proposed to at least once, and fell in love (or into a serious relationship) once. She also met her life's mentor, Dr. Louis S. B. Leakey, and, without fully noticing it herself, moved from one social circle to a second. Her first two or three months were spent within the privileged orbit of the White Highlands set. The currency of this group was horses — the breeding, racing, and riding of them — and Jane quickly shone as a superb horsewoman. Soon after meeting Louis Leakey, though, her attention shifted. She found some excellent and loyal friends among the museum staff — including entomologist Robert Carcasson, mammal expert Derek Fleetwood, ornithologist John Williams, technician Norman Mitton, and accountant Gerry Hillings — and by September of 1957 was becoming involved in an extended if stormy affair with Brian Herne, the son of a camp manager at Ngorongoro Crater in Tanganyika. Brian and Jane shared a love of adventure, animals, and wilderness, and with Brian and his family and friends she regularly explored the wilds of the Serengeti — as well as of Nairobi, where they danced, went to parties, frequented nightclubs, and in general behaved like young people of high spirits and great energy. The most serious problem with that relationship may have been Brian's love of hunting and his plan to become a "white hunter."

Her first meeting with the legendary anthropologist Louis Leakey happened simply. After Jane had been in Kenya for less than two months, Clo mentioned Leakey to her. "If you are interested in animals," so the words were later recalled, "you must meet Louis Leakey."* According to the second letter in this chapter, written on

---

* *My Life with the Chimpanzees* (1988), p. 35. Whether it was Clo or her father who said this, how the introduction actually happened, and other details are not perfectly clear. The letter of May 30 probably recalls the story as accurately as we can hope for.

May 30, Jane telephoned Dr. Leakey at his curator's office at the Coryndon Museum, told him "how interested in animals I was," and was invited to visit him at the Coryndon at ten o'clock on Friday, May 24. The meeting was momentous, arguably the single most important event of Jane's Kenya Colony experience.

Louis Seymour Bazett Leakey was born at Kabete Mission Station, Kenya, on August 7, 1903; he died on October 1, 1972. The son of one of Kenya's pioneering missionaries, he was raised in unusual circumstances. His playmates were members of the Kikuyu tribe, and Louis grew up fluent in their language, adept at their games and hunting skills, and entirely knowledgeable about Kikuyu culture. In early adolescence he underwent the secret Kikuyu circumcision rites, marking his manhood as an African and his entrance into the tribe. He was, as he put it in one early autobiography, a "white African."* Louis combined that unique experience with immense personal energy and considerable intellectual brilliance, graduating from Cambridge University in 1926 with top honors in anthropology and archaeology. He soon became convinced that, contrary to the prevailing wisdom of the time, *Homo sapiens* had first appeared in Africa, and he set as his life's work the uncovering of human origins on that continent. In that task he and his second wife, Mary, were supremely successful, digging up at various sites in East Africa tens of thousands of ancient stone tools and thousands of fossilized bones and skull fragments from hundreds of human precursors.

When Jane walked into the Coryndon in May 1957, Louis had already established his reputation as a great, if eccentric, anthropologist. He and Mary had already begun their pioneering excavations at Olduvai Gorge. And he had already begun speculating that long-term studies of humankind's closest living relatives, the great apes, would prove extremely useful for our understanding of how ancestral humans lived. Of the four great ape species still living, three — chimpanzees, gorillas, and bonobos — could be found in African forests. As early as 1945, in fact, Louis had been aware of the chim-

---

* He used the phrase as the title of a memoir published in 1937.

panzees living in a protected patch of forest on the eastern edge of Lake Tanganyika. According to Leakey biographer Virginia Morell, he may have tried to send a young man out there to study the chimpanzees around 1946.* A decade later Louis once again attempted to launch an ape research project, this time with mountain gorillas. He sent his secretary at that time, Rosalie Osborn, out to Mount Muhavura, Uganda, for four months to locate and observe the apes. Four months, unfortunately, was simply not enough time to produce significant results, and in January 1957 Osborn returned to England.†

By the spring of that year Louis was still actively pursuing the ape-studies idea, and thus the appearance on Friday morning, May 24, of an eager young Englishwoman with steady gaze and hazel eyes was fortuitous — for her and for him. As Louis soon recognized, Jane Goodall was superbly suited to and ready for the task, sharing with him a powerful fascination with animals and nature, an interest in paleoanthropology, and exceptional energy, endurance, and fortitude. Her lack of formal training was a plus, in his view, since she could begin her studies without any foolish academic preconceptions. That she was a woman was also positive, Louis believed, since a woman would be less threatening to a male-dominated ape community.‡

The latter theory was reasonable, but Louis also had a less rational fondness for women, particularly young and pretty ones, and his reputation for informal relationships with his young protégées had been well earned by then, as had Mary's burning jealousy. Jane started to hear the gossip only after she began work as a secretary at the museum in September, but it appears that her secretarial prede-

---

* See Virginia Morell, *Ancestral Passions: The Leakey Family and the Quest for Humankind's Beginnings* (New York: Simon & Schuster, 1995), p. 239.

† Osborn did succeed in tracking gorillas and making preliminary observations; her work was extended by a subsequent volunteer, Jill Donisthorpe (Morell, *Ancestral Passions*, p. 246).

‡ Male dominance is certainly a characteristic of chimpanzee and gorilla society. Among bonobos, males and females are codominant. That is to say, dominance is more a matter of social class (who your family and friends are) than of sex and politics (who your friends and allies are).

cessor, Rosalie Osborn, had nearly become, in the words of Richard Leakey, "the third Mrs. Leakey."* Thus Jane's description of Louis's special concerns about how Mary might react to his new candidate for secretary, as we read in the letter of July 3 or 4, 1957, takes on added significance. And Mary's heavy drinking and disturbingly erratic behavior during the safari to Olduvai (as recorded in the long letter written in late July) become more comprehensible. Quarrels in the Leakey household had become increasingly noisy and violent after 1955, when Mary began to realize that Louis's affair with Rosalie was "quite serious."†

Leakey recognized Jane Goodall as an extraordinarily promising candidate to undertake a study of apes. At the same time, his motivations in dangling that tantalizing opportunity to "study a strange tribe of chimpanzees" (mentioned in the letter fragment from early September 1957) must have been more complex than she first reckoned. When Louis began to assert his romantic interest directly (noted in the October 1957 letter), Jane's candid reaction was of alarm and disgust. She resisted directly, emphatically, and regularly until he finally gave up. The process took longer and was more complex than will appear in these pages, but over time Louis's relationship with Jane shifted satisfactorily from suitor to mentor.

A generally understated background to this group of letters includes Kenyan colonial politics, particularly the Mau Mau rebellion, the Emergency, and the independence movement. More than forty different tribal groups lived within the region called Kenya during this period, of whom the most powerful, rapidly growing, and politically attuned were the Kikuyu. By the late 1940s the tribe included some 1 million people — compared to around 32,000 white settlers — and they had particular reason for resentment, since from the earliest days of its colonial administration the British had reserved Kikuyu land in the highlands north of Nairobi for white settlers only. In the 1940s a radical group among the tribe created the Mau Mau, a movement that at first focused its energies

---

* As quoted in Morell, *Ancestral Passions,* p. 244.
† Ibid., p. 245.

on a secret, compelling loyalty oath. That oath eventually included a sworn agreement to kill Europeans, and soon it was being administered forcibly to any resisting Kikuyu. After several assassinations of prominent Kikuyu moderates, as well as a series of chilling attacks on whites living in isolated farmhouses near the forests of Mount Kenya and the Aberdares, in October 1952 the British colonial government declared the Emergency. That declaration justified invoking supraconstitutional powers and rounding up many alleged leaders of the Mau Mau, the best known of whom was Jomo Kenyatta.*

At the start of the Emergency, some 15,000 Mau Mau militants fled Nairobi and the Kikuyu tribal lands and formed a guerrilla army in the Aberdares, continuing from their hidden camps a reign of terror. The great majority of the victims were Africans who opposed the movement. Comparatively few European civilians were killed — perhaps fewer than three dozen altogether — but those murders were unusually brutal and certainly horrifying to the colony's whites. Among the white victims were Louis Leakey's cousin Gray Leakey and his wife, Mary. A gang of Mau Mau guerrillas broke into their farmhouse, strangled Mary as her elderly husband watched, then dragged him into the forest and buried him alive.

As both a prominent white and a distinguished Kikuyu moderate, Louis Leakey was a prime target for the Mau Mau. His sympathies for Kikuyu land claims were well known, but he could never have been sympathetic to the brutal and often bizarre methods of the Mau Mau. He publicized his vehement opposition to that movement in both deed and word — including the books *Mau Mau and the Kikuyu* (1952) and *Defeating Mau Mau* (1954) — and in return he received death threats during the Emergency. By the time Jane arrived in Kenya Colony, though, the Mau Mau rebellion had been crushed. The final significant leader among the forest guerrilla army, Dedan Kimathi, was captured in October 1956 and hanged on February 18, 1957. So the "emergency" was actually over by the

---

* Sources include Morell, *Ancestral Passions,* pp. 163–74, and Nicolas Best, *Happy Valley: The Story of the English in Kenya* (London: Martin Secker & Warburg, 1979), pp. 172–203.

spring of 1957, though officially the Emergency did not end until January 1960.

The penultimate letter in this sequence treats another subject: Jane's menagerie. This collection began within the first or second week after her arrival with the purchase of Levi, the bush baby, at a pet shop in Nairobi. Levi accompanied Jane to work at her first job, at the Nairobi engineering firm of W. & C. French, and then, starting in September, her second job, at the Coryndon Museum, where he usually slept curled up inside a large gourd in Louis's office. Later in the year Louis helped Jane set up a fish tank in her room at Nairobi Technical Institute; around the same time Brian Herne brought her an orphaned bat-eared fox, Chimba, from the Serengeti. Chimba, mentioned briefly in the letter of February 1958, was stoned to death by some ignorant passers-by in March. Then came Kombo, a vervet monkey; Kip, a mongoose; Tana, a cocker spaniel puppy; Nanki Poo, a Siamese cat; and eventually Boozy, a large bush baby; Dinkie, a hedgehog; Lettuce, another monkey; Mrs. Kip, another mongoose; and various other visiting critters, including snakes, spiders, a rat, and another dog or two — all living at one time or another in Jane's apartment at the Museum Flats. "But can you imagine," she asks in the letter of June 1958, "how paradisical (if that is the correct word?) it is for me having all these animals round?"

Years later Jane Goodall concluded that people should not take exotic animals as pets. "It is almost never a good thing," she noted in her autobiography for young readers, "to keep wild animals as pets. They are adapted to live in the wild. They can't cope with human ways as our dogs and cats can."* In point of fact, the Museum Flats menagerie seems to have been both delightfully amusing and mildly distressing. It was a personal zoo, a hothouse wilderness of sorts created by someone who intuitively, passionately, and obsessively intended to live "among the wild animals" but had not yet figured out quite how to do so.

Jane's mother came to visit in September 1958, bunking in with

---

* *My Life with the Chimpanzees,* pp. 43, 44.

Sally, Jane, and the menagerie at the Museum Flats. By the end of the year Jane, preparing to return home, had released some of her animals and found new homes for others. Only Kip and Boozy were sent on to England. In early December, possibly the 1st, Jane and Vanne sailed on the S.S. *Kenya* out of Mombasa north through the Suez Canal, arriving back at the Birches in time for Christmas. Sally stayed in Nairobi a few weeks longer. And Louis S. B. Leakey, now Jane's fatherly friend and mentor, worked diligently to find a sponsor who would enable her to live truly among wild animals.

*   *   *   *

[Around April 15, 1957]
Most Darling Family, and, in particular, Mummy, Danny, Olly, Audrey, Jif and Pickles,

Hail, one and all! Also, with a capitol HAIL, most beloved Rixy, greetings. (Sorry, I'm feeling rather mad!) Quite honestly. I really do simply adore Kenya. It is so wild, uncultivated, primitive, mad, exciting, unpredictable. It is also slightly degrading in its effect on some rather weak characters, but on the whole I am living in the Africa I have always longed for, always felt stirring in my blood.

Thank you for your letter Mummy which arrived yesterday. I was so terribly sorry about the exam again being a flop.* It's such a shame. However, they always say third time lucky so we'll all cross our fingers for the next shot.

Since last writing I have been having a very gay time — also the rains have started which does rather mean the <u>end</u> of a gay time. Now, I must apologize for the pencil, but Clo & I are baby minding for a charming couple — he is Danish & she Swiss. They have 4 small boys, the eldest about 5 — & there is another due in June. It is a lovely house, a beautiful garden, heavenly orchard — but no ink! So I hope you can read the pencil. We have to stay here the night as it is quite in the cards that they will get stuck on the way back from Nairobi — we did last night. It is rather a hoot — Tony is busily falling in love with me! Clo is quite fed up with him — in fact he

---

* Judy was auditioning for admission to the Guildhall School of Music.

never was in love with her — so she is thrilled. She couldn't go into Nairobi with him yesterday so I went — he said I was easily the nicest girl he'd met in Kenya & that the evening was by far & away the best he'd had during his year out here. He is going home on 9th May for 3 months & suggested, Mummy, that he should meet you in London to tell you how I was & how I was getting on. Also Clo is very keen to borrow "My First Two Thousand Years" and the two books of Prof. C. S. Lewis — 'Out of the Silent Planet' & "Voyage to Venus" — not the other one. So Tony can bring them out when he comes.

On Friday Ivor* had booked 4 seats for "The King & I." Clo, I, himself & his son, Hugo. Ivor, as I may have told you, has pots of lolly and a Merc. We set off, Ivor, Clo & I, at 9.30. . . . It was full moon & Clo told Ivor & Hugo how I went moon mad & worshipped arum lilies at midnight. So I said it was quite true & that if I didn't have the lily to worship I pretended my partner was one! So it was all very gay & jolly & Hugo was asking for tips on looking Arum-like. Then, quite suddenly, the engine stopped. Ivor & Hugo disappeared under the bonnet & were joined by an Indian. Ivor was busily issuing instructions to them both to suck different tubes & poor Hugo kept getting mouthfuls. In the end Hugo was sent on into Nairobi to fetch a breakdown lorry. We coasted downhill for a few miles before reaching the escarpment & then came to a woebegone halt. A Land Rover stopped & out got one of the chaps who works for W. & C. French.† He practically took the car to pieces & got old Ivor sucking petrol! He is very very handsome & Clo & I sat in the car admiring his bottom & feeling sorry for him because he was getting filthy & oily & we knew he was on the way to Nairobi to meet his girl friend. He was very much your type of masculine beauty Mummy — like the boy from the Eagle Hotel you fell for. He pulled the whole engine out & when he put it back it was 30% worse! So we then — Clo & I — stopped a lorry for a tow rope — Hugo had been gone about 5 hours by then. We got a rope &

---

* Ivor Yorke-Davis was a Mange family friend and neighbor.
† Jane started work at the engineering firm W. & C. French about three weeks after this event.

started off — me & the bottom man in his Land Rover & Clo & Ivor in the Merc. After a few miles we met Hugo — & had a ghastly trip — through pouring rain, thick fog, & clouds of huge flying ants into Nairobi. Our windscreen was half the time inches thick in red mud turned up by the lorry. . . .

We had to get up [the next morning] at 11.30 as some people came to see one of the horses which Clo wants to sell. We have been schooling her madly in the intervals between our gallivanting & the heaven's downpouring. The silly clots arrived in a real torrential cloudburst & could only see the horse in the stable. But they liked her & are coming again to ride her — which gives us longer to school & is therefore good. We are embarking on a 2nd youngster next week. It is absolute bliss riding here. Shoes are unheard of as one never meets a tarmac road — there is only one in Kenya!

When these people had gone we were invaded by 5 people from the Belgian Congo — all down for a meeting of the Pyrethrum Board — of which Clo's father is a member. This pyrethrum is a white plant for insecticide — grown by everyone on the Kinangop. The plan is that we should all go to the Belgian Congo in September — smashing if it comes off. And then after riding all afternoon, in the evening we went round to some charming people for dinner. They had a new record player — and a Hi-Fi speaker. Reproduction was just about 100% & we had a marvellous evening — Grieg Piano Concerto, Beethoven, Sibelius & some lovely popular stuff. They also had a projector & screen where we saw some marvellous colour slides of Big Game. . . .

It is evening at the moment & Clo & I are collapsed in exhausted heaps in front of the fire having worn ourselves out by playing with the children — I gave them all piggy backs, bucking, and started swinging them round by the hands & various other energetic tricks. They are now silent in their beds & we are just going off to ours. Ivor came this afternoon & asked Clo when she would like him to divorce his wife! So Clo said, Never & he said that if he died it would be her fault! What a thing to say.

When Tony & I were driving back last night it was ghastly —

thick fog & blinding sheets of rain. We had to stop several times & never thought we'd make it. We managed to get nearly up to the house & then got well & truly stuck. Tony had said we'd be back at 11 & it was only 12 — but Mrs. M was in a real state — said she felt responsible for me & all that. Tony, of course, had to stay the night & in the morning the old man was simply livid — in one of his real rages. Poor old Tony. I doubt if he will turn up again for some time now!

This really will make you think I'm daft. When we were in Nairobi — Clo & I & Tony — Clo & I went into the pet shop — & I saw some bush babies. Oh, they are such darlings. I simply had to keep the one she showed me — £4!!! But he was <u>so</u> sweet. Only about 2 months, hardly weaned. Everyone said he was too young & that the altitude of the South K would kill him. But he has a wonderful appetite & is doing fine. I have called him Levi, & will send a photo soon. He already takes flying leaps onto me from any strange place, & clings with his tiny hands. They have teeny-weeny nails.* He really plays with me, hiding behind cushions & leaping out at one's hand. He loves sleeping under my jersey. Clo & I have made him a sweet little cage.

Oh yes, I have seen some giraffe!! Very near the edge of the road — one was in the road & walked away in a most condescending & stately fashion. They are even taller and more impressive than I had imagined.

I must tell you one other thing. I have found a most romantic lover. Every night he wakes me up, very gently, at about 2.30. He then creeps into my bed and makes love to me until I want to go to sleep again. I'll tell you more about him later — but I feel Dora would appreciate this. Clo <u>is</u> very jealous about him because formerly he was her beau.

<u>Later.</u> We are now in Nairobi. Papa† is in a foul mood & has gone off with the car leaving us to cart mounds of shopping in the sweltering heat. I have an interview with the French branch manager af-

---

* Levi was *Galago senegalensis,* a lesser galago or lesser bush baby, a nocturnal prosimian (primate) widely distributed in Africa.
† Clo's father.

ter lunch,* but I think I am plumping for a very well paid job — up country at Kitale as by doing this I can save up more money in 3 or 4 months than I could in 6 months living in this very costly city of Nairobi.

I must stop now. Clo is discussing rabbit illnesses in a Veterinary store & I am finishing this at a table in the corner. I will write again soon & let you know about jobs, etc. And, to relieve your minds as to the propriety of my conduct in Kenya — my midnight lover is Patch — the dog. He has firmly adopted me — & I like him best.

Tons of love to <u>everyone,</u>

Jane.

P.S. You really shouldn't send me anything for my birthday, but if you do send me something, I do need, rather much, a dark coloured pullover — you know, a thing with long sleeves & v neck — well, any sort of neck, but a cheap sort of thing to muck around in & that won't get so dirty as my white one does. But I would much rather you didn't send anything at all. Honestly I would.

P.O. Box 30132

[May 30, 1957]

Most darling Family,

I was most upset when I kept getting letters from you saying you hadn't heard from me for months and months, because not one single week since I left home has passed without my writing home — not one week. However, now you have got them, or most of them I think, so all is well. You should have had three typed from here, this being the fourth. I can hardly believe I have been here one month already. Thank you all for your letters. I had a real feast of mail when I got here this morning — two from Clo enclosing one from you, Ma, and one from Brian. And then one from Keith, another from you, mummy, with Jif's inside. And on Monday I got your letters,

---

* W. & C. French was an English firm with a Nairobi branch. She had arranged to work for the firm before leaving England but had to have an interview with the branch manager.

Danny and Olly. So I feel very satisfied and spoilt. Keith is a conundrum — and I assure you I'm not pining for him, only you needn't tell him so!

Since I last wrote an awful lot has happened. For one thing I have had a great deal of work, now happily disposed of into various files and envelopes. Friday — when, as I believe I told you we have a bank holiday out here, only I had to work on Sat. morning and so couldn't go away — was my nicest day in Kenya. Here in Nairobi is one of the best Natural History Museums there is, with all the most up to date and modern methods of showing and arrangements, etc. The Curator, who is responsible for all this, is a man called Dr. Leakey. He is the expert on the Kikuyu tribe, being himself a first grade initiated elder of the tribe amongst whom he was brought up. Despite the fact that in the emergency they buried his brother* alive as a blood sacrifice, he still thinks they are the best tribe in Kenya. He is also considered to be the authority on most types of African animal — he is about 60 incidentally. Anyway, Clo told me about him, as they had taken an Aard Wolf to the museum to be stuffed — for the museum, not them! She promised to introduce me, having met him on one or two occasions, but of course, she didn't. So I rang up and asked to speak to him, told him how interested in animals I was, and left the rest to him. He immediately suggested I should go there on the Friday morning, at 10 o'clock — which I did. And for the whole morning he took me round the museum, pointing out why one species of antelope had its head set on at a particular angle, or one type of pig had horny developments in one place and another sort in another. He showed me all the snakes, about which I was naturally very interested. He has a snake park in his garden, and I am going there to see them. He told me about experiments they are carrying out on the lung fish, and how these remarkable creatures have been proved able to remain in their dried mud holes without a drop of water or a bite to eat for — you just couldn't guess — 3 whole years!!!!! They were still alive, but very weak, and Dr. Leakey decided it wasn't fair to try and make them survive longer. At first

---

* Gray Leakey was his father's brother's son.

he dried them up for one year — most people thought they could only last out the dry season at that time. They were full of energy and very lively when water was added. So, after a few good meals they dried them out again, and left them for two years at the end of which they were still lively, and a little more hungry. So then they were left for a further three years, and even survived this. Isn't it incredible. He told me so many fascinating things, that it would take me pages and pages to tell you, so I won't. We then had some coffee. Now comes the amazing thing — and it is just as amazing whether it comes off or not. You must realize that he had never seen me before, and knew absolutely nothing about me at all. Over coffee we were talking about Levi, etc., when he suddenly said "Can you ride?" So I said that I loved it, etc. etc. Then he looked at me intently and said "Are you good with dogs?" So I answered in the same vein. Then he said "Would you be interested in living at my house while my wife and I are away, exercising the horses and seeing that all the animals are all right?" It absolutely took my breath away. He has 5 horses. 3 dogs. Several bushbabies. A very rare animal from Tasmania. Tree hyrax. A 12 foot tame python. And snakes in the garden. I told him his house sounded my idea of paradise, and he said of course he couldn't definitely say whether or not this was possible, and he had to discuss it with his wife. He is taking me out into the National Game Park tomorrow evening. And I am being armed with collecting bottles etc to collect spiders for the museum as the entemologist is not frightfully keen on them. So there for you !!!!!!!!!!!! I havn't yet got over the shock. I was there yesterday evening talking to the entymologist who showed me all his most fascinating specimens. . . .

Tons & tons of love,
Your little Jane.

P.O. Box 30132.
[July 3 or 4, 1957]
Darlingest Family,
I really have slipped up badly and missed out a whole week without writing. I am so very sorry. Thanks tons for all your letters — or

rather, I have only had one from you Mummy, since I last wrote. There was a reason for my not writing. I wanted to make certain of my future plans before letting you know them as possibilities or no possibilities. In fact I have been living under great tension for a few days. But I suppose you may as well know all the details, now that it is all over.

I hadn't heard from Dr. Leakey for about a week last Friday. On the Friday I wrote to Bob* & told him I would go & stay up at the Falls during the last two weeks in July. He wanted me to go for a 10 day trip round Lake Victoria in August — which I wrote & said no to.

On Saturday I was supposed to be going for the day to Kisumu — 200 miles away — with Jim Grant — the chap with the put on Oxford accent who gave me a lift to Nakuru — remember. At 3.30 on Friday he rang to say the trip was off as he had to go to Nanenki on the Sunday, but we would meet at the New Stanley for a chat at 10.00 on Saturday. While I was talking to him & feeling most annoyed because it was by then too late to arrange to go to T. Falls (Bob having asked me to the Hunt Ball up there & me having said no because of going to Kisumu!) the telephonist (Win!)† came in with a scrap of paper — "There's another call for you on the other line". So I said goodbye to Jim, & it was Dr. Leakey. He had just that day got back from safari. He would come & collect me from French's to bring me some more chapters of his book & have a chat. I had absolutely given up any idea of safari-ing with him & was frantically thinking how best I could inveigle myself into some other expedition. I planned to ask him that evening. Well, he turned up at 4.30 in his safari waggon — a vast van with a ladder up to the flat roof where one can put a table & eat or something. He gave me 3 more chapters & then asked me if I still wanted to go with them to Olduvai if I could? Well, he said, he would talk about it to Mary that evening. If she said no at once then it was all off. If she thought

---

* Bob, who was briefly a boyfriend, lived outside Nairobi in the Thomson's Falls area. At one point he proposed marriage — and he was kind enough to take care of Levi while Jane went on safari to Olduvai.

† A telephone receptionist at W. & C. French.

it vaguely possible I must go over there on Sunday. There was a hunt for which he would try & get me a mount.

Well, you can imagine how I felt. He was going to meet me on Saturday morning to tell me which way the wind was blowing — at 8.o in the morning on his way to the museum. I felt in such a state of ghastly suspense, & yet all the time I felt sure it would fall through & almost hated him for raising my hopes again. Making a project given up once into a possibility. After tea I was sitting in my room trying to read to take my mind off my fate — which was possibly being decided as I sat there, powerless to waft the decision in either direction. Suddenly there was a knock at the door — Tony. I was in rather a vast rage with him for not having been to see you, but found he was very nearly engaged & so I forgave him.* Apparently the film was taken on the wrong exposure, so you couldn't have seen that anyway. I said I'd go out to dinner with him because he seems like an old friend & I thought there was such a lot to talk over that I might be able to stop thinking about things for a while.

We had a very pleasant evening. He really is mad, is Tony. He is madly in love with this Italian girl who is very nearly his fiancée. But when I told him I should have been going to Kisumu with Jim he told me it was just as well I wasn't because he wouldn't have liked it at all! We had a good dinner and then sat in the car & talked until about 11 o'clock. After which I went to bed & was most grateful that I should know my fate — or at any rate a part of my fate — early in the morning. I got up & had breakfast & went down to the bottom of the drive. I found a fascinating little scene amongst the grass stalks. A lady beetle was climbing up a grass stalk, purposefully followed by a prospective & hopeful husband. He caught her up & she turned round to say "hello". And then wanted to bustle on about her own concerns. He had other & more amorous ideas. But she was a woman of determination & character. She was busy, it being a Saturday morning, & very firmly told him that there was a time & place for everything. I was chuckling to myself when I looked up to see the huge safari van approaching. I put on a brave face & went to meet it. "Well, the answer is yes!" he said. "Yes to

---

* Tony, Clo's friend, had said he would visit Jane's family while he was in England.

what?" I nearly flung my arms round his neck. "Yes you can come out on Sunday, & if my wife likes you, you can come with us". He couldn't stop then, but said he was going out into the Masai reserve in the afternoon. . . .

[On Sunday morning] I had just finished grapefruit & a large helping of cornflakes when Paul* said "That wouldn't be Dr. Leakey peeping round the door would it?" And it was. Oh, he is such a darling, my Dr. Leakey. I fled out, grabbed my bag, & told him I'd just got back. He asked if I'd rather go to sleep & not go over there!!! There was a professor of anthropology just back from Oldoway Gorge, in the Land Rover & we had to go round to the museum to try & get some skulls out of their cases for him to study. But the keys were lost! How typical. And so the poor fellow — Dr. Tobias (isn't it lovely) had to be content with peering through the glass — and he had corduroy trousers & a beard!†

Dr. Leakey & I then set off for his house — 12 miles out. On the way he told me he couldn't call me Jane yet because his wife would think it dreadfully familiar. I wasn't to tell her he'd taken me in the Park. There had been a row about his last secretary because Mary (his wife) thought the secretary had been making eyes at him. I began to be petrified of meeting Mary. "She takes violent dislikes or likes to people for no reason at all" he said. And you know me & wives!

We stopped at the dukha (village shop) to buy pop for the pony club members — the Leakeys run the Pony Club. And then on to the house. I couldn't hunt because the other horse was lame, but we were going to follow in the Land Rover & I was going to ride Mary's horse home.

We got to their house & collected 2 children — aged about 7 & 8 — little boys — who were following with us. One was known as "Peanut"!‡ I was introduced to what seemed like hundreds of large bouncing Dalmatians — Mary Leakey has the champion of all

---

* A friend and fellow boarder at Kirk Road House, a hostel in Nairobi where meals were eaten communally.

† Philip Tobias was a professor of anatomy at the University of Witwatersrand.

‡ Louis and Mary had three sons, the youngest of whom, Philip, born in 1949, was nicknamed Peanut; the older boys were Richard, born in 1944, and Jonathan or Jonny, born in 1940. Jonny was the snake collector.

Kenya which is quite an achievement — that is, champion of all breeds, not just Dalmatians. Here again is a comic nick-name — "Bottom Pincher"! Actually there are 5, and two belonging to a next door neighbour. I was also introduced to the two hyrax — the twins. Then we dashed off to the meet. And there I met Mary — but only for a moment or two — a small, lean woman, with blackened teeth, a perpetual cigarette, & short wavy hair. A little distant. I had no time to judge, as the hunt moved off, whether she liked me or not. I also met Gillian Trace,* the other girl going to Oldoway. She is absolutely sweet — 19 & she looks — & behaves! — a bit like me. I liked her no end from the moment I saw her, & apparently she said to Dr. L "How did you find such a nice person" — & we'd only seen each other for 10 minutes. A mutual click.

It was wonderful fun following with Dr. L. I know Land Rovers can go where cars can't — Dr. L's goes where Land Rovers can't! No other car was able to get even to the place where hounds found — & this was a drag hunt because Dr. L wouldn't let any of his family hunt an animal. We only came up on the hunt 3 times — but that was an achievement. Speaking Kikuyu as he does we had no end of co-operation from the Africans. The sun shone — & I was so happy. We had to keep getting out & making surveys to see whether the gari† could possibly get through some quagmire or over some vast ditch. We lost the hounds right at the end & so went back to the meet — or vaguely in that direction and met them there. I mounted Mary's wicked little pony who made an exhibition by firmly walking backwards.‡ There is absolutely nothing one can do when a horse does this, but it does make one feel such a fool. It was a blissful ride home. I talked to Jonny, the son of the 1st Mrs. Leakey.§ He is 16 & the one who is dead nuts on snakes. We talked snake. There was a very nice girl — about 14 — who rides beautifully & wants to show jump. Her parents are rolling in lolly & are getting her a

---

* A friend of the Leakey family.
† Vehicle in Swahili.
‡ This was Shandy (see the letter of February 1958). Mary must have known Jane would have trouble with this retrogressive horse.
§ Actually the son of Mary, the second Mrs. Leakey.

horse from England, but she is quite unspoilt. Then another of Leakey's boys — 10 or so, another little fellow, another girl, & a friend of Jonny's over for the day. We rode back through divine country, Jonny occasionally leaping off for frogs for his snakes — he has about 30 — & the younger brother chasing butterflys. I nearly got a large furry bat!

We got back & found the others had started lunch because they were half starved. Dr. L, carving, asked if I was hungry. I said "fairly" & Mary said "That means 'starving' only she's well brought up". A good sign I thought.

After lunch I looked at the fish — 19 tanks in the house. And then the python was brought out — he is now a good 13 feet & was in a bad mood. He bit his master's arm. A Jackson's Tree Snake, harmless, & about 4 ft long was the next favourite — almost identical to look at with the deadly Boomslang, Africa's most poisonous snake. These two — the python & Jackson live in their own houses.

Then I was taken to the snake garden where Jonny, to his father's slight horror, walked barefoot amongst deadly night adders & puff adders. He is not a polite child — indeed, none of them are. They are treated rather as grown ups and a little spoilt.

As we were still snake-ing there had come an urgent phone call. 2 miles away a leopard had taken a man's Irish wolfhound. The boys* had tracked the dragged body & found it about 1/2 mile from the house. Would Dr. Leakey go & set the trap. This was because leopards are wanted in the Tsavo Park where the baboon & wild pig are getting out of hand owing to hunters practically wiping out the leopards. Two have been sent there already. So Dr. L & I leapt into the Land Rover with the two youngest boys who came with butterfly nets. First we had to collect the trap from a nearby farm. It is about 8 ft long & 4' 10" tall & wide. It is strong mesh all round, and doesn't look very heavy.

We got to the house where we were met by the dog's owner, an old boy with heart trouble, and his beefy son-in-law. 6 Africans

---

* "Boy" was commonly used at the time to denote a man, typically but not necessarily African, who worked in some comparatively menial capacity. The term was not then considered racist.

helped us with the trap & we set off into the forest. As we went over rocks, through thorn bushes, across streams, & forced our way through dense forest the trap got fairly heavy. But we were fresh. Also it was very hot. Suddenly the undergrowth became very thick & the boys told us that the dog was just ahead. So we put the trap down & Dr. L went to see the best way of getting the trap through. Great consternation — the dog was gone. And it is most unusual for a leopard to come back to his kill during the day. So the boys were sent on ahead to follow the track again. We followed more slowly behind — without the trap. Suddenly there were excited voices ahead — the boys had seen the leopard up a tree & trying to drag the dog up. It had buzzed off when they came upon the scene.

It must have been still hanging around because the son-in-law's Alsatian was looking into the forest, his hackles rising. It was really ghastly to see the great Wolfhound lying there, all its guts hanging out & two holes in his throat where the leopard must have killed him. The poor old boy was most upset. And he was such a huge dog that it took 2 Africans to drag him along the ground. So you can imagine the vast strength of the leopard.

At first Dr. L thought we would have to drag the dog back to the trap because the path was pretty impassable the way we had come. But one of the Africans thought he knew a better way. We left the old boy and his son-in-law behind. They thought I should stay there too. But no fear. We got back to the trap. 6 Africans, one an oldish man & one a little boy — & another only about 15 — [and] Dr. L & I. Honestly, I havn't worked so hard for ages, & the going was ghastly. But one thing pleased me no end. Sometimes there would be a large boulder or a very thick thorn bush to one side of the track — not really a track — simply the way we had come. Then the people on that side would push those on the other side further over to avoid the obstacle. On this occasion there was one on each side — & Dr. L pushed harder than me — since I couldn't go through, over or under a very thick spiny thorn I had to let go — & they dropped the cage. Which proved my worth. We had to put it down every 5 minutes as it was.

When we got to where the others were waiting, the young man did look a little ashamed — & helped us for the last 10 yards or so!

We set the trap, saw that it worked, and went back to the house. Dr L said "Thank you" & we two walked together, some way from the others — reward enough.

When we got back he said to Mary, "Well, she can work anyway". And on the way back he said to me "I think you've been approved". I was so, so happy. I can't tell you how happy.

After a large tea — & Dr. L. would keep leaping up & handing me things, Mary took me back — Jonny's friend had to go back to school & so I went at the same time. Before going I was introduced to the Tenrec — oh the funniest darlingest wee animal you ever saw in all your life. He is about as long as your thumb, & half of that length is nose. His head is this shape: —

A tiny weeney little eye & long long whiskers. The rest of him is a bit like a hedge hog — as yet his spines are like thin white hairs except for one or two thicker yellow ones. He runs very very fast & eats worms. He will eventually grow about the size of a hedge hog & is a relation to a shrew.

After dropping off the friend Mary said to me "I hear you might like to come with us to Olduvai". So I said I wanted . . . nothing else in the world so much. "Well" said she "I think it would be an excellent plan — providing Gillian doesn't mind". My happiness I then thought was complete. But she then suggested I should help her school her pony for jumping & go hunting on him the Sunday before we leave. Honestly, <u>no one</u> in the whole of this huge world is so lucky or so happy as me! Gosh I was happy.

I got back & went into Paul's room with him, Jack & Mike* & we heard Finlandia & I lay on the bed & still didn't feel sleepy — only wonderfully, beautifully tired.

On Monday he rang up & said "Louis here" & this gave me ridiculous satisfaction. He met me outside the hostel at lunch time & took me to the Museum — where the lunch club eat on the roof — & there we met Gillian & he told us what things we would need.

---

* Friends at Kirk Road House.

Because, my beloved family, this safari is imminent, it is almost upon me. And I am so unprepared. We start on the 16th July. I am going to the Leakeys' on the Friday evening to help get ready. Gillian has a birthday party on the Sat to which I am going. Hunting on Sun. morning. Oh, the bliss, bliss, bliss. On Monday afternoon I just couldn't keep the excitement at bay any longer. I had said to Dr. L that I couldn't believe I was really going, & he said the only reason that could possibly prevent my going now was that I should change my mind! And somehow that shook away my last fears. . . .

At lunch time yesterday — Tuesday — I met Gillian & we had a hot dog & coffee & talked. We are very alike. We both wanted to ask each other what we were going to do with our hairs — both being in the same state as regards length etc — & decided to turn ourselves very prim by tying it back — dirty greazey hair — we only get a bowl of water each per day, the nearest water being 50 miles away — looking better thus than hanging in strands if we cut it short.

We are on a dig, incidentally. We shall have to do a lot of plaster-of-paris casting. Dr. L. asked us whether we liked milk or plain chocolate — & if we wanted gin or brandy after dinner!! — I mean before. We said orange squash thank you. He wanted to know if there was anything we couldn't eat — & if we'd had our appendix out!! . . .

I am now sitting in the bathroom, which opens into the bedroom. Gillian* is asleep, but late at night is the only time I have for writing letters at the moment. Life is too full. I have a vast tome on archaeology which I am supposed to digest in less than a fortnight & I havn't even started it. And lunch times are out as I have to go into Nairobi to buy things. We actually have one bath per week! in a canvas bath. And I shall be able to write, & so will you, but I shouldn't write me more than 2 at the most because it may take ages to get to me. Letters are fetched & posted when the van goes in for water once a week — laundry is also taken in. . . .

---

* Two Gillians are mentioned in this letter: Gillian Trace, who would be going to Olduvai, and Gillian Garret, an acquaintance with whom Jane was temporarily sharing a flat.

I really think that I must go to bed now. It must be well after 12 o'clock & we have to get up at 6.30 in the morning. Also I can't afford more than 2/6 — & soon this letter will become a parcel! As it is I doubt whether it will go into an envelope.

Oh, one last thing — the nicest compliment I have ever been paid I think. I was telling Dr. L. on Sunday morning that we had watched the sun rise over the Rift Valley. He told me there was only one place in Kenya to watch the sun rise & be simply amazed by the breathtaking beauty. He has never taken any one there because, he says, people must talk when they see something beautiful — talk & ruin it. He described the beauty. And then he said "I don't know yet, but I think I am going to take you there with me one day". Wasn't it sweet.

If I'm not fixed up with Jean Hyde when I get back from Safari — I do hope I've written since I saw her? — I am going to stay with the Leakeys until we can fix the museum flat, or until I can go there — so I rather hope I can do that!!

And now, to bed. I am getting bitten, sitting here with nothing on.

Tons & tons & tons of love to you all. Good luck in your exams etc Jif. Hope you had a good holiday, O.

All my love,
Your Jane

c/o Dr. L.S.B. Leakey
c/o G. Harvey, Esq.,
Warden of Ngorangora Nat. Park,
Tanganyika Territory.
[Third to fourth week of July 1957]

Darling Family —

I simply can't believe that it is I who am writing to you from here. I don't think I've ever had such a marvelous time in my life. Just imagine. Here we are — a charming Dr. L (and he hasn't got a temper at all providing he likes you. He is never, never cross, no matter how bitchey his wife is. He is terrified of a row. But more of that later.) His wife, Mary, who can be sweet. Gillian, whom I like so much, & myself. Then there are 7 Africans* & the two dogs. Dalmatians whose correct names are Victoria & Flicker, but who are known as Toots and "Bottom Biter"! (This because he really does come up and nip one in the seat, just when you least expect it.)

We are camped right in the middle of the Serengeti Plains — no one anywhere nearer than 40 miles away, and that is the Ngorangora camp, on top of the crater rim.† The Harveys live there, & 2 more charming people it would be hard to find. Apart from them, & a few tribes of Masai, we are about 100 miles from any form of civilization.

I will go back to the beginning now, and let you know the story from the start.

We set out on the Monday morning after I wrote you that letter from Gillian's house. There was, as there always is, a certain amount of last minute shopping so we loaded everything into the Land Rover and went into Nairobi. By the time everything was in there was just a tiny space in the back for 1 person & 2 dogs. 3 sat in front & we took it in turns to go behind — Mrs L only went behind once & LSB drove, so it was mainly Gillian & I. Things were piled up all round — & the back part is twice as long — or 3 times even — as that of an ordinary Land Rover. The only place out of which one could see was the window between the back & the front compartment. We lay on a little nest of bedding rolls — with our feet in the dog baskets. The 2 dogs were really more nuisance than anything else. I didn't mind. I just lay in a muddle, sometimes on top of the dogs, sometimes underneath them, or even in between, like a

---

* The Kikuyu crew did not socialize very much with the Leakeys and their guests. Their leader was Heslon Mukiri, Louis's lifelong friend and, ultimately, scientific colleague, according to Mary Leakey in *Disclosing the Past* (New York: Doubleday, 1984), p. 57.

† The great Serengeti Plains and Ngorongoro Crater (the caldera of a long-extinct volcano, now a small, semi-isolated kingdom of wildlife) are in a general sense part of a single 15,000-square-mile ecosystem; they are, however, separately defined within legal boundaries protecting about one third that area. When this letter was written, Ngorongoro was within the eastern boundary of the Serengeti Park; today it is administered as the Ngorongoro Conservation Unit. Gordon Harvey, the warden in charge of the eastern Serengeti, lived with his wife, Edith, in a house at the extinct volcano's rim.

sandwich middle. Then we all three looked through the little window & were happy. I got the technique of sticking my head right through so that I looked out between Gillian & Mrs L, & then I could see just what was going on. Gillian didn't like being a dog pillow or eiderdown & so wasn't as well off. It was a lovely journey, the one sad thing being that we saw no big game at all — nor have we up to date. Poor LSB keeps promising me we will meet lions & rhino around every bush & all we see are tommies & dik-dik!* We stopped at a lovely hotel for lunch where the grounds were full of red head agama lizards, each proudly gazing out from his house top — a pile of stones. It was the most peaceful place. On we went, steadily climbing through Masai Reserve Country with Mount Kilimanjaro faintly visible on our right and Mount Meru in front, tall & jagged against the sky. We paused at Arusha to see if the lorry was all right. This had gone on ahead with the boys to collect some equipment. Unfortunately we let it go off ahead of us from Arusha & it went much too fast. We found a lovely place to camp but couldn't stop until we caught up with the lorry. And then, of course, we found nowhere so pleasant & it was nearly dark when we eventually stopped. We put up 2 little travelling tents — not so very small either — while Muli, the cook boy, got his fire going. We were soon sitting out under the stars — freezing cold — eating steak & kidney pudding. Gillian & I slept on mattresses in our little tent & loved it. We were woken by Muli with a pot of hot tea at about 6.30, when it was even colder. We were away as soon as breakfast was over, to start the long climb up to the rim of the Ngorangora Crater. As we climbed it got colder & colder, & we could only see a few yards in any direction because of the dense white mist. As we climbed the mountain side it was quite wonderful looking out into the swirling white clouds. The tops of trees appeared out of the dense whiteness below, strange & mysterious.

When at last we reached the famous Ngorangora Camp we got out to pick up the water trailer, which holds 200 gallons, & wait for the lorry which was following. While LSB fussed around, Mr.

---

* Tommies are Thomson's gazelles; dik-dik are small antelopes.

Harvey, the Warden, took Gillian & I to look over into the crater. We just had a glimpse of the bottom before the mist closed in again.

When the lorry did arrive it was with a broken spring. With great difficulty it was extracted & then as it couldn't be mended on the spot, LSB & Mrs L. went off to Olduvai* to get it mended, leaving Gillian & I to have the most wonderful day. As we said afterwards out of all the miles & miles we had covered, the lorry broke down at the one place where we could have chosen to spend some time. We were literally frozen stiff by this time, so Mr. Harvey took us back & sprung us on his poor wife. They were both utterly charming, & had the most delightful house & garden with a view across the mountain slopes. In the evening they told us they saw buffalo & rhino from the drawing room window. Strange that my first taste of Mango — <u>delicious</u> — should be hundreds and hundreds of miles from where it is grown!

After lunch Mr H took us in his Estates car — van rather — down the new road they are making to the floor of the crater. The present one is right round on the other side & it takes 3 hours to get from the camp to the bottom so there was not time! When the new road is finished it will take 1/2 hour. They have to pick through solid rock, the work being done by prison labour. They have been at it for 2 1/2 years & expect to finish it by the end of next year. We saw 1/2 way down & he showed us distant spots which, he assured us, were hippo, rhino, lions etc. We gazed through his very powerful binoculars, but were no wiser really! Then he took us up into the bamboo forest — along a very narrow track with the tall whispering bamboo trees on either side. Hundreds of dim buffalo tunnels led out to our main track, & he said one must be prepared to meet <u>anything.</u> Half way along we got out & walked the rest of the way — he was going to inspect the stream where the Camp's water supply came from. It was all such tremendous fun, especially going with him. The night before he had been keeping elephant away from some native shamba† & had no sleep. When he curled up for a few minutes

---

* Probably an error. Arusha would have been the likely destination for repairing a damaged vehicle part.
† Garden in Swahili.

on the floor of a store house, he felt something cold & clammy under his chin. He put on the torch & found a toad nestled there! Very Gerald Durrell-ish I thought!

We met the Leakeys as we were on our way back to the Harveys' for tea. They were in a great hurry to move on so that we could camp at a lower, slightly warmer altitude. So we leapt into the Land Rover & bade Gordon Harvey a fond farewell. (Subsequently, we both agreed that had he been a young & unmarried man we should have fought over him like cat & dog!)

After getting the spring back on it was about 5.15 & we were expecting the mist to rise at any minute. So off we went to get as far as possible while it was still light. We found a lovely place — still in the Serengeti National Park, of which Ngorangora is a part. It is a huge park, shared by Masai & animals, & one of the most famous parks in East Africa. Camping in it is not allowed except in special cases. As we drove along, Gillian & I kept thinking that this was what rich Americans paid £100 a week for doing!

Camping was again fun — but even colder. Thank goodness we didn't have to camp up at the top. The wind shrieked over the plains — which rise & fall and are covered in golden sun-baked grass and clumps of scrub & thorn trees. We heard the laughing call of a hyaena & had to put away shoes & anything leather or they may pinch it during the night. LSB had one story of when he was sleeping out in the open with one boy. He took his boots off & put them under his pillow. The boy merely unlaced his & left them on for warmth. In the middle of the night LSB was woken by a shout & in the moonlight saw a hyaena dashing off with a blanket trailing after him. He had smelt the pong-y leather, grabbed it through the blanket, & made off — the boot, being unlaced, slipping easily off its owner's foot! They never got either back!

We heard lions that night too. It was most exciting. And at dawn the next morning the red rising sun showed herds of Tommies, Grants & Eland — all right on top of us & grazing unconcerned.

The last 30 miles were tremendous as we had to make our own tracks. No one ever goes to the place where Olduvai Gorge is situated — very few people have heard of it. Unfortunately we never see many animals around here because there is no water except a very foul rhino wallow about 7 miles up the gorge from us. We did see a wild cat on the way — very rare. And the most beautiful cheeta who walked along beside the car, quite unafraid, before turning rather disgustedly from our noisy machine & bounding leisurely into the nearby thorn thicket. She was my first cheeta. We had a burst tyre at a place where a lioness has her cubs. Gillian & I explored & there were lion tracks everywhere — But unfortunately we did not see her. She was there all right because the dogs were most uneasy.

We arrived at about 11 & it took the rest of that day to organize camp. We camp at the bottom of the gorge — which runs, winding & twisting, for about 50 miles, with numerous side gorges running into the main one. The rainy season is only just over & everything is still very green. There are a lot of trees at the bottom of the gorge, which is about 3/4 mile across & roughly 30–40 feet deep. Sometimes the walls are precipitous — at all times steep. Often they are grass covered, but equally often they are composed of rock or shale.

I never, never dreamt that I would ever be out in the wilds excavating animal bones from thousands of years before. It is sometimes very hard work — we spent two solid days with pick-axes getting one of the sites ready before we could start digging. Then one uses a sheath knife until one finds a bone, after which you use a dental pick — really. You must tell Dibble! Often we are working in such hard rock — as at present — that we have to use a hammer & chisel. But digging out a perfect tooth or perfect bone is ample reward. The great aim here is to find the man who made all the tools — primitive pebble tools & the beginnings of the more evolved hand axe. So far 2 teeth have been found — 2 years ago. The day before yesterday, just as we were coming home, there was great excitement because I found what could — and still may — be a human tooth. LSB is not sure yet. It might be a female baboon. Then Mrs L found a ghastly moth eaten old femur, with no articular ends — which is almost certainly human — But with no ends it tells one nothing. It is most peeving. However, we still have a long way to go on this site, & our hopes are high. I spent one utterly fascinating day collecting minute mouse bones & teeth — LSB gives me a star for record eyes! This should amuse you as I seem to remember odd remarks about my mouse skulls at home! When a bone is <u>very</u> fragile it has to be exposed & then plastered before being taken out of the ground. To do this one first wets pieces of Bronco lav. paper & plasters them over the bone with more water. And then you mix the plaster of paris & coat the bone with strips of either plastered [illegible] or bandage, depending on its size. I can't make up my mind whether it's a good advert. for Bronco, or not!

I <u>do</u> so hope that if we find a definite piece of Man it is LSB who finds it. He is <u>so</u> sweet, so utterly adorable. Both Gillian & I adore him & would do anything for him. With his grey hair tousled & falling over his forehead & his grey eyes twinkling, he looks for all the world like a naughty little boy.

<u>Nothing</u> is too much trouble, & he is so sweet to us. He is a wonderful cook — he once did the cooking & catering for a boarding house with <u>40</u> people! There is <u>nothing</u> he can't do. Our cook, Muli, is also very good & we feed most tremendously. Tonight we had roast chicken (we brought live cockerel with us) & potatoes — think of it. Superbly cooked with stuffing & all, over a camp fire in the middle of wildest Africa! The site we are digging at present is about a mile from camp, so we cook our own mid-morning coffee & tea there, but come back for lunch. We get up at 6.0 — or 6.30. We are generally at work by 8–8.30. We have lunch at any time from 12.30–1.30. And then a very short rest time — mainly because Mary insists. Then we clean, sort & mark specimens during the hottest part of the day, & then back to the site until about 6.0.

After this Gillian & I climb the sides of the Gorge. And we can never get over the heaven of being able to wander around on the famous Serengeti Plains. Admittedly we <u>don't</u> meet lion & rhino around every bush. But we do see Gazelle and dear little dik-dik — klipspringers walking on the extreme tips of their one modified toe of each foot, jackals, mongooses, & an <u>occasional</u> snake. I am disappointed there are not more of these. I found the most adorable chameleon — LSB christened her Melone. We kept her for 2 days on a branch hung from our tent roof. But she was not really happy so we took her back & freed her. One of the things that appeals to me almost most is the fact that everyone here is the same about insects & things as me. If we see a spider or beetle while we are digging it has to be rescued & taken to safety. We all spend hours watching bees & strange flies eating off our [illegible]. And LSB knows about almost every thing. Nothing gets killed. If by some sad mischance an insect is damaged, none of us want to kill it, so LSB comes & takes it sorrowfully away from prying eyes & executes it with due regret. The atmosphere is friendly & joking & oh so pleasant — until dinner time. This should be best — but "Lovey One" or "Mary Mine" drinks brandy beforehand until she is reduced to the staggering stage. She totters up to the table, unable to focus across it, & is quite tiddly every night. She can only think of her darling dogs. She does not get jolly — just blotto. She always serves out the veg — a most hazardous occupation. One is liable to get 1/2 a bean & 6 potatoes — whilst all the cauliflower goes onto the table. Gillian & I think it tremendous fun, but we get so worked up for LSB's sake afterwards. He will do anything to avoid a row & really <u>panders</u> to her. She knows this, & plays up to it no end, while he maddens us by waiting on her hand & foot. Dear darling Louis. And all she can say a good word for is her wretched dogs.

For a solid week "Mary Mine" complained about the soup in the evening. She said Muli made it wrong. So LSB came to make it — & thickened it with milk powder. It poured out of the jug in a thick, solid sick-ey looking mess & Gillian & I thought it was foul. We discussed it afterwards. The next evening we suggested that the milk made it a little thick, so he gaily said perhaps it should have less. The point was that neither of us liked it at all — it went into lumps. That evening Mary was staggering about even more than usual, which made us giggly to start with. Then the soup was poured out — thicker than ever, & we caught each other's eye & had a hard job not to laugh. Then we caught eyes again when we were each squashing out a lump of milk powder — & we exploded. It was dreadful really. I pretended to cough & Gillian pretended she'd burnt herself on the soup. It was a hoot.

They sleep in the lorry which has two pull-down-ible bunks.

Gillian & I have a very large tent with a bathroom at the back. We only have the tiniest drop of water to wash in — & you've no idea how economical one learns to be — in 1/2 inch of water one first washes one's face, then sponges the thick layer of dust off the rest of one, & finally washes out pants or bras. So far we've had one bath in a canvas bath — really great fun. You hang out all round & only have a minute drop. In which you first rinse your hair . . . & then do masses of washing. It's great fun.

We sleep on our two beds outside under the stars. It gets pretty cold at night sometimes, & once, when it was so windy we both slept with our heads under the blankets, the jackals stole the bacon from the cupboard almost next door! Often LSB roams round at night with his torch. Once the lions roared quite close. Another time LSB & I both heard a large animal walking round — a rhino. He saw one the first morning, but when we got there it had gone.

There are thousands of ticks around here — & they all love me. I have such a reputation that when the others get a tick they ask me why I can't keep them to myself! 15 is my record after one of our walks! There are very few mosquitoes. The worst insect worry are thousands of minute flies that bite like stink. They arrive in clouds & get into one's hair & one's ears & nearly drive us quite mad. There is nothing one can do. Luckily we only get them when there is no wind — not very often.

It is very late now. Everyone is asleep — LSB is snoring in the lorry to my left. Gillian is sleeping outside to my right. I am at the entrance of our tent — literally "burning the midnight oil". I must stop now & get some sleep or I shan't feel like leaping out of bed to greet the dawn tomorrow. I have to have this ready by tomorrow evening for when the boys leave to get more water from Ngorangora, but I will try to do some more during rest time tomorrow. So I won't end now, but simply say "Goodnight" & creep into my little warm bed under the stars. Oh yes, there are scorpions here, but so far we have only seen two — one of Mary's & one of mine. Both of which were solemnly executed by the boys as their bites can keep one in bed for a day or two.

I must apologize. I have not yet thanked you Mummy, Danny &

Uncle Eric for your letters. I feel it a very great honour, Uncle E, to have had such a long letter from you all to myself. I will answer it when I get a moment. You wanted to know, Mummy, if I have changed & become a new Jane. Most certainly not! Why on earth should I? I am doing the things I have always dreamed of doing, but it is the same person doing them as dreamed of doing them — if you see what I mean. I do, very often, wonder if I am dreaming — & if not what I have done to deserve such luck. Because not only am I actually where I have always wanted to be, but ever since arriving here everything has gone right. It really is too good to be true.

Since I last wrote another day has gone by — & a really lovely day. Mrs. L was such a 'B' yesterday that Gillian & I were wild. Today she has been sweet. When we got back, very hot, at lunch time, we found our dear Mr. Harvey had arrived — with two girls who had been dumped on him for the day. The poor man was fed up with them — & I'm not surprised. One was very plain & obviously on the shelf. The other wasn't too bad — but honestly, their clothes! They were both in dresses with sandals all open showing nail varnished toes. And they had little heels, & posh handbags. I ask you! For a day on the Serengeti Plains! We took them into our 'bathroom' to wash their hands & gave them good measure. We produced 'Shekel', the little snake, from his box under our pyjamas. Then we tipped out a bowl of black! water in which we'd both washed our feet & our pants. And being canvas, when we put some water for them it was filthy because we didn't rinse the settled dirt sediment. Amongst our brushes, combs, nivea baby powder etc we casually pointed out some of my museum, emphasizing the porcupine & dik-dik dung! I am collecting dungs so as to learn them. There were some lovely skulls grinning there as well — quite probably all maggoty!

When Harvey's son, Hamish, comes out, he is coming here to do some work for a day or two. We think he is coming home for the long vacs from Oxford because he has had a sordid affair with a bar maid or something. As soon as Harvey first saw us he said he would send Hamish out to see us, & the Leakeys think he has a nice little plan that we are the answer to his prayer — we are the two girls, arriving as an answer to his distracted prayer, who will pull his son together & make him realize there are better things in life than the bar maids! So we have to be very glamorous. He is only 21, so I have given Gillian a free hand, but Mary thinks he may develop a passion for me. So they are going to have a sweep stake on the affair. All this discussion was at supper time. She was quite boozy as usual, but terribly sweet. She said she compared his "two girls" with "our two girls" & there was no comparison. Harvey himself would gladly have swapped! It is one of the highlights of camp life — pulling visitors to pieces when they're gone!

I really must stop now. We shall be up at crack of dawn tomorrow, & the water trailer leaves at 6 with the washing & mail so I must get it all ready — & it is late now as G & I have been planning an attack on poor Hamish!

This letter is most incomplete. There just isn't time to say all I want to say. But I <u>must</u> stop now, so tons & tons of love to you all, & I will send some photos — if any come out!

Tons & tons of love to you all

Jane.

Olduvai Gorge

[Around August 10, 1957]

Darling Family,

I am only going to write a little just now, but I must start this letter to tell you how marvelous it is to sit here and write in the <u>moonlight.</u> It is full moon tonight, & sleeping under it is quite glorious — knowing me & moons you can imagine the effect. Poor Gillian is quite worried! She says she feels responsible — fatal where I am concerned.

I am sitting half way up the slope leading up from our camp. All around the crickets are singing their nightly chorus — and so many different types of song it is hard to imagine. The wind, which has been very strong all day, blowing the dust into our faces, is now a gentle and caressing breeze — blowing my long tresses around in what I'm sure is a most romantic way! Gillian is in her little bed below me — beside my empty one. An owl is hooting about 1/2 mile down the gorge, and before supper we heard the weird call of the hyaena — which means His Lordship the Lion is around somewhere. I can just hear the murmur of the boys as they sit gossiping around their camp fire. The whole gorge, lit by the cold moonlight, is strange and very still. It looks so different from the hot, dry, sun bathed gorge that we know so well. It is 100 miles long altogether, & this is only a side gorge — but just now there is one little tiny speck in the vast wilderness that is "home". 4 little tents & the lorry — & the cho* (about which I will digress tomorrow, if there's time). At the moment I must stop, and after sitting up here, quite alone with the wind, the moon, the stars, the whole immense vastness of Africa and the Serengeti with the mysterious universe all around and very real, creep into my bed and build up enough energy in the minute atom that is Jane for tomorrow. And you will have to excuse the complexity & length of the preceding sentence. I am actually quite tired & it is very late, & we are getting up at 5.30 tomorrow to try & see rhino. So for now your tiny atom bids you goodnight.

* i.e. Lavatory!

[Early September 1957]
... I <u>adore</u> working for Louis! He wrote this letter for me to pop in this morning. You see what he says about me working to be a Research Assistant? Well, he is getting hold of a very wealthy man & is going to try & get enough money to create such a post for me to fill. Isn't it super! And there is the vaguest possible chance that little me <u>may</u> have the chance to go right out into the wilds of the Northern Frontier for two or 3 months to study a strange tribe of chimpanzees who may be a new species, or sub-species. That is too heavenly to even think about. He says (Louis) that it might be hard as I'm a woman & one has to get the help of the D.C.* there. So I said he was to leave that part <u>entirely</u> to me!! ...

---

* District commissioner.

P.O. Box 658,
Nairobi.
[Mid-September 1957]

Darling Mummy,

I have been going to write for the last few days, but have been waiting for a letter from at least one member of the family. Complete silence. I am writing to you particularly because it is your questions that I want to answer, and one or two things which I want to communicate to you. This is the very first moment to myself I have had since arriving at the Museum — it certainly makes a difference when one has a lot to do of the sort of thing one likes. But now we have caught up on the last two months' letters etc. and there is more time for even nicer things — Mr. Williams, the bird man is showing me about birds, teaching me the main groups, etc. Mr. Carcasson, the entomologist is helping me begin my study of spiders, Norman, the technologist is all set to teach me casting. And, naturally, Louis shows me everything! He is off to Nakuru this afternoon to give evidence at a hand writing case* — and, naturally, is taking his personal secretary with him! It should be great fun as he is going to show me a delightful sounding place called Hell's Gate on the way there, by Lake Naivasha. Then, after the case we are meeting the mayor and other high up members of Nakuru County Council to discuss the plans for making Lake Nakuru into a bird sanctuary.

Last week I had to entertain a charming Portuguese professor who came to see Louis who was out. I had to talk to him for three quarters of an hour, and at the end of it, when we had discussed art, archaeology, architecture, history, and music, he told Louis that he had had a wonderful time, that I was so interesting because I had such a wide outlook and so many interests, and he invited me out to lunch on Monday. Unfortunately he had to leave earlier than he had intended, and so wrote a charming note saying he would be delighted if I could join him for lunch in Rome!! Also he would love me to visit him in Lisbon, stay with him and his wife, and see the

---

* Handwriting analysis was one of Louis's many areas of expertise.

Museum there — the Arts Museum of which he is Curator. He studied in Oxford so we had long talks about it.

On Sunday I went out with Louis and another — and very weedy — V.I.P. seeing some of the prehistoric sites. It was a lovely day — Gamble's Cave in particular is most enchanting. They have excavated it and there are countless levels, one after the other, of all the prehistoric people who lived in the cave by the lake shore. . . .

As it is nearly lunch time and we are off after lunch, and as I want to post this before we leave, I must get down to the essentials. The rest can quite well wait until I write again to tell you all about Nakuru and the Mayor — and I am having dinner with Brian* the evening I get back.

What I am really writing about is this. You will have realized that I couldn't possibly come back before Christmas. It would not be fair to this wonderful opportunity I have to stay in this job only a few months. Dr. Leakey goes on home leave next year, probably about July, and the plan is for me to return with him. While he is there I may have to help him carry on with his fossil horse research at the Natural History Museum. As Judy will be in London too, the obvious answer is for you, Jif and me to have a flat there. But I am still jumping on past what I want to say. I have thought and thought about you coming out here. And I can't make up my mind that it would be the best way of spending the money I shall have saved up. You can still do that if you think you would love it — but would you like the heat? And what would you do while I was working? etc. etc. So I have thought of an alternative, which seems to me to be a better plan. And this is that I should meet you somewhere on the way home and we shall have one — or even two months holiday — and that will depend on whether you can save up any money too. I have worked it out that I shall need £300 for my return fare, your return fare to wherever it is and back, and the holiday. So far my thoughts have turned to Rome and possibly Venice as well, Spain — or, indeed, wherever else you would like. So would you please start

---

* Brian Herne. It appears that Jane had not yet explained to her family who Brian was.

thinking about this seriously and deciding where best you would like to go, which place or places best appeal to you — or whether you would still rather come out here. I still don't really think you would like it. Only I have been getting rather worried — a few months ago I wrote saying it was practically arranged for you to come out — since when you have heard nothing and so, naturally, will have presumed that it was just a passing fancy and one which I had then proceeded to forget just because a fascinating job came along and I was particularly happy. Although perhaps you know, really, that I am not a person like that. I hope so anyhow. So now you will please to think about it.

I am now really getting down to collecting instruments for the Mummerys* with Louis's help — I havn't ever forgotten them. Would they like a photograph of a very, very early paleolithic instrument — practically the first ever made — a type of whistle? I was hoping to get a cast, but the one here is a cast already, so that is not possible.

Lousi (sorry!) Louis has just come up and said that if you come out here you can go to his house boat on Lake Victoria for 3 weeks and I can come with you. Also he can think of lots of places up country where you could stay and I could come for weekends. I still worry about the heat. It's never hotter than a heat wave in London, but I know you and the sun. Anyway, I now leave every decision in your hand. It would be fun if you did come out — it would also be fun to meet en route for England. So please do think about it very seriously. Now I must quickly do some letters before we set out.

Tons & tons of love to all,

[Jane]

[Probably October 1957]

Darling Family,

"The cat's away"....... Not that he keeps his mice in great order when he's here, but it does mean that the work I have accumulated

---

* Family friends in England who collected old and rare musical instruments.

can stay in a pile unobserved. And it can worry about itself when he gets back and, for now, stay in obscurity. Anyway, thanks for all your letters. I had one from you, Olly, which you wrote ages and ages ago, and posted to Olduvai apparently without a stamp. So Hamish sent it on to me from there where it had arrived by sea! Anyway, thanks for it, and for the other one. I do hope that by now you have had another parcel from Hamish — I thought you and Douglas could nibble cakes off them at Sunday tea, or put out a few of the sweets from the little rustling paper bags. They are rather attractive, don't you think? Thanks also for your letters, Mummy and Danny.

My situation here is really getting more and more tricky every day. Old Louis really is infantile in his infatuation and is suggesting the most impossible things. I have absolutely no intention of getting involved with him in the ways he suggests. For example, this weekend he left for a handwriting case in Mombasa on Friday. And suggested I should meet him on the way back to see Savo National Park. But imagine my dismay when, just before leaving, he handed me a railway ticket and said he would meet the train at 12 MIDNIGHT!!! We were to camp at the entrance to the Park so that we could go in as soon as it opened in the morning! In actual FACT it would have been O.K. I know I can trust him. He's much too fond of me for any monkey business. But suppose it got round? Suppose Mary got to hear of it? And, more than all that, it is the principle of the thing that is the most important. Don't you agree? I couldn't tell him all this just before he left as the room was full of the Full Board of Trustees, whose minutes I had just been taking. He rang up yesterday, and Hillings was in the room so I had to make an excuse, saying I had flue — which was true, but it wasn't worse, as I told him, but better. I caught it from Brian last week — oh yes, there is a lot to come about this Brian who you seem to think I have not mentioned in my letters. But let me finish about this first. The Technologist, Norman, is an absolute sweetie — and he too is madly in love with me — really in love actually. He knows all about Louis — the other staff may guess, but he, because he likes me so much, knows. He is the one who made me the house outside for little Levi, and is always doing things for me. He told me, roaring with mirth, that it had gone too far when Louis came and asked <u>him</u> for mealworms (which he breeds for various technical reasons, for use in cleaning etc.) so that he (Louis) could give them to me for Levi. Norman said to me afterwards that if anyone gave me his mealworms for Levi it was going to be him! But the other Sunday morning, after I had been out late on the Saturday and was having a well needed sleep (no more getting to look like I did before leaving England thank you — my lesson was well learnt!), I was, as I say, sleeping peacefully, when I became aware of bang bang bang on the door. Eventually I shoved on my dressing gown and opened the door. A hand appeared round the corner with a red rose — a token of his love. I ask you! At 8.30 on a Sunday morning! He really does behave like a child over this — and I begin to see why Mary has taken to the brandy. The trouble is that one simply can't get annoyed with him. He is such a complete darling and so childish and means so well. But he has a horrid habit of making one feel a pig when really one knows it is for the best. For example, and this is typical, I was talking to Norman once instead of having a Kikuyu lesson with him, as I often do in the lunch hour. He was hurt. So instead of being annoyed or anything he went and hammered a lot of waterproofing over Levi's cage. You see! And then I felt quite mean. However, I have Norman on my side. It was he who took me to the station to fetch back the money.* I do feel also a bit mean about letting him know everything, but dash it all, I'm not going to have all the staff thinking I'm madly in love with Louis — it would be too sordid. . . . Forgive all this, but it is rather an important and fundamental problem I think — you will see vaguely what it is I am getting at when I tell you more about Brian — is your curiosity about Brian being aroused!

Right. I will now unwhet your curiosity and tell you about Brian from the beginning. And right away I must admit something I am ashamed of where Brian is concerned — I have judged a character wrongly from a first impression, and not only his, but those of his friends also. I don't like to do that. Mind you, I did not make a bad

---

* A refund for the ticket to Savo.

mistake — I did not take a nice person for a nasty one. I just took a negative point of view — decided that I did not particularly like a certain crowd of people who have now turned out to be the <u>nicest</u> and most sincere that I have met since arriving here — of young people that is.

So. Brian is the son of the camp manager at Ngorongoro — he was lying in plaster from head to foot when I first met him as he had been in a lorry that had gone over the edge of the escarpment there — we saw it on the way to Olduvai, when the breakdown lorry was trying to pull it up. The poor boy had both femurs jammed up into his abdomen, breaking the pelvis on both sides. He was in plaster for 4 months — should have been longer. As soon as he was out the madcap got straight into his brother's M.G. and drove to Arusha, stayed there for a week, and then came to Nairobi — still hardly able to walk more than 8 steps at a time (Incidentally it was not his fault, the accident. The lorry was being driven by an African. He was trying to change down and couldn't get into the lower gear — and the brakes went. He managed to steer it round about 8 of the sharp corners, but the slope is very steep coming down the mountain, and they were getting faster and faster. Just imagine the feeling. The African was killed). Anyway, Brian turned up at the Museum for Hamish's address — and <u>not</u> to see me. We hadn't clicked at all when we met at the Rest Camp at the Crater. But then he came to see me again, and then he asked me out. This was the occasion when I met some of his friends. An Italian couple, and a family of Afrikaans called Enough — (Eenoff). That evening I just didn't sort of get on with any of them — not even Brian very much. However, Brian persisted, and I went out with him on his own. He is a White Hunter — very young, and has an external layer of the typical hard bitten and tough white hunter about him. But when I got him on his own it was incredibly easy to get through that layer, and I began to realize that the character underneath — and by no means hidden by this external layer — is one of the very nicest I've come across out here. Loyal, honest, faithful, etc., etc. (Incidentally, I'm not saying all this prior to announcing an engagement or anything! It has just struck me that that is what it might all sound like.) Brian was only supposed to be in Nairobi for 10 days. He stayed 3 weeks or more — because of yours truly. And I went out with him quite a lot and found him nicer and nicer. Gordon — dear Gordon* — likes him very much apparently. . . .

I started [this] letter on Saturday morning. And had a funny day. Let me relate it because I had better. Just before lunch Gillian popped in to say "Jambo".† She knew that I should have been meeting Louis at Savo & wanted to know what I had said when he rang the day before. I was just telling her when we heard a familiar Land Rover (the silencer is broken). Louis! And (I regret to admit this) I quite lost my nerve & my head & obeyed blind instinct. I fled. Out through John Williams' room, through Bob Carcasson's room — before their astonished eyes — & down to Norman. My heart was literally pounding & my legs were shaking. I stayed there for 5 minutes recovering from the shock & then went up to face the music. (It all must sound incredibly stupid to you!) Anyway, he wasn't in the office but downstairs looking for me. Gillian had gone — she told me today (Monday) that she had fled so as not to answer any questions! John Williams must have got vast amusement out of the situation — he wasn't born yesterday, he has eyes, & he knows Louis. Then Louis came in. "Why did you lie to me?" & while I was telling him that the telephone is not always private both ends, he said, coldly, "You have let me down — let me down by not speaking the truth". And went. And here again I was childish & ran to dear Norman & cried just a wee bit on his shoulder & then got over it. I was just going to set off home when Louis drove up. "I've come back to apologize. I was rude & beastly & I'm sorry". So I told him he had [no] reason to be, & it was really I who needed forgiving. And we went out the lunch club gallery, raided the kitchen & had lunch together, & then he gave me a lift into Nairobi. He had bought 3 bunches of sweet peas & left them, with a letter (written on the Friday night when I should have met him) outside my door — before coming to the Museum. . . .

---

* Gordon Harvey.
† Hello.

Oh dear, there is such a lot to tell you. Next, about Mrs. Mitchel — I'm not sure of the spelling but the Scottish way. She is one of Hamish's aunts — sorry if I've told you.* She lives next door & has 3 children & is <u>sweet.</u> When Mish heard I wasn't having breakfast he said, "Oh, I'll fix you up with my Aunt". Which I took as a joke. Then I met her — at the Airport seeing Mish off — & she said "You're Jane? Well, you're coming to breakfast". It was most embarrassing but she persisted so now I have breakfast with her each morning. They are a delightful family — in return I am to baby sit for them. (Though 'Baby' is hardly correct as the youngest is 6 (Hilary), then Arnold, about 8, & Fiona who is, I should say, 9 or 10.) <u>Please</u> Mummy, will you write to her to say how kind she is, etc., etc. Please. And Louis is hurt because you havn't written before. Also, Olly, Clo was <u>most</u> upset because you never wrote to thank her for the hanky. <u>Most</u> upset. And so please will you, & if so congratulate her on winning with her mare & foal at the Royal Show. Thanks.

Last Monday — it now seems months ago because this weekend seemed <u>weeks</u> — Louis took me into the Kikuyu Reserve. And I had the most <u>wonderful</u> time. We went into a council of elders in "Chief Charles'" village, & there Louis spoke to them about the new Governmental plans for land consolidation — which are <u>wicked.</u> Then we went into Charles' house — a proper house, but small, & like a European peasant's house. Clean. We met his old mother. Her husband was a dreadful Mau Mau — former chief of the village. He is now a prisoner, & her elder son is a political one in England — he killed one of his brothers in front of her & very nearly her as well. But she is such a sweet old lady. She only spoke Kikuyu — but she says that although she knows her husband was wicked, if only he could come back to her she could die in peace, feeling God was with her. Charles' wife spoke a little English & was sweet, & their two daughters are both in London, one doing Domestic Science & the other training to be a Nurse. We had tea & sandwiches & bananas,

---

* Eve Mitchell lived in a house very near Jane's residence on Protectorate Road in Nairobi and became her good friend.

& then left them for Harry Thuku. Harry was one of Louis' boyhood friends, extremely intelligent. He began one movement & so inspired his followers that it ran away from him, as these things sometimes do. In order to convince his followers that they could gain nothing by being so wild he allowed himself to be deported to England — otherwise he would still have inspired fanatical followers. But the authorities knew he was not anti-British & have allowed him back. He now plays a very prominent role in African affairs — behind the scenes.* We were going there to meet several African V.I.P's so that Louis could discuss land consolidation, a very, very real problem just now, & incredibly tricky.

Well, his house, built himself, would have done credit to <u>any</u> middle class European, & was 50% better than most of them into the bargain. He has a lovely garden, & is starting coffee behind the house — he has 2,000 trees already. He was charming, & so were the others. There was a minister (a church one that is), the under minister for African affairs — really nice & most intelligent — a wealthy farmer (who spoke no English) & another one, looking <u>so</u> like William! — who did. And a young chap who was very good looking & most brilliant & witty. They had their talk — for 2 hours — in Kikuyu. But after that tea came in — 3 kinds of cakes, lovely china, & a little table each — and they all spoke in English for my benefit. I can't tell you how honoured I felt. I am now having Kikuyu lessons! The wife of the non-English farmer we had met beforehand. Louis had gone to his house to see him not realizing that he was going to be with Harry. She gave me 12 eggs. Wasn't it sweet?

Now, Harry's wife is at this moment in London to perfect her English so that she can better help her husband to entertain — Europeans often stay in his house you see. It would be rather nice if

---

* Harry Thuku founded the Young Kikuyu Association. In 1922, he urged his followers to protest the issuing of compulsory identity cards by the British and so was arrested. When several thousand supporters turned up at the Norfolk Hotel to protest his detention, frightened Kenyan police opened fire and killed at least twenty-five people. Thuku was exiled to the northern frontier, and his Young Kikuyu Association disintegrated — soon replaced by the more militant Kikuyu Central Association.

you went to see her, Mummy? Would you like to? If so I will send you her address & get Louis to write to her. She is called Tabitha, & very sweet according to Louis. She is going to be away for 18 months. . . .

Honestly, I <u>MUST</u> stop — though there is really more news. I will write it in another letter.

Lots & lots of love,
Jane

[November 1957]

Darlingest Family,

Thank you all for your letters — you can't imagine how eagerly I await them all. . . . I must apologize for not writing for so long. But all sorts of things have been happening, & your little Jane has scarcely had time to write letters — or even to do any washing or ironing so that she has almost been reduced to going to work in a birthday suit. . . .

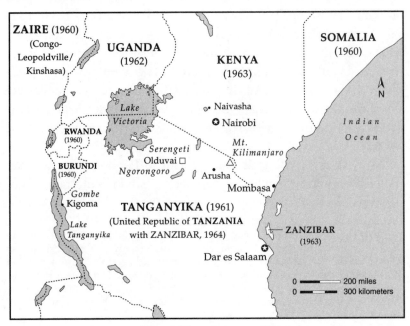

East Africa, 1957–1966

When I last wrote I think I was off to Ngorongoro. . . . Brian was meeting me in Arusha, half way, & I was lucky enough to get a lift — through Louis — with Noel Simon — a big wig, being the Director of the Wild Life Society of Kenya. He was going there for a big meeting on the Serengeti. On the way I saw one animal I'd not seen before, the beautiful Gerenuk. This is one of the antelopes, about the size — height rather — of an Alsatian, but with a very long neck. It loves to eat the leaves of trees, & by standing on its hind legs & reaching up with its long neck, it manages very well.

I was staying in Arusha that night — there are two hotels & I was in the best — a lovely room overlooking the garden. Hotels out here are not one compact building as they are in England — except in places like Nairobi. They sprawl, & usually are only one floor with gardens & courtyards in between. The New Arusha is, actually, fairly compact, but in a lot of the up country hotels a lot of the rooms are separate 'bandas' — round hut affairs with thatched roofs — very attractive.

That evening in Arusha was not particularly fascinating. We met David* & a photographer called André & had some dinner at this famous 'Beehive'. The 'Beehive' is the be-all & end all of Arusha. It is a restaurant, coffee house, bar — & even night club, all rolled into one. But there was no one very nice there that night, & we did not stay out late.

The next morning I was booked out & waiting for Brian by 8 o'clock. I chatted to a very charming American who had just got back from a Safari — photographic. His name is Mr. Pon, and I thought he was quite sweet — about 50, for your information! I havn't yet started falling for handsom rich young Yankees!

Before leaving Arusha we went out to David's farm. He is under manager of a big coffee estate, recently taken over by a large company, & managed by a very charming Italian count, Marco. He & David live there, & are just getting the place into shape, getting the house properly furnished, etc. David is getting good money for a lad of 20. David came back to Arusha with us — a 10 minute drive — & we had a cup of coffee — at the Beehive of course! — before set-

---

* David Herne, Brian's younger brother.

ting off. The drive to Ngorongoro was very hot & very dusty. The country round there is lower than Nairobi & very much more tropical. There are a lot of palm trees, sugar cane etc. around the little streams. In between are great stretches of the real true Africa — yellow grass, patches of scrub, and the still, patient green of the acacia trees. We arrived at about 2.30 & found a cold lunch all spread out & awaiting us. Mrs. Herne — her name is Peggy & so I am to call her — is simply sweet, & David senior is a charming man as well. Peggy has to work very hard up there, in comparison with other wives out here. She has no cook, and the business of looking after the camp never stops. No sooner has she got the garden ship shape than the Elephants & buffalo trample it down & break the fence. She never seems to have time to sit down — which makes their house seem much more like an English one than most of them out here.

After lunch & talking to them a bit, Brian found a spare Land Rover and we went out to look for animals. We drove well off the beaten track & saw eland & water buck. And then we drove up the track through the Bamboo Forest which I have described before — the one Gordon drove Gillian & I along the very first time I ever went to the Crater. It is the sort of place where you can feel, & even hear, animals close by, & know they are there watching you, but seldom see anything. But luck was with us in a very, very big way.

Suddenly, lying across the track ahead of us, we saw a large cat lying — a leopard. It lay there, not moving. So Brian decided to get closer to try & take a photo. We shut the windows, as their dog, Hobo, was with us, & slowly edged the car forward. He let us get fairly close — let us say the distance of the front door to the swing door, & then got up, looked at us, & disappeared into the bamboo. Did I say 'disappeared'. When we drew level with the place, there he was, one or two yards off the track, setting peering at us through one or two bamboo stems. Brian found it almost impossible to believe — he has never before met a leopard one could watch like that. He was a lovely creature — a large & dark-spotted forest leopard, and his green eyes gazed with calm & deliberate interest at Hobo moving about inside the car. After about 3 minutes he rose, and slowly padded away out of sight — we could only watch him for a few steps before he was swallowed up into the bamboos. We went on up to the water hole, stayed there about 5 minutes, & then turned back. And the most incredible thing happened. About 100 yards further down the track from the place where we had seen the leopard — we suddenly saw him in front of us again! We just glimpsed a dark form disappearing. This time, when we reached the spot, he was lying just off the track in one of the buffalo tunnels — so that we could see him even better. We watched him for another 3 or 4 minutes before he went. Do you know, only 65% of the people out here see a leopard at all. And of that 65% only about 2% have ever seen one as clearly as we did that day. It is obvious that I was intended to come out & see animals.

We saw nothing more that day. It was very unfortunate that while I was there Gordon was away — on an anti-poaching operation in the other part of the park. He left me a letter saying how sorry he was.

That evening we all were asked if we could give dinner to a V.I.P. who was arriving for 2 nights. Edith was coming to dinner anyway. And it turned out to be none other than Noel Simon. He hadn't ever been to the Crater, and as the meeting was very much connected with it, had decided to take the opportunity of coming to see it.

This proved lucky for me, as it was arranged that Brian & I should go down with him the next day — & this gave us the benefit of the very best driver & guide. Amtiye is a really nice African & he knows that Crater like the back of his hand. He also knows how to handle the Land Rover when a rhino charges etc — which makes quite a difference.

I woke up early & it was a lovely morning. So I dressed & jumped out of the window to run to the edge of the crater. This was unfortunate. When I got back I found I had created quite a scene. Poor Brian had been rudely awakened from a deep sleep, by his Mother shaking him & saying "Where's Jane? Where's Jane?" To which Brian, somewhat naturally, replied by saying how the hell should he know, he didn't have radar on me, & I was probably in the Crater. Things were calm again when I got back.

Then followed quite the most wonderful wonderful day. We saw

8 rhino. I suggested we should drive up the hill where we had lunch with Gordon that day & from where we had seen so many rhino. Sure enough we saw 3 from there. So we got Amtiye to drive down. This little hill is right at the edge of the floor of the Crater, & behind it the country is not suitable for driving — not even Land Rovers. How he got through at all I don't know, what with holes & tree stumps & fallen logs. I was up on the roof & how I stayed there I don't know. But we saw our Rhino. We were looking for the 3 of them, all together. Brian thought they were on the right, Amtiye on the left. It was me who saw them — directly behind us. One had a good long horn. They were coming straight for us — but until they got very close they didn't even know we were there. Then they suddenly snorted & tossed their heads — but were in no mood to fight. Just as they had gone we saw another, to the right, & I saw, from my elevated perch, that she had a baby. She was making for the open plains at a brisk trot — so we followed her — an incredibly bumpy journey, during which only by miracle was the car saved from overturning. But we got out at last & soon came up with Mamma & infant. She charged us, twice, & baby thought it was all a huge joke, capering round mum & making her more nervous than ever. Gosh, he was a darling.

The herds of zebra & wildebeest were quite fantastic in their numbers — it really gave one an odd feeling to be amongst so many animals all at once. And I then saw another animal new to me — the wild dog. These [are] pretty animals, a little like Alsatians. They hunt in large packs, & their method of hunting is very cruel. They have tremendous staying power & stamina & they just run after a poor animal until it tires & then close in, snapping off chunks of meat & beginning their meal even before the wretched prey is down. We came across a pack of 14 & were able to get pretty close.

We had lunch near the little cabin in the forest — known as Lerai. There is a cold stream & banana groves — & it is quite lovely. After lunch we stayed there for about an hour — at midday it is too hot to see animals. They are nearly all resting in the shade except for the plains herds. Brian was pretty tired. Although he is walking much better now, his hip still gets pretty sore, & it has a shocking jolting in the Land Rover. He went into the cabin & had a little sleep on one of the bunks. Simon read a magazine — & I climbed one of the huge & gnarled old fig trees growing over the stream. And then I got so near to a herd of Tommies that they were practically grazing all round me.

We set out again, by now the clouds were gathering & it looked a little like rain. We waited & watched 7 half-grown lions waking up from their daylight sleep, playing together like kittens. One of them, named by Brian the Spit, with the most beautiful eyes & the start of an absurd little mane, was playing with an empty tin. If one of the others tried to take it away, they got a smack over the ears from the Spit. We think that in a year or two he will be the most sought after young blood on the Serengeti!

We met one other old lion, a little scruffy in his mane, but quite handsom nonetheless. Then we came upon 3 altogether — A lion & two lionesses with a 3rd lioness some way away. One of them — the lion — let us go right up so that we were almost touching him. Simon, with his telephoto lens, got simply half a face in his view finder! After about 10 minutes he got up & peered in at Simon — nearly bumping his nose on the lens! He was a wee bit annoyed, & for half a second Brian thought he was going to bound onto the roof — where he & I were. Well, we wern't sitting on the roof — merely standing on the seat. But it was on the way out that we saw quite the most heavenly & beautiful lion. In fact I realized then that I hadn't really seen a lion before. He was huge, beautifully proportioned, sleek, glossy, & with a thick silky black mane, & elbow tufts about 4 inches long. And he was wild & unused to humans — he wouldn't let us anywhere near him. We were whizzing along the side of the Crater slope — Brian insisted we sit inside the car, because we really thought it was going over at any minute we were at such an angle. We only had to get one of the lower wheels into a hole — & over we'd have gone. But we didn't!

All we didn't see that day were elephants. And, in fact, I began to think the elephants didn't love me because though they were all round, we were never lucky. . . .

After lunch cum tea (at 4.30) [on Sunday] Brian did his first shooting since the accident as Peggy wanted some guinea fowl. He nearly killed himself by walking far too much on his leg — but men will be men. And David (senior) drove the car into a pot hole & tore a ligament in his arm, nearly fainted, & was in agony all the way home. So we were a subdued little party that got back rather late that night. David kept moaning and groaning all night. Suddenly I was woken from my sleep by an animal jumping through the window. There are no lights there of course — only lamps. And I had no torch. So I shouted out "Brian, there's something in my room". They all rushed in — Brian leapt out of bed so fast he nearly broke the other hip! Peggy found a torch as she ran — & standing in the middle of my floor was — "<u>Hobo</u>"!! I shall <u>never</u> live that one down!!

The next day was my last. Brian & I just messed around & enjoyed ourselves. In the afternoon we went out for a long drive, returning at about 4.30 & intending to collect Peggy & take her to see if the leopard was there. As we got to the camp gate David senior stepped out. "I've got a nasty shock for you — Leakey's here". They told me I went quite white. I had told Peggy that she <u>must not</u> let him start off with me late in the afternoon, whatever happened. (Actually, Brian & his father had concocted a lovely plan. L.S.B. was due to arrive on the Tuesday — not Monday as he did. And they were going to spread me out in bed, surrounded by bottles & medicine!) Anyway, we rushed over to Peggy, who said she'd seen him, & he had said "But Jane <u>must</u> have got my note saying I'd changed my plans & was fetching her today". He was very nearly saying he refused to believe that I hadn't! Just at that moment the lorry arrived from Arusha — & the driver handed L.S.B.'s note to Peggy — before his eyes! Lovely! Anyway, she had told him we were out & probably wouldn't be back till 6.30 or so — so we leapt into the Land Rover, Brian & I, and fled! That last drive through the Bamboo — & we heard a rhino but no more — was exceptionally vivid & very beautiful. When we got back LSB was there — very tired as he'd been driving since 4 am.

We planned to start at 6 the next morning. Peggy rushed in to me at about 6.5 to say she'd just heard the Land Rover door slam —

LSB was sleeping in one of the cabins. I was up & dressed & ready in a few seconds. Peggy said goodbye, & tactfully disappeared so that Brian & I could tenderly bid each other farewell!

And then came the beautiful climax to that heavenly holiday. We got outside, & I was just getting into the Land Rover when the chap at the gate rushed up. "You can't go yet, there's an elephant outside the gate." Brian & I rushed out — & that's the closest I've ever been — as near as the tall boy & the Drawing room window! It was feeding. When it heard us (Brian purposely going very close & LSB coming too of course — both trying to get nearer!) it turned round & moved a few steps towards us, ears outstretched. Oh, it was heavenly. There is something about the African elephant that captures the whole magic of Africa — something majestic, awe inspiring, giant & rugged. Something that one knows could be incredibly savage & terrifying. So departure, instead of being the normal anticlimax, was just the opposite. . . .

We got back, in a positive deluge, at about 9.30 on the Tuesday evening. On the Tuesday afternoon Brian had driven his father to Arusha — as he couldn't drive because of his hurt arm. He'd promised to ring me on Wednesday — which he did at 2.30. Imagine my horror when I heard "David (junior) has been beaten up by the Masai. He's in hospital & it's touch & go". It was ghastly. It had just happened & Brian knew no details. . . . [so] in desperation we rang the hospital. Thank God we got a sensible person who told us Dave had a very bad cut on his head from a knife wound, a suspected broken arm, & was under morphia & suffering from shock — but was off the danger list. He'd lost gallons of blood — had a [transfusion] lasting 6 1/2 hours. Poor, poor Peggy. She does have unfair things to cope with.

I rang all over the place next morning to try & get hold of Brian. No good. Then I heard a very welcome voice on the phone — André the little photographer, had just arrived from Arusha, laden with messages from Brian. . . . David had been driving the Masai cattle off the maize — & been deliberately set on by 10 Morani — ie, warriors. Thank goodness only one of them had a knife — or scemi — or young David would not be alive now. How he crawled away from them — he couldn't stand — no one is quite sure. Anyway, the police who went after them were driven off the first time — but they are all caught now.

Brian had set off back over the 100 miles to Ngorongoro, taking his Father back & fetching Peggy. She, poor thing, had just had a ghastly fall on the concrete floor, landing on her coccyx. The day before she had hardly been able to move from her bed. When Brian & David senior arrived she had heard nothing about Dave's beating up. Poor thing. . . .

Does my work fascinate me or is it the hearts thrown at my feet — oh, the work — the atmosphere & nice & interesting people at the Museum, staff & otherwise, the fact that I can have animals, talk animals, study animals. And also that I can get time off when I want or need it.

As for the questions of leave or permanency when I come home next year. That I don't know a bit as it depends on a plan which is afoot — & which you will know of first as soon as I know if it is going to work. Anyway, you, Mamma, whether you like it or not, are coming out here, about the middle of next year, & we are going home together. If my present plans work out, anyway.

I have been out with Peter this weekend. You would all approve of him vastly. Clever, won essay prizes, Chesterham, 6ft 5ins, dark, fairly good looking, likes music & literature, good manners, good job, money, nice to his mother, excellent dancer, dresses well — etc. ideal you would say I expect — 28 years old.

However, just now, Brian is No.1. And now I had better stop as it is late, & I got to bed at 3 last night after dancing at the Mogambourth & eating a chinese meal — I tried chopsticks! And we stalked some giraffe this afternoon in the Rift Valley.

Tons & tons of love,
Your little Jane

[February 1958]
Darling Family,

Thank you for all your letters. I do so apologize for making you weep & for wasting your rouge & valderma, Olly! I'm not feeling miserable just now at all. I am sitting in my bed having chatted to Mrs. Ellis — who <u>adores</u> me & is always giving me cake, bath salts, & meat for Chimba. I had a bath in her flat & then thoroughly cleaned my room, cleaned the bathroom, tidied & changed Chimba's earth box. He is lying contentedly on the bed beside me, & it looks as though he has been reading "The Oxford Book of Mystical Verse". (Actually I have!!) I am waiting for Brian who may not turn up for hours as he is trying to get his car going with Paul. He got back from his safari, & the poor chap got stuck for 3 days with no water and food. He had <u>some</u> of each, but no decent food (he couldn't leave the car because of Masai) and had to drink rusty water from the petrol tank. He also got knocked over by a wounded buffalo — luckily it was so weak it only tore his trousers — but it was a close shave.

I have been given a HORSE!! Let me hasten to explain this stupendous phenomenon. You know I have been riding Shandy & trying to school him in jumping. Well, Mary suggested I should go over with them on Sunday to the Pony Club meeting — a ride of about 10 miles — 15. It was a nice ride — a whole contingent of us. The chief instructors are Major & Mrs. Piper, whom I had never met before. Their P.C. doo's* are quite different from ours — <u>much</u> more fun. Gay & carefree & everyone happy. The kids have much bigger horses (you can't get them small) & they ride better, on the whole. More confidence. Anyway, they had a treasure hunt in the morning, & then, after feeding the horses, the kids had picnic lunches & all the grown ups went into the lovely old house for a <u>vast</u> spread — cold meats etc. There were at <u>least</u> 12 dogs of all kinds. (not to eat!!)

Then came jumping. Eventually I got on my devil & he knew <u>at once</u> that it was jumping. The day before I had jumped him & we got on <u>excellently.</u> But there had been no other horses. This time he decided to go backwards. People were laughing & leaping out of the way — & suddenly he wizzed, through a row of scattering old ladies, towards two tables laden with mugs of beer, tea, cakes, etc. The panic was comic. Everyone grabbed something from the table

---

* Pony Club events.

& by the time we hit them not much damage was done. Richard threw a bucket of water at our tail but Shandy didn't much seem to mind. So Major Piper came to the rescue with a hunting crop. That did the trick. We jumped fairly well — by which I mean relative to Shandy & not normal equestrian standards! i.e. we went over <u>all</u> the jumps but one or two were rather the worse for wear afterwards & I had a blister!

Eventually we rode home, & I talked to Mrs. Piper. She asked if I had a horse & if I wanted one. I said that when I <u>did</u> get one I wanted a really nice one I could school myself, & as I was going home this year it seemed silly.

Well, Mary Leakey rang today. The Pipers have a 15.2 thoroughbred. They were going to sell it, but would love me to have it & ride it until I go to England! Isn't it wonderful! It will have to be stabled at the Leakeys' at the moment, but later on I must find somewhere nearer Nairobi because petrol will be too expensive going all out there.

I have to leave my present place, which is a shame. I am going out to Jean Hyde for March, & then moving, with possibly Jean to share, into one of the Museum Flats — quite ideal. Did you know Sally <u>may</u> be coming out?!! If she does, you, Mummy, she & I will share this flat together. Your passage is booked for 1st September, Hurking Clan. I forgot the time it leaves London Airport. (I thought I'd better let you know!)

Tomorrow Mary & I want to save a pony that is to be shot as unmanagable. Muggins has volunteered to ride it & find out what all the nonsense is about! I have got the afternoon off, & we are going over to Limuru. If it is quite tractable we have an owner all ready for it. If not, Mary & I are going to school & sell it & share the profit! So your little Jane is getting into the horsey world again. The Royal Show is in September, so if this horse of mine is any good I shall enter it (don't know its sex yet!) & you, Ma, will feel it's like the good old days. The Pipers want me to be assistant instructress — which also rings a bell!!

I'm getting a car this month. I have to because of going out to live with Jean.

You ask for a snap of the Museum. Oddly enough I walked all round about 6 times the other lunch time & couldn't find a suitable place to get even one. I did take a shot, but it's so big & sort of straggly it won't fit in. But I'm blowed if I send any more photos until you send me some. So there!

Incidentally, Mummy, what did you write to Papa* about his being a boy friend of mine? I am highly intrigued to hear from you. He has been telling me all this about what you wrote to him, him to you & you back again, & I should be interested to hear your version of how it all started.

Now, one little remonstration to you, Ma. You can't have understood me properly over one thing re. Brian. You say that (a) I don't go out with other men because B wouldn't like it, (b) why don't I try peeling layers off what I call 'stuffy' young men. Well, (a) I am sure I said that at present I have no desire to go out with anyone else, except occasionally, & therefore I am NOT unnecessarily giving up my freedom of personality. I did go out with Ian the other day, & I had a horrible time trying to stop him kissing me — though I enjoyed driving the M.G. (b) there's no question of me peeling off layers (here's B. I think). It is, without exception, so far, they who try & do the peeling. I'm sure I've told you that all the young men out here have only one idea — to go to bed with one. (It's not B.). . . .

Oh, dear . . . I've done it again. Pip† on the telephone. He's got it too. What the devil am I to do with all these middle aged married men. They hang in multitudinous garlands from every limb and neck I've got, and most of them are so charming. Hey ho. What did you do some 24 years ago Mummy. I bet you never guessed when I lay so small and waxey in your arms!

Tons & tons of love,
Jane

---

* Louis Leakey.
† Major Piper, chief instructor of the Pony Club.

Most darling of families — Hail!

I hope you are all as hale and flourishing as I am. My family is growing still, but becoming more and more adorable. The puppy simply could not be more sweet and charming. I have christened her Tana (after a big river full of crocs where Brian is always saying he would take me if he had a Land Rover). She is inseparable friends with Kip now, and they sleep curled up in a box by my bed. Kombo, unfortunately, is still in my bed, but is moving out tonight as Sally is, at this moment (it being Saturday morning) buying him a hot-water bottle. We still havn't got our big cage, but plans for it are forging ahead, wire netting may be materializing from 3 different sources (or it may not!), plans are made for getting the wood on Monday, and Derek is going to help us build it, having just built a very nice one of his own — for his large bush baby, Boozy, who has now, somehow or other, become incorporated into our family. She simply adores Kombo, and the two sit, in each other's arms, and Boozy licks his face while he shuts his eyes in bliss. Poor little Levi is very out of it. Boozy was sleeping with us, in the animal room with Levi, but he was scared by her — for no reason, because she is very willing to love him as well. But as he refused and spurned her love, being all on edge after Kombo caught him when they were playing the other day, it seemed mean to leave him in anguish all night. So Boozy now visits us from about 6.30 to 10. All afternoon Kombo is tied up outside the flats, to the window, on a long string, and Kip and Tana play around with him. This is a highly satisfactory arrangement. It means we can thoroughly air the animal room, and clean it up, and also they get sunshine and fresh air. In this way we can keep the animal room under control — otherwise it's quite impossible. Then, at about 6 o'clock when it starts getting a bit chilly, they all go in. At first we used to have them all loose in the drawing room from about 7.0 onwards. But this got chaotic. I found it impossible to eat more than 2 mouthfuls of my own supper. There would be Kombo and Kip helping themselves from my plate, a bush baby stretching out and seizing handfuls from my fork as they sat on my shoulder, and two pleading eyes from such a charming little puppy face on the floor, that a few titbits had to be spared in that direction as well. So now they are fed in their own room while we have supper, except for Levi who can never eat when Kombo is around, so he has his little plateful in the sitting room, and the puppy, who has hers in the kitchen. In this way everything is well under control, and there is hardly any mess. They come out after supper, but Kombo, after breaking two vases and a picture, and getting very unmanageable in that he refused to be caught when it was time for him to go back, is now tied to the table from where he can do no serious damage. . . .

Sally and I are now really getting our flat organized a bit better. We had a thoroughly good go at cleaning up and polishing yesterday afternoon. Gerry sent me home at 4.0 as there was nothing whatsoever to do, and I polished all the furniture with O'Ceder polish, and Sally said the smell on the duster reminded her of the Birches. We still need a fridge, a toaster and some lamps. Brian and I got a lovely desk lamp the other day, from a queer old Indian who we are sure is a Receiver. This lamp — one of the ones with a wiggly bendy stem — we got for Shs 25. <u>Brand New.</u> The shop next door happened to be an electricity shop, and, as it so happened, there was <u>exactly</u> the same lamp there. So we marched in, leaving our identical one in the car, to ensure the cost. Shs 45!!! So we didn't do too badly I think.

Little Tana stays with me in the museum all morning. In the afternoons, except for twice a week, Sally is in the flat and can look after them all. She is terribly good. When she wants to do widdle she whines, so I carry her down. All the rest of the morning she sleeps in her box. She has just woken up now, as it is 12.30 and nearly lunch time. She isn't being a nuisance though — just gazing up at me with her brown eyes, resting her chin on the edge of the box. So sweetly melting in fact, that I have now picked her up and she is on my lap biting the typewriter rubber. For a purely bred dog I think she is going to be incredibly intelligent and sensible. You remember I told you I might have one of Clo's dogs, and that it fell through? Well, that little dog is the most highly strung creature imaginable. This little girl is really sensible and takes everything in her stride. She hasn't been homesick once. Sally has instructions to buy her a rubber bone this morning, and Kip a ping pong ball which he can crack against the wall. Kombo really should have artificial flowers to play with I think! Flowers have an irresistible fascination for him.

Incidentally, I must apologize for my ghastly typing today. I don't know what's happened, but I keep putting all my letters back to front. It should be worse than ever now because Tana is biting me with her sharp little teeth. Actually, I can't possibly get on, and as it's nearly lunch time I shall stop this now, and continue anon. . . .

But can you imagine how paradisical (if that is the correct word?) it is for me having all these animals round? Of course, they do make a hell of a lot of work, one can't get away from that. But once we have the cage it will be a lot less, and they are worth every minute of it. Kip insisted on coming into my bed last night, and flatly refused to sleep with Tana. This made Kombo jealous, but he just had to be jealous, because I was too tired to tackle Kip for long. And he was comical and wouldn't get up this morning. In the end I just stripped the bed and exposed him to the hard light of morning. Once up he had a lick and a stretch and felt fine and on top of the world. He wanted a real game with Tana — but poor Tana, who always wakes at about 6.0 was by then ready for another sleep! And so it goes on.

Sally really is a hoot. I was thinking about a Siamese the other day, and Brian said he thought that was a very good idea. So I asked Sally what she thought, and she thought it would be very nice. So then I began wondering how to go about getting one. "Oh, you don't need to worry" says Sal, "Now you've decided that you want one it will just turn up!" So she won't be very surprised when she hears that one is coming next week. . . . I hope Clo does come and share the flat because she will really be good fun. I now propose to end.

Tons & tons of love,

Jane

The Birches — etc.

[December 30, 1958]

My dear Sally,

Your letters come pouring in with all your news, and I am so dilatory. I do hope you had a merry Christmas — we, of course, had a simply wonderful one. We arrived safely back in England, to a smiling London — sunny & with a lovely nip in the air — crikey — of course I've written since getting back, surely? Anyway, we were welcomed with a red carpet & Union Jacks, & it was SUCH fun. On Christmas Eve Peter* rang up to say please could he come on Boxing Day with my Christmas present!! Eric also arrived on that day — & oh Sally, how lovely the house was. Jif's friend Rosemary arrived at 2.30 on Boxing Day, with her flute. Peter had his. There was music all day long. In between Peter & I sat in front of the fire, on the floor reading poetry and Shakespeare. Peter fitted so wonderfully into the family that we all — including him — felt he'd been here for ages & that we'd known him all our lives. Our room was the most fantastic sight — literally covered in books, music, & instruments. Peter discovered the violin and played that as well — & we got Jif castanets & a tambourine at Barcelona. Also an Arab pipe from Aden, & there is her Kenya drum! Eric has just had a tape recorder so we recorded Judy playing, solos, duets, singing and reciting. Funniest was when Rix had it on & we didn't know. It's the most wonderful toy. . . .

Gordon rang twice this afternoon, from London, but I was out, buying a coat — on the Never, Never! He told Danny he probably wouldn't ring again so I have to catch the 10.20 tomorrow & meet him at the Regent Palace at 1.30! Oh, I didn't tell you, but Peter brought me the most lovely skirt for Christmas. Wasn't it brilliant. Otherwise I'd have had nothing to wear. As it is I have that & a coat, & can borrow a jumper from someone, I hope. I have been living in my Barcelona trousers & boots & a jumper from the ship since I arrived home. Actually it is lovely warm & spring like

---

* She'd met Peter, a junior officer of the ship, on the voyage home.

weather mostly. Christmas Eve was the worst day — really raw &
freezing.

I had Leakey's letter about the animals arriving, & a cable, & so
am off to meet them. Gordon, Peter, Kip is my programme for the
New Year festivities. I admit that I am looking forward to meeting
the <u>last</u> of those gentlemen most!! Dear, dear, Kip. I am taking with
me a hot water bottle & blankets and Peter is driving us all home in
his car — he only went yesterday — & will be back the day after tomorrow!

Poor Olly is in bed with a stinking cold & I have a foul feeling
that I'm brewing one up myself. I have a stinking throat today & am
living on Gee's.

You & Nairobi & everything now seems so far away. I have slid
so easily back into the family that it is as though I had never left.
Nothing has changed. Danny & Audrey are the same as ever. Jif
hasn't altered more than a scrap, the house, the shops, Bournemouth — all is the same. It is lovely. And it is lovely to be in an artistic atmosphere again. I realize now, more than ever before, that I
can never live wholly without it. It feels so heavenly to be able to
just sit in front of the fire & talk for hours — of cabbages & kings
— poetry, literature, art, music, philosophy, religion. It's wonderful, marvellous, terrific. I wish Leakey would realize what it really
means to me. And I feel so lucky that I've met someone like Peter
with whom I can <u>share</u> <u>all</u> of these things. He is frantically artistic — crazily artistic. I am going to stay with them over this Ball
weekend, & am really looking forward to it. Dear old Peter.

He is the very first, of all my boyfriends . . . whom the family have
delighted to receive to their bosoms. I am longing for you to meet
him.

I wrote to Hans on the ship — he wants to see me on the 6th
Jan — which is, of course, quite impossible. I can't spend all my
time rushing up & down to London. But it really hurts me more
than anything to have to write and say 'No'. Still, there will be so
much time when I get to London.

Sally, I will stop now, because I must wash my hair. Thank you for
all that you've done — oh, if I asked you for Browning, forget it. I

have a Browning here. But an exercise book & odd things on paper you come across, please could you bring.

V. Imp. Please could you send all the animal stamps you can find from that cupboard. I find I've forgotten them. This is urgent as I have just been given 100 animal ones & the person wants to see my collection! I don't want the album but if there are any animal ones in it could you take them out. Please. Any news of Clo?

Tons & tons of love to you,

& — oh dear,

only to Kombo & Thimble!

Jane

4

✿ ✿ ✿

WAITING

1959–1960

It was a whole year from the time when I left Africa to the time
when I actually arrived among the chimpanzees. Sometimes . . . I
felt sure I would never get there. Surely, I told myself, it's all too
good to be true.

— *My Life with the Chimpanzees*

B
Y THE TIME Jane Goodall left Kenya Colony at the end of
1958, Louis Leakey had already seriously embarked on his
plan to send her out to study the group of chimpanzees living undisturbed in a comparatively small patch of forest known as
the Gombe Stream Chimpanzee Reserve along Lake Tanganyika in
Tanganyika Territory.

Tanganyika had once been part of the colony of German East Africa, but at the end of World War I the League of Nations designated
it a "mandate" territory, to be administered by the British with
the ultimate goal of self-government.* Thus Louis was corresponding with Geoffrey Browning, the British district commissioner in
Tanganyika's Kigoma region. Browning's response to Louis's request was somewhat ambivalent. Yes, it would be acceptable for a
young woman to go to the Gombe Stream Chimpanzee Reserve to
study the chimpanzees. No, it would not be acceptable for her to go
alone. For one thing, the wild apes were potentially dangerous. To
satisfy the authorities, Jane would have to have an assistant, a com-

---

* For an expanded historical discussion, see Brian Lapping, *End of Empire* (New
York: St. Martin's, 1985).

panion, a second official member of the expedition. According to Vanne's recollection, Louis mentioned this complication to her in Jane's absence; Vanne surprised herself by spontaneously volunteering to be the second member. The new proposed arrangement — two women going into the forest instead of one — was accepted.

So when mother and daughter returned home to Bournemouth in December 1958, Louis had already received official permission for the expedition. Now he needed to raise the money. And Jane, while she waited for Louis to work his magic, would begin her training as a zoologist.

After Christmas (and after Kip the mongoose and Boozy — or Boozey — the bush baby were settled in at the Birches, getting along as well as could be expected with Figaro the cat), Jane moved to London and began working at the film library of Granada Television (Zoo Television and Film Unit), headquartered at the London Zoo in Regent's Park. In subsequent months she informally studied primate behavior with Osmond Hill at the London Zoo and primate anatomy with John Napier at the Royal Free Hospital. Both men were friends and colleagues of Louis's.* While working at the film library, Jane also spent time getting acquainted with the animals inside the zoo. The first letter in this sequence was written soon after she began work at Granada Television as the assistant to Ramona Morris, the distinguished wife of the zoo's distinguished curator of mammals, Desmond Morris. Actually, the letter was written *during* work, within earshot of some of the zoo animals, on Granada stationery.

Jane found it convenient to live at her father's flat at Number 19, The Lodge, Kensington Park Gardens. Her sister, Judy, who was then studying piano at the Guildhall School of Music in London, also stayed at the flat. For transportation Jane bought a "cheap car" — soon named Fifi. And for entertainment the two sisters and some of their friends frequented an atmospheric coffee shop on Old Brompton Road called the Troubadour, a small dark place with

---

* Virginia Morell, *Ancestral Passions: The Leakey Family and the Quest for Humankind's Beginnings* (New York: Simon & Schuster, 1995), p. 242.

exposed beams overhead and antiques on the walls: a hangout where poets came to read, musicians to play, and earnest young people to hear poetry and music, sip exotic beverages, and notice each other. There Jane met a charming, classically handsome actor named Robert Young. The pair became involved, fell in love, and decided to follow their hearts and convention by getting married. The second letter of this sequence, probably written in January 1960, describes the moment when Robert asked Jane's father for permission to marry his daughter.

The announcement of an engagement between Mr. R. B. Young and Miss V. J. Morris-Goodall appeared in the social section of the *Daily Telegram and Morning Post* on May 13, 1960 — very bad timing, since almost simultaneously Louis Leakey informed Jane that her wait was over. He had gotten final permits from the Tanganyika Game Department, at last found a reliable sponsor for the research, and even received the grant money and purchased essential supplies, including a canvas tent, a small aluminum boat, and two plane tickets. Jane's plans for marriage to the glamorous Robert Young were thus abruptly postponed and then, gradually over the next several months, ended.

To most people, and to almost anyone connected with ordinary sources of scientific funding, Louis's proposal must have seemed bizarre: to send a very young woman, slight and delicate-featured, enthusiastic, but possibly too much so, completely untrained, no college degree — a secretary! — out to the "jungle" to live among the wild apes. The idea was improbable to the point of absurdity. Only Louis S. B. Leakey could have pulled it off. The sponsor he located, Leighton Wilkie of Des Plaines, Illinois, shared with Louis an excitement about paleoanthropology (the Wilkie fortune had been made in tools, and Leighton was interested in primitive tools) and an iconoclast's lack of concern over Jane's lack of credentials. The Wilkie Brothers Foundation came up with a $3,000 grant, enough funds to sustain the world's most unlikely scientific expedition for about six months.

On May 31, 1960, Jane and Vanne boarded a plane back to Nairobi. Upon their arrival, though, Louis appeared with bad news:

another delay, another wait. Disputes among fishermen camping along the shore of the chimpanzee reserve were making things unsafe for the present. To keep the two women occupied, and as a serious first experiment in field research, Louis packed mother and daughter onto a train to Lake Victoria, where they were met by Hassan Salimu, captain of Louis's forty-two-foot cabin cruiser, the *Miocene Lady*. Hassan took the two women out to Lolui Island in Lake Victoria, where every day Jane would watch the vervet monkeys living there and register her observations in a notebook. "The short study," Jane was later to recall, "taught me a good deal about such things as note-taking in the field, the sort of clothes to wear, the movements a wild monkey will tolerate in a human observer and those it will not."* On June 30 the women received a go-ahead radio message from Louis. They paused to bid farewell to the monkeys at Lolui — including a favorite one Jane had named Lotus and her baby, Grock — then returned to Nairobi with a book filled with Jane Goodall's first field notes.

Back at the Coryndon, Louis examined her preliminary report, an event briefly mentioned in the third letter of this chapter. Then they packed up the Land Rover and, from July 5 to July 8, were driven by Bernard Verdcourt (botanist at the Coryndon) around eight hundred miles south into Tanganyika Territory to the lakeshore town of Kigoma.

*   *   *   *

[Probably January 1959]

Darling Mummy,

Thank you so much for the letter. Both Jif and I were awake nearly all of last night, wondering and wondering about Kip.† We decided that he hadn't come back because we thought you would have rung if he had. In the morning I remarked to Jif that there would have been time to write and post a letter, so that if there was no good news in the post we should really have believed the worst.

---

* *In the Shadow of Man* (1971), p. 8.
† Kip had a habit of disappearing.

However, all was well, and good news came. I hear that only two photographs are expected to come out!

We had a very comfortable and speedy trip back — we got to Victoria at 9.5, and so were back at the flat at 9.30 and Pa was still up. I asked him about a cheap car, and he was useless. He said, in one breath, that I would never get one under £150. In the next that only last week his mechanic had been <u>given</u> one for nothing, and had sold it for £25. Hey ho! So please will you write and ask Sammy — SOON.

Please don't think that because I am typing this that I have no work to do. I have been HARD at it all day, and it is now 5.30. Ramona was out this morning, and I did some letters for the Zoologist, one Mr. Nicholas Guppy. There has been a vast row about this as Ramona doesn't think I ought to do any of his work, but as none of the indexing equipment has come yet, and so we can't start (the projectionist is away with flu') I am doing stuff for him to start with. He has just come in and told me my letters were beautifully typed. He's a queer fish, and I don't feel he's a super Zoologist. Rather the Fleetwood type, he appears, but I may be quite, quite wrong of course. Anyway, I did his letters, and typed them back. Well, I then looked at my watch — 2.45! When I went down with them, at 3.15 or so, the girl downstairs, Annabelle (and there is a Pauline too) was most concerned, and says she is coming to fetch me for lunch tomorrow. But after being used to starting work at 8.0 it just about made a normal morning — 10–3.0!

Since then I have done a lot of cards, and at the present moment should be typing a script for Ramona, but she is having a row with Nicholas Guppy about his proposed card to be filled in and filed, concerning each animal on each reel of film. I am entirely on her side — it is a ridiculous list, and if one had to put in all that detail, as she says, we should only get through about 1 reel per day — if that. She and I were discussing it when he came in. Which reminds me, he gave me a list to type for him, so I had better do it in case he appears from next door to demand it!

Well, I did it, but it ran off the end of the page, and anyway it ought to be on thick paper and I've only got flimsy up here, and I can't be bothered to go downstairs and fetch up the proper stuff. So he can jolly well wait until tomorrow for his old list!

All day long I have sat here, hearing strange sounds. The familiar roar, last heard across Serengeti Plains, of the hungry lion. The barking grunts of the deer, curious screeches and cries from the birds. Soon the hyaena will probably start laughing, and then I shall be really homesick!

I got here early this morning, not knowing how long it would take — which is about 3/4 hour — and wandered around looking at moose and elk, peacocks and various eagles and members of the crow family. There was the Fisheagle, looking so bedraggled compared to his lucky cousin that I saw, proud and free, on dear old Lolue.* And the Bataleur Eagle, seen so very often soaring over the African landscape. Strangely enough, the very first animal I saw was the Wolverine — the animal that so puzzled Sally and I on that stamp. And now it's time to go.

Tons of love to all,
Jane

P.S. <u>Please</u> get Boo some more meal worms. They won't be in until Wed — they'd run out on Saturday when I went in. 2/6 per oz — I'll pay you back. It's about the only thing she really loves — protein. Did you take back the flash gun?

[Probably January 1960]

Darling Mummy,

Many thanks for your letter — I'm glad you liked the record. I havn't met any of Bob's family yet, but we're off down there this evening. Bob† rang his Ma last night and she wasn't even expecting us. She said Bob didn't say definitely, and, thinking back on it, I think she was right. However, all is arranged now. She hasn't told Papa yet — so Bob said she was not to worry — he would tell him himself. It really is rather comic!

---

* Probably refers to a brief visit to Lolui Island in Lake Victoria in 1957 or 1958.
† Robert Young.

I have had Fifi "Aquatec'd" and she appears to be fine now.* No more trouble. Not that we have had such a lot of rain as last weekend, but still. I have written to Leakey to ask about money for the course, but not told him about getting engaged yet. I want to get everything settled first in case he goes queer — and there's not any chance of him getting to hear of it, because who would get to hear of it in Kenya? I told Sally not to tell anyone out there just yet. . . .

I had a letter from Napier when I got back on Sunday and he wants Boozey for a Television programme on primate hands. This is on 16th Feb — a Sunday. So we have a dance on the 14th — I think — and then have to collect Boozey on the Sunday — and may fit in Eileen and Stuart, who havn't answered my letter yet. Then I have to be at some strange studio by 2.30 although the programme is not until 6.30 — and then I have to go to Napier's house to meet his family and take Boozey to see how they get on with her since she will be staying there for a year. I think I'd better ditch Robert for the afternoon!

I went over to the Bird House yesterday to collect some food for Bishop, and, being bored, decided to wander round. Don, the head keeper, said I might as well feed the giant hornbill, Horatio, with some mealworms. Do you remember me telling you that I fed him before, on grapes — and how he puts them in your mouth if he likes you? Well, I didn't somehow imagine he would feel the same way about meal worms, but to my horror one was suddenly pushed lovingly into my mouth! It wasn't squashed at all, so in point of fact it really didn't matter! My nice gardener — not the cactus one, but [the] one who brings me roses in the summer, has brought me two lovely primulas. I am worried about them at the weekend because they need water every day or else they droop. Never mind, I'll just have to put them somewhere where it's cold.

Honestly, on Monday evening Daddy was in. I met Bob for a quick drink when he finished work, and then we went round to tell Chrispian and Annie we were engaged. We found poor Chris on his

---

* She had her car, Fifi, waterproofed.

own, a grass widower, Annie being away for the week. So I rang Jif, who was nobly coping with supper, and asked her to do the sausages and extra piece of liver. Anyway, we dashed back, and while Jif and I cooked, Chris sat in the kitchen and talked to us, and Bob actually went and said to Daddy "Can I have the hand of your daughter in marriage". We had told him to, but didn't think he would! So Daddy said "Which Daughter?"!! After this, Bob was very amused. He said he could see Daddy really didn't care two hoots about him, or what he was, but frantically thought of all the things which a father should say in like circumstances. When he told Bob his profession was rather precarious, Bob said he thought motor racing must be pretty precarious too, and when Pa said it had only been his hobby, Bob said that the fact that he might kill himself, made it even worse! Anyway, when we went in they were in deep and happy conversation. And then Daddy found out that Chris was going in for photography, and out came all his photographs — he was in his element, with Chris — who has wanted to take motor racing pictures for a long time — and Bob who is interested — both at his feet, while he produced pictures and anecdotes. Jif and I were very amused. Chris is a very charming person indeed — he was in the services in the Sudan, and has as much love for Africa as I have. He is terribly jealous of me, and is longing to go back himself. He immediately thought about being a photographer on my trip — not to begin with, but after it has established itself. But I had to point out that the money would be negligible, and, having a wife, he can't afford the trip for pleasure. Bob is going around his Studios reading "A Field Study of the Chimpanzee"* so as to get clued up — he says he wishes he never had as the more he reads the more worried about me he gets.

I think that is about all the news I can muster up this week — it seems to have flown by so very quickly. Thank you, and all the rest of the family, for a super weekend — and of course, not having done my new dress I now need it for the weekend. But not to

---

* A 1931 monograph by Henry W. Nissen, the only published study of wild chimpanzees at the time.

worry. The dark silk one or my skirt and white blouse will do very nicely. . . .

Anyway, must stop.

More love again,

Jane

P. S. Bob said last night that one of the nicest things about marrying me would be to gain a second family — with reference to <u>the</u> family he would be gaining.

[July 3, 1960]

Darling Family, Kip & Figaro,

I am frightfully sorry I havn't been writing long letters to you, but as Mummy may have explained I really have not been exactly <u>lazy</u> during the last few weeks. Oh, Lolui was a glorious beautiful place, and the monkeys so utterly charming that I <u>hated</u> to have to leave. Did Mum tell you about Lotus having her baby, Grock, and bringing him out to show all the others? How all the other children gathered round to peer at it, & one of them held its tail? And about them having a bathing party on the beach?

We are now back in Nairobi, and I have been working just as hard writing a preliminary report for Leakey, and, in between, rushing round shopping, paying social calls, and trying to develop some photos to send you! So far have had bad luck — the chemicals were faulty, it's Sunday, & I can't get anymore till tomorrow.

Judy, the spare keys to the flat — mine. Bob has. His address now is [blank space] Earl's Court Road. So if you don't see him you'd better drop him a line. He says he saw you in the Troupadour!

The scandals, scenes & situations at the Museum are the same as ever — I think they always will be. Dear old Museum. Little Ann* is thrilled to see me back & has just been ironing a dress for me! She begged to be allowed to!

Thank you for all your letters. I shall try to write more often at Kigoma. At this moment I am waiting for Leakey to finish reading

---

* Probably Ann Mitton.

my report. Great sighs are coming across the room — very fore-boding! However, I don't think I did too badly in 3 weeks — & Mummy got some very good insects. All in all I think our little expe-dition was very satisfactory.

This evening the Mittons, maybe Mum, & the Carcassons are go-ing to the elephant film — Roots of Heaven I think it's called.*

The journey to the chimp place, which commences on Tuesday, is going to take 4–5 days. We camp at nights, & it is going to be great fun. . . . Now my report is read, & I have been told it's fine. I have to go back & finish the job later!

Tons of love to you,

Jane

[July 5, 1960]

Darling Danny,

Many, many happy returns.† We are terribly worried about no present, but Mum will have told you we thought it was stupid to send a silly little nothing. But we shall be thinking of you — & drinking your health — in coffee no doubt! At this very moment Bernard is packing up the Land Rover. It looks quite impossible that all the stuff will fit in & leave room for us and the poor boy who has to do all the work when we camp at night. We both wish that either Bob or Norman was taking us instead of Bernard, but I dare say all will be well. Did Mummy tell you that I now have the ex-Governor of Kenya, Sir Evelyn Baring's revolver!!‡ Isn't it a hoot.

Leakey has just arrived so I must stop. I do hope you have a <u>very</u> very happy Birthday — wish we were with you.

With lots & lots of love,

Your little

Jane

---

* Norman and Marion Mitton and their two children, Ann and Christopher, lived on the museum grounds. Robert Carcasson, the museum entomologist, lived in one of the Museum Flats with his wife and son.
† Danny's birthday was July 13.
‡ The revolver was presumably lent her by Louis; Evelyn Baring was governor of Kenya from 1952 to 1959.

5

❧ ❧ ❧

FIRST DISCOVERIES
1960–1961

> I wanted to learn things that no one else knew, uncover
> secrets through patient observation.
> — *My Life with the Chimpanzees*

L AKE TANGANYIKA constituted a watery border between
Tanganyika Territory and the Belgian Congo. Upon their arrival in Kigoma on July 8, 1960, Jane Goodall and her mother
discovered a town struggling to handle the flood of refugees from
the Belgian Congo following its June 30 liberation from a repressive
colonial regime. On July 14 the two women boarded the *Kibisi,* a
launch maintained by the Tanganyika Game Department, and were
motored north about twelve miles to the Gombe Stream Chimpanzee Reserve. Their own little aluminum boat bobbed along behind.

Tanganyika Game Ranger David Anstey accompanied them, as
did Dominic Charles Bandola, whom they had hired in Kigoma to
be their cook. Dominic turned out to be a first-rate cook and a
pleasant companion; he was eventually joined by his wife, Chiko,
and their little girl, Ado.

Gombe Stream Chimpanzee Reserve was a rectangular stretch of
land on the eastern side of Lake Tanganyika stretching roughly ten
miles north to south. An erratic rock-and-pebble shoreline defines
the western boundary of Gombe; the edge of a 2,500-foot-high rift
escarpment marks the long eastern boundary. The reserve, in other
words, is an extremely rugged rectangle, with some fifteen or sixteen streams tumbling precipitously from the high eastern edge into

deep valleys and channels down to the lakeshore. The actual Gombe Stream is one of the southernmost of the streams.

The chimpanzee reserve was never very large, altogether perhaps only twenty square miles; today, as Gombe Stream National Park, it stands in severe ecological isolation, a forest island edged on one side by the lake and on the other three by stripped-down land resulting from overcultivation. In 1960, when the reserve was still part of a larger, semicontinuous wilderness habitat, chimpanzee populations existed to the south, east, and north of the boundaries; nevertheless, the reserve may have protected approximately as many individual chimpanzees then as it does today, around 160. The forest additionally protected (and still does) several other primate types: olive baboons; red colobus monkeys; blue, red-tailed, and vervet monkeys; and the needle-clawed bush baby. Some of the largest and most vulnerable mammals found at Gombe when Jane Goodall arrived in 1960 are now gone, including hippos and buffalo; other rare species — including the leopard and the serval cat — still survive. Bushbucks, bush pigs, civets, genets, and elephant shrews remain abundant, as do squirrels, mongooses, and various rodents. Crocodiles no longer swim along the lakeshore, but Nile monitor lizards are still found at Gombe, as are pythons and several seriously poisonous snakes: night adder, puff adder, spitting cobra, Storm's water cobra, black mamba, vine snake, and bush viper.*

The German colonial government first designated that rich piece of forest a reserve, limiting human intrusion, to protect chimpanzees. The English, upon taking over the administration of Tanganyika Territory at the end of World War I, were content to maintain the status quo.

Close to the center of this piece of forest, between Kasakela and Kakombe streams, the Tanganyika Game Department maintained a small camp — a convenient place for government officials to stop overnight during regular trips up and down the lake — as well as a modest, semipermanent station for the Tanganyika Game Scouts, who patrolled the reserve.

---

* *The Chimpanzees of Gombe: Patterns of Behavior* (1986), pp. 45–50.

Along with two or three game scouts, Kasakela camp included a few other Africans whose function seems to have been rather informal, to help maintain the camp or simply to keep the game scouts company. Among this group was Iddi Matata, an older man who served as unofficial "village headman." So when the *Kibisi* anchored offshore at Kasakela, the newcomers were welcomed by a small crowd headed by the dignified Iddi Matata. The crowd may have included Matata's two wives and six children, probably the game scouts stationed at Kasakela, certainly some local fishermen who were temporarily camping along the shore, and also possibly a few curious individuals from the fishing village just north of the reserve, Mwamgongo.

As David Anstey made clear, the game scouts could, if they wished, work for Miss Goodall as trackers. From the Game Department staff, Jane hired Adolf Siwezi; from the village of Mwamgongo she hired Rashidi Kikwale and his friend Mikidadi (described in the first letter home as "the chief's son").

Jane Goodall succeeded in *finding* chimpanzees very quickly. As we read in the first letter home, she saw one on July 14, her first day there. Of course, seeing the occasional wild ape — at a distance, disappearing in panic — was not enough. By the end of August (after she and her mother had endured the worst of an extended bout of malarial fever), Jane was able to write home with the excellent news that "I've discovered more — since my fever, in about 5 days, than in all the dreary weeks before." She kept up a grueling pace, rising before dawn, seldom returning to camp until after dark, eating starvation rations, trying to follow uncooperative creatures over jagged terrain through hostile undergrowth for what most people would regard as a distinctly unrewarding goal: to catch one or two fleeting glimpses of a hairy blob behind leaves. Her first three field assistants didn't last long. They were soon replaced by professional trackers brought to Gombe by a Tanganyikan farmer and hunter named Derrick Dunn, who seems to have been in love with Jane. Dunn's employees — Wilbert and Soko and then Short — arrived at various times in September and are mentioned in the letters probably written on September 19 and September 25.

Vanne returned to England in November. Jane left Gombe for a vacation in Kenya from December 1 to mid-January. By then her only field assistant was another game scout, Saulo David — but, as Jane notes in the letter postmarked February 6, "I now climb the mountains on my own, & Saulo comes up later on." Starting in mid-January, the staff also included Hassan Salimu, former skipper of Louis Leakey's *Miocene Lady*, who served as camp manager.

Once Vanne left in November, the Gombe human community was all African except for Jane. She worked on learning Swahili and came more and more to rely on the Africans, who over time became her close companions and colleagues. One gets the impression from several of these letters — for example, the one written on April 3 — that the camp was a very lively place. The arrival of Hilda, the hen, and Hildebrand, the cock, produced additional amusement in camp, along with a steady supply of eggs and, by early April, about fourteen baby chicks . . . then thirteen, then twelve, as the great Nile monitor lizards came out of hiding long enough to claim their share. Occasionally visitors from the outside arrived by boat. They included David Anstey, as well as, once or twice, friends and acquaintances from Kigoma, including (see the letter of February 6, 1961, for example) Robert and Alison Greenshields and Colin and José (pronounced "Josie") Lamb.

In early October 1960, Jane and Vanne were visited by the distinguished field zoologist George Schaller and his wife, Kay, who together had just completed a pioneering study of mountain gorillas in Rwanda. The letter written on October 31 and November 1, 1960, mentions that visit and credits Schaller with the following prophetic challenge: "George said he thought that if I could see chimps eating meat, or using a tool, a whole year's work would be justified."

Goodall made at least four momentous discoveries during her first year at Gombe. The two best known and perhaps most remarkable occurred within a week of each other and followed Schaller's challenge by about three weeks. On October 30 she saw chimpanzees eating meat, as described in the letter of October 31–November 1. Her first observations of chimpanzees using tools — fashioning and manipulating long twigs and inserting them into termite mounds to fish out termites — happened, according to the journal she kept, on November 4. Unhappily, though several subsequent letters refer to termite-fishing, I have not found any that describe her first observation.

The third momentous discovery, which took place after Jane's return from Christmas vacation in Nairobi, is described in dramatic detail and at some length in the wonderful if rambling letter postmarked February 6, 1961: "the chimpanzee rain dance."

The fourth great "discovery" of this first year is perhaps more event or accomplishment than discovery. But we see it referred to again and again and (in the letters written after September 1960) with increasing confidence: her brilliant success in overcoming the normal, natural wariness of these wild animals and eventually habituating them to her presence. No one ever had done this to such a degree.* Field zoology before Goodall arrived at Gombe typically consisted of specimen collection: shooting wild animals and measuring their remains. As for observations of living animals, the few researchers who tried it typically observed for relatively short periods at safe, comfortable distances, and inevitably with a narrower focus. By moving among the wild chimpanzees and immersing herself as fully as possible in their world, this young, scientifically naive woman had chosen to sail right off the edge of the map, to enter the terra incognita of scientific research. The results were astonishing. By her twenty-seventh birthday (letter of April 3, 1961), a few of the apes were actually wandering into camp.

Jane's extraordinary success at habituating the chimpanzees of Gombe was not, of course, the result of dumb luck. She labored at it, following the secretive creatures day after day after day, maintaining with great sensitivity the comfortable distance they defined by their actions, wearing dull-colored clothes, moving slowly, behaving in nonthreatening ways, and so on. But Jane also had help (as we can see from the letters of May 7 and May 16) from one individual chimpanzee she called David Greybeard. David was easily recognizable because of his distinctive gray beard, his calm disposition, and, soon, his curiosity about the strange and slender ape with

---

* George Schaller, who had begun to habituate wild mountain gorillas in the Virungas during his two-year stay there, was probably her most successful predecessor.

yellow hair. He became a quiet friend, and his calm, curious de-
meanor helped break through the fears of the other members of his
community.

The final letter of this sequence, written exactly one year after the
"Morris-Goodall Chimpanzee expedition" stepped onto the pebble
beach at Gombe, amounts to a first annual report from the field.
Jane summarizes her year's progress in getting to know the terrain
and the chimpanzees of Gombe with a deep sense of real achievement: "The challenge has been met. The hills & forests are my
home. And what is more, I think my mind works like a chimp's,
subconsciously."

* * * *

[July 16, 1960]
Darling Family, one and all, Douglas & Kip & Figs,

I'm really sorry to be such a bad letter writer, but there's so much
to be done. Ma says, anyway, that she tells you all the news in detail
so it would be silly to relate it twice, & I have to write it all to Bob,*
you see.

Anyway, after all the delays etc. which you will know about by
now, we have at last arrived. We got here, Danny, on your birthday†
& mentally had tea with you — just after I had seen my first chimpanzee! I could hardly believe I could be lucky enough to see one on
my very first day. We were quite far away, but at least close enough
to know it was a chimp & not a baboon. There are lots of Baboon
here — one Troop comes very close to the tent each morning to
watch us. I went out yesterday afternoon to do a little exploring
on my own and saw a beautiful bushbuck — a smallish animal, a
lovely reddish gold colour. He flew away almost from under my
feet, barking like a dog.

The country here is quite beautiful, but very rugged. The little
stream behind the tent rushes down the steep rocky valley, gurgling
and splashing down steppes of waterfalls. The water is pure and
sweet — doesn't even have to be boiled. 16 such streams flow down

---

* Robert Young.
† They actually arrived a day after Danny's July 13 birthday; Jane exaggerated the
coincidence of dates for her grandmother's amusement.

the valleys between the mountain ridges, & along their banks are the forest galleries, the home of the chimps. In between the mountain slopes are fairly bare — really it is ideal country for my job, though at the moment the task seems of a huge magnitude. Anyway, it's lucky I have more than 3 weeks!

At the moment I have 3 boys making a table with a shelter over it for Mummy to type in. They are really very clever at this sort of thing. The fishermen have just presented us with a large fish, an offer of friendship.

We hope to be able to send & collect mail about once a fortnight — the chief's son, named Mikidadi! will go in, either on one of the little motor boats which operates a passenger service along the shore — carrying about 10 Africans per trip, or else with my own boat, as he is supposed to be a fundi* with boats. David & I got the engine working yesterday & went right along the coast to the end of the Reserve. We saw 8 chimp nests in 2 trees quite close to the water, & he showed me the valley where he advises me to look first. I have 3 Game Scouts to choose from to take with me, & also a local fellow who was employed by a previous Game Warden as a guide when he marked out the reserve in 1947. He knows where the chimps are likely to be, & I shall pay him 2/- a day if the Scouts have other duties. I do hope it's all going to work.

David is just off back to Kigoma — taking Mikidadi who will bring back the few things we've forgotten.

Tons & tons of love,
Jane

Chimp Reserve.
[August 30, 1960]

Darling Family,

How are you all? and thank you for all your letters. I wanted to write you a long one this time, but what with fevers and journals and chimps life has been a bit hectic.

However, all is well now. I had a bit of fever again yesterday so am recuperating today. The D.C. & his wife, together with a White

---

* Expert.

Father, are all arriving at any minute now for lunch, after which they will be bearing these letters away.

Did Mum tell you how many chimps I have been finding, up behind our own mountain. I've discovered more — since my fever, in about 5 days, than in all the dreary weeks before. I've seen them walking along paths, I've seen them resting under trees, I've seen them playing. I've seen them 12 yards away, walking along, unconcerned. And, down in one of the cool river valleys I saw just a little baby, peering at me, & then he was joined by the most hideous female with jet black face & beetling brow ridge. She was <u>huge.</u> She swept him up & climbed down the tree. Then another came & peered at me, gazing down from a high fork. Quite pretty with a nice pale face, & ordinary size. Then the most <u>enormous</u> chimp I have ever seen came & peered at me. It was a she — old, with a half bald head & huge great arms. Her face, too, was black, & she was big as a gorilla. She came even closer & waved a tree at me, standing up & flinging her weight from side to side. And they never uttered a sound, & it was quiet except for the odd rustlings in the leaves and the distant rumbling of the thunder, all heard as a background to the gurgling of the little stream.

Oh — here they are. I will write a very long letter next time.

All my love to you all, Douglas,

& Sal if you're there, & Kip & Fig,

Jane

Chimp Reserve.

[Probably September 19, 1960]

Darling Family, Danny, Olly, Audrey, Eric — not you Jif unless you send that address — see further on in letter — I really <u>WANT</u> the book.

It's awful not having written for so long, but I just have not had time to write letters — I hope Mum has told you. Ever since my boys came I have been out every day from 6 am–7.30 pm. And then there's the punishing Journal to be written. That is <u>really</u> quite terrible. After climbing mountains all day, getting back & having a huge supper, one does <u>not</u> feel like writing several pages about chimps. But my chimps are so lovely now. I know where to find them, I know some of them by sight. I know the hideous Sophie with her son, Sophocles. I know the bearded grizzled old Claud, and an almost bald old lady whom, I think, must be Annie. They are getting used to us. When I was up on my own the other day I heard them in the trees down below & yards away — 15 perhaps. They retired, but only just out of sight. I could hear them moving about in the leaves. 10 minutes later 17 adults, 3 females carrying their babies, filed past — only 20 yards away. They all knew I was there, but didn't care a bit. They all sat down to look at me for a while, & then carried on up the slope, unhurriedly. It really is comical when 2 or 3 suddenly see you and stop, & peer, & then sit down, arms over their knees, chins on arms, and stare with intent interest. And then they often go round, under cover, & appear in a nearby tree, peeping through the leaves. The other day I saw 4 chimps being baited by a pack of baboons. It was like a play being enacted, in a little open clearing down below. The baboons got closer & closer until the chimps could stand it no longer. The 2 females climbed trees, the 2 males chased after the nearest tormentors. Then all was as before. One baboon came very close to the tree in which a female was — she leant down, waving her free arm up & down, & screaming at the top of her voice! The baboon moved sedately a couple of feet away. In the end the chimps walked off, & the baboons followed them to the edge of the clearing! But when the chimps — about 6 — were all feeding in a tree, & the baboons arrived, the chimps looked in alarm & swung out of the tree. It's terribly fascinating — I don't think anyone knew anything about the relationship between the two before, though I may be wrong.

Please JUDY — my ADDRESS book, or anyway Charles' address — I do think you're mean. You can always look up Burroughs Welcome in the London Directory. And now he's written to me & will never believe I wrote well over a month ago. Please make her, someone.

It's getting quite cold up on the mountains at dawn, now. An icy wind sweeps over the peaks, & one longs for the clouds to be swept away from the sun. Then, at 12 when the sun is hottest, the wind stops altogether & one nearly dies of heat! I am rapidly becoming like a piece of tough brown leather. Even when I slip down a few yards of shale, I find the skin on hands, elbows, legs, etc. is not broken! It's rather a hoot! Today is my day for doing paper work — the 1st for 2 weeks when I have not been out. It feels very strange to be staying in camp all day. But there is <u>such</u> a lot to do. I havn't written any letters for <u>weeks.</u>

I hope the news about your knee is good, Olly, poor you. I was pleased to hear from Sally that Kip is not too <u>fat!</u> And thank you, Dan, for looking after him so beautifully. We've only just had your letter about the washing machine & things — it had no stamp! We <u>adore</u> getting your letters. We hear all the news of everyone. Thank you. Love to all, Douglas & Kip & Fig.

Love,
Jane

<u>Chimp Reserve</u>
[September 25, 1960]

Darling Family,

We are supposed to be going to Kigoma this morning — in one of the little African boats because my engine is not working. But the man who was supposed to stop the 5 am one did not, & now we are loaded with the possibility of having to wait for hours & hours. Luckily — well, only in this respect is it 'luckily' — really it is awful, but my chimps have all but vanished. I have come to the end of my month's work on home ground, & am now all set for a great search party. Yet <u>another</u> of Derek's boys arrived for me yesterday! Ma & I are getting giggly — we expect all his labour will be here soon! The farm will then cease to run & he can come here himself! It is very grey & cloudy here this morning — typical of your English summer I should think. We have just heard that Sue & Ron went to Bournemouth for 3 days of their honey-moon — what a hoot — & spent all their time with you.[*]

Yesterday afternoon I went along the stream to collect the fruits

---

[*] Sue Cary (of the Alligator Society) had married Ronald Featherstone in August.

the chimps had been eating. I had Wilbert — one of the original 2 of D's staff, who is 6 ft 5 in — & the next one, Short — about 5 ft nothing! It was a hoot. I had them both nipping up trees after chimp food, & trees for our plant collection. We had an <u>enormous</u> polythene bag which, draped over Short's shoulder, reached the ground. Of course, they all had to be pressed that night — ready for our 5 am start! — so I laid them out in families & noted their description in hurricane lamp light while Ma bunged them into presses. Day before yesterday saw a Ma chimp lift her baby from the branch where it had been hanging while she ate, & hold it to her breast, human fashion, for its feed. It was the sweetest thing. And then, half an hour later, I saw it lying, face downwards, on her lap while she groomed its back. I love my chimps now — at first I was only homesick for little vervet monkeys. There are a lot of kinds of monkey here — & I've seen one very queer one that I've never seen before — or heard of. Wouldn't it be fun to have a Cercopithecus goodalli!*

Mummy is now rushing round in great agitation because we don't know how to preserve the large fruits which the chimps eat — for identification purposes. It's a job I don't like — collecting food plants. Another part of my job is messing around in dung, under their nests, to see what they've been eating! What a life, eh! Sometimes it suddenly comes over me how strange it all is, really. Here I am, an ordinary person, with my staff of 3, a camp, unlimited funds, and doing what I have always wanted to do. Not stuck away in some horrid office, out of the sunlight, but out in the open, sleeping under the stars, climbing the mountains, watching all the animals. Is it possible? Can it <u>really</u> be me? Or is it some strange hallucination? The only sad part is that it's so far away from all of you. If only you were all in Kigoma, or even Nairobi. Or if my chimps & their reserve were in the New Forest. But, of course, one can't have everything. You must look out for the Watney's advert — Bob's the chap drinking beer!!† He appears to have a bit of work now — about time too! Poor old Bob. It's now 9 am — seems <u>hours</u> since I

---

* Possibly she had seen one of the occasional hybrid blue/red-tailed monkeys.
† Robert Young, her former fiancé, had found temporary employment.

got up, ready for the non-existent boat. It is hours. Sometimes I love getting up at 5.30. Sometimes it's awful!

Love to all,

Jane

Chimpland.

[October 31 and November 1, 1960]

Darling Family,

I feel so guilty for not having written a long letter for such centuries. I console myself with the fact that Mum gives you all the news anyway. How are you all. How's the Bentley, Rix? You'll have to forgive my writing, but my hand is frozen stiff, & I'm sitting in a hurricane on a rock on a cliff top. When such a wind blows the chimps always stay on the ground, generally in the river valleys, so there is no hope of seeing them just yet. And I happened to have these rather scruffy bits of paper in my pocket.

I dare say Mum has told you about the visit of George & Kay Schaller? The American who has just done such a superb study of the gorilla. It really was nice to talk to someone who really understood what I was doing, and why, & who didn't think I was completely crazy. He did not envy me my mountains or my heat. He, poor man, had the most freezy wet climate. When in their little cabin they wore layers of sweaters & shivered, & he ate porridge for breakfast. It rained regularly every day — usually 4 times — often more. He said he sometimes used to sit on a branch & watch the gorillas below. The branches were all covered in long moss — it looked lovely & soft, but when you sat on it it went "squelch" & was cold, soggy and nasty. He used to get very embarrassed at presenting the boy, time after time, with pants that were a queer greeny brown colour!!

It was a pity all my chimps departed on his arrival, not returning till the day after he went! But he had only come to look at their habitat, the possibilities of the Reserve and, mainly, to spy on me! He admitted as much to me before he went! Which proves, I think, that he was not too horrified by my work.

Now I must recount two chimpy things. One I just mention because it is rather exciting. George said he thought that if I could see chimps eating meat, or using a tool, a whole year's work would be justified. Well, yesterday we were lucky enough to see a male chimp with a piece of pink meat. I think it was a baby animal of some sort. In the tree with him were a female with a tiny baby clinging round her, and a 6 year old child — and a small collection of baboons. It was the funniest thing. At first it was all rather noisy — the baboons & chimps were chasing each other. But it quieted down, leaving Pa with his meat, and all the others sitting round gazing at him. His wife beseechingly put out her hand, but he tucked the meat firmly under his arm. She made no other move — just sat, gazing longingly, & occasionally putting out her hand & touching his. No response. But he did let the child have a taste. The comical thing was that he sat with the meat in one hand & a bunch of leaves in the other, taking a bite at each, alternating. For all the world like a bloke with a pork pie in one hand & a stick of celery in the other! Then another male chimp, with his wife & tiny baby, climbed up the tree. And every time the lucky chap moved, they all followed him in a row, the baboons behind. It was both comical, fascinating, and scientifically valuable.

Oh dear, how cold it is. Soon it's going to rain I think. Then I shall retire under my polythene sheet (which George gave me).

Now my next item, which is far more exciting in a personal way. I was sitting, waiting for some chimps to arrive & climb into their fruit trees on the other side of a little stream. It was cold, & I had the aforementioned polythene sheet folded round my shoulders. I suddenly heard footsteps in the leaves behind me. Thought it sounded like a chimp, & did not want them to see me just there. So I lay down, half hidden by a tree. Kept very still. The footsteps approached. Then I heard very small, surprised, puzzled exclamations. "Huh" "Hoo hoo". High little sounds. The footsteps stopped. A few more comments. The leaves rustled nearer still. I closed my eyes — if they thought I was asleep, & did not know they were there, they probably would not bother unduly. "Huh" "Huh" — it sounded as though 4 or 5 chimps were conferring over this peculiar object, done up in polythene.

There was a silence. Then one voice behind me grew a little louder. Short sharp hoots, with an occasional little wimpery noise. I did not move. The sounds, I judged, were about 10 feet away. Then I heard branches shaking. For the first time I opened an eye. A few feet from the tree I was under was another little sapling. Up this a male chimp was climbing. He sat there & hooted at me. Screamed a few times. Then he climbed into my tree & sat on a branch not far above my head. For about 5 mins. he shrieked at me. He hit a leafy branch over me, & then hit the tree trunk with his hand, making a drumming noise. Then he seized the branch with both hands & shook it vigorously. I was showered with (rain!) twigs & buds & leaves. Then, back to the little tree, & out of sight. A second male climbed this tree & sat silently looking at me. And a female with her baby appeared, down the slope in front of me. Meanwhile my friend was behind me, hooting excitedly. He had worked up a lot of courage by now. The hoots were closer & closer. I heard breathing. Still I did not move. He retreated & paused for a moment. Then, with a last defiant hoot I felt his hand brush across my hair!! You see, if only you wait long enough, the chimps will establish "contact" with you!

Well, at this point I thought the old boy had got excited enough, so I slowly raised myself on one elbow & turned to look at him. He shut up at once, and retreated. The other male climbed rapidly down & joined him. The female disappeared discreetly. Extraordinary what an effect movement can have. A last defiant series of hoots & they all drifted away. Very excited. I heard him calling out to the other chimps, saying what a brave chap he was, drumming several times on the trees.

Wasn't that fun! And I can dine out on it for years. You wait till I tell Cliff Mitchalmore on Tonight, with full sound effects — I'm quite good at them by now.

We had another visitor here last week — David Anstey, the Game Ranger who greeted us on arrival & helped us to get set up. He was very nice, though he did come up on the mountain with me, which was annoying, & rather mucked up a morning. Still, by 12 am he'd had enough, so the afternoon was all right. He is removing the bane of my life, Adolf the Game Scout. How happy I shall be. And sending a well educated English speaking scout who has been trained by the Govt. Biologist. So he should be O.K.

Now that these rains have come the chimps seem to be going down to the lake shore, which is wonderful. Perhaps in the long rains I shall be able to take my tent to the beach & do all my observing from within!

It is a day since I started this — see change of pen! It is now about 10.30 pm, so that I must end or I shall be asleep before I'm in bed. I walked miles & miles today — & if I'd stayed at the camp there were chimps here all day!

Douglas, I wanted to write to you at Whipps, but by the time a chance & post arrived we guessed you'd be out again. I do hope the opp. went off O.K.

Danny, as for you & Douglas & the tree — well, we were quite stunned. What a work, & for you, Olly, too.

I meant to write more. About the exquisite wonder of the flowers which have sprung up like magic since the rain. You cannot imagine how strange it is. For months I have trudged through the heat on a parched dry soil, rocky & barren. Now, a magic wand is waved. Beautiful lilies, striped with pale purple, sway beneath the trees on the lake shore. Little bells, like hair bells, bloom delicately in the woods. White orchids push, leafless, from the damp moss. Beautiful scents wherever you go. And a really <u>fantastic</u> plant is a flower, rather like a yellow nasturtium, in the middle of a cone shaped, thick single leaf: cross section (too late to draw!!!)

Shall write a longer letter soon. When Ma goes, the official scribe of this expedition, having more time, I will make an effort.

Tons & tons of love,

Jane

Chimpland.
[Postmarked February 6, 1961]*
Darling family (except my ex-Sister whom I forthwith excommuni-
cate, disown, & cut from my will [i.e. she will not be left my super-
fluous gym shoes and my boxes of love letters!]),

I do hope you have had some letters from me by now. I was rather
a long time writing after Christmas — but so were you. I almost
sent you a cable to see if you were all right, until at long last, a letter
came. To which I immediately replied, only the reply was length-
ened out between Nairobi & Kigoma.

Anyway, thanks for yours, Mummy (2), and Olly and Dan. I'm
dreadfully sorry about the high blood pressure — I must tell Norman — that is his complaint. He has to have 'de-compression' pills!
Poor old you. And I'm sorry to hear you're under the weather Dan.
Hope you'll be O.K. by the time you get this. The dress, Olly, I
didn't have the chance to wear this time — being mostly at the
Coast where it was too hot for anything more than shorts. Also,
camping, we didn't wear dresses at all. But it will be smashing for
when I return to Nairobi in June — for my photography course —
if I have it.

News from here is mostly a trifle damp! Oh dear, Danny, I often
think of your horror when I plod around in wet cloths or sit on the
wet ground. Luckily, being Africa, it's not the sort of damp to give
you rheumatism.

I now climb the mountains on my own, & Saulo comes up later
on. I leave little notes in polythene bags saying where I shall be, so
that he has a sort of paper chase each day — rather fun for him!!
But just now, with the chimps so erratic, I see no point in two of us
getting wet all day, when one can get just as effectively damp, all on
one's own! So my mountain climbing cloths are now practical, if
slightly unconventional. I tie my trousers round my waist, & my
polythene sheet round my waist too, & there I am. The top half
doesn't get too wet. Occasionally, if I am forced to walk about in the
rain, I bare that to the elements as well! It's the same old polythene

---

* Written in stages between January 29 and February 4.

sheet — my new one is surrendered to Hassan who has a hole in the roof of his tent!

Well, José and the Kibisi arrived last Saturday with all my things, as planned + + +! Collin, the Greenshields, Dominic's wife, Hildebrand & Hilda, and 3 "Tobacco gentlemen" as they were introduced to me. Do you remember Mum, from Belbase days, a young man in the tobacco trade — Mike I think — Shawe or something? Well, he was one, & 2 others. Well, Robert went off for a baraza* with old Iddi Matata, & Colin & the 3 tobacco gents all whipped the tent up in no time, with Hassan & Rashidi helping. None of the others helped! They all returned to the huts — I think because Robert went there to talk business & they didn't want to miss anything. But Rashidi turned up real trumps and worked like a Trojan. We had tea, & then they departed, leaving me with a <u>superbly</u> erected tent, and absolute <u>chaos</u> around the place. Saulo appeared from the baraza, & he & Rashidi & Hassan & Dominic & the Askanzi father all helped me to pile everything into the tent. Hildebrand & his new wife had made themselves quite at home, & José had brought a large box for a hen house. She said he's had a <u>rotten</u> time with her — her cock had chased him all day long & he'd had to sleep, an outcast, on the woodpile. He is now in his element, & has learnt to crow very nicely.

That night the heavens descended. Of course, we hadn't got round to making a ditch, so the 'verandah' was like a toddlers' paddling pool! I struggled with the guy ropes with my failing torch, & was soaked to the skin when I got back. It was lovely to lie hearing the rain on my new roof. The next day I got back a bit earlier than usual, & made everything ship-shape. You would love it now Mum, really you would. I have a great box of surplus — coo — here are my chimps. Bye.

Well, after that interruption to the tune of 23 hours, here I am again. I had been sitting overlooking the Pocket — I am again, when I suddenly heard loud chimp screams. Baboons joined in. I didn't have a very successful time — I picked out two chimps — a

---

* A meeting.

long way away, & saw them make their nests, & Ma & baby climb into one & the other into the other. And this morning I got nearer & saw one getting up, but the other had already got up when it was light enough to see. And they silently vanished baby & all. So I've been working on Red Colobus all morning. Now, back to my vigil again.

Where was I — oh yes — a box of extra stores in the bathroom — which is now large! From this Dominic keeps a smaller box filled with day to day requirements. Hassan had made the most lovely hen house, door & legs & all. This lives at one side of the verandah & acts as a sideboard. On it, in a shining row, are 7 large tins from Bimje,* for sugar, flour, etc. The other side, low down, is Norman. He has cups & plates etc on him.† And in the middle — where there is still a lot of room, is my new little low camp table. This can be moved easily. I usually have supper outside unless it's actually raining (often is!). Also, after supper, it's just the right height for me to write at sitting on my bed (albeit balanced on two pillows & a folded blanket!). It is always kept quite clear except for whatever it is being used for.

Derrick gave me 3 tin ammo boxes. One is outside, by Norman, & has biscuits, spaghetti, cigarettes, etc. in it. One is at the top of my bed — all my books fit in it, backs upwards, so that it's like looking into a bookcase, only it's been lain on its back. The 3rd has oddments required daily, or fairly often, such as NIVEQUIN!!!‡ extra torch, batteries, etc. The blue trunk has all my papers in it. The black one contains only things likely to be wanted once in a blue moon, or not at all. On this is the clock, baby powder, Pier, and George. George is a beautiful white ivory elephant presented to me as a souvenir of days hunting of the real George. (I take it you did get my long letter all about the trip home? — about 18 pages?)§ Hassan has dug huge & beautiful trenches all over the place, direct-

---

* A shopkeeper in Kigoma.
† A storage cabinet named Norman, possibly made by Norman Mitton.
‡ Malaria medicine.
§ On her way to Nairobi during the Christmas holidays, Jane visited with Derrick Dunn in Arusha; together they went on a safari that included elephant "hunting" (without guns).

ing the flow of water, so I'm in no danger of being washed away. And with a piece of corrugated iron from Robert, Hassan has erected a fine banda* for the kitchen. And I am looked after as though I were a Queen. Terribly spoilt. . . .

Now I must tell you about the chimps. I saw 7 resting [in] a big tree for over an hour. The lady made a nest! Two old gents groomed each other. It was very nice indeed. Then, the same evening, I saw 2 chimps making nests in the Pocket. Next morning I was up close before light, & I saw a mama & her baby waking up. There were 3 others that I didn't see, only heard. They got up as soon as it was light & screamed & crashed around. Baby leaned along Ma's leg to see what they were doing, & then flopped back to bed. She was lying on her back. Babe went off for a walk, came back, & crawled on her chest, putting his face down to hers & lay on her tummy. At last Mum got up. She just sat in her bed. Looked round. Yawned. And sat. Babe kept going off having little walks. Then she sat at the side of her bed. Babe came & sat with his arms round her. Then she groomed him. Then he went past her & lay in the bed, & she held her hand over him & he played with it. It really was all too sweet for words. She never saw me till she was actually down on the ground, & even then I saw babe, sitting up on her back, & just appearing above the grass, very close before she saw me. It was a really good day — thank goodness for it, or I'd really be miserable by now.

Yesterday, right at the top of Sleeping Buffalo, in one of the open spaces, I saw at least 25!! There were too many to count accurately, anyway!! But they all disappeared again — didn't come down at all. So I'm left with the 2 & the baby, who move silently.

Hello again! Can't remember what page I got to so these are A, B, C etc. Now, I'm going to tell you something — it's raining! Honestly! I'm in the same place as before, but two days have elapsed — already both have taken on a dream-like quality & I find it hard to believe in their actuality. However, let me tell you about them — what a pity you arn't here now, Mum — for once you would have had a really excited Jane — more than the meat, more than the termites.

---

* Thatched hut.

The day started well. I heard chimps by Linda, went over, & saw them down by what I call the Bottom Bump — you know Mum, where the stream goes out into the lake, & the slope is all thick with trees. It's stopped raining. Well, I managed to get reasonably close — on the opposite side of the valley. One could easily see sex, face colour, etc. I watched them playing in the trees — mostly young ones, all morning. Then they vanished. I moved a little way down the slope, & heard the angry hoots & squeaks of the males. They'd seen me. I sat down, and soon saw them — 5 large males and one adult female. They were all feeding away in some trees opposite. This they did for 30 mins. Then they climbed down, & I first saw them climbing up through odd spaces in the trees & grass. They arrived at another tree and climbed up. There they rested peacefully. Suddenly the rest of the party appeared — seemingly out of thin air! All the children and at least one more male & a young lady of skittish temperament. The romping began all over again — the poor grown ups just had to lump it. The games went on for an hour. I could see better this time — wrestling, chasing — all silently, as it had been all morning.

Then it began to rain. I expected them all to get down to shelter under the trees. Not a bit of it. They stayed where they were. Then one old male climbed down. He has a pale face — I knew him of old. He sat on the grass under a tree & just looked around, hunched. A very young male (who rather hero-worships Paleface) ran over and sat very close. Slowly they all climbed down from the tree. Half of them came to join Paleface, the other half went and grouped themselves about 50 yards away. It was most organized. A mum with a child on her back headed Paleface's group — 5 all told. They began moving sedately, in line, up the hill. The other group also started off — just a little behind Paleface, & headed by 'Bare Bum' — you remember him, Mum?

(Interrupted there. Now next morning — and it's <u>raining!</u>)

Well, they were almost at the top of the slope. When they started off they left the tree, & there was about 100 yards or more of grass above, with single trees scattered around.

Suddenly Bare Bum left his troop and galloped, full speed, at the other line, swinging his body from side to side, arms flailing in a scything motion. There was an outburst of panting calls. He moved on up a hill & as he reached the top, stood up and swiped at a bush with his hand. Well, I thought that was that. But no. They all began to climb trees. Pale Face then turned & began to charge diagonally down the hill. As he went he snatched at the branch of a tree, tore it off, waved it above him, & charged on, dragging it with him. Then he dropped it & climbed a tree. But another large male was on the move, charging down, breaking off his branch. Then two hurtled down, one after the other, leapt into a tree, seized branches, & leapt to the ground — 30 ft. at least, taking their branches with them, charging on, reaching a tree, seizing it, swinging round & leaping up into the branches. I think only the males took part in this "Rain Festival". The others staying in their 'seats', watching.

I don't think I have ever watched any performance which gave me such a thrill. Mostly the actors were silent, but every so often their wild calls rang out above the thunder. Primitive hairy men, huge and black on the skyline, flinging themselves across the ground in their primaeval display of strength and power. And as each demonstrated his own majestic superiority, the women and children watched in silence, and the rain poured down while the lightning flashed brilliantly across the grey sky.

For thirty minutes this wild display continued — and as I watched I could not help feeling the display was for my benefit — it was to me they were proving their strength and might — me, the poor miserable weak human who dared to intrude upon their lives. The place of the Festival was a natural out of door theatre — a curve in the hillside, with trees all round. They looked so black and gigantic, slightly above me, against the brilliant green of the grass.

When it was over they all sat in trees — 3 in one, 2 in another — but Pale Face sat alone, centrally, reclining at ease in the branches. Eventually they began climbing down, one by one, and walking quietly to the brow of the hill. On the skyline they looked even larger. One or two climbed a tree for a moment, waiting for the others to catch up. But at last they had all gone — all save Pale Face. He was last, & before finally crossing the ridge he stood up, one hand on a tree, and looked back at me for a long minute. The actor taking his final curtain.

Can you begin to imagine how I felt? The only human ever to have witnessed such a display, in all its primitive, fantastic wonder? I fear I was not able to report it as exactly as science might wish. I had no thought for exact numbers, or seconds — nor could I write as I watched — a) for fear of missing one second, and b) because it was far too wet.

I was interrupted yesterday by a troop of Red Colobus, which I watched until Saulo arrived. This morning I gaily crested the peak — & there, not 15 yards away, was my sedate old gentleman friend, the bull buffalo. He was lying there so peacefully, chewing his cud & having 40 winks! He never even saw me. Ye gods — it is pouring! I'm endeavouring to keep the paper dry by holding a polythene bag over it — without overmuch success. If it had done this an hour ago I shouldn't have climbed till it was over. Hassan & I got the new pressure lamp going last night, & today he is erecting a frame for the large towel. So I shall be moth catching in a big way. He's quite a carpenter is Hassan. And Dominic is zealous with his dudu* catching. I've got the little net living up on the mountains now, so am able to do a bit myself in between the chimps — & the rains!

Well, I still havn't related the second day. When I climbed up there were chimps calling all over the place — one big group up Sleeping Buffalo, & more behind me, very close. These arrived from Linda at about 9.30, & I suspected they were my 'actors' of yesterday. Anyway, I set off to investigate. I decided to go into the forest, rather than climb up to look down. I could hear them close to me, but they seemed to be on the move. However, I kept on, even though I had a suspicion they knew I was there. Suddenly I found I was very close. And it began to rain. For a while I stayed still, under my sheet. Silence from the chimps. So I thought, to blazes with the rain, & moved off in the direction I thought they had gone. Well, the thing was, they hadn't gone. And suddenly loud angry hoots sounded, almost overhead. So I sat me down. I was in a bad place — a small clearing with thick undergrowth all round. For a few minutes I heard nothing. Then I saw branches moving — perhaps 15 yds away. I could only see by lying down. So I lay down. There was

---

* Insect.

a large female, eating away, about 20 ft. up. As I looked she turned round, gave me a contemptuous stare, & went on feeding. All at once my eye was caught by a bush moving, about 6 yards away. There was Bare Bum, on the ground, regarding me. He turned & moved into the thick undergrowth where I could only tell he was there from an occasional stirring leaf. There were sounds of other chimps moving in the trees, but I just could <u>not</u> see. Did not like to move again. Then came a low 'hoo' from Bare Bum. A reply came from the bushes to my right — even closer. But I could <u>not</u> see a chimp. These little "hoo's" went on for some time. Then the rain, which had paused, started up again. Suddenly there was a loud "hoo" & a deafening chorus of hoots & screams of defiance — almost all round me! Certainly on 3 sides. Well, I thought they'd better have something to keep their minds off how much they didn't like me, so I diligently dug for insects, making little grunting noises. This kept them quiet!

After this it was wonderful. A small child came down, looked at me, climbed a tree, & sat regarding me. (Maybe Spray). Another large black female came & stared at me through the bushes. For 3 hours the whole troop was round me, feeding. I could hear the smacking of their lips and the little pleasure grunts.

Where the ink starts* is another day — 2 days since I last started. Since when I have been working on Red Colobus — good work. Very close. Mating etc. And tonight the chimps came back.

Now Hassan has just informed me he's going to Kigoma tomorrow to send his wife some money, so I'm <u>frantically</u> finishing this off, together with other urgent ones — poor Norman will have been trotting vainly to the P.O. for weeks! At present I'm sitting by the big towel, erected in a large frame, under the pressure lamp, leaping up every now and then to catch dudus! Hassan has also made a frame for the mosy† net, so I sleep unmolested.

I met more buff. the day I stopped writing! Also, it <u>really</u> rained.

---

* She changed from ballpoint to blue fountain pen in the middle of the previous sentence.
† Mosquito.

And last night it never stopped. I wasn't able to get up the mountain until 11 — & I stayed in bed until z̲!!!

Well, tons & tons of love, and I'll drop a line again as soon as poss.

Jane

Chimpland.
3rd April [1961]

Hello all,

Thought I must pen a few lines on my Birthday. It is a funny one and no mistake — a nice one too. It started off with a mountain climb in the moonlight and 8 dear little chimps in their nests. One poor young lady, while it was scarcely light, was woken from a deep sleep by an amorous suitor. With a scream horrifying to hear she leapt out of bed — no time to make up or anything. Dear me! From the sound of things she was not permitted a peaceful breakfast either! They all went away after that. I sat up a tree over by Linda, and then came back to look at the nests. Had done half of them, & was busily poking about in dung, when I heard chimps. The trail led me back to camp! Where I saw 3 just up behind for a while.

Since then it has been raining hard. I found Dominic cursing the fire because it was spoiling my cake. No mere 'safari' cake this — it has everything on it — every egg D could lay hands on, tins of butter — my word. I have been left to put the icing sugar & candles on when it's cool. Jellies are made. And yesterday D, on his own bat, made a loaf of "sweet bread". Iddi and bibi,* and the Scouts —

Well!! W̲h̲a̲t̲ a birthday present (only one I might add). I had just penned the last word when I heard a noise, (I am i̲n̲ the tent, on bed, as it's cold) & saw a chimp hanging on the end of the frond of the palm tree outside. N̲o̲t̲ the bathroom one (anon) but the one where (I keep writing one letter of one word followed by first letter of n̲e̲x̲t̲ word!) we had that table Mum! He climbed up. I lay on my tummy & looked up at him. A second walked across to the frond. I suppose

---

* Wife.

it's 5 yards away. Then I think the one up there may have seen me. Anyway, he looked down & hooted at the one below who went across the grass & into the bushes opposite. Here he climbed a bush. Then both of them gave loud angry calls — at me? The old man up the tree went on stuffing nuts into his mouth. Made a funny little cross hoot to himself. The other climbed higher and ate some fruit. After 20 mins the old boy climbed down his frond, reached for the trunk, got to the ground, and went into the bushes. They're both gone now. It's still raining as hard as ever. This is the way to watch chimps! The bathroom episode was these same two. Chimps appear here every other day now. As it usually rains about 1 pm & there were no chimps up top I decided to try my luck here. And these two were already up the tall palm — nearer the lake. They saw me come & climbed down. I went into the bathroom & peered out — there was the old boy sitting in the rain scratching his chin. Suddenly he got up. Passed me by about 3 yards, no more. And re-climbed the palm! He was up there for an hour, but the trouble was I couldn't see him properly. The following day I spent another 2 hours on the bathroom floor, with no luck, so I abandoned the idea. WHAT a pity you're not here now Mum.

Ma. Must tell you a funny thing. You know the parcel of dawa* you sent? Well, it arrived via Adolf 2 days ago. (Just wondering if I've told you about the bathroom?) It's thundering now. I'm eating peppermints — got them as a treat — havn't had any choc this time — choc eats though! Anyway I thought to myself, seeing your writing, 'Good old Ma — at least she has got a present here in time'. I carefully didn't look at the declaration of course! So I opened it at lunch time — well, if 3 pm is lunch time, but I had opened a tin of bully beef, with D's new loaf — and how I laughed. — 'Can you send word back in time for me to send a present to reach you on THE day?' Well, old bean, I guess I can't! So sorry!!

It's thundering now. I'm very glad I am down here, apart from the chimps. I can't begin to tell you how wet everything is. I opened my camera — in case I got a chance to do the chimp — & it won't shut

---

* Medicine.

again. Everything is covered in mildew. What a life. All Bob's*
dudus are rotting away gaily.

I was tackling at least 2 hours of Journal last night when Iddi &
a troop came along with their lantern — giving the pigs a good
scare for once. Oh dear — an ill baby, an ill bibi — and two "kich-
was"† — I don't think! Long chats of course. He sent me some
meat today — don't know why. Mutton, D says.

Don't think I'll write any more now because this won't go until
Hassan does on Thursday. So I'll add. Who would be cross if I said
T.T.F.N.‡ Since I don't think I've ever said it, I wonder what put it
into my head. I hope by then (Thursday) there'll be a letter answering some of my questions. Can't remember what they were, but I'm
sure there were some. I've just iced the cake & stuck candles in it.
Dominic came to make me some coffee & disapproving 'cos I
hadn't done it! Hildebrand is crowing in my ear, & Hilda has wandered off with her 14 babies. I'm sure the monitor is eating them
all, but I can't leave her shut up anymore. (It <u>DID</u> eat one!)

Adieu.

Hi! Thought I'd better finish off today. It's 7 pm. Still very light
these days. It's just stopped raining though luckily it's only been
spitting since 5 pm. I'm sitting up by my deserted kitchen accompanied by Hildebrand. I couldn't face a meal tonight! The jelly wasn't
set, so, with great glee the kids are coming round tomorrow. My
party was a great success I think. Iddi and family sauntered up while
Dominic and I idly thought we had another hour. So they all sat &
watched me cut up the "sweet" bread. Dominic & Hassan arranged
the tea etc, & the oldest son was despatched to tell Saulo to bring
more cups & chairs. It was quite a gathering. Iddi with <u>two</u> bibis. 4
small watoto.§ 2 big ones. Saulo. And we 3. They consumed the loaf
and innumerable cups of tea, & I related the soko episode** — they
all said he came for my birthday. I had a weird fruit I found in chimp

---

* Robert Carcasson, the entomologist at the Coryndon Museum.
† Headaches.
‡ "Ta-ta for now," an expression her mother hated, used ironically by Jane.
§ Children.
** The chimpanzee episode described earlier in the letter.

dung which was handed round. No one knew it, but Iddi said his big son might. I think he's a bit dim! Anyway, he came back & I handed it to him & asked if he knew what 'tribe' it was. I JUST managed to stop him putting it into his mouth!! How everyone laughed. I had hit his hand hard, & we had quite a job to find the precious specimen! Hassan made a speech saying he wished me and my sister many happy birthdays. Then, the great ceremony of lighting the candles — which fizzled ominously in the rain — & D explained the custom of wishing for me — so they all — well, I wouldn't go that far — sat and wished. Then we thought the monitor was caught — but the trap had been sprung from the outside. Then we found Hilda only had 13 babies, not 14. Very sad. I solemnly dosed the small ill child — which seems a bit better. And presented Iddi with a bottle of orange juice.

The sunset is lovely. Hildebrand has just stalked off to join his wife & family in the henhouse. It is getting dark, and is peaceful and lovely. It's been an odd birthday, compared to all my others, but I must say I've enjoyed it. A wind is springing up and I shall probably go in in a minute. The Congo Hills are so clear nowadays you can see the valleys & the forests. It's fantastic. And as for Ruanda — you feel you could walk there in a couple of hours — right at the North of the lake I mean.*

The ointments, etc, which, in the joke of it, I forgot to say thank you for! — actually came just at the right time because I got bitten by a mosie last night — she was in bed with me! Oh yes — 2 more things. (1) did I tell you that D and Hassan respectively guessed I was 14 and 16!!!!

Iddi wants a picture of him & me to put in a large frame — an enlarged picture — to hang in his house! Isn't it sweet. Now, goodnight.

P.S. I havn't a clue I realize, of Sue's name!† Never heard it!! Can you address this envelope — making at least the NAME look like my writing!

---

* The territory of Ruanda-Urundi, which is now the nation of Burundi with Rwanda to the north.
† Sue Cary's married name.

Chimpland
4th April 61

Dear Bernard,

Sorry to plague you unmercifully, but I have to write when I think of these things. This one is, I imagine, quite out of the question, but it was just a notion I had — that it would be interesting to know the food value in the things the chimps eat — their main foods that is. Now, for instance, they seem to eat only a certain yellow blossom for whole days at a time. Is there any way of finding out such a thing? (I'm thinking of my thesis!)

I had the most lovely birthday present yesterday. It started off nicely when I climbed the mountain in the moonlight & saw all my chimps wake up in the morning. Then I came down early because of rain. And 2 chimps climbed the tree outside my tent & ate there for 30 mins! I just lay on the floor & watched them. They knew I was there too — just yelled at me! as though I had no right to be in my own tent!

And such a sweet little birthday party I had. Dominic had made "sweet" bread, a superb cake, & jelly, & I had the old boy who lives here, his two wives, 4 little boys, 2 big ones, & the game scout — a new & very nice one. Such a ceremony over lighting the candles on the cake, & they all had to wish for me when I cut it!

I now have 14 little chicks just out for Easter. At least I did, though now the vile monster has eaten two, despite Hassan & Dominic running after them like nannies all day, & specially made hen coops, etc. The old devil much prefers my chicks to the smelly piece of meat in his specially constructed trap!

Dear me, how it does rain. And rain. And how the grass grows. I've been treed by 2 buffaloes! And the day before yesterday was really thrilled to see my leopard — albeit a little too close for comfort. But he is so very beautiful.

I am frozen stiff at the moment, but luckily a nice hot curry is on its way. Let me know how things are with you. Incidentally, if you feel the need to sort yourself out, the mountains are the place to do it. I'm sorted out completely.

Love
Jane.

[May 7, 1961]

Have to write a few words, simply because it can't be true. It can't. David Greybeard is up the palm. I am sitting outside the tent. D. is washing up after my breakfast — which I ate sitting outside the tent. I have walked all round the tree taking pictures — sadness — only one film & that, I think, spoilt by damp. Even from directly underneath. We have talked. Can it be true? My filming difficulties, re. termites — are as good as over. I can just walk up to the ant hill & film David G. This is unique. I can get my own fabulous pictures. Only the sad thing is it's not salt he's after — it's palm nuts & they are nearly finished. Still, as I proved the other day, he doesn't mind me up in the mountains either. I keep looking up & not believing it's a chimp — not a real one. How I wish you were here Mum. He'd soon take food from your hands, come when you called! He's sitting contemplating now, scratching his chin. I have just been under the tree talking in a loud voice to him. He didn't even look! Rayed out below are: 1 tin baked beans, open. 1 plate salt. 1 plate sugar. 1 glass lime juice!!! I am drinking coffee! Isn't it too ridiculous for words? Better than George's "Junior"* who sat 25 yards away. This is not 25 feet. I'm longing for him to come down.

Sadness — it began to pour & he climbed down & vanished. Never mind — from 8–10 he was there.

Tons of love,
Jane

The Peak,
Chimpland.
16th May [1961]

Darling Family,

I'm up here waiting for a gale to subside so that I have a reasonable chance of hearing anything worth hearing, or seeing anything to be seen. It is 4.30, and I had a very nice time with chimps from 8 am–2.15, so I can't grumble. Horace and his girls, Sophie and Sophocles.

---

* A gorilla so named by George Schaller.

I simply don't know where to begin, telling you about David Greybeard. He is utterly fantastic. I think with this moment: I was staying down to try & take some pictures of David G. I was expecting him about 8.30–9. I was, therefore, still reclining in luxury at 7.30, & Dominic was just getting my tea — fancy! — early morning tea! My bed was about 4 ft from the palm — David's Palm. I was under my net, gazing through it at the grey sky. Suddenly I heard a rustling. David G. He glanced up casually at my bed, climbed 5 ft. up the trunk, reached out for his usual frond (which he then swarms up) & only then noticed me under the net. He gazed harder, then, almost visibly shrugging his shoulders, he ascended and sat above me, chewing nuts. Did not look at me again.

Another moment. Waking up at 6.15 and waiting for it to get light, peering up at the outline of the tree where David is sleeping. Still too dark to make anything out when I hear a sound like someone pouring a kettleful of water down from a tree top through leaves — which is almost what it amounted to, anyway! Then Olly's famous card cow-pats. Then silence. As it got lighter I was able to see David G. on his tummy, head sideways, eyes closed. Suddenly his eyes opened wide. He blinked. Gazed round. Glanced at me. I scratched. David G. scratched. Stretched. Closed his eyes once more. Then turned over out of sight. 10 mins passed. Dominic peered out of his tent, grinned, and walked along the path, avoiding my bed which lay across it, & went off to cook me a sausage! David G sat up & scratched. Then lay on his tummy, propped on his elbows, and gazed at me between hiccoughs! Then he slowly got up, stretched, sat nearby, & swung over my bed to his fig tree above Hassan's tent. H's face emerged, & said jambo to me and Bwana David. Retreated. I had my breakfast gazing at David G in the fig, having his breakfast. Then, I sat waiting for him. Up the path he strolled. Gathered up his bananas, & sat on the ground, facing me (on the ground) 12 feet away. Up his Palm. I laid out more bananas. He finished his nuts, climbed down, picked up 3 from the ground, sauntered over to the tent (I was opposite) helped himself to 3 from the table — right at the back of the verandah, walked upright with his haul to the tree where you, Ma, made your clinic sit, & ate them.

Another moment. I was climbing Ogre at 5 pm having waited

vainly at the salt lick. Just by the place which I think was your "1st plateau" Mum, I heard rustlings. I stopped. They approached. A black head emerged onto the path some 20 yards in front. Stood looking at me. I stepped aside. He stopped. So I turned round and went back along the path. Looked round. He was following! He did not follow me all the way back along the path, but used his own some of the way. He gave me 5 mins to get things ready for him, then strolled in from the kitchen!

Can you imagine it? We all keep saying how sad it is that Memsahib Mkubwa* isn't here.

He is a lovely specimen too. All his hair, scarcely any baldness of the forehead, long cheek hair, beautiful beard, dark handsom face — very handsom chimp. Rather like old Dick† at the zoo in fact, only I reckon he's bigger.

The time he made his nest we had all been watching him in his fig. He sat there, in the sunset, sucking away at the lump of pips in his lower lip. Dominic went off to start the supper, & Hassan & I lay on our backs & watched him cross over, climb the tree, and make his nest.

At 2 am Rashidi went to Dominic's tent with some dagaa‡ for me, with a lamp. David G. was most annoyed, & told everyone so! Rashidi, who did not know he was there, says he ran off to start with! Then put his lamp out & returned in the dark!

I think the rains are almost over. I thought they were 4 days ago, and then: — well, at 12 midnight I felt a few drops, decided it would pass, & so merely dropped my polythene sheet over the net & frame. This was fine. I dozed off. Was dimly aware of rain pounding on the roof of the tent — lovely sound. It wasn't till I was lying in a good several inches deep that I realized I was not in the tent, but in a sodden bed, lying in a river of water which was charging through the camp. Well, the bed was beyond hope, so I made a dash for the tent, pulled out the two spare blankets, rolled up in them, and spent the rest of the night on the floor. It did not stop. At

---

* "The senior madame," that is, Vanne.
† A chimpanzee at the London Zoo.
‡ Small sardinelike fish.

Valerie Jane Goodall, about two, out for a stroll in a London park.

Feeding the birds.

*Trying out
a horse.*

*Valerie Jane holding
Jubilee, her stuffed
chimpanzee, with her
younger sister, Judy,
and their nanny,
Nancy Sowden.*

Mortimer and Vanne Goodall with their daughters.
Mort joined the Royal Engineers in 1939.

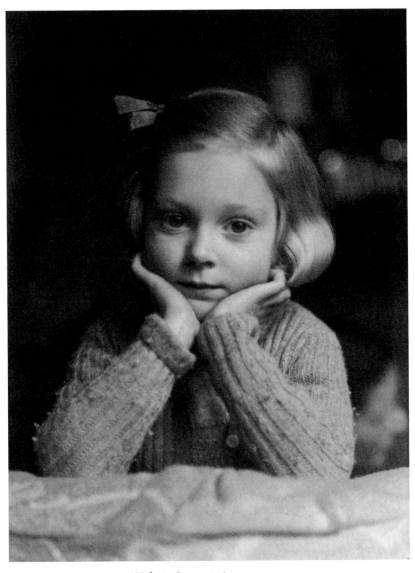

Valerie Jane at six or seven.

The Manor House in Kent, where the family stayed just before the war.

The family at Bournemouth. Left to right: Judy,
Aunt Olwen, Danny (Jane's grandmother), Aunt Audrey,
Valerie Jane, Uncle Eric, and Vanne.

The Alligator Society. From the top: Red Admiral (Valerie Jane),
Rusty the dog, Puffin (Sally Cary), Ladybird (Sue Cary),
and Trout (Judy).

Jane riding Daniel.

Jane as a teenager with her beloved dog.
"Rusty was the only dog I have ever known who
seemed to have a sense of justice."

The charismatic Reverend Trevor Davies.

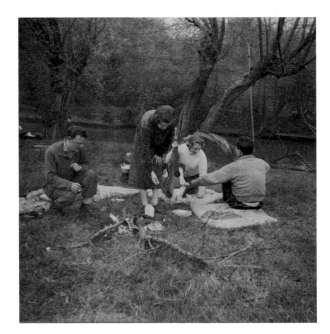

May Day picnic breakfast at Oxford.

Louis Leakey at Olduvai Gorge about 1957.

Dancing with Brian Herne at Ngorongoro Crater, Tanganyika, December 1957.

Jane Goodall, age twenty-three, Kenya Colony.

Jane drove Annabelle the orangutan to the Granada television
studio for a program by Desmond Morris.

*Flo and little Flint. Flo was "quite won over to the idea of
popping in for the odd banana."*

Jane's cartoon of life at Gombe Stream Reserve in the early years.

Jane and Hugo van Lawick were married on March 28, 1964.

Flo's Flint reaches out.

*David Greybeard was the first of the chimpanzees
to overcome the fear of human contact.*

9 am when D. appeared it had just begun to slightly ease off. He and I shrieked with mirth at the sight of my bed — it did look a mess. Earth had rushed over it & through it, with the stream, & the weight of the wet net had pulled the frame inwards. Added to which a large & v. poisonous centipede — about 8″ long & 2″ wide — was curled up under my pillow! D. says their bite is as bad as a snake — not fatal of course.

The rain continued until 4.30! David G arrived in a slight break, at about 3.30, and was still with us when it finally stopped. Yesterday we had a very heavy storm, with thunder. I suppose we shall get these odd deluges till the end of May.

My gale is still blowing. It would be dreadfully hot otherwise, and as I don't really expect to see any more chimps today, I'm not too sorry.

It seems quite amazing that we are over half way through May. And when I go to Nairobi I shall be half way through this year's watching. In some ways this is rather alarming. One thing's for sure — I shall not have seen all I want to see when I have to go. But one good thing — I can check up on all sorts of minor feeding points, etc, on David G. And he will be invaluable for filming the termites!

I don't know whether I shall be able to post this. I am putting it with one to José, & leaving it, in the hopes that a 'Rafiki'* will be going into Kigoma soon. Otherwise it will have to wait till end of May.

All the bibis are very friendly nowadays, including the one who had her baby. The husband, Yosef, is a good pal of Dominic's. Rashidi is now so willing & helpful. Because David employed him again as a porter & I think he knows it's thanks to me that he wasn't turned out of the Reserve. It's very nice for me — he cuts posts, & helps Hassan with things — & supplies me with fresh dagaa when I want it.

He also climbed David's palm with a dead rat! Which David G completely ignored, although nearly bumping his nose on it. He didn't even look at it — as though it was quite an everyday occur-

---

* Friend.

rence to find dead rats hanging on old shoe laces under his nose! You never told me if you got the photo of me and Colin that José took?

I'm sure that at some distant point I shall be asked what I want for Christmas. By when I shall have forgotten what has just occurred to me, so I will tell you now.

(1) Any of [blank space] Anthologies — I have "the Book of Love". There are 3 others — of Pleasure, of England — & Beauty! Beauty is the one I should prefer I think. But I don't know, as I've not seen them. (2) A reproduction, if there are such things, of a picture by [blank space] called [blank space]. I am utterly enchanted by the little girl in this picture.

Oh, I think it's going to deluge. What fun. I shall go if it does. I am now going on a tour to examine various chimp spots — with no expectation of seeing anything I might add! . . .

So tons of love,
Jane

Chimpland.
13th July [1961]

Darling Uncle Eric,

Please do forgive one of these nasty little things,* but I'm so busy nowadays that I can scarcely fit it all in. For one thing now that it has stopped raining I have no opportunities, or few, of writing letters up in the hills — as of yore, beneath my polythene sheet!

But it is really wonderful now the rain has stopped. Do you know, towards the end of the wet season I honestly wondered how I was going to exist through these last months. I didn't even feel like coming back after the week in Nairobi.† But oh, how different it is now. Already I feel the time speeding away, so much to do. Chimps are extremely friendly — I don't mind how far I scramble after them now because I know that there is a very good chance that they will not go away when I eventually reach them. At last I know most of

---

* The flimsy blue aerogramme on which the note was written.
† She took a brief holiday from Gombe in late May and early June.

the ♂ individually — as well as David G. (did you like his pictures?). There are Mike, Horace, Hollis, Huxley, Lord Dracula, the Hon. Mr. X, William, Winston and No. 3! What a collection of names! Women are <u>very</u> difficult & I can't usually get so close. Only to Barbara, Wilhemena, and Mrs. Maggs. Children are hopeless to recognize, except by the ♀ they are with. All the photography ahead alarms me considerably. The camera I have can only be used when one is almost shaking hands with the chimps, though it's the largest tele lens you can reasonably safely use hand held. Now Geographic have sent me all this complicated stuff — you will have seen from my other letter.

I meant to thank you for your letter to start off with. Anyway, I do thank you for it. It's jolly decent of you to find time to write because you're even busier than I am.

Next week — I hope — Derrick Dunn is bringing me a tape recorder. He's on a safari, & going to drop it in as he goes through Kigoma. This is another rather alarming aspect of the business, but one which I must cope with somehow. Though I've a feeling that the equipment isn't going to be good enough for the quality I want.

You heard of the Schallers — chap who did gorilla & came to visit Ma & I? They have a baby in a month & George is most anxious that Kay keeps it with her from the moment it's born — he feels the early mother/child relationship is particularly important — <u>after</u> studying his gorillas!! I only wish I could see a birth. <u>Most</u> unlikely.

Anyway, drop me another line when you have a moment.

Love to Peggy, lots of love to you,
Jane

<u>Chimpland.</u>
14 July [1961]

Darling Family,

If you can work this* out you will be clever. But I must write it on small sizes because of the gale. And small because all I have is this

---

* Her cramped handwriting on small pieces of paper.

thick paper. Oh, maybe biro will help. It's not meant to be blotting paper, but not much good for ink.

Mum, I do hope your colds & throats are <u>quite</u> better now. I wonder if there was a recurrence of our fever. When I told Dr. Grant about it, he said we should have made a blood slide. I told him Ugo said there was no malaria, and he said "B — " well, he said a rude word! And how horrid — about the machine needle going through your finger. Made me shudder all down my back. I hope that, too, is better.

Dan, your letter about Kip in Dennis's drawer — note, O & Jif, drawer, <u>not</u> with an S. What a time you all had to be sure. And there he was all snug & safe & laughing at you.

I am beginning to get in an awful flap about the way time is going. Do you know I have been back a <u>month,</u> already! And today is the anniversary of the first arrival of the Morris-Goodall Chimpanzee expedition! As a matter of fact it does seem a long time ago in many ways. Yet sometimes I can look at the peaks & valleys & see them with my early eyes, & how different they seem now. Then they were alien, strange, confusing — a challenge. And indeed, so were they in the rains. But now — now life is so wonderful. The challenge has been met. The hills & forests are my home. And what is more, I think my mind works like a chimp's, subconsciously. For when I take a track through the forest, selecting one from a maze of little trails — sure enough, if chimps are around, some old chap will be on the same road. It's happened <u>so</u> often. And I can't put it down to my cleverness at all — often it's a very <u>bad</u> track — for me. And often I choose one which I think I took before, & find it's another — & there is a chimp. It's most peculiar.

Although I'm not, at the moment, finding out anything startling, and <u>very</u> little that is new to me, none the less, life is good. Yesterday I made another friend. Another David G. Only this one is up in the hills and is all my own. I think it's the one we used to call Winston. I met him in my 'wood' the other day — he got to 4 or 5 yards from me, saw me, & bolted off. Not far. Anyway, yesterday I saw him plodding around the shoulder of Bald Soko so I decided to take a chance & go to his path in the wood. I only just got there when there was a rustle, & lo, a black face looking at me. Well, for one and a half hours he moved round me, picking up fallen mbula fruits from the ground. Sat in the sun with his back to me for ages — & this only 10 yards away. At times he came even closer to reach for a fruit. I prefer a tame chimp up in the mountains than in camp. I didn't take any photos — not the first time he honoured me with his company — because there are mbula trees ripe throughout this wood, so he definitely chose to be here because of me. I say "here" because I am now in the same spot. I don't think he'll come, because Mike & his woman, & another group, went across in his direction this morning & I dare say he has joined them. Still, I followed them for miles beyond Linda, but they wern't in a mood to hang about, so I left them. Then came the gale, so I thought I might as well wait here as anywhere. It is 4.30 pm.

You will probably all be delighted to hear that I have become ul-tra civilized. Now that Camp II is so very luxurious, I make myself a mug of coffee at some point during the day — when I get back from one of my safaris. Talk about the height of luxury!

I havn't yet mentioned, have I? that Derrick & Likens are coming here in 2 weeks with my tape recorder. I rather doubt it'll be good enough for the job, but I shall get D. to help me install the thing. They come just at the right time.

They come on 27th, & at the end of the month I have to go & look at the tree in Mitumba* — its name is lovely — Msululu. (The one you lost Mum!) So on the 28th we can play tape recorders, and on the 29th I can take D up Mitumba & get some hints on hide building, and on the 30th they can go, & if the tree is ready† I can organize my safari there. So it all fits in beautifully.

Robert & Alison come tomorrow for the night. They will hope to see a chimp on Sun. morning & then, I HOPE, Robert will drive the "Soko Muke"‡ back to Kigoma — if he will. Because Hassan is due back next week & can return with the boat & stores. Works very

---

* A valley at the northern end of the reserve.
† Ripe with fruits to attract chimpanzees.
‡ Jane's small aluminum boat. *Soko Muke* means "chimpanzee lady."

well. And if, for some odd reason, Hassan can't get here, it is not very long before Derrick can bring it.

The weather is <u>perfect</u> at this time — everything is late this year, because it's much cooler than when we arrived, & the grass still green in many places. I hope it doesn't affect the termites.

The dreadful morning gales have, at any rate for the moment, stopped. I say there is a gale now, but it's mild compared to what I have been coping with, & anyway it's not so bad in the middle of the day, because by then the chimps are either here, & you know where they are, or not here, as today, & you know they may come later on when the wind drops in the evening.

2 Lowrie birds are having a terrific flirtation just here. Such a flipping of wings and tail from the ♂, and a funny whirring chuckling call. I presume that I <u>did</u> tell you about my chimps all lying on the ground & grooming, etc? That was the start of my present mood — everything lovely. I don't know if it was obvious in my letters — I hope not too much so — but towards the end of the rains I began to wonder how I could exist through these next 4 months. The last few weeks before I went to Nairobi were the longest I can remember. I was not looking forward to returning. And when I first got back, I still expected to feel the same — so that I did for a few days. But now, as I say, the days are speeding along far, far too quickly. I think it was a combination of rain, grass, heat and general "unfitness" on my part. I don't know why I wasn't fit. I looked OK except for being rather skeletal. But everything was such an effort. Now I don't mind how far I go, how often I get up here before dawn, how often I return in the moonlight. I am just in love with the mountains & the chimps & the monkeys — Oh, & everything. Obviously I am still looking forward to coming HOME — but because it's home, and not, as before, because I near the end of my sojourn here. . . .

Sorry this is a measly letter, but I don't have much time these days. I always seem to be up in the mountains before dawn, & never down till dark fall — kazi!* Anyway, it's rather late now so I

* Work.

shall cease. The Greenshields won't be bringing mail as a Scout brought it yesterday, so there won't be anything to answer, so I'll end here.

Tons & tons & tons of love,

Jane

P.S. Ma, when the Ansteys come you might have a chat with Margaret about her Ma in Cambridge. Re. me.

Also, if you're in London, go & see Napier — & how can I find out why Ramona won't write?

Did I send any pictures of David G. in his fig tree — reclining, etc? Or just the 2 tent ones & one in the rain?

6

❧ ❧ ❧

PHOTOGRAPHING GOMBE
1961–1962

The National Geographic Society . . . wanted to send out a professional photographer, but I was terrified at the thought of a
stranger arriving on the scene and ruining my hard-won relationship with the chimps.

— In the Shadow of Man

B Y THE END of her first year in the forest, Jane Goodall had
gotten closer to wild chimpanzees, seen more, and learned
more about them and their daily lives than any other human
ever had. Louis Leakey's faith in the energy, endurance, passion,
and intuition of his young protégée was vindicated.

At least for him. For the rest of the world, the vindication was
more complex. The young Miss Goodall's lack of formal scientific
training may have been an advantage in terms of her raw field work.
She approached her task and subjects from a fresh point of view,
without the limits of a theoretical filter. In terms of communicating
her discoveries, however, that lack might actually become a great
disadvantage. Who would ultimately take her work seriously? And
so, to bolster the quality of her research as well as her credibility,
Louis Leakey lobbied the academic authorities at Cambridge University to admit Jane as a doctoral candidate in ethology, the science
of animal behavior, under the distinguished tutelage of Professor
Robert Hinde.* Louis's potent reputation, along with his summary

---

* Professor W. H. Thorpe was originally to have been her advisor at Cambridge.

of Jane's actual accomplishments during the first several months of field research, was persuasive; she became one of only a handful of students in the history of Cambridge enrolled in a doctoral program without having first completed the undergraduate degree.

Jane left Gombe in December of 1961, returned to England, and settled into a bed-sitter at 1 Magrath Avenue in Cambridge. During the subsequent university term she attended lectures, regularly met with her advisor, and produced various papers and reports. Meanwhile, she was invited to talk about her work at scientific conferences in London and New York and to submit papers for publication. She finished her first term at Cambridge in early June of 1962 and by early July was back at Gombe, where she remained until December.

If her first year in the forest (July 1960 to July 1961) had focused upon approaching the apes and making those great first discoveries, her second year (July to December 1961 and July to December 1962) concentrated on communicating the discoveries broadly through her own writing and through photography.

The National Geographic Society of Washington, D.C., had taken over the funding of Jane's research in the spring of 1961, starting with a grant of $1,400 to Louis Leakey earmarked as support for the work of his "chimpanzee research assistant" in the field. The grant was finalized in a meeting that took place on March 13, 1961. By the end of the month, William Graves, an editorial staff member of the Geographic, was visiting Louis in Nairobi and discussing the possibility of an article about Jane and the wild apes, complete with brilliant photographs, for which *National Geographic* magazine, of course, was famous.

Photography was the problem. Beyond the standard technical challenges anyone would need to master — the usual conflicts between light and lens, film and focus, shutter and aperture — a photographer coming to Gombe would have to deal with photonically elusive subjects: dark-haired creatures skittering through dark places, shy beings more likely to absorb than reflect light — shadows inside shadows. As well, a photographer would have to be concerned with the effects of high heat and penetrating moisture on delicate instruments. The heavy, clumsy equipment would have to be lugged up and down, back and forth. There would be the isolation, the confinement of camp, the supply limitations. There was the problem of potentially hostile fauna — poisonous snakes and such — and that of invariably hostile flora — thorns and thickets and mazes. Malaria was a likely problem. And the unavoidable treachery of the terrain, those steep ridges and plummeting chasms. Moreover, the chimpanzees were likely to be physically elusive — why should they stick around? Why would they pause and pose? The Gombe environment gave chimpanzees a vast physical advantage over humans, and if they chose not to be photographed, it would be almost impossible to do so.

Still, in the summer of 1961, Jane and the African staff optimistically built "hides" or "blinds" at a few critical spots in the reserve, hoping to predict where the chimpanzees might go and imagining that they might tolerate a person plus a big glassy eye on top of a pole if the person and glassy eye were half obscured. Chimpanzees inhabit pretty much the same perceptual world as humans. A blind would no more fool them than it would fool a person, but it might make the photographic snoopery seem less intrusive.

Partly because National Geographic was funding Jane through their larger grant to Louis, much of the early discussion about photographing Gombe initially took place in a loop of correspondence between Washington and Nairobi, with Jane remaining to some degree outside.

Louis was at first very optimistic. Jane's progress in habituating the chimps was successful enough, he informed Graves, that possibly a professional photographer could go out to Gombe by July of 1961; but, he insisted emphatically, that person would have to be a woman. As Graves paraphrased Louis's words in a March 29 letter back to Washington: "Miss Goodall spends unbroken weeks in the bush and for her own sake and for appearances it would be very unwise to send a man out there." So, yes, a woman photographer might be acceptable by July but "only if Miss Goodall agrees and things are going well."

Within a few weeks, the Geographic had assigned to the task a staff illustrations editor with photographic experience, Mary Griswold. But almost immediately the idea was reconsidered. "I know Mary is going to do a magnificent job," noted Graves in an internal memorandum, "but it occurs to me that her problems — at least for a short time — will be every bit as great as Miss Goodall's."

By the end of May, Melville Bell Grosvenor, president of the society and editor of the magazine, had written to Louis noting that the Geographic had "reluctantly come to the conclusion that it would be unwise to send someone inexperienced in working with wild animals." That meant Mary Griswold was out. But, Grosvenor thought, perhaps Louis's son Richard might be acceptable to Jane, "since he is no stranger to her." Additionally, Richard had photographic experience and also "knows the animals and would not be unduly alarmed about being alone with them in the jungle." Grosvenor concluded by noting that the Geographic had already air-expressed a wide-angle Rolliflex camera, a supply of high-speed Ektachrome film, and some special cartons to expedite the return shipments of exposed film. Ideally, the society would want enough photographs of the study to produce twelve to fifteen pages of "top quality" pictures.

Louis replied in a letter of June 7 that there was "no possibility" of sending Richard to Gombe. Jane arrived for her brief vacation in Nairobi soon after that first letter — and just after the wide-angle Rolliflex arrived. Thus, in a letter of June 12, Louis noted that Jane had tried the camera and found it "far too heavy and clumsy, and [therefore] will not take it with her into the field. What would you like me to do with it?" As an alternative, Louis had purchased a much lighter instrument with an easily portable telephoto lens. That could serve as the "camera round her neck" — but it would be important for the Geographic to send a second camera with much better telephoto lenses and a tripod to support them.

Jane returned to Gombe with the "camera round her neck," and National Geographic airmailed the additional camera, stronger lenses, and other equipment Louis had requested. In a letter to Gombe written on June 22, Joseph B. Roberts, National Geographic's assistant director of photography, informed Jane that he was shipping out a Nikon reflex 35mm camera with three telephoto lenses of 50mm, 105mm, and 300mm; an electric motor drive powered by eight Type C batteries in a battery case; a relay box; a fifty-foot extension cord for remote control operation; a General Electric light exposure meter; fifteen rolls of Kodachrome II film; a Globe Trotter carrying bag; aluminum tripod; and a set of caption cards and film shipping cartons. "Now," Roberts went on, "for the shortest correspondence course in photography ever written. I presume that you have had considerable camera experience on previous scientific expeditions."

The situation was absurd. Jane wrote her family about the letter, which she found "quite horrifying." And, after about five weeks of apparent anguish over the Geographic shipment, she responded to Roberts (her letter of August 14) with the declaration that "I am not proposing to use your equipment until nearer the end of my work here, as I feel that a determined effort at close-up photography will very definitely upset the animals."

She also sent at that time a "test roll" taken from the neck-hanging camera. That roll, when processed at the National Geographic laboratories in Washington, proved to be more disappointing than anyone had anticipated. "Of 37 exposures on this roll," noted an illustrations editor, Robert E. Gilka, in an internal memo, "16 are so underexposed as to be unreadable, 10 are spoiled because of camera motion, and 6 are not useable for other reasons. We are left with one picture we might possibly use, a shot of Miss Goodall sitting on a hillside scanning the area for chimps."

Meanwhile, Louis and Jane had come up with an alternate plan. Why not send out Jane's sister, Judy? She could take time off from her job — she was by then working at the British Museum. She had "already had some experience of color photography," as Louis noted in a letter of July 17 to Grosvenor. So would the society agree to pay her air fare and expenses, plus perhaps some compensation for her time off from work in London? The reply, sent by Frederick G. Vosburgh, the Geographic's vice president and associate editor, was quick and rather stiff, if not downright stuffy. "The production of satisfactory photographs for the National Geographic requires considerable experience as well as aptitude, and this assignment would tax the skill of even a professional photographer."

Louis persisted, however, and eventually — in spite of Vosburgh's continuing resistance — Judy did go to Gombe to work the big camera. Jane by this time was "obsessed with two things," as she noted in her letter to Aunt Olwen on September 4, 1961: to observe mating behavior and to get some good photographs. And when Judy arrived toward the end of September, for a brief period the weather and the chimpanzees cooperated enough to produce a wealth of solid photo opportunities. But soon the weather stopped cooperating, as did the chimps. Jane's November 9 letter to Louis (whom she was then addressing as "Fairy Foster Father" or "FFF") provides one indication of how discouraging the situation had become.

Jane and Judy both left in December: Jane to Cambridge to begin her first term at university, Judy to London to resume her job at the British Museum. Back in Washington, Illustrations Editor Robert E. Gilka was scanning the latest rolls of film. As he wrote in a January 2, 1962, letter to both Jane and Judy: "I wish that we were in a position to publish an article on your subject because it is an unusual and fascinating subject. However, there is a lack of good pictures of the animals in their natural habitat. This shortcoming is so serious as to preclude attempting to illustrate a story." Incidentally, Gilka went on, where are the camera, lenses, and tripod we lent you?

By this time, however, society president and magazine editor Melville Bell Grosvenor had become convinced that the Jane Goodall story was, as he noted in a letter to photographer David S. Boyer, "fabulous" and the Geographic "must make every effort to get it." He then wrote to Louis in Nairobi and Jane in Cambridge, proposing that the Geographic pay Jane a handsome sum to leave Cambridge for about three weeks during February and fly out to Gombe with Boyer to get those pictures. Both Louis and Jane wrote back and declared the idea impossible: too difficult for her to get out there in so short a time, too hard to find the chimps in February, Jane too busy with her studies, and so on.

Still, the Geographic had begun to support Jane's work seriously, both her studies at Cambridge and her continuing field work at Gombe. Additionally, at a meeting in March of 1962, the society's board of trustees voted to provide a travel grant so that Jane could fly to Washington and present her initial findings (which she did in April) and also to give her the Franklin L. Burr Prize for Contribution to Science (which included a cash award of $1,500). March was a good month, in short, and Louis's wonderful news made it even better. He reported to Jane that he had met an excellent professional wildlife photographer who ought to satisfy everyone involved. Jane mentioned this reassuring bit of information to a friend, zoologist and author Desmond Morris, in a letter of March 12.

About a month after Jane returned to Gombe in the summer of 1962, a handsome Dutch photographer, Baron Hugo van Lawick, showed up at camp. Vanne had been enlisted to come out that summer as chaperone, theoretically to salve any stung conventional sensibilities, but she showed up a few weeks after Hugo did. Back in Washington, Gilka was himself mildly concerned about convention. He described to Jane in a letter of September 14 an earlier photograph that, though it was not successful, still had been a nice concept. "I've told him [Hugo] in my letter of several shots I want him to try," Gilka declared. "One of these pictures is a picture of you washing your hair. It is possible Hugo might be too embarrassed to ask you to do this for him." Jane wrote back on September 26: "You will by now have had stills of me washing my hair — though Hugo is going to take some more in a more forested part. You needn't worry about him being embarrassed. I haven't noticed it yet!"

Hugo proved to be "just the right person for the job," as Jane wrote in early September to Melvin Payne, Geographic's executive vice president and secretary. And by the end of the season the National Geographic had enough superb color photographs to proceed with the chimpanzee article. Jane had virtually finished her first draft by December 19, as she noted in the brief letter to Vosburgh. And in August 1963, Jane Goodall's "My Life Among Wild Chimpanzees" appeared in 3 million copies of the glossy, flatbound magazine with the bright yellow frame around its front cover. The feature began with a romantic silhouette of Jane Goodall sitting in front of a campfire above Lake Tanganyika and proceeded to display three dozen extraordinary visions of Gombe life, including a remote view of a chimpanzee carrying meat (evidence of meat-eating), three closer pictures of chimps fashioning twigs and using them to fish for termites in termite mounds (tool use), a photo of Vanne dispensing medicines in front of the tent, a few more of the African staff and fishermen and other local people illustrating various local activities, some shots of David Greybeard and Goliath, an artist's conception of the "chimpanzee rain dance," a photo of Jane sitting on a hillside and scanning the distance for her quarry, and one of Jane standing knee-deep in a stream and washing her hair.

*   *   *   *

Chimpland.
[July 5, 1961]

Darling Family,

All hail! Wot, no chimps! Actually, there are some, but they are not nice to me these days.

Thank you, Mum and Dan, for your two letters. As I said to Jif, I am about to disown knowledge of an Aunt Olwen. And as for the Aunt Mary Audrey Gwyneth — never heard of her! I've certainly forgotten who she is! Now, Danny, you are <u>not</u> to write me letters with a hurting neck. I suggest you talk them into the tape recorder & Ma can type them!! Or else dictate them to Jif who is supposed to be learning short hand isn't she? You will by now have had various letters from me — since these 2 (yours Mum & Dan) were sent on to me from Nairobi. I think all you wanted to know you will now know.

May I mention a little business first? Mum, did you ever see Napier? Because he's now not answering my latest letter, though I suppose, actually, he's not had it long. But I just wondered if you ever did see him? Also, can you think of a way of finding out if Ramona is O.K.? You remember the long & sweet letter she wrote me? I've penned her two since then, & not a word. I hope she's O.K. I <u>did</u> have a letter from Poosh. DID YOU SEND ON SUSIE'S LETTER??

The only real news I have is quite horrifying. A long letter from National Geographic with details of the equipment they are sending me — camera with 3 lenses & 1 tripod & automatic controls. It makes me feel so utterly helpless & despondent. It's a good thing you wern't here when it arrived, Ma. I was still awake at 3.30, & taking painocils for a raging headache! Have recovered a bit now. The man presumed I was already an experienced photographer after photographing my other scientific studies! It's bad enough having to battle with mountains, heat, tired body and chimps — let alone tripods & lenses & lengths of wire etc., etc. If they only realized the conditions — & this includes dear L.S.B. For instance, yesterday I was inching my way up a mountain side, clinging onto rocks & roots. And I bumped into some chimps. Well, there they sat, yelled at me a bit, ate a bit, scratched a bit, & went on their way. Wonderful view. Super photos — if I could have taken them. But as I hadn't really enough hands & feet to secure me to the mountain's surface, how could I take out my one simple little camera? Let alone if I'd had millions of lenses & tripods stuck all over me!!

You remember when we first got here, Mum, how I went off to Mitumba with my "merry men!" Well, I set off — walking! — with Andreano and Rashidi 2 days ago, to have a look at the tree. Made me quite homesick for Mitumba Valley! But the tree is going to be at least a month late this year. No signs of fruit, or even flowers.

(Must interrupt here to say that I now feel quite homesick for you, Mum. One of my hens is snoring — & it sounds just like you!!! Did you know hens snored? Nor did I. Do please ask Douglas if he has heard this? It's the most incredible sound!)

However, we made a hide — a dear little wee house of palm fronds where I shall sit when and if they come — almost in the tree with them! . . .

It now feels very late — it isn't in fact, but for the last few nights I've just lain awake. Back to me old tricks! I've read recently on the Nivequin pamphlet that a side effect of that is insomnia! But I feel they meant that only when one was taking large dosages, not simply the small preventative amounts.

If the D.C. brings letters from anyone I may add to this, but probably not until Robert & Alison. So tons & tons of love — to all members of my family not yet ex-communicated!

Jane

c/o The District Commissioner
Kigoma
Tanganyika
14 August 1961

Dear Mr. Roberts,

Many thanks indeed for your letter of June and let me quickly offer you my sincerest apologies for the delay in replying. This is
partly due to the fact that it stayed in Kigoma for some time before
being sent to me here in the Reserve — since then I have been hopelessly trying to make arrangements concerning the equipment —
very difficult as Dr. Leakey had been away from the country.

You will have heard from him that I am not proposing to use your
equipment until nearer the end of my work here, as I feel that a determined effort at close-up photography will very definitely upset
the animals.

Has Dr. Leakey told you that for the present I am using a 35 mm
camera with 135 mm telelens? I am sending you, in one of your cartons, a test roll from this camera — which is very disappointing.
Since receiving the film from you I have had the worst month of my
entire research period! Not only no opportunities for photographic
chimps — scarcely a chimp at all. True, one comes to expect these
sort of set-backs when engaged on such a study, but it is a disappointment.

The main difficulties here, so far as photography is concerned,
are two. Firstly, the nature of the country (as you will see from the
couple of habitat shots on the test roll) renders the transportation
of equipment extremely difficult. The chimps are seldom in the
same place for more than an hour at a time. I must work and travel
about, alone if possible. And most of the time I have to be crawling through dense undergrowth or scrambling up and down sheer
mountain sides. However, the camera I am using at the moment, to
its possible detriment, accompanies me during all my wanderings.

Secondly, and even more trying, is the attitude of the chimps. I
cannot say that they are frightened any — far from it. But they do
not like to be watched. And to approach them within 50–100 ft.,
unless it be in bush so thick as to make observation, let alone pho-

tography, difficult, is often not possible. However, there are occasions when the troops gather together when a certain tree bears fruit. When all the big males are there, all will be well. Also I have established hides near these trees, in readiness, and shall set up the big telephoto lens there when your equipment arrives.

I have gone into all this, probably unnecessary, detail to put you in the picture a little and to let you know that I feel sure that I shall get the necessary pictures despite a somewhat unfortunate beginning.

As for general background pictures, these will be admirably provided by the dagaa fishing. The tribesmen are allowed to camp along the shores of the lake during the season and spread out the fish on the beaches. I plan to get some fascinating pictures. The canoes setting out at dusk, the lights on the lake, the giant "butterfly" nets which they use to scoop up the fish — all these are very attractive pictorially. And I have several other ideas for "local colour".

Again, my sincere apologies for the delay in answering, in fact this is only the second opportunity of sending out mail since your letter eventually got to me. Any further tips you can give me will be very welcome. I am not in the position of having had previous camera experience I'm afraid. None the less, I am quite certain that when my chimps return again I shall get the sort of pictures you are wanting — as well as the sort I must get for my report — habitat, nests, positions, etc.

Sincerely yours,
Jane Goodall

Chimpland.
10.30 pm.
[September 4, 1961]

Darling Olly,

Just had your <u>letter</u> — wonders will never cease! However, I was writing to you anyway to wish you a very, very happy birthday — I'll be with you next year & can give you a present properly, & everything. But for now, will you just have a whole heap of 'good wishes' from 'chimpland' — where <u>both</u> your nieces (by then) — by <u>now</u> — will be thinking of you & sending "Happy birthday dear Olly" resounding across the mountains like mad!

I only <u>hope</u> I'll be able to get this sent off so that it does get to you in time. It's the 4th Sept at the moment, but Hassan is away — child ill — & unless a Scout goes in, or some other trustworthy bod. — I don't see how I can send it. Still, I shall just <u>hope.</u>

The time is flying past so quickly — that August is over I find almost <u>impossible</u> to believe. It's horrifying really — I am now obsessed with two things — photographs and sex!! Sounds bad, doesn't it! A sort of "chimps' pornography dept!"!!

I'm sitting here, with my pressure lamp. Out on the lake the fishermen's lights are gleaming across the dark, still water. Every so often they bang on their canoes, making the fish jump. A very noisy pig is crunching up dry palm nuts — what a loud sound. The crickets have the orchestration to themselves now — the little tree frogs are silent for some reason. And way up the dark valley a baboon keeps barking — the sentry is uneasy — something is lurking in the black shadows — the unknown terrors of the mountains at night.

Dominic is out in my boat, busily fishing. He keeps me well supplied with delicious fish. Small, but tasty. He had a silver pile of dagaa for my supper tonight — the hens ate it all! My chickens will taste odd soon — they eat so much dagaa I shan't know whether I'm eating fish or fowl!

O — I must stop (not "oh" — "Olly"!). I'm really too sleepy to know quite what I'm writing. I saw my <u>darling</u> David Greybeard again this morning. He was in company. Mike, Hollis, Olly! — the "Terrible Twins" and an unknown lady & gent. It was <u>so</u> nice to meet him again. Don't know where he's been hiding away.

Anyway, I do hope you have a 'super' Birthday. Give my love to Douglas.

Tons & tons to you,
Jane

The Tent.
Chimpland.
[September] <u>14th.</u> [1961]

Darling Family,

You will probably be wondering if I am still alive — it seems ages since I last wrote, though I don't suppose it is really. The fact is that my chimps have come back, & I really, honestly & truly havn't had a single moment till tonight to pen a line, though I did have the chance of posting one, had I written it! Well, Judy will have arrived in Nairobi today — what a joke. Charles* (D.C.) sent me a note to say he had millions of letters & telegrams from Leakey, all cancelling each other out! She is apparently arriving on 23rd — at least, that is the latest telegram. (I've noticed my writing is turning into a sort of long short hand. It comes of my Journal — it's about 5 or 6 pages every night & these days I'm climbing & returning in torch light — still, I have got some chimps to watch.) But oh, what a tragedy. Two days ago I broke the camera — & today what <u>lovely</u> pictures I could have taken — William 12 ft away, standing up with one hand on a tree, saying, very gently, "hoo" & then sitting there gazing up at the trees looking for figs — Mike, the same distance, chewing a lovely pink wadge of palm nut fibres & fig pips. Mrs Maggs followed by her baby. It was no use for anything else — they were on a safari & did not stop. But superb for photos. And it is the first time in 2 months I've had the opportunity. Makes you weep. I frantically despatched the camera to Nairobi hoping Jif can bring it with her — the shutter's gone. One scout was in Kigoma, the other couldn't go till he got back, so I sent off Dominic's wife. I hope it got on the train O.K — she hasn't come back yet.

The Boma† has been secretary-less for 2 weeks, so I've not had any mail for ages & ages. There is a letter from you, Mum, to answer, & I will do so when I have it by me. I can't post this yet awhile, but decided I'd better start a letter to you all.

Poor Hassan has a very sick child & had to go off to Kisumu. I'm hoping he'll be back next Thursday.

---

* Charles Campbell-Whalley, the district commissioner.
† An old German fort in Kigoma, site of government offices, including the post office.

I saw 2 little children, 2 years old, <u>dancing</u> yesterday. I can't really call it anything else. They were pacing up & down, a distance of 4 yards or so, passing each other, turning, & re-passing, walking bipedally, & stamping down each foot — sort of Conga step, bringing the arm down in time, & nodding their heads. It only lasted a few moments, but was rather fun. All the gents are in fighting fettle just now — everywhere they go they charge around, swiping at trees & yelling & screaming and flinging their arms about. One, followed by a rather bewildered young ♀, came right down from practically the very tip top of Sleeping Buffalo, to the valley. About 1/2 mile I suppose. Yelling nearly all the way.

And oh, so funny. I saw a very neat little group of 3 — gentleman, old lady (in 'interesting' condition) and a pretty and glamorous 'teenager'. They were the same side of a valley as I. They vanished, down to the stream. Then the gentleman, followed by glamour-puss, appeared, walking rapidly up the other side. They did not pause, nor did they go by the usual route, but turned off sharply when they got to the top of the very steep part, & entered a karonga.* Vanished. About 4 mins later the old girl appeared. She was rather like a fat old lady wanting to catch a bus — every few yards she broke into a sort of loping run for a few steps — awful effort — it was <u>very</u> steep. Oh dear, she'd never catch them up. Her pink behind waggled ponderously from side to side. At last she got to the top & paused. Gazed upwards — where they <u>should</u> háve gone. Not a sign. She looked anxiously in the right direction, but obviously could not see them. Hurrying still, she climbed a bit higher to get a better view. Not a sign. Go up again. No good. So it went on, right up a completely bare hill side — 1/4 mile. Finally, she reached the trees at the top. She sat for a moment, still looking round. Not a sign. They <u>must</u> have gone up there after all — better hurry on. So she hurried on. But when the fat old lady spies some extra delicious home made pastries in the shop window — well, bit of a risk — bus might go — <u>must</u> have some of those. And so the old girl could not resist gathering some tasty fallen fruits & stuffing them in her mouth en route! Well, she got right to the top — no

---

* Ravine.

sign — so she climbed a tall tree & sat there for 30 mins. At last, wearily, she plodded off alone. "Oh well, boys will be boys — but talk about cradle snatching!" And she disappeared over the brow of the hill!

We have had the first heavy rain storm — do you remember, Mum, the first last year. It was earlier — just after my first fever, when I saw the two giant ladies in Linda, & you were whisked into the Kibisi by Audrey Knight* & Co? And then the second when I was with Wilbert — I thought we'd been <u>so</u> far — we walked back, early, along the beach, & Wilbert collected shells for you, & thought he'd get a fever from having got wet!

It has got incredibly hot again — though not quite so bad today after the rain. I was sick for 2 days — don't know what the matter was — some old bug or other. It was an effort getting round, but had to be done, and was worth it. Now I am fighting fit again — seem to be fitter than ever. (N.B. Not serious or I'd not have mentioned it!)

I despair of 2 things — (1) — seeing mating (2) Jif or I getting any photos — it's <u>not</u> a question of the capabilities of <u>taking</u> them — it's getting in the right place at the right time. Really one needs about 6 people, all with telephotos, all sitting in all possible places, in hides every day for a couple of months!! As it is, Jif will have to hopefully dash from hide to hide, & they'll never go the right way at the right time. What a life. Since I last wrote I found the home of some more Banded Mongooses, & got some pictures, 16 feet away, of them at their entrance. If <u>only</u> cameras didn't click I could have got many more, but at the 'click' they run for their lives. Surely someone could invent one that <u>doesn't</u> click? Also a ♂ bushbuck, 18 feet away, looking at me. He didn't mind the click. And a very grizzy frankolin† with his greedy, non-stop-pecking wife — 14 feet away. I think they're a new sub-species, or a west African race, & I'm hoping JGW can tell from photos. And now — no camera. (I must say it's <u>bliss</u> going around without having to lug the weight about).

---

* A friend in Kigoma.
† A kind of partridge.

I am now going to put out the light as it's late. Shall continue anon. . . .

<u>Next day</u>

Well, another 24 hours of my life have vanished — 25 actually. I had a delightful morning, with chimps all over the place — & very nearly saw mating — saw <u>mounting</u> anyway, & then, with her lover still clasping her amorously, the lady stood up & held onto a tree. Maybe they <u>did</u> mate, but I couldn't see properly — a most odd way of doing things if so! And then they did a sort of dance round the tree on their two legs, & joined by a 2nd ♂ also upright. It was most entertaining. They all vanished utterly at 10.30, so I did some work on 2 hides this evening. I am doing them myself so as to put them up gradually, a little more every day. . . .

It's now considerably later than it was last night, & I'm going to stop once more. Adieu. I'm going to bed now. My fingers are so sore with writing 11 pages of today's Journal, & it's awful late, & I may be able to post this tomorrow.

Saw about 30 chimps today — & oh where, oh <u>where</u> was my camera. It really is too bad — I was relying on this fig time for the best pictures — & how right I was. Chimps all around me. What a day — chimps near, chimps far, old men, young men, ladies, children, babies, teen-agers — the lot. I don't really like these days — it's <u>wonderful</u> to see them all, but <u>such</u> a muddle.

Like the Boma — they <u>are</u> the limit. Hassan got back today — he asked for my letters — they gave him <u>one</u> which arrived today. <u>What</u> have they done with my last 3 weeks mail. However, the Kibisi passed today & Dominic sent a stern message back to say I <u>wanted</u> my mail — wouldn't they send it via Kibisi when she comes back to collect the tsetse man from up the Lake.

It's too late to be coherent. Hassan's child is in hospital, but getting better. No more news anyway.

Tons & tons of love,
Jane

The Tent

11 pm

[Around September 25, 1961]

Darlings all,

Hail. How are you all? Well, Jif has arrived. It seems a <u>hoot</u> — yet in a way quite normal. She was waiting when I got back on Saturday. I wanted to be here to greet her, but Mike was mating, & I was involved — I don't mean what it sounds as though I do!!! Dominic is thrilled I think, & is working even harder. We eat outside with a fire. He makes puddings. His bibi made us an 'African Cake' today — <u>delicious.</u> Tastes like doughnut. He madly tips baths in & out, washes & irons, etc., etc.

As for Jif's introduction to chimps — more than 25, all spread out over the Pocket! Mating! Walking on hind legs! Dragging branches! And, today, making a nest! Not bad! She hasn't had a chance to take pictures yet as I'm taking the camera, close up to my darlings (mine is due back this week). It is a good thing — she is getting to know the lie of the land, & finding her feet. She is bearing up remarkably — excellent at spotting chimps, & <u>most</u> useful — I wish even <u>more</u> that I could have had an assistant for longer as one can get so much more out of it with 2.

Incidentally, Mum, in one of your letters you were looking over at your youngest, sleeping all pink & white & peaceful. You hoped she would sleep as well here. Well, she may be a little more pink than white!, but as to the peace of her sleep, that is unquestioned. She sleeps most blissfully as I lie wakeful. I have just finished my journal! And am having my customary late night nibble! (Bit of D's new loaf, tiny slither of the cake — well, I'll have the paw paw now, not tomorrow. Cup of coffee? May as well. Oh, there's the cheap choc Jif got in Kigoma — square or 2 would go well with coffee! Etc!)

I think I'd better stop for now. I have a <u>very</u> early start tomorrow. Though it will probably avail me little as it's such a complicated place to get to that I'll probably get lost & arrive at the time I would if I started later!! Goodnight.

Well — I didn't get lost. And Poosh woke up over my head and very nearly wee'd all over me! Just missed! Mike came along, hit a tree at me & climbed it — only 20 yards away. 2 days before he went to <u>sleep</u> on a branch 30 <u>feet</u> away!! And he & Poosh & Humphrey sat & groomed etc, quite unconcerned, for an hour. It really is fabulous. As for mating — you'd have really laughed the other morning. It was early. Few calls from the valley. Then a female jumped up into a big tree, followed by her 5 year old child. With yells & shrieks, full of the joys of life, 5 large males bounded up after her. All masculine strength and virility they swung from branch to branch, calling wildly, huge and black in the cool clear morning. One of them bounded up to the lady. She screamed — but she played the game all right. Well, she coped with No. 1. He sat beside her for a moment, then swung away, out of the tree. 2 of the others had vanished. No 2, allowing no decent interval, bounded up to the lady. Well, she saw nothing wrong with 2 before breakfast. She didn't even scream. Over quickly and he went happily away. No 3 wasted no time. Like a flash he charged across. The lovers passed each other en route — "Have a good time" says No 2. "Good stuff, eh?" says No 3. He evidently finds it so, for he repays her by laying himself at her feet, offering her the privilege of grooming his head. She accepts the invitation, and then they sit sociably side by side, passing the time of day. But what's this? More business by the look of things. "Well, it was nice while it lasted, but you must be on your way, my love". No 3 can take a hint — and No 4 is sitting on a branch at the bottom of the tree. "You sure like taking your time" he remarks, as No 3 swings down past him. Up he goes. He knows what they like — all women are the same. Cave man stuff & all that. Be forceful. Bursting with masculinity he charged to the fray, yelled, shook the branch. "Come on, Woman". She played up all right. Screamed, pretended to run away — but how quickly she succumbed and yielded when he grabbed her.

And, hello — No 5 is queing, down on the bottom branch. "Thanks Big Boy, but don't hang around". No 5 leaps out of the way as No 4 charges down. Then up for his turn. Soon over, & off he goes. Now perhaps a girl can have a bite of breakfast. She settles comfortably. The child comes up & sits beside her. "What's that, my dear? — oh, don't you worry your head about it — your turn will come, all in good time. Just eat your breakfast!"

Hello — what have we here? Another suitor? Well, a most embarrassed and coy young man. He peeps round the trunk. Takes a step towards her. Yes, he will. He takes another step — but oh dear, she's such a woman of the world, so experienced, while he — he dangles, bashful, by one arm. He looks away. He swings his legs. Perhaps he can get some Dutch courage. He hopefully shakes a branch to prove his superior strength, his budding malehood. He takes another step. No good — he just can't. <u>Next</u> time he will. It's too late now, anyway. Giving him a condescending look, my lady swings gracefully past. Young men nowadays — what are things coming to. Her daughter follows. "Let the men do all the chasing, dear" her mother always says. So she too gives the youth a haughty look. But he's rather good looking, all the same — she peeps back. He is looking after her — just a little wistfully — or is she imagining it?

I'm going to stop now. There's no more news, & any there is I dare say Jif has told you. I <u>can't</u> believe there are only 2 more months. Ma — can you find out <u>somehow</u> whether Newnham* will approve of my starting off with M's mother? 'Cos one must be in 'approved lodging'.

Tons of love,
Jane

October
The Tent.
[Probably November 3, 1961]

Darlings All,

How goes everything? All these preparations — really! What with new lino, straightened tiles, new covers, hoards (spent!) under carpets, & rows of permanent waves, I shan't know anything. Maybe I shall walk into O.R., view the covers, & burst into tears because they arn't the same old chairs.

---

* Her college at Cambridge.

Thank you so much for the last 2 letters, Mum & Dan. Danny, you say you are a "bad letter writer". I've <u>never</u> heard such rubbish in my life! You are a fabulous letter writer — & don't worry — I shan't breeze into the arctic house, leaving all doors & windows open in my wake for Kip to depart through in unaccustomed glee — which is what it sounds as though you fear will occur as soon as I set foot over the threshhold.

We are making plans too — at least, we are already saying — in 39 more days we shall be in the Birches. It doesn't seem possible. Where have the 18 odd months gone to I wonder? It is very mysterious.

Dear me, how it does rain here to be sure. I really have ceased worrying over photography & begin to laugh instead. Hordes of frogs, not even gracing Chimpland in the long rains, have arrived to celebrate the "water water everywhere". Only there are plenty of drinkable drops. Yesterday visibility was nil up top, & two very drenched — sorry — 3 — people dripped into camp at 4 pm. And there we remained. The rain was still coming down in buckets at 9 pm, & we cooked eggs, beans & corned beef on the primus. D was prepared but the poor fellow is dreadfully ill with — probably flu I should say.

Had a funny thing with John Napier — he wrote and asked me for a title for my paper in April. Which gave me a heart attack as I think I told you. Anyhow, I asked him what lines the symposium was being run on — to do with human evolution, or what. I suggested, if he was really desperate for a title, he invent one to fit the bill. Well, then Moshi* arrived & I wrote to him again — about 1 week later — to know if he wanted Moshi as a founder member of his new Primate Unit. And I thought I'd really been rather foolish & said, if he thought it O.K., I'd call my paper "Ecology & Behaviour of the Free-ranging Chimpanzee". (Jiff thought Free-<u>living</u> sounded immoral!) This crossed with John's answer to my original letter sug-

---

* When some fishermen brought a baby vervet monkey to Gombe one day, Judy named the monkey Moshi and "adopted" it for the duration of her stay. After Judy left, Moshi was given to people in Kigoma.

gesting we call my paper "Observations on the ecology & behaviour of the Free-living chimpanzee"!!!* Rather a hoot!

I am planning a farewell party — back to the <u>original</u> birthday idea of an evening curry. I have been discussing it with D — we think 2 hours will be enough. There will be 14 adults & goodness knows how many children. Iddi & 2 wives, Saulo, Rashidi, & Severino with their wives, H & D with Mrs. D, & Jiff & I. And then all the strings of infants. Quite a "doo" — Or am I only allowed one "o"?

What — do I hear someone saying "she hasn't mentioned a chimp yet!" A chimp — what, pray, <u>is</u> a chimp. I fear I've forgotten. Quite honestly, the last few weeks have been a waste of time except that we have termite pictures. And I should, of course, tell you about when David G came to the termitery. He sat on top of the hill, gave the hide a passing glance, & set to on the bananas. "Click" went the camera. He glanced across. Ate another banana. "Click". Another look. "Click". Banana. "Click". No attention. Etc. But, having finished the bananas he very slowly & deliberately climbed down & proceeded up the 30 feet of path to the hide. The "door" is a low hole across which grass is pulled. Slight pause outside — then a hand grasped the "door", pulled the grass to one side, & a face looked in. (The hide is <u>just</u> big enough for 2 people & you can't stand upright.) Well, he said "hoo", retreated a couple of steps, paused. Then marched solemnly back & got on with the main business — termite eating. But it got funnier. At one point I held out a banana to him: He didn't like me doing that. Anyhow, I threw it — it misfired & fell about 4 feet away. Well, I didn't think he'd paid much attention. But after 5 mins he began shaking a branch. This got more & more violent. Then he climbed the tree & shook that. Then, wildly hitting everything, he arrived in a small tree over the hide & shook that about till I expected him through the roof at any moment. Then he sat. Then he leapt down, drummed a few times, & returned to the hill. I could not decide what it was all in aid of.

---

* This paper, finally entitled "Feeding Behaviour of Wild Chimpanzees: A Preliminary Report," was given in 1963 at the Symposium of the Zoological Society of London.

Then, after 5 mins, he began to march up the path again. And got the banana. All that was because he was annoyed that the banana was too close to me for his liking!! Well, he vanished. The walls are very thick. I heard much rustling just outside, where there is a lot of long grass. But could not see. Silence. Then fingers appeared — literally 5″ away from my foot. Again, I wondered what on <u>earth</u> was going on. It was a banana skin Jiff had poked out through the grass, & he wanted it!! It was terribly funny. Then he went back to termite eating again!

We made an amusing discovery when C.W.* was here. He told us he had nearly been christened "William" but his Godfather said <u>anything</u> but that — with a surname like his he would be "Willy Whalley" (pr. "Wolly") for sure. We immediately decided to call him just that. And Jiff happened to announce that I'd once been "Weary Willy". We got quite hysterical & he said that if ever we met in public — "Hi Willy Wolly" — "Hello, Weary Willy" people would shrug "They've been in the bush too long"!! Did Jiff tell you the dirty fellow forgot his bath, refused ours, said he'd use the lake, and never did more than wash his hands & face?! D. was horrified. I've never known a "bush" person before who didn't have baths whenever possible.

Did I tell you I saw a Colobus clasping her dead baby? It was so sad & upset me dreadfully. It had been raining, and it was all sodden & limp, & she kept trying to groom its poor little coat. Oh, it was heart rending. I'm only so glad I've never seen a chimp with a dead baby. I just couldn't bear it.

Today, when I was inspecting a termite hill the termites were leaving — you know, on their nuptial flight — oh, sorry — I must not refer to "that certain behaviour" — even in the bees, the birds or the flowers?† Anyhow, I caught a lot and we ate them as "toasties" before supper! I gave them to Mrs D who de-winged them, & they arrived all crisp on a plate. You know those little tiny things you get

---

* Charles Campbell-Whalley.
† Danny had recently written to Jane saying that she hoped she could trust her granddaughter, when surrounded by erudite scientific gentlemen, not to disgrace the family by referring to "that certain behaviour."

at cocktails? Can't think if they're prawns or what. Well, the ants taste just like those — Jiff was rather horrified when she saw the plate, but having closed her eyes & munched a few she liked them, & polished off the plate. Moshi was in his element!

It is 10.30 pm. Still raining. I was a gorgeous brown when Jiff arrived. I am now rather lily-like! Perhaps 'old parchment' would be a better description!

We are starting to sing carols! We hum them as we go up & down Ogre. I laugh to think of Jiff "running up ahead of me"! Though she is a little less grampus like. But then, she doesn't lead an energetic life — her job is sedentary at present. If the cherry trees ripen she will need a bit more energy.

Must stop now. Hassan will go to Kigoma tomorrow — oh, Christmas lists — I sure <u>do</u> need a warm cardigan. Apart from that — I <u>will</u> try to think of some little things & let you know in next letter.

Tons & tons of love to you all,

Jane

Wish it was!

9th ~~October~~ November [1961]

My dear FFF,

You will have heard the news from Judy, who has explained <u>again</u> about the speed of the film — oh, unless you are reading this first, in which case see other letter.

I am <u>Shs 1,000!</u> overdrawn. This is most alarming, & due to the fact that the duka* forgot to send me any bills. How <u>is</u> the money situation? I hope it's better than the photographic one — see Judy's letter.

She has told you all the news, so I won't repeat. Life is depressing — wet, chimpless, and, it seems, impecunious. We are doing our best, but I cannot — repeat <u>cannot</u> — contend with FATE. What else is it that makes it <u>pour</u> when I get close to chimps, or else my camera fails — the new one. Had to send Judy into Kigoma to get it

---

* Store or shop.

repaired — mechanical fault. Cost 20/-. Will send bill for insurance? Fruit not fruiting. Chimps vanishing. Me being ill. Oh, just **** everything.

A despondent & sad
FC*

1, Magrath Avenue,
Cambridge.
12th March 1962

Dear Desmond,

I'm sorry to plague you, but I'm wondering if you can help me on one point. I'm suddenly faced with having to write a paper on nesting which is supposed to be finished by 19th March — most unlikely, but still!

I was thinking about the various reasons for the construction of a new nest every night — you know, greater protection from predators, or the fact that fresh leaves are softer and warmer than old ones. For various reasons these do not explain the behavior — even though they may have been the original cause of it. So I began to wonder whether, perhaps, it was simply habit, like a dog turning round and round before he lies down (and this is begging the question as to whether or not the actual nest making is learned behaviour or not). So I wondered if you had any idea as to whether a zoo chimp, if its straw nest is left quite undisturbed from one night to the next, will re-make its bed or simply climb into the old one? Schaller's theory that the gorilla probably makes a new nest each night because it fouls the old one obviously does not apply to the chimp which never, under any circumstances, mucks up his nest.

I have just seen Leakey and am feeling happier than I have felt for a very long time because at long last there is the prospect that I shall get a really suitable photographer. This man is, at the moment, climbing about mountain forests in Africa to see how much equipment he can reasonably carry, and is also experimenting with flashlight on various sorts of monkeys and other animals to see just how

---

* "FC," as in Fairy/Foster Child.

much effect it has on them, and how long they take to get used to it. The thought of someone like this, who is really desperate to [film] the chimps and who is, in addition to being a first class photographer, wonderful with animals — well, it's just too good to be true.

I'll hope to see you sometime next week if you have a minute to spare — which is a good day, sometime between Tuesday and Friday (inclusive), and when I might be able to see Jan too.

Give my love to Ramona,

Jane

1, Magrath Avenue
Cambridge
20 May 1962.

Dear Dr. Bell Grosvenor,

I am horrified that so much time should have elapsed since I returned from America — and still I havn't written to thank you for your wonderful hospitality in Washington. To me it only seems like a few days since I left America, but when I look at a calendar....! Anyway, please do accept my very sincere apologies for the lapse of time. I really do appreciate everything which you did to make my stay in Washington so memorable, and I only wish I could have stayed just a few days longer and seen a little more of your lovely city. It is so white and clean and green — I quite fell in love with it.

I still havn't got over the magnitude of your organization. I knew it was large before I came, but never dreamed of anything quite so tremendous and magnificent. I expect your new building has grown quite a bit since I left Washington.

The temperatures over here still continue below 45°. We have rather given up any hope of summer — we had no spring at all, and the spring flowers are still blooming in bits and pieces all over England, whilst the summer flowers which ought to be appearing now, have scarcely struggled out with an occasional bud. In a resigned way everyone blames atomic tests as they crouch over blazing fires or wrap themselves in thick winter clothes to brave the elements outside.

Thank you again, and I only hope that I can obtain sufficient chimpanzee pictures to justify all your kindness. If I fail I think I shall just quietly disappear into the forests of the Reserve because I shall never dare to show my face again!

I hope very much to see you next March, on my way to Stanford in Palo Alto, and give you the latest chimpanzee news.

Yours very sincerely,

Jane

Chimpland.

17 July [1962]

My dear FFF,

Safely here. I've not had much luck yet, but have had two opportunities for taking photos — 4 rolls in the first week isn't bad when compared with one roll in over a month last time! But, of course, whether they will be any good is quite another matter! And it was nice of David Greybeard to come and welcome me — the same old David as ever, and just as amenable, bless him. I couldn't help laughing when I saw him, sitting up there in the great fig tree, chewing peacefully on his fig wadge, of all the toasts we have drunk to him, of all the places where his name has been in the forefront, in England, Washington and New York. Dear old David G!

One bit of bad news concerns the boat. I thought Hassan had tested the engine before we left, but apparently he hadn't been able to get it out — as it was Sunday of course, and when he said it was all right, he meant it was all there. Anyhow, I despatched him to Kigoma yesterday with the first batch of film, as Geographic are most insistent that it should be sent off at once. And I found when I got down that he had been unable to start the engine and took it in a water taxi, and they don't know if they can repair it or must get a new part. Hassan got back today, and is returning the day after tomorrow to see if soaking it in oil has worked. Good old Jack Granham, the only European left from the "old days" is working on it, and there is a Tsetse man who takes a keen interest in my affairs and helps Hassan when he goes in. Also the African Town Foreman is the most charming and helpful of men, and the D.C. likewise.

Anyhow, if a new part has to be got, I am asking that it shall be got — I only hope that it doesn't because I desperately need the boat next week. The big tree at Mitumba valley, 4 miles up the reserve, should be ripe, and I plan to make a temporary camp up there — it's normally a simple matter to get there on foot, but I had the most hair-raising journey owing to the water of the lake having risen so much, and the way along the beach being, in parts, almost impassable. To carry any equipment along would not be possible. However, if I can't have the boat I shall send the kit with the Scout — or Hassan if he's back — in one of the boats, and myself go across the mountains (If I went with the stuff I'd be charged treble!).

I am industriously collecting your sackfuls of dung. Dominic thinks its a real scream, this "kasi ya mavi!"* But he quite understood when I told him that it was to find out about endoparasites and small things they'd eaten. He's good on that sort of thing which is a help, because he's industrious in the drying. Actually one doesn't find dung in a fit state to be of use very often. Usually the dung beetles, flies etc. have been doing their work.

My word, but it's good to be back here. Even when the chimps are scarce, it's still good. But I've already crashed down onto some rocks and jolly nearly broken the camera. Heaven help me if I do. It certainly hampers one's progress and speed — when one is continually wondering whether each leap or scramble will bash some vital piece of equipment against a rock. However, I've got the original camera (which Geographic were most scathing about!) if the worst comes to the worst.

I don't think there's any more news to relate, so I'll end now and go to bed, since it's a bit late. I don't know if you will have seen the letter I wrote to Mummy — but I don't think Ahamed's overhauled the tent at all. They did the poles — bas. Because there is a rip in the bathroom roof, and <u>none</u> of the guy ropes have been changed — well, some of them certainly havn't. And, into the bargain, there were scarcely enough pegs and the mallet had gone. So you can tick off dear Jimmy Ahamed† when you see him, for me.

---

* Working with dung.
† The Nairobi supplier who had promised to overhaul the tent.

Now I'll really close before I think of something else unnecessary.
Hope something has happened to my final feeding paper.

With love,
Your FC

Chimpland
17 August [1962]

Darling Family,

Thanks tons for all your letters which arrived with Bwanas
Samaki and Ndorobo (Fish and Tsetse).* Bwanas S and N to my
horror had come for the day. As chimps were gaily feeding all round
I couldn't very well say I had to go away, and, of course, they sent
away poor Charlie. Never mind. They brought stacks of mail, including a super Geographic letter of which more anon, and a hooting parcel from Derrick.† The rail service is still at sixes and sevens,
and things get landed at Tabora and dumped for a week or so. Such
was the fate of this box of vegetables — it was oozing vile liquid
when it arrived in Kigoma — it sat in the Boma for a week, and arrived with Bwanas Samaki and Ndorobo! It took a lot of courage to
open it — ugh!!!! A really vile sight — I've never seen such rotten
vegetables. So sad. I had to tell him because it would be foolish to
waste any more. Thanks for the photos Jiff — and for 2 letters
which all arrived at the same time. Staggering. You still haven't answered my letter properly as you will see if you re-read it. I also had
a weird telegram from Hugo saying "Arriving 15th". As it was
the 13th, I imagined he was arriving 2 days later to have a look
round. I was overjoyed as it would have meant getting David and
Co on cine, the chance to do which may not come again (grammar!). Anyway, I made complicated arrangement for his transportation — Bwana Fish said he'd bring him, and Bwana Tsetse is pass-

---

* Tanganyika became independent within the Commonwealth on December 9, 1961
(and would become the United Republic of Tanzania when unified with Zanzibar in
1964); the transition to independence was smooth enough to be almost unnoticed in
the backwaters of the country. One clear result of independence, however, was that
many civil service posts passed on to black Africans, including those in Fisheries and
Tsetse Control.
† Derrick Dunn was sending extra food from his farm near Arusha.

ing tomorrow and said if he came late he would bring him. Then my heart smote me when I thought that if he arrived today he would wait for the Kibisi tomorrow and it might be the last morning of David. So when he didn't appear with Bwana Fish by 10 this morning, I despatched Hassan. But it is now 11 p.m. so I imagine, after all, he meant 15 September. I really don't know. Why send a telegram? Anyhow, that's rather later than I feel he should come, but I don't suppose it matters — I really don't think we'll get much worthwhile cine whenever he comes, but so what. Now let me tell you about Geographic — I will quote. It's from the camera editor — no picture editor, beg his pardon. Bob Gilka. Who always seemed so horrid when beastly letters used to come from him saying everything was all wrong, but was so nice when I met him, and he realized what was what. Anyhow. "Your first shipment . . . is the best you've done so far. Good going! In the 4 rolls are the first really readable pictures of the animals in the trees. I feel sure that at least one of David G. will wind up as an illustration in your article, and there is a sequence of one chimp out near the end of a limb, reaching for food, which may also make the grade". He says even the shot of Ma and baby, though marginal as the babe is lost rather against dark coat of Ma, can be made usable with careful work if I don't get better! That is more than I dared to hope. "I am most pleased with the way in which you have mastered the photographic equipment we gave you. With this kind of progress I am sure you will end up with excellent coverage of the study". Isn't it super! The jinx must be over — pity you're not here this time Jiff. Between us we could do fabulously. What pleases me most is that the chimps in the dudu tree are O.K. — when I trailed the tripod and big lens along and all 5 came — the only time I had the lens there — the only time more than one fed in that tree at a time. You see — the jinx working the other way.

I had one bad show — took some fabulous pictures of David and Goliath grooming each other — found, at the end, that the film hadn't been winding on. A whole sequence — David in a bare tree, really close as well. Very sad. No matter.

Here, things go from strength to strength. I found David, Goliath and Charlie all huddled behind the huts the other day. They let me get right close, of course. (Oh dear, every boat I hear I have to run out and listen in case it's Hugo). No! I couldn't think what they were doing. Then I found that David and G. each had half a mat under their arms! Charlie had a little piece. They were tearing bits off, chewing them, and spitting it out. They are straw mats — something to do with dagaa and called Mrago. I've never seen anything so funny. Charlie tried to pinch a bit of David's, and when it was pulled away he screamed in temper — David charged off, holding the mat high above his head — unfortunately all behind branches because it would have been a lovely shot — Hugo could have done it with cine — and Charlie following. David sat, still holding the mat up, and Charlie went on making a scream face without a sound. Then he vanished into the grass and reappeared with a piece — may have got it from Goliath. Later on, Goliath having moved out of sight, David took his piece up a little tree. Charlie, having found, torn up, and chewed, a piece of very ancient patched trousers! — joined him. The end of David's mat was very near Charlie, and after 10 mins. Charlie just allowed one straw to stray into his mouth — a little guidance from one hand that just happened to be there. David didn't mind much. The straw is joined together with string, and he found much difficulty in pulling away the bits of straw near the string. He struggled with one bit for ages, and finally, with such a lordly air, he handed Charlie the part he couldn't manage! (Charlie's hand being outstretched.) He dispenses his cast off bits and pieces with regal condescension — today he dished out his finished banana skins to Goliath in exactly the same way! And today No. 3 (who is going to become Huxley, because I've always thought they were the same, and it means I can probably get Sir Julian* the photo he wants!) — with a pal, also came to camp — I just saw them. Would have had a super time if I wasn't so flippin' conscientious. But, of course, I trailed up Lower Kitanda Valley at dawn, and merely succeeded in seeing two chimps in a fig, who didn't like me and went. And when I got back, Huxley was sitting

---

* The biologist Sir Julian Huxley, whom Jane had gotten to know at Cambridge.

right behind Hassan's tent on the ground — about 10 feet away. Just looking. Most odd! His pal with a very droopy lip was up above, more snooty like. Poor Huxley never got a banana.

Now that 2 or even 3 chimps come here it really is rather fab — it means I can get little details of social interaction at first hand close up — oh, another boat. Hang on. No! The little touches of David handing out his spare oddments are quite charming — not to mention pictures, of course. But, unfortunately, my best ones of 2 together are the roll that didn't take! Still, I have got some with two. Even when they're feeding in the new shoot trees along the beach I can get quite a reasonable picture with the big lens — it's usually rather dark when they're there though. And did I tell you I even got some black and whites of David and Charlie early in the morning? And I got some divine baboon pictures this morning — they are black and white too. The weather is fantastic — for the past three days there hasn't been one single glimmer of sun, and low heavy clouds. Most peculiar. The new grass is alarmingly tall in places. I hope this all means I can get some good Red Colobus pictures. If this goes on much longer I shall find I'm getting camera conscious! Gosh — that was the boat.

And it was my boat — but without Hugo. I had decided, as I may have said, he must have meant 15th <u>Sept.</u> But a letter came from Shirley* saying she was giving him a pair of shoes to bring as he was starting up the next day. I believe the road is still very bad. It is so unlucky I could weep.

Actually I am just writing a few words now to tell you that today is the happiest, the proudest, of my whole life to date. Something has occurred — an achievement which I value far higher than any prize, degree, praise — oh, anything you like.

David G — yes — he has TAKEN BANANAS FROM MY HAND. So gently. No snatching. The first time I held one out he stood up & hooted, swayed from one foot to the other, banged the tree, & sat down. So I threw it him. The next one he came & took.

---

* Shirley Coryndon, a friend of Jane's from the days when they both lived at the Museum Flats.

Even when I stand upright he takes them. I even got Dominic to come & get a picture — unfortunately he was a second too late & D. had taken it from my hand.

Just now I got back — 12.30 — & David was eating bamboo grass near the lake. Then he trundled towards my tent. I waited for a moment & then followed. He was sitting in the tent trying to open the banana box! So I sat outside & held out a banana. He came out, took it, ran back in, & sat inside eating it!! I hope, Mum, you don't mind sharing a tent with a chimp! Also at dawn (having gone to sleep about 4.30 am) I was woken by Shaitani (Devil in Swahili). He was sitting happily by my bed eating a banana. He IS a devil! I shooed him off & closed my eyes. 5 mins later I heard a stealthy foot fall. When I shouted at him he spitefully gave the table a wham & knocked the thermos over! Now I must go & look for some of my other pals — but can you blame me for devoting time to David?

Hi! Super letters came from you, Danny and Mummy. Thanks tons. Danny, how you can say your letters are dull and uninteresting I just don't know. Far from it — I was breathless with suspense when reading of Kip's wasp, and horrified when you couldn't find him — though I knew it was O.K. cos I'd read the bit on the outside sending me a spit-y kiss from him. More to the point if I send him such a kiss I should think. Oh no — your letters are very very far from being dull. They are some of the nicest and most interesting and most well written that anyone ever sends to me.

Fancy Uncle E — you going all the way to Bournemouth in Annable! The typewriter always insists on corrupting her name! Good luck in your next test Jiff — I guess you'll have an English driving licence before me anyway!

Ma — I think you'll still be in England when this letter arrives, though as I don't know when I can post it I can't be sure. I shall probably write this to Nairobi as well — but don't bring a netting thing for the veranda. There's no room for it now. What I do suggest you get is a proper net for your bed — WITH PROPER FRAME! This will mean you can sleep under it — tuck it into the mattress and no dudus can creep into your bed or fly down your neck to cause those alarming upheavals and grunts as I'm about to drop off!

That is the answer. The other thing is a) quite expensive and must be properly made, and b) as I say, there's no room, we're so elegant with tables now, and c) it always gets eaten by something remarkably quickly. Maybe, if you go to Ahamed Bros. (De la Mere Avenue) and tell Jimmy Ahamed — the boss — you're my mother, he might fix you up a SINGLE piece of netting to go across the inner part of the tent — I. e. if you want to sit inside the tent and I'm on the veranda I can then draw this net down behind me. Get me? IF he made it the right shape — he knows the tent size — large officers — we can sew it on when you get here. That's if you really want it. But since we eat outside and so are not likely to want netting then, and I don't want it anyway — it would just be silly. But DO bring a net. We don't seem to have any here — the old ones may be in that box in Shirley's room! But get yourself a new one — white. Those green ones are dingy. But if they're there, please bring green one for me.

Had to send Hassan and Dominic off to Mwamgongo today — Hassan couldn't get any bananas for David in Kigoma. Luckily Vic* (he is a dear, but such a hoot — came to visit me in Trilby, lace ups, grey trousers, socks and jacket!!) had sent me two bunches of ripe ones — which, of course, was a great treat for David, and may be why he took them from me. Just think — it's taken about 2 years to get to this stage of almost perfect trust. Isn't it really simply and absolutely fabulous. I do hope we get a really correct picture tomorrow — with a bit more light than this morning. Apparently the rains are heavy in Ruanda Urundi now. And today it was so humid and overcast, with thunder and odd drops of water oozing from the water-logged atmosphere. Most sweaty sort of weather — most unseasonable. All the Africans say the rains are about to begin. You'd better bring more polythene bags from Nairobi, Mum — Man's Shirt Pack. Can't get that size in Kigoma. Not a gleam of sun again, all day.

---

* Vic Jones, a friend in Kigoma.

c/o District Commissioner,
Kigoma.
2nd September 1962.

Dear Mr. Payne,

I am enclosing an interim report for August which, as you will see, is encouraging.

One thing which I should like to mention specially is in connection with the taking of film simply for the scientific record. I have stressed to Hugo van Lawick that it is of extreme importance to film some things even when lighting conditions or distance of the subjects from the camera means that the results will be far from perfect. With this end in view I have suggested that we get some fast black and white film for use in the early morning or late evening so as to get records of nest making, etc. which is not possible with the commercial ektachrome. I do hope that the Committee is in agreement with this.

I must say that the filming is going far far better than I ever imagined possible, and if things go on as they are we should end up with some very exciting material both for a scientific record and the lecture film. Hugo van Lawick is managing wonderfully and I think he is just the right person for the job. He uncomplainingly carries huge weights to the most inaccessible places, and waits all day on the most uncomfortable slopes.

I'm afraid all this is a little incoherent as I am surrounded by Africans all talking and the Game Ranger who came to visit the reserve is packing up all round me. Not ideal conditions for writing reports, but it is the only opportunity I have had for a long time.

Please do give my regards to everyone.

Yours sincerely,
Jane

Chimpland.
26 September 1962.

Dear Bob,

Many thanks for your last two letters with the discards. I'm glad they are not too appalling. Just at present we are going through a very, very bad spell, and I'm able to get practically nothing, but I dare say things will come all right again soon. The trouble is that the fig season has failed, and during this time I hoped to get all the "intimate" pictures of chimp life. However, some other chance may occur. Provided we manage to get good frames of the termite eating, the main outstanding gaps seem to be a mother and baby, good social grooming, and a few shots showing a large number together. An awful lot really, when you stop to think!

There are one or two questions I must ask. The first is about the overexposing when I shoot into the sky. In fact, I should aim at a silhouette shot? I was trying to bring out the details of the chimp — a ditto for the exposure of the chimps on the Ridge. However, in the future I won't if you think not.

Secondly, although Hugo is horrified at the idea of my even asking you, is it ever possible to blow up frames from 16mm film? I ask this because Hugo has been able to film some scenes which I probably won't have the chance to get stills of. I don't expect it is, but I can't see any harm in asking!

For your personal information the chimp in rolls 16 and 17 written on the cards as "Ugly" has been renamed. He was due for another name as he isn't, in fact, Ugly. It was a misnomer. When he scratched his back on the tree trunk he made faces just like Hugo does when he's concentrating hard — so he is Hugo! I thought I'd better inform you or you might get confused with all the Hugos!

You will by now have had stills of me washing my hair — though Hugo is going to take some more in a more forested part. You needn't worry about him being embarrassed. I haven't noticed it yet!

Incidentally, I wonder if you could send some more of the small boxes for packing film. We seem to have both run out — I think perhaps some have got mislaid, though I never remember there being many. Anyway, I've hunted high and low and can't find any. The small boxes are definitely the most useful.

The last lot of film I sent off — well, it is going at the same time as this letter — will be pretty useless. Probably none of it worth looking at — I'm talking of mine of course, not Hugo's. But, as I've said, it's the bad spell. And don't worry — I shan't miss any opportunities of taking shots of Buffalo, etc. They don't appear until a bit later, when the rains are well under way, and I shall do my best. I really wish I had a bigger lens, but I'll manage somehow — they are rather shy around here, and it's very difficult to get close — except the one bull who charges on sight! Maybe I'll get some real close-ups of him, one day, from the tree he has made me climb!

Yours sincerely,

Jane

Chimpland.

30 September 1962.

Dear Bob,

Just a short note — sorry I have no stills to send off lately. This business is the most frustrating I can think of. Just lately I've been getting really in amongst my black hairy friends — 20 feet and closer. They stay there, that close, for an hour or more. And even I find it hard to believe that I have not been able to take pictures. There are so many twigs and things between them and me that it just isn't worth it, and, into the bargain, it is very dark. I've taken a few black and whites, but not even a complete roll. However, the closer they let me get . . . the more hopeful it is, because there is bound to be a time when there is not half the African jungle in the few feet between me and my elusive subjects!

I also want to say that I retract all my remarks about silhouette shots when I shoot into the sky — I now have new batteries for my viewer and so I can see clearly that the chimps as well as the sky and the leaves are overexposed! Please forgive me!

And the last thing — in Hugo's latest shipment which he is sending off at the same time as this there are a lot of stills of various African dagaa fishermen. When he first tried to take them they all demanded 5/- and were not very pleasant. However, I talked to them and told them that after all we gave them medicine for nothing when they were ill — and I then told them that if they let their pictures be taken they would be able to see them — at this their faces lit up — could you possibly send a few Polaroids? It means so very much to them, most of whom have never seen a photograph of anyone, let alone themselves. In particular the bloke with the net, the ones turning the fish, the one playing the pipe — and any others who have close ups. I hope you don't mind my asking — Hugo didn't like to ask you, but I feel sure you won't mind, especially as it helps so much with better feeling all round. If you do mind — just say so! And don't let Hugo know I told you he didn't like to ask you! — please. I wouldn't like to jeopardize my friendly relations with my cameraman in order to promote them with my fishermen!!

Shall try and send you more stills in the near future.

Sincerely,
Jane

c/o District Commissioner,
Kigoma,
Tanganyika.
21 October 1962

Dear Dr. Carmichael,

Thank you so much for your letter in reply to mine. I am sure you will have heard by now that the photographic side of this study has been far more successful than I ever dared to hope. The chimpanzees have become so much tamer since last year, and they have accepted the presence of Hugo van Lawick with his tripods and lenses in the most wonderful way. The method I have always followed — never hiding from the chimpanzees, never following them when they have moved away from me, and never appearing particularly interested in them — has, at long last, paid its dividends.

I understand that Dr. Leakey has already written to you saying that I do want, very, very much, to return next year. There are, of course, many reasons for this — not the least being that even if I spent my whole life here I should still have a tremendous lot to learn about chimpanzees! However, in particular, there are three main reasons for my wanting to follow up this year's field study as soon as possible.

Firstly, the way in which the chimpanzees now tolerate the presence of an observer is so remarkable that it seems wrong not to take as much advantage as possible of such an opportunity for learning more about the social interactions between the various individuals. This was a task which seemed formidable at the commencement of my research, and only now is the pattern really beginning to take shape. It took so many months of patience and frustration before these chimpanzees would, in fact, tolerate my presence, that I cannot bear to think of leaving them just when they really will allow me to remain within a few feet of them on almost every occasion when I am able to get close to them.

Secondly, my observations to date suggest that there may be an increase in carnivorous behaviour amongst the chimpanzee population in the area. I cannot as yet be sure that this is so, but if it is then you will realize that it is vital to return in the near future to find out if there is any further increase in the eating of meat. It would be an important development in the life of the chimpanzee — after all, many people think that it was the desire for flesh and subsequent development of the hunting technique which was so important in the history of the first men, or near-men.

My last point is in connexion with filming. As you know, Hugo van Lawick is with me now, and is doing a wonderful job. But we have had a spell of phenomenally bad luck. During September the chimpanzees usually move about, in large groups, over my main observation area. It is this area which is so ideally suited to filming with long lenses. Other areas are more thickly forested, and not only are opportunities for filming much less, owing to fewer valleys and open slopes which can be overlooked from any one place, but it is impracticable to carry heavy equipment for long distances across the mountains. It is one thing to crawl and slide along by oneself — it is another matter to do the same when loaded down with heavy and valuable equipment.

Two weeks ago the chimpanzees returned in force to my home area. Their return coincided with the start of the rains. Had the weather been fine Hugo could have shot some truly remarkable scenes — as it was he had to sit and watch, helpless in the pouring rain. The main consolation is the degree to which the chimpanzees accept his presence, either in some sort of hide (which seldom deceives a chimpanzee for long) or just sitting out in the open. I am hoping that you will have seen, or be able to see, some of the material which we have managed to get so far on chimpanzee behaviour and that, in view of the facts I have outlined, you will agree with me that it is tremendously important that we have a second chance next year. I cannot believe that such bad luck will occur for two years running.

Please do give my regards to your wife, and to my other friends in Washington.

Yours sincerely,
Jane Goodall

10 December 1962.

Dear Bob,

Very many thanks for your last letter with the black and white prints and the slides. They are simply splendid, and it was most kind of you to go to all the trouble of looking through everything for me.

By now you should have got the last shipment I sent — 12 rolls in all. I sure do hope that some of those come out all right, more than anything the ones in the nests. These really are unique pictures — well, so are the termite ones — so, I suppose, are they all! But I'm particularly hoping the nest ones will be all right. There is another roll of nest ones in this shipment. It's funny how one plods on for 2 years and suddenly all the photographic opportunities come right at the end!

I also hope that one of the ones of me in the field with a chimp will be better than the one you had before. Because, quite honestly, it rather looks as though I'm sitting in a field with an exceptionally tame cow! — or something! Do you agree?

There will be a lot of rubbish in some of these rolls — but I am desperately trying to capture some of the social gestures, and they always seem to make these in the most unphotographical places imaginable. It's most annoying. I hope the "chimpanzee tea party" comes out — I think it's the most delightful scene, but the light was awful — sorry about using ektachrome by the way, but I suddenly ran out of Kodachrome. Thought I had a lot more.

The missing roll I mentioned was black and white — the Polaroids you sent I seem to remember came from a Kodachrome roll — people's heads cut off because I had all my hands full of bananas which made picture taking tricky!

Would you like any of the pictures we shot last year sent over? Or not. Or did you keep any that were the slightest bit of use? I was thinking in terms of packing up camp, or things of that ilk.

I don't think I shall be able to get the buffalo — the grass is now about 10′ everywhere, and the buffalo just seem to have vanished. However, you never know.

Thanks again for the fine pictures.

Regards,
Jane Goodall

P.S. By the time you get this I shall almost be leaving. The safest address in England, at the moment, is the Bournemouth one, The Birches, 10 Durley Chine Rd, Bournemouth. Don't know what horrible digs I shall end up at in Cambridge.

Chimpland.
19 December 1962.

Dear Mr. Vosburgh,

Excuse the frivolous address, but as I shall have left here before I could receive an answer to this letter, my correct postal address seemed unnecessary.

I have nearly finished a first draft of an article for your Magazine. It will, of course, be too long! What I am writing to ask is this: would you prefer me to sit down when I get back to England and reduce it to the approximate length required? Or would you rather first see it as it is so that you can see the sort of material. I feel this might be better — it would be discouraging if all the parts which I decided needed shortening were the very incidents you subsequently might think in need of filling out! (Excuse grammar — It's too late I think).

However, I am very happy to do either. It would be best if you could send an answer to my home address in England as I am not sure yet what my Cambridge address will be. That is "The Birches, 10 Durley Chine Road, Bournemouth". I shall have to go home first, anyway, to sort myself out.

I expect you have heard from time to time how well things are going here. The season has been far more profitable than I hoped it could be. Have you also heard that I am returning next year? The family have given up — they imagine that I shall still be coming back to watch chimps when I'm old and tottering. But it's taken so long to get the chimps really used to me that really it's only just starting to be worth while. Well, perhaps that's putting it too strongly. It has occurred to me that this may alter your plans about when the article should be published. If it is decided to hold it over until the end of next year's research — well, the sooner I know the better!

It's too late to wish you a happy Christmas, but I can wish you a very happy New Year.

With best regards,
Jane

7

❧ ❧ ❧

CLOSE OBSERVATIONS
1963

> I must say . . . that throughout the . . . study of the chimps at the Gombe Stream, I have often felt like an anthropologist taking notes on a tribe of people, for chimpanzees can seem so human.
>
> — *My Friends the Wild Chimpanzees*

I NTUITIVELY, Jane Goodall chose a bias that happened to be rare among the scientific biases of the time. She thought of her study subjects as sensate beings who shared with her (and us) a significant array of similar, perhaps identical, emotions and perceptions. Her apes lived in a parallel universe, one might say, separated from hers (and ours) not by an uncrossable gap in feeling and perceiving but by a partly reversible failure of communication and understanding. Apes don't have language. They can't speak. And our own habits of thought and language had always kept us from understanding very much about them. Indeed, in spite of all we've learned between then and now, our language still retains that automatic and unexamined point of view. While humans are imagined to have character and personality, a quality or a value of being, a *personhood,* and as such are automatically dignified with the pronouns "who" and "whom," all nonhuman creatures are by unreasoned definition nonpersonal objects: "it" and "that." Only humans have "children"; other creatures have "offspring." Only humans include "men" and "women"; other animals are usually "adult male" and "adult female." Only humans, by definition, have "consciousness" and "minds" and "reason"; all other creatures possess "brains" and "instincts." And thus only humans have "souls" when alive and become "corpses" when they die, whereas animals have nothing equivalent to soul when alive and usually turn into a "carcass" or "meat" at death. Language is a scratched lens, yet such habits of expression are rooted so deeply in our speaking and thinking and seeing that we ordinarily accept them as unassailable measures of reality rather than as what they actually are: flawed expressions of perception, expectation, and habit.

Jane Goodall's imaginative respect for her study subjects as sensate beings with feelings, minds, and individuality may help account for the rapidity with which she gained their confidence and was able to approach them for closer observation. Soon enough, as we have seen from some of the earlier letters, a few individual chimpanzees — the one she called David Greybeard, most obviously — began approaching *her* for closer observation. Apes are curious, and it is easy to imagine that a few of the chimpanzees who paused, gazed at, and even perhaps vaguely approached that peculiar yellow-haired ape who had recently dropped into their forest were motivated by curiosity. But, of course, very few humans in history have been curious enough about apes to trip along in their wake, day after day — why should the apes show any greater interest in humans? Both Hugo van Lawick and Jane wanted the chimps closer, for better photographs and film, for more intimate and consistent and accurate observations. Jane wanted to penetrate beyond the random and still occasional glimpses she had so far been able to achieve. Her ultimate goal, as she suggests in some of the letters, was to "tame" the apes: to make them comfortable enough that she could move among them regularly, daily, and get to understand them thoroughly. If the human ape-watchers were to achieve this goal, their subjects would have to be motivated by more than mere curiosity.

What might entice them to come closer?

The banana feeding began accidentally and developed haphazardly. Bananas were sometimes left out in camp. David Greybeard one day bravely snatched one and ran. Soon after that, Jane found that if she offered David a banana, he would be bold enough to ac-

cept. As she wrote home on August 17, 1962, "David G has — yes
— he has TAKEN BANANAS FROM MY HAND. So gently. No
snatching."

Jane began to recognize the usefulness of leaving out a regular
supply of bananas — "provisioning" her study subjects — so she
established the camp as a site of temptation. Chimpanzees tend to
follow their food source, which can change drastically over the year.
When food is widely and sparsely distributed, the individuals making up any single community become widely and sparsely distributed as well. But with seasonal food concentrations — a large and
healthy fig tree that suddenly bears fruit, for instance — the chimpanzees of that community will concentrate nearby. When Jane and
Hugo began regularly leaving out substantial numbers of bananas,
they were creating the artificial equivalent of a very good fig tree.

The apes responded. Soon, as the following sequence of letters
written during 1963 shows, they were coming into camp and, "as
they daily get tamer," becoming increasingly easy to approach. First
appeared the adult males: David Greybeard and his friend Goliath,
then William, followed by six-year-old Evered and old Mr. Mc-
Greggor. Of course, once the apes lost some of their fear of camp,
they began to find many nonbanana objects also tasty or otherwise
interesting. Towels must have contained a provocative mixture of
sweat and soap; clothes were probably good to suck on for their
piquant trace of sweat; cardboard boxes may have provided an en-
ticing taste of glue. Even haversacks were interesting enough to
drag away and check out.

Females as well began approaching the camp, including the one
who arrived with Goliath (described in the June letter home); she
was a "very pink female" who was happy to escape Goliath's apparent coercion the moment his attention wavered from sex to
food. The famous Flo also arrived in camp around this time (first
mentioned in the letter of late May or early June), carrying her
three-year-old daughter, Fifi, followed by her older son, Figan. By
then, Flo had been "quite won over to the idea of popping in for the
odd banana." And Flo's presence in camp attracted even more of
the wild chimpanzee community, particularly during August when

Flo herself "developed her first pink swelling" and "trailed millions of men along here with her." (During estrus a female chimpanzee's genital region becomes swollen and pink, unambiguously advertising to the community's males her condition of sexual receptivity.)

Provisioning ratcheted up the research a notch. Jane was suddenly getting an explosion in the number and quality of observations. But, of course, provisioning also resulted in an increasing level of danger. For starters, the bananas attracted both chimpanzees and baboons, and soon individuals of the two species were competing in sometimes violent battles, including the classic fight (still featured in film clips about Gombe) described in the letter of April 25. The chimpanzees also displayed vigorously and sometimes squabbled violently among themselves, behavior that is normal for them around any good source of high-quality food. The dominant males get the best and the most the earliest, and they assert themselves in the process. Still, the displays and squabbles in camp were genuine cause for alarm. When, for instance, the chimpanzee Hugo "got a fright" and "rushed about with all his hair out" and threw a two-pound rock some twenty feet, Jane found that act "quite fantastic," as she noted in the letter of late May or early June — and she also recognized the danger that the apes would accidentally or unthinkingly or deliberately hurt one of their human observers. Pound for pound, chimpanzees are several times stronger than humans. A weak chimpanzee could tear the arm off a strong human. So large numbers of apes coming into camp brought an increasing danger of some unforeseen, unpleasant conflict between observers and the observed.

Other people recognized the dangers of banana provisioning, including Melvin Payne, executive vice president of the National Geographic Society (whom Jane felt she had to "hasten to reassure" in the letter of June 17), the Coryndon Museum botanist Bernard Verdcourt (letter of July 5), and Louis Leakey (letter of August 30). To mitigate the danger, Jane and Hugo had a steel cage built as a quick and easy retreat should the chimpanzees appear to be getting out of control. At the same time, the pair were working on various ways to limit the number of bananas each individual chimpanzee would be able to take. By 1964 they had developed a feeding area away from the original camp and also were experimenting with remote-controlled boxes to dole out bananas in a manner that ideally would reduce the squabbles.

But the advantages of provisioning, Jane insisted, far outweighed any disadvantages. As she forcibly asserted in her letter to Louis Leakey of August 30: "to be able to follow the interrelationships from DAY TO DAY, instead of simply seeing the same two animals together once a week or even once a month — well, I can really say, now, that I know chimps." Banana provisioning allowed astonishingly close observations, in short, and the superb quality of the subsequent epistolary reports during 1963 reflects this accomplishment. Several of these letters show the increasingly accomplished Jane Goodall at her most candid; they present altogether a set of powerfully detailed, deeply affectionate portraits of creatures who seem, suddenly, less like the "animals" we usually consider nonhumans to be.

The last in this sequence is her first extant letter to Paul Brooks of Houghton Mifflin Company, which was to become in 1971 the American publisher of her best-selling book *In the Shadow of Man.* To Brooks, Jane summarized the year's accomplishments at Gombe Stream: "I now know about 30 chimps really inside and out, characters and all — and there are some splendid characters." She also described, notably, her growing intention to establish a "permanent research center" in order that her study of those chimpanzees and their offspring might continue for "years."

*   *   *   *

[Early January 1963]

Best beloved family — Hail!

It is almost completely dark, and Hassan is having difficulty with my lamp. He has been up there for hours. Then he stalked off majestically, and has just gone up there with another one — I suppose it will be explained to me anon. It's lucky I learnt touch typing, because it's far too dark to see for anything else — even writing would be a strain on the eyes.

As for my chimps. They go from strength to strength — that is, David, William, and Goliath. The others have all vanished, except for Pooch* who occasionally appears, but doesn't follow David to camp — though she will come and look for termites on her own. Goliath now always takes bananas from my hand, not always gently. William ditto — but he now takes them gently. The other day Goliath came on his own. He wouldn't take anything from my hand. I threw them to him, and he dashed about in an agile fashion — rather like a heavy weight boxer dancing. He is, in fact, just like a heavy weight boxer, with the temperament of a thug! Anyway, I threw one very close, and he did all sorts of gymnastic leaps and springs on his way to get it — then carried straight on and took the whole bunch giving the table a great hit as he passed and knocking everything off. Dear old Goliath.

Must interrupt, while I think of it. Firstly I had telegram from Hugo to say termite eating fine.† Then a great package of photographs from Geographic which I had asked for to show the people at Dar — Ministers, etc. They are simply super. Hugo has a wonderful one of David jumping the stream — they sent some slides, and 12 huge black and white photos, and a letter from Bob saying to relax on the photographic side — between us we have achieved a "fine illustration package" for the article. Which is very nice, and especially as all that was written before my last 14 rolls — full of two or even three chimps termiting at once, lovely close-ups of William and Goliath, and, best of all, David and William in their nests.

To return. G, W, and E have all been coming together. The last time they all three made day nests and slept for 2 hours — right near camp too. David has brought Pooch twice, but she will not venture closer than the termite heap. As for darling William. He trailed along one day at 5. He wasn't feeling very well — had a runny tummy poor old boy — and at 5.20, all in the sun, just by camp, all visible, he made his nest. I climbed above and took pictures of him lying asleep, still in the sun. And then, after supper, I

---

* Jane had originally named this chimp Poosh, after her childhood riding instructor.
† Hugo had left Gombe and was reviewing the photographs in his possession; Jane was about to leave for her term at Cambridge.

went up there and spent the night with him, watching him in the moonlight. That day I saw him almost every minute until 6.30 — after that the 3 of them appeared up at the top — from the beach — and as that was time for nest building, I really did see him solidly, all day long, plus a night. That's a record for one chimp. Good old William. When he came yesterday, still with the boys, he was still under the weather. Goliath is foul to him. But I see some simply wonderful social gestures with those three — David even made them to me once — put his hand on my arm, with backs of his fingers, making soft hoo hoo noises, and then held my forearm very gently but firmly with his hand. This is how he placates Goliath — but unless he thought I was scared by a sudden crashing of a baboon I don't know why he did it to me. If he gets cross with me he makes louder hoo hoo sounds, and raises his right forearm. Once he was thoroughly fed up with me, and smacked my arm! Yes, he really did, with a lovely nonchalant attitude!

I have been photographing small deformities. I find William has a broken finger and deformed feet — they are just like orangs' feet. Goliath has a broken toe, and David must have once cut the end of one toe almost off. He also has a nick in one ear. William looks as if he had his ribs broken once too. Poor old skinny William. How I do love them all now. Even more than before. In between times I climb up through the ever lengthening grass, but I never hear anything or see much, so I run back to my most darling ones. After all, I tell myself, all during next dry season I shall be with the screaming hordes. I may as well make the most of my friends while I have them to myself with no one messing them about by filming them. Also, as they daily get tamer, Hugo should be able to film this social behaviour if he returns.

Hi again — because it's anon from when I finished the last page. In fact it's several days later, and I'm several days older, and several facts wiser — etc, etc. I'm also rather sleepy as I've spent two nights with William, with one night in my bed in between. He spent last night in bed — and in a bed he'd made two nights previously — with my towel. When I went up to him at 10, in the moonlight, he was there, sitting up and sucking away. David took the one you left,

Mum. I now only have that miserable red and yellow check rag! When William trailed along yesterday Dominic was replenishing his iron in the kitchen. William accepted the bananas I offered him, and then drooped off down the path to the boys. "Tell Hassan to watch the clothes" yelled D. But as I rounded the corner William was heading for the bushes with a white shirt and my towel in tow. He climbed a tree at the top of that ledge there. And do you know, from 4 until 6.30 he was up that tree sucking my towel! After 15 minutes he accidentally dropped the shirt, but though he nipped down smartly to retrieve it, I was smarter. Every time I met his gaze, after that, he rocked, almost imperceptibly. If I didn't know William I shouldn't have noticed it even! And then he climbed down, bundled the towel up carefully and held it behind him to take the one banana I had with me, and then wandered off on two feet and a hand to climb into his old nest. There he sat, sucking the towel, as the sun went down behind the Congo hills. He sucked it when I disturbed him, climbing up for my night's vigil, and then, first thing in the morning after waking up, stretching and rolling onto his back, he reached lazily for the towel and sucked it — an early morning suck. I was only peeved that the mean old fellow didn't bring it down with him as he left it up there in an unclimbble tree. (Good word, that — a climbble or an unclimbble tree!)

But William's evil doing was not over. The odd thing is that he knows it's evil, when he steals these things. I had a new haversack made in Kigoma. Three times already he has tried to take it. He always says "hoo" in an aggrieved way when I say no and hold onto it! Anyway, this morning after his bananas he looked so melting sitting there that I resolved to get him one from the bunch I had hidden in the tent. A shriek from Dominic who was making my bed warned me — too late. William had taken my haversack from the table and was dragging it off, bumpity bump, into the bushes. In it was my camera. Also the 300 and 150 mm lenses. Also exposure meter and my last 5 KII films. Well, I yelled at him and just charged after him. He dropped it just before getting to the bushes opposite the tent. Now this is the amazing thing. I told you he knows it's wrong — I quickly followed him with a banana, but was afraid that I might have scared him badly. Not at all. He came up at once, though he did pause and say "hoo" in a rather defiant way before taking it. And came out again, bold as ever, to try and push me off the box to see if there were more inside. Which proves most positively that he recognized my right to get my property back. He is a real menace — a real cleptomaniac. He stands in front of the tent gazing in to see what he can take. He will even put a tentative hand onto a jersey if I happen to be holding the other end. But if I say no, he simply looks sad and goes away. He is a real "card" is William. That describes him to a T. An old card!!

Yesterday David wandered into a thick patch of that bamboo grass on the lake shore. I was going after him as I havn't got a picture of that. Suddenly there was a tremendous explosion in the grass and a large red pig shot out, almost knocking me over. A startled silence from the grass, and then a bewildered black face peered out and said "hoo" in a very surprised voice. It was so funny. My three blokes all came singly yesterday. First David. Then Goliath. Then David again. And finally William. David was worried that he had lost Goliath and looked everywhere. William this morning was convinced David was coming, and hung around for ages. David never came. But the wretched Humphries did, with an Italian and hundreds of children of all ages.* Ugh! I was just too late hearing the engine to escape! And as it poured with rain most of the time it seemed foolish to announce my departure. They didn't see any chimps, and they did bring me meat and veg. which they wouldn't let me pay for, and had asked about mail. One up to them.

Hi! I intended to finish this epistle in a leisurely way this evening & send it, via Hassan, tomorrow. But Vic Jones passed — my only real friend in Kigoma — stopped the Kibisi especially to deliver mail — didn't come ashore but was rowed in to deliver it to Hassan in person — and is stopping again this evening to collect anything for the post. Really decent.

I am sitting companionably with William who is having a luncheon date with half a cardboard box! I was not invited. It is rain-

---

* Uninvited and unwelcome visitors arriving from Kigoma.

ing. William has been eating termites — they go on & on. Yesterday was wonderful — D, G and W all sat in my veranda sharing a cardboard box, & then Goliath begged from William later up in a tree over the tent — where they were joined by a 6 year old male — Evered! Having rushed up to the Peak & found nothing I went down the valley & said 'howdy' to Mr. McGreggor, & came back in time for the box party. I shall start a new fashion. Can't you imagine, say, William Goldsmith, Byron and Mr. Wilson all sitting round solemnly chewing cardboard & spitting the bits elegantly into a red wagger pagger!* The begging was best. And the little male coming along. And William, not allowed his share of bananas, suddenly running when he saw termites flying, so as to get some of the big juicy winged ones.

Oh — there may be a panic. I was invited to Peterhouse Ladies Day, or something. Evening dress. And at first I wrote & said no. Then I thought that the first night in Cambridge would be pleasanter at such a 'do' than with Mrs. Tweedie!† So I said yes. Well — I don't even know where my green evening dress is, or the whalebone crinoline — &, wherever they are, they are both dirty! The green dress might be with Mrs. Tweedie — in which case she might be asked to have it cleaned — if it's not at home it's with her — 14 Grantchester Rd. And it will mean buying some shoes. And my hair will just have to be tied back! You see, it's on the 14th!

My plan, anyway, was to spend what is left of 13th in London & go to Cambridge on the 14th. Then return to London on the Friday, go to B'mth with Jiff & Annabelle, & stay at home for several days — whilst ostensibly in Cambridge. . . . I do hope Louis is going to send more money. Time is running out & I don't know where he is. I asked him to.

I must stop as I have to scrawl various epistles to people like Tweedie.

Tons of love,

Jane

---

* Goodall family slang for waste paper basket.
† Jane's landlady in Cambridge.

[Second week of April 1963]
Darling Family, one and all, including, of course, Dido.

Many thanks Olly Danny and Mummy for Easter and/or birthday cards. I couldn't work out when Easter was — I no more knew of it than I did of my birthday! Anyway, your letter was a hoot, Mum — saying you had been thinking of me all day because it was my birthday, letter dated 4th April!* Hugo says that in Holland you do give presents to the person whose birthday it is — but only small ones, and the main presents are given to the parents. So the Victorian ladies would have done well, with 22 children!

The most fantabulous things are happening here. Guess who has been to camp twice, and got bananas we threw — why, none other but my adored Mr. McGreggor. I can hardly believe it. We have filmed more baboon fights, drinking and greeting. Yesterday, when David appeared at 7.30 on a brief lonely visit and hastened away I presumed that the others had decided not to come back and so took myself off up the horrible grassy trail to Mkenke. Ugh — foul, and not a chimp. I had started the day by going up Ogre pre-dawn to watch Evered leave his nest — just up Hassan's beautiful main road, which is now only a few yards off achieving its destination — the Peak. However, Evered, with scarcely a rustle to announce his departure, vanished into the dawn, so I wetly trailed down again. It was, unfortunately, (for Hugo) a grey cold day. I found a most comfortable tree way up the Watu path from which I could see both sides, and hear any possible calls for miles around. There were no calls and it was chilly, as I was buried in clouds. By using a vivid imagination I was able to hunch my back, close my eyes, and slowly the sun came out, warming my back with its happy glow. But, if I chanced to open my eyes — cold grey clouds enveloped me again, and the shy sun hid his face with miraculous speed. (I find it impossible to type these days. I guess I typed too much during the past 3 months.)

Well, I pushed down the track, and getting back along the beach was well nigh impossible. It was high tiede (you will have to sort out

---

* Jane's birthday is actually April 3.

the errors in future or I shall be all night at this!) and the waves were right up to the grass — the track along the beach further inland, of course, quite overgrown with impenetrable grass. So — I had to sort of run around outgrowing trees, racing the waves — all most dramatic and wet-making. I got back to a most excited Hugo. In the palm tree in camp (not the one with the water bags) two days before the little black weaver birds began building. Hugo is doing a bird film for Louis and filmed the making of the nests, the stealing by one bird from its neighbour's nest as soon as the neighbour's back was turned, the shredding of the palm fronds for weaving in strips, etc. We were amazed that in two days the nests were almost complete. Now, I read in Dominic's truly fabulous report that Goliath, once, seized two chickens and ate them in a tree — with leaves.* Also William took one. On another occasion William seized Hassan's hen who was sitting and dashed her out of the way, taking the poor dear's eggs. Well, this, as you can imagine, far from rousing feelings of false sentiment in evil minded Hugo and Jane filled us with high hopes for getting meat eating. Vile indeed are our plots for the slaughter of the innocent! When I saw these nests I said to Hugo, wistfully, "Wouldn't it be wonderful if William, when the palm tree is ripe, happened to notice those nests". Well, Hugo had been filming David and Goliath greeting, baboons attacking William, and throwing bananas to a yelling McGreggor who was lurking in the bushes. Suddenly, with his usual swift perspicacity he saw Goliath suddenly gaze up at the palm, his hairs all rising at the same time. With lightning speed the cameraman rushed to get the fronds in silhouette — Got the murderer climbing the trunk, pulling down a frond, hand over hand, and then, very carefully, with two fingers, feeling inside the nest on the end. He then repeated the process, let the fronds swing back, the nests undisturbed, and climbed down. Wasn't it super! The birds have not deserted, and we now see a contemplative expression come over Goliath's face when he looks at the nests — the same sort of expression as you see on the face of a

---

* While Jane was away at Cambridge, from mid-January to late March, Dominic stayed in camp and kept a running report of chimpanzee-related events.

housewife when she gazes towards the kitchen where her cake is in the oven, and looks at her watch. "When will it be done". In fact yesterday when Goliath returned he sat resting in a tree, one foot dangling, gazing with delighted anticipation at the little nests whose owners are working so industriously to provide the rapacious creature with a tasty h'oerdoevre (the effect of that sentence, I fear, is sadly lost by my inability to spell this common culinary dish!)

Well, I had scarcely got back, and was cursing fate that sent me drearily off up Mkenke when so many exciting things were going on, when I heard a crash in the bushes opposite — a little 5 year old girl with a cardboard box, and a year old infant. Lurking behind was Ma. The children were most unafraid, but mean old Ma — when I got out my binoculars she seized her infant and moved the family to a further back tree. The children went on playing, and then they all rested from 2 to 3.45. Suddenly, just as Ma appeared to look at us, a sudden yell — William, with a bit of cardboard appeared round the tent, followed by the other two — the scream was from McGreggor — still with the boys. He was quite happily walking about behind the kitchen for bananas which Hugo threw there. It was splendid. The other three climbed up a bare tree to feed, and McG remained up above the boys' tents feeding on his own. But he had quite a good taste of bananas. Finally they all trooped off — just 5 minutes too early — for we had run out of ripe bananas, and just as they had gone Hassan and Rashidi got back with them — with bananas I mean! I couldn't find them, though I looked in all likely places for the next hour until dark. Today I am determined to stay in case McG comes back. That is too good to miss. At 7.30 David came on his own, and was in such a bother. He kept looking for the others to come — we didn't give him enough bananas for his liking, I wouldn't let him have my sweater, he didn't like the only remaining box. He has gone off over the stream in a huff.

But something happened the other day that was quite fantastic. I hope one of my stills comes out because otherwise no one will believe me. I followed David and Goliath across the stream — where Hugo got them jumping and drinking — can you believe all this drinking when I only <u>saw</u> it once before! — and then they went into thick stuff. I after. David lay on his back under a low tangle of vines. Goliath flung himself beside him. After a moment I saw they were holding hands. They began to play with each other's fingers — at first gently, then more actively. And after about 4 minutes they began to wrestle. There they were, two old gents (and I believe now that David is much older than I had suspected) playing about like two year olds, roaring with laughter and tickling each other in the ribs. After a couple of minutes David couldn't stand it any longer and with a final guffaw he jumped up and ran round in a half circle. Goliath followed a little way and then sat to eat a reed. Then David sat down by a sapling with open space round it. Quite light. Goliath once more flung himself at D's feet and sprawled, face down. Suddenly he put one hand on D's foot and held it. D at once put a hand on G's hand. And the fun began all over again. I got one picture — oh how I hope it comes out — of David sitting up, leaning slightly back, head thrown back, and simply shrieking with laughter whilst Goliath, almost hidden behind, tickled under his arms. Twice again D broke away and ran in a circle — and twice again the playing started with holding hands and playing with each other's fingers. It was so completely fantastic that I simply couldn't believe it was actually happening. One of the most delightful things I've ever seen. I'm sad I can't find my hordes, but so much is going on here that I may as well make the most of it. Especially with Ma and infants, and other young ones, AND McGreggor. Oh — the day the two played was the first day dear old William arrived. I knew he had come because as David Goliath and I were dozing peacefully in the shade I heard William's high annoyed barking call from camp. D and G at once sat up and rushed to the edge of the stream. But they did not go to join Wm — after 10 minutes they lay down and went to sleep again. The bark was because Hugo moved a towel which William had his eyes on. He is a worse thief than ever — so is Goliath.

Tons of love,
Jane

[Postmarked April 25, 1963]

Darling Family,

This is the second letter I've started — one got sodden & illegible in my haversack & one is lost. It is simply pouring & blowing such a gale that typing is impossible. I've never known such rain. It was so bad yesterday I could no longer see from the Peak & so I thought I'd come down & see the boys. So I put my clothes in a polythene bag, just for fun, & walked nearly back naked. It was simply super! I was cross, though, that it rained. A child was poking into a hole in a dead tree stump with a stick & licking the end I could see beautifully with the telescope. Only it went when the rain started before I'd seen exactly what it was doing. I also found why they chew cardboard — I saw them pulling off dead wood, chewing it, & spitting it out. So cardboard is a type of dead wood for them. Of course, now remains — Why do they chew dead wood!! Still, it was interesting.

I am feeling very cross. Heard crashing outside, went out — & the baboons have destroyed 3 of the weaver nests. With eggs too. To hell with them.

David, Goliath & Hugo came this morning. Hugo waited up a palm the other side of the stream (now a roaring red torrent) & watched Hugo & I sitting with David & Goliath in the kitchen. I am hoping Mr. McG. will come with William. I met him on my path last night. Flo, Figan & Fifi are around too. In fact I was going to follow G & D hoping they'd lead me to the others when this storm began — there seemed little point in trying then. I prefer to wait for McGreggor. What a way to watch chimps — eh! Never mind. It took 18 months of slogging before I could!

I caught the 3rd rat last night. We decided to kill it & were trying to get it into a snake bag for the purpose. Suddenly — bingo — it was out! Like an arrow it rushed back to my tent! What they do is to collect food in my tent, carry it to Hugo's, & there make a nest. Only this one is trying to make a nest in my bird books in the bookcase.

Oh, Ma, before I forget. When you come, can you please bring the New York Conference book with nesting in it. I forgot.

Have just had a colour transparency of the 'Rain Dance'. It really is very very much better. Only the silly artist hasn't done it in the rain. Mr. Poggenpohl* said he wouldn't fault him, as I did say I'd seen it in good weather, but he thought it a pity. So do I.

We had the most <u>glorious</u> baboon fight. The cheeky baboon, Max, just deliberately ran at poor William who at once took himself up a tree. Then the baboon ran at David who chased it, upright, screaming — turned, ran to Goliath & flung his arms round him. After that the 2 attacked the baboon together — but after about 2 mins, it was Max who drove the chimps away. He is the only baboon who is so brave. <u>All</u> in good light. All filmed. And, believe it or not, the film ran out <u>just</u> as the fight was over! We have also filmed begging, beautifully, and nesting on the ground. Social grooming. Could have filmed Hugo in the palm this morning if it hadn't rained. Ugh — it is so cold.

Well — narrowly averted a disaster. I had just fetched water for coffee, & Hugo came over. Suddenly an extra violent gust of wind, frenzied flapping — 3 guy ropes came out & all the rest down one side almost out of the ground. So I held frantically to the main one in front while Hugo ran for aid. He flew back with Hassan, Anyango & Rashidi tearing after through the deluge, & Condo in the rear. Eventually my tent was safe again. Condo arrived yesterday with a large bald patch in the middle of his head in which was a <u>tiny</u> cut. He had cut himself with a panga while cutting a track! It was a microscopic cut! At first we thought he had miraculously shaved his hair off with the panga! So I had to put a strip of plastic on. Now he has shaved his whole head to match & it looks so funny! He still demands epsoms every other day. Oh — I <u>do</u> wish it would stop raining. New grass is shooting up. We'll never be able to burn it down. It is <u>sickening</u>. Incidentally, Mum, for purchase in Nairobi (or England) plastic table cloth for our table. . . . Can't get in Kigoma. Oh yes — do you know what David took? — your waste paper basket. I was so surprised when Dominic produced it intact — told him how pleased you'd be. Now the three old men have chewed it up.

---

* Art editor at *National Geographic*.

It is very touching how Goliath rushes to David's aid — whether or not this is necessary. Certainly, in the baboon fight, his assistance was most necessary. After I was peering at David's cut, & I put out my hand to groom his back. Suddenly "Look out!" said Hugo. I looked — there was G who had been resting about 20 yards away. He had advanced 1/2 way & was standing, eyes round, all his hair out. It was like an apparition in a nightmare! I have never seen him look so huge. I took my hand away & he returned to his seat. I had to test, so again I groomed David — at once G rose & advanced threateningly, & went back again when I stopped. Most spectacular & very touching.

Yes — Ma — I had a letter from Robert saying he was sorry he'd pestered you needlessly. I hope I've heard the last of the vile thing. He only asked me how a strongyle egg can turn into a hookworm or a roundworm! How on earth he thinks I should know! I have referred him to poor John — who did explain at some point — it went in at one ear, encountered a head full of dominance & sexual behaviour, turned round, and went out again!*

Did I thank you, Jiff, for your Christmas card? It was waiting for me when I got back. Also a letter from Peggy, & one from Pa. I now see what he meant when he asked me, on the phone, about the stamps — in his letter he asked me to spend up to £2 to buy him a set! No wonder I didn't know what he meant! Incidentally, I wonder if he ever got the giraffe tie? He never said.

Well, folks, I guess I'll sign off! There is no more vital news. Just prospects of more rain. The kitchen is <u>full</u> of baboons. All sitting sheltering. It looks so funny. Not friends with them now.

Anyway, tons of love to you all till next week. Don't forget 'nesting', Ma.

Jane

P.S. <u>Mum</u> Another item for you to bring — some of those salt pills — don't bother to bring whole tin — some in polythene bag. Also, from Nairobi, bandages.

---

* Robert Hinde was her tutor at Cambridge; John was probably the primate expert John Napier.

Chimpland.

[late May or early June 1963]

Darling Family,

I meant to write such a long letter — in fact I really looked forward to describing all the things which have been happening. But when Hassan returned from Kigoma, after posting my last mingy blue, he brought back various copies of chapters from Stanford — including mine,* Vernon's, one on Sexual Cycles, and one on Communicative Patterns in Primates. So I have been frantically busy each evening since making comments. . . .

What about my chimps. Oh, they are so fabulous and wonderful that it's hardly possible to believe it's true. Just to give a typical sort of day, let me say what happened today. Goliath arrived at a fig which I saw from a new look out post which scans the whole valley from near camp. Then he vanished. I went to see if he was in camp — he wasn't so I went back. Then I had a note to say others had come — well, Goliath actually, on his own. He clambered up the slope — the poor fellow has hurt his foot so much that he keeps losing his friends who travel too quickly for him. For 20 mins he sat waiting, hoping they'd come. Then he plodded on up. And about 1 minute after he had gone David arrived, leading Hugo and Evered. They all ate bananas. The most wonderful character, Hugo. He is a real gourmet — he just guzzles and guzzles, skins or anything will do. When one throws a banana his hair stands out and he runs for it. Rather jumpy, like Goliath. Evered tried to get one — he ran at it — screams. Evered got it, with wild fear grimaces presented, and was given a reassurance gesture. This is typical of Hugo. He hits out at everyone when he is excited, and then, when they scream and get scared, he is at once very sorry and sticks his hand towards them to reassure them. All his subordinates are continually being reassured. But he doesn't like to take time off eating and as he sticks one hand towards the other's lips or thigh he is stuffing skins into his mouth with the other. This morning, for example, a baboon was being irri-

---

* "Chimpanzees of the Gombe Stream Reserve," that she wrote for Irven DeVore's *Primate Behavior* (New York: Holt, Rinehart and Winston, 1965).

tating and threatening the chimps. As it chased Evered past him he hit out towards the scuffle — which was, after all, disturbing his eating. Then, as Evered ran behind him he hit out again, irritably — but was rather upset to find that in his preoccupation with his bananas he had hit out at the wrong animal!

Flo! Oh Flo! She is, as Hugo and I agree, a hoot! She has the most enormous nose. It is almost human, is Flo's nose, projecting forwards into a sort of beak. She has a small face and rather tight upper lip, with a small lower lip which, on occasions, droops down. She is scraggy and all her body seems out of proportion. She is devoted to Hugo* and, occasionally, we think he hands out some bananas to her. Slowly she is becoming tame — she is quite won over to the idea of popping in for the odd banana — ever since she got an entire bunch, in addition to my haversack. She is a funny beast. Yesterday Fifi was begging from David — how she loves David. She follows him round, sits on his knee, plays with his hand — and sometimes he puts his arms round her. Anyway, he gave her a skin, and Flo wanted it. Mother and daughter rolled over on the ground, Fifi holding the skin out of Flo's reach, and Flo determined to get it. It was very charming really — a sort of good natured scramble with no screams or upsets. Hugo again boobed — Fifi went up to beg from David. Hugo himself had just reached out a hand which David had gently but firmly pushed out of the way. When Fifi went up to beg Hugo hit out — not realizing who it was. A small whimper — Hugo looked round — prostrated himself on the ground as he leaned right back to reassure Fifi of his good heart by touching her on the thigh.

Evered and Pooch are wonderfully tame — and so is Flo's eldest, Figan.† Figan, far from being scared when we throw bananas, runs toward them with his hands out, trying to catch them!!

When he first came into the open Hugo was very rude. He got a fright when a banana was thrown, and because of this he rushed about with all his hair out. On one never to be forgotten occasion he

---

* Hugo the chimp.
† Flo in fact had an older son, Faben, but he was not much in evidence during this time.

stood completely upright when I threw one, and with a forward swing of his arm he picked up and threw, all in one movement, a 2 lb rock which happened to be right under his hand. It was quite fantastic — 19 1/2 feet he threw it. We tried to get him to do it again — he once tried to do the same with a dead palm frond, strengthening our conviction that it was not really throwing at us — simply a reaction.

Now Hassan is about to go — early. I got up at about 6 — but here he is. Continuation in 2 days.

Tons of love,
Jane

"Chimpland"
17 June 1963.

Dear Dr. Payne,

Thank you very much for your last two letters. The cheque has arrived safely in the bank, and I will certainly do as you say and keep a close watch on my funds. I am delighted to hear that there is a little money left from last year's work.

I must hasten to reassure you with regard to our safety here. I know you think that I am rather foolhardy in my attitude to the chimpanzees. In actual fact, although I do have implicit trust in David Greybeard, I do not have this trust for the other chimpanzees at all. In fact I mistrust Goliath very much! I have never pretended a friendship with him. He is slightly mad and not very intelligent. I am telling you this so that I can stress that Hugo and I do, in fact, take very great care not to alarm or upset him in any way. So do not go on thinking that I am just being completely foolish and presuming a friendship — which might terminate at any moment.

The enclosed interim report deals with only about half of the things which I am now finding out about these animals. I feel that I am only just beginning to understand them. One of the most important things with which I am becoming familiar is the <u>real</u> relationships which exist between the various chimpanzees in this community. Normally, under the everyday sort of conditions, it is not possible to observe these actual relationships except on the occasions when I am lucky enough to see meat eating or some other such situation. To see the behaviour evoked by throwing a desired food object amongst a large group is not studying natural behaviour. But, taken in conjunction with the many many hours of observation on normal behaviour, it provides a vital insight into the pattern of chimpanzee life. The only danger would be in describing this behaviour as normal — that is a danger I have seen well in advance and into which I shall not be guilty of falling.

You will have to excuse the terrible English in which I am trying to express myself. I can't seem to keep up with all my writing work these days — so much happens each day that it takes hours to type out each evening, and I am still having to cope with bits and pieces arising out of the chapter for the Stanford book.

I must just warn you that I had a letter from a Nan Russel-Cobb of Aldus Books Limited. They are publishing a book on Human Biology and want a picture of chimps in natural habitat. I suggested she contact you — I havn't the faintest idea whether it would be a good thing to have a picture in this book — they say it will be published in the United States and I thought maybe someone at the Geographic might know something about it. Anyway, I have to leave it to you to say yes or no, if, in fact, they do get in touch with you.

With warm regards,
Yours sincerely,
Jane

[June 1963]

Darling Family,

This is going to be rather messy. I have banana-sticky hands, bare feet, a kikapu* of bananas beside me, & I am with Hugo, Goliath & Evered who are sprawled asleep. We are on the 'pig path' side of the stream, just opposite camp. On the other side of the stream are

---

* A woven shopping basket.

Hugo II* and David. They (mine & David) missed each other by 5 mins — driven from camp by baboons. Blast them. . . . Honestly, if you'd seen McKnew† yesterday threatening Evered — going right up & keeping on opening his mouth in a threat yawn in the little fellow's face, & hitting bushes at him. Just taking it out on him because he couldn't cope with Hugo & Goliath together. Evered tried not to look at him but jumped each time McKnew hit a bush. Hugo charmingly reached out a hand & touched his scrotum in reassurance, & then hit at McKnew (who was not attacking him).

I am in such a muddle as to what I have and have not told you. I should have made a list. However, I do know I was just going to relate the tale of Goliath & his wench. He had been away for 2 weeks. The boys came to say Goliath was there but wouldn't come down. There he was, staring at the bananas. Most odd. He then set off towards camp, still up in the trees. From my veranda the mystery was explained. He appeared up the slope with a very pink female. With mouth — (4.0 Hugo starts eating leaves — ! That was for my note book!) with mouth watering he looked from the bananas to his female. She sat, hands on knees, chin on hands, gazing in the other direction, in a fork. After a moment or two G climbed down and took a couple of steps towards us — then, in sudden panic, rushed up another tree (they were in grass so otherwise he couldn't see her). She hadn't moved. He gazed at the bananas, at her. At b's. Climbed down. Ran a few yards — panic — up a tree. Gazed at her, b's. Her. She hadn't moved. Scratched. Suddenly climbed down and rushed nearly all the way down — ran to the right and stood upright — she was still there. He ran down — ran to the right, stood upright to look at her — she hadn't moved. Got to the banana box. Took a banana — ran towards the kitchen, stood up, gazed up. Still there. Hurried back, got to the veranda. Took 3 bananas. Simply charged back towards the kitchen. Stood up — she'd gone. With typical feminine cunning she'd waited until he was the farthest from her he was ever going to get — & then she'd made a dash for it. Goliath simply rushed up the slope. Bounded into the tree where she'd been

---

* Hugo van Lawick.
† A baboon.

— sniffed the fork, peered round. Leapt down. Ran in all different directions, flat out, all his hair out, appearing up various trees, standing upright to look over the grass. Hugo & I were in <u>hysterics.</u> And he never found her! After 10 mins he came down, seized bananas, crossed the stream, & met up with David who was waiting up a tree. They'd been apart for 2 weeks so there was a splendid greeting and a 2 1/2 hour grooming session.

This is another part of the letter or scrawl which is gradually multiplying in various parts over the reserve. I ought to quote you bits from letters from Geographic people. But one and all, even the most unlikely sort of people, say that the article is one of the most fascinating they have read in a long time, and is likely to be received with tremendous enthusiasm, etc., etc. They are saying this in letters to Hugo as well. I must say it is nice, after using their money and equipment for so long to have produced something which they think first rate, both manuscript and pictures. A pleasantly satisfying sort of feeling. And they are mad with enthusiasm for another article next year. . . .

Now, before I relate any more news — Mummy — millions of congratulations on passing your test.* I am now the only member of my family which has <u>not</u> passed a test!! Which is rather a hoot. Anyway, many congrats — Hugo told me to send his as well. I am being madly bitten as I write. It is early morning and I'm waiting here until they arrive as they left late yesterday, going north, and this usually means they arrive between 7.30 and 9. The trouble is, with Evered and Hugh† still not properly tame, I can't follow them. I hope your mouth is quite better Jif — though if I don't have a letter from you soon you may as well have rotted for all I know. I hear vague bits from the rest of the family, that's all.

Oh — you know how Louis pushes his lower lip forward whilst lecturing? This trait is becoming more pronounced in David every day. He has recently become, officially (though not yet with the approval of his — what is the other part of "namesake"?) David

---

* Driver's license test.
† Hugh (no relation to the chimpanzee Hugo) was a powerful young male who had recently appeared at the provisioning area.

Louis Greybeard. We feel, anyway, that he is of sufficient rank to warrant an extra name to all the other chimps. Let me also tell you — I do hope I havn't — about Mr. McGreggor and Hugh. We had had the most splendiferous afternoon in camp, with Flo and the whole lot. As soon as they'd gone we whizzed up to the mango. In one of the figs there were the two aforesaid gents. Funny thing — I'd come down from that tree for Flo, over an hour before — and Hugh had been there then! Anyway, he was still there, and had been joined by McG. Hugo (let him be I, and the chimp II) arrived, and had been filming for some time. Because Hugh is an absolute hoot. He droops his lip even more than William and, what's more, he doesn't close it when he eats, which gives a very strange effect — with each chew it sort of waggles about! Suddenly they both peered down, and their hair came out. We knew someone was coming. By enormous good luck Hugo I just happened to have them both in the screen — so that he could concentrate on whichever one did the best greeting. Suddenly McGreggor's hand went out towards Hugh — almost at the same time Hugh reached his hand toward McG — and they held hands. I've never known anything so simply amazing — no one would believe it, save that, right from the first movement, it is on film. They held hands for nearly two minutes, peering down. And then Hugo II bounded up, having got rid of Flo, and he and McGreggor embraced. All three groomed each other, and it was super. All in sunlight. We at last got some really good film showing McG's baldness.

I mentioned I'd seen chimps eating bushbuck. McGreggor was prominent in that feast — he had the whole skin and leg bones of the buck. He was dishing out large dollops to Huxley, and wadges, from his mouth, to two of the small children. Also Huxley was dishing out helpings to one of the small ones. And one little incident was charming. It concerned Mr. McGreggor and a female unknown. McG. had eaten or given away all the flesh from the skin except for a piece up at the top, so the whole rest of the hide was dangling down. The female reached out and touched it — she withdrew her hand. Then she reached out and tentatively held it, looking up at McG. All I could see of that gent, because of a leafy branch, was his feet on one branch, and the skin dangling down. The female was on a lower branch. Well, she gently pulled the skin — suddenly a large black foot was lowered, grasped the importunate lady by one wrist, and gently, but firmly, pushed her hand away! It was so funny — I just burst out laughing. But honestly, none of these observations would be anything but for my telescope. I cart it madly around with me. I can learn far more by watching from a good distance, when I can see who everyone is, than by creeping up close in the thick forest — which, super though it is, doesn't give me so much information. It used to be nice for the resting on the ground — but we have that daily in camp. And the telescope is 100 times better for Ma's and babies because they don't have to bother to sit behind thick vegetation, and so I can see exactly what is going on. But can you believe it that huge Fifi still suckles. It is amazing. Still rides on poor old haggard Flo's back.* (Hugo keeps calling her Clo!) Have I told you about Flo's nose? It is a real human nose — on a chimp is quite hideous. But what a beak.

I must now break what may be the most sad news in a long while. This concerns William. William has not been [seen] for well over a month — so long, in fact, that I simply dare not check on the exact duration of his absence. So long that we are full of terrible forebodings; so long that I can't believe we shall ever see William again. I just can't bear it. It has got to the stage when I feel all weepy when I think of him, and his darling groans when he doesn't like bananas, and his rocking — oh, and everything. True it would be worse if David disappeared — but we'd much rather that it had been Goliath. Goliath has given us wonderful things — both film-wise, photograph-wise, and observation wise. But he has not got a really nice character — not like darling darling William. There is just a chance, of course, that he has gone on a long trip, visiting an aged aunt perhaps, who lives outside the reserve. But that possibility becomes less likely with each succeeding day. Every evening we say — William just <u>must</u> come tomorrow — and he never does. Tonight is even

---

* Flo was a very tolerant mother. Her difficulties in weaning Fifi, as noted here, were repeated with disastrous results later with her son Flint.

worse than usual. "We shall never see William again". It's made worse by the fact that not a single chimp came to see us today, and I only saw 3 chimps vaguely from my mango — which is the worst day for a month. Trouble is, as we've agreed, we've been thoroughly spoilt — n.b. it is Hugo who is cheering me up these days!

Now — this, in fact, is the end of the letter, and comes after the other two typewritten pages. There is so much more to relate, and, as usual, simply no time to relate it. For instance, tonight Flo, Fifi, Figan, Hugo, Goliath and David and Evered are all sleeping just along the path. It is too good to be true. It started with David coming at 10.30 and going almost at once. Then, about 12.30 Flo and Fifi came. And this is what is so interesting. Last week Figan, Flo's eldest, wanted to go off with David, Hugo, Goliath and [Evered]. His mother was going in another direction. He went after them until he could just see them and also Flo. Then Flo climbed down and set off her way — Figan at once turned and ran after her. So, we presume that Figan, until now, has been tied to Ma's apron strings as it were. 3 days ago a whole group appeared in one of the figs in the valley, late at night. In the morning David, Hugo, Goliath, Evered and Figan arrived for bananas. Not Flo and Fifi. The "men" trouped off together. In the afternoon Flo came, with Pooch and Fifi. No Figan. She waited all afternoon and went off without him. The next day she came — we didn't see Figan — Goliath arrived. Today they all met up. It was so super. Flo and Fifi were here. Goliath arrived. No greeting. Then suddenly Goliath began standing up and being absolutely fabulous, swaying from foot to foot, all his hair out. Charging off to greet Hugo who was [following] a trail down the path. Unfortunately 4 strangers got so far and then turned and went off — before I even saw who they were. Anyhow, there was a lovely greeting of G. and Hugo. And then we saw Fifi stand upright and go up to her brother, put her arms around his neck and her face to his. Then Figan went up to Flo and they kissed briefly. A very filial and dutiful peck, but lips to lips. It was so wonderful. Fifi and Figan played in the open beside Flo, with Evered lying beside them, reclining on one elbow. Hugo ate so much that every time he moved he collapsed, sprawling, on the ground. Figan made wonderful fear grimaces and presented to Goliath. Fifi half rode on Goliath's back. Fifi cracked half a gourd. Fifi swung and played. Fifi jumped on her mother's back and rode across in the open. Fifi suckled. And then they trailed off. We went up to see if we could see them make nests. Missed the making, saw them in their nests. Hugo went down as it was late and too dark for filming — I heard my signal — went down — David had arrived and Flo and the children had come back with him. He was feeling belligerent and wanted the whole boxful of bananas for himself, but we managed to load Flo up, and the other two got plenty. They joined the sleeping, bloated, banana-full Hugo, Goliath and Evered. The other things that have happened are without number. It is so super. There just isn't time to write letters — I'll tell you more in the next. There has been a gap because Hassan didn't go in last week — my very urgent cable re final script of Geographic went with Ian and his family who came.* I am getting 500 reprints of my article, which is very nice. I asked for 50!

Tons and tons of love,
Jane

P.S. <u>Ma. When</u> are you coming? <u>How</u>!!?? To Nairobi? Dar? Train or air? v. imp. Can get clothes as presents in Africa. Chiko & Ado not here. Can you bring <u>ancient</u> sweater or cardigan — David took my yellow one.

P.S. <u>Please</u> Ma — do borrow Olly's ciné if she can spare it.

2 July 1963
Chimpland.

My dear FFF,

I gathered from Ma's last letter that you would be away when she was in N[airo]bi. I gather from Bernard you won't be. I hope she gets the notes I have written her at New Stanley where she said she might stay. This is really just to say: I think I told her to send a

---

* Casual visitors who came for the day, probably from Kigoma.

telegramme to McDonald <u>instead of</u> me. But I've now worked it out we can send it on the 9th & so, all being well, get her cable. So ask her to send <u>2</u> — one to McD & one to me.

Chimpland is still fine. I hear from Mary Griswold via Joanne* that you think you'll be able to stay on in Kenya. Will you? I hear most of your news & views via other people!

Still no William. Letters come from all over the world asking if William has turned up. He never will any more.

The bit on the back of the envelope — I just had a letter from Robert. <u>He</u> thinks the extra term a good idea — he is proposing it to the Board which doesn't meet till 1st week in August. He suggests I carry on on the assumption I shall be here till Christmas, but that I must be prepared to return, at short notice, to fulfill degree requirements. I think I'll write a chatty note to Huxley telling him how important the term is. He helped before — I don't mean I'll <u>ask</u> him.

Have I asked you if you can find out for me at what age a chimp's canines are full grown? Or who should I write to?

Incidentally, the most urgent note for Ma was asking her to arrange interflora flowers for Danny's birthday from me.

Filmed the most <u>super</u> greeting today. David Louis G. did 4 steps of the "greetings swagger", (upright, hair out) flung one arm round Olly, in front of the infant Gilka. Was just about to poke his finger into her backside when Gilka, most agitated, dropped from Ma's back & got in the way. So he stroked her little white tuft instead! It was super.

With love,
FC

"Chimpland"
5 July 1963

Dear Bernard,

Many thanks for sending the two extinguishers, and for your letter. Before reading the end of your sentence about water pistols

---

* Joanne Hess of the National Geographic had hand-delivered mail during her recent visit to Gombe.

filled with ammonia Hugo and I said to each other — "Why didn't we think of that. What a wonderful idea!" and you were about to be bamboozled with requests for millions of water pistols. Then I read the second part — that they are unobtainable! Of course they are. I remember Norman trying to get a toy gun into Kenya which he bought in U.K. for Christopher. Of course he couldn't get it in for love nor money. Still — it was a bright idea.

I trust that you will take everything off the blank cheque. If by any chance you cashed it before we wired for one of the expensive ones, then I trust you will let me know with all due speed and I will send you another. Only please let me know how much you have cashed it for so that I can keep my accounts in order — or Ma can for me!

You needn't worry about being careful. We are. We have a cage built!!!! For us! This is only for when Goliath comes with a group of other males early in the morning or when it rains. At these times his temper is terrible. The trouble is that ever since the baboon episode when Hugo threw a stone at him fearing he was going to join David in chasing me, Goliath has borne Hugo a grudge. He is really horrible to him, and has chased him 4 times. You know what he can be like in a rage, and I'm sure you and Helen both can imagine how unpleasant it must be to be on the receiving end of his rage!* Anyway, though if I'd been just on my own I'd never have considered something like a cage, with such a spite raging it seems only fair. Also with Ma coming out, it's best to be safe than sorry! Another tame one we've got who is still just a bit scared, luckily, has a worse temper than Goliath. That is Hugo. He would certainly join in if Goliath started anything, but wouldn't dare on his own.

However, enough of that, because otherwise everything is simply superb. We have two tame mothers, Flo, the most hideous chimp in Chimpland, and Olly (!). Olly has a darling daughter of about 1 year, and an elder son of about 8. Flo, with her huge nose, her sagging bosom, her ear with the piece torn out, and her skinny little legs, has a dear child of 3, Fifi, and a cute and most intelligent son

---

* Bernard and his friend Helen had visited Gombe and were familiar with the personalities involved.

Figan, who is about 7. Flo, although she's such an old bag, is very popular with the men. Particularly David, who sometimes greets her in the most fabulous way — did I tell you how he once kissed one of her nipples and pinched the other! The men also have a naughty habit of poking a finger up their lady friend's vagina when greeting her!

Honestly Bernard, I am learning so much in such a short time that I sometimes wonder how much longer it can go on. I mean — there must be a limit to the amount I can go on learning about chimps — such large amounts of new things, anyway. Of course, one would expect to go on learning in dribs and drabs for years and for ever — not so much. I have already applied for yet another term here — which means I wouldn't get back to England till Christmas. . . .

Why are you returning to England? Is it because of Africanization? Politics? Or what? And where will you try for a job. Kew? I'm sure you will find it dreadful, after being here, won't you.

Anyway, I hope you saw Vanne (I am having to call her this daily to get Hugo used to saying it. What a pair you are, to be sure!) She will be on her way by the time you get this. She's going to find it a very different camp from the one she knew. It is a camp completely taken over by chimps. The kitchen and choo have both been moved out of the way of photography. We keep cutting down various trees — well, bushes, which removed the light for Hugo's photography. The boys all vanish like lightning at the smallest whistle which indicates that chimps have come. Meals, half cooked, are abandoned on the fire. Bread cannot be made. The boys are in their seventh heaven — they never have to come up to make tea or breakfast, because Olly always comes about that time and mustn't be disturbed. Often they only appear after 7 p.m.! What a blissful life.

I must stop. Incidentally, Mummy may have asked you already, but I couldn't read your writing — the large prickly what growing on the foreshore? And what does it look like? And are those the seeds from the dung which I found whilst you were here? Sorry about all those questions, and there's no hurry with answers. Any old time will do — this year, next year, sometime. . . .

Thank you again, very very much, for all you've done. And all the bother. And please give my love to Helen. I hope Ma did manage to get out to have a meal with you — though somehow I rather doubt it.

With love,
Jane

c/o Box 8,
Kigoma.
20 July 1963

Dear Dr. Payne,

I am enclosing an interim report for 15 June to 15 July. I am sorry it is rather delayed. Although the report is not as long as usual it has, in fact, been one of the most fruitful periods of my research. With such a large group of "tame" animals details of interrelationships between different animals are acquiring more and more significance.

I must tell you now about our cage which, I hope, will finally set your mind at rest with regard to our safety in camp. This cage is designed for us — a retreat in case of emergency, and a more substantial one than the inside of Hugo's tent where we are protected only by mosquito netting! I hope that we shall never be forced to use this cage, but it does provide a really sound safety precaution.

There were several reasons which decided us finally to have such a cage made. Firstly: we now have so many "tame" males that they are inclined to excite each other — and chimpanzees, like humans, do things without thinking when highly excited. Secondly: Goliath bears a lasting grudge against Hugo (because Hugo threw a stone to dis-attract Goliath from chasing me on the day of the baboon fight which I mentioned in my last report). On several occasions since Hugo has been chased.

The cage is foolproof. It has two doors, one as an emergency. Projection forwards with a netting dropping down in front of the cameras while Hugo can nip into the cage and close the door. It was made by Hassan in Kigoma — all metal — and is a really first class job.

I next want to ask you what the position is with regard to my using photographs taken by Hugo in any subsequent books — both scientific and popular. This, of course, will not be for another two or three years, but I intend, ultimately, to write a popular book about my chimps. For one thing I think they deserve it, and it might well help their pathetic relations which are forced to live in captivity. Obviously I should need some pictures of myself doing various things, and, in addition, Hugo is taking a lot more stills of chimps now — many of which will be far better than any which I take. I'd be very grateful if you could let me know about this point.

There is one final point which I hate to worry you with. But I have received another letter from Aldus Books Ltd, which I have enclosed. Can you advise me as to how I should answer these people? Should I tell them to write to you, to wait till I return to England so that I can find out more about the book concerned — or what? Maybe this is the last request for the moment, but there might be others.

Joanne Hess was extremely lucky when she visited us for the day. We thought it was lucky at the time, when 21 or so chimps came to camp that morning. Since then we have realized that she was even luckier — for the following three days there were no chimps here at all — neither in camp nor anywhere in the surrounding country. They had all gone off on a long trek.

I have nearly forgotten the most important item of all! When I started thinking about the tame mothers with their children I realized that it was absolutely vital to get an extra term's leave of absence so that I could witness the behaviour of the infants during the termite season. Dr. Leakey immediately agreed (as you may well have heard by now) and so I wrote next to my Supervisor in Cambridge. He also agreed, but said that he could not give the answer of the Research Board until mid-August. However, he suggested that I plan to stay on until Christmas.

You told me I had a certain amount of money in hand from last year. Even without that I feel sure that I can carry on until Christmas with the money here in Kigoma. So that I feel sure that from your point of view there will be no objections to my staying here for a longer period than was originally planned. I myself am more happy about the prospect than I can say — as I dare say you can imagine!

My mother has arrived safely. And now, with all these chimps coming almost daily, we are finding a third person extremely helpful in all sorts of ways.

It is now well after midnight and I must close.

All best wishes,
Sincerely yours,
Jane

"Chimpland"
30 August 1963

My dear FFF,

I havn't yet had your long typewritten letter re the chimps, and am forstalling it. I know that part of your worry so far as WE are concerned is due to the film you saw in Washington. And that's fair enough because I WAS silly then — and I freely admit it. But as for the safety of the chimps — Louis, can you honestly think that I havn't thought and thought about the safety of my chimps. I have already talked about this very thing with the Game Department, before all these chimps came to camp. Bill Moore-Gilbert and I decided that the best thing would be to keep the fishermen from the little bit of beach where my boys are now — then there are no huts for a long way along the beach. Apart from this, only David ever goes up to the Africans — the others all keep well away.

The cage. This has been erected not really so much as a means of escape, but as a means of removing temptation from the chimps — if they get excited we do not have to try and get out of their way, which might excite them more, but simply sit still in the cage. From which — or outside which — Hugo films when he is here.

Tourists. So far as I can see the only way to safeguard these chimps in the future — I don't mean the immediate future during which I guess things will go all right, but the future beyond which no one can see — is to make the reserve pay just a little. I know that Government, at the moment, is keen on game. But local pressure is still strong, and this particular little Reserve is NOT safe. The game dept. once I have gone, might well change their minds and reconsider a suggestion which was once almost taken up — give this place back to the Africans and make Mahale Mountain area, south of Kigoma, a chimp preserve.

So. All is planned. The attraction is provided — the chimps themselves. Their safety is planned. I myself am planning to put back all the money from my lecture film into the Reserve, in the building of a place for — say — 4 people at a time. I plan to pay for the looking after of the chimps — and I feel some sort of arrangement can be made with Geographic whereby I can give lectures with the film for money for the chimps. The hut for the visitors is to be by the lake. A covered way leads to an observation cage, and a Scout lets them know when chimps are here. Mummy, Hugo and I have planned it in detail. Obviously hardly anyone will come, certainly not for ages. But if bananas are bought from the village which causes the trouble, that will slightly appease them. And if I employ one of their leading lights, as we do now, that will also appease.

Most important of all. If only you came you would see for yourself that things are not as Joanne and Richard painted them.* If you could only SEE my chimps for yourself. O.K. — we didn't quite know how to cope when 20 chimps arrived, the first couple of times. It is now so well taped that there is not the slightest danger of anything happening at all. I mean that. Mum will agree — I expect she'll tell you herself.

And if you are worried about chimps raiding huts after I've gone — they would (IF the banana supply stopped) simply look for a few weeks in the places they know and then presume the tree was out of season and move off. They will not look for them anywhere else. Why should they?

Louis — you had faith in me when the whole project was seemingly hopeless and futile (to me). Do not suddenly lose it just when things are better than I ever dared to hope. The results I am getting now are the sort of things I never dreamed of getting.

---

* Joanne Hess and Richard Leakey, who briefly visited Gombe, apparently commented on problems with the banana feeding regimen.

A few examples, which should be exciting enough. Flo, my mother with the 3 year old (approx). Still suckling. Flo developed her first pink swelling since the child has been born. She trailed millions of men along here with her. I was able to see for the first time the real effect of a sexual swelling on the other chimps, the duration of their interest, and the effect it had on the movements of Flo. I was able to see, close up, the effect of mating behavior, on the child, during the whole of the attractive period. (Throughout which she continued to suckle.) I was able to see the different treatments accorded to this old female and a very young female (Jane!) in the same pink condition (she was almost completely ignored when Flo was present). And another very, very interesting thing — the elder child, probably between 6 and 7, finally left his mother, for days running, during this first pink swelling since the birth of his younger sister. His whole behaviour is changing — he is becoming grown up!

As for the details of social behaviour — to be able to follow the interrelationships from DAY TO DAY, instead of simply seeing the same two animals together once a week or even once a month — well, I can really say, now, that I know chimps.

Louis — I beg you will try to come and see things for yourself. Anyway — I plan to come back here the moment I finish at Cambridge, even before the Pigmy Chimps* (if that is possible) because then Flo will have a new baby and I can see the effect on Fifi — the daughter — not to mention the 101 other things. I CAN'T tell you, in a letter, how simply fantastically exciting everything is. . . .

DO try and come. You would fall head over heels in love with all my darlings — never, never think that I will let anything happen to them through what I am doing. I KNOW it is right. I KNOW that I can work the Reserve the way it must. I KNOW that I shall come back here time and time again until the problems that remain are hardly worth mentioning.

It is after midnight. My journal is usually about 10 pages per

---

* Louis and Jane had planned that she would make comparative observations on bonobos (pygmy chimpanzees) in Congo; the plan was never realized.

night. There is seldom time for a good night's sleep. But the results will so justify it, and your faith — don't, please don't, lose it now. It hurts, you know.

With love,
F.C. Jane

P.O. Box 8,
Kigoma,
Tanganyika.
12 October 1963

Dear Dr. Payne,

I have just received a letter from Dr. Grzimek of 12 August — sent on from England by sea. He wrote after seeing the chimpanzee article in the Geographic Magazine. He is very anxious to publish a translation of a shortened version of this article in Das Tier — which he edits together with Professor Lorenz and Professor Hediger.*

Since August I have been busily refusing articles to hundreds of magazines. So far as this is concerned, however, I am not quite sure what I should do. It is certainly the best animal magazine in Europe. But, quite apart from this, I do not want to make an enemy of Dr. Grzimek. I am sure he was not to blame so far as the Kinloch episode† was concerned and I rather feel that, if we refuse to co-operate with him in this article he may feel that we are holding a grudge. I have a great admiration for his work in Africa — and, since I wrote to him explaining that the chimps would be badly disturbed

---

* Bernhard Grzimek, director of the Frankfurt Zoological Garden, was a great popularizer of animal behavior studies and conservation and, perhaps most significantly, one of the most powerful voices calling for the preservation of the Serengeti Plains; he was also a trustee of Tanzanian national parks. Konrad Lorenz, Austrian zoologist, director of the Max Planck Institute for Behavioral Physiology, shared a Nobel Prize in 1973. H. C. Heini Hediger was director of the Zoological Gardens in Zurich.

† A conflict with Tanzanian officialdom (as represented by Major Kinloch) over Jane's reluctance to cooperate with a Grzimek team hoping to film chimps in Gombe.

if he came here he has not attempted to press the matter further.

As I only posted my interim Report two days ago there is really no further news from here — oh, but yes. There is one thing I really must tell you as it is one of the most amazing things that has happened since I started working with the chimps. Yesterday David Greybeard and I set off along the valley together. He was in a lazy and tolerant mood — after he had vanished through a thick tangle of vegetation I found him sitting (seeming to wait) when I finally crawled through after him. We sat and ate leaves side by side. And then I found a palm nut, nice and ripe and red, and felt sure David would appreciate it. So I held it out on my outstretched palm. Now David is a past master at affecting to ignore completely what he considers foolish actions on the part of his would-be human friends. He gave my offering a scornful glance and turned away. I held my hand a little nearer. For a few more moments he continued to ignore me. And then, suddenly, he turned towards me, reached out his hand to the nut, and, to my astonishment and delight, held my hand with his, keeping a firm warm pressure for about 10 seconds. He then withdrew his hand, glanced at the nut, and dropped it to the ground.

I have explained in my reports how chimps sometimes hold each other's hands — normally the subordinate animal holds out its hand when wanting reassurance and the dominant animal, if feeling friendly, reaches out to clasp the hand of the other. David did not want the nut. But there was this strange creature, holding out its hand, making an offering. So he took it, reassured me, and then demonstrated his complete lack of interest in my offering by dropping it to the ground. If it had not happened to me I think I would never have believed it possible.

The rains are very late — already the chimps are inspecting the termite heaps, but as yet the insects are not ready to fly.

I must close. My mother can post this when she goes tomorrow.

Yours sincerely,

Jane

P.S. Dr. Grzimek wanted black and white stills for the article.

c/o P.O. Box 8
Kigoma, Tanganyika
27 November 1963

Mr. Paul Brooks,
Houghton Mifflin Company,
2 Park Street,
Boston 7.
United States of America.

Dear Mr. Brooks,

Please forgive this messy little "blue" (I hate them) but I felt I must write immediately, upon receiving your letter of 19 November, to express my horror on hearing that you never got my reply to your last letter. This is the third letter of mine which has gone astray in 4 months — including one marked "urgent" in huge red letters for Dr. Leakey. I really am sorry about this.

I am writing just a hasty note — your letter came with the mail today and because the mail brought us a terrible problem — the mail always does seem to! — we are sending in an African tomorrow to send off batches of cables. It is already midnight.

Anyway, thank you a second time for your original letter, and for the extremely kind gesture of sending John Williams' book — which is a very fine one, and has been most helpful. In comparison with Grant and Praed it is a handy book indeed! Grant and Praed is often quite useless unless you have the dead bird in your hand and can measure its various feathers!!

As regards a book — I really and honestly can't tell you anything about that just at the moment. I feel quite helpless about it. I had a letter from the Geographic Society (because a number of publishers wrote to them to ask about the possibility of a book) suggesting that I should make no commitments at the present because there was the possibility that the Society might wish to publish a book. This I should not be happy about for various reasons, but if they really insist there is little I can do about it, being, as I am, indebted to them so greatly. However, when I have sorted things out a bit more I will contact you again. I think the type of book Collins wants is something very different from that which the Geographic wants, and there might be no clash at all.* At present, however, I can only wait and see!

In the meantime — splendid news from "Chimpland". Results are so splendid this year, so much in excess of my wildest dreams, that I have got two more terms away from Cambridge next year, and shall be returning to the Gombe Stream in March. I now know about 30 chimps really inside out, characters and all — and there are some splendid characters. The sad thing is that dear William died — we think he must have caught pneumonia as a result of his cold which never properly cleared up — the last time he was seen he was coughing dreadfully.

However, the splendid thing is that I am pretty sure we can raise the necessary funds to set up a permanent research center here — so these individuals can be studied over a sufficient number of years to make the research really worth while. When you think of the amount of money poured into the social behaviour and psychology of captive chimps you realize how very worth while this scheme will be. After all, the psychological state of a captive chimp, in most instances, must be rather similar to that of a man in prison. The older chimps in captivity, that is.

I apologize again for my seeming rudeness, and I will write again when I can let you know anything definite about the possibility of a book. Incidentally, I was interested that you heard from Fairfield Osborn† about the conference in Nairobi. I am still waiting to hear about that Conference — at which this Reserve was discussed. No one, so far, has told me anything! However, I am so glad Osborn is optimistic about the future of the animals — and with you I certainly hope he is right.

Sincerely yours,
Jane Goodall

---

* National Geographic was to publish one "popular" book, *My Friends the Wild Chimpanzees*, in 1967; Collins in England and Houghton Mifflin in the United States published *In the Shadow of Man* in 1971.
† Osborn was with the New York Zoological Society.

8

MARRIAGE AND RETURN
1964

Hugo and I agreed afterward that we had never been
to a wedding we enjoyed more.

— *In the Shadow of Man*

JANE GOODALL and Hugo van Lawick left the camp at Gombe
in late 1963, he returning to Nairobi, she to Bournemouth for
Christmas and then to Cambridge to begin her third term. As
during her second university term, she lived in an old farmhouse
at Cross Farm, Comberton, a few miles outside the city of Cambridge. During her four months' absence from Gombe, Hassan and
Dominic managed the daily operations, and Dominic kept a continuing log of chimpanzee observations. Also present in the winter
of 1963–64 was a young Polish-born mycologist, Kris Pirozynski,
who had come to look at the local microfungi.

Jane and Hugo were by then, as she later wrote, "very much in
love," and the separation of early December was enough to convince them both that marriage should be the next step. Boxing Day
(the day after Christmas) at the Birches was therefore enlivened by a
telegram that said: "WILL YOU MARRY ME LOVE STOP HUGO."*

So the term at Cambridge was a very busy one, filled with the
usual pressing research reports and papers and meetings with her
advisor, as well as a quick trip to Washington, D.C., in February
to address a huge and enthusiastic audience at the National Geo-

---

* As quoted in *In the Shadow of Man* (1971), p. 90.

graphic headquarters — not to mention planning the wedding. Held at Chelsea Old Church on March 28, Easter Saturday, the wedding was done in yellow and white: daffodils and arum lilies, with the bride in white and the bridesmaids in yellow and white. Perhaps all weddings are exercises in anxiety, excitement, and frantic activity; this one may have been more so than most, as the letter of February 3 to "Kins" — that is, Sally Cary — suggests. In addition to all those "cables and express letters . . . whizzing between here and Africa, Africa and Holland, Holland and here" and the "frantic cables from Africa to Washington, Washington to Africa and to England and from England to Washington about files and tapes and more films," Jane suddenly developed some physical symptoms alarming enough to warrant a visit to the Tropical Diseases Hospital in London.

But Africa and the chimpanzees of Gombe were never far from her thoughts. The wedding cake was topped by a clay model of David Greybeard. Enlarged color portraits of several other Gombe chimps, including Goliath, Flo, and Fifi, looked out at the happy crowds at the reception. Louis Leakey, though unable to attend in person, gave a brief congratulatory speech by tape recording. A telegram from the National Geographic Society informed one and all that the bride had just been awarded her second Franklin Burr Award for Contribution to Science (which included an honorarium of $1,500). And the bride and groom, having thus tied the knot, then trimmed their honeymoon down to three days in order to race back to paradise at the edge of Lake Tanganyika, because Flo had just given birth to a young male (soon named Flint). The couple's return was in fact briefly delayed by a grand reception at State House in Nairobi. There, after a couple of power dinners and a brief side visit to the Leakey house at Langata, Baron and Baroness Jane and Hugo van Lawick showed their latest film on the Gombe research to "H.E." — His Excellency Malcolm MacDonald (governor general of Kenya) and several ministers and other dignitaries associated with that newly independent nation. In Nairobi also they met Edna Koning (a young Dutch woman living in Peru who had written asking for work and was hired as a research assistant) before pressing south, through seasonal rains and unreasonable floods, to "Chimpland" at last.

*   *   *   *

Cross Farm,
Comberton,
Cambridge.
27 January 1964.

Dear Dr. Payne,

I am writing mainly to tell you what you may already have heard — namely that Hugo and I have just got engaged! It must seem rather strange that we were together for so long and then got engaged by cable! — but that's typical of Hugo! Anyway, it is all very exciting and we plan to get married at Easter, after my "ordeal" in Washington.

The other matter, linked with wedding arrangements (plus an endeavour to acquire enough clothes to do credit to the Society in February!) is that I shall be very grateful if you could send me a cheque enabling me to draw about £300 of the money for my last article. I have not got the correspondence with me, but I think the sum is lodged with your London Barclay's Bank account.

Work is going ahead well, and I have broken the back of my paper on aggressive and submissive behavior. It is always a bit of a shock — returning from the chimps to Cambridge. Most exhausting but, I feel, very good for me.

Thank you, by the way, for sending me the cuttings about the chimp kidney transplants. It would feel very strange, I think, to wander around with ape kidneys inside one — it is a peculiar thought — and quite extraordinary that the man lived for so long.

I must close and get on with working out a system for my new filing cabinet — a horrible job!

I look forward to seeing you all again in February, although not to giving the lecture!

Yours very sincerely,
Jane

Cross Farm,
Comberton,
Cambridge.
3 February [1964].

My dear Kins,

I can't think of many people on whom I would dare use up this charming shade in writing paper. However, I seem to remember various daintily coloured pages — or was it red ink — or violet or something — from you in the past — so here goes.

Your letter arrived this afternoon and forestalled me by 3 hours — as tonight I planned to write and tell you the latest. This is that Hugo and I get wed on 28th March, Easter Saturday of all days. It is the only possible day free. I most sincerely hope you are not planning to be away for Easter, and that, if you are, you will give a priority to coming to the wedding. It should be great fun!

It was all decided on in a hurry, and you can't imagine the cables and express letters that went whizzing — and still whizz — between here and Africa, Africa and Holland, Holland and here. My goodness. 7 letters all at once from Hugo. 1 express — did I like emeralds!! So back went a cable — "love emeralds love you"!!! Back came a cable — what size was my finger? Back went an answer — No. J. Another cable — can't find J on the card I was given. Then an urgent one — please cable names and address of your parents for announcement of engagement (there are two cables, both saying this, one from Africa, one from England. They crossed!!) Then a cable to Holland — please what are Hugo's full names. Then a cable from Africa to Holland — have I got christening cards. A cable back to Africa — please cable Jane to ring me. Cable to me — please ring my mother tonight. Horrors! Was I panic stricken. I got through at last, and his mother sounded quite sweet — but the poor thing was in such a muddle, all Hugo's letters having contradicted each other. Was I going to see them before the wedding. Was it a white wedding. Did Hugo really need christening cards — they were burnt by the Japs in Indonesia?!! Oh, I can't tell you what a muddle. And in the middle of all this frantic cables from Africa to Washington, Washington to Africa and to England and from England to Washington about files and tapes and more films. My whole life since I last saw you has been snowed under by showers of express or registered letters and cables! Not to mention film and paper!! I am exhausted in the extreme. Have got the most SUPER wedding dress — white of course. Went home on a sudden inspiration — having booked an appointment for the Tropical Diseases hospital because everyone thought I was about to die. I decided there was nothing I wanted to do less, so I went home instead. Now everyone here thinks I've been looked over, so they do not think I look so ill!! I only hope I don't have any evil disease when I do go or I shall find it hard to explain why they have been so long in finding out! Anyway, went into shop called "Brides Corner". A most fantastic shop, tucked away half way up Pool Hill. They stock over 300 wedding dresses — if you like the skirt of one, top of another, and material of a third they have it made up for you. People go there from all over the south of England. And there I found a dress that would have been at least £50 — oh — sorry — 50 guineas of course! — at Harrods. It is really quite superb.

Wedding plans. Chelsea Old Church, on the Embankment, where I was christened. Mum and I went to see the Vicar, and he was simply charming. Reception — ? Don't know yet. We want somewhere where I can just hire the room, and not somewhere that "does" receptions. Or it will be far too expensive. Aunt Margery, who is a cordon bleu cook, is being asked to do the catering. Uncle E. can get booze cost price. I plan on a bubbling wine, with choice of still wine — I think champaign (I always do spell it that way, it amused the family so!) is just a snob value waste of money! Wedding cake made by Arlene's on top of Poole Hill. Honeymoon of 6 days in Holland before I go back to Africa. We go back to Africa rather!

Other news is quite limited. Flo is behaving well, and I am horrified to hear that Apple* broke down. How very wicked of her. Piston slap sounds vaguely obscene!

Sally, do write back quickly and say you will come to the wedding. It would not be complete without you. I think it will be a

---

* Sally's car.

"fun" reception — lots of booze! You can stay at the flat — there will be space for you, and we expect you to. Can you give me any idea as to whether your Ma and Pa will be back? It will indeed be tragic if they cannot come. Do you think Sue would be able to come?

I am sorry this is such a short and rather dull letter. But I don't have much else to write about — latest news from chimpland was very disturbing — from Dominic to say that Kris had been walloped on the head by a chimp but was O.K.! I simply must get on. I have just added a missed out line to 50 reprints of my nesting paper, and put "with compliments Jane Goodall" on the back, and typed out 50 labels on a long sticky perforated label roll — looks like a miniature toilet roll — and done the envelopes up. This has exhausted me, but I still have about 10 more official letters to do. It is 9.30. So forgive me for stopping, but please write immediately — use another sheet of the airmail pad! You won't feel so guilty every time you happen across it then!

With love,

P.S. Yes — I got to Cambridge that Monday.

Cross Farm,
Comberton,
Cambridge.
11 March 1964

My dear FFF,

Knowing how hectic you must be, I simply hate to bother you with this. However, I feel I must. So let me quickly set out the points I was not sure on before I tell you anything else.

Mum and I went through the expense sheet together. In the first part — costs per month — I have filled in all the costs except (1) food for 4 Africans, (2) Medical supplies, and (3) contingencies. I havn't a clue what to put for these.

The next section is all complete. The final section I just havn't a clue about, and I'm hoping that you just have enough of an idea in your head: 2 large tents, one boys', camp equipment, boat, transport of boat, outboard motor. It is all set out on the sheet.

Anything you think is wrong, too much or too little, please alter. I'm sure you can get a secretary — anyway, the committee won't mind if it's all ink corrections I'm sure.

You needn't worry about the banana bit — I said to the committee exactly what I have written on the report, only in more detail. They were all very happy.

There is one other point I have not mentioned. We are still looking for an assistant (other than my secretary whose salary I want to pay myself) to train during the second part of my stay, to carry on when I go. Should I include that somewhere? Or what? Also, should one mention the fact that the N.Y. Zoological Soc. is extremely interested in the research center — Osborn as good as said that he would be willing, almost definitely, to co-operate with the Geographic on the project.

That, I think, is all for that. I didn't put down film stock for me, because I get all that sent, from the magazine, automatically. I gave Hassan a rise in the estimate — 400/- a month, and Dominic 160/-. Then there are two of 120/- each.

They are taking me into the Tropical Diseases to see if I might have Bilherzia — or however you spell it — just the day before Hugo gets back, which is really mean and horrid of them. Anyway, I couldn't have the treatment now, cos of Flo's baby, so I shall have to go off for 2 weeks in July or August or something — probably it would be best to do it when I have to do the silly T.V. recording. Ugh! Anyway, I don't think I've got it.

The wedding plans are going ahead nicely — only Judy has the problem of somehow trying to get the piano out of the room!!! Because more people than we thought are coming.

I met Richard* in the Trop. Diseases Hosp!!!! I expect you must have heard by now that he was bitten by a flea and paralyzed all over. Wasn't it horrible. I was whisked off in the middle of talking to him and when I got out I couldn't find him or what had happened to

---

* Richard Leakey.

him. Must end as must write more letters. I do hope all goes well — though since you are obviously going to be more hectic than I was I just don't see how you can possibly survive.

> With love,
> F.C.
> Jane

[Early April 1964]

Darling Family,

Well — here we are again. Outside the rain is <u>pouring</u> down in buckets. It has been doing so on & off ever since we arrived — which has been a great bore as we have had to do <u>so</u> much shopping.

First, let me thank you all again for the super wedding and all that you did for it. Hugo has only just learned that the cake was a present & he sends many thanks. It really <u>was</u> a super wedding, wasn't it? And, I do hope you have all recovered & that we didn't leave <u>too</u> much mess behind.

Some news. We got our heavily overweight hand luggage safely to Nairobi. B.O.A.C. were fantastic — I have never had such excellent service since the time Jif & I went 1st Class. Food superb. Smiles & help from all Hostesses. <u>Fans</u> brought round at Khartoum! Iced eau de cologne towels in the morning to freshen up. Nuts, crisps & cocktail biscuits at 7. It was all quite amazing. And a really <u>good</u> breakfast — on the plane & not at a sordid airport.

We arrived & were met by <u>two</u> shining State House cars — one for us, one for our equipment. We were conducted, on arrival, immediately to H.E. — leaving our luggage in the hall. We ordered coffee & biscuits & they brought tea & no biscuits — which peeved him no end! We then had a quiet lunch on our balcony, the two of us — in the same sumptuous suite. And then began at once on our shopping. Dinner with Mrs. & daughter as H.E. was tied up with Prime Ministers. I saw Jonny's* new wife when we went out to Langata.

---

* Jonny Leakey.

Last night there was a dinner in honour of a retiring Air commodore — another MacDonald. There were 20 guests. I wore the new black dress (with loose hair) & everyone was most impressed. I had the distinction of sitting on the left hand of Malcolm — the Air Commodore's wife on the other side. We talked chimp nearly all through dinner — the wife joining in & being nice & interested. The ladies then retired & sipped coffee & liqueurs round the fire; the gents, to Hugo's enormous amusement, followed H.E. into the garden & wee'd in a row! He said he'd heard they did that in Kenya but never known it happen at an official party before.

Tonight is the film show. There are about 60 people coming, including Clo. Poor Clo, whom I spoke to on the phone, is in court all day tomorrow — the same old Erskine business. So we couldn't meet her for lunch. She sounded rather subdued. She is living in her "sordid" flat now — not with Petal any more.*

No word from Miss Peru,† which is worrying.

I have gone & got some VILE shingles. Isn't it sordid. They arrived in the middle of the night. I found one or 2 virugon but have left most with Lyn. The shingles are spreading, & sordid. Ugh.

We have bought the most super tent — super fast engine, super tiny weeny tape recorder, super portable filing cabinets, found the only typewriter like ours in Nairobi & got it for Miss Peru, & various other super things. Including the most smashing 8 mm camera. So you will receive super films. Wack O.

It is now next morning. Cable from Miss Peru, from London Airport last night, to say she was arriving at 8.30. We got the cable at 8.15!! She really must feel she's fallen in clover! What with Washington when she watched our giddy progress, the wedding, & news of Palaces in Holland — & now State House where she has been warmly invited. Later again — she is now sipping coffee with us. We are about to go off & do our last shopping.

---

* Clo, Jane's school friend who had invited her to visit Kenya in 1957, married Francis Erskine, son of the distinguished Kenyan Sir Derek Erskine; the marriage was a troubled one, as this comment suggests. Petal was Sir Derek's daughter and thus Clo's sister-in-law. By coincidence, Petal eventually married Robert Young, the actor who had been engaged to marry Jane in 1960.
† Edna Koning, who had been living in Peru.

The film show was a <u>great</u> success. The ministers were <u>all</u> impressed. Kenyatta was ill & couldn't come, but all the others were thrilled. I think it has done an <u>enormous</u> amount of good. We are having lunch with the most interested Ministers today. Courie was there — ugh! he is <u>revolting.</u> But it really was a good thing.

Must end now as it is getting late. Must put some more gauze over vile shingle.

Tons & tons of love to you all,
& again many many thanks.
Your little 'pudding',*
Jane

<u>P.S.</u> Please send Mrs. Mackenny — the address of Leakey's office — One reprint. Please send us, by sea mail, the tinned food cooking book from drawer in Vicki's room.

Box 8,
Kigoma,
Tanganyika.
21 April 1964.

Dear Dr. Payne,

You will have to forgive me for not writing before, but things got pretty hectic, as you can imagine. It was the most wonderful surprise to receive news of the Franklin Burr Prize on our wedding day — that cable caused quite a stir when it was read out amongst the other greetings telegrams! And I should have written earlier. I do indeed feel honoured to have been awarded this prize for a second time.

The wedding went off wonderfully, and the chimpanzee pictures which you so kindly let us have absolutely made the reception. We even had models of chimps on our wedding cake! We then had a delightful but brief honeymoon in Holland — not a very conventional one as the main purpose was for me to get to know Hugo's family better. I certainly have got some delightful in-laws.

---

* By marrying Hugo, Jane became a baroness. In celebration, Olly had persuaded Danny to make a special dish known as "Baroness Pudding."

We had a terrible time getting back to the chimps, over flooded rivers and broken down trains. But we made it. And my new secretary also has got here — by the last passenger train which is likely to run for some time — the lake has risen so much that the rails in Kigoma are 20″ under water. And they expect the level to go on rising!

Flo's baby — a little boy whom we have provisionally named Flint — is simply the most adorable little object you ever saw. Although I was heartbroken she didn't wait till we got back, reports from the "caretaker" suggest that, in fact, we didn't miss anything. For the first 5 weeks of its life he never saw it move at all — it just clung onto Flo. Then, two days before Hugo and I got here, it began to look around with intelligent focused eyes, and move its arms around, etc. So I think we were lucky and timed our arrival fairly well. He should take his first crawl in a couple of weeks!

The rest of the chimps are all fine and we have already observed one or two new behaviour patterns. Hugo filmed a delightful sequence of David playing idly with little Fifi.

I hope to start work on another article in the not too distant future. There are still a few pressing things to attend to first, and a little more training of my secretary so that I can hand over to her most of the typing out of my taped notes for the day. Should the article be about the same length as the last?

Please give our regards to everyone — and once more, my apologies for not writing before.

Yours sincerely,
Jane

9

❧ ❧ ❧

BANANAS AND BABIES
1964

Without doubt the most exciting thing that year was being able to
record on paper and on film the week-by-week development of a
wild chimpanzee infant — Flint.

— *In the Shadow of Man*

UPON THEIR RETURN, Jane and Hugo were informed by
Dominic and Kris that the situation with the chimps was
veering out of control. Several new chimps had begun wandering into camp from the forest — too many in their opinion. The
apes were stealing anything resembling food, as well as clothes and
other loose items, and had started chewing on canvas, such as tent
flaps, and wood, such as chair legs. Additionally, and most alarmingly, some of the apes had entered the temporary huts on the beach
that the dagaa fishermen used; the fishermen were not likely to be so
tolerant. There was a legitimate concern that someone, either human or chimp, would get hurt.

Hugo had in February ordered the construction of steel banana
boxes that would dispense limited amounts of bananas by remote
control (with underground cables that could be pulled by handles at
one end and would attach to latch releases at the other). But those
supposedly ape-proof steel boxes had not yet arrived, so in the
meantime, the couple planned to relocate the banana feeding operation away from the beach. "We discussed the problem far into
one night," Jane later recalled, "and eventually decided that as soon
as possible we would move the feeding area farther up in the val-

ley."* The successful move is thoroughly described in two letters from late April. A banana storehouse was constructed of corrugated iron, and a sleeping hut for some of the African staff was built. And then Jane and Hugo moved the chimpanzees to the new area by the delightfully simple expedient (as noted in the first letter) of waving an empty banana box at David Greybeard. "Good old David, immediately hoodwinked, gave screams of delight and anticipation."

The new provisioning area had the added benefit of providing a nice sense of romantic seclusion for the newlyweds, since their own tent had been moved up to the feeding area as well. But as we read in the letter of June 1, that seclusion was slightly compromised when the much-anticipated new tent finally arrived. The new tent became their work area at the feeding site during the day, and at night the back portion served as bedroom for Edna Koning, the research assistant. Still, one gets a sense from the fond lingering over domestic details — the new coffee percolator, the "dear little veranda" outside the new tent, and so on — how pleasant their life was that summer. And in spite of the continuing problems associated with banana provisioning — all the competition and squabbles over that rich source of food — we can note the extraordinary, continuing flow of new information about the behavior of chimpanzees. Jane enumerates some details of this new information in the long letters of July 9 and September 24 to Melvin Payne.

At some point during the summer, before the arrival of the steel boxes from Nairobi, Hassan built some "temporary" banana boxes of cement with steel lids and latches (mentioned in the July 9 letter). The steel boxes finally arrived in September (letter of September 24), but even they were not actually very chimp-proof. Within a few weeks an enterprising chimp named J.B. had figured out how to break the control cables.

Edna Koning had arrived at Gombe during the floods of April, within a few days of Hugo and Jane. She seems to have spent most of her early weeks transcribing Jane's behavioral notes from audio-

---

* *In the Shadow of Man* (1971), p. 93.

tape. Gradually, though, she took on other tasks, and in the fall was preparing to study the baboons. In December a second assistant, Sonia Ivey, arrived (briefly accompanied by her friend John Sankey); she was hired to work more specifically as a secretary and typist. Arrangements with the African staff continued pretty much as before; Dominic Bandola and Hassan Salimu, assisted by a cook named Anyango, were in charge of the camp's day-to-day operations. Dominic, though, became seriously ill in August and spent a few days in the hospital in Kigoma, while around the same time Hassan developed back pains of unknown cause and so returned to Nairobi. Other African staff during this period included Rashidi Kikwale (there from the first days), as well as Ramadhani Fadhili, Hamisi Matama, and Sadiki Rukumata.

Visitors to Gombe that year included Joanne Hess, from the National Geographic Society, who came in mid-June to oversee some final details of a film about the chimpanzee research; Malcolm MacDonald, the governor general of Kenya, who arrived in September; Vanne, who came for a brief stay late in the year; and two European researchers, Hans Hass, a biologist and diving pioneer, and Irenäus Eibl-Eibesfeldt, an ethologist at the Max Planck Institute, who probably arrived on August 11. Jane, as we can see from the letters home preceding and following that visit, was apparently flattered and delighted at the positive interest and support of these two important men "from the same establishment as Konrad Lorenz."

Jane and Hugo had been imagining a permanent research institution at Gombe at least since the summer of the previous year. In March of 1964 she had mentioned the idea to a National Geographic committee, hoping for support. She had even (as we see in the August 10 letter) located "THE ideal site for the future research building." The distinguished Drs. Hass and Eibl-Eibesfeldt were "tremendously impressed" by her work at Gombe and entirely supportive of the research institute idea. So was Louis Leakey, who endorsed the proposal for National Geographic funds to purchase and put into place the first prefabricated semipermanent structures (the "uniports" mentioned in the letter of November 6). By the last days of December, the foundation area for the largest prefabricated building had been leveled, and the stones and sand for making concrete had been hauled up.

More immediately compelling during that year were the chimpanzee mothers and their newborns. The appearance of Flo's infant, Flint, as we have seen, was exciting enough to divert Jane and Hugo's intended honeymoon in March. Flint provided them with their first great opportunity to observe chimpanzee infant development from the earliest weeks. And then Gombe was blessed by the arrival of another newborn on September 7: Melissa gave birth to an infant tentatively named Jane — until "she" turned out to be "he" and was then rechristened as Goblin (by October 26). By early November, yet a third newborn appeared: Mandy's Jane.

In sum, the year 1964 was a productive, prolific, and momentous one indeed.

*　　*　　*　　*

[Around April 21, 1964]

Darling Family,

This must again be rather short, as I have to get several most urgent things off by the replacement of the Owens* who is flying to Dar. The urgency is because the railway is now almost entirely out of action. For two weeks there have been no passenger trains because a driver went too fast and ripped away 100 yards of line just outside Kigoma. Kris was stranded in Kigoma because of this. And still the lake is rising. Two days ago the first passenger train crawled into the station over 20″ of water! It contained one 1st class, two 2nd and 3 3rd class carriages only! People in Kigoma anticipated a funny time on its return journey because there were 50 bookings on it for 1st class and one school teacher alone had 300 pupils supposed to be travelling 3rd! They apparently reckon they can cope with water up to 24″ over the rails, after that they give up. They have had to remove the generators which live under each carriage — as if they get wet the train stops. So everything is in darkness!

---

* Perhaps Mr. and Mrs. John Owen; he was soon to become director of national parks in Tanzania.

How I know all this is because of our film show. The Owens arranged for us to go in and show the film to all the people who mattered. When Edna arrived she brought with her a message to say
would we go in on Wednesday. So on Wednesday, at 4.0, the whole
group of chimps had just left, and we thought we would leave in 30
mins, because of engine trouble. Well, Hassan had been working on
the engine all day, and he was still working on it at 5.0. At 5.30 we
were able to start out — what a slow boat. Well, bit by bit the coast
line slid away, and we reckoned on arriving at 8.30, the show being
at 9. We felt that <u>perhaps</u> the Owens might come to look for us in
their fast boat. Then, just at the valley beyond Gombe, where is the
little whitewashed hut, the last valley of the Reserve, and one third
of the way to Kigoma, the engine stopped. Hassan tried everything.
So then Dominic began rowing us to shore. We landed. Dominic immediately took charge of arrangements, and in next to no time he
had mustered 3 of the 5 inhabitants, chosen the fastest canoe, ordered Hassan into it, then off they paddled, to the next village just
round the corner, to bargain for a boat — if one was there. So
Hugo, Edna and I were left with our broken boat, the film, and a
suit-case of cloths to be left in the dry of the Owens' house. So. After
30 mins we opened our provisions and had some coffee. The two remaining inhabitants were watching, so I poured some for them —
they didn't want it so I felt silly. One hour and 15 mins later we had
made ourselves at home. Edna had tried to set light to some damp
straw. One of the little boys turned up trumps and kept rushing up
with pieces of dry twig and palm frond, so soon a cosy little fire was
burning. Edna and I had put jeans on under our pretty dresses!!
"Pwitty dwesses" read. Then a boat was heard, heading for the reserve. A tiny light far out on the lake. Thinking of the dismal prospect of rowing back to the camp, Hugo asked for a light to wave.
They produced their sole illumination — a candle! Hugo held it up
and it went out. So it was relit and went out again! So the boy
brought a long bundle of dry straw, we thrust it into our fire, and
Hugo waved the flaming torch aloft. After three of these the boat
headed for us and eventually arrived. Full of Africans. To cut a very
long story short we persuaded them first to go and look for Hassan,

and then to take us home. So Hugo went with them, and we packed up and waited patiently by our dying fire. 10 mins later, having given the little boy a slice of bread — he licked off all the butter and then offered half to his friend! — we heard a boat. It was going straight by! Horrors! And a second boat, right behind it, was arriving towing Hassan's canoe. This doesn't sound ghastly — in fact we knew that the first one was the one with Hugo in it! However, all was well, and Hugo was with Hassan in a boat which, after one and a half hours of bargaining had agreed to take us into Kigoma and bring us back for Shs. 140. Well, by that time it was 9.15! It seemed rather pointless to go back to Kigoma and arrive at 10.30 p.m. for a 9.0 film show! So a lot more bargaining and they agreed to transport us and boat for 70/-. Sheer robbery! Still, we got back.

Well, the following day the sordid White Father stopped by. The one who always whizzes past in the fast boat without stopping. He was so foul and rude that we were not very nice to him. "Well," he greeted me "I have been passing this place for two years now, and never bothered to call in and stop, but Krus* told me a lot about the chimps, and everyone is talking about them, so I thought I'd spare half an hour". No asking if we wanted him to do anything, or anything. He even said that we should have spent a whole day in Kigoma for the film as one could never be sure of the weather on the lake.

However, Hugo and I decided that it would be a squish on all the foul Kigoma-ites if he went in by taxi, organized a new engine for us, and, at the same time, showed the film. So he went off the next day and said Owen was so rude he almost caught the next boat back. There are lots of stories to tell about how horrible are the Kigoma-ites. Owen even insinuated, apparently when everyone was waiting for us to turn up that night, that we probably just "hadn't bothered" to turn up. We were livid. Anyway, it is done now, and over. None of the important Africans came to the film — either the proper night or the night Hugo finally showed it.

Well, I started this letter at 6.30 this morning, and got to the top

---

* This may refer to Kris, with Jane imitating the White Father's distinctive accent.

of this page. Then came Huxley, J.B., Pooch, Goliath, David and Flo and family. The Owens arrived while they were still here — or anyway, Carlos* and his "take over" and the take over's wife. The two latter, though I only said hello to once, were the most soppy people. I hope they won't open this letter — they are taking it to Dar, chartering a plane, and posting it there. Edna has answered all 30 of my publishers' letters, so those will go off as well. These silly people we planned would take the mail today but, as usual, nothing was ready.

It is now early the next morning. I have lost the other part of this letter, temporarily, so I had better start on a new subject.

Flint is the name of the new baby, and he is simply adorable. He is now begining to look around with interest, watch things, make little pout greeting faces, and he scratched himself yesterday. FF† loves to play with his hands, and the other day was allowed to groom one little arm, but Flo usually gently pushes FF away from him. We saw an exciting thing the other day — what one would have expected, true, but nice to see. Flo picking leaves to wipe off dung — we couldn't see if it was off the baby or herself. The other adults disappointingly ignore the infant. But David, two days running, played most sweetly with FF — and as for FF herself — she is quite fantastic now, so tame is she.

We are started on work up the valley. It was all so difficult, trying to visualize the organization, safely, of another camp that we are ended up much nearer to this camp than the original plan. But we reckoned that, once the chimps know there are no bananas here, they won't bother to come anyway, especially if there are other tasty things for them there — blankets, shirts, etc! We should be grateful for any old clothes — used and unwashed. This is a serious request. Perhaps some could be sent by sea mail? Though that might be foolish in view of present postal conditions! Anyway, cardboard does the trick usually — even David, having had no bananas at all, was fobbed off with cardboard yesterday!

---

* Apparently a bureaucrat from Kigoma.
† Fifi, Flo's next-youngest offspring.

Saw the most funny thing. There is a strange kind of termite that circles round and round like a swarm of bees, round a tree. We cannot understand why they do this, but they do. And have now twice seen chimps trying to catch them. It is just about the funniest sight you ever saw — a chimp, standing right as far out along a branch as it can, holding on with one hand sometimes, and reaching out with a waving — or beckoning — gesture trying to sweep a termite into its mouth. I watched a stranger doing this yesterday, through my telescope. He made the most fantastic face as he was making these antics — mouth wide wide open, all upper gums and teeth showing, lower lip slightly pushed forward. It was so funny to watch. And sometimes, if they are on a secure branch, they sweep out with both hands, and sweep them to their mouths one after the other! The little chap I watched yesterday performed in this way for 2 whole hours, rushing from side to side of the tree after the swarm. He must have been quite exhausted.

Anyway, to return to the new camp. We have a superb spot, just beyond the little ridge, and all yesterday Hassan, the scouts, and our other trusty helpers made the banana/clothes store. For this Hugo bought large sheets of corrugated iron in Kigoma. We are having a hut built here, so that two boys can always sleep there, and be there in the day — and they can change around for this, taking turn and turn about. We have, finally, two tents there, and the original one will stay here. We eat and bath here in the evening — for the rest we live and work at the other camp. There is a lovely view of Sleeping Buffalo and although the scope is not as great as if we had gone further up the valley, I think it should work out fine.

At the moment only Ben is here. He is very nervy.* He has been several times, but never had any bananas till today, as he came with groups. Today we saw him in a tree over the stream, put out a pile, and he came over. He is in the tree behind the tent.

That was actually written as page 3, a part of the first part which I said was lost on the previous page! Because at the moment Edna is typing my Journal from tape, Hugo is removing his burrs,† and

---

* Nervous.
† Shaving.

sends his love, and the chimps have just gone. We went to inspect work up the valley just a moment ago, and it's coming on fine. The store nearly done, and the main structure of the boys' hut nearly ready.

Chimps here all day. And darling Olly. I don't think I told you. She came once before, goitre larger than ever. Worzle and Leakey were here. She was very nervy, and when we sneaked her three bananas she was attacked by both the horrid males and Worzle bit her in the arm. So it was very sad and pathetic. Kris told us she had only been twice since we left, but we feel sure that she came, in silent Olly fashion, peered down, and there was no one to love her and see that she was sneaked bananas. Anyway, today, although we had Goliath, David, Leakey, Huxley, Gregs, Charlie, Worzle, Flo and family, and Evered, we managed to sneak Olly 14 bananas, and no one attacked her. Hugo filmed FF holding Flint's little hand, and moving a tiny piece of food which had dropped onto his head from Flo's mouth. He is getting more of a handful for poor Flo every passing day!

Edna — Miss Peru — is turning out just fine. She is not "tough" yet, and I'm not sure if she ever will be really tough. But she is keen, interested, observant, intelligent, and great fun. So, all in all, we feel she is a great success. She adores the chimps, and we certainly feel that she will be able to cope at the end of the year. If she agrees to stay on, that is. We asked her, point blank, if she felt she wanted to go on with this sort of work, and she said yes. I hope she does. It is nice having chimps here absolutely all day long.

I'm sure there is so much to relate, but I really feel I must write some more wedding letters! Oh — a most important thing, which I forgot last time. We could not find that unbreakable china in Nairobi. Not anywhere!! What a bore — but it isn't here. So what do you suggest? Could you find out the price of the various things and then we could send a cheque for it. Do we have to have a special cheque book for our joint account? Or what? Mum.

The rain is fantastic. The stream really gets uncrossable for ages — a nuisance with the choo on the other side! Poor lone Palm is miles and miles out in the water now, and I can't imagine how it can still be standing. Hugo, now smooth, says please will I send his love to everyone. I hope Nick is well, give him our love, And tons and tons to all of you — we have had no mail yet from anyone except one from Catherine Hitchen!!!* She addressed that to the Boma!

Tons of love,
Jane

P.S. The "H" has just come off the typewriter!!

"Chimpland"
[Late April 1964]

Darling Family,

Well — we have moved our camp! At least, Hugo and I and half of the chimps have. Edna is left sort of floating between the old and the new, often trailing chimps along here with her, by luring them with bananas or pieces of cardboard!!

But let me start from the beginning. We searched around, Hugo and I, and found the most delightful shady place, palm trees overhead, and a lovely open space opposite where, we thought, when the long grass was trampled or cut down, Hugo would be able to film the chimps admirably. Accordingly we instructed Hassan to gather his forces and start off by building a banana store, of corrugated iron, and a small hut for two Africans to live in, at a spot not too far from our camp site. This took some time, but eventually was finished. And then, before moving all our things up the valley, we thought we should try and get at least some of the chimps accustomed to the new place.

So we filled the store with bananas, and I came here at crack of dawn ready to seduce early chimps which might pass with delicious bananas. No chimps passed. Our walkie talkies are still working, and we had arranged to contact at 9.0. We did so, and Hugo told me that all sorts of chimps were with them — including David himself, Goliath, J.B. — who is more horrible and beastly every day,

---

* An old friend of Vanne's.

McGregor,* and Flo and her family. Hugo asked if I thought he should try to lead some of them here. So I said yes, but neither of us thought anything would come of it. So he picked up an empty box — one they sometimes have bananas in, walked past them — they ignored him — and then held the box up and sort of waved it at David. Good old David, immediately hoodwinked, gave screams of delight and anticipation. To cut a long story short, I, in the new place, suddenly heard a frenzied voice yelling "They're coming". I flung bananas all over the place as the excited screams and calls approached — and they came — a long string of black creatures all rushing after a panting and disheveled Hugo who was still brandishing the empty box. With yells of pleasure they fell on the new banana supply. Since then we have managed to lure dear Olly and Gilka to our new place — they come every day now. Olly's goitre is bigger than ever.

Well, to return to the camping place. Having established it with the chimps, it was time to establish it for ourselves. The first thing was to flatten some of the very tall grass. So we instructed Hassan to hire an army of eager fishermen, and up the valley we trailed. Half of them cut the grass with pangas, the other half hit it with sticks and trampled it. The trampling method was much quicker — Hugo and I turned it into a sort of dance — we held hands and tramped it down sideways in a sort of St. Bernard's waltz! By nightfall all was ready. What we had not reckoned on was the fact that all the area which has been cut is now bristling with hard sharp stubble — the chimps simply hate it! They tiptoe over the hurtful area if they have to, to reach a banana — but all Hugo's dreams of the superb charges out in the open sunlight are shattered! Instead the chimps happily sit and lie in the shade of our palms, sitting around the tent, and do wonderful things where it is far too dark for filming!

To continue. The following evening we hired a longer string of fishermen porters, got the tent down, piled all the equipment into separate loads, and led our "foot safari" off along the steep little

---

* Jane often spelled this balding older male's name with a double "g"; he was named after McGregor, the old gardener in Beatrix Potter's *The Tale of Peter Rabbit.*

path and down into the valley. It was quite sort of romantic, looking back and seeing them in their rags and tatters in single file behind us, trailing through the long grass with their loads on their heads. We then set them to on making a level place for the tent. This was hard work, as everywhere here is so sloping. They had to dig about a foot down at the back of the tent and push the earth to the front. Then we had a fairly level floor, though we still find only our heads and shoulders in the bed in the morning, our feet and legs having slid off the end! This leveling had to be finished by the light of two pressure lamps as it took much longer than we had anticipated. Then we got the tent up, piled the equipment inside, and went back to the other camp.

Edna — Miss Peru — was to be left in charge there until the new tent arrives — more of that later. We had supper and then Hugo and I set off with our torch back to our new little home. It is really most super — we have our cosy supper and coffee round the fire — did I tell you we have bought a really elegant coffee percolator — one of those glass ones that push the coffee up and then let it down again? It is really most handy for out here because all you have to do is light a small flame, and remember to time it. And it makes good coffee. Then we come back to our cosy tent here. Luckily Anyango loves the trip down the valley in the evenings to make our bed and wash up the odd cups and spoons and things we have used during the day.

Next we had some drama. We suddenly noticed that there was a tall dead palm tree right behind the tent — which could have smashed everything and everyone right out of existence. After hearing from Kris about the dead palm that fell exactly where Hugo had been sleeping that night, we were taking no further chances. (We have even had our fire moved, in the old camp, from under the palm tree in case dead fronds should suddenly crash down). So we got Hassan to look at it the next evening. He at once employed a few more fishermen, one of whom had a long strong rope. The tree itself was so rotten that no one would climb up it, but luckily a good palm grew very close. So an expert palm tree climber was sent up this tree with the rope, which, by some magical manoevering, he managed to tie firmly near the top of the dead palm. Hassan and various fishermen then took the other end of the rope. The next problem was the cutting. Palm wood is really very hard indeed, so they wanted to take advantage of the big hollow quarter the way up the trunk. This made cutting difficult — they had to cling round the trunk like — well, like chimps! while they cut. They took it in turns, and by the end, though they didn't have to cut much, the sweat was pouring off them.

Hugo suddenly had horrors that the tree might, after all, fall the wrong way, and so decided to take everything out of the tent and lay it flat on the ground. This was duly done.

At last they decided they had cut through enough of the tree. The cutters scuttled off to a safe distance, and the pullers took over. We didn't think it would work, but, of course, they had judged it to perfection. There was a creaking, and splintering, and the whole tree seemed to bend as though it was made of rubber before the trunk broke at the wounded place and the tree fell gently amongst the fronds of a neighbouring palm, and there came to rest.

Yesterday Edna suddenly found a palm tree, even closer to the tent, which is quite alive but, in the middle, all the inside has gone. The whole top half is supported by three little thin pillars of hard bark! They are about 9 inches high! We are either going to put wire cable round the tree and peg it, so that if it falls it falls away from us, or else cut it down.

Gradually we are getting our belongings "chimp proofed". High time too. We have lost one sweater (and another to the rats!) a pillow and pillow case, a blanket, a sheet and various small items. In addition we occasionally may have files or notebooks literally snatched out of our hands by such cheeky individuals as Pooch, Figan or Hugo — chimp Hugo! We now have polythene hanging over shelves with books (or we are just about to!) or else they are enclosed in firmly locked wooden boxes and crates. First job in the morning is to dismantle the bed and lock up the bedclothes! I dread the day when they suddenly realize that the clothes we are actually wearing are as good to chew as the ones they steal from broken into boxes and stores!!

Whether or not you ever receive this letter is in the lap of the Gods. Kigoma is completely cut off by road and by rail. There is no mail link at all, and the only way we can get mail out is by having it sent on some small plane which has been locally chartered. The Owens have promised to send anything we let them have at the first possible opportunity. 130 mail bags are stuck somewhere on the way to Kigoma — this includes masses of equipment from the Geographic and — we hope — various letters from our families. Edna's new tent is among the delayed goods. In addition to lack of mail, Kigoma has now completely run out of butter, margarine, sugar, and various other not so important things. We have had no butter for weeks.

We had one day, last week, when it rained as I never imagined it could rain. Our little stream was transformed into a raging hurtling river, with enormous boulders being dashed along in the [remainder missing]

"Chimpland".
1st June [1964].

Darling Family,

It seems so long since I last wrote that I can't remember what I've told you of all our news. So forgive me if I repeat myself from time to time. . . .

Edna has now moved up the valley to the new camp to sleep. This is rather sad — better really, from work points of view, but not so nice and cosy for us in the evenings when we had our own special little tent. Never mind. This, of course, means that our new tent has arrived — it came through, together with the new engine, on the first mail train that was able to creep through the flood waters into Kigoma. It is the most heavenly tent imaginable, and Hugo and I plan to get one for ourselves for the future. It is more or less square — that is, it has tent poles in the middle and also at the sides of the tent, so you can stand upright everywhere inside. It has yellow mosquito netting windows all round — lots and lots of them, so that it is always beautifully cool. At the back is a little oblong which is in-

tended for a bathroom, but which is now Edna's bedroom, so that
the whole of the rest is a work tent. In the bedroom just fits the bed
and a lovely wooden stand made by Hassan for Edna's trunk and
other personal things. The bedroom has windows too. The yellow
netting gives the tent such a nice warm light all the time. We have
had white small stones carried up from the lake shore for the veranda, and from this dear little veranda one has the most lovely
view over the mountains across a great open space leading to the
stream, where we give the chimps their bananas. It is a simply wonderful tent. The only reason that Hugo and I did not immediately
move in, is that in our own tent we now have lovely lots of room,
having moved all papers etc, into the new tent. This means that as
soon as chimps arrive the tent is zipped up and all the contents completely safe. Which is wonderful after having to immediately hide
all papers, files, etc., as soon as we heard chimps anywhere near.
The tent also has a plastic washable groundsheet, completely leak-
proof, and nylon guy ropes. A palace. You should have seen the
faces of the Africans when they saw it standing upright in its full
glory. None of them had ever seen such a tent in their lives before!

When we get back to the base camp in the evening we usually settle down wearily to a tomato juice in front of the fire, only to be at
once brought to our feet by a string of patients.* One poor old man
almost cut his toe off. Funny thing is that one of the chimps, Ben,
has a cut in exactly the same place — just slightly worse than the
old man. But what I was really going to say was that every third evening or so an extra large mob arrives, all madly inventing ailments,
and then ask if Edna will play her guitar! The two who have guitars
of their own are the ringleaders, and the idea is that after Edna has
played for a while she hands the instrument over to one of them,
and then they sit there, surrounded by an admiring circle, and play
their own African tunes until supper is ready, and Dominic shoos
them all away. How they love it. As a result we are getting lots of
presents of eggs. We manage to eat some of the eggs, but it gets more

---

* Vanne had started an informal "clinic" in 1960, offering medicines and simple
treatments to anyone who showed up, including African staff, fishermen, and people
from villages just outside the reserve.

and more difficult. McGreggor has developed an absolute passion for eggs. If we even half open a container with eggs in it, when he is anywhere around, he simply rushes up, taking the shortest possible route even when this is straight through the tent and over someone's legs, scattering wadges and cardboard in his wake, and grabs the egg. The first time we noticed how strong his passion was was when we handed two to Dominic, down in the old camp, so that he could boil them for breakfast. Greggor, who was miles away calmly eating a pile of bananas, suddenly leapt to his feet, rushed, upright to Dominic (whom he is normally scared of) and snatched away the eggs — albeit with rather a trembling hand at his own audacity! Little Gilka will steal eggs too, but she is funny. The eggs are too big to fit into her little mouth, and when she cracks them she loses the entire contents, and then just chews and spits out the shell! Then there are other egg fans — Pooch will dare much for an egg. Fifi manages to get one very frequently. And, in fact, nearly all of them apart from David and Figan, will occasionally pounce on an egg they see lying around.

Our most exciting piece of chimp news concerns Madam Butterfly and her little daughter. They came to camp about 4 times last year, very nervy. Earlier this month — last month I mean — Madam B. became most attractive to gentlemen who all pursued her madly all over the reserve. This went on for two weeks, at the end of which a very exhausted and jaded party trailed wearily to camp exhibiting large bare patches where hair had been pulled out by jealous lovers, and all manner of cuts and bumps. In fact, they all came except for David. He was faithful to her even when her charms were on the decline. Then, two days later, he brought her with him. All calm and peaceful. She got lots of bananas. And then came the exciting discovery — that her little daughter, whom we have now called Little Bee — b for short! — has a club foot. Whether or not club feet are known in captive chimps I don't know. But even if they are, the fact that this little thing has survived in the wild is quite fantastic. She is now about 2 years old. She obviously can't grip properly — if at all — with the deformed foot. She walks with the foot upright on the backs of the bent toes. And it obviously isn't all that easy for her because she is constantly rushing to climb onto her mother — while Gilka, the same age, is now seldom seen on Olly's back. Even more fascinating, she is the most cheeky and impudent infant we have yet seen. She doesn't just go up to a big male and beg — she goes and grabs hold of whatever it is she wants, and pulls! She continues thus until either she gets it, or else she is firmly pushed right away — which causes her to scream in temper, rush to her mother, stare round sulkily — and then, in the next instant, she is back and trying again! No wonder she survived.

Flo's baby Flint is three months old now. He still doesn't crawl, nor has he got any teeth yet. But he takes such an interest in life, and greets any newcomer with little baby pants and hoots. Fifi is fascinated with him and spends hours and hours playing with his hands and feet — when Flo allows these liberties that is. But Flo allows it more and more often.

Hi! I'm sure there was lots more news — but no time to write it. Absolutely not. Chimps from dawn until dusk absolutely. Wack o! Thank <u>goodness</u> for Edna. She is now in the work tent typing the first of 6 sides of tape — 2 days! We have bananas hidden in millions of different containers — most of which are discovered by David, Figan, Melissa or Charlie. This afternoon we had a most charming party in the tent. Goliath sat on our stone on the veranda (Hugo & my tent) with one hand on the tent pole — sort of 'tent owner' style. Inside sat Flo — leaning on the tent pole with Flint cooing & gurgling on her lap; Fifi — draping the last shreds of the mosquito netting door over her head like a veil; & Figan — rocking because he knew Edna & I were 'banana pregnant' (i.e., b's under our shirts) & yawning. Flo & Flint both wee'd & then they went out. It was then super — Fifi wanted to play with Flint. Flo doesn't like that. Flo also wanted to play with Flint herself. So she play-bit Flint's face — making him give baby-choking gurgles of laughter — meanwhile sparring with Fifi — parrying her grabs at Flint. Then Fifi tickled Flo, making the old girl chuckle. And Figan sprawled in front of his family then played with Fifi, making her chuckle and giggle like mad! It was so gorgeous.

Hugo has just come in & we are going to hear these various

laughs — which we recorded — they were super! Especially Flint's. We brought our coffee here in a thermos tonight, so as to be quicker over supper. But we weren't quicker because Edna had been doing her garden & had not had her bath — & it takes her 30 mins! She is growing veg! Hugo is composing your cable, Olly! You will have had it by now! The "wispy-burr" in case you wondered, is true. You & your scissors much needed, Mummy Pineapple!

Lots more news next letter — v. soon as sordid Owens coming in 2 days — ugh.

Tons of love,
Jane

P.S. 'Nature' has not arrived. Please AIR MAIL reprint if they have.*
P.S. In next letter comes mailing list for Nature reprints.

c/o Box 8,
Kigoma.
9 July, 1964.

Dear Dr. Payne,

Please accept my most sincere apologies for the long lapse of time since last I wrote to you, and for the fact that the promised interim report has never been sent. In fact, I have been kept so busy here that I still have not found time to write an official report.

First I must thank you for your last letter — which, owing to Joanne having to return to Kigoma early with the horrible ulcer on her leg, arrived after she had left.

Certainly I understand that it is necessary to build up a story around "Jane Goodall", and we have cooperated with Joanne as much as we possibly could. However, I know she was hoping to return to Washington with all the additional footage "in the can", and this, unfortunately, was not possible. This was because Joanne's visit coincided with a period when the chimpanzees came to camp in large groups, stayed for long periods of time, and were unusually

---

* Jane's article "Tool-using and Aimed Throwing" had appeared in the March 28 issue of *Nature*.

excitable. Because of this we did not feel that it was really safe to leave my new assistant, Miss Koning, alone in the camp for long periods of time. As you know we have moved our camp, and the artificial feeding area, further up the valley and away from the lake shore. . . . In fact the whole situation has come about because the steel banana boxes, to be opened by remote control, have not yet arrived from Nairobi. These boxes were invented and ordered by Hugo in February, before he left Africa. He stood over the maker until the first of the order had been completed and tested, and then left urgent instructions that the others be finished and despatched with the utmost speed. And still not one has arrived, despite wires and messages.

However, with the help of Hassan we have constructed temporary boxes out of cement and already the situation is vastly improved, and we are able to cope relatively easily with the largest of groups.

During Joanne's stay Hugo got about three quarters of the necessary additional footage completed. We plan to finish the remainder as soon as possible. The scenes of me we have had to hold up at present because of another outbreak of my old skin trouble on my face — now nearly healed up. The scenes on the beach are held up until the fishermen get a good catch of dagaa. And the night scenes have been held up until now because the sun gun was not properly charged.

I also hope to tape a draft commentary for the TV film and despatch it very soon. I gather, from talking to Joanne, that a great deal of last year's film material may be changed for better material shot this year and so, in view of this, we are not trying to make an exactly timed commentary, but I think that all the information required is included and that this will form the basis for a second commentary to be written when the film is finalized.

I now feel that I must summarize the highlights of this year's research. I hope you will be able to see some of the film — that will tell you, better than any words of mine, how wonderful is Flo's baby, Flint. Flo is now so tame that we have been able to observe every small development of the infant since our arrival. And as you say, we are most excited about the pregnancy of Melissa since this will give us a chance to fill in the details of the missing six weeks.

As I may, or may not, have mentioned, I had to prepare a paper to be read at a conference in Nairobi. I have not yet discovered whether or not it was read (by Dr. Leakey!) but I enclose a copy as this will serve to show you how the research is progressing and how, gradually, the pattern is becoming clear. This paper, which was prepared as an oral talk only and not with a view to publication, concerns the development of the young chimpanzee from infancy until it becomes mature at the end of the adolescent period. It was completed when Flint was about 12 weeks old. Since then he has appeared twice on Flo's back. In addition his interactions with other members of the chimpanzee community have increased. Fifi now takes him more and more often, and is allowed to keep him for longer and longer periods. As she sometimes runs off with him and carries him up tall trees, with poor Flo puffing in pursuit, we can't help feeling that this might be one of the reasons for the suspected high rate of infant mortality! Best of all, Flint has taken his first few tottering steps — so far not more than two before collapsing. However, he progresses, because, at first, he cried as soon as he collapsed so that Flo gathered him to her breast immediately. Now he keeps quiet, gets up, and tries again.

Flo and her family are certainly great assets to this research. We actually saw Figan losing one of his milk teeth — one of the lower canines. So this is one way of checking up on whether the approximate ages we had fixed on for each of the youngsters are more or less correct. And it seems likely that they are more or less right.

We have also come to the conclusion that one of the adolescent males, some two or three years older than Figan, is also a son of Flo. This, of course, is not absolutely certain, but so many facts point to such a relationship that we have renamed Ben "Faben"! One important point is that Faben is the only adolescent male, with the exception of Figan, who is allowed to touch, and even play, with Flint. He is continually moving about with Flo, plays frequently with both Fifi and Figan and, believe it or not, with old Flo! The other day he was tickling her in the ribs until the old girl shrieked with laughter. And only yesterday we saw a never to be forgotten sight: Flo, Faben, Figan and Fifi (not to mention little Flint clinging on for dear life under his Ma) all chased each other round and round and round a palm tree, grabbing at each other's ankles as they went. We all agree that we have never seen anything funnier. . . .

Before leaving things appertaining to Flo entirely, I must mention that this same lady has shattered yet another generalization (it really is true that you can't generalize about chimps). I had come to believe that female chimpanzees never display in the fashion of the males — that is a charge, dragging at branches or vegetation and ending up with slapping on the ground or on a tree. But the other day Flo charged!! She even commenced with a male-type bipedal swagger, she dragged (or tried to drag) a huge log, she stamped the ground, and she swayed a sapling. She even put her skimpy hair out whilst doing all these masculine acts! And the following day she leapt at a tree and drummed on it!

There is one exciting thing which I am not sure whether we have mentioned to you or not. And that is that one of the small infants (about the age of Gilka) has what appears to be a club foot. Although I had frequently seen the mother and infant in the reserve before, and although they came to camp several times last year, not until this season, when the mother, Madam Butterfly, started coming here regularly, did we notice the club foot. Unfortunately the pair has now temporarily disappeared, but I feel sure they will reappear soon. It is amazing that a chimpanzee in the wild can survive with such a deformity — she cannot use the foot at all, and walks on the top of her bent in toes, the foot held upright in the same position as a club foot on a human.

We have now seen the chimpanzees react twice to large snakes. One was actually chased by Fifi, who moved along behind it shaking branches at it and hitting towards it. The other snake was a much larger one which moved slowly into a small chimpanzee group. On this occasion the chimps were definitely apprehensive, but showed none of the terror which is characteristic of all captive chimpanzees when they see snakes of any size. Most of the chimps made a few small worried sounds, Flo walked unhurriedly up the slope away from it, Melissa went towards it which made it streak away, and as it went Worzle gave a threat bark and hit in its direction.

We are fortunate in having a very fine drumming tree right near this camp, and I have been able to observe drumming almost daily. Previously I had seen chimpanzees stamp, in passing, on tree trunks, but never seen the actual drumming which can carry for at least a mile. A drumming tree must have large flat buttresses on which the chimpanzees stamp with their feet, either once or several times in succession. If we try stamping on the same tree we are able to produce merely a dull thud!

With regard to feeding behaviour various new insect foods have been discovered. Firstly we have seen them eating weaver ants in large quantities — and feel that they may have made quite a discovery here! They have a most exotic flavour, and we are planning ways of marketing them as tropical delicacies!! We have also seen them eating caterpillars for hours each day. Somehow this seems a strange diet for chimpanzees, but they apparently relish them. In addition we have seen them standing in the tops of trees and reaching out with one or both hands to try and catch a type of termite which swarms — rather like swarms of bees they look. The chimps look very strange when they feed in this way — rather as though they are signalling! The baboons and monkeys also reach out in this way.

Also with reference to dietary matters, we have devised a "dung swirling" technique whereby the contents can be washed easily and examined carefully. Lists of all these contents are being kept carefully.

In addition to the above I am learning a whole wealth of exciting new material concerning social behaviour — particularly with reference to one of the most fascinating of all aspects — communication. As yet all this is un-analyzed, but at last the pattern is becoming clear — the means by which one individual obtains the support of others (or at least tries to).

The new Nagra tape recorder is superb, and I should like to thank the Committee very much indeed for sending us this piece of equipment. At last we are building up a collection of calls which will be of inestimable value for analysis at a later date.

This then, is a summary of some of the fascinating data already revealed during the first three months of this year's research. If the future produces similar results — as it is bound to do — our work this year will be worth while indeed.

Before I close this letter I should like to ask your views about a proposal which I should like to put before the Research Committee requesting an additional assistant. Miss Koning is proving very valuable in helping me to keep up the scientific record — in making detailed notes of things which it is impossible to record when one is observing the behaviour of a group as a whole (such as scratching, details of individual charges, etc.) in checking the dung samples, and in keeping notes when I follow a group away from camp.

Now, however, the overall work has increased so tremendously that we are all three going flat out from about 6.30 a.m. until nearly midnight each day simply in order to keep everything up to date. I should be very happy to take over all Miss Koning's expenses if the Society would agree to completely finance another assistant who would be employed more or less entirely for secretarial purposes. At present Miss Koning spends the greater part of her time typing out part of the day's notes — usually about ten pages like this one. If we could have someone to take over this part of the work it would mean that she would be free to help me, at night, in the sorting out of at least part of these notes for analysis for my scientific reports. It is wonderful to be acquiring so much information — but horrifying when one thinks of analysing it!

This brings me to one final point. In view of this vast amount of work, and to the exciting results which we are obtaining, do you not think that it might be mutually advantageous if the writing of an article for the magazine could be postponed until the end of the year? This would certainly be a very great relief, and I feel certain that I could make a better job of the article if I was able to write it in slightly more peaceful circumstances!*

---

* The article, titled "New Discoveries," was published by *National Geographic* in December 1965.

I'm afraid this has been rather a long letter, but the contents were long overdue. Please give my regards to your wife, and to other members of the Society.

With warm regards,
Jane

Note from Hugo. He asks me to tell you that he is most happy to devote the greater part of this year to filming the chimpanzees, and that he is most grateful to the Society for thus prolonging his honeymoon! He will do his best to ensure that the Society is not disappointed with the results!

P.S. (from me) I would be very grateful, and there is no hurry at all, if you could have a few copies made of the enclosed paper, as this is the only one I have until I get back the one I sent to Dr. Leakey.

"The Hut"
Chimpland.
10 August 1964

Darling family,

It becomes more and more impossible to find any time to write decent letters to one's friends and relations! Somehow, although we daily get more organized here, the amount of work to be done increases and increases, and the more we do, the more there seems to be left to be done. All this is just to excuse the sort of letter this will be by the time it gets posted. Because I have resolved to type little bits, here and there, as a nice way of relaxing in between other things. This will be quite a short little piece as it is almost too dark to see already! The lamp is lit in the tent, but I am sitting in our new little hut so as to be at hand for Edna — who is checking over her daily "dung swirling" results. Once more we have found the chimps with meat — it was old Flo this time. I went after the group up the valley (Flo was not among them when they left camp). I found them all sitting in a cosy little huddle, gathered around Flo. As there was a new mother amongst them (new for us I mean, though hardly "new" in any other sense as she is old as the hills), I was unable to go very close, and they were almost obscured by leaves. Then Flo emerged to greet Mike, and, in her hand, was a large gory piece of red meat! I can only presume that she had stuffed herself to capacity, for she was not even eating it. The others must have been eating meat too, as they showed little interest, merely sniffing at the bloody hand from time to time. After some time, and still clutching her booty, Flo got up and set off in the direction of camp. I quickly rushed ahead to warn Hugo that Flo was bringing red, red meat to camp, not just an old dry bone or an old piece of skin. And, believe it or not, the old bag arrived without it! I don't know what can have happened — I quickly went back, going by one route and returning by another so as to cover all ways she might have come, but I couldn't see a trace. I think old Huxley must have stolen it as she got near the tree where he was eating dry leaves!

Today it has been really hot and humid. Twice I set off to follow the chimps when they left camp, but they must have felt the heat too. They just flopped down — so I flopped with them!

I am rather lost now, with what you all know and don't know. There is nothing really startling, but a number of very nice things, to tell you. First of all, our three new females. Marina, whose name you have heard, has a most adorable family. Her eldest son, we have discovered, is Peter Pan,[*] one of the two chimps here which beat their chests. Then there is the daughter Miff, about 6, and the most adorable little boy, Merlin. Merlin is the epitome of a mischievous and wicked little boy. His face is "little boy" all over. The way he moves — running all sideways and gangling so that he looks all the time as though he might overbalance and tumble down in a heap of long arms and legs. And he's super at walking upright. The other day he sat on the path, a tiny, self sufficient little fellow (he's only about 2), and gathered up a number of dried, black, banana skins. These he tried to shove into his "trouser pocket" (i.e. between his thigh and tummy), but there were so many that, every time he put the last one in, one of the others tumbled out. It was so funny. Then, finally, he gathered them all up in one hand, except for one, and tod-

---

[*] Subsequently renamed Pepe.

dled off down the path, very upright and with a completely straight back, and the one odd skin he held first over his shoulder and then over his head, so that it hung down behind — just like the tail of a little boy's red indian headdress! He looked so quaint. You have probably heard what terrible thieves are Marina and her children. She is the worst. Creeping into the tent and stealing a pair of shoes, two days running. She completely chewed up the uppers of 4 shoes! Miff took away my haversack one day. Hugo's binoculars the next because she likes the flavour of the strap! And Peter Pan, hoping to find hidden bananas, went off with two thermoses and one torch which he proceeded to bang against rocks until they smashed open! The latest craze is to lick Hugo's tripods — the whole family gathers round, pink tongues licking into all nooks and crannies, Merlin often reaching out from his Ma's back! It really is a very funny sight.

Then there is the "new" mother. Her family is most exciting to have. The daughter is about the age of Olly's Evered, and the son about the age of Gilka. The latter is the funniest little thing, though we don't know anything of his character yet as Sophie is most retiring, and has only been three times. She comes because the males insist — she being, at present, particularly interesting to them. Poor woman — if she wants to go off for a quiet drink, she has a long escort of gentlemen — if she wants to sneak off by herself for a while, one of them notices, hurries after her, hair out, and shakes branches at her until she meekly turns and follows him back to the group. There even seems to be some sort of competition for her, because all the less dominant males, including the adolescents, are in the most ghastly tempers, attacking smaller ones for no reason whatsoever.

Before I explain about this delightful new typewriter,* let me just tell you the last of Sophie and family. Her daughter, about 8, is called Sally, and she, at last, will fill in one of the big gaps in the knowledge (still not quite sure where dashes, etc, live on this typewriter!) — adolescent females. Then there is the little boy — the funniest little fellow imaginable — bold and cheeky too. His second day he came right up onto the veranda and even peeped into the tent

---

* A sudden change of typeface begins here, at the start of the letter's third page.

where we were all huddled. To remind us of Bobbie he is called Sniff!*

Yet another interruption — I have to go and try and eat I am told. So the story of the typewriter will have to wait yet a little longer. Now, back again. Well, Hugo had a cable to say he had to do all of the Kigoma shots again. You can imagine how gloomy we all were about this. There had been a piece of fluff stuck in the lens, or the camera, or something, so it all had to be done again. Anyway, he set off bright and early yesterday, with Hassan (who has to do the bargaining in the market) and Anyango who was to do the shopping while those two filmed, and Dominic. Dominic is another story which I will relate in a moment. He got all his filming done, had a nice day (for a Kigoma day that is) and came home laden with spoils of the trip. It was a nice home coming. He brought the most super watch for me, — a darling little one that doesn't need winding, and is water proof and shock proof. I simply love it. He also brought me a Parker fountain pen as mine has been lost for months, and anyway, didn't write any more. This is also automatic — you just dip it in the ink and it fills itself in a magical sort of way. It is blue and most elegant. He brought all sorts of other nice things that we wanted from Bimji, including a bottle of liqueur. And he asked for Cointreau. Bimje said that he found it impossible to get rid of a crate, and he couldn't buy in smaller quantities. "Oh, fine", says Hugo — and so he and Bimje are ordering a crate between them — 6 for us and 6 for Bimje***!!!! (How nice, I now know this machine has a *!) AND he brought this typewriter. It is a superb little machine — looks almost identical to the Diplomats that we have, is a Triumph — and we do so love this neat little type. It was cheap too, so far as typewriters go — and for once Bimje doesn't seem to have doubled the price.

Now, the Dominic story. Dominic got up yesterday — no, the day before — feeling fine. At 11 a.m. there was a whistle from the whistle tree. We went to see what was happening, thinking gloomily that perhaps we had visitors. It was Rashidi, to say that Dominic

---

* This refers to an obscure family joke concerning Hugo's sister-in-law.

was ill. He made expressive gestures with his hands, and said he'd been throwing water all over Dominic. Hugo had to go to the old camp anyway, for his battery, and to shoot some film on the boys. So he went at once to see what the matter was. Well, we still don't know the cause, but what happened was that Dominic, at 10, felt very sick. He went to the stream to get water, fainted, and fell headfirst into the water. By enormous good luck Rashidi just happened to be passing — else we should have had a corpse — he was out, and with his face in the water!! Since that he continued to feel sick, and blood was coming out from both ends, so to speak. So we thought he'd better go into hospital with Hugo — I mean in the boat when Hugo went! We still don't know the answer!

The messy ending of the previous page was due to the fact that our precious new machine went wrong! On its third page. Hugo wrestled with it valiantly, and finally, by courageously slicing bits off a plastic roller with a razor blade, got it to work. Else it would have been disastrous. So it is now some time since last I wrote, and in addition it is terribly late, as I have been writing pages and pages to an American judge* (most influential in wild life matters) all about our plans for the research station. This has hung heavily over me since our visit to Washington in February!!!

So I will not write much more now. Hassan is going in again tomorrow as we have some scientific visitors. We hope that they will be genuine and are not coming to steal all our hard-won facts. If they are nice they may do a great deal of good for us as they come from the same establishment as Konrad Lorenz.

Let me quickly tell you that we have found an ideal — THE ideal site for the future research building. It is some way up the valley, up a little slope, and there you are, right in the forest, above the level of the trees, and with the most magnificent view stretching right across the valley and over the distant mountain slopes. When I first went there I fell in love with it — I was contacting Hugo on the walkie talkie and told him I'd found the site! So he came in the evening, and we ecstacised over it together. We have all plans formulated now —

---

* Russell Train of the World Wildlife Fund.

the plans for the building, drawn by Hugo, the materials it must be made of, how it should be transported, where the people will eat, how the stuff will be carried up the valley (and at night so as not to disturb the chimps) — then Hugo and I return as the building reaches completion to see that nothing has been overlooked and to help get the chimps accustomed to their new haven. That first time I was there one of the lovely little hornbills, black and white with a red beak, came swooping down across the valley, calling his strange cry, and landed on a dead tree stump just a few yards from me. He sat there, shining in the sun and with the wind blowing his feathers gently, and peered at me, his head first on one side and then the other. Then he seemed to accept that I was all right and he pecked into the dead wood in search of insects. That seemed somehow to be an omen that all would be well with our plans.

We havn't told you yet about our bath. We go to the old camp so seldom nowadays, and we got sick of washing bits and pieces of ourselves each night in the old green plastic bowl. So we started going down to the stream. But we got a bit sick of trying to dry whilst perching and wobbling on sharp stones. And then, one night, we found a perfect bathing place. This was thanks to the pig. Do you all know about the pig? I just cannot remember. One of the scouts found a pig, freshly killed, floating in the lake. So it was carried straight here and we laid it out, hoping the chimps might eat it. The chimps didn't, but their reaction was interesting — nearly all of them were nervous, peered intently at the corpse, wouldn't go near it, but sniffed at leaves, twigs and the ground nearby. We feel sure that they suspected a leopard and were trying to detect traces of the killer. Anyway, how does this tie up with our nightly bath! Quite simple really. We dragged the carcass out into the open grass, hoping that perhaps a leopard might be attracted by the smell during the night. The following day we were all nearly sick all day long. The smell was absolutely ghastly. . . .

So we went upwind to look for a place for our baths. And came across the most charming little place, which might be made for a picture post card advertising the charm of some holiday resort. A tiny white beach from which you step down to the rushing little stream. A view to the opposite mountain. A little waterfall. So Hugo and I paddled about for ages, made a sort of dam, a lovely deep pool with white sand at the bottom, and the white white sand to stand and dry oneself on. It is particularly attractive in the moonlight.

Did Hugo tell you that he filmed a baboon eating the remains of a baby bushbuck. Poor little thing, we got the skin back afterwards — quite perfect, the legs all inside out, and the head, but no flesh left at all. Such a pretty skin. Then another baboon stole the skin away and rushed up the slope with it.

I think I must stop. It is after 11, and we still have to do the last banana work — hiding them in trees, and seeing that there are enough containers in all the big boxes so that we can nip them out really quickly and pop them under our shirts ready to smuggle to deserving chimps. Thank goodness, at long long last, the boxes Hugo ordered in Nairobi, before coming to England, have arrived. So, within the next week or so, we should have 13 chimp proof boxes — then we can stop this silly game of hiding bananas in all sorts of places where bananas shouldn't be hidden — such as under the ground sheet!

I will promise that one of us will write another letter very soon. . . .

Tons of love,
Jane and Hugo

Chimpland.
Early one morning
Approx. 21 August [1964]

Darling Families and Lyn,

This will be short, but I must write something now to tell you about the events of the past few days. I can't recollect whether or not I even mentioned, in earlier letters, the impending visit of two scientists from Konrad Lorenz's institution — viz. Dr. Eibl-Eibesfeldt and Hans Hass. The underwater Hans Hass himself. Well, we were dubious about their visit, wondering if Eibl. was the sort of person to steal facts (he is working on human greeting ceremonies which is why he wanted to come here) although we felt that, if to do with Lorenz, he couldn't be too nasty! We also wondered whether, in fact, they would ever get here when they found how far they had to come. (Sorry about the ends of all the lines.* More type-writer repair work for Hugo!). Well, they duly arrived. Rashidi blew his whistle from the whistle tree about 3 in the afternoon, when we had a whole large group here, including the new female Circe. So, we despatched Edna downstairs (old camp is always thus referred to!) to give our guests some tea, and inform them they were not allowed to arrive until Circe had departed. Duly they arrived. There were still some old hands here — David and Goliath and Charlie, so far as I remember. They were most impressed.

Well, the long and short of it was that they are both tremendously impressed with everything here — the work, the chimps, and the fu-ture plans. Eibl., which is almost better than anything, has com-pletely undertaken to send future Ph.D. students of his here to do certain specialized studies — and this is the sort of thing which will give life to the research station, give it standing, and keep it going. Even better, they were both enthusiastically plotting means of en-suring that Lorenz himself, together with Tinbergen, should some-how get here in the autumn.† The trouble is that Lorenz is doing his trip with Tinbergen who has difficulty in getting sufficient time off from Oxford. However, it will be really wonderful if they do man-age to get here. It will do us such a lot of good. They have promised to spread the news abroad — that the chimpanzee research station at the Gombe Stream reserve is a "must". In addition, which is very nice news indeed, he is assistant editor to one of the best journals on animal behaviour — German, but publishing in all the main Euro-pean languages. And he has undertaken to publish any papers I may write (with lots of photographs) within 6 months. That is really wonderful. He has told us all about the most wonderful behaviour film library. You edit single "units" (i.e. feeding; tool using; locomo-

---

* The characters were jamming together at the right margins.
† Nikolaas Tinbergen was, with Konrad Lorenz and Karl von Frisch, a founder of ethology, the scientific study of animal behavior. These three great pioneers shared a Nobel Prize in 1973. Although Lorenz became a friend of Jane's and an admirer of her work, neither he nor Tinbergen ever made it to Gombe.

tion; etc). They have a negative of this, give you a print, and have a print in their library for scientific use. They sell prints to universities, etc, who are interested, and loan them for lectures on comparative behaviour etc. With the film goes a paper, which is not only circulated with the film, but which serves as a publication, and appears — I think in the same periodical as Eibl helps to edit. But one of the good ones. Best of all, this place PAYS the costs of preparing the internegative, which is quite costly. So there is one way of saving the chimp material for ever, and for it to be put to the right purposes.

In addition to all this Hans Hass has promised to give Hugo millions of contacts in all the right television places. He strengthened our opinion that, even if the Geographic do sell their T.V. film to the European market, this will not in the least interfere with the sort of film we want to make. They are both sending us copies of their new books — they showed us these. Hans Hass's has the most superb underwater pictures. And Eibl's is about the Galapagos Islands, and also has beautiful pictures. He was funny though. There is an English edition, but he said he wouldn't send us that one because he thinks the quality is inferior!! So we have to have it in German!

We took them up the valley to show them the proposed site — most enthusiastic. What amused us about both of them was that they never listened to anything we said. It was really funny sometimes. They asked us, right at the start, what animals constituted a danger to the chimps. We explained carefully that, so far as we could see, no animals did. We explained why we felt that leopards were not dangerous predators apparently — because chimps walk around in the forest without really being alert at all, and would often bump into me, when I was quite visible, and only see me when they got to about 10 yards away, or less. Well, the following day Hugo came to me in amazement to say that Eibl. had asked him all about which animals predated on the chimps here. And my amazement (sorry, had to take the paper out as the wind had blown it into queer shapes) anyway, my amazement was even greater than his, on hearing that, because Hans Hass had just asked me the same thing!!!

I think there were two things that really impressed them. One was the fact that the chimps, after eating their bananas, don't immediately rush off back to the forests, or even into the dense bushes, but sit around and do nice things — such as "social preen". It sounded so sweet, instead of social groom, and I kept thinking of David and Goliath as two strange large very black and ungainly birds! Then Eibl. went up to Figan and held his hand out, as we do, and Figan responded by patting on it in play. Not very enthusiastically, true, but a response. Eibl was delighted. Then, this being evening of their second and last day, Hugo took Eibl up the valley to take some pictures of the proposed site. And Hans Hass stayed here with David. Now David has developed a new habit. When he wants more bananas, he knows that it is quite useless to pull on boxes. He knows it's a waste of his energy. (Which, having so little of, he needs desperately to conserve in order to impress his lady of the hour.) So he comes up to whoever is nearest to the nearest full box and, very gently, pushes with the backs of his knuckles. Well, on this particular day he had tried pushing me, had pushed me all round the veranda, but I had not responded. He sat for some time, looking determined. He then approached Hass, in his deliberate way, and proceeded to push him, gently, twice. Hass was quite overcome with amazement and delight. He now feels "part of it all". It was a most thoughtful gesture on David's part, bearing in mind how useful such people may well be to his descendents.

We had a very successful evening, for their last. We so seldom go down to the old camp, and when we do some of the fishermen are quick to come for medicine. The little boy, Petro, who always wants to play Edna's guitar, had asked, the night before, if Edna would bring it down so that he could play. Which she did. Eibl and Hass both wanted to purchase an African instrument each — those small wooden ones with the metal strips that you flick with your fingers. So two of those had arrived to be sold. And, best of all, the African who is so very, very good at playing the guitar also came. So, whilst we sat around a splendid camp fire, this African played, accompanied by the two small wooden instruments (lent back to their original owners) and Hans Hass was able to get out his tape recorder and tape some of the music. They both really enjoyed the evening. So, all in all, a most successful visit.

Since they left we have seen hardly any chimps. The big group has vanished, and are nowhere to be found. I went up to the Peak the day before yesterday, but only saw Flo and Olly on their way from camp! Today we have despatched Edna off to Mitumba valley, at the end of the reserve, so as to give her some practise in observing by herself, and because the valley is full of figs. I can hardly bear to do this — memories of the valley are so vivid, and these days it is all work work work with little time to roam through my mountains. I wouldn't wish it otherwise though. Being able to observe the sort of behaviour that we see these days, and beginning to understand so much about the social pattern, is worth everything.

Sophie was most disappointing. I met her up the opposite mountain two days after her brief visits to camp. Since then she has not been seen. I have a horrible feeling she may not visit us any more. Which will be so sad.

Apart from various sundry things, of little interest — such as the fact that the terrible Dominic is now out of the hospital three days and <u>still</u> not back (we plan to reduce his salary to what it was last year), that Hassan is continually complaining about his back and we don't know what to do, and that Anyango is so often in a bad mood and grumpy in the evening — probably because he has to do all Dominic's work as well. These are not interesting, and apart from them there is no more news. We have had our tent, our poor chimp invaded tent, thoroughly spring-cleaned. Luckily our dear little toad was "out" at the time when Anyango flung dettol and soap and water all over the floor! We hardly know it now. The chimps so seldom go in now, that we thought it was safe to give it a real good clean. And so, the very first day, Hugo's namesake, having been busy with females over the hills and far away for nearly a week, returned, and for old time's sake, and to christen the unpleasant smelling clean tent, sat on the floor, grunted happily, — and did a wee!!! (Excuse the sentence rather running away with me). It is suddenly excessively hot here. The bare trees with their huge red flowers are in full bloom. We couldn't have chosen a more lovely camp site. Our "field" has six of these trees, and half are now a blaze of red against the green palm trees and the yellow grass of the opposite mountain. The chimps, luckily, don't fancy these blooms, but the baboons simply love them. Our cheeky Stephanie, who still persists in visiting us despite being shone at with mirrors, narrowly missed by Hugo's stones, and chased up the slope by me, is always being caught with a prize blossom disappearing into her mouth. She is a funny baboon. We are thinking of starting Edna off on these baboons later on in the year — if I can get another secretary.

I will now end the letter. Still two days before Hassan goes in to collect Malcolm MacDonald. I wonder if he really will make it this time. Anyway, if anything startling happens I will continue later.

Lots of love from us both.

"Chimpland"
8 September, 1964

My dear FFF,

We have had your last letters, the long ones, about the buildings here, and the films, etc. First, thank you a million times for all your hard work and thought re. the buildings. We have a long letter to you which should go off by the next post — we are waiting to find out the prices of the various materials.

First, though, and urgently, and this, please, keep as a secret from Ma because it has to be a surprise for her when she arrives here, Melissa has had her baby. Yesterday! It is the most adorable little thing, sex not yet known, but Jane if it is a girl. I was able to see her [the infant] when she [Melissa] first met up with some of the chimps today — they stared and stared, and their behaviour towards her has changed considerably. She really hit out and grabbed the hand of one childless female who tried to touch it. She is not scared of us at all. Didn't see the birth — we have been expecting it so long, and it came as such a surprise.

However, the point is this. If I stay on here until March, as you suggested — well, until April I suppose, do you think a) the Geographic would agree to Hugo staying on to cover the baby, and b), and more important, will you mind if, in the end, and if the Geographic agree for Hugo to stay here, if he doesn't film any of your next lecture film? We must know about this first, before asking the Geographic, or making any other arrangements at all. The value would be firstly that we could cover Flint's development until he is one year old, and second, cover the new baby over the time when it has got to the stage at which Flint is now — just seeking social contact with individuals other than the mother. It might be most fascinating because Flint is a fourth child, and the new one is a first (or anyway, a first to survive).

If we did this we could still come out here to see the final stages of the building in the summer. Hugo's long letter to you explains everything about the building, and about its supervision, etc, so don't get confused by my saying we will see to the last stages. All will be explained.

Must tell you a fascinating thing. These chimps, anyway sometimes, don't break off, bite off, or eat, the placenta. Melissa had hers dangling for probably two days. It was off this afternoon. Flo, apparently, was seen by Dominic to drape the cord around Flint's neck so as to get it out of the way!

One final point. We have got a baboon person. Edna is now really keen, and she is shaping well. We are giving her a trial period on the baboons and, when this is written up, and with some film on them, we feel absolutely convinced that money will be forthcoming. Particularly as there is a most exciting development at the moment — one adult male — a really big dominant one, is going around with a stage 1 baby (black coat) on his back all the time. It is fascinating, and we are desperately trying to get a few facts and pictures of it — via Edna, as I have no moment to spare just now!

Forgive me ending now, but it's terribly late, and supper is getting cold. PLEASE don't tell Ma about the baby being here — you can, of course, mention we want to stay till March.

Much love,
F.C.
Jane

"Chimpland"
24 September 1964

Dear Dr. Payne,

Many thanks for your last letter and for relieving my mind about the article and next season's lecture. With reference to the Franklin

Burr prize money, I much fear that the letter I wrote to you about it must have been one of the many that went astray in the floods. At that time I asked if you could put that money together with the rest of the money which the Society is keeping for me. Hugo and I have now discussed the matter fully and have come to the conclusion that it would be best if you could send the money, in Hugo's name, to his account in Switzerland. We shall then transfer it to an account of my own there, once the formalities have been completed.

We are still continuing to get exciting results here with the chimps. As you so rightly said in your letter, there seems no end to the surprises the chimps have in store for us. Once more this letter will take the form of an interim report.

To start with, as you may already have heard, Melissa has come up to expectations and we have a new member of the chimpanzee community. We did not actually see the birth, but saw the infant when it was certainly not more than 48 hours of age, and probably only one day old. The mother seemed completely dazed as though she couldn't understand at all what had happened. She walked only a few yards at a time, supporting the infant carefully with one hand and also with her thighs — she walked all the time with very bent legs. The entire placenta was dangling from the umbilical cord — on one occasion this became entangled in the vegetation and Melissa had to stop and unwind it. I was able to watch her making her nest that night — it was made very quickly, with one hand only and with none of the customary crude interweaving of branches. She was originally seen in the company of a mature male, but she left him and made the nest completely on her own.

The following morning I was able to see what were almost certainly the first reactions of some of the other chimps to the baby. The 4 year old Fifi was particularly interested, and kept approaching closely, peering, and sniffing at the placenta. This last worried Melissa who quickly gathered the cord up. (And it was interesting to find out, from Dominic, that when Flo first appeared with her infant the placenta was likewise dangling, but Flo, old and experienced in child-birth, carefully wrapped the cord around Flint's neck!) David was also interested in the baby, went very close, and peered and peered. As did Flo. Another childless female, Circe, tried to touch the baby, at which Melissa immediately grabbed her hand, and rushed to Goliath for reassurance. Her first encounter with Flo's eldest son, Faben, we are lucky enough to have on film. Faben was tremendously curious and his continual peering worried Melissa who kept reaching out her hand to him, presenting and generally trying to appease him yet keep her distance.

Luckily for us Melissa did not at all mind our close scrutiny of her offspring for the first few days — in fact she was far less wary of us than of the other chimps. So we were able to observe and photograph the infant closely. Despite this we have been unable to discover its sex — it is provisionally named "Jane"! She is the ugliest little creature you can imagine and, from Dominic's and Kristopher's descriptions, completely different from Flint when he was a baby. Flint, apparently, had a very pale and pretty face, and was very sparsely covered in hair on his head and back, and more or less naked below. This infant has a strangely marked face, dark around her eyes except for pale eyebrow streaks, and pale around her mouth. In addition she has thick hair on her head, back, and outsides of legs and arms. We have not been able to see the underside yet.

Unfortunately Melissa is now going through a spell (which I hope will be of short duration) when she is a bit shy of our too close observation and is uneasy if I follow her. She likes to keep very close to one of the dominant males, but finds it difficult to keep up with them as she is continually pausing to sit for half a minute or so and so usually gets left behind and ends up alone.

With regard to our other small infant, Flint is now beginning to walk with more determination and more success. He is still extremely unstable and collapses after every four steps or so unless he manages to keep on his feet by going so fast he simply has not time to fall over! He now regularly rides on Flo's back, or else dangles from her side reaching back at vegetation with his free hand in a most annoying way (for Flo that is). He actively seeks social interaction with all other chimps, who, for the most part, ignore him (mainly because of fear of Flo I suspect). Figan now occasionally carries him ventrally for a few steps, as does Gilka (now 2 1/2 years old). Fifi, on the contrary, although she is continually playing with him, almost to the exclusion of all other chimps, carries him around seldom — mainly, I think, because she finds him a bit much to cope with now he has such a mind of his own. She still picks him up and cuddles him when he is asleep.

Flint went through a short period when he would whimper whenever a chimp, who had been sitting or standing near him, walked away. With his little lips pushed forward he cried pathetically as he staggered and slithered after the retreating individual — it was as though he wanted to be the center of all attention. The younger chimps all responded to his crying by returning to him.

He is getting very expert in climbing, which he does much more skillfully than walking. He is also beginning to respond to Flo's "moving away signals", and to cling or clamber onto her when she reaches out to him or pauses with bent knees near the twig he is climbing on.

It is proving extremely interesting to compare the behaviour of a male infant, Merlin, with that of the female Gilka. Merlin really is "little boy" through and through. His playing, whether alone or with others, is far more "rough and tumble" than Gilka's ever was (he is about a year younger). He literally "flings" himself into games, onto other chimps, and, in fact, into everything he does, including begging food from his mother. In this latter he is invariably successful which is a measure of his persistence since Marina is extremely fond and possessive of her food!

Gilka herself is going through a most difficult period. Until the birth of Flint she was very frequently seen playing with Fifi, but now Fifi has time for no one but Flint. As Olly seldom goes around with mothers other than Flo, this leaves Gilka more and more to her own devices. Her brother, Evered, is not, at present, moving about very often with Olly and Gilka so she is also deprived of his companionship. In addition to all this, Olly is apparently trying to wean the child. I have never before observed any weaning behaviour in wild chimpanzees, and it may be that this is an exceptional case. Certainly no weaning behaviour was observed between Flo and Fifi, and Fifi was about a year older than Gilka when Flo's milk finally dried up. This weaning has a very marked effect on Gilka. When the breast is denied to her she whimpers, and she usually approaches Olly, when she wants to suckle, stands in front of her, and whimpers. If Olly does not want her to suckle she stands up and either gently bites her wrist, or "play bites" and nuzzles at the child until she stops whimpering to laugh. If the whimpering continues (and this I saw for the first time two days ago) Olly takes Gilka ventrally, carries her a few steps, sets her down, and again tickles her until she laughs. Several times that worked, but twice Gilka continued to cry. This seemed to affect Olly considerably — she returned to the child, gathered her up in an embrace and sat holding her on her lap. Then, when Gilka tried to suckle and the breast was again denied, Gilka moved away crying. But she had only gone a few steps when Olly reached out, drew Gilka back by one arm, embraced her, and allowed her to suckle very briefly. I am hoping to get more details on this fascinating behaviour within the next few days.

Three times, in the last month, we have seen Gilka playing, just as she might with a chimpanzee agemate, with a young baboon (almost certainly the same individual). It is fascinating to speculate as to whether this "friendship" has perhaps arisen from the difficult social situation described above. Young baboons and young chimps often play together, but this play is normally rather one-sided as the baboons when small are usually rather afraid of the young chimps. But Gilka and "Goblin"* play extremely gently, and on one occasion we saw most exciting interactions between the two. Firstly the baboon presented to Gilka, tail up, and she carefully inspected his little bottom. She then presented to him and he actually mounted her and gave a few thrusts, as small baboons will do in play. Next he went round and they nuzzled each other in the neck, play biting, and he then embraced her from behind and tickled her in the ribs, she throwing back her head and laughing. She tickled him in a similar way. The last time I saw the two playing was when Olly and Gilka were up the valley. Gilka left her mother feeding when she

---

* The young baboon had tentatively been named Goblin; when Melissa's infant, Jane, was discovered to be male, he was renamed Goblin. Presumably the young baboon was then rechristened.

saw the baboons approaching, crossing the valley, ran up to the small baboon that I am sure was "Goblin" and the two played gently together until the baboons had passed and Goblin scampered off after them. I hope that we shall soon be able to make a positive identification of the baboon. If, in fact, it is the same individual, this will represent a most amazing "friendship" between young wild animals of different species.

In addition to the facts relating to infant behaviour above, we have been able to make several more observations of infants pushing away males mating with females in oestrus. And this includes pushing away males from females other than the infants' mothers.

In this latter respect the little male infant, Merlin, was particularly amusing. He found the large pink bottom of Circe tremendously fascinating, and was continually running up to embrace it, and even tried to mount her by half climbing up her legs! And when one of the big males approached, Merlin appeared like magic to rush up and push the bounder off "his girl".

Before leaving the subject of infants completely, I should add that one more female, Mandy, seems to be pregnant, but we do not expect the event until next April or May.

Just recently we have seen three superb examples of masculine tyranny over females. The first two were perfectly understandable as the females were in oestrus, but it was interesting to observe how the two males concerned just <u>forced</u> the females to follow wherever they went. By shaking branches at them or hitting at the grass and then, if the females still refused to follow, or if they tried to escape, charging at them flat out and beating them up. The third example occurred when J.B. arrived closely followed by an old female with an infant on her back. This female was in oestrus some two months ago, but when seen with J.B. had not the very slightest suggestion of a swelling. Yet J.B.'s behaviour was exactly as though she was at the height of her sexual attraction. The measure of her fear of him was well illustrated, since she is not "tame" having only visited the camp once before — when she was in oestrus and accompanied by a large number of males. Yet, although very nervous of approaching the camp he went on "branching" and charging at her until she finally followed him right up to the tent. To give him his due, he did share a very large bucket of bananas with her! And when she finally and whimperingly refused to come right onto the veranda (with us all huddled inside the tent with the flaps down) and despite the fact that he had already attacked her and pounded on her because of her unwillingness, he finally gave in and led her and her infant away.

The dung swirling technique continues to give excellent results — the latest find was the remains of bees and wax. During the first year of my study I came upon a group of chimps in thick undergrowth which I felt sure was raiding a bees' nest. I was unable to examine the place closely afterwards because of the bees swarming angrily around, and the chimps were not tame enough then for me to approach closely enough to see. In addition there are reports of chimpanzees eating honey in other areas. We now have nice proof that they do, in fact, raid nests, but the method is still unknown. Bees' nests are far from common in the Reserve.

Also, in connection with feeding behaviour, I have twice more observed meat eating. Once was almost certainly a baby bushpig. The previous day when I was following a group, they plunged into almost impenetrable undergrowth from which, after a few moments, emerged the most ghastly sounds of tumult. I was quite unable to find out for sure, but guessed that they had either stumbled across a bad tempered pig, which was "roaring" and charging heavily through the undergrowth, causing chimps to scream and race up trees. (And I did see several males displaying up in the trees and then leaping back into the undergrowth.) Or, and I thought more likely, they had been trying to catch a baby pig. Then, the following day, I heard similar sounds, but of short duration. Again I was unable to see what was going on, but some time later I found a group gathered around a male who was eating some sort of small animal (and a baby pig is very tiny).

On the other occasion the prey was a young bushbuck. It is interesting, in this connection, that Hugo was able to film a male baboon, closely attended by another, feeding on a young bushbuck. They had almost certainly caught the animal. It may well be the first time that baboons have been filmed actually eating meat (unless Professor Washburn shows this in his film which I cannot remember).

Also in relation to the hunting techniques of the chimps, we have come to the conclusion that monkeys are mainly caught during the breeding season. This might well tend to make them an easier prey. This theory is strengthened by the fact that remains of a very tiny baby (either just born, or, more probably, unborn) redtail monkey were found, together with bones and skin of the mother, in one day's dung swirling. It is possible that the mother, just before birth, may be slightly separated from the main troop. Certainly the one kill I have observed occurred when the colobus actually caught was one of a group of four. Last week a group of chimpanzees approached a large resting group of red colobus. Not only did the colobus seem unconcerned at the approach of the chimps, but several males could be observed leaping from their branches and bounding down towards the chimps. What followed took place out of sight, but produced loud screams from young chimps. And then, shortly after a prolonged outburst of angry and frightened chimp sounds, an old male chimp, Mr. McGregor (our greatest meat eater) was observed literally running down the mountain with a mature male red colobus in hot pursuit! I have seen young chimps running from colobus before, but should never have believed that a mature chimpanzee would do the same!

We had an excellent opportunity to test the reaction of the chimps to a freshly killed bushpig. The Game Scout found a young pig, which seemed to have been speared, floating in the lake early one morning. It had obviously only just died as the blood was still running from its wounds. We accordingly laid it out and awaited the chimps' arrival.

We had, of course, hoped (though not expected) that they might eat the meat, since it was so fresh. Instead a most unexpected and interesting reaction was obtained, and from nearly all the chimpanzees. They were afraid of the carcass. They were interested in it. They gave small worried sounds, and climbed trees at varying distances (according to each one's degree of boldness), and they then proceeded to <u>smell</u> at everything all around, without actually approaching the carcass. They sniffed at leaves, twigs, trunks and branches of nearby trees. And not only once or twice, but many times and in many places.

The only conclusion we could come to as to the meaning of this strange behaviour was that they suspected that the pig might represent the kill of a leopard and were smelling everywhere for leopard smell. Even if this was not the case, they were certainly trying to get some sort of clue as to how the pig got there or who put it there. Olly and her family, together with two other males, actually saw us handling the carcass, and they did not go around smelling for clues. But apart from those, all chimps sniffed around with the exception of one.

The above facts are among the most interesting observed since I last wrote to you. Many others, of course, have been seen and re-corded — in particular we are now getting a much fuller picture of female behaviour. For instance, I have now seen two other females, besides Flo, perform masculine type displays, charging and drag-ging on vegetation. And as for Flo — about three weeks before Me-lissa's baby was born, and for no apparent reason, Flo went under a tree into which Melissa had just climbed, Fifi took Flint, and Flo had all her hair out. Melissa climbed a little way down the tree, un-der which Fifi and the baby were sitting. All at once Flo moved closer. Melissa whimpered and held her hand towards Flo. No re-sponse, and so Melissa climbed higher. Then Flo all at once shot up the tree, shaking the branches, and Melissa leapt out into a next door tree, down to the ground and away. And Flo was after her, flat out, for about 100 yards. Then she stopped. And just sat, her lip drooping and all her hair out, and a rather mad glaze to her eyes. After about half a minute she seemed to recollect her poor baby, and returned to where Fifi had taken refuge up a tree. Poor little Flint looked quite dazed, and pushed his lips forward in a little whimper and reached out to his mother. Her hair gradually lay flat again as she climbed up and took him back. The reason for this was never known — the next day they were as they always had been.

I think that covers the main points of interest. But I should add that the boxes from Nairobi have arrived, and we have also fixed up additional cement ones. All work superbly, and we have no problems at all now with our feeding. Everything goes smoothly, and we havn't had one crisis since all were ready. We have one or two boxes more to come, and these should cope with our ever increasing number of visitors.

Dr. Leakey wrote to us to ask whether he should himself put forward a grant request for observations to be continued here during 1965. We decided it would be as well if he continued to do this, and sent him a draft estimate for Edna with the assistance of Sonia Ivey (see attached sheet) to carry on next year. I am sure that you appreciate the urgency of maintaining sustained and uninterrupted observations on the chimps here. We have been very lucky in finding Edna to assist in the work here and I am quite sure that, if the Society continues to sponsor the research here, she will do a very good job in continuing the observations on our behalf during 1965.

I think this letter is long enough now, and so will close.

With kindest regards to you and your wife.

Yours sincerely,
Jane

"Chimpland".
26 October, 1964

Dear Dr. Payne,

I am sorry that we seem to be burying you in an avalanche of letters all at once. This one concerns the possibility of my remaining here for the first three months of 1965.

The main reason for this is to enable us to make a fuller comparative study of our two infants, Flo's and Melissa's. The latter has be rechristened, by the way. I tentatively guessed it was a girl after a good look from the rear. However, a close up view from the front left no room for further doubt. "Goblin" is a little boy! In actual fact this, in itself, makes the comparison between the two infants even more interesting. To what extent, for instance, is Flint's social development influenced by the constant attention he received from sibling Fifi? Flint started to become really interesting when he was three months old as, from that time, his social contacts began to extend beyond those with his immediate family. It will be most important to follow Goblin's progress during these same months.

In other ways it is already interesting to compare the two babies. When we first saw Flint he was six weeks old, and even then Flo was continually having to support him as he had great trouble in gripping with his feet. Goblin, however, was able to cling on unsupported for quite long periods even during the first week of his life. In addition, he is far more active and seems to take more interest in his surroundings than did Flint at a similar age.

As you know, I have to keep two further terms' residence at Cambridge next year. I now feel that, from all points of view, it would be most profitable if I remained here until April and then worked flat out on my analysis for the rest of the year, with as few interruptions as possible.

We do hope that the Research Committee will approve of this plan which has been included in Dr. Leakey's grant request for this research for next year. You may have already received this. I should like to stress, at this point, how much Hugo and I appreciate the Society's generous support so far. The facts which are coming to light as a result of this support are, as you remark yourself, truly amazing.

Please give our best regards to Mrs. Payne.

Yours sincerely,

Jane

P.S. I quite forgot to thank you for your last letter with its entertaining enclosure. It was so kind of you to make such appreciative comments about my reports — which I always feel are far too brief.

Chimpland.
6 November [1964].

My dear FFF,

What super news about the grant, uniports, and everything going through so quickly and without question. I felt it would all be O.K. Many thanks for your help over it.

First — the question of what to do with the money. The amount for the Uniports . . . should certainly go to the fund which you operate so that you can pay all the expenses for them. For which, again, thank you a thousand times.

We suggest that, for the present, you keep the second sum in Nairobi but without, as yet, making any definite arrangements for it. We don't need any money here just at present, and Hugo is going to work it all out and then let you know. I feel so lucky having him to cope with all the horrid financial side of things — which I simply loathe as you may remember.

Things here are splendid — as usual. Mandy has had her baby — the most gorgeous little girl — which is splendid after the two little boys. I should be able to get really first class comparative material now. The social development of the fourth infant of one female (Flint) as compared with that of two first infants of young mothers, one male, one female. Both the latter, Goblin and Jane, are doing fine. We are rather worried about Flint — it seems he may either have something wrong with one leg or, less likely, something wrong with his sense of balance. He has been on his feet now for over 4 months, and he still wobbles and collapses all the time. Apart from that he is quite enchanting.

It would be nice if Tinbergen could come here — I rather feel he won't be able to. But I daresay we shall know by the time you get this. It was Lorenz we really wanted to see here.

Must stop — it is dark and the Africans are using the light to put in some pipes — dear J.B. found out how to break the wire of the boxes* and no Hassan to splice them for us! Hope he is O.K. Do let us know what was wrong with the poor man.

With love from us both, and many, many thanks.

Love
F.C.
Jane

---

* The latches on the steel banana boxes were controlled by wires running through buried pipes.

"Chimpland"
14 December 1964

My dear FFF,

Thank you so much for your last letter — it was so nice to have. It is such a wonderful idea of yours but, as you probably know by now, Hugo has not been granted permission to go to England with me next year — they want him to get on with the animal stills, etc. It is so sad, but do let's hope that at least they agree to one of the plans Hugo has told you about. I'm sure they must.

I wish I could see the genets — they must be lovely little things — Hugo had one that he adored, as you may remember. But we have an adorable pet too — a little mouse bird brought in when it was so tiny I never thought it could live. But it did, mainly thanks to Edna who spent a lot of time on it. I never would have thought that a tiny bird could have so much character. Did you know that mouse birds held their food with one foot when eating a large object, just like a parrot? . . .

Our new baby, Jane (species <u>Pan!</u>) is adorable. So we now have — Hugo, Leakey, Miff (Mummy's nickname in case you didn't know), Olly, Jane, and Rix (Eric's nickname)! Quite a good collection. No Jiff as yet — though we do have a Sniff. And, of course, there is a Sally. Oh yes, and a brand new mother, completely tame from the day she arrived, who is "Bessie". I'm sure Danny was jealous not to have a chimp called after her. And you know there's a MacD?

Anyway, I was going to say that Mandy is such a good mother as compared to Melissa. But I may have already told you that? Mandy is so concerned for the well being of her infant that, when eating and therefore having two hands in use (or, rather, if she is eating and happens to need both hands for the job!) she holds Jane pressed closely to her by means of her foot — which she may hold in the most uncomfortable looking position for ages. Melissa never goes out of her way to make things easy for the baby.

It will be fascinating to see whether Mandy's solicitude has the effect of retarding the baby's development, or the opposite. Certainly Goblin, who at first seemed much more lively than Flint, is apparently less advanced than Flint — and I am sure that this is because Goblin has no brother or sister to help him onto his feet.

I do hope there will be good news of Hassan. We are getting rid of the new boat boy at the end of the month, and Hugo's Anyango is going to take over the boat. Hassan did actually admit, on the day he left, that perhaps, after all, his stand in was not such a good bet.!

We are much wondering whether Payne and co. will venture this far. I do hope so. Perhaps, by then, all will be well.

I must stop now. Hugo and I both wish you a very happy Christmas, and please wish Mary and the rest of your family a happy Christmas from us too.

With love,
FC.
Jane

[December 31, 1964]

Darling Family,

Well, we are nearly at the end of the last day of 1964. What an impossible thought. What a day it has been too. Dear darling David displaying through the tent, using me as a pole first to swing round and then to drum on! His finger is hurting him a lot poor thing. Goliath back. He returned on Boxing Day which was so nice of him. Also on boxing day came dear Sophie and Sniff. Sniff now so tame that we can walk around and towards him and he doesn't bat an eyelid. And, talking of eyelids, Mum — you know Leakey's wart — we always called it a wart, on his left eye, lower lid, where the lid was torn? Well, I was gazing at his eye, and suddenly discovered that instead of being a wart sprouting black hairs, it is the skin that was torn from the lid, and the black bristle of hairs — I mean the bristle of black hairs is none other than — the eyelashes! There are no more on that lid — something must have torn it and pulled the skin to one side, and there it all healed up. The tent really stinks, as Mike and J.B. both weed into it.

Enough of chimps. How are all of you. Happy New Year. How did the tape go — we are dying to hear. No letter yet from you

Mum, though I guess one will be in the post. Bimje's niece and nephew, together with 2 friends, and Senter, came to visit us yesterday. NO MAIL!!!!!! How can they be so sordid.

Special thank you to you Danny for the calendar. How nice. It is hanging in the sitting room with the other cards. They are all absolutely super, the cards. I adore the tiger. Hugo's card from you, Olly, is an absolute hoot!

There is quite a lot to say, and I don't quite know where to begin. With "John" perhaps. Well, we sent Sonia off to meet him. That evening she did not return. We were peeved because, not knowing when they would return we had to put off our Staff party until Christmas Day. John and Sonia were scheduled to arrive on the 23rd, the party should have been on the 24th. However. On the 24th, during the afternoon, they arrived. What had happened was that poor John had omitted to report to the immigration in Kigoma. He had been told at the border that there was no more he need do. They nearly didn't let him come here. So their 23rd was spent in John taking a policeman to show him where he had slept, in the car, for the night (luckily he remembered there was orange peel there!) and Sonia weeping in the police station. Finally word came through from Dar that he could proceed, and so they arrived, with all the Christmas list we had ordered.

Hugo and I spent most of Christmas Day wrapping up presents and blowing up balloons and typing sweets into little coloured paper bags. — I mean, tying! John and Hugo went down to the beach in the morning for John to look at the engine. . . . John mended the engine, as he knew at once what was wrong with it. Being a very engine minded young man. They selected a shrub for Rashidi to put in a debe.* And that was our Christmas tree. A rather sadly drooping one by the evening when Hugo and I went down to decorate it. We had about 30 balloons, all of which we tied in a lovely bunch from a guy rope. The tree was just in the veranda there, in case of rain. And, by the way, it rained, non stop, all day until 4.30. Very worrying. We gave the presents to our boys — they were very delighted —

---

* A large tin.

thanks for thinking of the blankets Mum — and they loved the shirts. The little girls (and there were 3 so we had had to get one more of everything!) adored their tops and carried away the cases without unwrapping them. So we still don't know if they liked them! But obviously they did. They were all three very much little madams. We had bought a knife in Nairobi for a present for someone, and never given it, so we gave that to Petro. He was quite overcome. We then finished off the tree. We even had silver balls for it — real ones from Bimje!

Then Hugo and I came back here for a quick sip of wine to start off the evening, and wait until the work up here was finished. Then down we went. Mbrisho was already there.* The two scouts came with their wives. Our own boys. (Hamisi excepted as he was getting married!) And two of the hired boys who are carrying kerais† of sand and stones for the cement bases for the uniports. Of those more anon. Then, altogether, there were 8 little children, and Petro. It got off rather badly, as partys so often do — no decent music on the wireless. Rashidi and co an extra long time doing bananas. Everyone sitting round. We amused them with balloons — they loved making the air come out so that it squeaked. And then, as it got later and later, we began stripping the tree. First they each got a water pistol — the children. Then everyone got one of the little sweet packets. And then the ceremonious meal. Hugo and I were on the ground. Sonia and John on chairs, together with the scouts, Mbrisho — yes, the scouts and Mbrisho. Hugo and I were using our hands — like you and I did Jiff. So we were brought water to dip our hands into before the fray. The food arrived on enormous sort of tray like dishes, and there was a great to do sorting it out — the women in one circle, children in a group where they had to wait until their elders had finished — Sonia and John ceremoniously served onto their plates. Then the dishes brought down

---

* Petro was a regular visitor to the research station from a neighboring village. Mbrisho was a distinguished older man, formerly a fisherman, living in the village of Bubango outside the eastern boundary of the reserve. He was a long-time friend and a regular visitor.
† Baskets.

for Hugo and I — I assure you we came off better than they did! Nice music started, and Chiko's cooking was simply super. A really first class super duper chicken curry. After it came the cutting of Dominic's nice but rather blackened looking cake. First he made a little speech thanking us for the food.

Then we stripped the tree. A biro each for the scouts, D and A. For each of the adults apart from the scouts, who got 10/- each, a packet of tea and a tin of corned beef. More sweets. Smarties for all the children. Lollipops. And then the toy trumpet things. Sonia got more from Bimje, but instead of 8 he only had 7 — I mean however many more it needed to get to 7 over what you got, Mum. So we handed them round. I gave the last one to Petro and suddenly noticed that there was the most darling little boy, who was standing all the time by Richard (his father) and was about 2 probably — perhaps three. He was gazing wide eyed at everything. And no blower left for him. All the others blew theirs. His eyes got wider. They never grouse, these African children. If it had been European children of that age they would all have been shouting, and some crying, because many of them didn't get one toy or another. There weren't enough to go round. But after a while Hugo and I couldn't bear this dear little boy any longer. So Hugo took Petro's trumpet — he had his knife, and anyway, he plays real life instruments. And it made that little boy's day. For the rest of the evening he chirped like a tree frog, on and on and on. He had a super time.

And so the evening drew to its close just as things were warming up. We toasted you all at only 2 mins after the right time. Mbrisho made a long speech about the usual things. The balloons were distributed and, mostly, popped. And amidst laughing, music, and the peep poop peep of the trumpets, punctuated by the popping of balloons, we left them. And returned to coffee, quantro and, as Hugo suggested, more toasts to our families!

So that was Christmas Day. Apart from the party, it was not unlike the tape, so far as chimps went. They came and went and hung around. We were awaked, and how, by Mike. He and J.B. slept with us on Christmas Eve. Gregor got his Christmas egg. So did Flo and so did Fifi.

Since then I have been working hard on the article — which, I am happy to relate, is three quarters done, first draft that is. But it is coming on. Otherwise I would have written more. . . . There only remains to tell you about the new site. We found the perfect place — near where we went that night, Mum. Just the right distance up. They have now piled, on the ridge, sufficient stones and sad. — sand. And this is the 4th and last night of the leveling of the site for the large uniport. That is the main work. We have employed 4 people, and so, with Rashidi, Ramadthani and those we have 6 people at work. Sadiki and Hamisi do the bs. This is the first evening I have not been up to the site. Hugo is up there now. . . . I must close. I must find the bird — Dodo, and put him to bed as it is dark. I will close in pen.

It is very late. Hugo is smoking a cigar that is twice as big as he is — one of the Winston type! Must end. Happy New Year to you all.

Love, Wisp

With love — Cigar Burr, Hugo

10

◦❧ ◦❧ ◦❧

COMING OF AGE
1965–1966

When I first set foot on the sandy beach of the Gombe Stream
Chimpanzee Reserve I never imagined that I was taking the first
step toward the establishment of the Gombe Stream Research
Centre: that, nine years later, there would be ten or more students
not only studying different aspects of chimpanzee behavior but
also observing baboons and red colobus monkeys.

— *In the Shadow of Man*

B Y THE START of 1965, Jane Goodall had already accomplished much. Thirty-one years old, she was well respected in
the scientific community and — primarily by virtue of the
first *National Geographic* article, published in the summer of 1963
— was beginning to acquire her mature fame among the larger
American public. She had already made the first discoveries —
chimpanzee meat-eating and tool-using — that would forever un-
derpin her public and professional reputation. And she had managed to habituate to an astonishing degree almost an entire social
community of wild apes. She was then, as Dr. Leonard Carmichael
(chairman of the National Geographic Society's Committee for Research and Exploration) declared in a committee meeting of early
1966, "probably the best qualified person in the world today to
speak on the subject of chimpanzee behavior in the wild." Profes-
sionally she had come of age.

Carmichael's opinion was particularly important because Jane
had by then developed a vision of her future as a chimpanzee con-
servationist and researcher. She wanted to establish a series of chimpanzee reserves in West Africa, and she emphatically intended to

continue the research at Gombe on a long-term basis. National Geographic, with its wealth, influence, and abiding interest in pursuits geographical and anthropological, seemed precisely the organization to help.

National Geographic *was* helping, of course, but nevertheless, the January 1965 visit to Gombe by three alpha males from that institution — Dr. Carmichael, along with Dr. Melvin M. Payne (executive vice president of the Society) and Dr. T. Dale Stewart (member of the Committee for Research and Exploration and director of the Smithsonian's Museum of Natural History) — obviously was an occasion of paramount importance. As Jane wrote home (in the first letter in this sequence), "What paraphernalia went into their visit, what preparations, what work, what worry." Even the chimpanzees themselves, she noted in a casual flight of fancy, appeared to recognize the visit's significance: "It was as though they all knew that, perhaps, their future depended on the impression they made." It is thus noteworthy and even, I think, surprising that a quite young woman still without formal scientific credentials had the nerve and poise and self-confidence — the maturity — to stand up to all three proud and powerful senior men. She argued heatedly and earnestly with Payne, who at one point "nearly exploded with rage" at her apparent insolence; Carmichael she cut short; and Stewart she forthrightly disagreed with. In the end the visit was a great success. At least two of the men seem to have appreciated her assertiveness, and Dr. Carmichael made the reassuring pronouncement that "this place MUST be put on a permanent footing."

While 1965 marks the beginning of Jane Goodall's professional maturation, it also marks the start of her withdrawal from an intensely intimate, day-to-day association with life at Gombe. That withdrawal she regretted. "Yet there were times," she recalled a quarter of a century later, "when I thought back to my early days at Gombe with real nostalgia. . . . But change had been inevitable: there was no way in the world that one person, no matter how dedicated, could have made a really comprehensive study of the Gombe chimpanzees. Hence the research centre."*

---

* *Through a Window* (1990), p. 26.

By March of 1965 the first buildings of the center were complete — including two prefabricated aluminum units (floored with concrete and, for insulation and aesthetics, covered with palm-frond thatch and bamboo siding) and a smaller hut to store bananas. The two buildings were, by 1966, furnished, painted, fully in use, and even given names. The larger, which included a main workroom and two smaller rooms for sleeping quarters, was called Pan Palace (a punning link between aluminum pan and *Pan troglodytes,* the scientific name for chimpanzees). The smaller, consisting of a single room to be used as Jane and Hugo's sleeping quarters, was named Lawick Lodge. By May of 1966 a third semipermanent building was begun down toward the beach, constructed partly from pieces that had originally been a veranda for Pan Palace; this building, a dining hall for the research staff, was finished by June and named Troglodytes Taverne (mentioned in the letter of June 23, 1966).

The research staff during 1965 and 1966 consisted of two or three persons who did not have scientific credentials. Edna Koning, who had arrived at the start of 1964 and remained until the winter of 1965, began the baboon studies. Sonia Ivey, who stayed, along with Edna, for about a year, from late 1964 to the winter of 1965, labored mostly on secretarial duties, of which there were plenty. Edna and Sonia were replaced by Caroline Coleman, an American Ph.D. candidate in psychology, who took over as a researcher at the start of 1966, and, in March, by a woman who came to work as secretary, Mrs. Sally Avery. A few other people arrived for short stays at Gombe during this time, including a woman named Milly or Millie (referred to in the letters of October 2, 1965 and May 1966), who helped with the secretarial work for about four months, and John MacKinnon, who came for a time to study insects.[*]

Jane and Hugo, meanwhile, had been forced to leave Gombe Stream for more than a year — from March 1965 to early May 1966 — and in separate directions. Hugo followed his camera. National Geographic was funding him to photograph animals else-

---

[*] John MacKinnon, grandson of British Prime Minister James Ramsay MacDonald and nephew of Malcolm MacDonald, came to Gombe officially as an entomologist, but he was clearly interested in the chimpanzees. He studied zoology at Oxford and went on to conduct an extended, pioneering field study of orangutans in Borneo.

where in East Africa. Jane returned to Cambridge, living once again at Cross Farm in Comberton and working, as she expressed it in a letter of November 5, "flat out on the final stages" of her doctoral dissertation. At the same time, the many enticements and demands of her astonishing professional success were starting to pour in. She finished a draft of her second *National Geographic* article (letter of February 3, 1965); turned in the typescript of her first popular, nonscientific book (late July 1966); continued a correspondence with Paul Brooks at Houghton Mifflin, the American publisher that hoped to publish her second popular book; delivered a lecture for the prestigious Wenner Gren conference in Vienna, held within the walls of the castle Burg Wartenstein; and, after a "delightful month on the Serengetti" that included a very brief visit to Gombe, she returned to "horrible oral exams, lectures, lectures, and more lectures." The lectures were given during a whirlwind tour in the United States, where her visibility was rapidly expanding, thanks to a cover appearance for the second *National Geographic* article and a CBS television special, "Miss Goodall and the Wild Chimpanzees," both in December 1965. The tour began with three sold-out lectures in National Geographic Society's Constitution Hall in late February. After a quick return to England for, among other things, a March 9 lecture in Bournemouth, the tour ended in California with Jane ceremonially cutting and consuming the first of 30,144 pieces of a 320-foot-long birthday cake celebrating San Diego Zoo's fiftieth birthday (letter of April 23, 1966). At the end of April she received formal notification from Cambridge that henceforth she was qualified to be known as Dr. Jane Goodall. Finally, back in Africa, she and Hugo showed their latest chimpanzee film to Julius Nyerere, the distinguished first president of Tanzania.

There is little doubt that Jane — and Hugo as well — enjoyed the attention brought by this new-found fame, but she took greater pleasure in returning to Africa to be with the chimpanzees. Certainly the letters written from Gombe, filled with daily news and views from that small paradise, include the most fully detailed and emotionally engaged writing of this chapter. The business and professional letters mailed from Cambridge and elsewhere pale in comparison. The Gombe correspondence continues the story of hope and excitement, including the births of two new infants (Circe's Cindy and Little Bee's Tiny Bee) at the start of 1965, and of despair, such as the horrible death of Mandy's baby, Jane, in early February 1965.

Among the notable chimpanzee events of 1966 was Jane's first observation of an entire meat-eating sequence, as reported in the final letter from May: "MEAT-EATING. Saw Hugo (chimp) hitting a baboon (young, not baby) in camp!! He had it by leg and was bashing its head up & down on the ground. Saw the whole meat-eating sequence." The event, both dramatic and gory, was fully reported and even illustrated in the book Jane was just then finishing for National Geographic — except that chimpanzee Hugo was renamed Rodolf to avoid confusion with husband Hugo. One other compelling, if depressing, set of observations from the same period has to do with the decline of "poor little Merlin." After his mother, Marina, died in 1965, Merlin fell into a deep depression, losing weight, obsessively grooming himself, and neurotically plucking out his hair, until he seemed merely "a skeleton with a pot belly" (May 7, 1966). His sister, Miff, allowed him to "climb in and snuggle up" into her sleeping nest at night, but Merlin died before the year ended.

Some long-term management problems developed and continued during this period at Gombe. In the early years Jane had spontaneously touched — in grooming and play — a few of the chimpanzees, but as research assistants began to take over the running of the center, she and Hugo recognized the importance of keeping human observers from making physical contact with the ape subjects. For one thing, there was a reasonable concern about spreading disease. And, there was the issue of physical safety. Chimpanzees are vastly stronger than humans, and it seemed like a good idea to keep them from discovering that fact. Thus Jane and Hugo made it a rule that "no student should purposefully make contact with any of the chimpanzees."* And thus we note the alarm and concern in Jane's very first letter home after her return to Gombe in May 1966: "The

---

* *In the Shadow of Man* (1971), p. 139.

chimps are fine — except that, so far as we can see, even Caroline has been touching them."

A second persistent problem had to do with the banana feeding. Upon their return in 1966, Jane and Hugo were, as she recollected in her book *In the Shadow of Man*, "shocked by the change we saw in the chimps' behavior. Not only was there a great deal more fighting than ever before, but many of the chimps were hanging around camp for hours and hours every day."* The ultimate solution was to limit much more strictly and carefully the dispersal of bananas. In the meantime, the banana boxes were found to be not very functional. The original steel boxes were operated remotely, with levers pulling underground cables that drew open latches. But over time Fifi, Figan, and Evered figured out how to remove the locking pins from the lever mechanism. Hassan replaced the pins with threaded screws — which the chimps soon learned to remove. Then the threaded screws were held in place with tightened nuts, but those didn't last long either. By the summer of 1966 Hugo had decided to go hi-tech, ordering from Nairobi a number of steel boxes that could be locked and unlocked electronically via battery-operated radio control (as mentioned optimistically in the last letter, of late July 1966). At last, Jane enthused, those new boxes ought to "really fox cunning little devils like Fifi!" With the boxes just about ready, a wealth of "grand" safari equipment, including their "Folkswaggen" modified to serve as a traveling office, and "the fact that for the first time in 6 years I do not have a weighty work hanging over my head," Dr. Jane Goodall was ready to go: leaving with Hugo for a photographic assignment in the Serengeti and the "icy fastness" of Ngorongoro Crater and entering at last the mature phase of her brilliant career.

*   *   *   *

[Late January 1965]

Darling Family,

What ages since I wrote. But you must forgive me — I havn't had any seconds to do anything until now — now that the dear trio

---

* *In the Shadow of Man*, p. 141.

from the States have left us. What paraphernalia went into their visit, what preparations, what work, what worry. And how are we left as a result. In many ways their visit couldn't possibly have gone off better. There were lots of chimps, doing nice things. We have made the hut joined to the work tent by a great fence, with roll down mats across an opening where the path goes. So that the great men could walk from their tents to the hut, to their choo, etc. We had gone to enormous trouble with this fence, to buy and dye yards of mosquito netting so that no chimps took fright and ran away. We moved the salt block from its place on the path to the trees outside the work tent so that there was some incentive to keep the chimps, at least for a little while, in their sight. We had cut down vegetation so that by dint of peering they could see chimps by our tent from the work tent and the hut. We decided that, one by one, they could be allowed to our tent to see the chimps from close, unmosquitoed quarters. So. They arrived, with Hugo, when Sonia and I had had such a busy day that things were not really ready. We had been in hiding for over 2 hours because a very pink Sally had been in camp all afternoon. The hoot of Hugo rang through the air. Sonia and I like two frantic bees rushed to the sitting room and the work room tents and emerged laden with all the bits and pieces that we had instructions to tidy away during the day. All were dumped in Hugo and my tent and the flaps closed! Then the party was whistled on. No sooner had they been escorted by the back door into the hut than the next group came. Super arrival display by Mike and Hugo. Lots of other chimps. A very heavily preg. Circe strolled around. A few chimps peered at the four vaguely visible objects in the hut, all madly clicking.* But none of them bothered. And, the next day, one by one our resolutions were overcome as, one by one, all the chimps accepted our VIP's with a nonchalant stare and a turned back. It was quite unbelievable. It was as though they all knew that, perhaps, their future depended on the impression they made. Olly couldn't have cared less. Figan straight away brushed past Payne, nearly pushing him off his chair. Mac D, timid little Mac D, gave

---

* The visitors were taking photos.

them a noncommittal stare and continued to scrounge in the tent for bananas. Circe didn't mind. And even little Jomeo, our new latest little male who was christened Romeo until I found he was none other than Jo — even he, for whom we still hide in tents, came bouncing along the path whilst we were all standing out in the field! So. Our gentlemen from the States enjoyed two complete days of complete freedom. They were very good. Did what they were told. Didn't complain about cups without handles, cold breakfasts (because chimps always came in the middle and they wanted to take pictures and watch and we couldn't keep it all hot) and were quite happy to drink stream water in its pristine unboiled state. Carmichael, that great giant of a man, when I asked him if he would like hot water to wash with, or a bath, said I please wasn't to worry because he made his thermos top of shaving water go a long way — in fact he had almost bathed in it. Thinking of the little bird in the glass I had a hard job not to laugh out loud. Anyway, to speak of other things. Payne, dear Payne . . . nearly exploded with rage when I told him I wasn't happy about the lecture film being shown to scientific audiences. I was livid too. We let it be. And then, later that evening when we were all together, Carmichael mentioned to me that he had had the honour of showing it, and how successful it had been. I said nothing. Payne turned to me and asked if that didn't completely set my mind at rest. My opportunity, and all unasked for. So I regaled Carmichael and Stewart with the examples of unscientific things which had crept into the film. Stewart was on my side in a flash. Carmichael looked into the fire for a long time, and could only say that anyway it served to interest people in the chimps and in conservation. . . .

However, let me turn to the bright aspect of the visit. And it was very bright. For one thing we won over Carmichael, hook line and sinker. And are dying to hear, Mum, any report you may hear from Louis as to their comments when they left. When he arrived Carmichael was so pompous and so ready to pounce on every word I said — how did I know — why did I say so — was this justified — etc, etc, etc. We got almost hysterical — and this is not just Hugo and I — Payne and Stewart were usually on our side too — that we couldn't keep our faces straight. He was, in fact, being silly!! For instance, when I asked if he could remember at what age a laboratory chimp walked first, he spent 5 minutes giving a discourse on the origin of walking, and how infants new born walked by movements of their limbs through space, and walking originated by the C and then the S shape of swimming organisms — and it went on and on. And in point of fact he didn't obviously know the answer to the question, but he would never admit it! However, we had one long discussion about the meaning of a movement of Flint's, or Figan's or something. And he kept saying that when I was writing a scientific paper or my thesis I should say this or this, and not that or that. Until, in exasperation I said that I wasn't writing a thesis, but talking to him. And do you know, from that moment onwards, he was a changed man. He stopped being terrified that every opinion he gave would appear in reference to his name in some or other of my papers. He became human. He talked about chimps like we do. He commented on a satisfied expression on Gregor's face. He began extasising about Flint (only I'm sure he spelt it differently!) And we had fun. I think he rather likes it that I stood up for our views, and wouldn't be talked down, and even ventured to disagree with him on more than one topic! Stewart, the Director of the American Museum of Natural History, was also won over. He started off in a very critical vein. But changed quicker than Carmichael. In fact his turning point was when I ventured to disagree with his theory that man became man simply because an erect posture freed the vocal organs of some pressure which was the consequence of a quadrupedal gait and enabled man to talk. Anyway, the next morning he happened to mention that he had been thinking and thinking about the vocal organs and — this, that and the other. And next Carmichael appeared and said he'd been thinking during the night of something or other we'd been talking about. So both learned gents had had food for thought. And began to enjoy themselves, and relaxed, and told jokes, and we grew to really like Carmichael. And what a brilliant man he is to be sure.

Two things happened. The day before they came Faben came to camp with a whole, complete, and certainly baboon, skull. Of course, Hugo was meeting them so no record is made except in my notes and a few very poor stills — because Ben was so nervy and so certain that I wanted to steal his skull, that I couldn't get anywhere near him. The other thing is even more exciting. CIRCE HAS HER BABY! We don't know the sex. If it's a boy we are undecided as to whether we should call it Leonard, in honour of the great man's visit. Or Winston in honour of the even greater man's sad death.* How sad, but he was so old that it had to come soon I suppose. But we thought a little chimp Winston would be rather nice, and one little tribute we could give. It was Sonia who thought of it, and we thought it was a good idea. However, from the very brief glimpse of the relevant portion of its anatomy, both Hugo and I suspect a girl!

I forgot to tell you the research news. Carmichael is so impressed that he feels this place MUST be put onto a permanant footing. He feels he might get us some of the money that is available to primate research from the U.S.A. government. Countless millions of dollars. He feels sure he can find qualified people to come here and take over, because he feels as we do that there must be a continuity of observations, and the records must be kept. He was, in fact, wildly enthusiastic. He thought the Smithsonian might well finance an expedition to Liberia, such as we used to talk about. As it is an American — well, something, I've forgotten what — it sounds good. He is great friends with the President. Who is very keen on animals. . . .

So, our plans for next year are sadly changed, and Hugo will just be in England for about a month in July or August. Then he must be back for the birth session of the plains animals — and I hope that I shall be able to join him for a short time between Christmas and the Geographic Lecture which we have fixed for 10 Feb. What a relief it will be to know that I shall not need shingles for the lecture — that even though it will not be our film, the film of films, it will be a scientifically accurate film.† Please can someone find out when, if I do get a PhD, I would be expected to receive it, or be awarded with

---

* Winston Churchill died on January 24, 1965.
† She realized that she wouldn't break out in shingles from worry because, unlike an earlier film presented at a Geographic lecture, the current film was scientifically correct.

it, or whatever does happen? <u>URGENT</u> Also, Mum, <u>please</u> can you get Jiff, next time she is home, to look out one of her pictures of Priscilla termiting, which shows her <u>face.</u> This is URGENT — as we want to put it side by side with a strange new female who has now been twice, and who looks rather but not quite like the Priscilla of old.

Next thing, Mum. This is no urgent request — it is just something which I'd be most grateful if you could keep your eyes open for, or your ears. While I am at Cambridge I shall need someone to help me with charts, tables, etc. The work Edna should be doing if she was here now, but isn't. Otherwise I don't think I can get all the work done. If it was someone good at maths so much the better! Someone who had left school and had some odd time to fill in and wanted some pocket money — that sort of thing. You see, it COULD be someone in London, that I could meet every other weekend, or something. I shall also ask Lyn to keep her ears open in Cambridge, because, of course, that would be far more satisfactory. I could, also, take someone to Cambridge with me — could easily find them somewhere in Comberton, I should think, that would not be too expensive — that would be really ideal. Maybe you could ask Uplands [School] or something. Anyhow, just in case you do hear of such a thing.

Help — end of page. I will write again soon, now all panics over.

Tons & tons of love to all,

Jane

Hugo sends his love to all.

c/o Box 8,
Kigoma,
Tanzania.
3 February 1965

Dear Mr. Vosburgh,

Here at last is the promised manuscript! I have been trying to get it finished, in the few spare moments available, for several months, but couldn't manage it any earlier than this.

I do want to impress upon you that this is a <u>DRAFT.</u> There are several passages that I want to rewrite, particularly towards the beginning. However, I am sending it to you in this form because I feel sure you will find it too long and I should appreciate your advice on which parts to shorten. If you could write back, at some time, and let me know what you feel might be omitted or reduced I should very much like to do as much of this as possible myself.

I don't know if you were one of the members of the Research Committee to visit East Africa — if so I do hope that you enjoyed your 'safari'. I am sure you will have heard by now how well the chimps behaved for our Geographic visitors here.

Hugo joins me in sending our best regards,

Yours sincerely,
Jane van Lawick

P.O. Box 8
Kigoma, Tanganyika,
E. Africa
[Received February 8, 1965]

Miss Mary Griswold
National Geographic Society
Washington 6, D. C.
United States of America
Dear Mary:

I have received a letter from Professor Pronko of Wichita State University asking for permission to publish some photographs in a book of readings in general psychology he is compiling.

I have spoken to Dr. Payne concerning this and he agrees that we can let Professor Pronko have some photographs. He is, of course, particularly interested in tool using, and as I do not have contact sheets of termiting stills with me I should be most grateful if you could choose some for him. If you still have the list of the ones which were used in the Stanford book I would suggest the same would do for Pronko. In addition, from 1964 contact sheets — sheet No. 14A — No. 6, Sheet 19A, No. 2. (i.e. playing and grooming). The former is a female juvenile playing with nearly mature male, approx 10–11 years. The latter — mixed group social grooming.

Have you heard our latest news — that Circe has a baby? Still don't know the sex because after her first visit she has not been. But you have not heard our even more astounding news. Madam B. arrived here 1 hour ago, after an absence of 5 months, with a tiny, new born infant! We had been talking about her and saying we felt she must be dead only minutes before she arrived, because I dreamed about her <u>last night</u>!! Little Bee was still well, but Mama was very nervous. The new infant is "Tiny Bee". It really is most exciting — the 5th baby this season — the 2nd this year!

I do hope all goes well — we haven't heard from you for AGES.

With regards,

Jane

"Chimpland"

13 February 1965

Dear Dr. Payne,

What a wonderful surprise we had to receive your present — you can't imagine what a difference it has made to our meals out here — or perhaps you can! It was so kind of you to think of it, and you couldn't possibly have sent us anything we should appreciate more. Many many thanks from all of us.

You timed your visit here just right. If you had come two weeks later you would have been in Chimpland for the most horrible tragedy. Mandy came down the slope with a big group, and when she was way up we heard agonized screaming. And then we saw it — little Jane, her 3 month old infant you remember — had one arm dangling loose, all the inside of the lower arm torn off from the elbow and dangling down over the little hand. And every time Mandy moved she screamed in agony. She turned to the comfort of the nipple and suckled, but could find no relief. Mandy, of course, didn't understand at all, and when Jane screamed she pressed her close, adding to the infant's pain. It was about the most ghastly thing I've seen in a long while. It must have happened only a very short time before Mandy arrived, for blood was still dripping, and Mandy's own ear was torn and still bleeding.

Mercifully death came far quicker than we had dared to hope. She didn't, thank goodness, come here again with the baby. But two days afterwards we saw her opposite, carrying the body, hitting away the flies that seethed all over it. She didn't bring the body here, which we hoped she would, horrible though it would have been. It would have been interesting to see the reactions of the others. And then, two days after that, she arrived here, alone again. Her breasts very tight and swollen, but otherwise showing no ill effects. But sometimes she sits and stares and stares at one or other of the other infants.

The buildings are, to all intents and purposes, finished. Hugo has asked me to tell you that he will send the cost of the cement bases and the labour in the next mail. By then we shall know this down to the last cent. We are now busy getting banana boxes put there, and then we shall be able to leave the girls with a happy heart. The bamboo on the outside looks wonderful, and one is being thatched tonight. And with the linings inside they really are going to be nice looking buildings.

Poor Edna is still stuck — she is now in Dar es Salaam! But she is due back, definitely, on Tuesday next, just in time to help us start to organize the move to the new camp.

I do hope that the rest of your safari in Africa was successful and enjoyable, and that you had a good trip back to Africa. — sorry — America! Thank you again so much for your present, from all of us.

Yours sincerely,
Jane

c/o Box 8
Kigoma, Tanzania
20 February 1965

Mr. Paul Brooks,
Jpigjtpm ?off;om !!
Houghton Mifflin Company,
2 Park Street, Boston 7.
United States of America.

Dear Mr. Brooks,

It was nice to get your Christmas card and message. I do apologize for not writing — but for one thing we are so hectic here that it is hard to find even a moment to compose oneself sufficiently to write letters. For another thing, there is nothing I can say except that I still can't commit myself to a publisher. The Geographic is being a bit awkward as they want to publish a book themselves, and there is some question of their not liking another book on the market. I think this will resolve itself, but have heard nothing from them since I wrote about it.

Things here are going superbly. We have got two semi permanent buildings set up on the most magnificent site. They are just about ready now, and although Hugo and I have to leave in a month (me back to England and he, lucky fellow, filming in the game parks) we have two girls to leave here who will look after things while I finish my PhD. After that I hope to do another year here myself, and then perhaps our scheme will be working — that students should come here to make specialized studies. We have received enthusiastic promises of help from all sorts of sources — the Smithsonian, Professor Lorenz and Julian Huxley amongst them. I think we shall manage to find the finance somewhere.

Hugo and I also have a plan to establish a string of chimpanzee reserves throughout their range, so that, eventually, behaviour studies in the different areas may reveal cultural differences. The project has been taken up by the World Wild Life Fund, so that seems promising too.

Forgive hasty note, but I hope it's better than nothing.

Yours sincerely,
Jane van Lawick

July 25, 1965

Dear ~~Mr. Brown,~~ Andrew!

Excuse haste, but I want to answer your questions — or Dr. Carmichael's — before the post goes.

1. By all means qualify the statement that Faben is Flo's son, in the way you suggest. It is quite certain, but if people might object, we may as well qualify it.

2. No absolute proof, in positive form, that chimps KILL baboons. But, as I have said, we have seen them hunt baboons. I have seen one eating meat from a baboon skull. And I have no hesitation in asserting, dogmatically and with assurance, that chimps will not, under any circumstances, eat something that has already been killed.* We have tested them out in this respect, on several occasions, and the result was always negative, even though we had seen them kill and eat the same animals or birds.

3. No one from the Geographic had a hand in getting Edna to us. She read the article and wrote direct to me, and Hugo and I decided that, since she was so keen and was willing to get out to Africa under her own steam we would give her a try.

4. I do not consider the last paragraphs too anthropomorphic. I am not trying to attribute human motives to David. What he did was what he would do to another chimp. What I hoped I had conveyed, and what I want to convey, is the impression, purely subjectively, that this action had upon me. I think, on suddenly thinking about it, that the one wrong part is right at the beginning where I say that "he not only tried to communicate with me, but actually succeeded" — or words to that effect. In fact it would be better to omit the "tried". Something like — On this occasion my old friend, D.G. actually established communication with me, by using a chimpanzee gesture (or the chimp gesture before the actually established).

Do forgive haste — and I see I've torn the paper!!

Yours sincerely,
Jane Goodall

---

* The behavior has since been observed on a very few occasions.

Austria.

14 September [1965]

My dear FFF,

Well, here we are, on holiday at last. I think you would already be surprised if you saw me as I look about 80% better — even to myself!

We have just got to our chalet having stayed on to the bitter end of the Wenner Gren conference. It really went off fantastically well and we had a wonderful time. . . . I think the conference has done a lot of good all round. The film went down excellently and the principle of 'reassurance' was accepted without protest from anyone. They all immediately realized they had seen it in their own animals. We planned to stay 3 days and stayed 7! Isn't it a fantastic place for a conference. We had music in the chapel garden (no one talked, but we did all freeze). Liberal wine flowed and thousands of concepts were evolved round the dinner table. In the middle of the Conference part of the Board of Directors arrived and they came in to a session. Apparently the first time they have attended any meeting in session. Primates would get in first! Lorenz didn't come, which was a pity, but a lot of other interesting people were there — Mason, Marler, and Hamburg especially.*

On the last evening DeVore & Sherry sang a song about chimps to me which, I gather, was instigated by remarks made by you some years ago but which you had not heard! It was strictly censored!

With reference to the request for money for the drawings from film. These are not only for my thesis, not by any manner of means. But we got them all out — or Hugo did — while he was going through the film, & they may just as well be all done together. Certainly I will pay if the Geographic refuse, but I see no harm in asking. Especially in view of the <u>very</u> large return they will get from the television film.

We got the M.G. for our holiday. Grossly extravagant but as we are going to sell it we shouldn't lose any more than if we had got any

---

* The "interesting people," all of whom were distinctly promising or already distinguished academics with a direct interest in primate studies, included William Mason, Peter Marler, David Hamburg, Irven DeVore, and Sherwood ("Sherry") Washburn.

other car, & the open air is just wonderful. Sorry about change of pen but we can't find anything else at hand!

Well, I will end for now. I bet you are relieved that Sonia has gone back, all signed and all! It is raining hard here!

Will write again soon.

> With love,
> FC.
> Jane

> Don Quixote
> Kitzbuhel
> October 2, 1965

My dear FFF,

Well, just a few words. We are nearing the end of our holiday. We have had superb weather, and I feel 100% fitter than when you last saw me. It will be sad to leave Austria and the cows and deer and nearly black squirrels.

We went to see Lorenz last week, and showed him the film. He was delighted with it all. Poor man is not at all well — has something or other wrong with his insides and is about to give up paper work for a spell and calmly watch his geese. He made a superb remark about Pooch when she was investigating the dead rat* — "Ah — there is the first Zoologist"!!!

There are a list of questions I must ask you, and to clarify matters I will give each one a number.

1. Have you still got Edna's signed agreement? If so, can you send it back to me. Edna is unhappy about it and only signed it thinking it concerned chimps.

2. Did you get, direct from Caroline, her passport number? Is anything working out for her? Is there anything we should be doing from here to see that she can get through quickly?

3. We hear from Edna that she is to — or was to — pay Milly's salary from the Kigoma fund. The only source from which this was possible was the "emergency fund" which she was not supposed to

---

* A scene in a film made by Hugo.

touch unless in trouble. This money was the accumulation of several months of my stipend. If she paid 4 months of Milly's salary from it it will not cover emergencies, which is why we want to know. If so, then we can arrange something else for that fund. Edna also said that you said that the Nairobi fund was depleted. What is the financial situation for the end of the year? I suppose that Edna's salary is still all right, because she will be going on holiday early next year, and will presumably want it.

4. Has the new grant request gone off yet? If so, we'd be most grateful for a copy of it as it finally stood.

5. Hugo tried for insurance (medical) for the girls from England but was unable to succeed. He therefore can do no more about it until he sees you again in Nairobi. Also none of the African staff are insured yet either.

6. A final message from Hugo. Would it be all right if he camped at Olduvai for a couple of months when he gets back — quite self contained of course. If so, could he hire your truck for getting petrol there, for 2 days — I mean hire the truck for 2 days.

There — that is all the points I think. And I am keeping the letter brief because I am now working on "reassurance and touch, etc" and must get on with my lists. I hope you got my brief scrawl after the Wenner Gren which went off superly.

Hugo sends his regards,

With love,
F.C.
Jane

1, York Mansions,
Earl's Court Road,
London, S.W.5.
5 November 1965.

Dear Dr. Wolff,

I apologize for the delay in answering your letter of 23 September, but I have been away and only recently returned.

As I am working flat out on the final stages of my PhD thesis, and shall be kept busy until my arrival in Washington in February, I feel that I shall be unable to prepare a lecture for you with the first lecture film. However, if you could persuade the National Geographic Society to allow me to lecture with the new lecture film, after the lectures to the Society, I shall be very happy to accept your invitation to speak for the Maryland Academy of Sciences.

As an alternative, perhaps the Geographic Society might be more willing to allow me to show simply a half of the new lecture film — for the other half of the programme I should be happy to introduce the work being done at the Gombe Stream Reserve and show a number of colour slides.

If you or the Geographic agree to either of the above the best date for me would be February 22nd.

Yours sincerely,
Jane van Lawick-Goodall

Ngorongoro Crater Lodge, Ltd.
P.O. Box 751
Arusha, Tanzania
1 February 1966

Mr. Paul Brooks
Houghton Mifflin Company,
2 Park Street,
Boston 7.
United States America.
Dear Paul Brooks,

Just a short note, on our way back from a delightful month on the Serengetti to horrible oral exams, lectures, lectures, and more lectures, to say thank you for the book — which we got yesterday, together with your letter.

We havn't, of course, read the book yet, but it looks fascinating, and we look forward to doing so — perhaps on our flight to the States in two weeks time!

I think we are coming to Boston to show the film there. If so it will be during the week starting 7th March. Any chance of meeting you there? It would be fun, and I'm sure there is a lot we could talk about.

If you want to know our plans, contact Miss Joanne Hess of the National Geographic Society — but she will not know the Boston dates yet, since we do not know ourselves! Roy Little has invited us — I'm sure you know him. We met him in Seronera, and he is very interested in the chimpanzee work, and our plans to make Reserves, or Parks, in West Africa — for the chimps I mean.

Hoping to see you,
Jane van Lawick

Ainsworth
Nairobi.
23 April, 1966

Darling Family,

How are you all. We had a jolly good flight back — plane almost empty, and it didn't stop after 10.30 p.m. until we got to Entebbe in the morning. We were able to sprawl out on a seat each — in fact, almost everyone could, so few seats were filled. It was a B.O.A.C. plane — the service was fantastically good — nice polite people, super food, gorgeous huge blankets — really looking up. Much better than on any of the Pan Am flights, or TWA in America.

Poor old Hassan trailed along here yesterday. Come to see Louis about what he is supposed to do in Victoria. Another of his children died. He asked Mrs. Crisp for a bit of money, and Mary, since he had none at all. They both lost their tempers with him, and sent him off to Mike Richmond.* Of course Mike didn't know what to do — it was lucky we were here. His [Hassan's] back is bad again — we are taking him to the doctor who was so good with Hugo, this morning. Mrs. Crisp is vile. In a most flying into tempery mood (notice that this typewriter too is beginning to overtype, Mum!!!!!). In

---

* Mrs. Crisp was Louis Leakey's secretary. Mike Richmond, a businessman with East African Film Services in Nairobi, came to serve, with a small retainer fee, as their factotum and general contact in Nairobi.

fact, so many things are disturbing. Caroline is making things very difficult for herself. She wrote to us to say she was sorry her last letter sounded cross — but she had been cross with us for several reasons. (1) Mrs. Avery had arrived, and been horrified at the set up, and said that she had not been at all prepared for what she found. For weeks had been terrified of the chimps but was beginning to settle down now, and was most efficient. (2) Much worse. She said she had been most cross not to hear that Mrs. Avery was arriving until she got a wire from her from Dar. Then we found two letters, written by Caroline, written about 3 weeks before Mrs. Avery got to Africa, saying she had heard a Miss Avery was arriving, and could she please take to the Reserve a long list of items!!!! What muddles we do get into. . . .

We have ordered our travelling office — Carmichael calls it a "portable" office!* He is a hoot. It is a super thing — the only one they had in stock. We have also ordered the radio telephones. Mike Richmond is the agent for them, and apparently the mountains won't affect them at all. Never recommend anyone to buy an Alder typewriter! The bus is a pale grey, and absolutely super inside. We can't get an air conditioning to work except by running on the battery, but we can apparently have a fan fitted — this would probably be sufficient to keep the temperature bearable.

There are two things which it would be wonderful if Anthea or Shirley could bring. I should forget the little white case — I really don't need the things from it. (1) the case of cups you gave us, Mum (which are in the little white case). (2) the telescope. It's not heavy, and is in the flat, with its tripod, in our cupboard in the studio. We are happy to pay the overweight which this might involve, if either of them could bear to. Also one pot of Boots Moisturising cream — No. 7 I think it is.

I had better stop now, but will write again soon — either whilst we are at Manyara, or when we get back.

Tons and tons of love to you all,
Jane

---

* A Volkswagen bus.

c/o P.O. Box 2818,
Nairobi, Kenya.
23rd April, 1966

Dear Dr. Carmichael,

Thank you very much indeed for your letter of 24 March. We were, of course, delighted to hear that our grant request had been approved, and are extremely grateful to the Society for its continued generous support of the chimpanzee research.

I understand that the Chimpanzee Research Account at Kigoma has already received $3560 for the maintenance of staff etc. until the end of April. We should be grateful if an additional $3204 could be sent to this account as soon as possible — this should be sufficient for a further four months. Could this be sent to the National Bank, Kigoma, to A/C no.10640 Caroline Coleman Chimpanzee Research A/C. We shall be in Kigoma ourselves in two weeks time.

We should also be grateful if the $3976 for the metal buildings, their transport, etc, and the $7056 for the Volkswagen portable office etc. could be sent to the Chimpanzee Research Account, in my name, in Nairobi — General Bank of the Netherlands. We should appreciate it if this could also be sent off as soon as possible. . . .

Hugo and I had a fantastic time when we returned to San Diego for their Zoo's silver jubilee celebrations. It happened, by coincidence, that the Zoo's birthday was on the same day as mine! They had made, for the occasion, a 100 yards long birthday cake, laid out along a great row of end to end tables in the zoo. The cake was for 30,000 children — and anyone else who came along! I had to cut the first piece! It was quite a performance, and the children loved it — as did all the great apes who were all given pieces as well!

We had to do heaps of television interviews while we were there and you would have been delighted if you had seen the number of times that the December issue of the National Geographic Magazine was held up before T.V. viewers, and the pages slowly turned!! We also aroused a lot of interest, and quite a bit of support, for our chimpanzee reserves plan. We have been in touch with Professor Bourliere about this, and I will write further when we have followed up his suggestions.

It is wonderful to be back in Africa — and it will be good to see all the chimps again. I'll write from the Reserve to say how things are going.

Hugo joins me in sending best wishes to you and your wife.

Yours sincerely,

Jane

[Around May 7, 1966]

Darling Family,

A hasty hasty note — we are just off, flying with Mike Richmond 'cos the road is out. So we'll be with the chimps this evening. I meant to write heaps of times — but we have been <u>frantic</u> — I have just got the paper off to Phyllis — who hasn't received from England — (Peter's) photos. I hope you got the list Mum? If not, please CABLE — & I will send you the list. Been struggling with Geographic book outline, rushing to show film to Nyerere & Tanzania Society in Dar — lots of love from Caroline Sassoon* — showing it twice in Nairobi — drama with Owen (re Park status of Reserve) — great time in Manyara with elephants <u>when</u> I went out. It was mean — we were there for 6 days — I went out only 2 afternoons!! Rest of time battling with the Wenner Gren.†

Havn't had <u>any</u> letters from you, so presume they're in chimpland?! Has Judy sent the copy of Mrs. Avery's agreement? It is rather urgent, but is really too late now to be useful as we wanted to consult a solicitor here in Nairobi.

Apparently poor little Merlin is dying — steadily and irreversibly he gets thinner & weaker, and goes blue with cold. A skeleton with a pot belly. Sad & horrible. Caroline told us that when they had a scheme in West Africa to <u>stop</u> the Mum's breast feeding for 3 years there was a drastic increase in infant mortality. This they put down to the fact that the mothers were too ignorant to know what the children should eat. Why we have to be so interfering I don't know.

---

* Caroline and Hamo Sassoon were friends living in Dar es Salaam.
† That is, with the paper she gave at the Wenner Gren conference, which she was preparing for publication.

<u>URGENT</u>. Hugo left some keys in his <u>brown</u> suitcase — the large one that opens in half. <u>Please</u> could these be given to Anthea — or Shirley — for us. They are for the safe & the filing cabinet. Can be left at the office or with Louis. We are <u>dying</u> to hear about the trial of Nigel. How is the book getting on?

Love,

Jane.

[May 1966]

Darling Family,

This will be a rather queer letter — I am in a crouvched position on our matress, on the floor of Lawick Lodge, with the typewriter on the matress in front of me. And, guess wha t — it is my very original dear little typewriter. It has gone through 4 years of tropical humidity, typed several papers and 2 Geographic articles — not to mention the Stanford chap ter. It ha s endured being typed on by me, you Mum, Edna, Sonia, Millie, and "Sally" Avery — and it is still quite super to typ e with. It's faults, as you see, are jjumping and a crooked margin. But neither of these effect the speed of one's typ ing, nor make it impossible to read as overtyping does. Good old Diploma t. And the new one, so generously given to us for whatever it was, is simply hopeless. So hopeless that I ahve left it in Nairobi, and we shall try to sellit and get another when we get back. Most of the mis takes, incidentally, are due to the strrange position in which I am typing — but we don't even have a proper table in here yet. The girls are in luxury, but we have our matress and a pile of old boxes in the corner — and our luggage in another. It was even worse yesterday, since all our belongings were strewn absolutely all over the floor — but dear Benjamin arrived from his holiday — you know, the one Hugo and I had on the Serengitti. He, unasked by us, at once tidyed up the whole place.

Well, I will start with first things first. The chimps. A nd the wset up. the chimps are fine — except that, so far as we can see, even Caroline ha s been touching them. It really is hopeless. Anyway, David is absolutely impossible — when he comes he takes one by the hand and leads his victim to a box. He is too dim to realize that the person should be taken to the handle — so you sit with him at the box held in his iron grip, and he gets progressively more livid because you don't open the box. So, a fter he has had h is box he is left outside and everyone ha s to remain in the buildings until he has gone! Talk about being in a cage!!!!!! But the others are fine. Flint is a n absolute little dear mischevous wicked imp. Never still for more than a few moments at a time, and a lways up to some mischieve. And Fifi is worse than ever. Really wicked. She has developed a pashion for throwing, with very bad aim (I know I spelt that wrong!) But she doesn't just throw one stone. She collects stones until her hands are full and then goes stamping off towards the poor female she is about to attack, scattering her stones all round her. Merline is a most pathetic and sad little cha p. He is actually sma ller than Flint, except that his limbs are longer. But, even worse than his skeletal form, is his ap athy. We watched Master Flint trying to play with him this afternoon — it was quite horrid. Flint jumping all over him, and Merlin just crouching down, taking it all — ra ther like a mother being attacked by a male. He does all sorts of peculiar things — for instance, when he grooms himself which he does all the time, he pulls his hairs out by the roots, with his teeth. H e is like an old neurotic little ma n.

Next — the staff. Ca roline seems to be doing excellently. She is a very conscientious and neat person, just as we thought. Very thorough, and everything is kept quite up to date and ship shap e. She is rat her extravagant in her tastes, but we don't think she is spending more money than she should. And she certainly likes the chimps. She is a bit tired at the moment as they have been having a terrible two months — chimps here the entire day through with scarcely a moment to even have a cup of tea or visit the choo! And Sally — we find it so hard to get used to "Sally". She seemw to be w orking out fine after all our worries. She is sweet a ctually, and also loves the chimps. Very quick typist, does shorthand so Caroline dictates the notes which saves the tapes. She seems to love trailing into Kigoma for a day to do the shopping, and since Caroline doesn't mind being on her own with a n A frican for a day, and since Sally is simply sup erb a t getting everything that can be got in Kigoma, we think that, after all, it is proba bly a pretty good idea. She is ra ther upset a t the moment because her Mother has just died — not that she shows it, but she mentioned that she couldn't sleep, and told me a bout it when I asked her why she couldn't sleep. But she trots off swimming in the lake every night, and we are having supper on the ridge as planned. . . .

Well, our flight was tremendous fun. Hair raising on 3 occasions because we were much too overloaded: Taking off, cross the Ngorongoro mountains (the ones near the crater) in thick cloud when we could not climb as high as we should because of the load. We nea rly turned round and went back a t tha t point! But made it. And, a bit, landing — beca use we went down much faster than we should have, again because of the weight. But we did a superb landing. And actually managed to get out of Kigoma quite fast. We did not get ba ck in the boat — we had told the girls we should be a rriving a dsy later, but got permission to go early when it was toolate to let them know. Anyway, apart from having to wait for ages and ages at the immigration nothing held us up.

The radio telephone is fantastic. xxxxxx Nairobi. a parantly, as clear as a bell. The aerial is a fantastic t hing, all held up withx guy ropes and 40 feet high. It is not with the chimp s, for obvious reasons, but near the ridge. Hardly visible from nywhere, really. Beautiful thing. A lso, when we were in Dar, we got a nice typewriter — were all most excited to try it out. But, believe it or not, despite its packing it had had a jolt. And one of the tab stops had got pushed up out of place so that the carriage wouldn't move past the middle. Well, Hugo managed after much difficulty to get the carriage off — then got the naughty tab stop out of the way — then the carriage wouldn't come off. — I mean, of course, it wouldn't go back on, but it is getting rather late at night! Also I am getting stiff from my wierd postion, and it is dark since the shadow of me is over the page. So I will just say, now, that the new typewriter now workds superly, and will then finish tomorrow. Page 3

Well — it's now morning. A very very windy moirning indeed. I have turned myself around for work today — instead of facing the opposite mountain where I kept thinking I saw Madam Bee, I can just see bits of blue lake through the trees. Outside are Flo, Flint, Fifi and Melissa with Goblin. I should be doing the book, but am not in the mood. The pa per is blowing all over the place in the most irritating ma nner. Hugo is getting his equipment ready and drinking coffee — and it is superb to have a typewriter that I can type fast on without it sticking. Last night Hugo and I followed Miff and Merlin. S aw Miff making a nest, and Merlin, after eating caterpillars for 30 mins, climb in and snuggle up beside her for the night. Caroline Sassoon — we stayed with them in Dar as I'm sure I already said, told us an interesting thing. That when, in West Africa, they had a scheme for stopping mother's breast feeding their infants after one year, the infant mortality rate simply shot up. Jolly interesting. But Merlin has simply GOT to live. It would be too awful if he died.

Well — as I huirriedly told you in my blue, we rushed off to Dar and showed the film to Nyerere and then to the Tanzania Society — where Hugo met an old army friend of his. As I told you, Nyerere loved the film, but it wasn' to successful a show as last time because no one else was xxxxx invited, and it is never so good when you see a film with a small audience as with a large one. The Tanzania Soc. showing was a great success — the Museum hall was packed — approximately 40% of the audience were standing or sitting on t he floor!!!!! We sa w poor Hassan in Nairobi — his back is awful — he ha s osteo-arthritis in the lumbar spine. If it is very bad for him to work you should write and tell Louis — who will otherwise put him to any sort of work he fancies. He is not very compassionate where his staff are concerned, simply because he is not for himself. But when you are doing your own work it is different. . . . Caroline and Hamo Sassoon send their love to you — Caroline was most intrigued by the story of Nigel mum. Oh — have I thanked you for your letter, telling us at last about the trial. Well — it was waiting for us when we got here, and a blue. Someone else who wanted very much to be remembered to you, Mum, was Philip Tobias. He too was intrigued by the tale. We took him out to dinner. We had fondue and the poor man burnt his lips most terribly by clsoing them on a red hot fork. Huge white blisters leapt up, and you could hear his lip sizzle. Ugh. We also took Louis and Mary and Philip out to dinner!!!! Mary is wierd — she is always so charming to our faces!! Philip is now quite O.K. so far as she is concerned — she also told C. Sassoon she planned to meet him with a horse whip. I think I must end now — I may add to this, but it is cool, and no chimps, and peaceful, and I must tackle this sordid book. So xxxxx au revoir for the present. . . .

Tons of love from us both,

Jane

Chimpland

[May 1966]

Darling Family,

Just a note to let you know that all is well — very very well re. chimps. Not so well re. book since I havn't yet had much time to write it yet! <u>Chimps.</u> MEAT-EATING. Saw Hugo (chimp) hitting a baboon (young, not baby) in camp!! He had it by leg and was bashing its head up & down on the ground. Saw the <u>whole</u> meat-eating sequence. Hugo being selfish. Mike chasing all others away from him — & getting the liver — JB begging from Mike & crying when he couldn't get any. Hugo carrying the carcass over his shoulder to drink. Lying asleep with it. Suddenly getting up & leaving it on the ground. The others, his faithful persistent followers, staring in disbelief & then all with one accord <u>pouncing</u> on it. Mike, Goliath, JB & Huxley & David. They <u>all</u> grabbed it & pulled. Mike attacked them all & finally got it. Rushed off, flailing it. But the others rushed after him and grabbed it again. Guess who got the best bit? — David!! Up a tree with rump & one leg. Then JB — one arm. Then Huxley. Other arm. Then Goliath — small bit of bone. Then Mike — head and bit of shoulder. All were allowed to share with Mike when they'd eaten their little bits (Hx, Gol & JB). But David turned his back on people. He gave Gol a <u>tiny</u> splinter. And, right at the end, let Mandy have 3 tiny bits of cartilage, & Flo a nearly bare bone! But the best is to come. When Mike's was nearly finished he stopped letting JB share. JB gave up & reclined above Mk, further along the branch. Suddenly he rushed past Mike, shot down the tree, & was gone. I peered, wondering what he had seen. Mike was staring after him with 1/2 open mouth. Then I saw. Mike's share was gone! The prettyest bit of snatch & run robbery I ever saw! He took it up a tall tree & no one bothered him! One horrid part was when Mike lay on his back, held the head above him with one foot, &, with one hand, groomed the head!!

Another thing. Sniff had been coming alone for 2 months. We thought maybe Sophie was dead. But she came, 4 days ago. And, as luck would have it, we saw the re-union. Sniff rushed up & they groomed fanatically. Sophie, Mandy, Pallas & Athaena are all pregnant!

We like Sally — still too talkative though! The new "dining room" on the ridge will be superb — it has been begun. We are painting the inside of Pan Palace — hardly know the place — cream & sky blue.

Will write proper letter anon.

Love from us both to all,
Jane

[Postmarked June 23, 1966]

Darling Mum — dear drunken Pineapple,

Have just read your letter — or at least the start of it — to all. Hoots of mirth, but secret commiseration that I have an old soak as a mother. Love from all, before I forget. Hugo is looking at Playboy — full of nude women. I didn't see a joke he showed me, so he said I was taking after you in my old age. What a reputation. He keeps interrupting with Olly-type jokes. Well — Olly. No — surely by now you have heard how Hugo and I went off to Mtumba, hoping to see Olly. No chimps at all. My old original tree where I saw the first chimps with Rashidi and Adolf and Mikidadi — it was full of fruit but not yet ripe. So we got back — who came that afternoon. Mandy with a new baby. And — Olly. Wasn't it fantastic. It is now three times that Olly has come back, as a regular person, soon after Hugo and I got back. Once when Kris was looking after the camp — and she didn't come for three months. Once when we got back in Jan. And now now. Can't see the page — it is in pitch darkness. So we have dear Olly with us — and a heavily-pregnant Olly. Hugo is going in a week — going to Sambura park, towards the Northern Frontier area. Where I have always wanted to go. But we felt that if I stayed here I could a) finish the book, and b) see Olly's baby. Sophie also any minute now. And a new mother, Spray — we think the original daughter of Mrs. Maggs — with a dear little girl, aged 2 — Sparrow. Another new mother — Jessica — with a little tiny baby, and a daughter of about 6 called Lita — after Lita Os.* We havn't told her yet as we are waiting to get a picture.

Pan Palace is now quite fantastic. All painted. Carpenters here for 2 days, shelves, bookcases, fantastic deck for Sally to type at. It really is super. Poor Sally fell over the other day, caught her hand probably on a tin, and cut huge flap of skin on her finger. This won't heal and is hurting, and so she is going to Kigoma tomorrow to have it looked at again. She has managed to make up 4 long, long back days of tapes with [illegible] in pictures of Flint, Fifi and Figan — for their files. They really do look super now. In fact, I suddenly thought, as I stuck in some hair of Figan's that was pulled out by Mike on 8 July 1964, that our research is the most super in the world. Oh — do you know the latest on the John Owen thing.† I suppose I did write to say that he had proposed Tinbergen for my <u>supervisor</u> if the research here came under the Serengeti Research Institute? Well, we were planning all sorts of drastic measures — he has now decided to ask Robert to act as advisory scientist to the Board of Trustees of Tanz. Nat. Parks. If Robert accepts all should, I hope, be well. We have had 2 Americans staying here all week — actually for 10 days. We thought it was going to be two boys — we met one in San Diego and he asked if he could come for a couple of days when he was travelling round — just to look. So we said yes. Well — he came for 10 days — and with him was a girl — she spells her name — Chryssee. Honestly! They slept all cosy in Trog-

---

* Lita Osmundsen of the Wenner Gren Foundation.
† There seem to have been several points of tension between Jane, as director of Gombe Stream Research Centre, and John Owen, then director of Tanzania's National Parks.

lodytes Taverne! The beds got a bit closer together every time we had supper we thought! That's when we noticed it I mean!!

We shall keep our fingers crossed for Jiff as well — hope that you will let us know when a decision is reached. I can't get over the sermon.* Am dying to hear all about it. Did Danny know in advance! Or do you mean it wasn't really about me, but an allegory. Am rather mystified. Can see down to Hugo's sordid magazine. Page filled with over ripe bosoms and buttocks. Not at all in Hugo's style really, but still. Better than James Bond which has been with us sev. nights and many days during past few weeks!!! Merlin doesn't seem to be getting any livelier or more normal. Sad though it is, it really is quite fantastically interesting — and important. I should think many psychologists will be more interested in him than in almost anything else. Flint is just superb. A real wicked naughty little boy. His whole face is one wicked little impish mask. And Fifi is more wicked too. She doesn't just throw stones when she's angry — she unobtrusively collects up handfulls and throws the whole lot together. Only female known to throw in aggressive context. Would be Fifi. She has taken on Flo's job as chief baboon chaser. Flo is really a bit too old. 2 new tools!! One a stick used to investigate — poked in and then end sniffed. Once my pocket to see if b. in it. Once stick when wasp grubs in hollows inside. Other tool — Flint and a — nose pick!!!! Mandy's baby, by the way, clings like a limpet. So her behaviour with Jane really was because of a weakness in the baby. Do hope Old Men are going well.†

Tons,

me

---

* In a sermon preached at Bournemouth's Richmond Hill church, Reverend Trevor Davies mentioned Jane's life story as an exemplary case.
† Vanne had been working with Louis on a coauthored book exploring "ten decades of thought about human evolution." Entitled *Unveiling Man's Origins* (but privately referred to as "The Old Men"), the book was published in the United States in 1969.

Chimpland
[Early July 1966]

Darling Danny,

I do hope that this letter will arri[ve] for your birthday — if it doesn't, you will [know] it was meant to, but that Tanzanian posts decid[ed] otherwise. If it does — well, very happy birth[day.]

It is early in the morning. I had meant to do more book, but I think I must have been too late at it last night — I don't seem to be able to [do] any now, anyway. It's as bad as the thesis all over again. Even to the extent of grass-widowing me all over again!

Two days ago Mike Richmond flew down, in his little plane, to collect Hugo and Michael.* We had decided that if I went too, what with messing about in Nairobi with no fixed address, driving all over the place, camping — well, I should never get the book ready for when the old Geographic wants it. So I am staying here.

There are compensations of course. Olly is pregnant, we are pretty sure, and it will be wonderful if the baby comes before I go. To see whether Gilka behaves like Fifi did with Flint, always trying to steal the baby. Also Pallas and Sophie are both pregnant too.

You would love to see the babies playing together. There are so many now, all little furry bundles — the smaller ones so gentle and sweet — the elder ones, like Flint and Goblin, little wicked and mischievous imps. Flint is really terrible — Goblin is super. In fact we have added onto his name — he is now Goblin Grub. Because he always, always has a dirty face. Hugo filmed him the other day eating a large banana. It was too much for him. He pushed the whole lot into his mouth and it was so much it fell into his hands again. So then the little grub slapped his hands onto his face, again and again — covering his face with sticky banana! It was just like a small human child let loose with ice-cream!

I followed Flo and Melissa the other day, and they both climbed a tree to feed — with their two infants, Goblin and Flint. Then they climbed down, leaving the children playing. Then Flint climbed down, and went to Flo to suckle. Goblin, half a year younger than

---

* Hugo's brother.

Flint, was left all alone. He stared down, and began to cry, very softly. His cold Mama stared, and decided he was old enough to fight his own battles. But little Flint stopped his suckling and hurried back to the tree. Up he went, flung his arms round little Goblin, and then climbed oh so slowly down, looking up at Goblin and every so often reaching up to touch the little one with one hand, as though encouraging him. Finally they got to the ground, and Flint more or less waved Goblin past him, and the two returned to the adults, Flint in the rear with one hand on Goblin's rump! It was so charming!

Our buildings really are smart now — well, Pan Palace is, but Lawick Lodge has not really been touched. It is furnished now, though, with the left overs from the newly furnished and fitted Pan Palace! Pan Palace has long bookshelves down one wall, over which is a huge framed colour print of the picture in the last article of Flo, Fifi and Flint, Fifi kissing Flint. It has two new tables, one a really good and super desk for Sally to type at. And, as you probably don't know, we already had a four drawer filing cabinet. Then the kitchen has been fitted with new table and shelves all down one wall and above the table. The store has super shelves at one end, and down the side (kitchen and store are only tiny weeny little rooms). The girls each have shelves, and proper beds. Just imagine it all — I still find it hard to believe. They, of course, take it all for granted!

We now have the most beautiful table for the supper house, Troglodytes Taverns. It is dark polished wood with two cutlery drawers, and very heavy. We were absolutely staggered when we saw it — we had never meant such an elaborate thing to be made! But it is super, in the evenings, to sit at it with candles. And for the girls, who, after all, are not here doing their life's work, I think it is an excellent thing that they should have some feeling of civilization! I, personally, preferred the early days when Mum and I, and then I, were "roughing it" — but things have changed so since then, and it's difficult to live in a tent with 50 tame chimps around!

Oh — the chimps killed another baboon. We heard the sudden excitement way down the valley, the chimps in camp simply ran, and Hugo and I hurried after. When we got there Mike had the baboon — it was very different from the time when Hugo had it. Mike shared much more liberally. And then, near the end, Hugo arrived — chimp Hugo we are talking about! He took hold of a piece of the skin of the bab, wanting to pull it off. Mike didn't mind. But Hugo couldn't tear the skin, so he just held onto it! Mike got frenzied, pulling and twisting and turning — Hugo just sat, quite motionless — even with Mike's hardest pulling Hugo's hand scarcely moved. It was the most wonderful demonstration of his enormous strength I have ever seen, and was most impressive. Finally he got a bit off. Then David came up to beg, and, just as a mother tickles her child to distract it from some naughty plan, so Mike began to tickle David. In the middle, when the two old men were rolling over and over and roaring with laughter, Hugo returned having eaten his piece. And he held on again and sat, motionless until the game had ended — just holding on! I do wish Hugo could have filmed it, but it was dense undergrowth. The final episode was Mike with the skull. He poked his index finger into the hole where the top vertebrae goes in order to pick out the brains!

I wonder if you are having a "flaming July" for your birthday. Probably cold and wet, as usual. Am dying to get your letter about the sermon!

Well — the day wears on. They have just called me over to eat a boiled egg, and then, whether I feel like it or not, I must get on with the old book. Only one more month to get it finished. Tell Mum that the first installment for you ALL to severely criticize, particularly from American public's point of view, will be in the mail after this letter. Also that the reprints and her last letter with letter from Nature, etc, arrived safely, and many thinks.

Once again, happy birthday, and I shall be thinking of you.

Tons and tons of love to all,

Your Jane

Please tell Mum — Olly v. pregnant and Gilka most independent — slept a good 50 yards away from Olly — in a different tree! P.S. Did the San Diego 8mm films ever arrive? If so, please, what were they like?

Nairobi
[Late July 1966]

Darling Family,

Just seen Shirley,* who looks terribly happy to be back here in Nairobi. She had the things you gave her to bring — what super, duper little slippers. I adore the sorts of striped ones — not stripes, but I can't think of the word for those things. The others are gorgeous too. Thank you very much whoever sent them.

We are just ready to set off to Ngorongoro for three weeks. We then return here to collect Phyllis Jay and take her down to the chimps to install the 40 electric boxes.† The four that arrived down with Hugo are not ready yet, but he fixed them up inside the building for us — you should have seen the boys' faces when we showed them! They are super — you just have a car battery — which we can charge ourselves by a generator that Hugo and I got — and this works all 40 boxes. We are having 4 panels of 10 switches each, and the boxes can be up to 100 feet away. They open towards the building, so that you can see the number of the box from the window, and press the corresponding number on the pannel. It all seems most weird, — but should really fox cunning little devils like Fifi!!

We were having a birthday party, combined for both girls, just when Hugo and the two Mikes were there. It was quite spoilt and made sad because we got this cable, when in Nairobi, to say that Caroline's brother had been killed. Her only brother, whom she adored. She took it very well — but it hadn't really sunk in at all. I am glad we were able to leave her with an older sensible person like Sally. Poor Sally met J.B. head on — the moment his head left her leg, her leg swelled up — rather like Rod's. I've got a feeling I've told you this before.

The enclosed cheque is to help me celebrate the fact that for the first time in 6 years I do not have a weighty work hanging over my

---

* Shirley Coryndon.
† Phyllis Jay, an anthropologist from the University of California at Berkeley, had organized the 1965 Wenner Gren conference on primate studies.

head. Please will you buy something for all of you that the Birches needs — or something small for each of you that each of you wants — or just anything you like.

Our safari equipment is so grand now that we shan't recognize our own camp when we see it. The new Folkswaggen is absolutely super. Our first little house. We are taking pictures, and will send to you. We have no money left in the bank, but decided that it was more fun to have nice things now and enjoy ourselves, whilst we are still able to be in Africa, than to wait until it was too late. We have taken on another African — supposed to be a driver for our second vehicle, but he's not good enough, so Hugo will give him lessons, meanwhile I shall drive it. Also he is going to help Benjamin with everything on safari — which will be necessary when we have Phyllis. After the chimps, we take Phyllis to Murcheson — where there are chimps and patas monkeys, then to another park, then to see some colobus, then we take Michael to Mombasa to catch a boat, because Hugo has to photograph Sable antelope down near the coast. Then Phyllis leaves East Africa, and Hugo settles down on the Serengeti with me. I start analysing in earnest, and he films lions with George, and hyaenas with Hans Kruuk.*

I mustn't write long now. We have to dash a last minute dash into Nairobi for last minute things. Collect various things, and buy some things, and Michael have his hair cut. We have to have lunch with Judge Russell Train — the world wild life man from America. And then depart to get to Namanga to show them the chimp film this evening. Oh — I never said about our flight back from Kigoma. Smoke, smoke, smoke all the way. Poor Mike Richmond had sore eyes — and it made it very bumpy. He didn't dare take his eyes off his panels at all, or one wing went up or down. He is an excellent pilot. You will see the plane at Kigoma airport on next 8mm films. HAVE YOU SEEN THE AMERICAN ONES YET? ALSO, did the Sunday Times thing ever materialize?

Must stop, as Hugo is fussing around and although he's not say-

---

* George was George Schaller. Hans Kruuk was a Dutch scientist studying hyenas in the Serengeti.

ing anything I know he's rar'in to go — or should it be rarin' to go? Anyway, he's anxious to be off!!!!!!!

Will write again from the icy fastness of Ngoro — will be really freezing there. It will be best if you write to 2818 Nairobi and Mike forwards, rather than to Ngorogoro. For one thing, we can contact him about changes by means of the radio telephone.! What a thought.

Tons and tons of love to all — hear the proofs are done Mum — jolly good show. Dying to read your book.

Jane

Hugo sends his love too. How is your knee Olly? Thanks tons for your letter — will write to you soon. How is Dido? And Figgy?

ILLUSTRATION CREDITS

Illustrations not otherwise credited were provided by the Goodall family.

The manor house in Kent: Dale Peterson
May Day at Oxford: Jane Goodall
Jane dancing with Brian Herne: Brian Herne
Jane Goodall at twenty-three: Brian Herne
Annabelle gets a ride: Jane Goodall
Flo and Flint: Jane Goodall and Hugo van Lawick
Cartoon by Jane Goodall: Jane Goodall
Jane Goodall and Hugo van Lawick: Jane Goodall
Flint reaches out: National Geographic Society
David Greybeard: National Geographic Society

INDEX

No. 7.

The Peak,
Chimpland.
16th May.

Darling Family,

I'm up here waiting for a
gale & subside so that I have a
reasonable chance of hearing anything
worth hearing, or seeing anything to be
seen. It is 4.30, and I had a
very nice time with chimps from
8am - 2.15, so I can't grumble.
Horace and his girls, Sophie and
Sophocles.

I simply don't know where to
begin, telling you about David
Greybeard. He is utterly fantastic.
I think with this moment: I was
staying down to try to take some
pictures of David G. I was expecting
him about 8.30 - 9. I was,
therefore, still reclining in luxury
at 7.30, & Dominic was just
getting my tea — fancy! — early
morning tea! My bed was about
4ft from the palm — David's Palm.
I was under my net, gazing
through it at the grey sky. Suddenly
I heard a rustling. David G.

ALSO BY HÅKAN NESSER

Borkmann's Point

The Return

Mind's Eye

Woman with Birthmark

Woman
with Birthmark

AN INSPECTOR VAN VEETEREN MYSTERY

Håkan Nesser

Translated from the Swedish by Laurie Thompson

PANTHEON BOOKS, NEW YORK

Translation copyright © 2009 by Laurie Thompson

All rights reserved. Published in the United States by Pantheon Books, a division of Random House, Inc., New York.

Pantheon Books and colophon are registered trademarks of Random House, Inc.

Originally published in Sweden as *Kvinna med födelsmärke* by Albert Bonniers Förlag, Stockholm, in 1996. Copyright © 1996 by Håkan Nesser.

Library of Congress Cataloging-in-Publication Data
Nesser, Håkan, [date]
[Kvinna med födelsemärke. English]
Woman with birthmark : an Inspector Van Veeteren mystery / Håkan Nesser ; translated from the Swedish by Laurie Thompson.
p. cm.
Originally published: Stockholm : A. Bonnier, c1996.
ISBN 978-0-375-42504-2
1. Thompson, Laurie, 1938– II. Title.
PT9876.24.E76K8513 2009
839.73'74—dc22   2008032385

www.pantheonbooks.com

Printed in the United States of America

First United States Edition

2 4 6 8 9 7 5 3 1

To Sanna and Johannes

And then, of course, there is a certain type of action that we can never leave behind us, nor buy ourselves free from. Perhaps we can't even beg forgiveness for such deeds.

W. Klimke, therapist

I

December 23–
January 14

I

She felt cold.

The day had started with a promising light snowfall, but as lunchtime approached, the strong wind blowing off the sea had turned the precipitation into diagonal, driving rain of the very worst kind. It chilled you to the bone, forced the stall owners down by the harbor to shut up shop hours earlier than usual, and in Zimmermann's bar they were serving about three times as many hot toddies as on a normal December day.

To make matters worse, the cemetery was facing southwest, on a gently sloping, treeless hillside, totally exposed to every kind of weather and wind. When the little group finally reached the newly dug, muddy grave, a thought struck her.

At least it was sheltered down there. At least you didn't have to take the wind and this damned rain into the grave with you. Every cloud has its silver lining.

The clergyman snuffled, and his accomplice—or whatever you should call him—struggled with the umbrella. Tried to make it cover both the man in black and himself, but the gusts were capricious and the correct angle shifted from second to second. The bearers dug their heels into the soaking wet soil and started to lower the coffin. Her bouquet on the lid already looked a mess. Like a dollop of vegetables that had boiled for too long. One of the bearers slipped but managed to regain his balance. The clergyman blew his nose and started to read the liturgy. His accomplice fumbled with the spade. The rain grew even worse.

It was typical. She couldn't help acknowledging that as she clenched her fists in the pockets of her overcoat and stamped on the ground in an attempt to warm up her feet.

Absolutely goddamned typical. A ceremony just as shambolic and undignified as the rest of the dead woman's life had been. So she couldn't even be granted a decent burial. The day before Christmas Eve. A patch of blue sky, or the light snowfall lasting into the afternoon—would that have been too much to ask? Would that have been too much trouble?

Of course it would. Her mother's life had been littered with defeats and messy failures; to be honest, all this was both fitting and expected, and she felt herself having to bite her lip so as not to burst out crying.

A totally consistent and logical conclusion, then. In the same key all the way through. And no crying. Not yet, in any case.

For some inscrutable reason her mother had urged just that. Don't cry. Whatever you do, don't stand there bawling at my funeral. Tears have never been any use in any circumstances, believe you me. I've sobbed bucketfuls in my lifetime. No, do something, my girl! Take action! Do something magnificent that I can applaud up there in heaven!

She had squeezed her daughter's hand with both her own chafed, weak ones as she said that. Fixed her with her dying eyes, and it had been clear that for once, this was serious. For once, her mother was begging her to do something; it was a bit late and the wording was hardly crystal clear, but there could be no doubt about what she meant. Or could there?

Half an hour later she was dead.

Do something, my girl. Take action!

The clergyman fell silent. Looked at her from under the dripping umbrella, and she realized that he was expecting her to do something as well. What? It wasn't easy to tell. It was only the second time in her life that she had attended a funeral; the first time, she had been eight or nine years old, and she was there for her mother's sake on that occasion as well. She took several cautious steps forward. Stopped a safe distance short of the grave to avoid the farce of slipping and joining her mother down below. Bowed her head and closed her eyes. Clasped her hands in front of her.

I expect the bastards think I'm standing here praying, she thought. Or at least, they're pretending to. Goodbye, Mom! You can rely on me. I know what I have to do. You'll be able to warm the palms of your hands up there with the angels.

And so it was all over. The clergyman and his accomplice each held out a cold, damp hand to shake hers, and ten minutes later she was standing under the leaking roof of a bus shelter, longing for a hot bath and a glass of red wine.

Or a brandy. Or both.

One mourner, she thought. At my mother's interment there was only a single mourner. Me. So that was that.

But I sincerely hope that several more will be mourning soon.

That was quite nicely put, and as she stood there fighting against the cold and the damp and her desire to cry, it was as if those words had lit a small flame inside her. Set fire to something combustible at last, something that slowly began to heat up all the old frozen and stiff lumber lying around in her soul.

A conflagration, no less, that soon enough would spread, consuming others in its flames . . . making them fear this sea of anger that in due course would surround and destroy them all!

She smiled at that thought as well. Something she had read, presumably; or perhaps it really was true what one of her very first lovers had maintained. That she had a gift. A sort of aptitude for poetry and putting things into words.

For the truth, and passion. Or suffering, perhaps. Yes, that was more like it. She had suffered all right. Not as much as her mother, of course, but she had endured her due share. And more.

I'm freezing cold, she thought. Come on, you fucking bus!

But there was no sign of the bus. No sign of anything, and it dawned on her as she stood stamping her feet in the gathering dusk in the leaky shelter that this was exactly what her whole life had been like. This was the ideal image for what it was all about.

Standing waiting for something that never came. A bus. A good man. A proper job.

A chance. Just one damned chance to make something sensible of her life.

Standing waiting in the darkness and wind and rain. And now it was too late.

She was twenty-nine years of age, and it was too late already.

My mother and I, she thought. One mourning at the side of the grave. The other lying in it. We might just as well have changed places. Or lain down beside each other. Nobody would have minded. If it weren't for . . .

And she felt the flame set fire to her resolve once more, and everything inside her welled up and filled her with warmth. A strong, almost tangible warmth, which caused her to smile in the midst of her grief and clench her fists even harder deep down in her overcoat pockets.

She took one final look at the long bend but there was no trace of a headlight. So she turned her back on it all and started walking toward the town.

2

Christmas came and went.

New Year's came and went. Rain shower followed rain shower, and the blue-gray days passed in a state of monotonous indifference. Her doctor's certificate ran out, and she had to sign on for unemployment benefits. There was no noticeable difference. Off work from what? Unemployed from what?

Her telephone had been cut off. When she received the warning in October, she had purposely failed to pay the bill, and now the company had taken action. The wheels had turned.

It was pleasant. Not only did she not have to meet people, she avoided having to listen to them as well. Not that there would have been all that many for her to put up with. There was no denying that her circle of acquaintances had shrunk recently. During the first fourteen days after the funeral she spoke to a grand total of two persons. Heinzi and Gergils; she had met both of them by accident in the square, and within thirty seconds they had both tried to cadge something off her. Heroin or a bit of hash, or a bottle of wine, at least—for fuck's sake, surely she had something to give to an old mate? A shower, then, and a quick screw, perhaps?

Only Gergils had gone so far as to suggest that, and for half a minute she had toyed with the idea of letting him have her for half an hour. Just for the pleasure of possibly infecting him as well.

But, of course, it couldn't be guaranteed that he would get it. On the contrary. The chances were small. It wasn't easy to catch it, despite all the stories you heard; even the doctors had stressed that. But on this occasion she had managed to hold herself in check. Besides, there were quite a few people who had survived whose behavior entailed a much higher risk factor than hers.

Risk factor? What a stupid expression. Hadn't she spent the whole of her life taking one damned risk after another? But it was no doubt true what Lennie used to tell her many years ago: if you were born on the edge of a barrel of shit, you had to accept the likelihood of falling into it now and again. That was only to be expected. The trick was clambering out again.

And, of course, eventually you didn't. Didn't clamber out. You just lay down in the shit, and then it was only a matter of time.

But that was old hat now. Thought about and fretted about and left behind. October had changed a lot of things. And her mother's death, of course.

Or rather, her mother's story. The words that came tumbling out of her like a thirty-year-old miscarriage the week before her time was up. Yes, if the news she had been given in October was what made her want to be alone, her mother's story did the rest. Gave her strength and determination. Something had suddenly become easier. Clearer and more definite for the first time in her troubled life. Her willpower and drive had grown, and her drug addiction had ebbed away and died without her needing to exert herself in the least. No more of the heavy stuff. A bit of hash and a bottle of wine now and again, no more, but most important of all—no more of that accursed and desperate contact with all the rest of them perched on the edge of the shit barrel. It had been easier to shake them off than she could ever have suspected, just as easy as the drugs, in fact, and of course each of those developments had assisted the other. Maybe what all the quacks and counselors had been droning on about all those years was actually true: it all came down to your own inner strength. That alone, nothing else.

Courage and resolve, in other words.

And the mission, she added.

The mission? She certainly hadn't been clear about that from the start; it sneaked its way in later on. Difficult to pin it down precisely, and just as difficult to say where it came from. Was it her mother's decision, or her own? Not that it mattered all that much, but it was interesting to think about.

About cause and responsibility, things like that. About revenge, and the importance of putting things right. The fact that her mother had ten thousand guilders hidden away came as a surprise and also, of course, a helping hand. It was a nice round figure, and no doubt would come in very useful.

Had done already, in fact. On January 12 she had spent two thousand of it; but it wasn't wasted money. In a drawer of her bedside table she had a list of names and addresses and a fair amount of other information. She had a gun, and she had a furnished room waiting for her in Maardam. What more could she ask for?

More courage? Resolve? A pinch of good luck?

The night before she set off she prayed to a very much unspecified god, asking him to stand by her and grant her those precise things, and when she turned off the bedside light she had a strong feeling that there wasn't very much in this world capable of placing obstacles in her way.

Nothing at all, probably. That night she slept in a fetal position, warm and with a smile on her face, and in the knowledge that she had never felt less vulnerable in all her life.

3

Finding a room was one of the things that had not taken much effort. She had simply answered an ad in *Neuwe Blatt*—but when she saw the result, she realized she could hardly have done better.

Mrs. Klausner had been widowed early—at the dawn of the 1980s, in her middle-aged prime—when her husband the major had a sudden and unexpected heart attack. Instead of selling her charming old two-story house in the Deijkstraa district, she had adapted and refurbished it to suit her new circumstances. She retained possession of the ground floor together with the garden, two cats, and four thousand books. The upper floor, comprising the old children's rooms and guest bedrooms, had been transformed into studio apartments: four rooms in all, each with running water and limited cooking facilities. Plus a shared bathroom and shower room in the hall. The staircase was supplied with its own entrance in a gable wall, at a safe distance from Mrs. Klausner's bedroom; and even if she had the occasional butterfly in her stomach when she launched her new enterprise, she soon found she could congratulate herself on an excellent setup. She let rooms only to single women, and never for more than six months at a time. Most of them were students in the latter stages of their courses in the Faculties of Law and Medicine who needed peace and quiet for their studies. Or nurses on short sup-plementary courses at the nearby Gemejnte Hospital. Two or more of the rooms were often vacant during the summer, but she earned enough during the rest of the year to satisfy her needs. Major Klausner would have had nothing against the reor-ganization, she knew that, and sometimes when she was waiting in line at the bank to pay in the rents she had received, she thought she could see him nodding approvingly up there, on the final battlefield.

As agreed, the new tenant moved in on Sunday, January 14, the evening before she was due to begin a three-month course for finance managers at the Elizabeth Institute. She paid for six weeks in advance, and after receiving the necessary instructions (explained in a most friendly manner and lasting less than a minute), she took possession of the red room. Mrs. Klausner knew the importance of respecting her tenants' privacy: as long as she was not disturbed in her reading or during the night, and they didn't fly at each other's throats, she found no reason to interfere in whatever they got up to. Everything was based on unspoken mutual respect, and so far—after thirteen years in the business—she had not experienced any serious disappointments or setbacks.

People are good, she used to tell herself. They treat us as we treat them.

There was a mirror hanging over the little sink in the kitchen alcove, and when she had finished unpacking her bags she stood in front of it for a couple of minutes and contemplated her new face.

She had not changed much, but the effect was astounding.

With her hair cut short and dyed brown, with no makeup and wearing round, metal-framed spectacles, she suddenly looked like a librarian or a bored handicrafts teacher. Nobody would have recognized her, and just for a moment—as she stood there making faces and trying out angles—she had the distinct feeling that she was somebody else.

New features and a new name. A new town and a mission that only six months ago would have seemed to her like the ravings of a lunatic, or a bad joke.

But here she was. She tried one more time—the last one?—to see if she could find any trace of doubt or uncertainty, but no matter how deep the soundings she made into her soul, all she came up against was solid rock. Solid and unyielding ground, and it was clear to her that it was time to begin.

Begin in earnest. Her list was complete in every respect, and even if three months can be quite a long period, there was no reason to mark time in the early stages. On the contrary: every name required its own meticulous planning, its own specific treatment, and it was better to make full use of the early days and avoid being under stress toward the end. Once she had started on her mission, and people had caught on to what was happening, she would naturally need to be on the alert for problems. Everybody would be on the lookout—the general public, the police, her opponents.

That was the way it had to be. It was all dictated by the circumstances.

But she was already convinced that she would not have any worries. No insurmountable ones, at least, and as she lay on her bed that first night and examined her gun, she could feel that the scale of the challenge would doubtless make the allure that little bit stronger.

That little bit more exciting and more enjoyable.

I'm crazy, she thought. Completely and utterly mad.

But it was a daring and irresistible madness. And who could blame her, after all?

She looked at the list of names again. Studied them one by one. She had already decided who would be first, but even so, she pretended to reconsider it one more time.

Then she breathed a sigh of satisfaction and drew two thick red lines around his name. Lit a cigarette and started to think through how she would go about it.

II

January 18–19

4

It was not a part of Ryszard Malik's normal routine to drink two large whiskeys before dinner, but he had a good reason to do so today.

Two reasons, in fact. The contract he had long been negotiating with Winklers had collapsed, despite two hours of intensive telephone discussions during the afternoon, and when he finally left the office he discovered that a sudden cold snap had transformed the streets, soaking wet after all the rain, into an ice rink. If it had been exclusively up to him, there would, of course, have been no problem—not for nothing did he have thirty years of blameless driving behind him, and he had often driven on slippery roads. But he wasn't the only one out. The rush-hour traffic from the center of town to the residential districts and garden suburbs was still in evidence. It happened just before the roundabout in Hagmaar Allé: a white, Swiss-registered Mercedes going much too fast slid into the back of his Renault. He swore under his breath, unfastened his safety belt, and got out of the car to survey the damage and argue about what to do next. Right taillight smashed, rather a large dent in the fender, and two deep scratches in the paintwork. Various unlikely excuses, some forced politeness, an exchange of business cards and insurance-company details—it all took a considerable time, and it was over forty minutes later when he was able to continue his journey home.

Malik didn't like coming home late. Admittedly, his wife rarely had dinner ready before seven, but an hour, preferably an hour and a half, with the newspaper and a whiskey and water in his study was something he was reluctant to miss.

Over the years it had become a habit, and a necessary one at that. A sort of buffer between work and a wife growing increasingly conscious of her importance.

Today there was time for only a quarter of an hour. And it was to go some way toward compensating for the loss—of both the precious minutes and his taillight—that he skipped the newspaper and devoted all his attention to the whiskey instead.

Well, not quite all. There were those telephone calls as well. What the devil was it all about? "The Rise and Fall of Flingel Bunt." What the hell was the point of phoning somebody and then playing an old sixties hit? Over and over again.

Or once a day, at any rate. Ilse had answered twice, and he had taken one of the calls. It had started the day before yesterday. He hadn't mentioned to her that whoever it was had called again yesterday evening. . . . No need to worry her unnecessarily. No need to tell her that he recognized the tune, either.

Quite early in the sixties, if he remembered rightly. The Shadows. 'Sixty-four or 'sixty-five, presumably. Irrelevant anyway: the question was what the hell it signified, if it signified anything at all. And who was behind it? Perhaps it was just a loony. Some out-of-work screwball who had nothing better to do than to phone decent citizens and stir up a bit of trouble.

It was probably no more than that. Obviously, one could consider bringing in the police if it continued, but so far at least it was no more than a minor irritation. Which was bad enough on a day like today.

A pain in the ass, as Wolff would have put it. A scratch in the paintwork or a shattered taillight.

There came his wife's call. The food was on the table, it seemed. He sighed. Downed the rest of the whiskey and left his study.

"It's nothing to get worked up about."

"I'm not getting worked up."

"Glad to hear it."

"You always think I'm getting worked up. That's typical of the way you regard women."

"All right. Let's talk about something else. This sauce is not bad at all. What have you put in it?"

"A drop of Madeira. You've had it fifty times before. I listened for longer today."

"Really?"

"A minute, at least. There was nothing else."

"What else did you expect there to be?"

"What else did I expect there to be? A voice, of course. Most people who make a phone call have something to say."

"I expect there's a natural explanation."

"Oh yes? What, for example? Why ring somebody and just play a piece of music?"

Malik took a large sip of wine and thought that one over.

"Well," he said. "A new radio station, or something of the sort."

"That's the silliest thing I've ever heard."

He sighed.

"Are you sure it was the same song both times?"

She hesitated. Stroked her brow with her index finger, the way she did when a migraine attack was in the offing.

"I think so. The first time, I put the phone down after only a few seconds. Like I said."

"Don't worry about it. It's bound to be just a mistake."

"A mistake? How could that be a mistake?"

Hold your tongue, he thought. Stop nagging, or I'll throw this glass of wine in your face!

"I don't know," he said. "Let's drop the subject. I had a little accident today."

"An accident?"

"Nothing serious. Somebody skidded into me from behind."

"Good Lord! Why didn't you say something?"

"It was a minor thing. Nothing to speak of."

"Nothing to speak of? You always say that. What shall we speak about then? You tell me. We receive some mysterious telephone calls, but we should just ignore them. You have a car accident, and you don't think it's even worth mentioning to your wife. That's so typical. What you mean, of course, is that we should just sit here every evening without saying a word. That's the way you want it. Quiet and peaceful. I'm not even worth talking to anymore."

"Rubbish. Don't be silly."

"Maybe there's a connection."

"Connection? What the hell do you mean?"

"The telephone calls and the car crash, of course. I hope you took his number?"

My God, Malik thought, and gulped down the rest of the

wine. There's something wrong with her. Pure paranoia. No wonder the hotel wanted to sack her.

"Have you heard anything from Jacob?" He tried to change the subject, but realized his error the moment the words left his mouth.

"Not for two weeks. He's too much like you, it would never occur to him to phone us. Unless he needed some money, of course."

The hell he would, Malik thought, and hoped that his grim inner smile wouldn't shine through to the outside. He had spoken to their son a couple of times in the last few days, without having to shell out a single guilder. And although he would never admit it, he regarded his son's passive distancing of himself from his mother as a healthy development, and a perfectly natural one.

"Ah well," he said, wiping his lips with a napkin. "That's the way young people are nowadays. Is there anything worth watching on the box tonight?"

When the fifth call came, he was lucky enough to be able to answer it himself. Ilse was still watching the Hungarian feature movie on Channel 4, and when he answered it on the bedroom extension he was able to tell the anonymous disturber of the peace to go to hell in no uncertain terms, without a risk of her hearing him and guessing what it was about. First he established that it really was "The Rise and Fall of Flingel Bunt"; then he listened to it for half a minute before delivering a series of threats that could hardly be misunderstood before replacing the receiver.

However, he had no way of knowing if there really was somebody listening at the other end.

Maybe there was somebody there. Maybe there wasn't.

But that tune? he thought. Was there something? . . . But it was just a faint shadow of a suspicion, and no clear memories at all cropped up in his somewhat overexcited brain.

"Who was that?" asked his wife as he settled down again on the sofa in the television room.

"Jacob," he lied. "He said to say hello to you, and didn't want to borrow a single nickel."

5

On Friday he made a detour past Willie's garage to discuss repairs to his car. Having been guaranteed absolutely that it would be ready for collection by that evening, he left it there and went the rest of the way to his office on foot. He arrived fifteen minutes late, and Wolff had already gone out—to negotiate a contract with a newly opened hamburger restaurant, he gathered. He sat down at his desk and began to work his way through the day's mail, which had just been brought in by Miss deWiijs. As usual, most of it was complaints about one thing or another, and confirmation of contracts and agreements that had already been fixed on the telephone or by fax, and after ten minutes he realized that he was sitting there humming that confounded tune.

He broke off in annoyance. Went out to fetch some coffee from Miss deWiijs's office instead, and became involved in a conversation about the weather, which soon came around to focus on four-footed friends. Cats in general, and Miss deWiijs's Siamese, Melisande de laCroix, in particular. Despite the regular ingestion of contraceptive pills and despite the fact that the frail creature hardly ever dared to stick her nose outside the door, for the last couple of weeks she had been displaying more and more obvious signs of being pregnant.

There was only one other cat in the whole of the block where Miss deWiijs lived—a thin, arthritic old tom that as far as she knew was being taken care of by a family of Kurdish immigrants, although he preferred to spend the waking hours of day and night outdoors. At least when the weather was decent. How he had managed to get wind of the shy little Madame Melisande de laCroix was a mystery, to say the least.

A mystery and an absurdity. To be sure, Miss deWiijs had not yet been to the vet's and had the pregnancy confirmed. But all the signs pointed very clearly in that direction. As already indicated, and unfortunately.

Malik liked cats. Once upon a time they had owned two, but Ilse hadn't really been able to put up with them, especially the female, and when they discovered that Jacob was apparently allergic to furry animals, they had disposed of them by means of two rational and guaranteed painless injections.

He liked Miss deWiijs as well. She radiated a sort of languid feminine warmth that he had learned to prize highly over the years. The only thing that never ceased to surprise him was that men had left her unmarried and untouched. Or rather, there was nothing to suggest that this was not the case; and the indications were that she would stay that way. She would be celebrating her fortieth birthday next May, and Malik and Wolff had already begun discussing how best that occasion should be celebrated. Needless to say, it was not a day that could be allowed to pass unnoticed. Miss deWiijs had been working for them for more than ten years, and both Malik and Wolff knew that she was probably more vital to the survival of the firm than they were.

"What are you thinking of doing if you're right about the state of your cat?" he asked.

Miss deWiijs shrugged, setting her heavy breasts a-bobbing under her sweater.

"Doing?" she said. "There's not much else one can do but let nature take its course. And hope there won't be too many of them. Besides, Siamese cats are easy to find homes for, even if they are only half-breeds."

Malik nodded and finished off his cup of coffee. Clasped his hands behind his neck and thought about what else needed to be done today.

"I'll drive out to Schaaltze," he decided. "Tell Wolff I'll be back after lunch."

It was only when he was in the elevator on his way down that he remembered he didn't have a car. He recited an elaborate curse under his breath, wondering how he could be so absentminded, and considered briefly going back up. Then he recalled that it was possible to get there by bus. It was unusual for him to travel by public transportation nowadays, but he knew that Nielsen and Vermeer sometimes used to travel in on the Number 23 from Schaaltze, and if the bus goes one way, surely it must go the other way as well?

The bus stop was on the other side of the shopping center and post office, and he was about halfway there when he had the feeling that somebody was following him.

Or observing him, at the very least. He stopped dead and

looked around. The sidewalk wasn't exactly teeming with pedestrians, but nevertheless, there were enough of them to prevent him from detecting anybody behaving oddly. He thought for a second or two, then continued toward the bus stop. Perhaps he was just imagining things, and in any case, it was probably best not to make it too obvious that he suspected something. He quickly convinced himself of this, lengthening his stride and trying to keep all his senses on the alert.

He was amazed by his reaction, and how quickly and almost naturally he'd accepted the feeling and the suspicion. As if it were an everyday occurrence, almost.

Why on earth should anybody be following him? Ryszard Malik! Who the hell could be interested in such an everyday and insignificant person?

He shook his head and thrust his hands into his overcoat pockets.

What kind of stupid imagining was this? Ilse must have infected him with her silly nonsense, that must be it!

And yet . . . he knew it was true. Sensed it, rather. There was somebody behind him. Not far away. Somebody dogging his steps. Perhaps it was somebody who'd walked past him, he thought, and then turned around and started following him, some ten meters or so behind. You would be bound to notice such a maneuver in some vague, intuitive way. . . . Or had there been somebody standing in the foyer when he went out into the street? Somebody who'd been waiting for him? Good God, that would be worrying.

He came to the bus stop and paused. The bus had evidently just left, as there was nobody waiting. He backed into the little shelter and began surreptitiously watching passing pedestrians. Some were walking fast and purposefully, others more slowly.

Occasionally somebody would stop and step into the shelter beside him to wait for the bus, shielded to some extent from the wind. Stand there with that half-friendly, half-distant air that strangers on the same mission usually adopt. A young man with a black-and-yellow-striped scarf that was almost brushing the ground. Two old women in threadbare coats, carrying shopping bags. A slightly younger woman in a blue beret, with a slim leather briefcase. A boy in his early teens with some kind of facial tic, scratching his groin continually without taking his hands out of his pockets.

Not especially likely candidates, he had to admit, none of them. When the bus came, everybody got on apart from the two old women. He let the others go first, paid somewhat awkwardly, and managed to find an empty seat right at the back.

So that he wouldn't have anybody behind him, he told himself.

During the journey, which took barely twenty minutes— more or less the same as by car, he noted with a degree of surprise—his mind indulged in an unequal struggle with refractory and importunate questions.

What the hell am I doing? asked his thoughts, soberly. This is utter lunacy! Madness!

But there is something, insisted his emotions. Don't try to convince yourself otherwise.

I'm going crazy, maintained his thoughts. My life is so damned monotonous that I'll clutch at anything that might introduce a bit of excitement.

You are in danger, countered his emotions. You know you are, but you daren't admit it.

He looked out the filthy window. The Richter Stadium with its pompous clock tower was just passing by.

Why do my thoughts say "I" and my emotions "you"? he asked himself, confused. No doubt it has something to do with my macho syndrome, or so Ilse would . . .

Then he suddenly realized that he was sitting there humming that tune again under his breath.

"The Rise and Fall of Flingel Bunt." There was something about it. About that as well. Something quite specific. A memory of something he'd taken part in that was now drifting under the dark surface of the well of forgetfulness, without his being able to pin it down.

Until he got off the bus and was on his way across the street to the factory. Then it struck him, and as it did so he realized that he would do well not to dismiss suspicions and threats out of hand in the near future.

That was as far as Ryszard Malik's imagination and powers of insight stretched; but as his son would say afterward, the less he knew and suspected, the better, no doubt.

And what happened to Melisande de laCroix's presumed pregnancy and Miss deWiijs's fortieth birthday were questions that, as far as Ryszard Malik was concerned, also disappeared rapidly into the dark void of the future.

6

Although it was a year and a half since Ilse Malik had resigned from her job at Konger's Palace, she still hadn't managed to develop much of a social life. She played tennis with an old girlfriend once a week—on Tuesday afternoons. She went to visit her sister in Linzhuisen when her husband was away on business, which was at least once a month. She was a member of the association Save Our Rain Forests, and every spring and fall she used to sign on for one of the evening study circles but she always left after the first meeting.

And that was all—apart from the season ticket for the theater that all the hotel employees were given and which she still made use of even though she was, strictly speaking, no longer entitled to it.

But nobody wanted to be strict, and this particular Friday (they always went on the Friday after the premiere) she was going to see *A Doll's House*. She didn't know how many times she'd seen it already, but it was one of her favorites, and it would have taken a lot to keep her from going.

Perhaps there might be a glass of wine and a bite of cheese afterward, and a chat with Bernadette, the only one of her former colleagues with whom she had had and still had any kind of close contact.

As it turned out, she had more than just one glass of wine. The part of Nora had been played exceedingly well by a young and very promising actress on loan from the Burgtheater in Aarlach, and a new managing director had taken over at the hotel less than a month before. There was much to talk about. When Ilse Malik clambered into a taxi outside Kraus a few minutes after half past eleven (Bernadette lived close by, and preferred a short walk and a breath of night air), she felt unusually contented with the evening and with her existence in general, and promptly started a conversation with the cabbie about movies and plays. Unfortunately it ebbed out after a minute or so, when it transpired that he hadn't set foot inside a theater since having been forced to attend a play by an overzealous drama teacher at college more than thirty-five years before. Of all the movies he had lapped up in recent years, he hadn't come across a single one that could measure up to *The Creature from the Black Lagoon*.

In any case, shortly after twenty minutes to twelve he pulled up outside the Maliks' house in Leufwens Allé—the temperature had risen by some five degrees, thank goodness, and the roads were good. Ilse paid, and added a generous tip, rounding it up to fifteen guilders despite the cabbie's distressing lack of culture, and got out of the car.

The house was in darkness, which surprised her somewhat. Malik seldom went to bed before midnight, especially on a Friday night when he had free run of the place. There wasn't even a light on in his study upstairs; but of course, it was possible he was sitting in the darkened TV room, which was at the back facing the garden.

But the fact that he'd switched the light off in the hall when he knew that she hadn't come home yet was sheer stupidity. She made a mental note to tell him so as she fumbled in her purse for her keys. He didn't normally lock the outside door when she was out, but something told her he'd done so this evening.

At least, that's the way she told herself she had been thinking. Later.

Afterward. When she was trying to relive what had happened, and when everything was in chaos and one big black hole.

She inserted her key into the lock. Turned it and found to her surprise that the door wasn't in fact locked. Opened it. Reached out her hand and switched on the light in the hall.

He was lying just inside the door. On his back with his feet almost on the doormat. His white shirt was dark red, as was the normally light-colored pine floor. His mouth was wide open, and his eyes were staring intently at a point somewhere on the ceiling. His left arm was propped against the little mahogany chest of drawers used to store gloves and scarves, looking as if he had put his hand up in school to answer a question. One of the legs, the right one, of his gray gabardine trousers had slid up almost as far as his knee and exposed that ugly birthmark that looked like a little crocodile—she had been so fascinated by it when they were engaged. By the side of his right hand, half-clenched, next to the shoe rack, was the *Telegraaf,* folded to reveal a half-solved crossword puzzle. A fly was buzzing around his head, evidently unaware that it was January and that instead of being there, it ought to have been hidden away in some dark crack, asleep for at least three more months.

She registered all this while standing with her keys dangling between her thumb and index finger. Then she closed the door behind her. She suddenly felt dizzy and automatically opened her mouth to gasp for more air, but it wasn't enough. It was too late. Without a sound she fell headfirst, diagonally over her husband, hitting her eyebrow against the sharp edge of the shoe rack. Her own warm, light-colored blood started trickling down to mingle with his, cold and congealed.

Sometime later she came around. Tried in vain to shake some life into her husband, and eventually managed to crawl five more meters into the house, staining the floor, carpets, and walls with blood, and phoned for an ambulance.

It was only after it had arrived and the crew established what had happened that the police were called. By then it was six minutes past one, and it was half an hour after that before the real police work got under way, when Detective Inspector Reinhart and his assistant Jung arrived at the crime scene with forensic technicians and a police doctor. By then Ilse Malik had lost consciousness again, this time as the result of an injection administered by the older and more experienced of the two ambulance men, with a modicum of necessary force.

By this time Ryszard Malik had been dead for more than five hours, and when Inspector Reinhart announced in some irritation that "we're not going to solve this shitty mess before dawn, gentlemen," nobody even raised an eyebrow in protest.

III

January 20–29

7

He could have sworn that he'd disconnected the phone before going to bed, but what was the point of swearing? The telephone—the devil's own invention—was ensconced on his bedside table and was intent on etching its blood-soaked sound waves onto his cerebral cortex.

Or however you might prefer to express it.

He opened one reluctant eye and glared at the confounded contraption in a vain attempt to shut it up. It kept on ringing even so. Ring after ring carved its way through his dawn-gray bedroom.

He opened another eye. The clock on the aforementioned table indicated 7:55. Who in hell's name had the nerve to wake him up on a Saturday morning when he wasn't on duty, he wondered. Who?

In January.

If there was a month he hated, it was January—it went on forever with rain or snow all day long, and a grand total of half an hour's sunshine.

There was only one sane way of occupying oneself at this lugubrious time of year: sleeping. Period.

He stretched out his left hand and lifted the receiver.

"Van Veeteren."

"Good morning, Chief Inspector."

It was Reinhart.

"Why the flaming hell are you ringing to wake me up at half past five on a Saturday morning? Are you out of your mind?"

But Reinhart sounded as incorruptible as a traffic warden.

"It's eight o'clock. If you don't want to be contacted, and refuse to buy an answering machine, you can always pull out the plug. If you'd like to listen, Chief Inspector, I can explain how you—"

"Shut up, Inspector! Get to the point!"

"By all means," said Reinhart. "Dead body in Leufwens Allé. Stinks of murder. One Ryszard Malik. The briefing's at three o'clock."

"Three?"

"Yes, three o'clock. What do you mean?"

"I can get from here to the police station in twenty minutes. You could have phoned me at twelve."

Reinhart yawned.

"I was thinking of going to bed for a bit. I've just left there. Been at it since half past one. . . . I thought you might like to go there and have a look for yourself."

Van Veeteren leaned on his elbow and raised himself to a half-sitting position. Tried to see out through the window.

"What's the weather like?"

"Pouring down, and windy. Fifteen meters a second, or thereabouts."

"Excellent. I'll stay at home. I suppose I might turn up at three, unless my horoscope advises me not to. . . . Who's in charge now?"

"Heinemann and Jung. But Jung hasn't slept for two nights, so he'll probably need some rest soon."

"Any clues?"

"No."

"How did it happen?"

"Shot. But the briefing is at three o'clock, not now. I think it's a pretty peculiar setup. That's why I rang. The address is Leufwens Allé 14, in case you change your mind."

"Fat chance," said Van Veeteren, and hung up.

Needless to say it was impossible to go back to sleep. He gave up at a quarter to nine and went to lie down in the bath instead. Lay there in the half-light and thought back to the previous evening, which he'd spent at the Mephisto restaurant with Renate and Erich.

The former wife and the lost son. (Who had still not returned and didn't seem to have any intention of doing so.) It had been one of Renate's recurrent attempts to rehabilitate her guilty conscience and the family that had never existed, and the result was just as unsuccessful as one might have expected. The conversation had been like walking on thin ice over dark waters. Erich had left them halfway through dessert, giving as an excuse an important meeting with a lady. Then they had sat there, ex-husband and ex-wife, over a cheese board of doubtful quality, going through agonies as they tried to avoid hurting each other any more than necessary. He had seen her into a taxi shortly after midnight and walked all the way home in the pious hope that the biting wind would whip his brain free from all the murky thoughts lurking inside it.

That had failed completely. When he got home he had slumped into an armchair and listened to Monteverdi for an hour, drunk three beers, and not gone to bed until nearly half past one.

A wasted evening, in other words. But typical, that was for sure. Very typical. Mind you, it was January. What else could he have expected?

He got out of the bath. Did a couple of tentative back exercises in front of the bedroom mirror. Dressed, made breakfast.

Sat down at the kitchen table with the morning paper spread out in front of him. Not a word about the murder. Naturally enough. It must have happened as the presses were rolling. . . . Or whatever the presses did nowadays. What was the name of the victim? Malik?

What had Reinhart said? Leufwens Allé? He had a good mind to phone the inspector and ask a few questions, but pricks of conscience from his better self, or whatever it might have been, got the upper hand, and he refrained. He would find out all he needed to know soon enough. No need to hurry. Better to make the most of the hours remaining before the whole thing got under way, perhaps. There hadn't been a murder since the beginning of December, despite all the holidays, and if it really was as Reinhart said, an awkward-looking case, no doubt they would have their hands full for some time to come. Reinhart generally knew what he was talking about. More so than most of them.

He poured himself another cup of coffee, and started studying the week's chess problem. Mate in three moves, which would presumably involve a few complications.

. . .

"All right," said Reinhart, putting down his pipe. "The facts of the case. At six minutes past one this morning, an ambulance driver, Felix Hald, reported that there was a dead body at Leufwens Allé 14. They'd gone there because the woman of the house, Ilse Malik, had phoned for an ambulance. She was extremely confused, and had failed to contact the police even though her husband was as dead as a statue. . . . Four bullet wounds, two in his chest, two below the belt."

"Below the belt?" wondered Inspector Rooth, his mouth full of sandwich.

"Below the belt," said Reinhart. "Through his willy, if you prefer. She'd come home from the theater, it seems, at about midnight or shortly before, and found him lying in the hall, just inside the door. The weapon seems to be a Berenger-75; all four bullets have been recovered. It seems reasonable to suspect that a silencer was used, since nobody heard anything. The victim is fifty-two years old, one Ryszard Malik. Part owner of a firm selling equipment for industrial kitchens and restaurants, or something of the sort. Not in our records, unknown to us, no shady dealing as far as we are aware. Nothing at all. Hmm, is that it, Heinemann, more or less?"

Inspector Heinemann took off his glasses and started rubbing them on his tie.

"Nobody noticed a thing," he said. "We've spoken to the neighbors, but the house is pretty well protected. Hedges, big yards, that sort of thing. It looks as if somebody simply walked up to the door, rang the bell, and shot him when he opened up. There's no sign of a struggle or anything. Malik was alone at home, solving a crossword and sipping a glass of whiskey while his wife was at the theater. And then, it seems the murderer just closed the door and strolled off. Quite straightforward, if you want to look at it from that point of view."

"Sound method," said Rooth.

"That's for sure," said Van Veeteren. "What does his wife have to say?"

Heinemann sighed. Nodded toward Jung, who gave every sign of finding it difficult to stay awake.

"Not a lot," Jung said. "It's almost impossible to get through to her. One of the ambulance men gave her an injection, and that was probably just as well. She woke up briefly this morning. Went on about Ibsen—I gather that's a writer. She'd been to the theater, we managed to get that confirmed by a woman she'd been with . . . a Bernadette Kooning. In any case, she can't seem to grasp that her husband is dead."

"You don't seem to be quite with it either," said Van Veeteren. "How long have you been awake?"

Jung counted on his fingers.

"A few days, I suppose."

"Go home and go to bed," said Reinhart.

Jung stood up.

"Is it okay if I take a taxi? I can't tell the difference between right and left."

"Of course," said Reinhart. "Take two if you need them. Or ask one of the duty officers to drive you."

"Two?" said Jung as he staggered to the door. "No, one should do."

Nobody spoke for a while. Heinemann tried to smooth down the creases in his tie. Reinhart contemplated his pipe. Van Veeteren inserted a toothpick between his lower front teeth and gazed up at the ceiling.

"Hmm," he said eventually. "Quite a story, I must say. Has Hiller been informed?"

"He's away by the seaside," said Reinhart.

"In January?"

"I don't think he intends to go swimming. I've left a message for him in any case. There'll be a press conference at five o'clock; I think it would be best if you take it."

"Thank you," said Van Veeteren. "I'll need only thirty seconds."

He looked around.

"Not much point in allocating much in the way of resources yet," he decided. "When do they say his wife is likely to come around? Where is she, incidentally?"

"The New Rumford Hospital," said Heinemann. "She should be able to talk this afternoon. Moreno's there, waiting."

"Good," said Van Veeteren. "What about family and friends?"

"A son at university in Munich," said Reinhart. "He's on his way here. That's about all. Malik has no brothers or sisters, and his parents are dead. Ilse Malik has a sister. She's also waiting at the Rumford."

"Waiting for what, you might ask?" said Rooth.

"Very true," said Van Veeteren. "May I ask another question, gentlemen?"

"Please do," said Reinhart.

"Why?" said Van Veeteren, taking out the toothpick.

"I've also been thinking about that," said Reinhart. "I'll get back to you when I've finished."

"We can always hope that somebody will turn himself in," said Rooth.

"Hope springs eternal," said Reinhart.

Van Veeteren yawned. It was sixteen minutes past three on Saturday, January 20. The first run-through of the Ryszard Malik case was over.

Münster parked outside the New Rumford Hospital and jogged through the rain to the entrance. A woman in reception dragged herself away from her crochet work and sent him up to the fourth floor, Ward 42; after explaining why he was there and producing his ID, he was escorted to a small, dirt-yellow waiting room with plastic furniture and eye-catching travel posters on the walls. It was evidently the intention to give people the opportunity of dreaming that they were somewhere else. Not a bad idea, Münster thought.

There were two women sitting in the room. The younger one, and by a large margin the more attractive of the two, with a mop of chestnut-brown hair and a book in her lap, was Detective Inspector Ewa Moreno. She welcomed him with a nod and an encouraging smile. The other one, a thin and slightly hunch-backed woman in her fifties, wearing glasses that concealed half her face, was fumbling nervously inside her black purse. He deduced that she must be Marlene Winther, the sister of the woman who had just been widowed. He went up to her and introduced himself.

"Münster, Detective Inspector."

She shook his hand without standing up.

"I realize that this must be difficult for you. Please understand that we are obliged to intrude upon your grief and ask some questions."

"The lady has already explained."

She glanced in the direction of Moreno. Münster nodded.

"Has she come around yet?"

Moreno cleared her throat and put down her book. "She's conscious, but the doctor wants a bit of time with her first. Perhaps we should . . . ?"

Münster nodded again: they both went out into the corridor, leaving Mrs. Winther on her own.

"In deep shock, it seems," Moreno explained when they had found a discreet corner. "They're even worried about her mental state. She's had trouble with her nerves before, and all this hasn't helped, of course. She's been undergoing treatment for various problems."

"Have you interviewed her sister?"

Moreno nodded.

"Yes, of course. She doesn't seem all that strong either. We're going to have to tiptoe through the tulips."

"Hostile?"

"No, not really. Just a touch of the big-sister syndrome. She's used to looking after little sister, it seems. And evidently she's allowed to."

"But you haven't spoken to her yet? Mrs. Malik, I mean."

"No. Jung and Heinemann had a go this morning, but they didn't seem to get anywhere."

Münster thought for a moment.

"Perhaps she doesn't have all that much to tell?"

"No, presumably not. Would you like me to take her on? We'll be allowed in shortly in any case."

Münster was only too pleased to agree.

"No doubt it would be best for her to talk to a woman. I'll stay in the wings for the time being."

.   .   .

Forty-five minutes later they left the hospital together. Sat down in Münster's car, where Moreno took out her notebook and started going through the meager results of her meeting with Ilse Malik. Münster had spoken to Dr. Hübner—an old, white-haired doctor who seemed to have seen more or less everything—and understood that it would probably be several days before the patient could be allowed to undergo more vigorous questioning. Assuming that would be necessary, that is.

Hübner had called it a state of deep shock. Very strong medicines to begin with, then a gradual reduction. Unable to accept what had happened. Encapsulation.

Not surprising in the circumstances, Münster thought.

"What did she actually say?" he asked.

"Not a lot," said Moreno with a sigh. "A happy marriage, she claimed. Malik stayed at home yesterday evening while she went to see *A Doll's House* at the Little Theater. Left home about half past six, drank a glass of wine with that friend of hers afterward. Took a taxi home. Then she starts rambling. Her husband had been shot and lay in the hall, she says. She tried to help him but could see that it was serious, so she called an ambulance. She must have delayed that for getting on an hour, if I understand the situation rightly. Fell asleep and managed to injure herself too. She thinks her husband is in this same hospital and wonders why she's not allowed to see him. . . . It's a bit hard to know how to handle her: the nurse tried to indicate what had happened, but she didn't want to know. Started speaking about something else instead."

"What?"

"Anything and everything. The play—a fantastic production, it seems. Her son. He hasn't time to come because of his studies, she says. He's training to be a banking lawyer, or something of the sort."

"He's supposed to be arriving about an hour from now," said Münster. "Poor bastard. I suppose the doc had better take a look at him as well."

Moreno nodded.

"He'll be staying with his aunt for the time being. We can talk to him tomorrow."

Münster thought for a moment.

"Did you get any indications of a threat, or enemies, or that kind of thing?"

"No. I tried to discuss such matters, but I didn't get anywhere. I asked her sister, but she had no suspicions at all. Doesn't seem to be hiding anything either. Well, what do we do next, then?"

Münster shrugged.

"I suppose we'd better discuss it on Monday with the others. It's a damned horrific business, no matter which way you look at it. Can I drive you anywhere?"

"Home, please," said Ewa Moreno. "I've been hanging around here for seven hours now. It's time to spend a bit of time thinking about something else."

"Not a bad idea," Münster agreed, and started the engine.

Mauritz Wolff opted to be interviewed at home, an apartment in the canal district with views over Langgraacht and Megsje Bois and deserving the description "gigantic." The rooms were teeming with children of all ages, and Reinhart assumed he must have married late in life—several times, perhaps—as he must surely be well into his fifties. A large and somewhat red-faced man, in any case, with a natural smile that found it difficult not to illuminate his face, even in a situation like this one.

"You're very welcome," he said. "What an awful catastrophe. I'm really shocked, I have to say. I can't take it in."

He shooed away a little girl clinging on to his trouser leg. Reinhart looked around. Wondered if a woman ought to put in an appearance from somewhere or other before long.

"Not a bad apartment you have here," he said. "Is there anywhere we can talk in peace and quiet?"

"Follow me," said Wolff, clearing a way through a corridor to a room that evidently served as a library and study. He closed the door and locked it. Invited Reinhart to sit down on one of two armchairs by a low smoking table, and sat down heavily in the other one.

"Too awful," he said again. "Have you any idea who might have done it?"

Reinhart shook his head.

"Have you?"

"Not the remotest."

"Did you know him well?"

"Inside out," said Wolff, holding out a pack of cigarettes. Reinhart took one. "Would you like anything to drink, by the way?"

"No thank you. Go on."

"Well, what can I say? We've worked together for sixteen years. Ever since we started the firm. And we knew each other before that."

"Did you mix privately as well?"

"Do you mean families and so on?"

"Yes."

"Well, not really. Not since I met Mette, my new wife, at least. It must be absolutely awful for Ilse. How is she? I've tried to call her . . ."

"Shocked," said Reinhart. "She's still in the hospital."

"I understand," said Wolff, and tried to look diplomatic. Reinhart waited.

"She can be a bit nervy," Wolff explained.

"I've heard it said, yes," said Reinhart. "How's the firm going?"

"So-so. We're keeping going. A good niche, even if it went better in the eighties. But what the hell didn't?"

He started laughing, then checked himself.

"Can it have something to do with work?" Reinhart asked. "The firm, I mean?"

The question was badly formulated, and Wolff didn't understand it.

"Can the murder of Malik have some connection with your business?" Reinhart spelled it out.

Wolff shook his head uncomprehendingly.

"With us? No, how could that be?"

"What do you think it could be, then? Did he have a mistress? Any dodgy business deals? You knew him better than anybody else."

Wolff scratched the back of his head.

"No," he said after a while. "Neither of those things. If Malik had been seeing other women I'd have known about it. And I can't imagine him being involved in anything illegal."

"So he's a model of virtue, then," Reinhart established. "How long have you known him, did you say?"

Wolff tried to work it out.

"We met for the first time about twenty-five years ago . . . that was through work as well. We were both with Gündler and Wein, and eventually we pulled out and started up on our own. There were three of us to start with, but one left after six months."

"What was his name?"

"Merrinck. Jan Merrinck."

Reinhart made a note.

"Can you remember if anything unusual has happened recently? If Malik behaved oddly in some way or other?"

Wolff thought it over.

"No. No, there hasn't been anything as far as I can recall. I'm sorry, but there doesn't seem to be all that much I can help you with."

Reinhart changed tack.

"What was his marriage like?"

"Malik's?"

"Yes."

Wolff shrugged.

"Not all that good. But he hung in there. My first was worse, I reckon. Malik was strong. A confident and reliable man. A bit dry, perhaps. My God, I can't understand who could have done this, Inspector. It must be a madman, don't you think? Some lunatic? Have you got a suspect?"

Reinhart ignored the question.

"What time did he leave the office yesterday?"

"A quarter to five," answered Wolff without hesitation. "A bit earlier than usual as he had to collect his car from a repair shop. I stayed there on my own until half past five."

"And he didn't behave unusually in any way?"

"No. I've said that already."

"This Rachel deWiijs, who works for you. What have you to say about her?"

"Rachel? A treasure. Pure gold, through and through. Without her we wouldn't survive for more than six months. . . ." He bit his lip and drew at his cigarette. "But everything has changed now, of course. Hell."

"So Malik didn't have anything going with her, then?"

"Malik and Rachel? No, you can bet your life that he didn't."

"Really?" said Reinhart. "Okay, I'll take you at your word, then. What about you yourself? Did you have any reason to want him out of the way?"

Wolff's jaw dropped.

"That was the most fucking—"

"There, there, don't get overexcited. You must realize that I have to ask that question. Malik has been murdered, and the fact is that most victims are killed by somebody they know. And you are the person who knew him best, I thought we'd agreed on that already?"

"He was my business partner, for Christ's sake. One of my best friends . . ."

"I know. But if you had a motive even so, it's better for you to tell us what it is yourself rather than leaving us to find out about it later."

Wolff sat in silence for a while, thinking about that one.

"No," he said eventually. "Why the hell should I want to kill Malik? His share in the firm goes to Ilse and Jacob, and all that will do is to make a mess of everything. You must understand that his death is a shock for me as well, Inspector. I know I sometimes sound a bit brusque, but I'm grieving over his death. I'm missing him as a close friend."

Reinhart nodded.

"I understand," he said. "I think we'll leave it at that for today, but you'll have to count on us turning up again before long. We are very eager to catch whoever did this."

Wolff stood up and flung out his arms.

"Of course. If there's anything I can do to help . . . I'm at your disposal at any time."

"Good," said Reinhart. "If anything occurs to you, let us know. Go back to the kids now. How many have you got, incidentally?"

"Six," said Wolff. "Three from before and three new ones."

"Go forth and multiply, and replenish the earth," said Reinhart. "Isn't it a bit of a strain? Er, looking after them all, I mean."

Wolff smiled and shook his head.

"Not at all. The tipping point is four. After that, it makes no difference if you have seven or seventeen."

Reinhart nodded, and resolved to bear that in mind.

8

In their eagerness to sell a few extra copies to casual readers with nothing better to do over the weekend, the Sunday papers made a meal of the Ryszard Malik murder. Bold-print headlines on billboards and front pages, pictures of the victim (while still alive, smiling) and his house, and a double-page spread in both *Neuwe Blatt* and *Telegraaf*. Detailed and noncommittal, but needless to say they were pitching it right—what the hell did people have to keep them occupied on a damp and windy day in January apart from sitting indoors and lapping up the story of somebody who had suffered even more than they were doing?

Van Veeteren had a subscription to both papers and had no need to stick his nose outside the door in order to buy one. Instead he stayed in all day, reading selected chapters of Rimley's *Famous Chess Games* and listening to Bach. He had paid a brief visit to Leufwens Allé on Saturday evening and established that there was nothing useful for him to do there. The technicians and crime-scene boys had run a fine-tooth comb over both house and garden, and for him to imagine he would be able to find something they'd missed would be to overestimate his abilities. Although it had happened before.

And in any case, it was not even certain that he would need to bother about it. Hiller would no doubt decide when he emerged from the sea on Monday morning; perhaps he would judge it best for Reinhart and Münster to continue pulling the strings. That would be good, he had to admit. A blessing devoutly to be wished, he thought—if he'd been able to choose a month in which to hibernate or to spend in a deep freeze, he would have gone for January without hesitation.

If he could pick two, he would take February as well.

On Monday his car refused to start. Something to do with damp somewhere or other, no doubt. He was forced to walk four blocks before he was able to scramble into a taxi, soaking wet, at Rejmer Plejn; and he was ten minutes late for the run-through.

Reinhart, who was in charge, arrived a minute later, and the whole meeting was not exactly productive.

The forensic side was done and dusted, and had uncovered nothing they didn't know already. Or thought they knew. Ryszard Malik had been shot at some time between half past seven and half past nine on Friday evening, with a 7.65-millimeter Berenger. As none of the neighbors had heard a shot, it could be assumed that the killer had used a silencer.

"How many Berengers are floating around town?" asked Münster.

"Le Houde guesses about fifty," said Rooth. "Anybody can get one in about half an hour if he has a bit of local knowledge. There's no point in starting to look, in any case."

Van Veeteren sneezed and Reinhart carried on describing the wounds, the angles, and similar melancholy details. The murderer had probably fired his gun at a distance of between one and one and a half meters, which could suggest that he hadn't even bothered to step inside first. The door opened inward, and in all probability he'd have been standing ready to shoot the moment Malik opened it. Two shots in the chest, then, each of which would have been fatal—one through the left lung and the other through the aorta. Hence all the blood.

And then two below the belt. From a bit closer.

"Why?" asked Van Veeteren.

"Well, what do you think?" said Reinhart, looking around the table.

Nobody spoke. Heinemann looked down at his crotch.

"A professional job?" asked Münster.

"Eh?" said Reinhart. "Oh, you mean the fatal shots. . . . No, not necessarily. A ten-year-old can shoot accurately with a Berenger from one meter away. Assuming you're ready for a bit of a recoil, that is. It could be anybody. But the shots below the belt ought to tell us something, or what do you think?"

"Yes, sure," said Rooth.

For a few seconds nobody spoke.

"Don't feel embarrassed on my account," said Moreno.

"Could be a coincidence," said Münster.

"There's no such thing as coincidence," said Reinhart. "Only a lack of knowledge."

"So the shots in the chest came first, is that right?" Heinemann asked, frowning.

"Yes, yes," sighed Reinhart. "The other two were fired when he was already lying on the floor—we've explained that already. Weren't you listening?"

"I just wanted to check," said Heinemann.

"It doesn't seem to make much sense, shooting somebody's balls off after you've already killed him," said Rooth. "Seems a bit mad, I'd say. Sick, in a way."

Reinhart nodded and Van Veeteren sneezed again.

"Are you cold, Chief Inspector?" Reinhart wondered. "Shall we ring for a blanket?"

"I'd prefer a hot toddy," grunted Van Veeteren. "Is the forensic stuff all finished? I take it they didn't find any fingerprints or dropped cigarette butts?"

"Not even a grain of dandruff," said Reinhart. "Shall we run through the interviews instead? Starting with the widow?"

"No, starting with the victim," said Van Veeteren. "Even though I assume he didn't have much to say for himself."

"I beg your pardon," said Reinhart, producing a loose sheet of paper from his notebook. "Let's see now. . . . Ryszard Malik was fifty-two years of age. Born in Chadów, but has lived in Maardam since 1960 or thereabouts. Studied at the School of Commerce. Got a job with Gündler & Wein in 1966. In 1979 he started his own firm together with Mauritz Wolff and Jan Merrinck, who jumped ship quite early on—Merrinck, that is. Aluvit F/B, and for God's sake don't ask me what that means. Malik married Ilse, née Moener, in 1968. One son, Jacob, born 1972. He's been reading jurisprudence and economics in Munich for several years now. Anyway, that's about it. . . ."

He put the sheet of paper back where it came from.

"Anything off the record?" Rooth wondered.

"Not a dickie bird," said Reinhart. "So far, at least. He seems to have been a bit of a bore, as far as I can see. Boring marriage, boring job, boring life. Goes on vacation to Blankenbirge or Rhodes. No known interests apart from crossword puzzles and detective novels, preferably bad ones. . . . God only knows why anybody should want to kill him, but apart from that I don't think there are any unanswered questions."

"Excellent," said Van Veeteren. "What about the widow? Surely there's a bit more substance to her, at least?"

Münster shrugged.

"We haven't been able to get much out of her," he said. "She's still confused and doesn't want to accept what's happened."

"She might be hiding something, though," said Heinemann. "It's not exactly anything new to pretend to be mad. I recall a Danish prince. . . ."

"I don't think she is," interrupted Münster. "Neither do the doctors. We know quite a lot about her from her sister and her son, but it doesn't seem to have anything much to do with the murder. A bit pitiful, that's all. Bad nerves. Prescribed drugs on and off. Taken in for therapy once or twice. Finds it hard to get on with people, it seems. Stopped working at Konger's Palace for that reason, although nobody has said that in so many words. . . . As far as we can see, Malik's firm produces enough cash to keep the family going. Or has done until now, I should say."

Van Veeteren bit off the end of a toothpick.

"This is more miserable than the weather," he said, spitting out a few fragments. "Has Moreno anything to add?"

Ewa Moreno smiled slightly.

"The son is rather charming, actually," she said. "In view of the circumstances, that is. He flew the nest early, it seems. Left home as soon as he'd finished high school and he doesn't have much contact with his parents, especially his mother. Only when he needs some money. He admits that openly. Do you want to know about the sister as well?"

"Is there anything for us to sink our teeth into?" asked Reinhart with a sigh.

"No," said Moreno. "Not really. She also has a stable but

rather boring marriage. Works part-time in an old folks' home. Her husband's a businessman. They both have alibis for the night of the murder, and it seems pretty unlikely that either of them could be involved—completely unthinkable, in fact."

All was quiet for a while. Rooth produced a bar of chocolate from his jacket pocket and Heinemann tried to scrape a stain off the table with his thumbnail. Van Veeteren had closed his eyes, and it was more or less impossible to make out if he was awake or asleep.

"Okay," said Reinhart eventually. "There's just one thing I want to know. Who the hell did it?"

"A madman," said Rooth. "Somebody who wanted to test his Berenger and noticed that the lights were on in the house."

"I reckon you've hit the nail on the head," said Heinemann.

"No," said Van Veeteren without opening his eyes.

"Oh, really?" said Reinhart. "How do you know that?"

"By the prickings of my thumb," said Van Veeteren.

"Eh?" said Heinemann. "What the hell does that mean?"

"Shall we go and get some coffee?" suggested Rooth.

Van Veeteren opened his eyes.

"Preferably a hot toddy, as I said before."

Reinhart checked the time.

"It's only eleven," he said. "But I'm all for it. This case stinks like a shit heap."

On the way home from the police station that gloomy Monday, Reinhart stopped off at the Merckx shopping center out at Bossingen. It was really against his principles to buy anything in such a temple of commerce, but he decided to turn a blind eye to the crassness of it all today. He simply didn't feel up to running around from one little shop to the next in the center of town, after rooting about in the unsavory details of Ryszard Malik's background.

Half an hour later he had acquired a lobster, two bottles of wine, and eleven roses. Plus a few other goodies. That would have to do. He left the inferno and a quarter of an hour later went through the front door of his apartment in Zuyderstraat. Put away his purchases in their appointed places, then made a phone call.

"Hi. I've got a lobster, some wine, and some roses. You can have them all if you get yourself here within the next hour."

"But it's Monday today," said the woman at the other end.

"If we don't do anything about it, it'll be Monday for the rest of our lives," said Reinhart.

"Okay," said the woman. "I'll be there."

Winnifred Lynch was a quarter Aboriginal, born in Perth, Australia, but raised in England. After a degree in English language and literature in Cambridge and a failed and childless marriage, she'd landed a post as guest lecturer at Maardam University. When she met Reinhart at the Vox jazz club in the middle of November, she'd just celebrated her thirty-ninth birthday. Reinhart was forty-nine. He went home with her, and they made love (with the occasional pause) for the next four days and nights— but to the surprise of both of them, given their previous experiences, it didn't end there. They carried on meeting. All over the place: at concerts, restaurants, cinemas, and, above all, of course, in bed. As soon as the beginning of December it was clear to Reinhart that there was something special about this slightly brown-skinned, intelligent woman, and when she went back to

England for the Christmas holidays he felt withdrawal symptoms, the like of which he hadn't experienced for nearly thirty years. A sudden reminder of what it was like to miss somebody. Of the fact that somebody actually meant something to him.

The feeling scared him stiff, no doubt about that; it was a warning, but when she came back after three weeks he couldn't help but go to meet her at the airport. Stood waiting with a bunch of roses and a warm embrace, and of course it started all over again.

This Monday was the fifth—or was it the sixth?—occasion since then, and when he thought about it he realized that it could hardly have been more than ten days since she'd returned from vacation.

So you could bet your life that he had something special going.

"Why did you become a policeman?" she asked as they lay back in bed afterward. "You promised you'd tell me one day."

"It's a trauma," he said after a moment's thought.

"I'm human, you know," she said.

"What do you mean by that?"

She didn't answer, but after a while he imagined that he understood.

"All right," he said. "It was a woman. Or a girl. Twenty years old."

"What happened?"

He hesitated, and inhaled deeply twice on his cigarette before answering.

"I was twenty-one. Reading philosophy and anthropology at the university, as you know. We'd been together for two years.

We were going to get married. She was reading languages. One night she was going home after a lecture and was stabbed by a lunatic in Wollerim's Park. She died in the hospital before I got there. It took the police six months to find her killer. I was one of them by that time."

If she has the good sense to say nothing, I want to spend the rest of my life with her, he thought out of the blue.

Winnifred Lynch put her hand on his chest. Stroked him gently for a few seconds, then got up and went to the bathroom.

That does it, then, Reinhart acknowledged in surprise.

Later on, when they'd made love again and then recovered, he couldn't resist asking her a question.

"What do you have to say about a murderer who fired two shots into the groin of a victim who's already lying dead?"

She thought for a moment.

"The victim's a man, I take it?"

"Yes."

"Then I think the murderer is a woman."

Well, I'll be damned, Reinhart thought.

9

The weekend spent by a stormy sea had had an invigorating effect on Police Chief Hiller, and when he returned to work on Monday morning he promptly ordered full steam ahead on the Malik case.

What that meant in practice was no fewer than six officers of the Criminal Investigation Department, with Van Veeteren in charge, plus whatever foot soldiers were around, all of them expected to work full-time on finding the murderer. Senior officers in addition to Van Veeteren were Reinhart, Münster, Rooth, Heinemann, and Moreno. Jung had succumbed to influenza after his succession of sleepless nights and was expected to be sidelined for several more days yet. DeBries was on vacation.

Van Veeteren had nothing in principle against having so many people working on the case. The only problem was that there wasn't very much for them to do that made sense. Trying to trace the murder weapon via narks and contacts in the so-called underworld was a hopeless, Sisyphean task, as he knew. In order to increase the chances of success to twenty-five percent, it would mean assigning a hundred police officers to that job for a hundred days—plus generous overtime money. That kind of staffing was resorted to only when a prime minister had been murdered. It was widely believed by the senior officers that Ryszard Malik had not been prime minister.

That left the wife. Van Veeteren charged Moreno and Heinemann with keeping an eye on Ilse Malik's gradual return to full consciousness and emergence from the shadows. It was decided that they might as well have somebody at the hospital around the clock, seeing as they had enough officers available for once. You could never tell, and if there was anybody who might be able to come up with something relevant to this business, she was the one.

The only other thing to do was to cast bread upon the waters. That was always a possibility. Call on anybody who had any kind of link with Malik—neighbors, business acquaintances, old and new friends—and ask them questions, in accordance with the proven method used with pigs searching for truffles; i.e., if you continue rooting around in the ground for long enough, sooner or later you'll come across something edible.

Van Veeteren gave this less than stimulating task to Rooth and Reinhart to begin with (together with at least three otherwise unoccupied probationers of somewhat variable ability). Van Veeteren was naturally well aware that there was little point in telling Reinhart what to do, but as Hiller was revelling in his newly awakened zeal and wanted a sheet of paper on his brightly polished desk no later than Tuesday afternoon, that is of course what he would get.

Despite a rather troublesome cold, Van Veeteren himself went to play badminton with Münster. This was not mentioned on the list of duties on the document placed before the chief of police.

.   .   .

By the time Hiller's full steam ahead was throttled back on Friday and the team was reduced, due to an armed robbery resulting in a fatality in the suburb of Borowice, nothing much had been discovered. Under the supervision of Rooth and Reinhart—and later Münster as well—some seventy interviews had taken place, and the only outcome was that the image of Malik as a somewhat wooden but also reliable person used to taking responsibility had been fully established. Eighty kilos of decency with two left brains, as Reinhart preferred to express it.

And precisely in line with Dr. Hübner's forecast, Ilse Malik had begun to float up toward the surface of the real world out at the New Rumford, even if it was a somewhat precarious journey. In any case, on Wednesday morning she had finally accepted as fact the murder of her husband. Her memories of that Friday evening consequently became a little more consistent in outline, and she was also able to tell them relatively coherently what she had been doing during the day of the murder. It is true that she occasionally relapsed into attacks of hysterical sobbing, but what more could one expect? Her son, Jacob, was present by her side more or less all the time, and if what Moreno had suggested was true—that he had cut himself loose from his mother's apron strings somewhat precipitately—he now seemed to be making up for his youthful rebellion. Of course, he had little choice but to make the most of the hand fate had dealt him.

On Thursday morning something new crept into Ilse Malik's memory. To be sure, the son maintained immediately—in conversation with Heinemann and Moreno, who had also taken up residence at the bedside, with at least one of them permanently present—that it was a typical example of his mother's paranoia. He had heard about similar things before and recommended strongly that the officers shouldn't pay too much attention to it.

However, what Ilse Malik claimed was that somebody had clearly had designs on her husband's life in the week before that fatal Friday. To begin with, they had received strange telephone calls, on two different occasions: on Tuesday and Thursday, if she remembered rightly. Someone had phoned without saying a word—she had only heard music through the receiver, despite the strong words she had used, especially the second time. Ilse Malik had no idea what the music was and what it was supposed to mean, but she was pretty sure that it had been the same tune both times.

Whether or not her husband had received similar calls she had no idea. He certainly hadn't said anything about it.

The other evidence of a plot to take Ryszard Malik's life was that a white Mercedes had attempted to kill him by crashing into his Renault as he was on his way home from work. For want of anything else to follow up, this information was also checked; but in view of the relatively slight damage done to Malik's car, both Heinemann and Moreno decided that the suspicions had no foundation in fact. The owner of the Mercedes in question was a sixty-two-year-old professor of limnology from Geneva, and when they contacted the Swiss police they found no reason to suspect that he might have had murderous intentions when he skidded into Malik's rear end.

As for the rest of Mrs. Malik's revelations, they were mainly a distinctly humdrum description of a humdrum life and marriage, and in view of the changed circumstances with regard to staffing, Van Veeteren decided on Friday to cancel the hospital watch. By this time both Heinemann and Moreno were so bored by the job they had been given that they both volunteered to join the bank-robbery team, which was being led by Reinhart, who was also released from the Malik case—for the time being, at least. Jung and Rooth were also transferred to the newly established team, despite strong objections, especially from the latter, to the prospect of having to work over the weekend.

Which left Van Veeteren and Münster.

Also left was the necessity of attempting to achieve something vaguely reminiscent of a result.

"Have you got any ideas?" ventured Münster as they sat over an early Friday evening beer at Adenaar's.

"None at all," muttered Van Veeteren, glaring at the rain pattering against the windowpane. "I don't normally have any ideas in this accursed month of the year. We'll have to wait and see."

"Yeah, I guess so," said Münster. "Funny, though. Reinhart thinks the killer is a woman."

"It's very possible," sighed the chief inspector. "It's always hard to find a woman. Personally, I've been trying to find one all my life."

Coming from Van Veeteren and on an occasion such as this, that was almost to be regarded as a heroic attempt at humor. Münster was obliged to cough away a smile.

"At least we can have the weekend off," he said. "What a relief that we didn't have to go after the bank robber."

"Maybe. It's a relief for him, too, not to be pestered by us."

"I expect they'll get him all the same," said Münster, draining his glass. "There were witnesses, after all. Anyway, I'd better be heading for home. Synn will have left for work by now, and the babysitter gets paid by the hour."

"Oh dear," said Van Veeteren. "There's always a cloud on the horizon."

On Monday it became clear that Münster's prediction had been correct. The bank robber—an unemployed former traffic warden—had been arrested by Rooth and Heinemann early on Sunday morning, following a tip from a woman who had been extremely well dined in one of the best restaurants in town on Saturday evening. The confession came after less than an hour, thanks to some unusually effective interrogation by Reinhart, who was evidently keen to get home as quickly as possible as something important was awaiting him there.

There had been no developments in the Malik case, apart from the fact that Jacob Malik had returned to his studies in Munich. His mother had been on a short visit to her sister's, where she would also be staying until the funeral, which had been fixed for February 3. Some twenty tips had been received from the general public, but none of them was considered to be of any significance for the investigation. When the general run-through and reports took place in the chief of police's leafy office, it was decided to reduce the level of activity to routine, with Van Veeteren in charge. On Saturday there had been a robbery at a jeweler's in the city center—this time, luckily, nobody had been injured; a racist gang had run amok through the immigrant district beyond Zwille and caused a certain amount of damage; and in the early hours of Monday morning an unhappy farmer out at Korrim had shot dead his wife and twelve cows. Obviously, all these incidents required careful investigation.

By now Ryszard Malik had been dead for nearly ten days, and just about as much was known about who had killed him as on the day he died.

Absolutely nothing, zilch.

And January was still limping along.

10

The feeling of satisfaction was greater than she had expected.

More profound and genuine than she could ever have imagined. For the first time in her adult life she had discovered meaning and equilibrium—or so she imagined. It was hard to put her finger on exactly what it was, but she could feel it in her body. Feel it in her skin and in her relaxed muscles; a sort of intoxication that spread among her nerve fibers like gently frothing bubbles, and kept her at a constantly elevated level of consciousness, totally calm and yet with a feeling of being on a high. As high as the sky. An orgasm, she thought in a state of exhilaration, an orgasm going on for an absurdly long period of time. Only very slowly and gently did it ebb away, subsiding lazily into expectation and anticipation of the next occasion. And the one after that.

To kill.

To kill those people.

Some years ago she had been touched by religion, had been on the point of joining one of those religious sects that were springing up like mushrooms from the soil (or like mildew from the brain, as somebody had said), and she recognized her state from the way she had felt then. The only difference was that the religious bliss had passed over. Three or four days of ecstasy had given way to regret and a hangover, just like any other intoxication.

But not now. Not this time. It was still there after ten days. Her whole being was filled with strength, her actions with determination and significance; on every occasion, no matter how trivial—like eating an apple, cutting her nails, or standing in line at the checkout of the local supermarket. Awareness and determination characterized everything she did, for even the most insignificant action was of course also another step on the way, another link in the chain leading ultimately to the next killing.

To kill, and to kill. And eventually to close the circle that had been her mother's past and her own life. Her mission. There was a point to everything, at last.

She read about her first deed in the newspapers. Bought the *Neuwe Blatt, Telegraaf,* and several others, and lay in her room studying all the speculations. She was surprised by all the attention it had attracted. How much would they write next time? And the time after that?

She was slightly annoyed at the fact that she didn't have a television set; she even toyed with the idea of buying a little one, but decided not to. Or at least, to postpone doing so; perhaps she would be unable to resist the temptation of seeing and hearing about herself on the news on the next occasion, but it was best to bide her time. She could have sat in a café and watched, of course, but that didn't feel sufficiently attractive. Not sufficiently private.

Because no matter what—this was a private affair, all of it. Between herself and her mother.

Just her, her mother, and the names on the list.

She had crossed one of them out now. Drawn a red circle around the one next in line. Late on Monday evening, she decided that the period of waiting should come to an end now. The scene was set. The stage design completed. Time to go out again. First the preludes, and then the act itself.

The killing.

A feeling of well-being spread underneath her skin, and when she closed her eyes, through the yellowish, fading glimmer, she could make out her mother's face.

Her tired, but imperative, expression.

Do something, my girl.

IV

January 30–
February 1

II

When Rickard Maasleitner woke up on Tuesday morning, the headmaster's words were still ringing in his ears; and there was reason to suspect he had been dreaming about them all night.

"You must understand that your being off work sick is not only a result of your allergy problems. It is also an opportunity for you to think things over. I want you to consider—and to consider very carefully—whether or not you really want to continue working here."

He had pushed his glasses down to the tip of his nose and leaned forward over his desk as he talked. Tried to look as fatherly and understanding as possible, despite the fact that they were more or less the same age and had known each other since they had first joined the teaching staff. During the Van Breukelen era.

"You have plenty of time," he had added. Put an arm around Maasleitner's shoulders for a moment as he left the room, and mumbled something about idealism and upbringing. In bad taste.

Plenty of time?

He turned over and checked the alarm clock in the bookcase. A quarter to ten.

A quarter to ten on a Tuesday morning in January. Still in bed.
A strange feeling, to say the least. Off sick for three weeks with
allergy problems. Ah well—what it really meant was that he had
been suspended from teaching for dragging a cheeky fifteen-
year-old out into the corridor and telling him to go to hell. Or
back to the country he came from, wherever that was. And
boxed the ears of another one of similar ilk.

And not regretted it for one moment.

That was the crux of the matter. He had not apologized.
Refused to crawl up to the cross. Both incidents had taken place
during the hectic exam period at the beginning of December,
and since then the wheels had been turning.

Protests by pupils. The parents' association. A couple of articles in the newspapers. All the time there had been a door open
for him, and, of course, he had been well aware of it—an escape
route which would have enabled everybody concerned to draw a
line under the whole business, if he would only acknowledge his
guilt and beg for forgiveness.

If he would regret it, in other words.

Everybody had expected that to be what happened. Needless
to say. Maasleitner would do the sensible thing, do the decent
thing, and give way. If not before the Christmas holidays, then
during them. Obviously . . . he would be filled with misgivings
after due consideration, and all that.

But that was not what happened at all. He had come to a dead
end instead. At quite an early stage he had known that he was not
going to back down this time. He had done that before, pleaded
guilty and begged to be forgiven for actions he knew deep down,
and without a shadow of a doubt, were correct and justified.

This time that was more obvious than ever. In the case of
both of those young thugs. They had received only a fraction of

the treatment they really deserved. An ounce of justice for once. And now he was suspended, more or less. As yet they weren't calling it that, and he was still being paid, but, of course, it was only a matter of time before the whole thing was a bit more official. The sack, in other words.

Three weeks, to be precise. Rickard Maasleitner knew the rules of the game. Understood them and didn't like them. Never had. A safety net for cretins and blackguards. Hell and damnation, he thought as he kicked off the covers. Justice!

He had barely gotten out of bed when the telephone rang.

If it's somebody from school, I'll hang up on them, he decided.

But it wasn't somebody from school. It was a woman's voice. A quite low-pitched and slightly gruff voice.

"Do you recognize this tune?" it said.

That was all. Then the music started. Something instrumental. Or a long intro, perhaps. A bit long in the tooth, by the sound of it. But a nice tune.

"Hello," he said after listening for about ten seconds. "Is this some kind of quiz?"

No answer. The music kept on playing.

He held the receiver some way from his ear and thought for a moment.

"If you think you can throw me off balance with this kind of bullshit, you're wrong!" he said, and hung up.

Scum of the earth, he thought. What the hell's this world coming to?

He put on his dressing gown and went to the kitchen to make breakfast.

. . .

During the rest of the day he received at least eight more telephone calls—he lost count sometime in the early afternoon.

The same music. No singing, just a band playing, something from the sixties, he thought—he seemed to recognize it vaguely, but couldn't remember what it was called. Or the band playing it.

Several times he considered pulling out the plug and putting a stop to it, but for some reason he didn't. Instead, each time the phone rang he broke off his reading or his work on the index of the textbook he was busy with. Answered, listened to the music, and stared out over the rooftops and the naked black trees, wondering what the hell was going on. Didn't say a word from the third call onward.

At first he had been convinced that it had something to do with school, that there was probably some pupil or other behind it; but the longer it went on, the more doubtful he became. Strangely enough his irritation seemed to drain away . . . drain away and change into something else, an equal mixture of curiosity and another ingredient he didn't quite want to acknowledge. He was reluctant to admit that it was probably fear.

There was something disturbing about the whole business. Something he couldn't grasp or understand. Sophistication, perhaps? The woman's voice from the first call never came back, only the music, nothing else. The same pop tune, no words. . . . Quite well played, that had to be said, and, he thought, from the early sixties, if he wasn't much mistaken.

But even if the voice never returned, he remembered what the woman had said.

"Do you recognize this tune?"

It was something he ought to remember. Isn't that what she implied? The music meant something, and of course the point was that he should know what it meant. Surely that was what she implied?

Hell and damnation, he muttered as he replaced the receiver for the fifth or sixth time. What is it all about?

It would be some time before Rickard Maasleitner became fully aware of what it was all about. But on the other hand, by then it was all the more obvious.

12

Enso Faringer was nervous. That was beyond question. The moment they sat down at their usual table at Freddy's, he had started squirming around and scratching at the ugly rash on his neck he always had in the winter. He also gulped down his beer, and managed to smoke two cigarettes before the food was served.

The conversation was floating around in circles, and Maasleitner could see that his colleague didn't quite know what leg to stand on. Or rather, what chair to sit on. He had tried to get Faringer to eat out with him on Tuesday evening, but had been given what was obviously an excuse—an old friend was visiting, something like that.

So he was supposed to believe that Enso Faringer had friends? Maasleitner had a good mind to inquire further about the alleged visit while he had him trapped on the line; but he had swallowed the lie with a wry smile. No point in stirring things up. He played with the idea of putting his colleague on the spot now as well, but let it pass. He didn't want to be awkward. Faringer was a contact, after all. Somebody who had insight into what was going to happen at the Elementar school, even if he was hardly capable of drawing conclusions of his own. Or influencing them in any way.

Come to that, Faringer was his only contact. There was nobody else he could rely on. In a situation like the one he was in, Maasleitner would have to make do with whatever was available.

They had kebabs, as usual, and Faringer gossiped tentatively about a few pupils and teachers he knew Maasleitner didn't like. A bit about his aquarium as well, and his father, who had been in a mental hospital for several years, but never wanted to die despite the fact that he was more than ninety-five years old. Enso was in the habit of visiting him about four times a week.

That was also a sign of his nervousness, of course. The fact that he was gossiping. Faringer's mouth seemed to be ticking over in neutral, as if he were talking to his fish, or to a classroom of pupils when he didn't need to think too hard about what he was saying. Maasleitner was tired of his company after only ten minutes.

"Whose side are you on?" he asked when Faringer had been served and taken a swig of his third beer.

"What do you mean?"

"You know what I mean."

"No . . . well, yes, maybe. No, you'd better explain. I'm not quite with you."

"I'm going to get the sack three weeks from now. Or two and a half, to be precise. What do you say to that?"

Faringer swallowed.

"You can't be serious? That can't be allowed to happen. I must have a word with . . ."

He fell silent.

"Have a word with whom?"

"I don't know. But you're surely not going to leave? It'll sort itself out somehow or other."

"Don't talk rubbish. Don't try and tell me you don't know the score. It's as clear as day, for Christ's sake."

"Well . . ."

"I'm going to get the boot because I gave those fucking thugs what they deserved, haven't you grasped that? What the hell do you mean by sitting here mumbling on and pretending you don't know what's going on?"

His anger had spilled over much sooner than he'd expected, and he could see that Faringer was scared. He tried to smooth things over a bit.

"There must have been some sort of reaction among the staff. Are they just going to stand by and let things take their course, or . . . or am I going to get some sort of support? What are they saying? That's all I want to know."

"I see."

Faringer looked relieved.

"So if you could keep your ear to the ground . . . listen to what's going on. I mean, you're good at interpreting moods. You have more insight than a few of the others, there's no need to hide your light under a bushel. . . ."

It was a very clumsily expressed compliment, but he could see that it was effective. Enso Faringer leaned back in his chair and lit another cigarette. Narrowed his eyes and tried to look like he was thinking hard.

Maybe he really is, Maasleitner thought.

"You'd like me to make a few soundings, is that it?"

Maasleitner nodded.

"Maybe start a little . . . campaign?"

"Well, why not?"

It was obvious that the beer was starting to affect his colleague's confused mind now, and it dawned on Maasleitner what a waste of time it all was. Needing to turn for help to the likes of Enso Faringer! Sitting here and asking for favors from this universally despised and ignored laughingstock. *Herr Fräulein*, the pupils called him.

Besides, he wasn't at all sure what he hoped to get out of it. Just a chance to let off steam, presumably. Give vent to his irritation and his feeling of being trampled underfoot. A stubborn old fool with a bee in his bonnet, was that what he would end up becoming? Slowly but surely he could feel exhaustion and pointlessness grasping him by the throat, and when he saw the little German teacher frown and take a ballpoint pen from his inside pocket, he had the feeling that everything was being enacted in the theater of the absurd.

A farce.

Was Faringer going to work out tactics on his paper napkin? Sketch out a manifesto, perhaps? An appeal?

Bloody hell, Maasleitner thought. Who are all these people I'm surrounded by?

Or are they all like this, if you scrape a bit at the surface?

It was not a new question. Barely even a question, come to that.

More of a statement.

More beer, he thought. Might as well blur a few edges. Inertia, come and embrace me!

When they staggered out of the little basement restaurant some considerable time later, the mood was significantly more relaxed. Maasleitner even found it necessary to place his arm over his colleague's shoulders in order to assist his attempts to negotiate the steps leading up to street level. Faringer missed one step altogether, grabbed hold of the iron rail, and roared with laughter; and when they shortly afterward managed to flag down a taxi, it transpired that he had left his wallet on the table. Maasleitner went back to retrieve it while Faringer lay slumped in the backseat, singing a rude song for the scarcely amused but decidedly unimpressed driver.

As Maasleitner watched the cab's rear lights vanish around the corner by the printing works, he wondered how on earth Enso Faringer would be able to summon up the strength to face his classes the next day.

As far as he was concerned, that was no longer a consideration that he needed to take into account, and thanks to the alcohol flowing sweetly through his veins he suddenly had the feeling that despite everything, all was well with the world. A nice, comfortable lie-in was in store for him the next morning, and then perhaps a little excursion. To Weimarn? Why not? Provided the weather turned out to be reasonable, of course.

It wasn't too bad at the moment. The rain had died away. A warm, gentle breeze caressed its way through the town, and as he slowly began to wander through the familiar, narrow alleys that would lead him home to Weijskerstraat, he had the strong impression that there was not really much point in worrying about the future.

As if to confirm this feeling, at about the same time a lone figure emerged from the dark shadows enveloping the Keymer Church a little farther down the same street.

It followed him about thirty paces behind; discreetly and silently, as Maasleitner walked over the rounded cobbles, across Wilhemsgraacht, into Weijskerstraat, and right up to the front door. Maasleitner was somewhat surprised to find that it was standing ajar, and that there appeared to be something wrong with the lock. Despite his euphoric state, he paused for a few moments to mutter away about the circumstances—while his pursuer waited patiently in another doorway diagonally across the narrow street. Then Maasleitner shrugged, stepped inside, and took the elevator up to the fourth floor.

He hadn't been home for long, hadn't even had time to get undressed, when there was a ring at the door. The clock over the stove in the kitchen said a few minutes past midnight, and as he went to open up he wondered who on earth it could be, visiting him at this time of night.

Then it dawned on him that it must be Enso Faringer, whose euphoric state had doubtless enabled him to come up with some crazy idea or other, and there was a tolerant smile on his lips as he opened the door.

Some sixteen hours later his seventeen-year-old daughter opened that same door, and if the circumstances had not been so grotesque, it would probably have still been possible to see traces of that smile on his face.

V

February 1–7

13

"So there's no doubt, then?" said Heinemann.

"Not really," said Münster. "Same ammunition—7.65 millimeter. The technical guys were more or less certain that it was the same weapon, but we won't know that for sure until tomorrow."

"Two bullets in the chest, two below the belt," said Rooth, looking at the photograph lying on the table in front of him. "I'll be damned if it isn't the same thing all over again, more or less. A copy of Ryszard Malik."

"Of course it's the same culprit," said Moreno. "There hasn't been a word in the papers about the bullets below the belt."

"Correct," muttered Van Veeteren. "Sometimes the muzzle we put on journalists actually works."

He looked up from the document he was holding and had just read. It was a very provisional medical statement Miss Katz had popped in to hand over, and it suggested that Rickard Maasleitner had probably died between eleven and twelve o'clock the previous night, and that the cause of death was a bullet that had penetrated the heart muscle. The other shots would not have brought about instant death; not taken one at a time, that is—possibly in combination, as a result of blood loss.

"A bullet in the heart," said Van Veeteren, passing the sheet of paper on to Münster, who was sitting next to him.

"He didn't leave Freddy's until shortly after half past eleven," said Moreno. "It takes at least a quarter of an hour to walk to Weijskerstraat. The murderer can hardly have struck before midnight."

"Between twelve and two, then," said Rooth. "Ah well, we'll have to find out if anybody saw anything."

"Or heard," said Heinemann.

Rooth stuck his index finger into his mouth, then withdrew it with a plopping sound.

"Did you hear that?" he asked. "That's about as much noise as is made when you use a silencer. He must have used one, or he'd have woken up the whole building."

"Okay," said Heinemann. "We'll assume that, then."

Van Veeteren broke a toothpick in half and looked at the clock.

"Nearly midnight," he said with a deep sigh. "We might as well go home now and get some sleep, but so help me God, we'd better make some progress tomorrow. We have quite a few threads to pull at, this time around; and there's no reason why we should be left floundering. The sooner we solve this business, the better."

He paused briefly, but nobody took advantage of the opportunity to speak. He could see in his colleagues' faces the same mixture of intense concentration and weariness that he could feel inside his own head. Best to rest for a few hours, no doubt about that. Besides, there wouldn't be much point in waking people up in the middle of the night to answer a few questions. The police had a bad enough reputation as it was; there was no need to make it any worse.

"This is what we'll do tomorrow," said the chief inspector. "Reinhart and deBries will continue interviewing the neighbors. The whole block, if there's time. I assume they're still at it now, and I suppose they might as well carry on. It could be that somebody has seen something—the murderer must have called round twice, for God's sake. Once to tamper with the lock, and once to kill. It might be that nobody noticed anything, but we'll have to see. . . . Heinemann."

"Yes."

"I want you to dig into the background. We have details of the whole of Malik's life. Find out when his and Maasleitner's paths crossed. There must be a link."

"Let's hope so," said Heinemann.

"Münster and Rooth will take his family. Or rather, the family that used to be his. I have a list of them here. Moreno and Jung will go to the Elementar school. . . ."

"Oh my God," said Jung. "That's the school I used to go to. . . ."

Van Veeteren raised his eyebrows.

"When was that?" he asked.

Jung tried to work it out.

"Eighteen years ago," he said. "Just one term in the seventh grade, then we moved in the spring. I hardly recall a single teacher. I didn't have Maasleitner in any case."

"A pity," said Van Veeteren. "Talk to the headmaster and some of the staff even so, but tread carefully. They're usually very wary of anybody who intrudes on a seat of learning like that. Remember what happened at Bunge?"

"I certainly do," said Münster. "Lie low, that's my advice."

"I'll bear it in mind," said Jung.

"But leave that Faringer character alone," said Van Veeteren. "I intend to have a little chat with him myself."

"A bit of an oddball," said Münster.

"Of course," muttered Van Veeteren. "All teachers are. If they're not odd to start with, they become so as the years go by."

He rummaged in his empty breast pocket and looked around the room.

"Any questions?"

Rooth yawned, but nobody spoke.

"Okay," said the chief inspector, and started collecting his papers together. "We'll meet for a run-through at three o'clock tomorrow afternoon. Make sure you make the most of the time until then. This time we're going to get him."

"Or her," said Münster.

"Yes, yes," said Van Veeteren. "*Cherchez la femme,* if you really must."

When he got home and had gone to bed, he realized that his tiredness had not yet overcome the tension in his brain once and for all. The image of Rickard Maasleitner's bullet-ridden body kept cropping up in his mind's eye at regular intervals, and after ten minutes of vainly trying to fall asleep, he got up and went to the kitchen instead. Fetched a beer from the refrigerator and sat down in the armchair with a blanket around his knees and Dvořák in the speakers. He allowed the darkness to envelop him, but instead of the unease and disgust he ought to have felt, in view of the two unsolved murders they were struggling with, another sensation altogether took possession of him.

It was a feeling of movement. Of hunting, in fact. The feeling that the drive had begun now, and that the prey was somewhere out there in the hustle and bustle of town, and it was only a matter of time before he would be able to get his teeth into it. Bring down the murderer.

Oh, shit! he thought as he took a swig of his beer. I'm beginning to lose the plot. If I weren't a police officer, I'd probably have become a murderer instead.

It was only a random thought, of course, but nevertheless, somewhere in some obscure corner of his brain, he realized that there was more meaning in it than would be sensible to acknowledge. It had something to do with the concept of the hunt. . . .

In the beginning, at least.

Only in the beginning, if truth be told. Somewhere along the line came the peripeteia, the volte-face, and when he eventually—usually much, much later—stood there with his prey, with the perpetrator, what generally possessed him were exclusively feelings of loathing and disgust. The excitement—the stimulation—was only theoretical.

And in the beginning.

For when you had dug down sufficiently deep into dire reality, his stream of thought told him, when you had dug down as deep as the soil layer of the crime itself, all there was to see was the black and hopeless dregs. The causes. The maggot-ridden roots of warped society.

The back side.

Not that he believed the society in which he lived had higher or lower moral principles than any other. It was simply the way things were—two to three thousand years of culture, and law-making bodies were unable to do anything about it. The veneer of civilization, or whatever you preferred to call it, could begin to crack at any moment, crumble away and expose the darkness underneath. Some people might have imagined that Europe would be a protected haven after 1945, but Van Veeteren had never been one of them. And then things had turned out as they did. Sarajevo, Srebrenica, and all the rest of it.

And of course it was in the same underlying darkness that his own hunting instincts originated. In any case, he had always found it difficult to associate his police activities with any kind of noble deeds. Nemesis, rather. The inexorable goddess of revenge with blood on her teeth. . . . Yes, that was more like it, there was no denying it.

And at some point, the game always turned deadly serious.

In this particular case it had taken two murders for him to begin to feel involved. Were his senses becoming duller? he wondered. What would he be like a few years from now? What would be needed by then to start the notorious Chief Inspector Van Veeteren firing on all cylinders?

Butchered women? Children?

Mass graves?

When would cynicism and world-weariness have overcome his determination to fight once and for all? For how much longer would the moral imperative have the strength to continue screeching in the darkness of his soul?

Good questions. He felt his self-disgust rising and cut off the train of thought. No doubt it had been the contrary nature of January that had made him a little sluggish at the start. Now it was February. February the second, to be precise. What was this Maasleitner business all about?

He started thinking about what had happened that afternoon.

The alarm had sounded just as he was preparing to pack up for the day. Half past four. He and Münster had been at the apartment in Weijskerstraat a quarter of an hour later, more or less at the same time as the forensic guys and the medical team. Rickard Maasleitner was lying in exactly the same posture as Ryszard Malik had been some . . . how long ago was it now? Two weeks, more or less? Yes, that was correct.

He had been convinced from the very first glance that it was the same killer. And that the method had been the same.

A ring on the doorbell, and then shots the moment the door opened.

A sound method, Rooth had said.

Most certainly. Once it was done, all that remained was to close the door and walk away. What sort of time was involved? Ten seconds? That would probably be long enough. You could fire four shots from a Berenger in half that time, if need be.

He emptied his glass.

And then?

Well, then everything got under way, of course. Police tape around the crime scene, a thorough search, taking care of the poor daughter who had found him. And so on.

Questions.

Questions and answers. No end to it already. And yet it was just the beginning. As already stated.

But if one were to look a little more closely at the whole business, one thing stood out, of course. Only one so far, that is. There was an enormous difference between the risk involved in the two murders.

In the case of Malik, the chances of being seen were as minimal as it is possible to be; but yesterday, all it needed was for somebody to happen to go out with a garbage bag, or to glance out through a half-open door.

It had been nighttime, of course; but even so.

Ergo: either there were witnesses or there weren't.

Perhaps, and this was much to be desired, somebody (or several people) had seen the killer on one of the two occasions when he must have visited the apartment block—while he was fiddling with the lock (because it must surely be the murderer who was responsible for that?), or when the shooting took place. Either on the way there or while leaving.

Or while he was standing waiting?

A case of either-or, then. If Reinhart and deBries did their job properly, we should know tomorrow. And even if the neighbors, or Reinhart and deBries, had missed something, there was still a good chance of striking lucky. A press release had been issued at ten o'clock, and it would be in all the main newspapers and in the radio and television news bulletins later this morning. Everybody who thought they might have some relevant information, or had merely been in the Weijskerstraat area around midnight on Wednesday evening, was urged to get in touch with the police immediately.

So there were grounds for hope.

Having come thus far in his deliberations, Van Veeteren gave in to temptation and lit a cigarette. It was time to address the big question, and that would no doubt need a bit of extra effort.

Why?

Why in hell's name should anybody march up to somebody's door, ring the bell, and shoot whoever opened it?

What was the motive?

What was the link between Ryszard Malik and Rickard Maasleitner?

And furthermore: What would have happened if somebody else had opened the door? Could the murderer be one hundred percent certain who it would be? Was it all the result of meticulous planning, or was coincidence involved?

There's no such thing as coincidence, Reinhart had once said, and that was no doubt basically true. Nevertheless, there was a hell of a difference between some causes and others. Between some motives and others.

Why had Malik and Maasleitner been singled out by the murderer?

Dvořák fell silent, and Van Veeteren could feel the weariness behind his eyes now. He stubbed out his cigarette and heaved himself up out of the armchair. Switched off the CD player and went to bed. The blood-red digital numbers on the clock radio showed 2:21, and he realized that he had less than five hours' sleep to look forward to.

Ah well, he'd been through worse situations in the past, and no doubt would be faced with worse in the future as well.

When Detective Inspector Reinhart snuggled down under the covers on his big iron-frame bed, the night had ticked its way through twenty more red minutes; but even so, he considered phoning Miss Lynch and asking her if she felt like popping over. In order to exchange a few words, if nothing else; and to remind her that he loved her.

However, something—he was confident it had to do with his good character and upbringing—restrained him from submitting to his desires, and instead he lay for a while thinking about their efforts during the course of the evening, and the way in which people seemed to notice nothing of what was happening round about them.

Or their stupidity, as some would doubtless have expressed it.

In any case, a lack of awareness. In the old, well-maintained 1930s apartment block where Rickard Maasleitner lived, there were no fewer than seventy-three inhabitants. In apartments off the relevant staircase—26B—there were seventeen tenants at home at the time of the murder, in addition to the victim himself. At least eight of those had been awake when the murderer fired the fatal shots (assuming that the incident took place before two in the morning). Five of those had been on the same floor. One had come home at ten minutes to twelve.

Nobody had noticed anything at all.

As for the front-door lock, which the murderer had sabotaged by jamming a piece of metal between the bolt and the drum, at least three persons had noticed that there was something amiss, but none of them had done anything about it, or drawn any conclusions.

Stupid idiots! Reinhart thought.

There again, of course, he knew that this was not an entirely fair judgment. He himself hadn't the slightest idea of what his neighbors got up to of an evening—he hardly knew what they were called, never mind anything else—but after seven hours of interrogation, and with so many possible witnesses among them, one would surely have been justified in expecting a rather more positive outcome.

Or any outcome at all, to be honest.

But there had not been any.

What was pretty clear, however, was the time sequence. The front door of Weijskerstraat 26 was locked automatically at 2200 hours every evening. In order to tamper with the lock in the way the murderer had done, he (or she, as Winnifred Lynch maintained) must have waited until after that time, presumably somewhere inside the building. And then, when the automatic locking took place, he or she must have calmly opened the door from the inside and inserted the piece of metal. The alternative was that the murderer stood hidden somewhere in the shrubbery outside the front door, and slipped in when one of the residents went in or came out. A pretty risky operation, and hence not very likely, as deBries and Reinhart had agreed.

What the murderer did after that was impossible to say, of course; but when Maasleitner came home at about midnight after his night out with Faringer, he (or she) had presumably wasted no time hanging around. Everything suggested that Maasleitner hadn't been at home for more than a few minutes before the doorbell rang.

And then four bullets. Two in the chest, and two below the belt. Exactly the same as on the previous occasion. Close the door and melt away. And no witnesses.

Good God, thought Reinhart with a shudder. It was so simple, enough to make you afraid of the dark.

Nevertheless he stretched out his arm and switched off the light. And as he did so he remembered that there were a couple of straws to grasp. Two of the apartment owners had been at home during the night in question, but had not been available for an interview. What is more, one of them—a certain Mr. Malgre—lived next door to Maasleitner; for want of anything better, Reinhart made up his mind to attach his best hopes for the next day's interviews to the one with him. This was scheduled for midday, when Malgre would be back from a conference in Aarlach. DeBries was due to interrogate him.

Now, if Malgre was the type used to attending conferences, Reinhart thought, he was bound to be a person with a high level of awareness. Not your usual thickie.

As he registered that thought, the usual flag of protest was raised in the back of his mind, condemning such prejudiced thoughts. But his exhaustion had the upper hand. Reinhart sighed, turned onto his side, and fell asleep.

By that time the minutes had ticked their way forward to 3:12. All evening and night he hadn't devoted a single second to thinking about the motive.

That would have to wait until tomorrow.

He'd been working today. Tomorrow he would start using his brains.

14

Baushejm was only a few stone's throws away from the suburb where Münster lived, and he drove straight there on Friday morning. If for no other reason than to save time. Wanda Piirinen (formerly Maasleitner) had to get to work—she was a secretary at one of the town's most reputable attorneys' offices—and despite the murder of her ex-husband, she had no intention of taking any more leave than necessary. Half a day, to be precise.

The children—three of them, aged seventeen (the girl who had found her father murdered the previous day), thirteen, and ten—had been allowed an extended weekend, and when Münster was shown into the well-kept villa, they had just been collected by an aunt, and would be spending at least two days with her and their cousins out at Dikken.

"We divorced eight years ago," explained Wanda Piirinen. "It was not a good marriage, and relations have not improved since then. I don't have any feelings, although I know I ought to have."

"You have three children together," said Münster, devoting a rapid thought to his own two.

She nodded and gestured toward the coffeepot on the table. Münster poured himself a cup.

"That's the only reason why we still remain in contact. Or used to, perhaps I should say."

Münster took a sip of coffee and observed her covertly over the edge of his cup. An elegant lady, that was for sure. Round about forty-five, he thought; fit-looking and suntanned despite the time of year, but also displaying signs of ruthlessness which she had difficulty concealing.

Perhaps she doesn't want to, Münster thought. Perhaps she wants her independence and strength to be noticed immediately. To deter men from getting any inappropriate ideas or taking liberties. Her thick, ash-blond hair was skillfully done in a French braid, and her makeup seemed to be fastidious and understated. He guessed that she spent rather a long time at the dressing table every morning. Her nails were long and well manicured, and it was a little difficult to believe that she had been solely responsible for bringing up three children. On the other hand, of course, this is what people working in an attorney's office should look like— efficiency and well-directed energy radiated from her like an aura, and he realized that he would have to deal with what Reinhart generally called a modern woman.

Or possibly postmodern?

"Well?" she said, and he became aware that he had lost himself in thought.

"Describe him!" he said.

"Rickard?"

"Yes, please."

She gave him a searching look.

"I don't think I want to."

"Why not?"

"I would only have negative things to say. It doesn't seem

appropriate for me to disclose my feelings about my former husband when he has just been murdered. Please excuse me."

Münster nodded.

"I understand. How was contact with the children? Between him and the children, I mean."

"Bad," she said, after a moment's hesitation. "At first they used to go and stay with him occasionally. Every other weekend, and sometimes during the week. We live in the same town, after all. It ought to have been a practical possibility to arrange something along those lines, but after a year I realized that it would be better for them to live with me all the time. They needed *a* home, not two homes."

"Did he protest?" Münster asked.

"Not really. Just a little bit, for appearances' sake. He no doubt thought it was a bit of a nuisance, having them in his house. That is . . . was . . . his attitude toward quite a lot of people."

"What do you mean?"

"I'm sure you understand. If you talk to some of his colleagues, you will soon get a clear idea about that. And his friends, always assuming that he has any left . . ."

"We'll do that, of course," said Münster.

He looked around the modern kitchen. There was very little to show that four people had recently had breakfast there, but no doubt there are painless routines for cleaning up, he assumed.

Why am I feeling so aggressive? he wondered, slightly surprised. What's the matter with me?

He had managed to find time to make love to Synn, take a shower, and have breakfast before leaving home, so he ought not to be so irritated. Surely she wasn't all that dangerous?

"What do you think about it?" he asked.

"About the murder?"

"Yes."

She leaned back and gazed out the window.

"I don't know," she said, and for the first time there was a trace of doubt in her voice. "A lot of people don't like Rickard, that is no secret; but that anybody would want to murder him . . . no, I'd never have thought that."

"Why didn't people like him?"

She thought for a moment, searching for the right words.

"He could see no further than himself," she said. "Contemptuous of everybody and everything that didn't suit his taste. Or didn't fit in with his way of thinking."

"And what was that?"

"Excuse me?"

"His way of thinking."

She hesitated slightly again.

"I think it can be traced back to his upbringing," she said. "He was an only child from the age of ten onward. He had an elder brother who drowned at the age of fourteen. After that, his parents devoted all their care and attention to Rickard, but they were totally blind to the fact that he might have any faults or shortcomings. Yes, that was the basis of it all, of course."

"Why did you marry him?" Münster asked, wondering if he might be being impertinent.

But she smiled for the first time.

"Feminine weakness," she said. "He was handsome and I was young."

She took a sip of coffee and sat for a few moments with the cup in her hand.

"He was overflowing with manly attributes," she said eventually. "They are best in the early stages. By the age of forty they have somehow changed. I hope you don't mind my saying that."

"Not at all," said Münster. "I'm forty-three. But that isn't what we should be talking about. You don't have any suspicions, I take it?"

She shook her head.

"And he hadn't mentioned anything?"

"No. But we didn't talk to one another all that often. A telephone call once a week, perhaps. He had a life of his own."

"What was your daughter doing there? When she found him, that is."

"She'd gone to fetch some books. She was the one most in touch with him. They could talk to each other, I think, and her school is only a couple of blocks away from Weijskerstraat. She used to go there to study sometimes. When she had a free period, for instance."

"And she had a key?"

Wanda Piirinen nodded.

"Yes. It's worst for her, that's for sure. It'll take time. . . . A pity she should have to be the one who found him as well."

She bit her lip.

"Please be gentle with her, if you have to interview her several times. She didn't sleep much last night."

Münster nodded.

"We talked to her quite a lot yesterday. A smart girl."

Suddenly Wanda Piirinen had tears in her eyes, and he wondered if he had misjudged her slightly. He felt it was about time to take his leave.

"Just one more thing," he said. "Ryszard Malik. Does that name mean anything to you?"

"He's the one who was shot on the previous occasion, isn't he?"

"Yes."

She shook her head.

"No," she said. "I've never heard the name before, I'm quite sure."

"Okay, many thanks," said Münster, rising to his feet. "I hope you'll get in touch if you think of anything you consider might be of interest to us."

"Of course."

She showed him out. For some reason she remained in the doorway until he had clambered into his car in the street outside. When he started the engine, she raised her hand as a sort of farewell gesture before disappearing into the house.

That's that, then, Münster thought. Another insight into another life. And as he did a U-turn in the deserted suburban street, he suddenly felt something dark and somber stick its claws into him.

"Hell and damnation," he muttered. It must be something to do with the time of year. . . .

"Fired!" said Jung. "Can you believe that he was actually in the process of being fired? For Christ's sake, I thought it was impossible for a teacher to get the boot!"

They were in the car again, on the way back to the police station. The visit to the Elementar school had taken up three hours of their time, but the outcome was not bad at all. After a short introductory conversation with Greitzen, the headmaster, they had spent most of the time with the school's so-called staff welfare group—three women and three men—and the picture of Rickard Maasleitner that had emerged was undoubtedly a colorful one.

He was evidently one of those pedagogues who should have chosen a different career. That was soon clear to Jung. A job in which he didn't have such good opportunities to take advantage of his position. To use and misuse his power.

The incidents in December had not been the first ones. By no means. Maasleitner's twenty-five-year teaching career had been littered with similar intermezzos. What had kept him in his job were esprit de corps, misguided solidarity on the part of colleagues, interventions by school leaders and others; but it was crystal clear that many people were sick and tired of him. Not to say everybody.

"There are two types of teacher," a hardened, chain-smoking counselor had explained. "Those who solve conflicts, and those who create them. Unfortunately, Maasleitner belonged to the latter category."

"Belonged to?" a gently ironic but confidence-inspiring woman, a language teacher, had commented. "He was their uncrowned king. He could hardly walk across the school playground without stirring up trouble. He could pick an argument with the flagpole."

Moreno had wondered if Maasleitner had enjoyed any kind of support from the staff even so, and what the outcome of his suspension would have been, if it had progressed to a natural conclusion, as it were. Needless to say the problem had been discussed in the staff welfare group—whose function was to deal with delicate matters like the problems caused by Maasleitner—and there was a surprisingly firm agreement that they would have let it take its natural course. They would have left Maasleit-ner to dig his own way out of the hole he had created himself, as best he could.

That indubitably said quite a lot about the situation. And about Maasleitner.

"But he must surely have had a few allies?" Jung had suggested.

But not a single name was mentioned. Perhaps that was a way of presenting a united front, it had occurred to Jung afterward. Perhaps it was only natural. But there again, it was rather odd. Maasleitner had just been murdered, after all. . . . Don't speak ill of the dead, and all that. But here the opposite seemed to be the case.

Terrible, he thought. If the people you have been working with every day—in some cases for more than twenty years—had nothing but shit to throw at a man lying helpless on the ground, well . . . It indicated that he hadn't been anybody's favorite, that was definite.

They had spoken to some of the pupils as well. Six of them, to be precise; one at a time. These somewhat younger witnesses displayed rather more consideration and respect for the dead. To be sure, Maasleitner had been a pain, but it was going over the top for somebody to go and shoot him. Kick him—yes! Kill him—no, no! as one young man put it. A couple of the girls had even tried hard to find the odd nice thing to say about him, although their efforts gave the distinct impression of being rather strained and forced.

He was knowledgeable, and sometimes fair, he didn't have any particular favorites—those were among the good qualities they mentioned. (In other words, he thought just as badly about all of them, Jung thought to himself.)

In the end they had gone back to the headmaster's study

again. He served them coffee and wondered if they needed any further information—and hoped that if so, they could arrange to dig deeper outside school hours.

Neither Moreno nor Jung thought they had much more to ask about at this stage. Apart from what could have caused his murder and who did it, of course; but the headmaster had merely shaken his head in response to that.

"You mean, can I think of anybody who would want to eliminate him? No. I assume you are not looking for a young murderer. Our oldest pupils are sixteen years of age. I can't imagine that any member of our staff would . . . No, that's out of the question. He wasn't exactly well liked, but it's completely out of the question."

"What do you think?" asked Moreno as they waited at a red light down by Zwille.

"Well," said Jung, "I wouldn't like to be the headmaster and need to say a few words at the funeral. Good Lord, no."

"It's wrong to tell lies in church," said Moreno.

"Exactly."

"And Malik doesn't seem to have had any connection with the school at all. No, I think we can leave them in peace and let them get on with their studies."

Jung said nothing for a while.

"How about going for lunch somewhere instead?" he said as the police station loomed up in front of them. "There's two hours to go before our meeting."

Ewa Moreno hesitated.

"Okay," she said. "At least they won't have us getting in the way if we do that."

.   .   .

DeBries started the tape recorder even before Alwin Malgre had settled down in the visitor's chair.

DEB: Welcome, Mr. Malgre. I'd like to ask you a few questions about Wednesday evening.

M: So I understand.

DEB: So, your name is Alwin Malgre, and you live at Weijskerstraat 26B?

M: That's correct.

DEB: Would you mind speaking a bit louder, please?

M: Why?

DEB: I'm recording our conversation on this tape recorder.

M: Oh . . .

DEB: Anyway. I take it you are aware that a murder was committed in the apartment block where you live at some time between midnight and two in the morning last Wednesday night?

M: Maasleitner, yes. It's terrible.

DEB: Your apartment is next door to his, I understand. Can you please tell me what you were doing the night before last?

M: Er, let me see. . . . Yes, I was at home, reading. . . .

DEB: Do you live alone in the apartment?

M: Yes, of course.

DEB: And you didn't have any visitors?

M: No.

DEB: Please go on.

M: I was at home reading all evening. Cramming, perhaps I should say. I had to attend that seminar because Van Donck didn't have time. . . .

DEB: Who's Van Donck?

M: My boss, of course.

DEB: What is your work, and what exactly was
       this conference? Is that where you were
       yesterday?

M: Yes, in Aarlach. I work at the Stamp Center. Van
       Donck is my boss. . . . Well, there's just the two of
       us in the firm. You could say that I'm his assistant.

DEB: You sell postage stamps, is that right?

M: And buy. Are you interested in philately, Mr. . . .
       Mr. . . . ?

DEB: DeBries. No. What was this conference all about?

M: More of a seminar, really. Seminar and auction.
       About the problems resulting from the collapse of
       the Soviet Union. This time it was mainly the
       stamps issued by the Baltic states that we were
       discussing. I don't know if you realize the chaos
       that has been caused in philately by the formation
       of all these new states. . . . It's a gold mine for us as
       well, of course, depending on how speculative you
       want to be.

DEB: Naturally. Anyway, we can go into that some other
       time. Back to Wednesday evening, if you wouldn't
       mind.

M: Well, I don't know what to say. I came home at half
       past six or thereabouts. Had my evening meal and
       started reading. Had a cup of tea at about half past
       nine, I should think it was. . . . Watched the nine
       o'clock news on the telly as well, of course. Well,
       and then I suppose I sat up until about half past
       eleven, roughly.

DEB: So you were asleep from half past eleven, is that right?

M: No, I carried on reading until about a quarter to one. In bed, that is. Van Donck had acquired two new books that same afternoon, and obviously, I didn't want to go to Aarlach underprepared. I'd have a bit of time on the train as well, naturally, but . . .

DEB: Did you notice anything?

M: Excuse me?

DEB: Did you notice anything unusual during the evening?

M: No.

DEB: You didn't hear anything around midnight?

M: No. . . . No, I was in bed by then. The bedroom faces the courtyard.

DEB: So you didn't notice when Mr. Maasleitner came home?

M: No.

DEB: Nothing else around that time either?

M: No.

DEB: Do you usually hear noises from inside Maasleitner's apartment?

M: No, the building is extremely well insulated.

DEB: We've gathered that. Were you well acquainted with your neighbor?

M: Maasleitner, you mean?

DEB: Yes.

M: No, not at all. We said hello if we bumped into each other on the stairs, but that's all.

DeB: I understand. Is there anything else you saw or heard that you think might be connected with the murder?

M: No.

DeB: Nothing you noticed that you think we ought to know about?

M: No— What are you referring to?

DeB: Anything at all. Something unusual that has happened recently, for instance?

M: No . . . no, I can't think of anything.

DeB: You don't know if Maasleitner had any visitors these last few days?

M: No, I've no idea. You'd better ask the other neighbors. I'm not all that observant. . . .

DeB: We can't very well expect you to be. Anyway, many thanks, Mr. Malgre. If anything occurs to you, please get in touch with us without delay.

M: Of course. Thank you very much. This was most interesting.

Extremely productive, deBries thought after Malgre had left the room. He lit a cigarette, stood by the window, and gazed out over the town.

Three hundred thousand people, he thought. There sometimes seemed to be pretty high walls between all of them. While one of them gets shot and killed, his neighbor is in bed ten meters away, reading up on Estonian postage stamps.

But no doubt that's what was meant by the concept of privacy.

. . .

It took Van Veeteren about a minute to discover that having lunch while reconstructing what had happened was not a good idea. When he entered Freddy's bar and restaurant through the low door, Enso Faringer was already sitting at their reserved table, and his nervousness was obvious from a distance.

Van Veeteren sat down and produced a pack of cigarettes: Faringer took one and dropped it on the floor.

"So," the chief inspector began, "we might as well have a bite to eat, seeing as we're sitting here."

"Sounds good."

"So this is where you spent Wednesday evening, is it?"

Faringer nodded and adjusted his spectacles, which evidently had a tendency to slide down his shiny nose.

"I understand you are a German teacher."

"Yes," said Faringer. "Somebody has to be."

Van Veeteren was not sure if that was meant as a joke or not.

"You presumably knew Maasleitner well?"

"Er . . . not really, no."

"But you used to meet, I gather?"

"Only sporadically. We'd go out for a beer now and then."

"Such as last Wednesday?"

"Yes, like last Wednesday."

Van Veeteren said nothing for a while in order to give Faringer an opportunity of saying something off his own bat; but it was a waste of time. His eyes were moving ceaselessly behind his thick glasses, he was wriggling and squirming in his chair and fiddling with the knot of his tie.

"Why are you so nervous?"

"Nervous?"

"Yes. I have the impression you're frightened of something."

Faringer emitted a very short laugh.

"No, I'm always like this."

Van Veeteren sighed. The waiter came with the menu and they spent a few minutes perusing it before deciding on today's special.

"What did you talk about on Wednesday?"

"I can't remember."

"What do you mean?"

"I don't recall. We had a bit too much to drink, and I often get these black holes in my memory."

"But you must remember something, surely?"

"Yes, I know that Maasleitner asked me about the situation at school. He was in a bit of a mess. He asked me to help him."

"How?"

Faringer scratched at his neck, where he had some kind of a rash.

"Oh, I don't know. Keep my eyes open, I assume."

"He didn't ask you to take an initiative?"

"An initiative? No. How would I be able to take an initiative?"

No, Van Veeteren thought. That would be out of the question, of course. Enso Faringer wasn't the type to take initiatives.

The lunch lasted for forty-five minutes, despite the fact that Van Veeteren canceled dessert and coffee; and by the time he sat down in the driver's seat of his car, he was convinced of one thing. Faringer had been telling the truth. The little German teacher had no recollection of the measures he and Maasleitner had drawn up to save the world during the evening of the murder. Van Veeteren had also talked to the staff at Freddy's, and nobody found it the least bit strange that the "little Kraut" had lost his memory. On the contrary.

It had simply been one of those evenings.

So that was that, Van Veeteren thought. Deep down he was also rather grateful—having to sit there and listen to Enso Faringer's account of a whole evening of drunken rambling would hardly have constituted an unmissable experience.

When he was about halfway back to the police station, he found himself with something else to think about. It had started raining again, and it was clear that if he didn't do something about replacing that damned windshield wiper as soon as possible, something nasty was likely to happen.

But then again, he knew that the moment he did something about replacing a broken part, something else would break.

His car was like that, that's all there was to it.

A bit reminiscent of life itself.

15

"Why did you give Heinemann the job of sifting the background?" wondered Reinhart. "I mean, he needs a week in order to have a shit."

"Could be," said Van Veeteren. "But at least he's meticulous. Let's start without him. Somebody pour out the coffee. Miss Katz promised to serve us something tasty."

"Sounds good," said Rooth.

"Let's start with the scientific guff," said the chief inspector, distributing a set of photocopies. "I don't think you'll find anything sensational there."

The seven detectives present each read through the brief reports from the pathologist and the forensic team (all apart from Van Veeteren, who had already digested them, and Reinhart, who preferred to fill his pipe); and the consensus was that sure enough, they didn't contain anything new. Generally speaking, they merely confirmed what was already known—cause of death, time of death (now made more precise, assigned to the period between 2345 and 0115), the weapon (a 7.65-millimeter Berenger, ninety-nine percent certain to be the same gun used for the murder of Ryszard Malik). No fingerprints had been found, no trace of anything unusual; the piece of metal used to jam the lock was made of stainless steel, available all over the place and impossible to trace.

"All right," said Van Veeteren. "Let's record the crap, so that Heller can use it as a lullaby to send him into dreamland over the weekend."

He started the tape recorder.

"Run-through of the case of Rickard Maasleitner, Friday, February second, three-fifteen p.m. Those present: Van Veeteren, Münster, Rooth, Reinhart, Moreno, deBries, and Jung. Reinhart and deBries first."

"Pass," said Reinhart.

"We've got nowhere," deBries explained. "We've interviewed over seventy people at number 26 and the building opposite. Nobody's seen or heard a squeak. The light over the front door of 26B had blown out, by the way, so it would have been hard to get an image of the murderer anyway."

"Did he smash that as well?" asked Moreno.

"Probably not, but it's hard to say. It's been out of order for the past six days."

"Nothing else?" asked Van Veeteren.

"No," said Reinhart. "The transcripts of the interrogations are at your disposal if you want something guaranteed to send you to sleep over the weekend."

"Good," said Van Veeteren. "Well done."

"Thank you," said deBries.

The rest of the meeting proceeded in more or less the same way. As far as the character and general reputation of the deceased was concerned, a number of reports came up with the same conclusion. Rickard Maasleitner was a shit. A bully and a self-centered know-it-all of the very worst sort, it seemed. Even so, it was difficult to see that anybody would have had sufficient cause to kill him. As far as was known he hadn't had any affairs—indeed, it was not at all clear if he'd had a single relationship with a woman since his divorce eight years earlier. He might possibly have resorted to prostitutes occasionally, but this was pure speculation that couldn't be confirmed or disproved. He had no debts. No commitments. No shady deals.

And nobody had been close to him.

His former wife had nothing positive to say about him, nor had anybody else. His children were naturally a bit shocked, but any sorrow they might have felt would no doubt be able to be assuaged successfully, according to both amateur and professional diagnoses.

Both of Rickard Maasleitner's parents were dead, and one could be forgiven for thinking that his last real ally had been buried three years ago, in the shape of his mother.

"A right bastard!" was Reinhart's summary of the victim's character. "He sounds so awful, it would have been interesting to meet him."

Van Veeteren switched off the tape recorder.

"A good finishing line," he explained.

"Wouldn't it be possible to track down the weapon?" Jung asked.

Van Veeteren shook his head.

"DeBries, tell the assembled masses how one goes about getting hold of a gun. You've been looking into this."

"By all means," said deBries. "Pretty straightforward, in fact. You get in touch with somebody who gives the impression of being just outside the reach of the law—some seedy-looking type hanging around the Central Station or Grote Square, for instance. You say you need a gun. He tells you to wait, and a quarter of an hour later he comes back with an envelope. You slip him a hundred guilders for his services, then you go home and open the envelope. The instructions are inside. You have to send money—let's say a thousand guilders—to a general delivery address. Müller, General Post Office, Maardam, for instance. You do as bidden, and a week or so later you receive a letter with a key inside it. It's for a safe-deposit box at the Central Station. You go there, open the box, and presto!—you find a little box containing a gun. . . ."

"Then all you need to do is get off your ass and start killing," said Van Veeteren.

"A sound method," said Rooth again.

"Devilishly clever," said Reinhart. "But we have to assign Stauff or Petersén to the job of looking into that. Just to be sure."

Van Veeteren nodded. Reached over the table and took a cigarette out of deBries's pack.

"And what are the rest of us supposed to do, then?" asked Münster.

"Jung," said the chief inspector, when he'd finally managed to light his cigarette. "Could you go and search for Heinemann? It'll be a real mess if we can't nurse a single horse over the winning line."

"Sure," said Jung, rising to his feet. "Where is he?"

Van Veeteren shrugged.

"Somewhere in the building, I assume. In his office, if you're lucky."

. . .

Ten minutes later Jung returned with Heinemann in tow.

"Sorry," said Heinemann, flopping down onto an empty chair. "I was a bit delayed."

"You don't say," said Reinhart.

Heinemann put a large envelope on the table in front of him.

"What have you got there?" asked Münster.

"The connection," said Heinemann.

"What do you mean?" wondered Rooth.

"I was supposed to look for the connection, wasn't I?"

"Well, I'll be damned!" said deBries.

Heinemann opened the envelope and took out an enlarged photograph. He handed it to Van Veeteren.

The chief inspector studied it for a few seconds, looking bewildered.

"Explain," he said eventually.

"Of course," said Heinemann, taking off his glasses. "The photograph is of the leaving class—that really is what they call it—from the United Services Staff College in 1965. Third from the left in the bottom row is Ryszard Malik. Second from the right in the middle row is Rickard Maasleitner."

You could have heard a pin drop. Van Veeteren passed around the photograph of thirty-five formally dressed young men in gray-green military shirts with innocent expressions on their faces.

"Did you say 1965?" asked Münster when everybody had seen it.

"Yes," said Heinemann. "They were called up in April '64, and left at the end of May '65. Anyway, that's what I've found. . . . Apart from the fact that they have the same initials, of course, but I expect you've thought about that?"

"What?" said Rooth. "My God, you're right!"

"R.M.," said Reinhart. "Hmm, I don't suppose it means anything."

"Have you got the names of all of them?" asked Van Veeteren.

Heinemann dug down into the envelope and produced a sheet of paper.

"Just the names and dates of birth so far, but Krause and Willock are working on more. It'll take a while, as you'll appreciate."

"The main thing is that it's done scrupulously," said Reinhart.

Silence again. Münster stood up and walked over to the window, turning his back on the others. Van Veeteren leaned back and sucked in his cheeks. Moreno took another look at the photograph.

"Well," said deBries after a while, "this is worth thinking about, I reckon."

"Presumably," said Van Veeteren. "We'll take a break now. I need to contemplate. Come back here half an hour from now, and then we can decide where to go from here. DeBries, can you let me have a cigarette?"

"Where exactly is this military college?" asked Moreno when they had reassembled.

"Up in Schaabe nowadays," said Heinemann. "It was moved from here in Maardam at the beginning of the seventies—it used to be out at Löhr."

"Did you find any other connections?" Münster wondered.

"No, not yet. But I think this one is spot-on. If there are any others, they will probably be further back in the past."

"How should we go about this, then?" asked Rooth.

Van Veeteren looked up from the list of names.

"This is what we'll do," he said, checking how many of them there were. "There are eight of us. Each of us will take four names and track them down over the weekend. It ought to be possible to find at least two out of four. You can check addresses and suchlike with Krause and Willock. They can distribute the names among you as well. On Monday morning I want comprehensive reports, and if you come across anything significant before then, get in touch."

"Sound method," said Reinhart.

"Exactly what I was going to say," said Rooth. "When will Krause and Willock be ready?"

"They'll be working all evening," said Van Veeteren. "Joensuu and Klempje have been roped in as well. You can all go home and then ring here and get your four names tonight, or tomorrow morning. Okay? Any questions?"

"One more thing, perhaps," said Reinhart.

"Of course, dammit," said Van Veeteren, tapping at the photograph with his index finger. "Tread carefully. It's by no means certain that these are the guys we're looking for. Don't forget that!"

"Should we release this information to the general public?" Münster asked.

Van Veeteren thought for three seconds.

"I think we should be extremely careful not to do that," he said eventually. "Bear that in mind when you ask your questions as well—don't say too much about what's going on. I don't think Hiller would be too pleased if thirty-three people suddenly turned up and demanded police protection all around the clock."

"Mind you, it would be fun to see his face if they did," said Reinhart.

"If they did," said Van Veeteren.

Russian roulette? Münster thought as he was sitting with the kids on his knee an hour later, watching a children's program on the TV. Why do the words "Russian roulette" keep coming into my head?

It could be a coincidence, of course, Van Veeteren thought as he settled down in the bath with a burning candle on the lavatory seat and a beer within easy reach. Pure coincidence, if Reinhart hadn't already banned that expression. Two people living in the same town might well end up sooner or later in the same photograph, whether they want to or not.

Wasn't that more likely than their not doing so?

God only knows, Van Veeteren thought. In any case, we'll find out eventually.

16

Saturday, February 3, began with warm southwesterly winds and a misleadingly high and bright sky. Van Veeteren had already made up his mind in principle to attend Ryszard Malik's funeral, but when he stood in the balcony doorway to check the weather situation at about nine o'clock, he realized that he also had the gods on his side.

Still standing there, he tried to establish what had led him to make that decision. Why he felt it was so necessary for him to be present at the burial ceremony in the Eastern Cemetery, that is. And, to his horror, it dawned on him that it was because of an old movie. Or several movies, rather. More specifically that classic introductory scene with a group of people dressed in black around a coffin being lowered slowly into a grave. And then, a short distance away, two detectives in their crumpled trench coats observing the mourners. They turn up their collars and begin a whispered conversation about who's who. . . . Who is that lady with the veil, half-turned away from the grave; why isn't the widow crying, and which of the bastards is it who pumped a bullet into the head of the stinking-rich Lord Ffolliot-Pym?

What reasoning! Van Veeteren thought as he closed the balcony door. Downright perverse! But then, there's nothing one won't do. . . .

Out in the windswept cemetery later that day there seemed to be a distinct shortage of possible murderers. The one who behaved most oddly was without doubt a large man in a green raincoat and red rubber boots; but he had been instructed to attend by the chief inspector.

Constable Klaarentoft was known as the force's most skillful photographer, and his task on this occasion was to take as many pictures as he possibly could. Van Veeteren knew that he had stolen this idea from another movie, namely *Blow-Up*, from the mid-sixties. Antonioni, if he remembered rightly. The theory was, of course, that somewhere among all these faces, which would slowly emerge from the police photographic laboratory, would be the murderer's.

Ryszard Malik's and Rickard Maasleitner's murderer.

He recalled seeing the film—which was a pretty awful mishmash—three times, simply to observe how the face of a killer could be plucked out of the lush greenery of an English park.

Another kind of perversion, of course, and Klaarentoft had evidently not seen the film. He traipsed around between the graves, snapping away to his heart's content, totally ignoring Van Veeteren's instruction to be as unobtrusive as possible.

The fact that he managed to take no less than twelve pictures of the clergyman conducting the ceremony suggested that he might not have grasped the point of his contribution.

On the other hand, of course, the group that followed

Ryszard Malik to his final resting place was on the sparse side, so there was a shortage of motifs. Van Veeteren counted fourteen persons present—including himself and Klaarentoft—and during the course of the ceremony he was able to identify all of them, apart from two children.

He was unable to detect furtive observers keeping some distance away from the grave (there were a few persons tending other graves in the vicinity, of course, but none of them behaved strangely or alerted his famous intuition in the slightest), and when the rain started to fall and he had managed to give Klaarentoft discreet instructions to go away and snap something else, he had long been aware that there was not much point in his hanging around.

And an hour or so later, when he had finally managed to drink a glass of mulled wine at the Kraus bar, he realized that the cold he had succeeded in keeping at bay over the last few days had now gotten a second wind.

The next funeral will be my own, he predicted.

"It's Saturday. Do you really have to do that today?" he had asked.

"Today or tomorrow. Don't you think it's best if I get it out of the way as soon as possible?"

"Yes, of course," he'd replied, and turned over in his bed. "I'll see you this evening."

It wasn't an especially unusual exchange. Nor unexpected. As she sat in the bus she felt a nagging pain at the back of her head, like a bad omen. She had been with Claus Badher for fifteen months now—maybe sixteen, it depended on what criteria you used—and it was probably the best relationship she'd ever been involved in. In fact, it certainly was. It involved love and mutual respect, shared values and interests, and everything else one could reasonably expect.

Everything in the garden was lovely. Pure bliss. All their friends thought they ought to take things further. Move in together permanently, with all that implied. Claus thought so too.

There was just that little irritation. That tiny little snag that frightened her. That might be rooted in contempt, despite everything, and if so was destined to grow and become even more worrying. She didn't know. Contempt for her job. Needless to say he was extremely careful not to make it obvious—probably didn't even realize it himself; but sometimes she couldn't help but notice. It just crept up on her, flashed briefly on the surface, then vanished: but she knew it was there. As in the little exchange they'd just had, for instance, which wasn't really significant in itself as yet. . . . But she suspected it could grow into something really threatening as the years passed by.

A threat to their equal status. And to her life.

Claus Badher worked as a foreign-exchange broker in a bank, and was on his way up. She worked as a detective inspector and was on the way . . . where was she on the way to?

She sighed. At the moment she was on the way to a house in Dikken, where she was due to meet a fifty-two-year-old lawyer and ask him about his time as a National Serviceman.

Absurd? Yes, it was absurd. She often thought that Claus was absolutely right. Always assuming that that was what he was thinking, of course. . . .

She got off the bus and walked the hundred meters or so to the house. Went in through the gate and was greeted by two boxer puppies, enthusiastically barking and wagging their stumpy tails. She paused on the gravel path to stroke them. Looked up at the big two-story house in dark brown English brick with green shutters. Behind one of the gable ends she could just make out a swimming pool, and some wire netting she assumed must be surrounding a tennis court.

Why not? she thought. If I really had to, I suppose I might manage to cope with living like this.

"Ewa Moreno, detective inspector. I'm sorry to trouble you. I just have a few questions I'd like to ask you."

"No problem. I'm at your disposal."

Jan Tomaszewski was wearing something she assumed must be a smoking jacket—and indeed, the rest of him seemed to belong to another age. Or in a movie. His dark hair was powdered and immaculately combed, and his slim body gave the distinct impression of being aristocratic. Leslie Howard? she wondered. He reached out over the smoke-gray glass table and served her tea from a charmingly sculpted silver pot.

Another world, she thought. I'd better get going before I swoon.

"Thank you," she said. "As I mentioned, I need to ask you about the time you spent during your National Service at the Staff College in Löhr. I think that was 1964 to 1965—is that right?"

He nodded.

"That's correct. Why on earth should you be interested in that?"

"I'm afraid I can't tell you that. And I'd appreciate it if you would be discreet about our conversation as well. Perhaps we can meet again at a later stage if you want to know more."

That was a formulation she had thought out in advance, and she could see that it had fallen on fruitful ground.

"I understand."

"Anyway, we are mainly interested in a couple of your fellow students at the college. Ryszard Malik and Rickard Maasleitner."

She took the photograph out of her briefcase and handed it to him.

"Can you point them out?"

He smiled and took a pair of glasses from his breast pocket. Scrutinized the photograph for some thirty seconds.

"Maasleitner isn't a problem," he said. "We were in the same barrack room nearly all the time. I'm not so sure about Malik, but I think that's him."

He pointed and Moreno nodded.

"Correct. Can you tell me what you remember about them?"

Tomaszewski took off his glasses and leaned back in his chair.

"I can hardly remember Malik at all," he said after a while. "We were never in the same group and we didn't mix when we were off duty. He was a bit introspective and pretty anonymous, I think. I should mention that I'm not completely unaware of what has happened. . . ."

Moreno nodded.

"Do I take it that you think this is the link? The connection between the two of them, I mean?"

"We're following up several different lines of inquiry," Moreno explained. "This is just one of them. Obviously, we need to follow up every possibility."

"Of course. Anyway, I recall Maasleitner in a bit more detail. We were frequently in the same class during training—

telegraphy, general staff work, and so on. I have to say I didn't much like him. He was a bit dominant, if you see what I mean."

"How do you mean, dominant?" Moreno asked.

"Well . . ." Tomaszewski flung out his arms. "Bigmouthed. Young and arrogant. A bit unbalanced—but he probably wasn't all that bad."

"Was he generally disliked?"

Tomaszewski thought that one over.

"I think so. Not that it was a real problem. It was just that he had something about him that could be a bit trying. But, of course, there's bound to be one or two like that in such a big group."

"Did you mix at all when you were off duty?"

Tomaszewski shook his head.

"Never."

"Do you know if Malik and Maasleitner did?"

"I've no idea. I wouldn't have thought so, but, of course, I can't swear to it."

"Do you know if any of the others were close to them? To either one of them, that is?"

Tomaszewski studied the photograph again. Moreno produced a list of names and handed it to him. Drank a little tea and took a chocolate biscuit while he was thinking about it. Looked around the whitewashed walls, crammed full with rows of colorful, nonfigurative paintings, almost edge to edge. Her host was evidently something of a collector. She wondered how much money was hanging here.

Probably quite a lot.

"Hmm," he said eventually. "I'm afraid I can't be of much help to you. I can't think of any link between them. I can't associ-

ate Malik with anybody else at all. I think Maasleitner occasionally hung around with them."

He pointed to two faces in the back row.

"Van der Heukken and Biedersen?" Moreno read the names
from her list.

Tomaszewski nodded.

"As far as I can recall. You realize that it's over thirty years
ago?"

Moreno smiled.

"Yes," she said. "I realize that. But I understood that time
spent on National Service had an ineradicable effect on all young
men who underwent it."

Tomaszewski smiled.

"No doubt it did on some. But most of us try to forget all
about it, as far as possible."

"Charming" was the word that stuck in her mind after the visit to
Tomaszewski. The discreet charm of the middle classes, she
recalled, and she had to admit that on the whole, there were
worse ways of spending an hour on a Saturday morning.

She had not expected her trip to Dikken to produce anything
substantial for the investigation, and the same applied to the next
name on her list: Pierre Borsens.

When she got off the bus in Maardam, she had succeeded in
thrusting aside the morning's gloomy thoughts and made up her
mind to call in at the covered market and buy a couple of decent
cheeses for the evening meal. Pierre Borsens lived only a block
away from the market, and it wasn't yet quite half past twelve.

.   .   .

The man who sat down at the table brought with him an aroma that Jung had some difficulty in identifying. It had the same crudely acidic quality as cat piss, but it also had an unmistakable tang of the sea. Rotten seaweed scorched by the sun, or something of the sort. Most probably it was a combination of both these ingredients.

And more besides. Jung hastily moved his chair back a couple of feet, and lit a cigarette.

"I take it you are Calvin Lange?" he asked.

"I certainly am," said the man, reaching out a grubby hand over the table. Jung leaned forward and shook it.

"My place is a bit of a mess at the moment," the man explained. "That's why I thought it would be better to meet here."

He smiled, and revealed two rows of brown, decayed teeth. Jung was grateful to hear what the man said. He would prefer not to have been confronted by the mess.

"Would you like a beer?" The question was rhetorical.

Lange nodded and coughed. Jung gestured toward the bar.

"And a cigarette, perhaps?"

Lange took one. Jung sighed discreetly and decided it was necessary to get this over with as quickly as possible. It was always problematic to arrange reimbursement for beer and cigarettes; that was something he'd discovered a long time ago.

"Do you recognize this?"

Lange took the photograph and studied it while drawing deeply on his cigarette.

"That's me," he said, placing a filthy index finger on the face of a young, innocent-looking man in the front row.

"We know that," said Jung. "Do you remember what those two are called?"

He pointed with his pen.

"One at a time," said Lange.

The waitress arrived with two glasses of beer.

"Cheers," said Lange, emptying his in one gulp.

"Cheers," said Jung, pointing at Malik in the photograph.

"Let's see," said Lange, peering awkwardly. "No, no fucking idea. Who else?"

Jung pointed at Maasleitner with his pen.

"Seems familiar," said Lange, scratching his armpit. "Yes, I recognize that bugger, but I've no idea what he's called."

He belched and looked gloomily at his empty glass.

"Do you remember the names Malik and Maasleitner?"

"Malik and . . . ?"

"Maasleitner."

"Maasleitner?"

"Yes."

"No, is that him?"

He plonked his finger on Malik.

"No, that's Malik."

"Oh, shit. What have they done?"

Jung stubbed out his cigarette. This was going brilliantly.

"Do you remember anything at all from your year as a National Serviceman?"

"National Service? Why are you asking about that?"

"I'm afraid I can't go into that. But we're interested in these two people. Staff College 1965—that's right, isn't it?"

He pointed again.

"Oh, shit," said Lange, and had a coughing fit. "You mean this picture is from the Staff College? Fuck me, I thought it was the handball team. But there were too many of 'em."

Jung thought about this for three seconds. Then he returned the photograph to his briefcase and stood up.

"Many thanks," he said. "You're welcome to my beer as well."

"If you twist my arm," said Lange.

Mahler advanced a pawn and Van Veeteren sneezed.

"How are things? Under the weather again?"

"Just a bit, yes. I was out in the rain at the cemetery for too long yesterday afternoon."

"Stupid," said Mahler.

"I know," sighed Van Veeteren. "But I couldn't just walk away. I'm rather sensitive about that kind of thing."

"Yes, I know how you feel," said Mahler. "It was that Malik, I gather. How's the case going? They're writing quite a lot about it in the newspapers."

"Badly," said Van Veeteren.

"Have you found a link yet?"

Van Veeteren nodded.

"But I'm not sure it's the right one. Well, I suppose I am, really. . . . But that doesn't mean very much yet. You could say that I'm looking for a stone and I've found the market square."

"Eh?" said Mahler.

Van Veeteren sneezed again.

"For Christ's sake," he said. "Looking for a star and I've found a galaxy, how about that? I thought you were supposed to be the poet."

Mahler chuckled.

"I know what you mean," he said. "But isn't it an incident that you're looking for?"

Van Veeteren picked up his white knight and sat there for a few seconds, holding it in his hand.

"An incident?" he said, placing the knight on c4. "Yes, that's probably not a bad guess. The problem is that such a lot is happening."

"All the time," said Mahler.

17

Of the four people eventually allocated to Inspector Münster, it turned out that one lived in central Maardam, one in Linzhuisen, barely thirty kilometers away, and one down in Groenstadt, a journey of some two hundred kilometers. On Saturday afternoon, Münster conducted a short telephone interview with the last—a certain Werner Samijn, who worked as an electrical engineer and didn't have much to say about either Malik or Maasleitner. He had lived in the same barrack room as Malik and remembered him most as a rather pleasant and somewhat reserved young man. He thought Maasleitner was a more cocksure type (if the inspector and the man's widow would excuse the expression), but they had never mixed or gotten to know each other.

Number one on the list, Erich Molder, failed to answer the several phone calls Münster made to his house in Guyderstraat; but number two, Joen Fassleucht, was available; Münster offered to drive to his home late on Sunday afternoon.

Münster's son, Bart, aged six and a half, objected strongly to this arrangement, but after some discussion, it was decided that Bart could go along in the car, provided he promise to stay in the backseat reading a *Monster* comic while his father carried out his police duties.

It was the first time Münster had agreed to anything of this nature, and as he sat in Fassleucht's living room nibbling at cookies, he became aware that it did not have a particularly positive influence on his powers of concentration.

But perhaps that didn't matter so much on this occasion—it was hardly an important interrogation, he tried to convince himself. Fassleucht had mixed with Malik quite a lot during his National Service: they were both part of a group of four or five friends who occasionally went out together. Went to the movies, played cards, or simply sat at the same table in the canteen and gaped at the goggle-box. After demobilization, all contact had ceased; and as for Maasleitner, all Fassleucht could do was confirm the opinion expressed by Samijn the previous day.

Overbearing and rather cocky.

Münster had been apprehensive, of course, and when he returned to his car after about half an hour he saw immediately that Bart had disappeared.

A cold shudder ran down his spine as he stood on the pavement wondering what the hell he should do; and, of course, that was the intention. Bart's disheveled head suddenly appeared in the back window—he had been lying on the floor hidden under a blanket, and his broadly grinning face left no doubt about the fact that he considered it an unusually successful joke.

"You really looked shit scared!" he announced in glee.

"You little bastard," said Münster. "Would you like a hamburger?"

"And a Coke," said Bart.

Münster drove toward the center of town in search of a suitable establishment for the provision of such goods, and decided that his son would have to grow several years older before it was appropriate to take him along on a similar assignment.

"There's an in-depth article about your case in the *Allgemejne* today," said Winnifred Lynch. "Have you read it?"

"No," said Reinhart. "Why should I do that?"

"They try to make a profile of the perpetrator."

Reinhart snorted.

"You can make a perpetrator profile only in the case of a serial killer. And even then it's a decidedly dodgy method. But it sounds good in the press, of course. They can write and make up stories about murderers who don't exist. A green flag for any fantasies you like. Much more fun than reality, naturally."

Winnifred Lynch folded up the newspaper.

"Isn't it a serial killer, then?"

Reinhart looked hard at her over the edge of his book.

"If we go and take a bath, I can tell you a bit more about it."

"Good that you have such a big bathtub," commented Winnifred ten minutes later. "If I do take you on, it'll be because of the bathtub. So don't imagine anything else. Okay?"

"The murderer?"

"Yes."

"Well, I don't know," said Reinhart, sinking down further into the bubbles. "Of course it's possible that there's going to be a series, but it's almost impossible to judge after only two. And then, what kind of a series is it? Continue this series of numbers: one, four . . . then what? There are all kinds of possibilities."

"And the former National Servicemen have nothing useful to say?"

Reinhart shook his head.

"I don't think so. Not the ones I spoke to, in any case. But the key might well be there somewhere, even so. It's so damned easy to hide something, if you want to. If there's something you don't want stirred up, then all you do is say nothing about it. It was thirty years ago, after all. . . ."

He leaned his head against the edge of the bath and thought for a while.

"It's going to be extremely difficult to solve this case, no matter what. If there are no more after these two, that is. There's a bit of difference in the work input, I can assure you."

"What do you mean?"

Reinhart cleared his throat.

"Well, hypothetically. Let's say I make up my mind to kill somebody, anybody at all. I get up at three o'clock on a Tuesday morning. I get dressed in dark clothes, hide my face, go out and find a suitable place, and wait. Then I shoot the first person to come past and go home."

"Using a silencer."

"Using a silencer. Or I stab him with a knife. What chance is there of my being found out?"

"Not a lot."

"Next to none. But if I do it even so, how many working hours do you think it costs the police? Compared with the hour it took me."

Winnifred nodded. Stuck her right foot into Reinhart's armpit and started wiggling her toes.

"That's nice," said Reinhart. "When war breaks out, can't we just come here and lie like this?"

"By all means," said Winnifred. "But what about a motive? That's what you're getting at, I take it?"

"Exactly," said Reinhart. "It's because of this imbalance that we have to look for a motive. A single thought on the right lines can save thousands of working hours. So you can see why I'm such a trump card at the police station."

She laughed.

"I can imagine it. But you haven't had that thought on the right lines in this case, is that it?"

"Not yet," said Reinhart.

He found the soap and started lathering her legs.

"I think it's a wronged woman," said Winnifred after a while.

"I know that's what you think."

He thought for half a minute.

"Would you be able to fire those other two shots?"

She thought about it.

"No. Not now. But I don't think it's impossible. You can be driven to it. It's hardly inexplicable, let's face it. On the contrary, in fact."

"A madwoman who goes around shooting the willies off all men? With good reason?"

"For specific reasons," said Winnifred. "Specific causes. And not just any old willies."

"Perhaps she's not mad, either?" said Reinhart.

"Depends on how you look at it, I suppose. She's been wronged, as I said. Affronted, perhaps. . . . No, let's change the subject, this is making me feel unwell."

"Me too," said Reinhart. "Shall I do the other leg as well?"

"Yes, do that," said Winnifred Lynch.

. . .

Van Veeteren had arranged to meet Renate for a while on Sunday afternoon, but when he got up at eleven o'clock, he was pleased to discover that his cold had gotten so much worse that he had a perfectly good excuse for canceling the meeting. All his respiratory passages seemed to be blocked by something thick and slimy and more or less impenetrable, and the only way in which he could breathe at all was by walking around with his mouth wide open. For a few painful seconds he observed what this procedure looked like in the hall mirror, and he recognized that today was one of those days when he ought not to force his presence on another human being.

Not even an ex-wife.

It was bad enough putting up with himself, and the day progressed in a fashion reminiscent of a seal traveling through a desert. At about ten in the evening he slumped over the kitchen table with his feet in a bubbling footbath and a terry towel draped over his head—in the vain hope that the steam from an aromatic concoction in a saucepan would banish the slime in his frontal cavities. It certainly had an effect: fluid poured out from every orifice, and he was covered in sweat.

Bugger this for a lark, he thought.

And then the telephone rang.

Van Veeteren recalled Reinhart's early morning call the other day and formed a rapid but logical conclusion: if I didn't wish to receive any calls, I ought to have pulled out the plug.

I haven't pulled out the plug, and therefore I'd better answer.

"Hello. Enso Faringer here."

For a few blank seconds he hadn't the slightest idea who Enso Faringer was.

"We met down at Freddy's and talked about Maasleitner."

"Yes, of course. What do you want?"

"You said I should give you a call if I remembered anything."

"And?"

"I've remembered something."

Van Veeteren sneezed.

"Excuse me?"

"It was nothing. What have you remembered?"

"Well, I remember Maasleitner talking about that music."

"What music?"

"Somebody had telephoned him over and over again, and played him a tune, it seems."

"A tune?"

"Yes."

"Why?"

"I don't know. It had annoyed him, in any case."

A diffuse memory began to stir in the back of the chief inspector's brain.

"Hang on a minute. What kind of music was it?"

"I don't know. He never said what it was—I don't think he knew."

"But why did this person call him? What was the point?"

"He didn't know. That's what irritated him."

"Was it a man or a woman?"

"I don't think he said. I think it was just music, all the time."

Van Veeteren thought for a moment.

"When exactly was this?"

Faringer hesitated.

"The same day we went to Freddy's, I think. When he was shot. Or maybe the day before."

"And this call was repeated several times?"

"Yes, it seems so."

"Did he try to do anything about it?"

"I don't know."

"And he didn't know who it was behind it?"

"I don't think so. No, he was angry, mainly because he'd no idea what it was all about."

Van Veeteren thought again.

"Mr. Faringer," he said eventually. "Are you sure you remember this correctly? You're sure you haven't got hold of the wrong end of the stick?"

He could hear some coughing at the other end of the line, and when the little German teacher's voice returned, there was no doubt that he was rather offended.

"I know I was slightly drunk, but I can remember this as clear as day."

"I understand," said Van Veeteren. "Is there anything else you remember?"

"Not yet," said Faringer. "But if I do, I'll be in touch again."

"I'll probably be in touch again as well," said the chief inspector before hanging up.

Well, what the devil does this mean? he wondered as he poured the liquid from the footbath and the concoction of herbs down the sink.

And what was it he almost remembered that somebody had said a few weeks ago?

18

It was late on Tuesday afternoon before they succeeded in tracking down all the remaining thirty-three staff NCOs (which was their official military status) of the 1965 vintage. Thirty-one of the group were still alive, the youngest of them now fifty, the eldest fifty-six. Five of them turned out to be resident abroad (three in other European countries, one in the United States, one in South Africa), fourteen were still in the Maardam police district, and the remaining twelve in other parts of the country.

Heinemann was in charge of this side of the investigation and kept a register of all those concerned. He also made an effort to systematize the results of the interrogations, without finding an entirely successful method. When he handed the documentation over to Van Veeteren at about half past six in the evening, he devoted some considerable time to an attempt to enlighten his boss about all the cryptic signs and abbreviations, but in the end they both realized that it was a waste of time.

"You can explain it orally instead when we meet tomorrow to run through the current situation," Van Veeteren decided. "It'll be just as well for everybody to get the information at the same time."

. . .

There had been a rumor to the effect that the chief of police himself intended to turn up for this meeting, which was due to take place at ten a.m. on Wednesday; but when the time came he was unable to attend. Whether this was due to something important that had cropped up, or the desire to repot some plants in his office, was something nobody was in a position to say—but the fact that February is the most sensitive month for all plants was something that Reinhart at least was fully conversant with.

"Eight wise heads is a good score," he said. "If we had Hiller's as well, that would reduce the number to seven. Let's get started."

Heinemann's summary—with questions and interruptions and comments—took almost an hour, despite the fact that there were no real links or justifiable suspicions to report.

Opinions of Ryszard Malik had been more or less unanimous. A rather reticent, somewhat reserved person; friendly, reliable, without any striking characteristics or interests—that seemed to be the general impression. His social intercourse with his fellow students had been restricted to a group of four or five, generally speaking; but even among those there was nobody able to give any interesting tips of use to the investigation.

Needless to say, it was not easy to have any idea about what any such tips might have constituted; but without denigrating anybody's efforts, it would be fair to say that comments made about Malik failed to bring the question of who murdered him a single centimeter closer to a solution.

The same could probably also be said of Maasleitner. The perception of him as a somewhat overbearing, self-centered, and not very likeable young man was universal. He had belonged to a group of eight to ten people who frequently went around together, in their free time as well as during duty hours. Quite an active group, it seems, with a few questionable escapades on the program for some evenings, not to say nights, as Heinemann put it.

"Questionable evening and night escapades?" said Reinhart, raising his eyebrows. "Is that a formulation you made up yourself?"

"No," said Heinemann unexpectedly. "It's a quotation from the Koran."

"I don't believe that for a moment," said Rooth.

"Go on," said Van Veeteren, clearly irritated.

"It must also be pointed out," said Heinemann, "that not a single one of those questioned managed to think of any links at all between Malik and Maasleitner, which surely undermines our hypotheses to some extent. We need to ask ourselves two questions. First: Is this really the background to the murders? Were Ryszard Malik and Rickard Maasleitner really murdered because they were on the same course when they did their National Service thirty years ago?"

He paused. Van Veeteren blew his nose into a paper tissue, which he then dropped on the floor under his desk.

"Second: If we say yes to the first question, what form does that connection take? There are two possibilities. Either the murderer is one of the others in the photo"—he tapped on the photograph with the frame of his spectacles—"or there is an outsider who has some kind of relationship with the group."

"Who intends to murder all thirty-five of them," said Rooth.

"There are only thirty-one left," deBries pointed out.

"Great," said Rooth.

Heinemann looked around, waiting for comments.

"Okay, we've made a note of that," said Reinhart, clasping his hands behind his head. "Where do we go from here, then?"

Van Veeteren cleared his throat and leaned forward over the table, resting his head on his clenched hands.

"We have an extremely important question to ask ourselves," he said, speaking slowly to emphasize the significance. "I know it's a bit of hocus-pocus, but never mind. Anyway, did any of you smell a rat when you spoke to these people? Something they weren't telling us about? Just a little trace of a suspicion, you know what I mean. . . . No matter how illogical or irrational it might seem. If so, speak up now!"

He looked around the table. Nobody spoke. Jung looked as if he were about to, but changed his mind. DeBries might also have been on the way to saying something, but decided to hold back. Moreno shook her head.

"No," said Reinhart in the end. "I usually recognize murderers, but this time I saw no trace of one."

"There were several of them we interviewed over the phone," said Münster. "It's almost impossible to get the kind of impression we're talking about if we don't have them sitting in front of us."

Van Veeteren nodded.

"Perhaps we should have another chat with the lads who were a bit familiar with Maasleitner. It couldn't do any harm. If the murderer is an outsider who nevertheless has some sort of link with that group . . . well, there are all kinds of possibilities, needless to say. I think we should try to find out if there was something that happened . . . something that could have been traumatic, somehow or other."

"Traumatic?" said Rooth.

"It ought to have cropped up during our interviews, if there had been anything like that," said deBries.

"Possibly," said Van Veeteren. "But you never know. We have a few more interviews to conduct, in any case. I have an old colonel and a couple of company commanders in store."

"Where?" asked deBries.

"One here," said Van Veeteren. "Two up in Schaabe, unfortunately."

"I know a girl in Schaabe," said Rooth.

"Okay," said Van Veeteren. "You can take those two."

"Thank you," said Rooth.

"What about that music?" said deBries.

"Yes," said Van Veeteren with a sigh. "God only knows what it means, but it seems that both Malik and Maasleitner received strange telephone calls shortly before their time was up. Someone who didn't say a word, just played a tune. . . ."

"What kind of a tune?" wondered Jung.

"We don't know. Mrs. Malik evidently took two such calls; she mentioned it when she was in the hospital, but we didn't take her all that seriously. I went to see her yesterday—she's still staying with her sister, and won't be leaving there anytime soon, I suspect. She confirms that it actually happened, but she had no idea what the music was, nor what it might signify."

"Hmm," said Reinhart. "What about Maasleitner?"

"He evidently also received lots of calls the same day, or the day before. He told that little Kraut teacher about it, but he was wallowing in alcohol up to his armpits more or less, and doesn't remember all that much about it."

"But it must have been the same music, no matter what," said Münster.

"Yes," muttered the chief inspector. "We can take that for granted. But it would be interesting to know what the point of it was."

Nobody spoke.

"Didn't they understand, at least?"

Van Veeteren shook his head.

"It seems not. Maasleitner didn't, in any case. We don't know if Malik received any calls himself. He didn't say anything to his wife, but that's understandable."

"Very understandable," said Rooth.

Reinhart took out his pipe and stared at it for a while.

"It seems we have a worthy opponent this time, don't you think?"

Van Veeteren nodded glumly.

"We certainly do. Anyway, I have no intention of mentioning this telephone music to the media . . . not yet, at least. But obviously, we have to warn the remaining thirty-one."

"Those who have still survived," said deBries.

"Münster can write a letter that we can send to them. Be careful about the wording, and I want to see it before it goes out."

"Of course," said Münster.

"I suppose we'll have to cut back on the number of officers on the case," said the chief inspector, blowing his nose for the twentieth time in an hour. "Let's discuss how to divide the jobs after coffee."

"There's a right time for everything," said Reinhart.

. . .

Reinhart sat down opposite the chief inspector and stirred his coffee slowly.

"It feels a bit worrying," he said.

Van Veeteren nodded.

"Do you think there'll be more?"

"Yes."

"So do I."

They sat in silence for a while.

"It might be just as well," said Reinhart. "We'll never solve it otherwise."

Van Veeteren said nothing. Rubbed his nose with a paper tissue, breathing heavily. Rooth came to join them, carrying an overloaded tray.

"What's preferable?" Reinhart continued. "Two victims and a murderer who gets away with it? Or three victims and a murderer who gets caught?"

"Or four?" said Van Veeteren. "Or five? There always has to be a limit."

"Or at least one has to be imposed," said Reinhart. "That's not quite the same thing."

"It would be best if there weren't any victims at all," interposed Rooth. "And no murderer, either."

"Utopia," Reinhart snorted. "We deal with reality."

"Oh, that," said Rooth.

That evening, ensconced in an armchair and wrapped up in two blankets with Handel in the speakers, Van Veeteren thought back to the conversation in the canteen. He noted that it was almost exactly a week since Rickard Maasleitner was murdered. Nearly three since the first murder.

And he also noted that the police had hardly earned any laurels thus far. Had he used the resources available to him as best he could?

Should he not have arranged some kind of protection? Ought he not to have put more resources into tracing the weapon? Should he not . . . ?

He picked up the photograph and studied it for the thousandth time since Heinemann first produced it. Studied the faces of these formally dressed young men, one after the other.

Thirty-five young men full of optimism as they began to make their way into the world. Every one of them looking with confidence as far into the future as it was possible to see, or so it seemed.

The future? he thought.

Was one of them next in line?

He thought so. But who?

VI

February 8–14

19

When the call finally came, Karel Innings had been waiting for six days.

Ever since he had sat reading his newspaper that morning and drawn the horrific conclusions, he had known that it must come.

Something had to be done. He had twice tried to get in touch himself, but Biedersen had been away. The message on his answering machine said he would be home by the sixth, but the same message was there when he tried to phone again on the seventh.

The most obvious course would be for Biedersen to make the first move. Without needing to think any further about it, he knew that to be the case. That's what the relationship had been, quite simply—Biedersen and Maasleitner, Malik and Innings. Insofar as there had been any relationships at all, that is.

The next most obvious course—and for every hour that passed during these ominous, gray February days, he could feel that this solution was becoming more and more inevitable—was to contact the police. The timid detective inspector who had been to see him inspired warmth and confidence, and he acknowledged that in different circumstances he would scarcely have hesitated before telling all.

Perhaps he also realized that the special circumstances were really just an excuse. There were always special circumstances. You always had to take things into account. Things like consideration for others—false and genuine—and, naturally, awkward situations were a constant possibility. But who could cope with something like this becoming public knowledge? A horrendous skeleton suddenly falling out of the cupboard after more than thirty years of silence. Probably nobody. When he lay awake at night and felt Ulrike's warm body by his side, he knew that at this moment it was an impossibility.

She must be spared this.

And, of course, it was not only his life with Ulrike that was at stake, even if she was beyond doubt the most important part. The whole of his new life, this incredibly placid and harmonious existence that was now beginning its second year, with Ulrike and their three children—his own and her two . . . no doubt it could have tolerated crises, but not this. Not this nauseating, abhorrent bombshell from the past.

It had evidently decided to haunt him yet again. It never gave up, and could never be atoned for.

The two-edged fear gnawed constantly at him during these waking hours. On the one hand, the fear of being exposed, and on the other, something even worse. During the day, the thought gave him hardly a moment of peace. It was as if every part of his body, wound up like a spring by worry and tension and lack of sleep, was in acute pain as he sat in the newspaper's editorial office and tried to concentrate on the routines and tasks he had known inside out for more than fifteen years. Was it obvious to the others? he kept asking himself more and more frequently. Could they see?

Probably not. Given the nonstop hustle and bustle and stress, it was possible for a colleague to more or less collapse on the spot under the weight of personal problems without anybody else noticing a thing. It had actually happened. It was even worse with Ulrike and the children, of course. They lived in such close contact, and they cared. He could blame it on his bad stomach, and did so. Sleepless nights need not necessarily mean that something serious was wrong.

And simply belonging to the group was an acceptable reason for being worried. The group originally comprising thirty-five National Servicemen. For the uninitiated, that was no doubt bad enough.

He was still managing to keep control of himself, then. But it was inevitable that things would get progressively worse; and when at last he heard Biedersen's broad dialect over the phone on Thursday afternoon, he had the feeling that the call had come in the nick of time. He couldn't have kept going for much longer.

Not much longer at all.

Even if it was not easy to take everything seriously, he had entertained the thought that his telephone might be bugged, and evidently Biedersen thought so as well. He didn't even say who was calling, and but for the fact that Innings had been expecting it and recognized Biedersen's dialect, he would have had little chance of identifying the voice.

"Hi," was all Biedersen said. "Shall we meet briefly tomorrow evening?"

"Yes," said Innings. "It would probably be as well."

Biedersen suggested a restaurant and a time, and that was that.

It was only after Innings had replaced the receiver that it

occurred to him that there was an unanswered question in this disturbing game.

What exactly would be involved if he entered into discussions with Biedersen?

And later that night as he lay awake in bed, wandering through the no-man's-land between sleep and consciousness, it suddenly dawned on him.

The new image for his fear was a trident.

20

Rooth had set off early and was in Schaabe by noon. As his first meeting was not until two hours later, he treated himself to a long and nourishing lunch at the railroad restaurant before heading to the Staff College.

Captain Falzenbucht turned out to be a short, thin little man with a strange low, husky voice. (He'd no doubt been standing too long on the barrack square, shouting his head off, Rooth thought.) He had passed the age of sixty several years before, and so ought to be leading a life of leisure in retirement—but as he pointed out several times, as long as the college needed his services, it was naturally his duty to stay on. As a good soldier. As a man. As a citizen.

As a human being? Rooth wondered.

Oh yes, of course he could recall the cohort of 1965. They had been his second brood as a sublieutenant, and when Rooth produced the photograph, he proceeded to identify several individuals by name.

So he's had enough sense to do his homework, thought Rooth, whose own military career was not suitable to be brought into the light of day on an occasion like this. Nor on any other, come to that.

"Anyway, the ones we are most interested in at this stage are Malik and Maasleitner," he said. "Can you point them out?"

Falzenbucht duly did so.

"I take it you know what's happened?"

"Of course," croaked Falzenbucht. "Murdered. A shocking story."

"We've spoken to all the rest," said Rooth.

"Are they all still alive?" Falzenbucht wondered.

"No, but we concentrated on those who are. Nobody can think of a link between Malik and Maasleitner, and nobody has any idea what might lie behind it all."

"I understand," said Falzenbucht.

"Have you any ideas?"

Falzenbucht assumed an expression that suggested deep thought.

"Hmm. I'm not surprised to hear that nobody could come up with anything. There is nothing. It has nothing—absolutely nothing at all—to do with the college and the education we provide here. I ought to make that clear."

"How can you know that?" said Rooth.

"We'd have known about it if it had."

Rooth considered this military logic for a few seconds.

"So what you don't see doesn't exist?" he said.

Falzenbucht made no reply.

"What do you think it's about, then?"

"I've no idea. But find out, you police officers."

"That's why I've come here."

"I see. Hmm."

For a few brief moments Rooth toyed with the idea of putting his foot down—picking up this growling, poker-backed little man, putting him in the car, and subjecting him to a thorough interrogation in some poky, smelly little cell at the Schaabe police station—but his good nature won out in the end, and he let it pass.

"Is there anything," he said instead, "anything at all, that you can tell me that you think might be of use to us in this investigation?"

Falzenbucht stroked his thumb and index finger over his well-trimmed mustache.

"None of the others in this group can have done it," he said. "They're lovely lads, every one of them. The murderer is somebody from the outside."

The devil himself, perhaps? Rooth thought. He sighed discreetly and checked his watch. There was over half an hour to go before his next appointment. He decided to waste another five minutes on Falzenbucht, and then find the canteen for a cup of coffee.

Major Straade proved to be roughly twice the size of Falzenbucht, with rather less of a military bearing, but he had just as little to contribute to the investigation. Nothing, zilch. Like the captain, he was inclined to think that the background to the affair was to be found outside the barrack gates—the now closed-down barracks at Löhr, on the outskirts of Maardam, that is.

Something that happened outside working hours. In the men's free time. Somewhere in town. Always assuming that the link really did have to do with the Staff College. Was that certain?

Had it been confirmed? Why imagine that the Staff College had anything to do with it at all?

They were questions that Straade kept coming back to, over and over again.

When Rooth had returned to his car and sat in the parking lot, he tried to assess all these guesses and judgments, but, needless to say, it was not easy to decide what they were really based on.

Sound and experience-based intuition? Or merely an anxious and boneheaded determination to protect the good name and reputation of the college?

Whatever it was, he found it hard to comprehend the military code of honor, and the obvious conclusion to draw was that the visit to Schaabe had resulted in absolutely nothing of value at all.

As far as the investigation was concerned, that is.

He checked the time and spread out a map of the town on the empty seat beside him.

Van Kuijperslaan, is that what she'd said?

She opened the door, and he noted immediately that her warm smile had not cooled down over the years.

He removed the paper and handed over the bouquet. She smiled even more broadly as she accepted it. Showed him into the hall and gave him a hug. He responded gladly and with as much enthusiasm as he considered advisable at this early stage, but then he noticed from the corner of his eye a dark-haired man—about the same age as himself—coming out of the kitchen with a bottle of wine in his hand.

"Who the hell's this?" he hissed into her ear.

She let go of him and turned toward the man.

"This is Jean-Paul," she said cheerfully. "My boyfriend. I'm so glad he managed to get home in time for you to get to know him."

"Great," said Inspector Rooth, trying to smile as well.

As Innings was about to enter Le Bistro, he was stopped at the door by a porter who gave him an envelope and suggested that he might like to go back out into the street. Somewhat bewildered, Innings did as he was told, opened the envelope, and found inside the address of another restaurant.

It was located some three blocks up the street, not far from the church, and as Innings made his way there he thought over the fact that Biedersen was evidently approaching the situation in a serious frame of mind, and leaving nothing to chance. He tried to come to terms with his own attitude, to think about what to say, but when he got there and saw Biedersen sitting in a booth about as far away from the door as possible, his dominant emotion was relief—and a strong desire to leave everything in somebody else's hands.

There didn't seem to be any doubt that Biedersen was willing to provide those hands.

"Long time no see," he said. "You are Innings, I presume?"

Innings nodded and sat down. Closer inspection suggested that Biedersen had changed rather less than he had expected. The last time they'd met had been by pure chance some ten years earlier—but they hadn't really spent time together since those days in June 1976.

The same powerful, sturdy figure. Rugged face, sparse reddish hair, and eyes that seemed to burn. They were never still. He recalled that some people had been afraid of them.

Perhaps he had been one of them.

"So, here we are," he said. "I tried to get hold of you several times. Before you rang, that is."

"Have you gathered what's going on?" said Biedersen.

Innings hesitated.

"Yes, er, well, I don't know. . . ."

"The other two have been murdered."

"Yes."

"Somebody has killed them. Who do you think it is?"

Innings recognized that somehow or other, he had succeeded in avoiding that question so far, goodness knows how.

"Her," he said. "It must be her. . . ."

"She's dead."

Biedersen spoke the words just as a waiter came to take their orders, and there was a pause before he was able to expand on what he had said.

"She's dead, as I said. There must be somebody else acting on her behalf. I think it's her daughter."

To his surprise, Innings noticed a trace of fear in Biedersen's voice. The same broad, off-putting dialect, certainly, but with the addition of something forced, a touch of nervousness.

"Her daughter?" he said.

"Yes, her daughter. I've tried to trace her."

"And?"

"She doesn't exist."

"Doesn't exist?"

"Impossible to pin down. She vacated her apartment in Stamberg in the middle of January, and nobody knows where she's gone to."

"You've tried, you say. . . ."

"A bit." He leaned forward over the table. "That bloody bitch isn't going to get us as well!"

Innings swallowed.

"Have you received any of these music calls?"

Innings shook his head.

"I have," said Biedersen. "It's a right bastard. But you must have had a letter from the police?"

"This morning," said Innings. "It looks like you're next."

It slipped out of him before he could stop it, and he was well aware that the relief he felt for a brief moment was a very transitory phenomenon.

First Biedersen. Then him. That's what was planned.

"You could be right," said Biedersen. "But don't feel too secure, that's all. We have to put a stop to her—I mean, that's why we're sitting here."

Innings nodded.

"We've got to get her before she gets us. I take it you're on board?"

"Yes. . . ."

"Are you hesitating?"

"No, no, I'm just wondering what we ought to do."

"I've already thought that through."

"You don't say. What do you mean?"

"Like with like. There's a bag under the table, can you feel it?"

Innings felt around with his feet and hit against something next to the wall.

"Yes," he said.

"Your weapon's in there. You owe me eight hundred for the trouble."

Innings felt a wave of dizziness envelop him.

"But . . . er, haven't you thought about . . . er, another possible alternative?"

Biedersen snorted.

"Huh. What might that be?"

"I don't know. . . ."

Biedersen lit a cigarette. A few seconds passed.

"Shall we go and look for her?" Innings said. "Or just sit here and wait?"

"For Christ's sake!" Biedersen snorted. "We don't even know what she looks like! But if you're prepared to travel to Stamberg and try to get hold of a photo of her, by all means. But how the hell do we know that she's not wearing a wig? And other stuff? You must know how easy it is for a fucking woman to change her appearance!"

Innings nodded.

"It could happen tonight, do you realize that? Or tomorrow. The next person to ring your doorbell could be her. Have you thought of that?"

Innings didn't reply. The waiter came with their food, and they started eating in silence.

"That music . . . ?" said Innings after a while, wiping his mouth.

Biedersen put down his knife and fork.

"Twice," he said. "Somebody's called a couple of times and

hung up when my wife answered. But it's that bloody tune in any case. . . . I can't remember what it's called, but we were playing it all the time. But I suppose I don't need to tell you that—you were pretty sober."

"I wasn't sober," said Innings. "You know I wasn't, I'd never do anything like that—"

"All right, all right, we don't need to go through all that again. What was the band called?"

"The Shadows?"

"Yes, that's it. You remember it. I've looked, but I don't seem to have the record anymore."

"Isn't it possible to trace the phone calls?"

"For God's sake," said Biedersen. "You don't seem to understand this. Naturally we can bring in the police and get as much bloody protection as we like—I thought we'd agreed not to do that?"

"Okay," said Innings. "I'm with you on that."

Biedersen stared hard at him.

"I don't know what your circumstances are," he said, "but I've got a family, have had for twenty-five years. A wife, three kids, and a grandchild as well. I have my own firm, good friends, business contacts. . . . For Christ's sake, I have a whole world that would collapse like a house of cards! But if you're doubtful, just say so. I can manage this on my own if need be. I just thought it would be beneficial if we collaborated a bit. Shared the responsibility."

"Yes . . ."

"If you don't want to play along, just say so."

Innings shook his head.

"No, I'm with you. Sorry. What do you think we should do?"

Biedersen flung out his hands.

"Maybe just wait," he said. "Be ready with the gun. You'd hardly need to explain why you acquired it, either—everybody will believe us. A man must have the right to protect his life, for God's sake."

Innings thought for a moment.

"Yes," he said. "It would be self-defense, of course."

Biedersen nodded.

"Sure," he said. "But we have to keep in touch as well. We have no other allies, and there could come about a situation in which it wouldn't do any harm if there were two of us. We might get wind of her, for instance. Malik and Maasleitner never had a chance, really."

Innings thought about that.

"How?" he said. "Keeping in touch, I mean."

Biedersen shrugged.

"Telephone," he said. "We have to take a chance, anything else would take too long. If we get through, all we need do is to arrange to meet somewhere. If necessary, spell it out. . . . I mean, she must be hanging around us for some time first, and . . . well, if you notice you're being followed by a woman, all you need to do is phone."

"It takes two hours to drive up to where you live, is that right?"

"About that," said Biedersen. "An hour and three quarters if you're lucky. Yes, it might well be my turn next, so you can stand by to set off."

Innings nodded. They continued eating in silence. Toasted each other without speaking, and when Innings swallowed the cold beer, he again felt a moment of dizziness. Carefully, he placed his foot on the bag with the ominous contents, and wondered how on earth he would be able to explain something like that to Ulrike.

A gun.

If he was forced to use it, he'd have to tell her the same story he told the police, of course—she would naturally be upset, but his precaution would have been proved to be justified, so why the hell should there be any reason to think otherwise?

But for the time being he decided to keep its existence a secret. That would be the easiest way.

And hope he would never have to use it.

Rely on Biedersen to do his duty.

"I must pay you," he said. "I don't think I've got as much as eight hundred on me, though. . . ."

"All in good time," said Biedersen. "If we can take care of this lunatic, we'll settle what we owe as well."

Innings nodded, and they sat quietly for a while.

"There's one thing I've been thinking about, and that bothers me a bit," said Biedersen, when they had been served with coffee and each lit a cigarette. "She's behaved in exactly the same way twice now. Surely she can't be so bloody stupid as to do so again?"

No, Innings thought as he left the restaurant five minutes after Biedersen. That's right. Surely she can't be as stupid as that.

22

The persistent cold—in combination with the occasional beer and too many hot toddies during recent days—meant that it didn't turn out to be much of a match. Perhaps also an accumulated and unsatisfied need for more sleep played a role as well.

In any case, during the third set Münster toyed with the idea of changing hands and playing with his left for a few games; things were not normally as bad as that. However, he knew that if he did so it could be interpreted as an insult, and so he refrained.

Be that as it may, the final scores were 15–5, 15–5, 15–3, and afterward the chief inspector looked as if he needed to be placed on a respirator as quickly as possible.

"I must buy a new racket," he croaked. "There's no spring left in this old mallet."

Münster had nothing to say about that, and they made their way slowly to the changing rooms.

After a shower, a change of clothes, and a walk up the stairs to the reception area of the badminton hall, Van Veeteren suddenly felt that he was incapable of staggering as far as his car unless they paused for a beer in the café.

Münster had no choice, of course. He looked at his watch and sighed. Then he rang the babysitter, announced his delayed arrival time, and slumped down opposite the chief inspector.

"Hell and damnation," announced Van Veeteren when his face had resumed its normal color with the aid of a copious swig of beer. "This case annoys me. It's like a pimple on the bum, if you'll pardon the expression. It just stays where it is, and nothing happens. . . ."

"Or it grows bigger and bigger," said Münster.

"Until it bursts, yes. And when do you think that will be?"

Münster shrugged. "I don't know," he said. "Haven't Rooth and deBries discovered anything new?"

"Not a dickie bird," said Van Veeteren. "The military types seem to be a bit worried about the college's reputation, but they don't appear to be holding back any information."

"And nobody has reported any phone calls with musical accompaniment?"

Van Veeteren shook his head.

"A few have asked for police protection, that's all."

"Really?"

"I said we'd keep an eye on them."

"You did?" said Münster. "Shall we, in fact?"

Van Veeteren grunted.

"Needless to say, we keep an eye on all citizens. It's part of a police officer's duty, if you recall."

Münster took a swig of beer.

"The only thing that's actually happening in this confounded case," Van Veeteren continued, lighting a cigarette, "is that Heinemann is sitting in some closet searching for a link."

"What sort of link?"

"Between Malik and Maasleitner, of course. It seems that he's feeling a bit guilty because the Staff College connection was so unproductive. Ah well, we'll see."

"I expect we shall," said Münster. "He's good at stumbling over things and finding gold. What do you think?"

Van Veeteren inhaled deeply and blew out the smoke through his nostrils. Like a dragon, Münster thought.

"I don't know what I think. But I think it's damned inconsiderate of a murderer to take such a long time. Something has to happen soon, that's obvious."

"Is it?" Münster wondered.

"Can't you feel it?" asked Van Veeteren, raising an eyebrow in surprise. "Surely you don't imagine it's all over after these two? Malik and Maasleitner? The vaguer the link between the two of them, the more likely it is that they must be a part of a broader context—you don't need to complete the whole jigsaw puzzle in order to discover if it comprises a hundred or a thousand pieces."

Münster thought that one over.

"What is it, then? The broader context, that is."

"A good question, Inspector. There's two guilders for you if you can answer it."

Münster finished his beer and started buttoning up his jacket.

"I really must be going now," he said. "I promised the babysitter I'd be home in half an hour."

"All right," sighed the chief inspector. "All right, I'm coming."

"What shall we do?" Münster asked as he turned into Klagenburg. "Apart from waiting, I mean."

"Hmm," said Van Veeteren. "I suppose we'll have to have another chat with the group comparatively close to Maasleitner. Given the absence of anything else so far."

"More questions, then?"

"More questions," said the chief inspector. "A hell of a lot more questions, and no sign of a good answer."

"Well, we mustn't lose heart," said Münster, bringing the car to a halt.

"Ouch," said Van Veeteren as he started to get out of the car. "I'll be damned if I haven't pulled a muscle."

"Where?" asked Münster.

"In my body," said Van Veeteren.

23

It gradually dawned on him that he'd seen her for the first time at the soccer match on Sunday. Even if he didn't realize it until later.

He'd gone to the match with Rolv, as usual, and she'd been sitting diagonally behind them, a couple of rows back—a woman with large, brown-tinted glasses and a colorful shawl that hid most of her hair. But it was dark, he remembered that distinctly: a few tufts had stuck out. Thirty years of age, or thereabouts. A bit haggard, but he didn't see much of her face.

Later on, when he made an effort to think back and try to understand how he could recall her, he remembered turning around three or four times during the match. There had been a trouble-maker back there shouting and yelling and insulting the referee, making people laugh part of the time, but urging him to shut up as well. Biedersen had never really established who it was; but it must have been then, when he kept turning around and was distracted from the game itself, that he saw her.

He didn't know at the time. Even so, he had registered and committed to memory what she looked like.

She was wearing a light-colored overcoat, just like when she turned up the next time.

. . .

Apart from that, almost everything else was different. No glasses, no colorful shawl, her dark hair in a bun, and it was astonishing that he could know nevertheless that it must be her. That was the moment he reacted. The new image was superimposed over the old one, and the penny dropped.

Monday lunchtime. As usual, he was at Mix, with Henessy and Vargas. She came in and stood for ages at the desk, looking around—trying to give the impression that she was looking for an empty seat, presumably, but she wasn't. She was looking for him, and when she'd found him—which must have been at least a minute after he'd seen her—she continued to stand there.

Just stood there. Smiled to herself, it seemed, but continued looking around the premises. Pausing to look more closely at him now and then, for a second or two; thinking back, he found it hard to recall how long this had gone on. It could hardly have been more than a few minutes, but somehow or other that short period felt longer, and afterward, it seemed to him longer than the whole lunch. He hadn't the slightest recollection of what he'd been talking to Henessy and Vargas about.

Insofar as there were still any doubts, they were cast aside by what happened on Tuesday morning.

It was about half past ten when he went to the post office in Lindenplejn to collect a parcel—and also to send advertising material to a few prospective customers in Oostwerdingen and Aarlach. Miss Kennan had been off work with the flu since the previous Monday, and there were things that couldn't be allowed to fester forever.

He didn't see when she came in—there were a lot of people in the lines formed in front of the various windows. But suddenly he was aware of her presence—he sensed that she was somewhere behind him, just as she had been at the soccer match.

He slowly turned his head, and identified her right away. In the line next to his. A few meters behind his back, three or four at most. She was wearing the shawl and the glasses again, but had on a brown jacket instead of the overcoat. She stood there without looking at him—or at least, not during the brief moment he dared to look at her—but with a slight, introverted smile. He chose to interpret the situation almost as a secret signal.

After a short discussion with himself, Biedersen left his place in the line. Walked quickly out through the main entrance, continued across the street, and entered the newsagent's on the other side. Hid inside there for a few minutes, head down and leafing through a few magazines. Then he returned to the post office.

She was no longer there. There was no other change in the line she'd been standing in. The man in the black leather jacket who'd been in front of her was still there. As was the young immigrant woman behind her. But the gap between them had closed.

Biedersen hesitated for several seconds. Then he decided to put off whatever it was he was going to do, and returned to his office instead.

He double-locked the door and flopped down behind his desk. Took out his notebook and a pen, and started drawing more or less symmetrical figures—a habit he'd formed while still at school and had resorted to ever since when faced with a problem.

And as he sat there, filling page after page, then tearing them out, he asked himself if he'd ever been confronted by a bigger problem than this one. His conclusion that this woman was in fact following him—that it must be her—did not mean that the outcome was a foregone conclusion, no way. Having identified her meant he had a chance: a trump card he must be careful not to waste. The main thing, he convinced himself, was that he didn't let on that he had noticed her. Didn't let her realize that he knew who she was, and what was involved. That was obvious.

The fact that he would have to kill her was another conviction that came early to him. The inevitability of this conclusion became clearer the more he thought about it—although you could say he had known from the start. He phoned Innings, but there was no reply. Perhaps that was just as well. He wouldn't have known how much to tell him, or what to have him do.

It would be better to continue on his own to start with, he decided. The first couple of steps or so, at least. But no rush—the whole business was so delicately balanced. The main thing was to keep a cool head. The fact that he would have to kill her before she killed him didn't mean that he should just shoot her at the first opportunity, in broad daylight. He soon realized that there were only two possible alternatives: either he would have to shoot her in self-defense—wait until the last moment, as it were, with all the implied risks and uncertainties—or else . . . or else he would have to find a way to get rid of her without anyone suspecting him.

Murder her, in other words.

It didn't need much in the way of consideration before he concluded that the latter was the best way to proceed.

That's simply the kind of man I am, he decided. And this is simply that kind of situation.

He could feel something inside come alive as he reached these conclusions. A new source of energy, a new source of inspiration. In fact, he had known this all the time. This is what he had to do. He opened his desk drawer and took out the bottle of whiskey he always had concealed there. Took two deep swigs and felt the determination spreading throughout his body.

This is the sort of man I am. . . . A new source of inspiration?

It hadn't been hard to make up his mind, but it would be much harder to decide how to proceed. Nevertheless, when he left his office at four that afternoon, he thought he had a good idea of what he was going to do.

In outline, at least.

It could hardly have been more than a pious hope on the part of Biedersen that he would come across her again that same evening; but when she turned up in the rain outside Kellner's, he had the feeling that something had short-circuited inside him. As if his heart had skipped a beat or two.

He closed his eyes and took a deep breath. Raised his newspaper so that it hid his face, and hoped that she hadn't seen him through the window.

After a short pause she came in through the revolving doors. Looked around the quite large and well-attended restaurant, and eventually found a vacant table so far back that it was almost out of sight for Biedersen. Nevertheless, by turning his chair a fraction and leaning back, he could keep an eye on what she was up to. It was obvious that she intended to eat—Biedersen had only ordered a beer. He watched her hang her jacket over the back of her chair, subject the menu to lengthy scrutiny, and eventually order something complicated from the Indian waiter.

Meanwhile, Biedersen paid his bill, and when the Indian waiter came to serve her meal, Biedersen made the most of the opportunity to slip into the men's room with his bag. He locked the door and proceeded to make use of the contents of his bag: a wig (it had been packed away in his cellar ever since he'd taken part in a jokey charade when a good friend had gotten married more than twenty years ago), an American military parka (which he'd forbidden Rolv to wear when he still lived at home), and a pair of round glasses of uncertain origin.

And also a pistol: a Pinchman, loaded with six bullets.

He checked his appearance in the scratched mirror, and, as far as he could make out, his disguise was just as effective as it had been when he tried it out in the bathroom mirror at home a couple of hours earlier.

There was no obvious reason to assume that this superannuated hippie was in fact identical with the locally well-known and successful businessman W. S. Biedersen.

No reason at all.

For safety's sake he decided to wait for her in the square outside. For almost an hour he wandered up and down in the wind and the light, driving rain. After a while he bought a pack of cigarettes at a kiosk, and a hamburger shortly afterward. Called Innings from a phone box as well. Got through without delay but restricted himself to saying that something might well be about to happen and he would ring again later. Since meeting Innings the previous Friday, he had been unable to decide if his former colleague was a help or a hindrance, and he wondered if it would be best to ignore him altogether. That was his inclination at the moment.

There were not very many people out on a wet, windy evening like today, and his appearance and behavior seemed not to attract curious looks. He realized that people took him for a drifter, a natural if regrettable background figure in any town or any street scene anywhere in the world. The perfect camouflage. At one point he was even greeted by another of the same sort—an unpleasant-smelling elderly man with one hand in an incredibly dirty bandage—but he only needed to tell him to piss off in order to be left in peace without more ado.

The clock on St. Mary's Church had just struck nine when she came out. She looked left and right several times, then walked rapidly across the square, passing by only a few meters away from him, and boarded one of the buses waiting outside the station.

Biedersen hesitated for a few seconds before getting on the bus as well. He gathered it was going to Hengeloo, and bought a ticket to there. He had barely sat down six rows behind her when the bus shuddered and set off.

It struck him how close he had been to losing her altogether, how small the margins were in this kind of situation, and he made up his mind to stick as close to her as possible in the future.

They were traveling westward. Through Legenbojs and Maas. There were about a dozen passengers on board from the start, mostly elderly women with bulging plastic carrier bags and shopping baskets in their laps. A few youths were half asleep at the back with personal stereos turned up so that the high notes hovered over the muffled rumble of the engine like a cloud of buzzing insects. The driver occasionally stopped to pick up new passengers; a few got off as well, but not many—until after twenty-five minutes or so they came to the square at Berkins-

haam, when more than half the passengers stood up and prepared to alight.

He lost sight of her for a moment as a pair of old women
stood up and fumbled around with their bags and baskets, and
when they finally moved away he saw to his dismay that her seat
was empty.

He stood up and scanned the front part of the bus, but it was
clear that she must have left via the doors next to the driver.
When he tried to look out through the side windows, all he could
see was his own unrecognizable face and other items reflected
from inside the bus.

As panic welled up inside him, he made a dash to get off the
bus. Emerged into the dimly lit square and was lucky enough to
see—what he assumed was, at any rate—her back as she turned
into a narrow alley between high, dark gable ends.

He slung his bag over his shoulder and rushed to follow her;
when he came to the narrow entrance, once again he just caught
sight of her back turning into another alley some twenty meters
ahead. He swallowed. Realized that it was hardly a good idea to
go careering after her now. He also managed to overcome his agitation and slow down his pace. He put his hand into his bag to
check that the pistol was still there. He released the safety catch
and left his hand in the bag.

When he came to the inadequate streetlamp on the corner,
he found that what she had turned into was a twenty-meter-long
cul-de-sac culminating in a fire wall. The tall building on the left
appeared to be a factory or a warehouse, without a single illumi-
nated window. Nor could he make out an entrance or doorway
on that side of the street; the only entrance of any description
was a portal leading into the four- or five-story-high property on
the right-hand side. He investigated and discovered that it was

the entrance to a sort of tunnel running through the building and emerging into an inner courtyard, dimly lit by lights from various windows.

Biedersen paused. Took a few steps into the tunnel, then paused again. An unpleasant smell was forcing its way into his nostrils. Something rotten, or at least damaged by damp. He listened, but all he could hear was rain falling on a tin roof somewhere in the courtyard. And the faint sound of a television set evidently standing close to an open window. On one of the upstairs floors facing the street, presumably. A cat appeared and rubbed up against his legs.

Oh hell, he thought, clutching the pistol.

And he acknowledged that the feeling bubbling up inside him was fear, nothing else.

Pure, unadulterated fear.

24

When Innings got home after the restaurant meal with Biedersen, the first thing he did was to hide the bag containing the gun in a chest of drawers full of odds and ends in the garage. He knew that the risk of Ulrike or the children finding it there was more or less negligible, and he hoped sincerely that it would remain hidden forever. Or at least until he had an opportunity to get rid of it.

His mind felt like a playground for a mass of the most divergent thoughts and ideas. As he sat on the sofa with Ulrike, watching a Fassbinder film, he tried to assess the most likely outcome of—or escape from—this nightmare. It seemed even harder now than it had been before. His thoughts were being tossed around like a straw in the wind, and he soon began to wish that he could simply switch off his brain. For a little while at least, in order to gain some breathing space.

When it came to wishes and hopes, the situation was more straightforward. The most welcome development from his point of view would be for Biedersen to simply sort the whole business out by himself. Track down this madwoman and render her harmless, once and for all. Without any involvement on Innings's part.

In view of what he discovered at the restaurant—regarding the telephone music and so on—surely this was not an altogether unlikely outcome?

Innings came back to this conclusion over and over again, but his assessment of it, like the rest of his thoughts, kept swinging back and forth between hope and something that was most reminiscent of deepest despair.

In fact—and, gradually, this became the only consolation he could find—there was only one thing he could be absolutely sure of.

Something would happen soon.

This period of suspense would come to an end.

In a few days—a week, perhaps—it would all be over.

Any other outcome was unthinkable.

Given these hopes—which Innings began to cherish even before he went to bed on Friday evening—there is no denying that it was very stressful to have to accept that nothing in fact happened.

On Saturday and for half of Sunday they had visitors—Ulrike's brother with his wife and two children—and the practical things that needed to be done and the conversation helped to keep the worry at a distance. For part of the time, at least. But things became much worse after they had left, and peace and quiet returned to the house on Sunday afternoon.

It was worse still on Monday, which floated by in a cloud of listlessness and worry. That night he had barely a wink of sleep, and when he left the editorial office at about four on Tuesday afternoon, he had the distinct impression that several of his colleagues were wondering about the state of his health.

He had told Ulrike that he was a bit upset because of the murder of two of his former colleagues when he was a National Serviceman, and she seemed to accept this as a reasonable explanation for his occasional preoccupation.

And then, on Tuesday evening, the telephone call came at last from Biedersen. Something might be about to happen, he said, but there was no reason for Innings to do anything. Not yet, at least.

That was all he said. Promised to ring again later. And even if this call more or less corresponded to what Innings had been hoping for deep down, it increased his nervous tension even more—with another sleepless night as the outcome.

Needless to say, his sensitive stomach reacted accordingly; when he phoned in sick on Wednesday morning at least he had a legitimate physical excuse.

Perhaps he also felt emotionally calm when he settled down with his newspaper after Ulrike and the kids had left, but it didn't last long. He realized that subconsciously he'd been hoping to find something in the paper—the discovery of a woman killed in mysterious circumstances up in Saaren, or something like that—but, of course, there wasn't a single word about any such incident. Besides, it was obvious that the morning papers wouldn't have had time to carry such news. Biedersen had phoned at about half past eight. No matter what had happened next, the papers wouldn't have had time to print it. Innings had been working in the trade for nearly thirty years, so he should know.

The broadcast journalists would have had a better chance. He switched on the radio and didn't miss a single bulletin all morning. But there was nothing. Not a single word.

Something might be about to happen, that's what Biedersen had said.

What?

I'll be in touch.

When?

Minutes passed. As did hours. It wasn't until five minutes past twelve that the telephone rang.

It was the police. For one confused second this fact almost caused him to lose control of himself. He was on the point of coming out with the whole story, but then he realized that, of course, this was how he would be informed of what had happened.

If this woman really had been found shot up in Saaren, and there was even the slightest of links to the other murders, this was naturally how the police would react.

They would be in touch with all thirty-one and try to winkle out if anybody knew anything.

He came to this conclusion while talking to the police officer, who asked to come see him, and then when he sat waiting, he was pretty confident that he hadn't given himself away.

He had expressed surprise, obviously. Why would the police want to question him again? Routine questions? Okay, fair enough.

But while he waited, the other possible scenario dawned on him.

Biedersen might not have succeeded in killing the woman.

If the opposite had been the case—if it was Biedersen who had been killed—well, there was every reason for the police to come visiting.

Every reason. He could feel his guts tying themselves in knots as this possibility became a probability.

Even more reason, in fact, than if Biedersen had succeeded in what he had set out to do, and when he opened the door and let in the woman who identified herself as a detective constable, he was convinced he knew why Biedersen hadn't been in touch later, as he had promised.

I must keep a straight face, he thought. No matter what has happened, I must keep a straight face.

It felt like clutching at straws. Thin and worn-out straws. But he knew that there wasn't anything else to clutch at.

She sat down on the sofa. Held her notebook at the ready while he served up tea and cookies. She didn't seem to be about to come out with something devastating, and he succeeded in calming down a bit.

"Help yourself!"

He flopped down into the armchair opposite her.

"Thank you. Well, there are a few questions we'd like you to answer."

"Has something happened?"

"Why do you ask that?"

He shrugged. She took a tape recorder out of her bag.

"Are you going to record this? That's not what happened last time."

"We all have our own ways of working," she said with a little smile. "Are you ready?"

He nodded.

"Okay," she said, switching on the tape recorder. "Do you recognize this music?"

VII

February 15–23

25

If there was anything that Chief Inspector Van Veeteren hated, it was press conferences.

The similarity with sitting in the dock during a trial was striking, and the kind of defense you managed was a bit too reminiscent of a guilty man's dodgy evasions. There was something about the very atmosphere on these occasions that seemed to him to express both the general public's latent (and now often openly expressed) fear of the violence inherent in modern society, and its lack of faith in the ability of the police force to put an end to it.

It was just the same this time around. The conference room on the first floor was full to overflowing with journalists and reporters, sitting, standing, taking photographs, and trying to outdo one another in the art of asking biased and insinuating questions.

He had been press-ganged to accompany Hiller and sit behind a cheap, rectangular table overloaded with microphones, cords, and the obligatory bottles of soda water that for some unfathomable reason were always present whenever high-ranking police officers made statements in front of cameras—Reinhart maintained that it had something to do with sponsorship, and it was not impossible that he was right.

Reinhart was often right.

However, the sponsorship Van Veeteren received from the chief of police was virtually nonexistent. As usual, once the questions started to come, Hiller leaned back in his chair with his arms crossed and a sphinxlike expression on his face. He was only too happy to leave all the answers to the chief inspector, who, he was careful to stress, was the person responsible for the investigation. Hiller was merely the administrator and coordinator.

But he provided the introductory information himself, formally dressed in his midnight-blue suit and emphasizing each point by means of forceful tapping on the table by a silver ballpoint pen.

"The murder victim is a certain Karel Innings," he explained. "According to what we have been able to ascertain, he was shot dead in his home in Loewingen at some time between half past twelve and half past one yesterday, Wednesday. Innings happened to be alone in the house, being home sick with a stomach complaint, and so far we have no definite clues concerning the killer. The victim was hit by a total of five bullets—three in the chest and two below the belt—and the weapon appears to have been a Beringer-75. There are clear indications that the gun was the same one as was used in two previous cases during the last few weeks . . . the murders of Ryszard Malik and Rickard Maasleitner."

He paused for a moment, but it was obvious that he had more to say, and no questions were fired at him yet.

"It is thus possible that we are dealing with a so-called serial killer; but there is also a clear link between the people who have lost their lives so far. All three are members of a group who spent their military service in the years 1964 and 1965 at the Staff College here in Maardam, an institution that was later relocated to Schaabe. Our efforts are currently concentrated on trying to discover the precise significance of this link, and of course also providing the best possible level of protection for the remainder of that group."

"Have you any clues?" interrupted a young woman from the local radio station.

"All questions will be answered shortly by Chief Inspector Van Veeteren, who is sitting here beside me," Hiller explained with a smile. "But before I throw the meeting open to the floor, just let me point out that you will be given access to all the information we possess at present, and I sincerely hope that we are all on the same side in the hunt for the ruthless murderer we are evidently up against. Thank you."

The chief of police had said his piece. Van Veeteren leaned forward over the table and glared at the audience.

"Fire away," he said.

"Was it the same method in this case as well?" said somebody.

"How come the police didn't provide some kind of protection, if it was known that the victim would be one of that group?" wondered somebody else.

"With regard to the method . . . ," Van Veeteren began.

"Has the level of protection been increased?" interrupted a third.

"With regard to the method," Van Veeteren repeated, unperturbed, "it was a little different this time. The victim, Innings, that is, evidently invited the perpetrator into his house and offered him tea. . . . Or her. This naturally suggests . . ."

"What does that suggest?" yelled a red-haired reporter in the third row.

"It can suggest that he was acquainted with the murderer. At any rate, it seemed that he was expecting him to call."

"Is it one of the others in the group?" asked somebody from the *Allgemejne*.

"We don't know," said Van Veeteren.

"But you have interrogated the whole group?"

"Of course."

"And will do so again?"

"Naturally."

"Protection?" somebody repeated.

"We don't have unlimited resources," explained Van Veeteren. "It obviously requires vast manpower to keep thirty people under observation all around the clock."

"Is it a madman?"

"A person is presumably not totally sane if he goes out and kills three people."

"Was there any sign of a struggle at Innings's place? Had he tried to defend himself or anything like that?"

"No."

"What theories do you have? Surely you have more than just this to go on?"

"Do you have a suspect?" the redhead managed to interject.

Van Veeteren shook his head.

"At this stage we don't have a suspect."

"Is it a man or a woman?"

"Could be either."

"What's all this about music being played over the telephone?"

"There are indications that suggest the murderer keeps calling his victims for some time before shooting them. He calls them and plays a particular tune over the phone to them."

"What tune?"

"We don't know."

"Why? Why does he ring?"

"We don't know."

"What do you think?"

"We're working on various different possibilities."

"Had Innings received one of these phone calls?"

"We haven't clarified that as yet."

"If he had, surely he'd have contacted the police?"

"You would think so."

"But he hadn't?"

"No."

There was a pause. Van Veeteren took a sip of soda water.

"How many police officers are working on this case at the moment?" asked Würgner from *Neuwe Blatt*.

"All available officers."

"How many is that?"

Van Veeteren did the calculation.

"About thirty. Of various ranks."

"When do you think you'll be able to close the case?"

Van Veeteren shrugged.

"It's not possible to say."

"Has it got something to do with the armed forces? The link seems to suggest that."

"No, I would hardly think so," said Van Veeteren after a moment's thought.

An elderly and unusually patient editor of a crime-magazine program on one of the television channels had been waving his pen for a while, and now managed to get his oar in.

"What exactly do you want help with? Pictures and stuff?"

Van Veeteren nodded.

"Yes," he said. "We'd like you to publish photographs and names of all the men in the group, and to write about the telephone calls. Ask the general public to pass on to us any possible tips they may have."

"Why didn't you release the pictures and so on earlier? You must have known about it after the second murder, surely?"

"It wasn't definite," said Van Veeteren with a sigh. "It was only an indication."

"But now it's definite?"

"Yes."

A gigantic man with a long, gray beard—Van Veeteren knew him to be Vejmanen on the *Telegraaf*—stood up at the back of the room and bellowed in a voice reminiscent of thunder: "Okay. The interviews with Innings's relatives and friends! What results have they produced?"

"We are still conducting them," said Van Veeteren. "You'll get the details tomorrow."

"How kind of you," thundered Vejmanen. "And when do you think we'll have the next victim?"

Van Veeteren blew his nose.

"Our intention is to pick up the killer before he strikes again," he explained.

"Excellent," said Vejmanen. "So shall we say that you are in no particular hurry? This business is going to be newsworthy for four or five days at least. . . . Possibly a whole week."

He sat down, and appreciative laughter could be heard here and there in the audience.

"If I understand it rightly," said a woman whose clothes and makeup suggested that she was attached to some television program, "you will be providing some kind of protection to all the remaining members of this group. But at the same time, one of them might be the murderer. Won't that be a pretty intricate task?"

"Not really," said Van Veeteren. "I can promise you that we shall cease to protect the murderer from himself the moment we know who he is."

"Have you made a profile of the killer?" shouted somebody from the back.

"I can't say we have."

"Will you be making one?"

"I always make a profile of the perpetrator," said Van Veeteren, "but I don't normally send it out into the ether."

"Why not?" asked somebody.

The chief inspector shrugged.

"I don't really know," he said. "I suppose I hold the old-fashioned view that one ought to stick to the facts when it comes to the media. Theories are best suited to the inside of my head. At least, my theories are. Any more questions?"

"How long is it since you failed to solve a case?"

"About eight years."

"The G-file?"

"Yes. You seem to know about it. . . . As you can all hear, the level of questioning has sunk. I think we'd better leave it at that."

"What the hell?" exclaimed the red-haired reporter.

"As I said," said Van Veeteren, rising to his feet.

"For Christ's sake, this is incredible!" said Reinhart when he, Münster, and Van Veeteren gathered in the chief inspector's office ten minutes later. "The murderer rings the doorbell, is let in, sits down on the sofa, and drinks a cup of tea. Then takes out a gun and kills him. Incredible!"

"And then simply goes away," Münster added.

"Conclusion?" demanded Van Veeteren.

"He knew him," said Münster.

"Or her," said Reinhart.

"You mean the bullet in the balls suggests a her?"

"Yes," said Reinhart. "I do."

"But it's hardly any less incredible if it's a woman," said Münster.

There was a knock on the door and Heinemann came in.

"What are you doing?" he asked as he perched cautiously on the window seat.

"These two are standing here saying it's incredible all the time," muttered the chief inspector. "I'm just sitting and thinking."

"I see," said Heinemann.

"What's everybody else doing?" asked Reinhart.

"Rooth and deBries have gone off to interview the neighbors in a bit more detail," said Heinemann. "Moreno and Jung were going to take his workplace, I think you said."

"That's right," said Van Veeteren. "There doesn't seem to be much point in looking for a murderer among his relatives and friends in this case, but we have to hear what they have to say. Somebody might have noticed something. You can take this little lot, Münster. . . ."

He handed a list to Münster, who read it as he walked slowly backward through the door.

"Heinemann," said the chief inspector, "I suggest you continue searching for links. . . . Now you've got an extra one to work on. Let's hope there's a lower common denominator than the whole group."

Heinemann nodded.

"I think there will be," he said. "I'm thinking of asking Hiller for a bit of help in getting me permission to look at their bank details."

"Bank details?" said Reinhart. "What the hell for?"

"There's no harm in having a look," said Heinemann. "If these three have been up to something, the odds are it won't withstand all that much daylight. And such things usually leave traces in bank accounts. Is there anything else you want me to do, Chief Inspector?"

"No," said Van Veeteren. "You might as well keep on doing what you've been doing."

Heinemann nodded. Put his hands in his trouser pockets and left Van Veeteren and Reinhart on their own.

"He's not so thick," said Reinhart. "It's mainly a question of tempo."

Van Veeteren took out a toothpick and broke it in half.

"Reinhart," he said after a while. "Will you be so kind as to explain something for me?"

"Shoot," said Reinhart.

"If it's as Heinemann says and these three have had some kind of criminal past together, and that they know very well . . . er, knew very well . . . who the perpetrator is, why the hell did Innings let him in and serve him tea before allowing himself to be shot?"

Reinhart thought for a while, digging away with a matchstick at the bowl of his pipe.

"Well," he said eventually. "He—or she, I mean—must have been in disguise, I assume. Or else . . ."

"Well?"

"Or else they know who it is, but don't know what the person looks like. There's a difference. And it was a long time ago, of course."

Van Veeteren nodded.

"Have you any cigarettes?"

Reinhart shook his head.

"Afraid not."

"Never mind. Just a few more questions, so that I know I'm not barking up the wrong tree. If it really is just a small group that the killer is after, Innings must have known that his turn would be coming. Or suspected it, at least. Isn't that right?"

"Yes," said Reinhart. "Especially if he was going to be the last one."

Van Veeteren thought about that for a few seconds.

"And must have known who the killer is?"

"Who's behind it all, in any case. A slight difference again."

"Is there any possibility, do you think, that Innings wouldn't recognize one of the group?"

Reinhart lit his pipe and thought that one over.

"They haven't seen one another for thirty years," he said. "We know what they all look like nowadays, but they don't. They may just have that old photograph to go on. . . . And their memories, of course."

"Go on," said Van Veeteren.

"Even so, I think I'd recognize the blokes I did National Service with. Without any trouble at all, in fact."

"Same here," said the chief inspector. "Especially if I'd been prepared for it. So, conclusion?"

Reinhart puffed away at his pipe. "If we're talking about a small group," he said, "then the murderer is an outsider. It could be a contract killer, of course, but I think that's hardly likely."

Van Veeteren nodded.

"Yes," said Reinhart. "As I've said before, I'm inclined to think that the murderer is a woman, and as far as I know, there isn't a woman in the group."

"You're sometimes bloody brilliant at observing things," said the chief inspector.

"Thank you. There's one thing we mustn't forget, though."

"What's that?"

"There's nothing to stop it being a woman who intends to kill the whole lot of 'em."

"There's nothing much to stop a woman doing anything at all," sighed Van Veeteren. "Apart from us. Shall we get this thing solved now, then?"

"Let's. It's about time," said Reinhart.

26

The distance to Loewingen, the latest murder scene, was not much more than thirty kilometers, and as he settled down in the car, he regretted that it wasn't a bit farther. A few hours' driving wouldn't have done him any harm; even when he got up, he'd felt the unfulfilled need for a long and restful journey. Preferably through a gray, rain-sodden landscape, just like this one. Hours in which to think things over.

But in fact it was minutes instead—he managed to stretch it to half an hour by taking the alternative route via Borsens and Penderdixte, where he had spent a few summers as a seven- or eight-year-old.

There were two reasons why he had postponed his visit until Friday. In the first place, Münster and Rooth had already spoken to Ulrike Fremdli and the three teenagers on Wednesday evening, and it might be a good idea not to give the impression that the police were hounding them every day. And in the second place, he'd had plenty to occupy himself with yesterday even so.

You could say that again. During the afternoon he and Reinhart had addressed the delicate business of organizing protection for the as-yet-not-murdered (as Reinhart insisted on calling them).

The five living abroad were without doubt the easiest ones to sort out. After a brief discussion it was decided quite simply to leave them to their own devices. This was made clear in the letter circulated to everybody concerned, which urged them to turn to the nearest police authority in whatever country they were living in, if they felt threatened or insecure in any way.

There are limits, after all, Reinhart had said.

As for those still in the country but outside the Maardam police district, something similar applied. Reinhart spent more than three hours telephoning colleagues in various places and simply instructing them to protect Mr. So-and-So from all threats and dangers.

It was not a pleasant task, and afterward Reinhart had gone to Van Veeteren's office and requested a job with the traffic police instead. The chief inspector had rejected this request, but told Reinhart that he was welcome to throw up in the wastepaper basket if he felt the need.

It was one of those days.

In the Maardam police district there were now thirteen possible victims left, and to look after them Van Veeteren assembled— if one were to be honest—a ragbag of constables and probationers, and left it to the promising and enthusiastic Widmar Krause to instruct and organize them.

When he had done that and leaned back for a moment, Van Veeteren tried to make a snap judgment of how effective this expensive protection would really be, and concluded that if it had been a condom he'd been assessing, to put it brutally, they might just as well have gone ahead without it.

But fictitious—or simulated—protection was nevertheless preferable to nothing at all, he tried to convince himself, with covering his own back in the forefront of his mind.

Then Van Veeteren, Reinhart, and Münster spent the rest of the afternoon and evening discussing the murderer's character and identity, and working out a system for how the interviews with the as-yet-not-murdered should be conducted (and in this context as well, they decided to leave those living abroad to their own devices, at least for the time being). Increasingly frequently they were interrupted by the duty officer or Miss Katz, rushing in with so-called hot tips from the general public, which had started flowing in despite the fact that the press conference was only a few hours old.

By about eight, Reinhart had had enough.

"Fuck this for a lark!" he exclaimed, and threw away the sheet of paper he'd just read. "It's impossible to think if we have to keep beavering away like this all the time."

"You could buy us a beer," said Van Veeteren.

"All right. I expect you'll want cigarettes as well?"

"Just a few at most," said the chief inspector modestly.

This was in fact what occupied his thoughts for the first half of the drive to Loewingen.

I ought not to smoke, he thought.

I drink too much beer.

Neither habit is good for me, certainly not the cigarettes. In connection with an operation for bowel cancer almost a year ago, an innocent doctor had said that an occasional glass of beer wouldn't do him any harm—Van Veeteren had immediately committed this advice to memory, and he knew that he would never forget it, even if he lived to be a hundred and ten.

Incidentally, wasn't it the case that an occasional cigarette could stimulate the thought processes?

Whatever, I ought to play badminton with Münster more often, he thought. Go out jogging now and then. If only I could get rid of this damned cold!

It was only after he'd passed the farm in Penderdixte where he'd spent some of his childhood that he changed tack and started thinking about the investigation. This accursed investigation.

Three murders.

Three men shot in cold blood.

In rather less than a month.

This last one was without doubt more than a bit rich. No matter how much he thought about it, changed the angle or reassessed it, he simply couldn't make it add up.

The questions were obvious.

Was there in fact a smaller group within the group? ("I hope to God there is!" Reinhart had let slip over a beer the previous evening; and, of course, that was significant. Reinhart was not in the habit of placing himself in the hands of the sacred.)

If not, and if the murderer was intending to kill all of them—well, they must be dealing with a lunatic. With an incomprehensible, irrational, and presumably totally mad motive. Nobody can have an acceptable (in any sense of the word) reason for killing thirty-three people, one after the other.

Not according to Chief Inspector Van Veeteren's yardstick, in any case.

A cold and calculating lunatic like that would be the opponent they feared more than any other; they had all been touchingly in agreement on that.

But if there really was a smaller group?

Van Veeteren fished up two toothpicks from his breast pocket, but after tasting them, he dropped them on the floor and lit a cigarette instead.

In that case, he thought after the first stimulating drag, Innings should (must?) have known that he belonged to that little group and was in danger. Without doubt.

But nevertheless he had invited the murderer into his house, and allowed himself to be shot without raising an eyebrow. Why?

And that wasn't all—he knew he could extend the argument further without exploding it: there was another crux.

If it was implausible to believe that Innings would invite in somebody he knew was intending to kill him, he can't have suspected anything. But if he knew he was in danger, it seemed beyond the bounds of possibility that he would invite a stranger into his house.

Ergo, the chief inspector thought as he slowed down behind a farmer on a tractor, the person Innings invited to tea and allowed himself to be murdered by must be somebody he trusted.

"That must be right, okay?" he said aloud to nobody in particular as he overtook the enthusiastically gesticulating farmer. "Somebody he knew, for Christ's sake!"

That was as far as he got.

He sighed. Inhaled deeply but was repulsed by the taste. He felt like a poor idiot who had been released from the asylum but was now drooling over a three-piece puzzle that had been thrust into his hand as a test to pass before being allowed back into society.

It was not an attractive image, but the images that flitted through his mind rarely were.

Hell and damnation, Van Veeteren thought. I hope Reinhart can solve this one.

Loewingen was a sprawling little town with a few industries, even fewer apartment blocks, and masses of individual houses and villas. Despite an ancient town center from the Middle Ages, this was one of those towns you simply lived in—one of many insufferable, monocultural wastelands of the late twentieth century, Van Veeteren thought as he finally found the housing development he was looking for. Uniform, boring, and safe.

Well, the extent to which it was safe might be arguable.

Ulrike Fremdli welcomed him, and ushered him to a seat on the same sofa the murderer must have sat on exactly two days earlier. She was a powerful-looking woman with neat brown hair and a face he reckoned must have been beautiful once upon a time. She seemed to be reticent and somewhat prim, and he wondered if she was taking sedatives—he thought he recognized the symptoms.

"Would you like anything?" she asked curtly.

He shook his head.

"How are you?" he asked.

She gave him a penetrating look.

"Bloody awful," she said. "I've sent the kids to my sister. I need to be alone."

"You'll manage?"

"Yes," she said. "But please ask your questions and get it over with."

"How long had you known each other?"

"Since '86," she said. "We moved in together eighteen months ago. We had a lot of trouble with his former wife before that."

Van Veeteren thought for a moment. Decided to skip as much as possible and not beat about the bush.

"I'd like to make this as brief as possible," he said. "I take it you think the same way. I aim to catch whoever murdered your husband, and I'd like some answers to a few very specific questions."

She nodded.

"It's important that I get honest answers."

"Fire away."

"All right," said Van Veeteren. "Do you think he knew he was in danger?"

"I don't know," she said after a tense pause. "I honestly don't know."

"Was he worried, these last few days?"

"Yes, but you might say there were reasons why he should be."

Her deep voice trembled slightly, but not much.

"I'll tell you what I think," said Van Veeteren. "I think Innings was one of a smaller group, and it's the members of that group the murderer is out to kill."

"A group?"

"Yes, a few of the National Servicemen who got up to something thirty years ago. . . . Possibly later as well. In any case, there must be a link between some of the thirty-five. What do you think?"

She shook her head.

"I've no idea."

"Did he ever talk about his military service?"

"Never. Well, we spoke about it recently, of course, but not much."

Van Veeteren nodded.

"If you think of anything that might suggest a link of the kind I've mentioned, will you promise to get in touch with me?"

"Yes, of course."

He gave her his business card.

"You can phone me direct, that's easier. Anyway, next question. Can you tell me if your husband was in touch with any new contacts during the week before it happened? Did he meet anybody you didn't know, or people he didn't normally mix with?"

She thought it over.

"Not as far as I know."

"Take your time. Think it through day by day, that usually helps."

"He met people at work as well. . . . We see each other only in the evenings, really."

"Let's concentrate on the evenings. Did he have any visitors these last few days?"

"No . . . no, I don't think so. Not that I noticed, at least."

"Did he go out at all in the evening?"

"No. Hang on, yes: last Friday. He went out for a few hours last Friday."

"Where?"

"Somewhere in town. Some restaurant or other, I think. I was asleep when he came back home."

"Who was he out with?"

She shrugged.

"I don't know. Some friends from work, I expect. Burgner, perhaps."

"He didn't say anything about it?"

"Not as far as I recall. We had visitors—my brother and his family—who arrived quite early on Saturday, so I don't think we ever got around to discussing it."

"Did he often go out on his own?"

She shook her head.

"No. Once a month, at most. The same as me, in fact."

"Hmm," said Van Veeteren. "Nothing more?"

"Do you mean, was he out any other evening?"

"Yes."

"No, he was at home . . . let me think . . . yes, Sunday, Monday, and Tuesday."

Van Veeteren nodded.

"Okay," he said. "Do you know anything about those telephone calls?"

"I've read about them," she said. "The officers who were here on Wednesday asked me about that as well."

"And?"

"No, nothing."

"Do you think he received any?"

"I don't know."

"Okay," said Van Veeteren, leaning back on the sofa. "Then I have only one more question. Do you suspect anybody?"

"What?" she exclaimed. "What the hell do you mean?"

Van Veeteren cleared his throat.

"One of the things that confuses us," he explained, "is that he invited the murderer in without any more ado. That suggests he knew the person concerned. If he did, then you might as well. You've been together for ten years, after all."

She said nothing. He could tell by looking at her that this hadn't occurred to her until now; but he could also see that she didn't have an answer.

"Will you promise me to think about it?"

She nodded.

"Please think as well about whether he might have felt under threat. That's an extremely important question—and it could be that the tiniest detail gives us a clue that'll put us on the right track."

"I understand."

He stood up.

"I know you're going through hell," he said. "I've been stomping around in tragedies like this for more than thirty years. You're welcome to contact me even if you only want to talk. Otherwise I'll be in touch again in a few days."

"Our life together was so good," she said. "I suppose we ought to have realized that something that worked so well couldn't last forever."

"Yes," said Van Veeteren. "That's more or less the way I look at life as well."

When he paused in the street outside and tried to imagine the route the murderer would have taken, it struck him that he rather liked her.

Quite a lot, if truth be told.

"Knowing what I know now," said the editor in chief, Cannelli, "quite a lot of things fall into place."

"What, for example?" Jung wondered.

"That there was something bothering him."

"How was that noticeable?"

Cannelli sighed and gazed out the window.

"Well," he said, "I had a few longish chats with him . . . about headlines, pictures, and suchlike. That was routine, several times a week. But there was something about his concentration that struck me. He seemed to be thinking about something else all the time. . . ."

"How long had you known him?"

"Five years," said Cannelli. "Since I took charge of the newspaper after Windemeer. He was good—Innings, that is."

Jung nodded.

"Do you know if he met anybody outside his usual circle of contacts lately? If somebody—or something—cropped up here at work that could possibly be connected with his unease?"

He realized that this was a pretty silly question, and Cannelli responded to his apologetic smile with a shrug of the shoulders.

"We produce a newspaper, Inspector. People are running in and out all day long. . . . I'm sorry, but I don't think I can help you.

Jung thought for a moment.

"Okay," he said eventually, closing his notebook. "If you think of anything and all that . . ."

"Of course," said Cannelli.

Moreno was sitting in the car, waiting for him.

"How did it go?" she asked.

"Pretty pointless."

"Same here. How many did you talk to?"

"Three," said Jung.

"Four for me," said Moreno. "But I think one thing is crystal clear."

"What's that?"

"He knew he was in danger. He was behaving oddly, that's what everybody says."

Jung nodded and started the car.

"At least, that's what they all say with hindsight," he said. "What a shame that people never react in time."

"Yes indeed," said Moreno. "Mind you, if we were to take care of everybody who seems a bit worried, we probably wouldn't have much time to devote to anything else."

"Absolutely right," said Jung. "How about a coffee? It's good for the nerves."

"Okay," said Moreno.

27

She dithered for a day and a half.

She had read about it for the first time on Thursday evening—in one of the newspapers on the bus on the way home—but it wasn't until much later the same night that her suspicions were aroused. In the middle of a dream that vanished immediately into the shadows of the subconscious, she woke up and could see it in her mind's eye.

The occupied telephone booth in the hall. The back pressed up against the tinted gray glass. The tape recorder pressed against the receiver.

It had happened only once, and that was at least three weeks ago now. But the image persisted. That Tuesday evening. She had intended to phone a fellow student to ask about something, but had seen immediately that it was occupied. It can't have lasted more than three or four seconds—she had simply opened her door, noted that the phone booth was occupied, and gone back into her room.

Five minutes later, it was free and she'd been able to make her call.

It was remarkable that this brief, totally meaningless sequence should have stayed with her. Now, when she had been woken up by it, she couldn't recall having thought about it before at all.

And, of course, it was precisely that—these vague, unlikely circumstances—that made her hesitate.

On Friday afternoon she had bumped into her on the stairs. There was nothing unusual about that, either—it was a banal, everyday occurrence—but when she woke up with a start early that Saturday morning, the two trivial images had somehow combined.

Melted into each other and roused a horrible suspicion.

She ought really to have consulted Natalie first, but Natalie had gone home to her parents for the weekend, and her room was empty. However, after an early jog in the park (which was cut short because of the rain), a shower, and breakfast, she had made up her mind.

Something prevented her from using the telephone in the hall (was it fear? she asked herself later), and instead she used a public phone booth by the post office to call the police.

It was 9:34, and the call and her information were registered by Constable Willock, who promised to pass it on to the senior officers on the case and report back to her eventually.

She returned to her room to study and wait.

Her conscience was clearer, but she had a nagging feeling of unreality.

Reinhart sighed. He had spent the last ten minutes trying to perform the trick of half lying down on a standard office chair, but the only notable result was that he now had a backache. At the base of his spine and between his shoulder blades. Van Veeteren was sitting opposite him, slumped over his desk, which was littered with paper, files, empty coffee mugs, and broken toothpicks.

"Say something," said Reinhart.

Van Veeteren muttered and started reading a new sheet of paper.

"Hot air, nothing else," he said after another minute and crumpled it up. "There's no substance in this, either. Loewingen is a suburb for the middle classes, in case you didn't know. All the wives work, and all the kids attend nursery school. The nearest neighbor at home when the murder took place was six houses away, and she was asleep. This case is not exactly gliding smoothly along the rails."

"Asleep?" said Reinhart, with a trace of longing in his voice. "But it was one in the afternoon, for Christ's sake!"

"Night nurse at the Gemejnte Hospital," Van Veeteren explained.

"So there are no witnesses, is that what you're saying?"

"Exactly," said the chief inspector, continuing to leaf through the papers. "Not even a cat."

"He certainly seems to have been worried," Reinhart pointed out after a moment of silence. "Everybody has commented on that. He must have known that he was in trouble."

"Certainly," said Van Veeteren. "We can assume we're looking at a small group."

Reinhart sighed again and abandoned the chair. Stood gazing out the window instead.

"Bloody rain," he said. "I ought to be reborn as a swamp. Haven't you found anything at all to work on?"

There was a knock on the door and Münster came in. He nodded and sat down on the chair Reinhart had just vacated.

"He was out last Friday night," said Van Veeteren.

"Innings?" asked Münster.

"Yes. Maybe we should check up on what he was doing. He was probably having a beer with a few colleagues, but you never know."

"How can we check up on that?" asked Reinhart.

Van Veeteren shrugged.

"Hmm," he said. "We'll put Moreno and Jung on it. They can ask a few questions at his workplace again. See if they can find somebody who was with him. And then, I wonder . . ."

"What do you wonder?" asked Reinhart.

"In town, I think she said. . . . He was at a restaurant in town, his wife thought. Did she mean Loewingen or Maardam?"

"Loewingen's not a town, it's a dump," said Reinhart.

"Could be," said Münster. "But there are a few restaurants there even so."

"Yes, yes," muttered Van Veeteren. "That'll be Jung and Moreno's headache. Where are they, by the way?"

"At home, I expect," said Reinhart. "I've heard it said that it's Saturday today."

"Go back to your office and ring them and wake them up," said Van Veeteren. "Tell them I want to know where he was and with whom by Monday afternoon at the latest. How the hell they do that is up to them."

"With pleasure," said Reinhart, walking to the door. Just then Miss Katz appeared with two bundles of paper.

"Tips from the detective known as the general public," she explained. "A hundred and twenty since yesterday afternoon. Constable Krause has sorted them out."

"How?" asked Münster.

"The usual categories," snorted Van Veeteren. "Daft and slightly less daft. Can you run through them, Münster, and come back to me an hour from now?"

"Of course," sighed Münster, picking up the papers.

Ah well, the chief inspector thought when he was alone again. The wheels are turning. What the hell was it I'd thought of doing myself?

Ah yes, an hour down in the sauna, that was it.

28

"I'm going away for a bit," said Biedersen.

"Oh, are you?" said his wife. "Why?"

"Business," said Biedersen. "I'll probably be away for a few weeks, at least."

His wife looked up from the burners on the stove she was busy cleaning with the aid of a new product she'd found in the shop yesterday and which was said to be more effective than any other brand.

"Oh, will you?" she said. "Where are you going?"

"Various places. Hamburg among others. There are quite a few contacts I need to follow up."

"I understand," said his wife, and started scrubbing again, thinking that she didn't at all. Understand, that is. But it didn't matter, of course. She had never interfered in her husband's affairs—running an import company (or was it two now?) was a complicated and not especially appealing business. Nothing for a woman like her. Ever since they married, they had been in agreement about one thing: they would each look after their own side of family life. He would look after the finances, and she would take care of the home and the children. All of whom had fled the nest now, and formed their own families on more or less similar lines.

Which in turn gave her time to devote herself to other things. Such as stove-top burners.

"How's it going?" she asked.

"How's what going?"

"Well, your business. You seem to have been a bit stressed these last few days."

"Nonsense."

"Are you sure?"

"Yes, of course."

"That's good to know. But you'll keep in touch, won't you?"

"Naturally."

But when he'd left, she found herself still wondering if there hadn't been something wrong nevertheless. Ever since—she worked it out—Tuesday evening, when he'd come home rather late and in a bit of a nervous state, he had been unusually irritated and touchy.

And then they had found one of his old National Service mates murdered, and that had knocked the stuffing out of him, she could see that. Even if he hadn't wanted to admit as much, of course.

So perhaps it was a good thing for him to get away from it all for a while. Good for all concerned, as they say. There were things she also didn't want to admit as well, such as not objecting to having their large house to herself for a change. She had nothing against that at all, she decided, and put a little extra elbow grease into her scrubbing.

. . .

When the chief inspector came back from the sauna, Münster was already sitting in his office, waiting. It looked as if he'd been there for quite a while, in fact, as he'd had time to supply himself with a mug of coffee and the morning paper.

"So," said the chief inspector as he sat down at his desk. "Let's hear it, then."

Münster folded up his newspaper and produced three pale yellow cards.

"I think it would be best if somebody else went through the material as well," he said. "It's a bit difficult to keep awake when you have to read so much rubbish. One guy has evidently called three times and claimed that his mother is the murderer."

"Really?" said Van Veeteren. "And you're sure he isn't telling the truth?"

"Pretty sure," said Münster. "He's well into his seventies, and his mother died in 1955. And then there's somebody who claims to have been present at the time . . . in Innings's house, that is . . . and seen exactly what happened. The killer was a gigantic immigrant with a scimitar and a black patch over one eye."

"Hmm," said Van Veeteren. "Do you have anything a bit more credible to tell me?"

"Yes, I certainly do," said Münster. "Several things we ought to follow up. These three are probably the most interesting ones."

He handed over the cards, and the chief inspector read them while working a toothpick from one side of his mouth to the other.

"I'll take this one," he said. "You can check the other two. Give the rest of the interesting ones to Reinhart, and he can arrange follow-ups."

Münster nodded, drank up his coffee, and left the room.

Van Veeteren waited until the door was closed, then looked at the card again and dialed the number.

"Katrine Kroeller?"

"Just a moment, please."

There was a pause of half a minute or so, then he heard a girl's voice in the receiver. No more than nineteen or twenty at most, he thought.

"Hello, Katrine Kroeller here."

"My name is Chief Inspector Van Veeteren. You've reported an observation in connection with an investigation we are busy with. Can I come and have a chat with you?"

"Yes . . . yes, of course. When will you be coming?"

"Now," said Van Veeteren, looking at the clock. "Or at least in twenty minutes or so. Your address is Parkvej 31, is that correct?"

"Yes."

"Okay, I'll see you shortly, Miss Kroeller."

"Yes . . . you're welcome. I hope . . ."

"You hope what?"

"I hope you're not just wasting your time."

"We shall see," said Van Veeteren, and hung up.

If only she knew how much of our time is wasted, he thought. Then he wriggled into his jacket and set off.

She was waiting for him at the gate. As he thought, she was about twenty—she looked very Nordic, with a blond ponytail and a long neck. She was carrying an umbrella, and she escorted him carefully along the paved path to the front door at the gable end of the large two-story house, making sure he didn't need to step on the soaking-wet lawn.

"It's not all that easy to find your way here," she explained. "There are four of us renting rooms. Mrs. Klausner, our landlady, lives on the ground floor."

Van Veeteren nodded. Both the house and the garden suggested well-heeled upper middle class; but, of course, there were always people hovering at the edge of their social class, he reminded himself. People who had to take in lodgers and resort to similar ways of making ends meet.

"Let's hear it," he said when he had sat down in her room, with its sloping ceiling and blue wallpaper. "If I understand the situation rightly, you saw a woman using a tape recorder in a phone booth."

She nodded.

"Yes, outside here in the hall. It's there for the tenants to use. I saw her inside there, holding a tape recorder against the receiver. . . . One of those little cassette things."

"Who?"

"Miss Adler, the woman who lives next to me."

"Adler?" said Van Veeteren.

"Yes. Maria Adler. There are four of us, but I don't know her at all. She keeps to herself."

"When was this?"

"Three weeks ago, or thereabouts."

"Just the once?"

"Yes."

"How come you remember it?"

She hesitated.

"I don't really know, to tell you the truth. I hadn't given it a second thought. But then it came back to me when I read about those murders in the newspaper."

Van Veeteren nodded and thought for a moment. She seemed

to be a reliable witness, that was obvious. Calm and sensible, not inclined to exaggerate or be hysterical.

And slowly, very slowly, the thought began to sprout in his case-hardened consciousness. That this could be it. If this pale girl knew what she was talking about—and there was no reason to think she didn't—it was not impossible that the murderer was right here. Ryszard Malik's and Rickard Maasleitner's and Karel Innings's murderer. In the very next room. He could feel his pulse beating in his temples.

In this respectable villa in the respectable district of Deijk-straa. Surrounded by doctors, lawyers, successful businessmen, and God only knows who else.

A woman, then, just as Reinhart had predicted—yes indeed, there was a lot to support that thesis. . . . Perhaps most of all this feeling he had, which he always seemed to have when something was happening. A little signal saying that now, now things were suddenly getting serious, after all those days of hard work and despair.

And it was winking at him this very moment.

The signal. That red warning light.

Naturally, there were plenty of other reasons for using a tape recorder in a telephone booth; he was the first to admit that. It was simply that he didn't want to believe them, had no desire to do so. He wanted this to be the breakthrough, that was the bottom line.

"So she's in there?" he said, indicating with his head.

She nodded.

"Maria Adler?"

"Yes."

"Do you know if she's there at the moment?"

Katrine Kroeller shook her head. Her ponytail waved back and forth.

"No. I haven't seen her today. But she's very quiet, so it's possible she's in."

Van Veeteren stood up and tried to work things out. If he were to follow the police rule book, the correct procedure in this situation would naturally be to phone for reinforcements. There ought to be several officers involved. The woman in that room could very well be the person who had shot dead, in cold blood, three of her fellow human beings during the last month. She had a gun, and presumably ammunition, and she didn't normally miss.

He didn't even have his police weapon with him. As usual, it ought to be said.

So of course he ought to phone. It wouldn't take long for a few more officers to get here.

He looked around.

"May I borrow this?" he said, picking up an oblong-shaped wooden statuette standing on a bookshelf. Presumably African. Easy to handle. Three-quarters of a kilo, or thereabouts.

"Why?"

He didn't answer. Stood up and went out into the hall. Katrine Kroeller followed him hesitantly.

"The next door here?"

She nodded.

"Go back to your room."

She reluctantly did as she was told.

With his left hand he slowly depressed the door handle. His right hand was clutching the statuette. He noticed that he was still sweating a little after the sauna.

The door opened. He burst in.

It took him less than two seconds to register that the room was empty.

More than empty.

Abandoned. The tenant who had been living here had left and had no intention of returning.

She had moved somewhere else.

"Shit!" he exclaimed.

Stood motionless for a few more seconds, looking at the barren room.

No personal belongings. No clothes. No dishes drying in the kitchenette alcove. The bed made in such a way that you could see there were no sheets. Just a pillow, a blanket, and a quilt.

"Shit!" he muttered again, and went back out into the hall.

Miss Kroeller peeped out through her door.

"She's done a runner," said Van Veeteren. "Go and fetch . . . what's the name of your landlady?"

"Mrs. Klausner."

"Yes, that's the one. Tell her I want to speak to her in your room immediately. When did you last see Miss Adler, by the way?"

Katrine Kroeller thought for a moment.

"Er, yesterday, I think. Yes, yesterday afternoon."

"Here?"

"Yes, on the staircase. We just happened to pass."

Van Veeteren pondered that.

"Okay, fetch Mrs. Klausner. Is it possible for me to use this telephone?"

She opened the door of the booth and keyed in her personal code.

"It's all yours," she said.

"Thank you," said Van Veeteren, and dialed the number to the police station.

Two minutes later, he was talking to Reinhart.

"I think we've found her," Van Veeteren said. "But she's done a runner."

"Oh, shit!" said Reinhart. "Where?"

"Deijkstraa. Parkvej 31. Get yourself here with some of the forensic guys. Fingerprints, the lot. Münster as well. I'll be expecting you twenty seconds from now."

"We'll be there in ten," said Reinhart, and hung up.

29

"What time is it?" asked Van Veeteren.

"Half past five," said Reinhart.

"All right. Let's have a summary, Münster. And those of you who've been lounging around at home, sit up and listen carefully."

For the last half hour the investigation team had been all present and accounted for—apart from Jung and Moreno, who had succeeded in remaining incommunicado all afternoon. It was still Saturday, February 17, and they had achieved a breakthrough.

Or a possible breakthrough, at least.

Münster leafed through his notepad.

"This woman," he began, "calling herself Maria Adler, moved into Mrs. Klausner's house—into one of the four rooms she has to let—on Sunday, January fourteenth. A month ago, in other words. She said she had enrolled for a three-month economics course at the Elizabeth Institute. There is in fact such a course, which started on January fifteenth, but it lasts for only six weeks, and they've never heard of Maria Adler. When she moved in she paid the rent for half the occupation in advance, she never mixed with any of the other tenants, and she seems to have vacated her room once and for all yesterday afternoon, or possibly yesterday evening. The reason why we know about her is that Katrine Kroeller—one of the other tenants—had seen her with a tape recorder pressed up against the receiver in a phone booth, and she let us know about it after having read in the newspapers about that telephone music. . . . Well, that's about it, more or less."

"Is that all we have to go on?" asked deBries after a pause. "It doesn't sound all that convincing. . . ."

"That's all we have so far," said Reinhart. "But she's the one, I can feel it in my bones."

"So far we've found four different Maria Adlers nationwide," said Münster, "but she's not any of them. I expect we'll find another one or two, but I've no doubt we can assume that she has been using a false name."

"Didn't this landlady check up on what kind of people she let rooms to?" asked Rooth.

"Mrs. Klausner assumes the best in people," Reinhart explained. "She doesn't know how old she was, nor where she came from—nothing. . . . She assumed the best because her prospective tenant paid half the rent in advance."

"Our technicians have gone over the room with a fine-tooth comb," said Münster. "So we can take it that we have her fingerprints, at least. And if she's on our database, we can identify her."

"Are you saying she simply cleared off?" asked Heinemann, holding up his glasses against the ceiling light to check that his polishing had been effective.

"Yes," said Van Veeteren. "That's what's so damned frustrating. If only that girl had phoned us yesterday instead, we'd have had her by now."

"Typical," said Rooth. "What does she look like?"

Reinhart sighed.

"That bloody artist is in my office with Mrs. Klausner, the girl who rang us, and another of the tenants. He's been sketching away for over an hour now, but he says he needs a bit more time. . . ."

"A photofit picture?" said deBries. "Don't we have an actual photo?"

"No," said Münster. "But it's not really what you would call a photofit picture. They've seen her every day, more or less, for over a month. It will be just as accurate as a photograph."

"And it will be in every damn tabloid tomorrow morning," Reinhart growled.

"Hmm," said Heinemann. "But what if it isn't her after all? It could just be somebody who's run away from her husband. Or something of the sort. As far as I understand it, there's nothing definite. . . ."

Van Veeteren blew his nose, long and loud.

"Damned cold," he said. "Yes, you're right, of course. But we'll take the risk. I also have the distinct impression she's the one."

"If she's innocent, no doubt we'll be hearing from her," Reinhart said.

"But the opposite also applies," said deBries. "If we hear nothing from anybody, we can assume that she's the one."

"We can also assume that she'll change her appearance a bit," said Münster.

"I'm sure you're right," said Van Veeteren.

Nobody spoke for a while.

"I wonder where she's gone to," said Rooth.

"And why," said Reinhart. "Dammit all, there are so many important questions. Why did she do a runner just now?"

"The day before we received the tip," said Münster.

"Interesting," said Rooth. "But it could mean that she's finished what she set out to do, of course."

"A possibility," said Van Veeteren, contemplating a toothpick bitten away beyond recognition. "Her task might have been to kill these three, and she's done just that."

"Has anybody checked her alibi?" Rooth asked. "Just in case. Might she have been away at precisely these times?"

"We've started," said Van Veeteren. "We'll let the artist finish his drawings first, then we'll have another go at these ladies. But I don't really think they are going to be of much help. They don't seem to have any idea of what the rest of them in that house are up to. The landlady reads two novels per day, and Maria Adler didn't mix with the others. If anybody were to bump into her at the relevant time, it would be pure coincidence. Or an unfortunate happening, one should perhaps say."

"I get you," said Rooth.

"How much longer does that artist need?" asked Reinhart. "Surely he doesn't need half a day to create a face? Is there any more coffee?"

"Rooth," said the chief inspector. "For Christ's sake, go and find out what's happening. Tell him we have to have a picture soon if we're going to be able to place it in the newspapers."

"Okay," said Rooth, rising to his feet. "Wanted, dead or alive."

"Preferably alive," said the chief inspector.

"That was the last one," said Jung, looking at the list. "What do you think?"

"I suppose we'll have to hope it was Klumm's Cellar," said Moreno. "If not, he must have been in Maardam."

"Good God," said Jung. "How many restaurants are there in Maardam? Two hundred?"

"If you include pubs and cafés, it's probably twice as many as that," said Moreno. "It's a great task, this one. It was such fun talking to all his workmates before we were given it. Why did you join the police?"

"People who are no good at anything become police officers," said Jung. "Anyway, shall we see if we can find this waiter? We might just get lucky. Then we'd better ring round and see if we can find somebody who was with him. . . . Before we start on Maardam, that is. Or what do you think?"

Moreno nodded and consulted her notebook.

"Ibrahim Jebardahaddan," she read. "Erwinstraat 16. . . . That's just before you come to that sports field, I think."

Fifteen minutes later Jung rang the doorbell of an apartment on the first floor of a rather shabby three-story block. Fifties, or early sixties. Crumbling plaster and mainly foreign names on the list in the entrance. A bronze-skinned woman on the far side of middle age opened the door.

"Hello . . . who are you looking for?" she said with a timid smile and a pronounced foreign accent.

"Ibrahim Jebardahaddan," said Jung, who had been practicing both in the car and on the stairs.

"Please come in," she said, ushering them into a large room containing about a dozen people of various ages, sitting on chairs and sofas. Some children were playing on the floor. Faint music in a minor key played by stringed instruments was coming from hidden stereo speakers. A low, square table was laden with bowls of exotic-looking food emitting warm, aromatic fragrances that seemed almost tangible.

"Smells good," said Jung.

"Perhaps we ought to mention that we are police officers," said Moreno.

"Police officers?" said the woman, but there was no trace of fear in her voice. Only surprise. "Why?"

"Routine inquiries," said Jung. "We're trying to find out about a certain person who might have had a meal at the restaurant Ibrahim evidently works at. . . ."

A young man had stood up and was listening.

"That's me," he said. "I work at Klumm's Cellar. What's it all about? Perhaps we should go to my room?"

His accent was less pronounced than the woman's. He led them through the hall and into a small room containing not much more than a bed, a low chest of drawers, and some large cushions. Jung showed him the photograph of Innings.

"Can you say if this person visited your restaurant last week, on Friday evening?"

The young man cast a quick glance at the photograph.

"Is that Innings?"

"Yes."

"Yes, he did. He had a meal at our place last Friday. I saw on TV that he'd been killed. And in the newspapers. I recognize him."

"Are you sure?" asked Moreno.

"A hundred percent. I've already told my friends that I saw him there. I was the one who served him as well. A few days before he was shot. Yes, Friday it was."

"Good," said Moreno. "Do you know who was with him?"

Jebardahaddan shook his head.

"No, I didn't see him so clearly. It was a man, but he had his back toward me, if you see what I mean. . . . I don't know if I'd recognize him again."

Jung nodded.

"It doesn't matter. Presumably it was one of his friends—we can check on that in other ways. Anyway, thank you very much."

The woman who had let them in appeared in the doorway with the same timid smile.

"Have you finished? Then you must come and eat with us. This way, please."

Moreno looked at the clock. Then at Jung.

"Why not?" she said. "Thank you very much. We'd love to."

"We certainly would," said Jung.

Van Veeteren stared at the picture. Reinhart, Münster, and deBries were crowded behind him.

"So this is what she looks like?" said the chief inspector.

It was a very well-drawn portrait, no question about it. A woman somewhere between thirty-five and forty, it seemed. Quite short, straight hair. Thin lips and a somewhat bitter expression around her mouth. Round glasses, a slightly introverted look. Straight nose. Quite a few wrinkles and marks on her skin.

"He says the eyes were the most difficult," said Rooth. "So much depends on the moment. Her hair is brown . . . mousy, if you like."

"She looks a bit haggard," said Reinhart. "With a bit of luck we might find her in police records."

"Have they finished fingerprinting?" Heinemann asked.

"I think so," said Münster. "There must be masses of them; she's been living there for a month, after all. I suppose it'll be best if deBries takes care of that, as usual?"

DeBries nodded. Van Veeteren picked up the picture and scrutinized it from close quarters.

"I wonder . . . ," he muttered. "Manon's spring . . . yes, why not?"

"What are you on about?" Reinhart wondered.

"Nothing," said Van Veeteren. "Just thinking aloud. Anyway, Münster: make sure this picture goes out to every damned newspaper in the land."

He rummaged around among the papers on his desk.

"Together with this communiqué," he added. "Apart from that, I think the best thing we can do now is to go home and get some sleep. I want you all back here tomorrow morning at ten o'clock. We'll be swamped with tips and speculations. With a bit of luck, we'll get her tomorrow."

"I wonder," said Reinhart.

"So do I," said the chief inspector. "I'm just trying to spread a little optimism and a belief in the future. Good night, gentlemen."

30

Sunday, February 18, announced itself with warm breezes and a vague promise of spring. For anybody who had time to detect promises.

Van Veeteren got up at six, despite the fact that he had been listening to Sibelius and Kuryakin until late into the night. He fetched the *Allgemejne* from the letter box and established that the picture of Maria Adler was on the front page. Then he went to the bathroom and took a long shower, constantly adjusting the tap to make it increasingly cold, and tried to envisage the coming day.

That it would be long—another in a succession of long days—was beyond all doubt, of course; but he also knew there was a little chance. A possibility that it might be the last day of this investigation. Regarding the arrest, that is. Actually capturing the murderer. Then other things would kick in, other wheels would begin to turn—interrogation, charging, custody, and all the other formal procedures of the legal process, but that was a different matter. The hunt would be over. It would mean that his own role had come to an end, somebody else would take over ultimate responsibility. Other officers, better equipped for such a role. Was that really what it was all about? he wondered. Was it really just those ingredients that drove him—getting his teeth into the prey and placing it at the feet of the red-jacketed hunter, black-robed judge? The bloodhound instinct?

Nonsense! he decided, and had a final rinse in icy cold water. These arbitrary analogies.

He left the shower and turned his attention to breakfast instead. Freshly brewed coffee, yogurt, and four slices of toast with butter and strong cheese. He had always found it difficult to feel really hungry in the morning, but today he forced himself. He knew he shouldn't begin today with coffee and a cigarette, as had been his custom for many years when forced to get to grips with the world and life at daybreak.

But on the other hand, he thought as he studied the picture in the newspaper, this chance, this suspicion he had that today might be crowned with success was not particularly strong. Perhaps no more than a pious hope, a chimera, something he needed in order to raise the strength to go to work on a Sunday morning in February.

Who the hell wouldn't need such a stimulus?

In any case, the woman he knew so far only as Maria Adler aroused his respect. If "respect" was the right word to use in the context.

There was something impressive about her. And frightening, of course. The feeling that she had full control over what she was doing was incontestable. Her way of striking and then withdrawing, over and over again, suggested both coldness and decisiveness. She had remained concealed in Mrs. Klausner's house for a month, had carried out her operations with unerring precision, and now she had disappeared. And as he stared at her everyday, slightly enigmatic face, he tried to analyze what this disappearance might imply.

Perhaps—as somebody had pointed out—it simply meant that she had finished. Her intention had been to murder just these three persons, for some reason the police as yet had not the slightest idea of, and since the task was accomplished, she had chosen to leave the stage.

Or—he thought as he scattered a generous amount of muesli over his yogurt—she realized it would be too risky to stay in the house. She knew (how?) that it was time to leave her hiding place.

Or—a thought one couldn't dismiss out of hand—she had chosen to move a little closer to her next victim. Take up a better striking position, as it were. Malik and Maasleitner and Innings had all been within easy distance of Deijkstraa—the first two in Maardam itself, the third only a few miles away. If it was in fact the case that Miss Adler had several more people on her list, and they belonged to the group who lived in different parts of the country (or even abroad), well, there was naturally a good reason for finding a new base from which to operate.

Van Veeteren started on the toast. If there were any other possibilities in addition to those three, he hadn't been able to think of them. He realized that number two did not necessarily exclude numbers one or three, of course; none of them seemed to him any more probable than the others.

Perhaps she had finished murdering.

Perhaps she had sensed the closing in of her pursuers.

Perhaps she was on her way to victim number four.

By a quarter past eight he had finished both his breakfast and his newspaper. When he contemplated the pale and by no means especially threatening sky through the balcony door, he decided to walk to the police station for a change.

His cold seemed to have given up the ghost, and he thought

he had good reason to extend the good start to this day of rest—especially as he was unlikely to get much of that.

Things turned out to be rather worse than he had feared.

By lunchtime the picture of the wanted woman calling herself Maria Adler had reached every nook and cranny of the whole country, and those who had managed to avoid it could only have been the blind and anyone sleeping off the effects of their Saturday night boozing.

According to Inspector Reinhart's understanding of the situation, that is.

By as early as eleven o'clock, the number of calls had passed the five-hundred mark, and by not much more than an hour later, that figure had doubled. Four operators were at the switchboard receiving calls; a couple of officers made a preliminary assessment and sorted them into two (later three) groups according to urgency, whereupon the material was sent upstairs to the fourth floor, where Van Veeteren and the others tried to make a final assessment and decide on what further action to take.

Another three women (to add to Münster's four) had called to say their name was Maria Adler. None of them had anything at all to do with the murders and could prove it, and none of them seemed to be too happy at being called Maria Adler at the present time. A poor woman up in Frigge, the wife of the lord mayor, was called something entirely different, but evidently looked exactly like the picture in the newspapers—she had been reported by four different people in her hometown, and had phoned the police in tears, both locally and at the headquarters in Maardam. The lord mayor himself was intending to sue.

However, the majority of all the calls came from the Deijkstraa area. All of them claimed—no doubt correctly—that they had come across this Miss Adler in various places during the month she had been living in Mrs. Klausner's house. In the supermarket. At the post office. In the street. At the bus stop on the Esplanade . . . and so on. No doubt most of these sightings were also correct; but, needless to say, they were of little value to the investigation.

What they were looking for were two types of information, as had been stressed in the press release and repeated in the newspapers and the broadcast-news bulletins.

First: information that could (directly or indirectly) link the wanted woman to any of the murder scenes.

Second: evidence to indicate where Miss Adler had gone after leaving Mrs. Klausner's house on Friday afternoon.

By noon only a regrettably small number of calls had been received in those categories. There might have been indications suggesting that Maria Adler had taken a northbound train round about six o'clock on Friday evening. One witness claimed to have seen her in the station, another standing on a platform where he was waiting for a friend—a woman who didn't quite look like the picture of her in the mass media, but might well have been her even so.

If these two claims were correct, the train in question must have been the 1803, and shortly after half past noon Van Veeteren decided to send out a follow-up message to the mass media, urging anybody who had been traveling on that train and might have seen something to get in touch with the police.

A few hours later a handful of passengers had contacted the police, but what they had to say was hardly of significance. It sounded more like a collection of irrelevant details and guesses, and there were therefore grounds for believing that the train line (as Reinhart insisted on calling it) was not very promising.

By three o'clock, the officers in charge of the investigation were beginning to show the strain. They had spent the day in two rooms, Van Veeteren's and Münster's offices, which were next to each other, and the piles of paper and empty coffee mugs had increased steadily for six hours.

"Hell's bells," said Reinhart. "Here's another call from the old witch who's seen our woman in Bossingen and Linzhuisen and Oosterbrügge. Now she's seen her in church at Loewingen as well."

"We ought to have a better map," said deBries. "With flag pins or something. I think we've had several tips from Aarlach, for instance. It would make things easier. . . ."

"You and Rooth can fix one," said Van Veeteren. "Go to your office so that you don't disturb us."

DeBries finished off his Danish pastry and went to fetch Rooth.

"This is a real bugger of a job, sheer drudgery," said Reinhart.

"I know," said Van Veeteren. "No need to remind me."

"I'm beginning to think she's the most observed woman in the whole country. They've seen her everywhere, for Christ's sake. In restaurants, at football matches, parking lots, cemeteries . . . in taxicabs, buses, shops, the movies . . ."

Van Veeteren looked up.

"Hang on," he said. "Say that again!"

"What?" asked Reinhart.

"All those places you chanted."

"What the hell for?"

Van Veeteren made a dismissive gesture.

"Forget it. Cemeteries . . ."

He picked up the telephone and called the duty officer.

"Klempje? Get hold of Constable Klaarentoft without delay! Yes, I want him here in my office."

"Now what are you onto?" asked Reinhart.

For once things went smoothly, and half an hour later Klaarentoft stuck his head around the door after knocking tentatively.

"You wanted to speak to me, Chief Inspector?"

"The photographs!" said Van Veeteren.

"What photographs?" wondered Klaarentoft, who took an average of a thousand a week.

"From the cemetery, of course! Ryszard Malik's burial. I want to look at them."

"All of them?"

"Yes. Every damned one."

Klaarentoft was beginning to look bewildered.

"You've still got them, I hope?"

"Yes, but they've only been developed. I haven't printed them out yet."

"Klaarentoft," said Van Veeteren, pointing threateningly with a toothpick. "Go down to the lab this minute and print them! I want them here within an hour."

"Er, yes, of course, will do," stammered Klaarentoft, and hurried out.

"If you can do it more quickly, so much the better!" yelled the chief inspector after him.

Reinhart stood up and lit his pipe.

"Impressive issuing of orders," he said. "Do you think she was there, or what are you after?"

Van Veeteren nodded.

"Just a feeling."

"Feelings can be helpful at times," said Reinhart, blowing out a cloud of smoke. "How are Jung and Moreno doing, incidentally? With Innings and that Friday evening, I mean."

"I don't know," said Van Veeteren. "They've found the right place, it seems, but not whoever was with him."

"And what's Heinemann doing?"

"He's in his office nosying into bank-account details, apparently," said Van Veeteren. "Just as well, this would be a bit much for him."

"It's starting to be a bit much for me as well, to tell you the truth," said Reinhart, flopping back down on his chair. "I have to say I'd prefer her to come here in person and give herself up. Can't we put that request in the next press release?"

There was a knock on the door. Münster came in and perched on the edge of the desk.

"Something occurred to me," he said. "This woman can hardly be older than forty. That means she would have been ten at most when they were at the Staff College. . . ."

"I know," muttered Van Veeteren.

Reinhart scratched his face with the stem of his pipe.

"And what are you trying to say in view of that?"

"Well," said Münster, "I thought you'd be able to work that out for yourself."

It took Klaarentoft less than forty minutes to produce the photographs, and when he had put them on Van Veeteren's desk he lingered in the doorway, as if waiting for a reward of some kind. A coin, a candy, a few grateful and complimentary words at least.

The chief inspector grabbed hold of the pictures, but Reinhart had noticed the hesitant giant.

"Hmm," he said.

Van Veeteren looked up.

"Well done, Klaarentoft," he said. "Very good. I don't think we need you anymore today."

"Thank you, Chief Inspector," said Klaarentoft, and left.

Van Veeteren leafed through the shiny photographs.

"Here!" he bellowed suddenly. "And here! I'll be damned!"

He skimmed quickly through the rest.

"Come here, Reinhart! Just look at these! That's her, all right."

Reinhart leaned over the desk and studied the pictures of a woman in a dark beret and light overcoat tending a grave not far from Malik's; one was in profile, the other almost full face. They were evidently taken with only a short interval between: the photographer had simply changed his position. She was standing by the same grave and seemed to be reading what it said on the rough, partly moss-covered stone. Slightly bent, and one hand holding back a plant.

"Yes," said Reinhart. "That's her, by God."

Van Veeteren grabbed the telephone and called the duty officer.

"Has Klaarentoft left yet?"

"No."

"Stop him when he appears, and send him back up here," he said, and hung up.

Two minutes later Klaarentoft appeared in the doorway again.

"Good," said Van Veeteren. "I need enlargements of these two, can you do that?"

Klaarentoft took the pictures and looked at them.

"Of course," he said. "Is it . . ."

"Well?"

"Is it her? Maria Adler?"

"You can bet your life it is," said Reinhart.

"I thought there was something odd about her."

"He has a keen nose," said Reinhart when Klaarentoft had left.

"Yes indeed," said Van Veeteren. "He took twelve pictures of the clergyman as well. We'd better arrest him right away."

"At last," said Reinhart when he snuggled down behind Winnifred Lynch in the bath. "It's been a bastard of a day. What have you done?"

"Read a book," said Winnifred.

"A book? What's that?" said Reinhart.

She laughed.

"How's it going? I take it you haven't caught her?"

"No," said Reinhart. "More than thirteen hundred tips, but we don't know where she is or who she is. It's a bugger. I thought we might even solve it today."

"Hmm," said Winnifred, leaning back against his chest. "All she needs is a wig. No suspicions, even?"

"She's probably gone northward," said Reinhart. "She might have taken a train. We'll be talking to a guy tomorrow who thinks he might have been in the same coach as she was. He rang just before I left."

"Any more?"

Reinhart shrugged.

"I don't know. We don't know about the motive, either."

She thought for a moment.

"You remember I said it would be a woman?"

"Yes, yes," said Reinhart, with a trace of irritation.

"A wronged woman."

"Yes."

She stroked his thigh with her fingers.

"There are many ways of wronging a woman, but one is infallible."

"Rape?"

"Yes."

"She was ten years old at most when they left the Staff College," said Reinhart. "Can't be more than forty now—what do you think . . . ?"

"No, hardly," said Winnifred. "Awful, but there's something of that sort in the background, believe me."

"Could well be," said Reinhart. "Can't you look a bit deeper into your crystal ball and tell me where she's hiding as well? No, let's forget this for a while. What was the book you read?"

"*La Vie Devant Soi,*" said Winnifred.

"Emile Ajar?"

"Yes."

"And?"

"I think I need a child."

Reinhart leaned his head against the tiles and closed his eyes. Sensed two completely irreconcilable images flashing through his brain, but it all happened so quickly that he never managed to grasp their significance.

Assuming they had any.

"May I give you one?" he said.

"If you insist," she said.

31

"She could well have taken that train," said Münster. "He seems pretty sure of what he's talking about."

"Good," said Van Veeteren. "Where did she go to?"

Münster shook his head.

"Alas," he said. "He got off in Rheinau, but she didn't. So . . . somewhere farther north than Rheinau, it seems."

"There must be more people who saw her?" said Reinhart.

"You'd have thought so. In any case, there was somebody else in the same coach, according to Pfeffenholtz."

"Pfeffenholtz?"

"Yes, that's his name. There was somebody else there all the way from Maardam. A skinhead. And it seems he was still there after Rheinau."

"Wow," said Reinhart.

"Dark glasses, Walkman, and a comic book," said Münster. "Between eighteen and twenty, about. Eating candy all the time, and a cross tattooed over his right ear."

"A swastika?" Reinhart asked.

"Evidently," sighed Münster. "What should we do? Send out a 'wanted' notice?"

Van Veeteren grunted.

"A swastika and candies?" he said. "Good God, no. Somebody else can go chasing after neo-Nazi puppies. But this Pfeffenberg . . ."

"Holtz," said Münster.

"Okay, okay, Pfeffenholtz. He seems to know what he's talking about?"

Münster nodded.

"Okay," said Van Veeteren. "Go back to your office and pick out the ones from the Staff College who might fit in. The ones who live north of Rheinau, in other words. Fill me in when you've done that."

Münster stood up and left the room.

"Have you thought about the motive?" Reinhart wondered.

"I've spent the last month wondering about that," muttered the chief inspector.

"Really? What do you reckon, then? I'm starting to think in terms of rape."

Van Veeteren looked up.

"Go on," he said.

"It must be a woman looking for revenge for something or other," Reinhart suggested.

"Could be."

"And rape would fit the bill."

"Could be," repeated the chief inspector.

"Her age makes it a bit complicated, though. She must have been very young at the time. Only a child."

Van Veeteren snorted.

"Younger than you think, Reinhart."

Reinhart said nothing and stared into thin air for a few seconds.

"My God," he said eventually. "That's a possibility, of course. Sorry to be so thick."

"No problem," said Van Veeteren, and reverted to leafing through papers.

DeBries arrived at the same time as Jung and Moreno.

"Can we take mine first?" said deBries. "It won't take long."

Van Veeteren nodded.

"She's not in criminal records."

"A pity," said Reinhart. "Still, as things are now it probably wouldn't help us if we knew who she was. But it could be interesting, of course."

"Innings?" said Van Veeteren when deBries had left the room.

"Well," began Moreno. "We've fixed the restaurant. He had a meal at Klumm's Cellar out at Loewingen, but we haven't managed to find out who he was with."

"Good," said Van Veeteren. "That was no doubt the intention. How carefully have you checked?"

"Extremely carefully," said Jung. "We've spoken to all his colleagues and friends, and all his relatives up to seven times removed. None of them was out with Innings that Friday evening."

The chief inspector broke a toothpick in half and looked pleased. As pleased as he was able to look, that is, which wasn't all that much. Nevertheless, Reinhart noticed his state.

"What's the matter with you?" he asked. "Don't you feel well?"

"Hmm," said Van Veeteren. "But you have the witness from the restaurant, I gather?"

"Only a waiter," said Moreno. "And he didn't get to see much of the person Innings was with. A man aged between fifty and sixty, he thought. He had his back toward the waiter most of the time, it seems."

"You can bet your life he had," said Van Veeteren. "Anyway, take those photographs of the group who attended Staff College together. The new ones, of course. Ask him if he thinks he can point anybody out."

Jung nodded.

"Do you think Innings was eating with one of them, then?"

Van Veeteren looked inscrutable.

"Moreover," he said, "be a bit generous when you ask him if he can identify anybody. If he's not sure, get him to pick out the three or four most likely even so."

Jung nodded again. Moreno looked at the clock.

"Today?" she asked hopefully. "It's half past four."

"Now, right away," said Van Veeteren.

Shortly after Van Veeteren got home, Heinemann phoned.

"I've found a connection," he said.

"Between what?"

"Between Malik, Maasleitner, and Innings. Do you want me to tell you about it now, over the phone?"

"Fire away," said Van Veeteren.

"Okay," said Heinemann. "I've been going through their bank

records, all three of them—it's more awkward than you might think. Some banks, Spaarkasse, for instance, have some routines that are highly peculiar, to say the least. It can't be much fun dealing with financial crimes, but I suppose that's the point. . . ."

"What have you found?" asked Van Veeteren.

"Well, there's a similarity."

"What, exactly?"

"June 1976," explained Heinemann. "On June eighth, Malik takes out ten thousand guilders from his savings account at the Cuyverbank. On the ninth, Maasleitner draws an identical amount from the Spaarkasse. The same day, Innings is granted a loan by the Landtbank for twelve thousand. . . ."

Van Veeteren thought for a moment.

"Well done, Heinemann," he said eventually. "What do you think that implies?"

"You can never be sure, I suppose," said Heinemann. "But a spot of blackmail might not be out of the question."

Van Veeteren thought again.

"You see where we need to go from there, I suppose?"

Heinemann sighed.

"Yes," he said. "I suppose I do."

"You need to check and see if anybody else in the group made a similar transaction at the same time."

"Exactly," said Heinemann. "I'll start on that tomorrow."

"Don't sound so miserable," said the chief inspector. "You can start with the ones who live up north—with a bit of luck that might be enough. Have a word with Münster, and he'll give you a list tomorrow morning."

"All right," said Heinemann. "I have to go and look after the kiddies now."

"Kiddies?" asked the chief inspector in surprise. "Surely your children are grown up now?"

"Grandchildren," said Heinemann, and sighed again.

Well, well, Van Veeteren thought as he replaced the receiver. We're getting there, the noose is tightening.

He fetched a beer from the fridge. Put on the *Goldberg Variations* and leaned back in his armchair. Placed the photographs on his knee, and began to study them with a slight feeling of admiration.

Thirty-five young men.

Five dead.

Three of them thanks to this woman's efforts.

This woman in a dark beret and a light overcoat, with the trace of a smile on her face. Leaning over a gravestone. A birthmark on her left cheek—he couldn't recall seeing that on the picture the artist had drawn, but then it was no bigger than a little fingernail.

Klaarentoft had made an excellent enlargement in any case, and as Van Veeteren sat in his chair, studying her face, he suddenly had the impression that she had raised her gaze a little. Peered over the top of the gravestone and looked at him.

A bit cheeky, he thought. A little bit roguish even, but at the same time, serious.

And very, very determined.

How old are you, in fact? he wondered.

And how many do you have on your list?

32

But then everything came to a dead stop.

The distinct feeling that the investigation, which was now entering its second month, had been on the right track over the weekend—caused by such developments as the discovery of Maria Adler in the house in Deijkstraa and the visit to the restaurant by Innings—turned out to have been a little hasty. Instead of gathering pace and culminating in the capture of the man—or rather, woman—behind the three murders, the sum of all the efforts being made gave the impression of something slowly but inevitably trickling out into the sand.

"We're drifting out to sea," asserted Reinhart on Thursday morning. "Land behind!"

And the chief inspector was forced to agree. The so-called train line—suggesting that Maria Adler had traveled on the 1803 northbound train from Maardam Central Station—could be neither confirmed nor disproved. Pffeffenholtz's evidence, strong as it was, was uncorroborated. No candy-eating skinhead had been in contact. Nor any other passenger. Perhaps Miss Adler had indeed traveled to somewhere north of Rheinau, or perhaps not.

But even if she had, as Reinhart pointed out, what the devil was there to say that she was still there? And that her move was because of the intentions imputed to her?

Nothing at all, he announced, answering his own rhetorical question.

On Tuesday afternoon, in accordance with Van Veeteren's instructions, Jung and Moreno interviewed Ibrahim Jebardahaddan again in Leuwingen. The young Iranian was at first very doubtful about his ability to pick out anybody, but when Moreno explained that it was especially important and serious, he picked out five people from the Staff College group that he thought might possibly have been sitting opposite Innings on the Friday in question.

When the chief inspector saw the list of names, he did not appear pleased with the result, and so Jebardahaddan was summoned to the police station on Thursday for another session with the photographs.

This time the five photographs he had picked out were mixed with not only some of the others from the group, but also pictures of about thirty other people who had nothing to do with the case, and the witness managed to pick out only two of the five faces he had chosen previously. Both of them lived south of Maardam, one of them as far distant as South Africa.

After Ibrahim Jebardahaddan had left the police station on unsteady legs, Moreno remarked that this was the first time she had seen him wearing glasses. The general consensus was that the restaurant line was a dead end, at least for the present.

As for contact with the as-yet-not-murdered (to use Reinhart's term), the group had now been reduced to twenty-five (excluding those living abroad), and on Wednesday the investigation team was due to hear the results of the latest interviews with them. The judgment that Karel Innings had been a person roughly halfway between Malik and Maasleitner was more or less universal. A generally liked, sociable, and positive young man, most of them recalled. With no strong links to either Malik or Maasleitner.

As far as anybody could remember.

Some of the group had declined to make any comment at all for some unknown reason, according to the local police authorities. Some had also declined the offer of some form of protection or guarding, and three had been impossible to contact because they were not at home.

The link between the three victims was thus restricted to the banking transactions in June 1976, unearthed by Heinemann, but as yet he had been unable to find any similar transactions entered into at that time by any other members of the group.

"Much more awkward than you would think," he explained when he reported to the Friday meeting reviewing the case. "Generally speaking we have to get specific permission for every single account we want to investigate."

"Ah well," sighed the chief inspector. "We know whose interests they're looking after. Where are we now, then? What does Reinhart have to say?"

"We haven't moved from the same spot," said Reinhart. "It's nine days since Innings was murdered. And a week since Miss Adler flew the coop from Deijkstraa. She's had plenty of time to hide herself away, that's for sure."

"I think she's finished," said Rooth.

"I don't," said Reinhart.

"We could keep a special eye on those on Münster's list," suggested deBries. "The ones who live up north, that is."

"Do you think it's worth the effort?" asked the chief inspector.

"Of course it isn't," said Reinhart. "The only thing we ought to be concentrating on at the moment is a long, free weekend."

"Is there anybody who objects to Inspector Reinhart's proposal?" asked Van Veeteren wearily, whereupon a gravelike silence descended on the senior investigative team.

"Okay," said Van Veeteren. "Unless anything special turns up, we'll assemble again here on Monday morning at nine o'clock. Don't forget that we have over two thousand more tips to work through."

A few hours later, when the chief inspector was about to enter the club in Styckargränd, he was met in the lobby by the manager, Urwitz, carrying in his arms a hopelessly drunk consultant from one of the local hospitals, a specialist in infectious diseases.

"We have to send him packing," he explained. "We can't stop him from singing and weeping and upsetting the ladies."

Van Veeteren nodded and helped the manager to lug the doctor up the stairs to a waiting taxi. These things happen, he thought. They dumped their burden in the backseat.

"Where to?" asked the driver, looking skeptical.

Urwitz turned to Van Veeteren.

"Do you know him?"

"Only in passing," said Van Veeteren with a shrug.

"He maintains that his wife is entertaining her lover, so he can't go home. Can that be true?"

"No idea," said the chief inspector. "But if he has a wife, it's probably as well not to send him home in this state no matter what."

The manager nodded, and the driver looked even more thoughtful.

"Make up your minds, or take him out again," he said.

"Take him to the police station at Zwille," said Van Veeteren. "Pass on greetings from V.V. and tell them to be nice to him and let him sleep it off."

"V.V.?" asked the driver.

"Yes, that's right," said Van Veeteren, and the taxi moved off.

"*O tempora! o mores!*" sighed Urwitz, and escorted Van Veeteren down into the basement.

"You look a bit miserable," remarked Mahler as the chief inspector sat down at the table. "Are you fasting for Lent already?"

"I lead an ascetic life all year round," said Van Veeteren. "A match?"

"Of course," said Mahler, starting to set up the pieces. "So the elusive lady continues to be elusive, according to what I've heard."

Van Veeteren made no reply, but drank half a glass of beer instead.

"And that incident we spoke about," said Mahler. "Have you found it?"

The chief inspector nodded and adjusted his pieces.

"I think so," he said. "But until I can fix the date, all I can do is be miserable and mark time."

"I understand," said Mahler. "Or rather, I don't," he added after a while.

"It doesn't matter," said Van Veeteren. "I've decided to lie low and wait for a few days in any case. Let her make a move. . . ."

"Shoot another one?"

"I hope not," sighed Van Veeteren. "Speaking of moves . . ."

"All right," said Mahler, leaning forward over the board and starting his concentration routine.

When Van Veeteren left the club, shortly after half past midnight, he had two draws and a win under his belt, and since it wasn't raining, he was inclined to think—despite all the setbacks in the current investigation—that life was just about managing to keep its head above water.

When he came to Kongers Plejn, however, he had it brought home to him that this was a somewhat hasty judgment. He had just turned the corner and found himself in the midst of a gang of bellowing young men who had evidently been lying in wait for a suitable victim.

"Gotcha, you fucking ancient old bastard!" growled a broad-shouldered youth with close-cropped red hair as he forced Van Veeteren up against the wall. "Your money or your prick?"

My prick, Van Veeteren had time to think before another youth slapped his face with the back of his hand. The chief inspector could taste the blood on his tongue.

"I'm a police officer," he said.

This information was greeted with roars of laughter.

"Police officers are our favorites," said the youth pressing him up against the wall, and the others sniggered in delight.

The one who had hit him tried again, but this time Van Veeteren parried, at the same time thrusting his knee up between the close-cropped redhead's legs. The youth doubled up and groaned.

Van Veeteren delivered a right hook and succeeded in hitting somebody in the nasal region. He heard clearly how something gristly was rendered even more gristly, and as far as he could judge, the damaged area was not in his own hand.

The injured youth retired, but that was naturally the end of Van Veeteren's successes. The three remaining—and uninjured—youths forced the chief inspector down on all fours and began beating him up.

Van Veeteren curled up like a hedgehog, and as the punches and kicks were landing on him, all he could think of was: Silly little brats! Where are your daddies now, damn them?

After a while—it probably was no more than ten or fifteen seconds—they went away and left him. Ran off shouting and yelling.

"Hell and damnation . . . ," muttered Van Veeteren as he slowly got to his feet. He could feel he was bleeding from his lips and from a wound over his eyebrow; but when he started moving his arms and legs, he was able to establish that he was relatively unharmed.

He scanned the empty square.

Where the hell are all the witnesses? he thought, then resumed his walk home.

A little later, when he examined himself in the bathroom mirror, it occurred to him that it had been absolutely right to put the investigation on ice over the weekend.

An officer in charge looking like this could hardly be a source of inspiration for his team.

Then, in his capacity as a private citizen, he phoned the police and reported the assault. He also insisted, in his capacity as a detective chief inspector, that he should be the one to interrogate any of the young delinquents the police managed to find.

"Were they immigrants?" asked the duty constable.

"No," said Van Veeteren. "Bodybuilders, I'd say. Why should they be immigrants?"

He received no answer.

When he had washed and gone to bed, he was surprised to note, on reflection, that he hadn't felt in the least bit scared during the whole of the incident.

Indignant and annoyed, but not scared.

I suppose I'm too old for that, he thought.

Or perhaps it needs something worse than that to put the wind up me.

Or then again—it occurred to him just as he was about to fall asleep—perhaps I'm no longer scared of anything on my own account.

Only for others.

For society. For future developments.

For life?

Then he recalled a silly riddle Rooth had come up with the other day:

QUESTION: How do you make a random-number generator nowadays?

ANSWER: You pour two beers into a bodybuilder.

Then he fell asleep.

VIII

February 16–
March 9

33

The Pawlewski Hotel had seen better days, but then, so had Mr. Pawlewski.

And better guests.

More specifically, he had seen them sixty years ago and more, when he had to stand on a blue-painted and scratched stool in order to be able to see over the edge of the reception desk. When it was still Pawlewski senior and Pawlewski grand-senior running the show. And his mother and grandmother ruled the roost in the restaurant and linen store, and kept the cooks and pomaded bellboys in good order. While the century was somewhat younger.

A lot of water had flowed under the bridge since then. An awful lot of water. Nowadays the stool stood under a tired palm tree in his own den, the former so-called bridal suite on the fifth floor of the hotel.

Everything has its day.

Biedersen spent the first three evenings in the bar in the company of numerous whiskeys and the assortment of doubtful characters that comprised the clientele, roughly half of them one-night guests and the rest introverted regulars. All of them were men. All had thinning hair and almost all had drooping shoulders, some kind of beard or mustache, and vacant expressions. He didn't waste a minute on any of them, and from Monday night onward he drank from the bottle he had in his room instead.

This made the days monotonous and indistinguishable. He got up about noon. Left his room an hour later and spent the afternoon wandering around the town, so that the chambermaid had an opportunity to come in and mark the commencement of a new day. He would drink black coffee in some café or other, preferably Günther's near the town center, try to read a newspaper or perhaps several, go for a long walk, and buy some cigarettes plus the evening's bottle, which he would choose with a degree of care that struck him as unjustified but nevertheless essential. As if it were one of the basic rules in a game—he was not sure if he was playing it or if he was one of the pieces, but for the moment it was the only thing taking place. There was nothing else at all.

He returned by devious routes to the Pawlewski the moment he noticed that the dirt-gray dusk was beginning to fall. It happened early in a town like this, accompanied by acid rain and the smog from coal fires.

Stretched out on his newly made bed, with sick-looking pigeons cooing outside on the roof, he drank his first whiskey of the day before taking a bath, with number two within easy reach on the floor. Went down to the restaurant for dinner, usually as one of the first diners, occasionally completely alone in the oversized, mouse-brown room with uninspiring crystal glass chandeliers and tablecloths that had once been white. Drank beer with the food, coffee and cognac afterward, and each night he remained sitting there a little longer.

He tried to last out for a few extra minutes; to shrink and cut back as much as possible the accursed boredom of what remained of the waking day. And it was as he returned from these meals—on his way to the bar or up to his room—that Mr. Pawlewski saw him. Pawlewski spent virtually all his waking hours more or less invisible behind the reception desk; from there he could observe and pass judgment and as usual ascertain that most things had seen better days.

Who this particular guest was, and what the hell he was doing in this lugubrious town in a month like February, were the kind of questions that, in his capacity of observer and man of the world, he had ceased to ask forty or more years ago.

At first the intoxication and numbing of the senses was an aim in itself. Simply to get away, to run away and put distance between himself and what was happening, had been the primary, not to say the only, goal he had had when he left home. The idea that eventually he would have to adopt a different strategy, would have to work out practical new tactics and courses of action, was as yet merely a thought dormant in the back of his mind; or at least was not something hanging over him, demanding that he should do something. Even so, these days were filled with the complicated actions and routines necessary to enable him to enjoy the blessing of sleeping in a state of unconscious intoxication.

Dreamless sleep for eight hours. Dead to the world. Beyond reach of everything and everyone. In the morning he would wake up sweating profusely, and with a headache strong enough to keep all other sensations miles away. Then, simply by taking a couple of tablets and preparing himself yet again for the afternoon hours spent on the streets and in cafés, he had set the warped wheels of time turning once more. Gained another day.

By the seventh night it was over, this purifying, cauterizing alcohol bath. The desired distance had been achieved, his fear was in check, and he needed to apply himself to the strategies once more.

Scrutinized and filtered through a week of turbid, soothing whiskey, the proportions of his opponent had become possible to assess accurately. He could envisage her again. His faux pas and the fiasco in Berkinshaam, followed by the shocking murder of Innings, had elevated her out of the real world—the murderer was a phantom that couldn't be stopped, a superwoman; the only thing he could possibly do was go into hiding and wait. Vanish. Go underground, and hope.

That is why he had run away. Made himself invisible. Not just stuck his head in the sand, but dug down and concealed all of him. Away from everything and everyone. Away from her.

But on the tenth day he weighed his gun in his hand and began to look ahead again.

First of all, it was necessary to reject two possibilities.

The first was the police. To abandon his self-defense. Give himself up and tell them the whole story. Allow the bitch to win.

It took him two drams of whiskey to dismiss that thought.

The other was to remain in hiding. For as long as was necessary.

That took him a bit longer. Four drams, maybe six. But he managed it.

So what should he do?

He drank more. A lot more.

Days. All the rest of the days he stayed at the Pawlewski Hotel, to be precise. Needless to say, this had been his original thought, the one that had been lying dormant in the back of his mind—to find a place like this, and to stay there. To stay in this damned, filthy, bad-smelling hotel until he was ready and knew what he was going to do next.

Stay here and wait for the strength, the determination, and the ideas.

There must be a way.

A way of killing this damned bitch. And the more he thought about it, the clearer it became that this wasn't just about himself. Not just his own skin. That strengthened his resolve. All the others . . . the friends she had murdered, the widows and children, and the lives she had destroyed in the course of her blood-stained campaign, just in order to . . .

All the people who had suffered. Just in order to . . .

His duty. His duty, for God's sake, was to kill her. Challenge her on her own terms, then outwit her and obliterate her from the surface of the earth once and for all.

Eliminate this accursed bitch.

The anger inside him grew into hatred. Powerful, incandescent hatred coupled with the feeling of having a mission to accomplish, a duty to perform—he was filled with the strength he needed to carry it out.

Courage. Strength. Determination.

And the method?

Was there more than one?

Two drams. Let it circulate in the mouth, as if it were cognac. The same question over and over again. One evening after the other. More whiskey? The method? Was there more than one?

No. Only one.

Lower his guard. Leave himself open.

Give her the chance to strike first.

Then parry and kill her.

That was the way.

Yes, the Pawlewski Hotel had seen better guests.

How and where?

Where? That was the most important thing. Where the hell could he find a corner into which he could entice her without giving her too much of an advantage? He still didn't know what she really looked like—naturally, he had studied the pictures of her printed in the newspapers, but the only sure thing was that she was never going to approach him with an expression like the remarkably peaceful one she had there.

Another woman this time. No matter what she looked like. Unexpected and completely unknown. But where? Where the hell would he be able to set the trap?

And how?

It took a whole night to sketch out the plan, and when he eventually fell asleep in the gray light of dawn, he didn't believe it would still hold water in the cold light of day.

But it did. On Tuesday, he had lunch in the restaurant for the first time, and when he checked through the plan with the aid of two cups of extra-strong black coffee, he found the occasional crack, but nothing that couldn't be papered over, and nothing wide enough for him to fall through.

It was watertight.

.   .   .

Biedersen left the Pawlewski Hotel at about two in the afternoon on Wednesday, February 28. His gaze met that of Mr. Pawlewski behind the reception desk for only a fraction of a second, but that was enough for him to be sure that those remarkably all-seeing yet nothing-seeing eyes would never recall a certain Jürg Kummerle who had spent twelve nights in Room 313.

In view of this, for the twelve days and nights that had never existed, he gave Mr. Pawlewski an extra hundred-guilder note.

If she had found him during this dreadful period, she would have won—he knew that. But she hadn't, and now he was ready again.

34

"The first of March today," announced the chief of police, snapping off a withered leaf from a hibiscus. "Take a seat. As I said, I'd like to hear some kind of summary, at the very least. This case is gobbling up a lot of resources."

Van Veeteren muttered and flopped down into the shiny leather armchair.

"Well?"

"What do you want to know? If I had anything significant to tell you, I'd have done so without your needing to ask me."

"Is that something I can rely on?"

The chief inspector made no reply.

"We've been guarding and protecting twenty people for two weeks now. Would you like me to tell you how much that costs?"

"No thank you," said Van Veeteren. "You can call them off if you like."

"Call them off!" exclaimed Hiller, sitting down at his desk. "Can you imagine the headlines if we cancel the protection and she then clobbers another one? We're in a big enough mess as it is."

"The headlines won't be any better if we leave things as they are and she picks one off even so."

Hiller snorted and started rotating his gold watch around his wrist.

"What do you mean by that? Are you suggesting that the guards are of no significance? They could be the very thing that's holding her back."

"I don't think so," said Van Veeteren.

"What do you think, then? For Christ's sake tell me what you do think!"

The chief inspector took out a toothpick and examined it critically before inserting it into his lower row of teeth. Turned his head and tried to peer out the window through the dense expanse of greenery.

"I think it's raining. For instance."

Hiller opened his mouth. Then closed it again.

"It's not possible to say," Van Veeteren continued, after a pause for effect. "Either she's finished, or she's intending to kill more. Whatever, just at the moment she's lying low. Perhaps she's waiting for us to lower our guard . . . and for the next victim to do the same. Clever. That's what I'd do."

Hiller made a noise that the chief inspector was inclined to associate with a horny but unhappy seal.

"But what are you doing?" he managed to say eventually. "For God's sake tell me what you are doing about it!"

Van Veeteren shrugged.

"We're working through tips from the general public," he said. "Quite a few are still coming in, despite the fact that the newspapers have lost interest."

Hiller breathed deeply and tried to look optimistic.

"And?"

"Not much there; I'm wondering whether we ought to go out on a limb, although that would involve a bit of a risk, of course.

We could concentrate on a few possible candidates and leave the rest to their fate. That might give results."

Hiller thought about that.

"Are there any? Ones who are more likely than the others, that is?"

"Could be," said Van Veeteren. "I'm looking into that now."

The chief of police stood up and went over to his plants again. Swayed back and forth with his back to the chief inspector, using his thumbs and index fingers to remove specks of dust from some leaves.

"Do that, then," he said, turning around. "Use that blasted intuition of yours and make something happen!"

Van Veeteren heaved himself up from the armchair.

"Is that all?" he asked.

"For now," said the chief of police, gritting his teeth.

"What did he have to say?" asked Reinhart.

"He's nervous," said the chief inspector, pouring some coffee into a plastic mug. Raised it to his mouth, then paused.

"When was this brewed?" he asked.

Reinhart shrugged.

"February, I should think. This year, in any case."

There was a knock on the door and Münster came in.

"What did he have to say?"

"He wondered why we hadn't arrested her yet."

"You don't say," said Münster.

Van Veeteren leaned back, tasted the coffee, and pulled a face.

"January," he said. "Typical January coffee. Münster, how

many have we failed to get in touch with yet? Of the as-yet-unmurdered, that is."

"Just a moment," said Münster, and left the room. Returned a minute later with a piece of paper in his hand.

"Three," he said.

"Why?" asked the chief inspector.

"They're away," said Münster. "Two of them on business, one on holiday, visiting his daughter in Argentina."

"But surely we can get in touch with her?"

"We've sent her a message, but they haven't replied yet. We haven't been pressing all that hard, to be fair. . . ."

Van Veeteren produced the well-thumbed photograph.

"Which of them is it?"

"His name's Delherbes. He lives here in Maardam. It was deBries who talked to him last time."

Van Veeteren nodded.

"And the other two?"

"Biedersen and Moussner," said Münster. "Moussner is in Southeast Asia somewhere. Thailand and Singapore and so on. He'll be back home before long. Sunday, I think. Biedersen is probably a bit closer to home."

"Probably?" said Reinhart.

"His wife wasn't very sure. He often goes off on business trips, maintaining contacts now and then, it seems. He runs an import company. England or Scandinavia, she thought."

"Scandinavia?" said Reinhart. "What the hell does anybody import from Scandinavia? Amber and wolf skins?"

"Of course," said Van Veeteren. "Has anybody seen Heinemann today?"

"I spent three minutes with him in the canteen this morning," said Münster. "He seemed pretty worn out."

Van Veeteren nodded.

"Could be the grandchildren," he said. "How many tips have we left to go through?"

"A few hundred, I'd say," said Reinhart.

The chief inspector forced the remainder of the coffee down, with obvious reluctance.

"All right," he said. "We'd better make sure we've finished plowing through that shit by Friday. Something had better happen soon."

"That would be helpful," said Reinhart. "As long as it's not another one."

Dagmar Biedersen switched off the vacuum cleaner and listened.

Yes, it was the telephone again. She sighed, went to the hall, and answered.

"Mrs. Biedersen?"

"Yes, that's me."

"My name is Pauline Hansen. I'm a business acquaintance of your husband's, but I don't think we've met?"

"No . . . no, I don't think so. My husband's not at home at the moment."

"No, I know that. I'm calling from Copenhagen. I've tried to get him at the office, but they say he's away on business."

"That's right," said Dagmar Biedersen, rubbing a mark off the mirror. "I'm not sure when he's coming home."

"You don't know where he is?"

"No."

"That's a pity. I have a piece of business I'd like to discuss with him. I'm sure he'd be interested. It's a very advantageous deal, with rather a lot of money involved; but if I can't get hold of him, well . . ."

"Well what?" wondered Dagmar Biedersen.

"Well, I suppose I'll have to turn to somebody else. You've no idea where I might be able to contact him?"

"No, I'm afraid not."

"If you should hear from him in the next few days, please tell him I've called. I'm certain he'd be interested, as I said. . . ."

"Just a moment," said Dagmar Biedersen.

"Yes?"

"He phoned the other day and said he'd probably be spending a few days at the cottage as well."

"The cottage?"

"Yes. We have a little holiday place up in Wahrhejm. It's his childhood home, in fact, although we've done it up a bit, of course. You might be able to catch him there, if you are lucky."

"Is there a telephone?"

"No, but you can phone the village inn and leave a message for him. But I can't swear that he'll be there at the moment. It was just a thought."

"Wahrhejm, did you say?"

"Yes, between Ulming and Oostwerdingen. Just a little village. The number is 161621."

"Thank you very much. I'll give it a try—but even so, if you hear from him, I'd be grateful if you mentioned that I've called."

"Of course," said Dagmar Biedersen.

Verbal diarrhea, she thought as she replaced the receiver; when she started the vacuum cleaner again, she'd already forgotten the woman's name.

But the call was from Copenhagen, she did remember that.

35

Dusk was beginning to set in as he drove into Wahrhejm. He turned right at the village's only crossroads, passed the inn, where they had already lit the red lanterns in the windows—the same lanterns, he thought, that had been hanging there ever since he was a child.

He continued past the chapel, Heine's house, and the pond, whose still water looked blacker than ever in the failing light. Passed Van Klauster's house, Kotke's dilapidated old mansion, and then turned left into the little road between the post boxes and the tall pine trees.

He drove in through the opening in the stone wall and parked at the back, as usual. Hid the car from the gaze of the street—an expression his mother used to use that he had never been able to shake off. But today, of course, it was appropriate. The kitchen door was at the back as well, but he didn't unload his food supplies yet. He got out of the car and examined the house first. Outside and inside. The kitchen and the three rooms. The loft. The outbuilding. The cellar.

No sign. She was not here, and hadn't been here. Not yet. He applied the safety catch on his pistol and put it into his jacket pocket.

But she would come. He started unloading the provisions. Switched on the electricity. Started the pump. Allowed the taps to run for a while and flushed the lavatory. Nobody had set foot in the place since October, when he had invited a business acquaintance to spend the weekend there, but everything seemed to be in order. Nothing had given up the ghost during the winter. The refrigerator was humming away. The radiators soon felt warm. The television and radio were working.

For a second or two the pleasure he felt at returning home succeeded in ousting the reason for his visit from his mind. Most of the furniture—as well as the pictures and the tapestries, the hundreds of other little things—were still there and in the same state as when he had been a young boy, and the moment of arrival, the first sight of the place again, always brought with it a feeling of leaping back in time. Vertigo-inspiring, instantaneous. And it happened again now. But then, needless to say, the circumstances caught up with him.

The circumstances?

He switched off the lights. He felt at home in the darkness inside the house, and he knew that no matter what happened, he would not need a flashlight in order to find his way around. Neither indoors nor out of doors. He knew every nook and cranny. Every door and creaking stair. Every path, every bush, and every root. Every stone. Everything was in its place, had always been there, and that gave him a feeling of confidence and security—something he might have hoped for during the planning stage, but had hardly dared count on.

Anyway, the outbuilding.

He unhasped the door. Dragged the mattress up the stairs as best he could. Placed it carefully by the window. Not much headroom up there. He had to crawl, crouch down. He went back to collect pillows and blankets. It was colder in the outbuilding, there was no source of heat at all, and it was clear that he would have to wrap himself up well.

He adjusted the mattress to an optimal position under the sloping roof. Lay down, and checked it was all as he'd foreseen.

Perfect, more or less. He could look out through the slightly rippled, old-fashioned glass pane and see the gable end of the house, with both the front door and the kitchen door in his field of view. The distance was no more than six or eight meters.

He opened the window slightly. Took out the gun and stuck it out through the opening, moved it back and forth, testing. Took aim.

Would he hit her at this distance?

He thought so. Perhaps not accurately enough to kill her outright, but he would probably have time for three or four shots.

That should be sufficient. He was not a bad marksman, even though it had been several years since he'd been out with the hunting club up here.

He returned to the house. Ferried over a few more blankets and some of the provisions. The idea was that he would spend his time lying here. Spend as much time as possible in the correct position in the outbuilding loft.

He would be lying here when she came.

He would ambush her and give her the coup de grâce.

He would finish off the mad bitch once and for all through this open window.

Pure luck, he would tell the police afterward. It could just as easily have been she who got me instead. . . . Good thing I was on my guard.

Self-defense. Of course it was self-defense, for God's sake—he didn't even need to lie.

But he would not reveal the real reason. The root of the evil. The reason he knew he was next on the list.

He had done all he could. Went back to the house and listened.

It's strange how quiet it is, he thought, and remembered that this was what he always felt here. The silence that came rolling in from the forest and obliterated every slight sound. Wiped out everything with its enormous, silent soughing.

The armies of silence, he thought. The Day of Judgment . . .

He checked his watch and decided to pay a visit to the inn. A short walk there and back, along the familiar road.

Just for a beer. And, maybe, the answer to a question.

Any strangers around lately?

Any new faces?

When he got back, the darkness lay thick over the house and its environs. The buildings and the scraggy fruit trees could just about be made out against the background of the forest—rather better here and there against the somewhat lighter sky over the treetops. He had drunk two beers and a whiskey. Spoken to Lippmann and Korhonen, who had charge of the bar nowadays. Not a lot of customers, of course: a normal weekday at the beginning of March. And not many strangers, not recently, either. The occasional one who had passed through and called in, but nobody who had been there more than once. Women? No, no, not as far as they could remember. Neither Lippmann nor Korhonen. Why was he asking? Oh, business reasons. Nudge, nudge. Did he really think they would swallow that? Pull the other one. Tee hee. And cheers! Good to see you back here in the village.

Homecoming.

He tiptoed over the wet grass. It hadn't rained at all this evening, but damp mists had drifted in from the coast and settled down over the open countryside bordering the forests like an unseen presence. He kept stopping and listening, but all he could hear was the same impenetrable silence as before. Nothing else. He withdrew behind the outbuilding in order to rid his body of the remnants of the beer. Carefully opened the door, which usually squeaked a bit but didn't on this occasion. He would oil it tomorrow, just in case.

Crouched down in order to negotiate the cramped staircase again, and crawled over to his bed. Fiddled around with the blankets. Wriggled in and snuggled down. Turned over on his side and peered out. The house was dark and inert down below. Not a sound. Not a movement. He slid the pistol under his pillow, and placed his hand over it. He would have to sleep lightly, of course—but then, he usually did.

Always woke up at the slightest sound or movement.

Would no doubt do that now as well.

Blankets wrapped around his body. Face close to the windowpane. Hand over the gun.

So. Bring her on.

36

"I don't know," said the chief inspector. "It's just an opinion, but if these three were up to no good together, you'd think that at least some of the others ought to have known about it. So it's more likely that something of this sort would happen toward the end of the course. But then, that's only speculation, pure and simple."

"Sounds reasonable, though," said Münster.

"Anyway, rapes in 1965. How many have you found?"

"Two," said Münster.

"Two?"

"Yes. Two cases of rape reported, both of them in April. The first girl was attacked in a park, it seems. The other in an apartment in Pampas."

Van Veeteren nodded.

"How many rapists?"

"One in the park. Two in the apartment. The pair in the apartment were sentenced, the one in the park got away with it. He was never found."

Van Veeteren leafed through his papers.

"Do you know how many rapes have been reported so far this year?"

Münster shook his head.

"Fifty-six. Can you explain to me how the hell the number of rapes could shoot up so drastically?"

"Not rapes," said Münster. "Reported rapes."

"Precisely," said the chief inspector. "How do you rate the chances of tracking down a thirty-year-old unreported rape?"

"Poor," said Münster. "How do we know it's a matter of rape anyway?"

The chief inspector sighed.

"We don't know," he said. "But we can't just sit here twiddling our thumbs. You can have another job instead. If it gets us somewhere I'll invite you to dinner at Kraus."

Mission Impossible, Münster thought, and so did the chief inspector, it seemed, as he cleared his throat somewhat apologetically.

"I want to know about all births registered by the mother with the father given as unknown. December '65 to March '66, or thereabouts. In Maardam and the surrounding district. The names of the mothers and the children."

"Especially girls?" Münster asked.

"Only girls."

That evening he went to the movies. Saw Tarkovsky's *Nostalgia* for the fourth, or possibly the fifth, time. With the same feelings of admiration and gratitude as usual. The masterpiece of masterpieces, he thought as he sat there in the half-empty cinema and allowed himself to be gobbled up by the pictures; and he suddenly thought of what the vicar had said at his confirmation service—a gentle preacher with a long white beard, and there were doubtless many in the congregation who considered him a very close relation of God the Father himself.

There is evil in this world, he had declared, but never and nowhere so much that there is no room left over for good deeds.

Not a particularly remarkable claim in itself, but it had stuck in Van Veeteren's mind and occasionally rose up to the surface.

Such as now. Good deeds? Van Veeteren thought as he walked home after the showing. How many people are there living the sort of lives which don't even have room for nostalgia?

Is that why she's murdering these men? Because she never had a chance?

And room for good deeds? Was that really always available? Who exactly decided on the proportions? And who started off the relentless hunt for a meaning in everything? In every deed and every happening?

Things occur, Van Veeteren thought. Things happen, and perhaps they have to happen. But they don't need to be good or evil.

And they don't need to mean anything.

And his gloom deepened.

I'm an old sod, an old, tired detective who's seen too much and doesn't want to see much more, he thought.

I don't want to see the end of this case that's been occupying me for the past six weeks now. I want to get off the train before we get to the terminus.

What were all those vile thoughts about flushing out and hunting that were so noble and meaningful at the start?

I don't want to get to the point where I'm staring at the bleak and grubby causes of all this, he thought. I know the background is just as ugly as the crimes. Or suspect that, at least, and would like to be spared everything.

A futile prayer, he knew that—but isn't futility the home ground of prayer? What else could it be?

He turned into Klagenburg and wondered briefly if he ought to call in at the café. He failed to reach a conclusion, but his feet passed by the brightly lit doorway of their own accord, and he continued his walk home.

Things happen, he thought. I might just as well have gone in.

And as he lay in bed, there were two thoughts that overwhelmed him and kept him awake.

Something is going to happen in this case as well. Just happen. Soon.

I must think about whether I have the strength to last for much longer.

And then the image of Ulrike Fremdli—Karel Innings's wife—popped up in his mind's eye. Hovered there in the dark mist between dream and reality, between slumber and consciousness, and was gradually interleaved by and combined with Tarkovsky's ruined church and Gorchakov's wading through the water with a flaming torch.

Something's bound to happen.

37

"Hello?"

Jelena Walgens's hearing was not what it had once been. She found it especially difficult to understand what people said on the telephone—and needless to say, she would have preferred to discuss whatever the topic was over a cup of coffee. With something freshly baked on the side. A little chat about this and that. But the young man was persistent, sounded pleasant, and of course it would be possible to settle matters over the phone even so.

"How long did you say? A month only? I would prefer to have a tenant for a bit longer than that. . . ."

"I could pay you a bit extra," argued the young man. "I'm a writer. Alois Mühren, I don't know if you've heard of me?"

"I don't think so."

"What I'm looking for is a nice, quiet hideaway where I can write the final chapter of my new book. I certainly don't need more than a month. All the people and the hustle and bustle of a city make things so difficult for a writer, if you see what I mean."

"I certainly do," said Jelena Walgens as she searched through her memory.

But she couldn't think of anybody by that name. She read quite a lot, and had always done so; but he was a young man, and maybe she hadn't quite heard the name right. Alois Mühren? Was that what he'd said?

"One month," she said. "Until the first of April, that is. Is that what you want?"

"If possible. But perhaps you have other prospective tenants?"

"A few," she lied. "But nobody who's committed themselves yet."

In fact this was the third week in succession that she'd placed the ad in the newspaper, and apart from an off-putting German who seemed to have misunderstood everything it was possible to misunderstand, and no doubt stank of sauerkraut and sausages, he was the only one who'd called. What was the point of hesitating? A month was a month, after all.

"Would you be happy with five hundred guilders?" she asked. "It's a bit of a nuisance having to advertise again when you move out."

"Five hundred guilders would be fine," he said without hesitation, and the deal was done.

After lunch she drew a map and wrote instructions. One kilometer after the church in Wahrhejm, take a left when you come to the hand-painted sign. Two hundred meters through the trees toward the lake, no more. Three cottages. The one nearest the lake on the right was hers.

Keys and an explanation of how to make the awkward water pump work. The stove and the electric mains. The boat and the oars.

She had only just finished when he arrived. Rather a pale young man. Not very tall, and with polished manners, she thought. She offered him coffee, of course—it was already brewed. But he declined. He couldn't wait to get out there and start writing. She understood perfectly.

He wasn't the least bit impolite or cocky. On the contrary. He was courteous, as she would explain later to Beatrix Hoelder and Marcela Augenbach. Courteous and polite.

And a writer. When he'd left, she tasted the word several times. "Writer." There was something sweet about it, that had to be admitted. She liked the idea of having somebody sitting and writing in her little cottage by the lake, and perhaps she even entertained the hope that at some point in the future he would remember her and send her a copy of the book. When it was finished, of course. That would take time, she imagined. What with publishers and all the rest of it. Perhaps he would dedicate the book to her, even? She made up her mind to go to the library before long and see if he was represented on the shelves.

Mühlen, was that his name? Yes, that's what it said on the contract they had both signed. Alfons Mühlen, if she had read it correctly. He seemed a bit effeminate, she had to say, and she wondered if he might be homosexual. A lot of writers were, even if they pretended not to be, according to what Beatrix had maintained once. But then again, she maintained all kinds of things.

She'd never heard of him, that was for sure. Neither had Beatrix nor Marcela, but he was a young man, after all.

Still, he'd paid in cash, without quibbling. Five hundred guilders. She would have been satisfied with three.

So, it was an excellent deal, all things considered.

Alfons Müller?

Ah, maybe she had heard the name after all.

38

He felt cold.

For the fifth morning in succession, he was woken up by feeling freezing cold.

For the fifth morning in succession, it took him less than one second to remember where he was.

For the fifth morning in succession, he felt for his pistol and looked out the window.

The house was still there in the hesitant light of dawn. Just as untouched, just as unvisited and unaware as when he had fallen asleep at some point during the night.

Unmolested. She wasn't coming. She hadn't come last night, either. The cold made his body ache all over. It was inconceivable how impossible it was to keep warm up here, despite the abundance of quilts and blankets. Every morning he had woken up in the early stages of dawn, frozen stiff. Checked the state of everything by looking out the window, then gone downstairs and into the house and the warmth created by the stove. He always made a big fire in the evenings when he came back from the inn. A really roaring fire in the iron stove in the kitchen, making sure that it would retain its heat until well into the following morning.

He followed the same routine this morning. Carefully scrutinized the whole area, outside in the raw morning air and inside the house. Gun in hand. With the safety catch off.

Then he sat down at the kitchen table for coffee. Took a couple of drams of whiskey as well, to drive the cold out of his body. Listened to the seven o'clock news on the radio while he made plans for the coming day. Pistol close at hand on the worn, fifty-year-old waxed tablecloth. Back against the wall. Invisible from the window.

Getting through the day was becoming harder and harder. He couldn't endure more than three or four hours at a time in the forest, and when he came back in the early afternoon, on the alert as ever, he generally sat down on the sofa again. Or lay down in the loft for an hour or two, waiting.

He would sit or lie there and glance through something from his father's library, which was not exactly voluminous and not particularly varied. Adventure stories. Brash, cheap literature bought by the meter at auctions or at sales time. He would quite like to read the occasional one, to be honest, but found it hard to concentrate.

Other things nagged and disturbed him. Other things.

Then he would go out for another walk, for an hour or so. As dusk drew in he would come back home in the dark. It felt like something he was waiting for, this darkness: a confidant and an ally. He knew that he had the upper hand as soon as night fell. If they were to confront each other while it was dark, he was at an advantage. He might need it.

Then he would have dinner in the dark kitchen. He never switched on a light—the worst-case scenario would be if she came across him in a lit-up window.

He had been into the village only once, to do some shopping. He tried to avoid it, during daylight hours at any rate. Nor did he go there during the evenings those first few days, but he soon realized that the isolation would be intolerable if he couldn't at least spend an hour at the inn with a beer.

He went there on the third evening. He made a risk assessment before setting out, and realized that the dangerous part would be returning home. On the way in, he could make sure he was walking behind hedges, through private gardens, or along the village street, which had no lighting. Inside the inn, lots of the drinkers had a clear view of the door. That fact would hardly present her with an opportunity, even if she found out where he was.

But walking back home was a different matter. Dangerous. If she knew he'd been at the inn, she had every opportunity of setting up an ambush, and so he took every possible precaution on his walk back to the house. Avoided the road. Dashed out of the inn and around the corner of the building, staying in the shadows there for quite a while. Then he would head for home cross-country, over terrain he had known in detail since he was a boy—changing direction, zigzagging irrationally, and approaching the house from a different direction every night. Extremely carefully, and gun in hand. Every sense on red alert.

But nothing happened.

Night after night, and absolutely nothing happened.

Not a single dodgy incident. Not the slightest indication. Nothing suspicious at all.

Two things nagged at him when he went to bed.

The first was a headache, caused by a whole day of tension and strain. To cope with that, every night he would take two tablets, washed down with a swig of whiskey in the dark kitchen.

That helped to some extent, but it didn't cure it.

The other thing was a thought. The thought that she might not come at all. The possibility that while he was spending these days in isolation and on red alert, she was actually somewhere else. Somewhere a long way away.

In an apartment in Maardam. In a house in Hamburg. Anywhere at all.

The possibility that this was the punishment she had decided to give him. Simply to let him wait. Wait for the murderer who never came. Wait for death, whose visit had been postponed.

And as one evening followed another, both these things grew in stature. The headache and the thought. A little bigger every evening, it seemed.

And neither tablets nor whiskey could do anything to help.

She pulled up beside an elderly man walking along the side of the road. Leaned over the empty passenger seat, wound down the window, and attracted his attention.

"I'm looking for Mr. Biedersen. Do you know where his house is?"

This was the second time she'd driven through the village. Dark outside. Quite dark inside the car as well, hat pulled down over her eyes, and a minimum of eye contact. A calculated risk, that's all. As they say.

"Yes, of course."

He pointed out the house and explained where it was. It wasn't far away. Nothing in the village was far away. She memorized what he had said, thanked him, and continued on her way.

It's all so easy, she thought. Still just as easy.

She knew that the car gave her all the camouflage she needed; and it was indeed from inside the car—the hired Fiat that had been another expense but also a necessity—that she discovered him. That same evening. Parked in the darkness and drizzle opposite the inn. It was still a calculated risk, but there wasn't much of an alternative. In a place like this a stranger couldn't turn up many times before questions started to be asked. Who? Why?

Unnecessary, and dangerous. There was no point in driving around, looking for him. But it was important to find him even so. Before he found her.

This time she had an opponent, not merely prey. There was a difference.

She watched him go in. Didn't see him come out.

The next evening, the same thing. While he was in there, she paid a visit to the house. Scrutinized it from the road for several minutes before driving back.

Thought about how to go about it.

He must know.

He had gone out of his way to entice her here; she had realized that from the start.

The third evening she went a step further. Drove into the village and parked the car behind the church. Walked down to the inn. Went in without hesitation and bought some cigarettes at the bar. She could see him sitting right at the back, out of the corner of her eye. A beer and a whiskey. He seemed alert and tense, but paid her no attention. There were more people in there than she'd expected, in fact. Twenty or so, half of them in the bar, the rest in the restaurant.

Three evenings out of three, she thought.

That meant that in all probability, it would be the same on day four and day five.

It was obvious what to do next. She had the upper hand again.

It was about time. All the waiting and the passage of time had been to her advantage, that was clear. But now things were coming to a head. The money she had left was committed, down to almost the last guilder. Every day cost money, and she no longer had the option of holding back, for the sake of it.

Just one opportunity. She wouldn't get another. Making a mistake was no longer a possibility either. It was clear that she would have no second chance of putting things right, if she made a mess of it.

So: what she must do was arrange things the best way she could. In line with the others, and making this a worthy conclusion.

It was quite a long time since she had started out on this mission. There was only one of them left. Just one of them still alive, she thought as she returned to the little cottage by the lake.

And in the flickering light of the paraffin lamp she arranged his death.

Later, at first light, she woke up and was unable to fall asleep again. So she got up and dressed. Went down to the lake and walked out onto the jetty. Stood there for quite a while, gazing out over the dark water and the mists, and trying to recall the almost ecstatic rapture she had felt in the beginning. Trying to weigh that against the calm she felt now.

The superior feeling of perfection and control.

She could find no real balance—but nor could she find any

objections. Everything was falling into place. Soon it would be over. Everything.

Two more days, she decided. In two more days. That might be a good time, bearing in mind the date as well.

Then she went back indoors, and sat down at the table. Started writing.

At my mother's interment . . .

39

Melgarves? Something about this Melgarves rang a bell. . . .

Jung fished around among the papers cluttering up his desk.

"Did you serve Maureen breakfast in bed today, then?"

Jung looked up.

"Eh? Why on earth should I do that?"

"You mean you don't know what day it is today?" said Moreno, glaring at him.

"No."

"International Women's Day. March eighth."

"Good God," said Jung. "I'd better buy her something. Thank you for letting me know. Did you get breakfast in bed?"

"Of course," said Moreno with a smile. "And a bit more besides."

Jung wondered for a moment what that might imply, then returned to his lists of incoming tips.

"This Melgarves character," he said. "I don't understand why he's ended up on this list."

"André Melgarves?"

"Yes indeed. He's one of the group. He's phoned in and passed on some information or other, but he's been bracketed with all the others. . . . Krause must have missed his significance."

"That's not like him," said Moreno.

She crossed the room and read the brief notes over Jung's shoulder, frowned, and started chewing the pencil she had in her hand. . . . A certain Mr. André Melgarves had phoned from Kinsale in Ireland and announced that he had information that could be of interest to the ongoing investigation. They were welcome to give him a call. His address and telephone number were duly recorded.

"When did this come in?" Moreno asked.

Jung looked at the back of the card.

"The day before yesterday," he said. "I think it's probably as well for the chief inspector to take this himself—what do you reckon?"

"I think so," said Moreno. "Go and show him now—but don't mention that it came in two days ago. He seemed a bit grumpy this morning, I thought."

"You don't say?" said Jung, getting to his feet.

The young man was dressed in jeans and a T-shirt with "Big Is Beautiful" printed on it. He was very suntanned, and his short-cropped hair looked like a field of ripe wheat. He was chewing away at something, and staring at the floor.

"Name?" said Van Veeteren.

"Pieter Fuss."

"Age?"

"Twenty-one."

"Occupation?"

"Messenger."

"Messenger?"

"For a security company."

I see, thought Van Veeteren. Almost a colleague. He swallowed a feeling of impotence.

"Anyway, I'm not the officer in charge of your case," he explained, "but I have a few things to say about it and I'd like to have an answer to a question. Just one."

Pieter Fuss looked up, but as soon as he caught the chief inspector's eye he reverted immediately to examining his sneakers.

"On Friday, February twenty-third," said Van Veeteren, "at half past midnight, I was walking toward Rejmer Plejn. I was on my way home after an evening with some good friends of mine. I suddenly found my way blocked by you and four other young men. One of your friends pushed me up against a wall. You punched me in the face. You eventually forced me down onto the sidewalk. You hit me and kicked me. You had never seen me before. My question is: Why?"

Pieter Fuss's expression did not change.

"Have you understood my question?"

No reply.

"Why did you attack an unknown person? Punch him and kick him? There must be a reason, surely?"

"I don't know."

"Can you speak a little louder? I'm recording this."

"I don't know."

"I don't understand. Are you saying you don't know why you do things?"

No answer.

"You were five against one. Do you think that was the right thing to do?"

"No."

"So you do things that you think are wrong?"

"I don't know."

"If you don't know, who does?"

No answer.

"What do you think your punishment ought to be?"

Pieter Fuss mumbled something.

"Louder!"

"I don't know."

"All right," said Van Veeteren. "Listen to me. If you can't give me a sensible answer to the question why, I shall see to it that you get at least six months for this."

"Six months?"

"At least," said Van Veeteren. "We can't have people running around who don't know why they do what they do to their fellow human beings. You can have two days to think about this in peace and quiet. . . ."

He paused. For a moment it looked as if Fuss was about to say something, but then there was a knock on the door and Jung poked his head inside.

"Are you busy, Chief Inspector?"

"No, not at all."

"I think we've had a tip that could be of interest."

"What, exactly?"

"One of the group has rung from Ireland. We thought you might like to follow it up yourself?"

He handed over the card.

"Okay," said the chief inspector. "Can you escort this promising young man down to the duty officer? Be a bit careful—he's not all that sure what he's doing."

Fuss stood up and slunk away with Jung. Van Veeteren read what it said on the card.

André Melgarves? he thought with a frown.

Then he contacted the switchboard and asked them to phone him. Ten minutes later he had Melgarves on the line.

"My name is Van Veeteren. I'm in charge of this case. You've said that you have information to give us."

"I don't really know if it's significant," Melgarves said, and his doubt seemed more obvious on the crackly line than the words themselves.

"Let's hear it," said Van Veeteren. "It would help if you could speak a bit louder, I think we have a bad line."

"Ireland," explained Melgarves. "The tax is advantageous, but everything else is rubbish."

"I see," said Van Veeteren, pulling a face.

"Anyway, something occurred to me. I've received your letters and instructions. And I spoke on the phone to somebody. I've got some idea of what's been going on, despite being miles away. My sister has sent me some newspapers and cuttings. And, well, if I can be of any help, then obviously, I'm at your disposal. It's an awful business."

"It certainly is," said Van Veeteren.

"What struck me," said Melgarves, "is only a minor detail, but it's something that Malik, Maasleitner, and Innings were mixed up in. It might be irrelevant, but if I understand the situation aright, you've had trouble in finding a link between them."

"We have had certain problems," admitted Van Veeteren.

"Well, it was in connection with our demob party," said Melgarves.

"Demob party?"

"Yes, we had a big farewell do in Maardam. Arno's Cellar—I don't think it exists any longer. . . ."

"No, it's closed down," said Van Veeteren.

"Just two days before we were released. Yes, it was a party that everybody attended—and some of the officers and lecturers as well. No women, men only. We'd rented the whole place and . . . well, there was quite a lot of drinking going on, obviously."

"The link?" wondered the chief inspector.

Melgarves cleared his throat.

"I'm coming to that. We kept going until rather late—two, half past two, I'd say; quite a few were pretty drunk. Some passed out. To be honest, I wasn't completely sober myself, but it was one of those evenings, you might say. And it was allowed—we didn't have any duties until the following afternoon, and . . . well, only two more days before demob, and all that. . . ."

"I understand," said Van Veeteren with a trace of irritation in his voice. "Perhaps you'd like to come to the point, Mr. Melgarves?"

"Well, afterward," said Melgarves, "that's when I saw them. Those of us who'd stayed on to the very end staggered out of Arno's. We were in groups, and kicking up a bit of a row, I'm sorry to say. Making our way back to Löhr—and that's when I happened to see them. I'd gone into an alley to, er, relieve myself, and when I'd finished I ran into them. They were in a doorway, and they had this girl with them—no more than seventeen or eighteen, I'd say. And they were giving her a rough time."

"Giving her a rough time? What do you mean by that?"

"Well, trying to talk her into it, I suppose."

"Talk her into what?"

"Oh come on, you know."

"I suppose so. And?"

"Anyway, they were standing around her. They were pretty

soused, and I don't suppose she was all that interested, or however you might put it. In any case, they were going on at her, and laughing, and wouldn't let her go."

"Did she want to go?"

Melgarves hesitated.

"I don't know. I think so, but I don't really remember. I've thought about it, of course, but I stayed there only a few seconds, and then I ran to catch up with the others. Not that they would have been what you might call desirable company."

Van Veeteren thought it over.

"And she wasn't a prostitute?" he asked.

"Could be, but maybe not," said Melgarves.

"How come you remember all this after thirty years?"

"I can understand why you ask me that. I suppose it's because of what happened the next day."

"The next day? What happened then?"

"Well, it was as if something had happened. Innings was really the only one I was acquainted with, just a bit, and he didn't seem to be himself for a couple of days afterward. He just wasn't himself, somehow. . . . He seemed to be evasive. I recall asking him what had happened to the girl, but he didn't answer."

"What do you think happened?"

"I don't know," said Melgarves. "I mean, we were demobbed the following day, and we had other things to think about."

"Of course you had," said Van Veeteren. "When exactly was this party, can you remember that?"

"It must have been May twenty-ninth," said Melgarves. "We were demobbed at the end of the month."

"May 29, 1965," said the chief inspector, and suddenly felt his temples pounding as he prepared to ask his next question.

And anticipated the answer. He cleared his throat.

"So, Malik, Maasleitner, and Innings," he said. "Was there anybody else?"

"Yes," said Melgarves. "There were four of them. That Biedersen was with them as well."

"Biedersen?"

"Yes. He and Maasleitner were probably the ones behind it all. Biedersen rented a room in town as well."

"A room in town?"

"Yes. For the last few months we were allowed permanent night leave, as they called it. In other words, we didn't need to be in our billets at night. Biedersen had a student room. He threw a few parties there, I gather, but I didn't go to any of them."

The line started crackling something terrible, and the chief inspector was forced to bellow out his final questions in order to overcome the noise.

"These three, plus Werner Biedersen. Is that right?"

"Yes."

"With a young woman?"

"Yes."

"Did anybody else see this?"

"Could be. I don't know."

"Have you spoken to anybody else about it? Then or now?"

"No," said Melgarves. "Not as far as I recall, at least."

Van Veeteren thought for a few more seconds.

"Many thanks," he said eventually. "Thank you for some extremely useful information, Mr. Melgarves. I'll get back to you."

He hung up.

Now, he thought. We're almost there.

"What the hell do you mean?" he roared ten minutes later. "Do we still not know where he is?"

Münster shook his head.

"Hell and damnation!" bellowed the chief inspector. "What about his wife?"

"Not at home," Münster explained. "DeBries keeps on phoning all the time."

"Where do they live?"

"Saaren."

"Saaren?" said Van Veeteren. "Up north . . . it all fits in. How far is it to there? A hundred and fifty kilometers? Two hundred?"

"Something like that," said Münster.

Van Veeteren took out four toothpicks. Broke them in two and threw the bits on the floor. Reinhart appeared in the doorway.

"Have we got him?" he asked.

"Got him?" roared Van Veeteren. "Have we hell! He's been off the map for several weeks, and his missus is out shopping!"

"But it *is* Biedersen?" said Reinhart.

"Biedersen," said Münster. "Who's next, that is. Yes."

"Have you got a cigarette?" asked Van Veeteren.

Reinhart shook his head.

"Afraid not. Just my old briar. What do we do now, then?"

The chief inspector clenched his hands and closed his eyes for two seconds.

"Okay," he said, opening his eyes again. "This is what we do. Reinhart and I drive up to Saaren. The rest of you keep on chasing after his wife from here. If you find her, tell her to stay at home until we come, or she'll be jailed for life. Then we shall have to see what happens next."

Reinhart nodded.

"Ask her if she knows where he is," he added. "And keep us informed. We'll try to find her as well, of course."

Münster made a note.

"So, we're off now," said Van Veeteren, gesturing toward Reinhart. "Go down to the pool and collect a car. I'll be at the entrance five minutes from now. I just need to collect a few things first."

"Are you sure that it's so damned urgent?" asked Reinhart when Van Veeteren had settled into the passenger seat.

"No," said Van Veeteren, lighting a cigarette. "But when you've been in a straitjacket for seven weeks, I'll be damned if it isn't time to stretch a bit."

40

He woke up with a start and fumbled for his pistol. Took hold of it and looked out the window. Noted that everything looked the same as before—except that the sun was shining.

He realized that it must be the sun that had warmed up the loft. He was lying just underneath the ceiling, but it wasn't at all the same all-pervading chill he'd experienced so far. On the contrary, it was nice and warm—and it was a few minutes to ten.

Ten! It dawned on him that he had slept for over nine hours on end. He had snuggled down in bed shortly after half past twelve the previous night, and he didn't recall having lain awake for very long. No sleepless periods during the night, either.

So he'd been lying here for nine hours. And what had been the point? He'd have been much more of a helpless victim than a guard dog, that was for sure. Would he have even woken up if she had come creeping up the stairs?

He rolled over onto his side and opened the window wide. The sunshine was very bright out there. Small birds were fluttering around in the shrubbery outside the kitchen door. The sky was blue, dotted here and there with tufts of scudding cloud.

Spring? he thought. What the hell am I doing here?

He recalled the previous evening. He'd stayed at the inn until eleven o'clock, and then thrown caution to the wind on the way back home. He'd simply stood up and left. Taken the main street—the chapel, Heine's, Van Klauster's—and then the narrow lane home to his cottage.

He'd had his pistol in his hand all the time, to be sure—with the safety catch off. But still . . .

He'd even entertained the thought of using the real bed, but something had held him back.

It was a week now. Eight days, to be precise, and as he brewed some coffee and buttered some bread in the kitchen, he decided that this would have to do. Today would have to be the last day. He would have to face up to the facts and acknowledge that he was wasting his time. It wouldn't bear fruit. He would have fuck-all to show for it, so that was that.

He might just as well have left right away, before lunch; but Korhonen had promised to show him some pictures of his new Thai girlfriend, and so he'd said he would be there tonight as well.

But after that, he'd draw the line. The realization that it had been a mistake to come here had been growing inside him for some time now—the realization that it was pointless, and that these weren't the circumstances in which she intended to confront him.

His telephone call to his wife four days ago—and her mention of the woman from Copenhagen who had been trying to contact him—had naturally been an indication and a confirmation. But not that she intended turning up here. Merely that she knew where he was.

It must have been her—he'd realized that right away: he didn't have any female business contacts in Copenhagen. Nor any male ones, come to that. But this delay . . . these days that passed by without anything happening. The only way he could interpret it was that she had declined his invitation. Refused to meet him on his terms.

The cowardly bitch, he thought. You murdering whore, I'll get the better of you, no matter what!

Nevertheless, he didn't relax his safety procedures this final day. Despite his recognition of the fact that his calculations had failed, he spent his accustomed hours out in the forest. Ate his meals as usual, did a bit of packing after dark, and was aware of the fact that he mustn't be reckless.

On his guard, as usual. His gun was always within reach. And he kept himself hidden.

Only one more night. Just one.

He didn't bother to think about how he would go about things in the future. He didn't have the strength, after all those efforts that had led nowhere.

He would leave here tomorrow.

He would make some new decisions tomorrow.

He listened to the eight o'clock news, then sneaked out into the darkness. Paused as usual outside the front door, pistol in hand, eyes skinned and ears cocked; then he set off for the village and the inn. The air was still warm, and it seemed to him that the spring he'd woken up to that morning had decided to stay on. At least for a few more days.

"Shouldn't we contact the police in Saaren?" said Reinhart when they'd been driving for forty kilometers and the chief inspector hadn't said a word.

"Have you forgotten who's chief of police there?" asked Van Veeteren.

"Oh my God! Yes, of course. Mergens. No, it would be best to keep him out of this."

Van Veeteren nodded and lit his third cigarette within twenty minutes.

"What the hell would we say to him, anyway?" he said after a while. "Ask him to come down like a ton of bricks on Mrs. Biedersen, and lock her up until we get there?"

Reinhart shrugged.

"He'd like that," he said. "No, you're right. We'll deal with this ourselves."

"Can't you go a bit faster?" Van Veeteren wondered.

It was a quarter past eight before deBries managed to get through to Dagmar Biedersen. She had just gotten back from a shopping spree and a last-minute visit to the hairdresser, and she sounded tired. When contact was made with Van Veeteren and Reinhart, it transpired that they were only about ten minutes away from Saaren, and so it was decided that it wasn't necessary to involve other police districts at this stage.

"Good timing," said Reinhart. "We'll go straight to her place. Tell her we'd like a couple of beers."

"But what exactly are you implying?" wondered Mrs. Biedersen, placing two protective hands over her new hairdo.

"Can't we sit down somewhere and discuss the whole business quietly and calmly?" Van Veeteren suggested.

Reinhart led the way into the living room and sat down on a red plush sofa. The chief inspector invited Mrs. Biedersen to sit down in one of the armchairs, while he remained standing.

"We have reason to believe that your husband is in danger," he began.

"In danger?"

"Yes. It's connected with those earlier deaths. Can you tell us where he is at the moment?"

"What? No . . . well, perhaps, but surely it can't be . . ."

"I'm afraid it can," said Reinhart. "Where is he?"

Without warning, Dagmar Biedersen burst into tears. Something had given way inside her, and her meager chest was convulsed by sobbing. Tears came flooding forth.

Oh, hell! Van Veeteren thought.

"My dear Mrs. Biedersen," he said, "all we want to know is where he is, so that we can sort everything out."

She took out a handkerchief and blew her nose.

"Excuse me," she said. "I'm being silly."

You certainly are, Van Veeteren thought. But answer the question, for Christ's sake.

"He's probably . . . up at the cottage, I assume. That's where he called me from a few days ago, at least."

"The cottage?" wondered Reinhart.

"Yes, we have a holiday cottage, or whatever you'd like to call it—it's where he grew up, in fact. We go there sometimes. He often spends time there on his own, as well. . . ."

"Where?" asked Van Veeteren.

"Oh, excuse me. In Wahrhejm, of course."

"Wahrhejm? And where is Wahrhejm?"

"Excuse me," she said again. "It's between Ulming and Oostwerdingen. Just a little village. It's about a hundred kilometers from here."

Van Veeteren thought for a moment.

"Are you sure he's there?"

"No, as I said. . . . But I think so."

"Is there a telephone in the cottage?"

"No, I'm afraid not. He usually phones from the inn. He likes to be undisturbed when he's up there."

Van Veeteren sighed.

"Just our damned luck," he said. "Would you mind leaving us alone for a couple of minutes, Mrs. Biedersen? The inspector and I need to exchange a few words."

"Of course," she said, and vanished into the kitchen.

"Now what?" asked Reinhart when she was out of earshot.

"I don't really know," said Van Veeteren. "I have the feeling that it's urgent—but, of course, there's nothing to say that it really is."

"No," said Reinhart. "I have the same feeling, of course. But you're the boss."

"Yes, I know that," said Van Veeteren. "And you're the one who does whatever I say. Go and phone the police in Ulming—they must be the nearest—and tell them to get out there and nab him."

"Nab him?"

"Yes, arrest him."

"On what grounds?"

"I couldn't care less. Make something up, whatever you like."

"With pleasure," said Reinhart.

While Reinhart was doing what he'd been told to do in Biedersen's study, the chief inspector turned his attention to the worried wife, in the hope of extracting further information.

"To be absolutely honest with you," he said, "it's probable

that this woman is aiming to kill your husband, Mrs. Biedersen. Naturally, we hope to stop her."

"Oh my God," said Dagmar Biedersen.

"When did you last see him?"

She thought for a moment.

"A couple of weeks ago—almost three weeks, in fact."

"Does anybody else know that he's there?"

"Er, I don't know."

"Is there any possibility that this woman has found out that he's there? Somehow or other?"

"No—but . . ."

He could see how the realization suddenly dawned on her. The color drained from her face, and she opened and closed her mouth several times. Her hands wandered back and forth over the buttons of her rust-red blouse without finding a resting place.

"That . . . er . . . that woman," she said.

"Well?"

"She phoned."

Van Veeteren nodded.

"Go on!"

"A woman phoned from Copenhagen. She claimed to be a business acquaintance of my husband's, and then . . ."

"And then?"

"And then she asked if I knew where he was. Where she could get in touch with him."

"And so you told her?" asked Van Veeteren.

"Yes," said Dagmar Biedersen, slumping back in the armchair. "I told her. Do you think . . . ?"

Reinhart returned.

"Done," he said.

"All right," said Van Veeteren. "Let's go. We'll be in touch, Mrs. Biedersen. You'll be staying at home tonight, we hope?"

She nodded, and was breathing heavily, her mouth open wide. Van Veeteren gathered that she would be barely capable of getting up from the sofa, never mind anything else.

"The place is full of women," said Biedersen, looking around the bar.

"Don't you know what day it is today?"

"No."

"International Women's Day," said Korhonen. "This is what usually happens every year. Every woman in the village turns up."

"A damned silly invention," said Biedersen.

"Of course, but it's good for business. Anyway, you can sit here in the corner as usual, and avoid having to get too close to them. A beer and a whiskey chaser, as usual?"

"Yes please," said Biedersen. "Have you got the photos of your Thai girlfriend?"

"I'll come and show you them in just a minute or two," said Korhonen. "I just have to serve the ladies first."

"Okay," said Biedersen. Took both his glasses and sat down at the empty table in the corner between the bar counter and the kitchen door.

Hell and damnation, he thought. This is an opportunity for camouflage if ever I saw one. I'd better play it safe tonight.

And he felt in his jacket pocket.

41

"What the hell's going on?" wondered Ackermann.

"I don't know," said Päude, starting the car. "In the middle of the match as well."

"The match?" said Ackermann. "Fuck the match. I was just about to start pulling her panties down when he phoned. That delicious little Nancy Fischer, you know."

Päude sighed and switched on the radio to hear the end of the soccer report, instead of having to listen to an account of his colleague's love life—he was treated to enough of that on a regular basis.

"Halfway in, you might say," said Ackermann.

"What do you think of this Biedersen character?" asked Päude in an attempt to change the subject.

"Cunning," said Ackermann. "Do you reckon we should just arrest him for vagrancy and wait for further orders? You don't think he's dangerous, do you?"

"Munckel said he wasn't."

"Munckel can't tell the difference between a hand grenade and a beetroot."

"Okay, we'd better be a bit careful then. How far is it to Wahrhejm?"

"Eighteen kilometers. We'll be there in ten minutes. Shall we put the siren on, or the light at least?"

"Good God, no! Discretion, Munckel said. But I don't suppose you know what the word means?"

"Of course I do," said Ackermann. "Discretion is the better part of valor."

"Another one?" said Korhonen.

"Yes, of course," said Biedersen. "Must just go and take a leak first. But that's a good-looking piece of skirt you've got there. A hell of a good-looking piece of skirt."

"Easy to maintain as well," said Korhonen, smirking.

Biedersen stood up and noticed that he was a bit tipsy. Perhaps it'll be as well to cut out the whiskey and stick to good old beer, he thought as he worked his way past a contingent of women sitting at two long tables and disturbing the peace. Laughing and singing. Apart from himself there were only two male customers in the whole of the bar. The old school janitor who was sitting at his usual table with a newspaper and a carafe of red wine. And an unaccompanied man in a dark suit who had arrived a quarter of an hour ago.

All the rest were women, and he held on to the gun in his jacket pocket as he passed them, with his back to the wall.

Women's Day, he thought as he stood and allowed the beer to take the natural way out. What a bloody silly idea!

The door opened and the man in the dark suit came in. He nodded at Biedersen.

"At least we can get a bit of peace in here," said Biedersen, gesturing with his head at all the commotion outside. "I've nothing against women, but . . ."

He broke off and reached for his jacket pocket, but before he had a chance to grab his pistol he heard the same plopping sound twice, and knew it was too late. A dark red flood washed over his eyes, and the last thing he felt, the very last thing of all, was a terrible pain below the belt.

Päude pulled up outside the inn.

"Go in and ask the way," he said. "I'll wait here."

"Okay," said Ackermann with a sigh. "His name's Biedersen, right?"

"Yes," said Päude. "Werner Biedersen. They're bound to know where he lives."

Ackermann got out of the car and Päude lit a cigarette. It's a relief to be rid of him for a few minutes, he thought.

But Ackermann was back after ninety seconds.

"Stroke of luck," he said. "I bumped into a guy on his way out who knew where he lives. Keep going straight ahead, a hundred and fifty meters or so."

"All right," said Päude.

"Then turn left," added Ackermann.

Päude followed the instructions and came to a low stone wall with an opening in it.

"Looks dark in there," said Ackermann.

"But there's a house there in any case. Take the flashlight and have a look. I'll wait here. I have the window open so you only need to shout if you need me."

"Wouldn't it be better if you went?" wondered Ackermann.

"No," said Päude. "Get going."

"Okay," said Ackermann.

I'm seven years older, after all, thought Päude as Ackermann got out of the car. With a wife and children, and all that.

The radio suddenly crackled into life.

"Hello. Päude here!"

"Munckel! Where the hell are you?"

"In Wahrhejm, of course. We've just gotten to his house. Ackermann's gone in and . . ."

"Get him out again! Biedersen's been shot dead in the john at the inn. Get your asses there and cordon the place off!"

"Oh, shit!" said Päude.

"Make sure that not a soul leaves the premises! I'll be there in fifteen minutes."

"Roger," said Päude.

More crackling, then Munckel vanished. Päude shook his head.

Oh, shit, he thought again. Then he got out of the car and shouted for Ackermann.

42

It can't be true, I'm dreaming! was the thought that Van Veeteren had sat wrestling with for the last twenty-five minutes. Ever since he heard the report on the radio.

This kind of thing simply doesn't happen. It must be a hoax, or a misunderstanding.

"I swear to God I thought I was dreaming!" said Reinhart as he pulled up. "But we're there now. It looks as if what they said was right."

Two police cars were already in place. Nose to nose diagonally across the road, with their blue lights flashing. Presumably to inform everybody in the village who had the good fortune to miss the news broadcast, Van Veeteren thought as they hurried into the inn. A uniformed officer was guarding the door, and several others were inside the premises, where the mood of fear and anxiety seemed to be tangible. The customers—almost exclusively women, he was surprised to see—had been herded together behind two tables, and their whispers and low-voiced discussions reached Van Veeteren's ears in the form of an unarticulated but long-suffering lament. A fleeting image of cattle about to be slaughtered flashed before his eyes. Or prisoners in concentration camps on their way to the showers. He shuddered, and tried to shake off any such thoughts.

Stop it! he commanded his own thoughts. It's bad enough without you making it any worse.

A man with thinning hair about the same age as Van Veeteren came up to him.

"Chief Inspector Van Veeteren?"

He nodded and introduced Reinhart.

"Munckel. Well, this is a cartload of shit if ever I saw one. He's in there. We haven't touched anything."

Van Veeteren and Reinhart went to the men's room, where one of the constables was stationed.

"Ackermann," said Munckel, "let these gentlemen in."

Van Veeteren peered inside. Studied the lifeless corpse for a few seconds before turning to Reinhart.

"Ah well," he said. "Exactly the same as usual. We might as well leave him lying there until the forensic team gets here. We can't do anything for him."

"The silly bugger," muttered Reinhart.

"When did it happen?" asked the chief inspector.

Munckel looked at the clock.

"Shortly after nine," he said. "We were alerted at a quarter past—it was Mr. Korhonen who phoned. He's the bartender."

A dark-haired man in his fifties stepped forward and introduced himself.

"It happened less than an hour ago," said Van Veeteren. "How many people have left the premises since then?"

"I don't really know," said Korhonen hesitantly.

"Who found him?"

"I did," said an elderly man with a loud voice and a checked shirt. "I just went to the john for a pee, and there he was. Shot in the balls as well. A cartload of shit . . ."

A shudder seemed to pass through the group of women.

Oh yes, dammit! It had eventually dawned on Van Veeteren. International Women's Day, March 8. That was why they were all here. Macabre—she couldn't have hit upon a better day.

"So when did Biedersen go in there?" Reinhart asked.

Korhonen cleared his throat nervously.

"Excuse me," he said. "I think I know who did it. It must have been that other guy."

"Who are you referring to?" said Munckel. "Why haven't you said anything before now?"

"That other guy," he said again. "The one sitting over there . . ."

He pointed.

"He went to the bathroom immediately after Biedersen—I remember now."

"A man?" said Van Veeteren.

"Yes, of course."

"Where is he?" said Reinhart.

Korhonen looked around. The man in the checked shirt looked around. All the women looked around.

"He's left, of course," said Munckel.

"He's gone!" shouted one of the women. "I saw him leave."

"You can bet your life he didn't hang around," muttered Reinhart.

"Is one of you called Van Veeteren?" asked a dark-haired woman in her mid-thirties.

"Yes, why?"

"This was lying on his table. I noticed it just now."

She came up and handed over a white envelope. Van Veeteren took it and stared at it in bewilderment.

I'm dreaming, he thought again, and closed his eyes for a moment.

"Open it!" said Reinhart.

Van Veeteren opened it.

"Read it!" said Reinhart.

Van Veeteren read it.

"Where is there a telephone?" he asked, and was directed to the lobby by Korhonen. Reinhart went with him, signaling to Munckel that he should keep everybody where they were in the restaurant.

"What the hell's going on?" he whispered as the chief inspector dialed the number. "Give me the letter!"

Van Veeteren handed it over, and Reinhart read it.

I'm waiting for you. Jelena Walgens
can tell you where I am.

Two lines. No signature.

What the hell? thought Reinhart. And then he said it out loud.

43

They parked at what seemed to be a safe distance, and got out of the car. It wasn't completely dark yet, and it was easy to pick out the outlines of the houses at the edge of the lake. The wind was now no more than a distant whisper in the forests to the northeast, and the air felt almost warm, Van Veeteren noticed.

Spring? he thought, somewhat surprised. Reinhart cleared his throat.

"It must be that cottage farthest away," he said. "There doesn't seem to be anybody at home in any of them."

"Some people occasionally manage to sleep at night," said Van Veeteren.

They continued walking along the narrow dirt road.

"Do you think she's in there?"

"I don't dare to think anything about this case anymore," said Van Veeteren, sounding somewhat subdued. "But no matter what, we need to get in there and take a look. Or do you think we should summon Ryman's heavy tank brigade?"

"Good God, no," said Reinhart. "It takes four days to mobilize them. Let's go in. I'll lead the way if you like."

"The hell you will," said Van Veeteren. "I'm oldest. You can keep in the background."

"Your word is my command," said Reinhart. "For what it's worth, I don't think she's at home."

Crouching down, and with quite a long distance between them, they approached the ramshackle gray house with the sagging roof. Slunk slowly but deliberately over the damp grass, and when there was only another ten meters or so still to go, Van Veeteren launched the attack by rushing forward and pressing himself up against the wall, right next to the door. Reinhart followed him and doubled up under one of the windows.

This is ridiculous, Van Veeteren thought as he tried to get his breath back, keeping tight hold of his standard-issue pistol. What the hell are we doing?

Or is it serious business?

He forced the door open with a bang and charged in. Ran around for a few seconds, kicking in doors, but he soon established that the cottage was just as empty as Reinhart had anticipated.

If she was going to shoot us, she'd have done so long ago, he thought, putting his pistol away in his pocket.

He went into the biggest of the three rooms, found a switch, and turned on the light. Reinhart came in and looked around.

"There's a letter here, addressed to you," he said, pointing to the table.

The chief inspector came forward to pick it up. Weighed it in his hand.

The same sort of envelope.

The same handwriting.

Addressed to the same person.

Detective Chief Inspector Van Veeteren, Maardam.

And the feeling that he was dreaming simply refused to go away.

. . .

The precision, Van Veeteren thought. It's this damned precision that makes it all so unreal. There's no such thing as coincidence, Reinhart had said; but in fact the reverse was true. He understood that now. When the feeling of coincidence suddenly disappears completely, that's when we find it difficult to rely on our senses. To have faith in what they tell us about happenings and connections.

Yes, that must be how things work, more or less.

There were two basket chairs in the room. Reinhart had already sat down on one of them and lit his pipe. The chief inspector sat on the other one and started to read.

It took him only a couple of minutes, and when he had finished, he read it once again. Then he looked at the clock and handed the letter to Reinhart without a word.

At my mother's interment there was only a single mourner. Me.

Time is short, and I shall express myself briefly. I don't need your understanding, but I want you to know who these men were, the men I have killed. My mother told me—a week before she died—about how I was conceived.

My father was four men. It was the night of May 29–30, 1965. She was seventeen years old, and a virgin. They raped her repeatedly for two hours in a student room in Maardam, and in order to stop her screaming they had stuffed one of the men's underpants into her mouth. One of the other men's tie was knotted around her mouth and the back of her neck. They also played music while I was being made. The same record, over and over again—afterward she found out what the tune was called, and bought it. I still have it.

Once they had finished impregnating my mother, they carried her out and dumped her in some bushes in a nearby park. One of my fathers said that she was a whore, and that he'd kill her if she told anybody what had happened.

My mother duly kept silent, but after two months she began to suspect that she was pregnant. After three, she was certain. She was still at school. She tried to kill me, using various tricks and methods she had heard about, but failed. I just wish she had managed it better.

She spoke to her mother, who didn't believe her.

She spoke to her father, who didn't believe her and gave her a good hiding.

She spoke to her clever elder sisters, who didn't believe her either, but advised her to have an abortion.

But it was too late. I wish it hadn't been.

My grandfather gave her a small sum of money in order to get rid of us, and I was born a long way away in Groenstadt. That's also where I grew up. My mother had found out my fathers' names, and was given some money by them when she threatened to expose them. When I was ten, she threatened them again, and received some more money, but that was all. They paid. They could afford it.

I knew from an early age that my mother was a whore, and I knew that I would become one as well. And the same applied to drinking and drug-taking.

But I didn't know why things were as they were, not until she told me about my fathers shortly before she died.

My mother was forty-seven when she died. I am only thirty, but I've been whoring and taking drugs for so long that I look at least ten years older. I received my first clients before my fifteenth birthday.

In addition, I have the urge to kill inside me. I was told the facts in October, and when I got to know my fathers a bit later on, I made up my mind.

It was a good decision.

My mother's life was a torment. Torment and indignity.

So was my own. But it was good to understand, to understand at last. I could see the logic. What else could possibly be the outcome of a night of lovemaking like the one when my fathers brought me to life?

What life?

I am the ripe fruit that grew out of a gang bang. It is that same fruit that is now killing its fathers.

That is completing the circle.

To be sure, that sounds like a sort of dark poetry. In a different life I could have become a poet instead. I could have written and read—I had the ability inside me, but never had the opportunity.

When I have finished, nothing living involved in that night will have survived. We shall all be dead. That is the logical outcome.

My mother—who had my father's underpants stuffed into her mouth while the act of love took place—gave me the task, and in her name I have murdered them all. Doing so has given me great joy, more joy than anything else in my life. At no point have I felt any guilt or regret, and nobody will ever come and call me to account.

I am also pleased that my mother saved some of the money she extracted from my fathers. It has been a great help to me, and I like the thought that in this way they have paid for their own deaths.

I say again: it has given me great satisfaction to kill my own fathers. Very great satisfaction.

I have been very precise all the time, and want to continue in that way to the very end. I am writing for two reasons. In the first place, I want the real reasons to be known. In the second place, I need to gain time—that is also why I left a note at the inn as well. If you are reading this letter at the time I intended and am hoping for, I have achieved my aims.

At ten p.m. I shall be on the ferry that leaves Oostwerdingen and heads for the islands; but I shall not be on board when it calls at its first port.

I shall be carrying substantial weights that will drag me down to the bottom of the sea, where I hope the fish will soon have chewed away my tainted flesh.

I never want to come to the surface again. Not one single part of me.

Reinhart folded the sheets of paper and put them back into the envelope. Then he sat for some time without speaking while he lit his pipe, which had gone out.

"What is there to say?" he said eventually.

The chief inspector was leaning back in the chair and had closed his eyes.

"Nothing," he said. "You don't need to say anything at all."

"No signature."

"No."

"It's a quarter to one."

Van Veeteren nodded. Sat up and lit a cigarette. Inhaled a few times. Stood up, walked across the room, and switched off the light.

"What's the first port of call?" he asked when he had sat down again.

"Arnholt, I think," said Reinhart. "At around one."

"Yes," said Van Veeteren. "That sounds about right. Go out to the car and try to make contact with the ferry. They can search the ship when it docks. She might have changed her mind."

"Do you think she did?" asked Reinhart.

"No," said Van Veeteren. "But we must continue playing our roles to the very end."

"Yes, I suppose so," said Reinhart. "The show must go on."

Then he went out and left the chief inspector alone in the darkness.

44

She locked the door, and almost immediately the ferry set off. Through the oval, convex porthole she could watch the harbor lights glide past before disappearing. This was her final extravagance: a single cabin up on B-deck. It had cost her more or less everything she had left; but this was no mere whim. This too was a necessity, and a logical requirement. She needed to be alone in order to make the final preparations, and there was no other way of ensuring that.

She checked her watch: seven minutes past ten. She sat down on the bed and felt the newly laundered sheet and the warm, red blanket with the shipping line's logo. She unscrewed the bottle and threw the cap into the waste bin, then drank directly from the bottle. Half a liter of cognac. Four star. An inferior sort would have served the same purpose, of course, but there had been just enough money. Four-star cognac. Single cabin with a wine-red blanket and wall-to-wall carpet. The final extravagance, as mentioned.

She had two hours to spare; that was in accordance with her timetable. Calculated from the moment she had seen the police car on the road outside the inn. No matter how efficiently they worked—and hitherto they hadn't exactly displayed much in the way of proficiency—it would be impossible for them to trace her here before midnight. First of all there was the crime scene, and the chaos at the inn; then they would have to find Jelena Walgens, conduct a confusing conversation with her, and then drive back to Wahrhejm—she was convinced that this chief inspector wouldn't delegate anything of this nature to his subordinates. Then the telephone call to the ferry. . . . No, anything less than two hours was out of the question.

Half past eleven, to be on the safe side. Ninety minutes in her own cabin on B-deck, that would have to be enough. It felt remarkably satisfying to be able to plan her own demise at last, not only that of others. She tipped the contents of her bag onto the floor. It would be as well to prepare things right away, in case anything went wrong. She found the end of the steel chain, and pulled up her sweater in order to expose her torso. Took another swig of cognac. Lit a cigarette before starting to wind the pliable steel around her waist. Slowly and methodically, round and round, exactly as she'd done it when practicing.

Heavy, but easy to handle. She had chosen the chain carefully. Seven meters long and eighteen kilos. Steel links. Cold and heavy. When she had finished winding she tightened it a little bit more, then fixed it in place with the padlock. She stood up and checked the weight and her ability to move.

Yes, everything was in order.

Heavy enough to make her sink. But not too heavy. She needed to be able to walk. And clamber over the rail.

Another cigarette.

A drop more cognac.

A warm and conclusive wave of intoxication had started to

flow through her body. She leaned her head against the wall and closed her eyes. Listened to, or rather felt, the vibrations of the heavy engines that were transmitted through her skull like a distant and pointless attempt at communicating. Nothing else. The drink and the smoke, nothing more. And the vibrations.

One more hour, she thought. It will be all over in another hour.

Just one more hour.

The wind took hold of her and threatened to throw her backward. For a moment she was afraid that she might have miscalculated, but then she caught hold of the stair rail and recovered her balance. Stood up straight and closed the door.

The darkness was compact and the wind roared. She slowly worked her way into the wind, down the narrow, soaking-wet passageway along the length of the ship.

Farther and farther forward. The rail was no more than chest high, and there were crossbars to climb up on. More or less ideal, for whatever reason. All that remained was to choose the right place. She continued a bit farther. Came to a staircase with a chain across it; a sign swaying and clanking in the wind indicated that passengers were forbidden to venture up the stairs.

She looked around. No sign of a soul. The sky was dark and motionless, with occasional patches of light. The sea was black; no reflections. When she leaned out and looked down, she could barely make it out.

Darkness. Darkness everywhere.

The muffled vibrations of the ship's engines. Gusts of wind and salt spray. Waves whipped up by the rotating propellers.

All alone. Cold, despite the cognac.

No other passengers had been bold enough to venture out on deck at this time of night. Not in this weather. They were all inside. In the bars. In the wine-red restaurant. At the disco or in their warm cabins.

Inside.

She clambered up. Sat on the rail for a second before kicking off with all the strength she could muster and flinging herself outward.

She entered the water curled up in the fetal position, and the slight fear she had had of being sucked in by the propellers faded away as she was rapidly—much more rapidly than she had been able to imagine—dragged down into the depths.

45

While they were waiting for the expected call, two others came.

The first was from the duty officer in Maardam and concerned information from Inspector Heinemann about another possible link on the basis of bank-account information. It was by no means certain, but there was evidence to suggest that a certain Werner Biedersen had made an unmotivated transaction transferring money from his firm to a private account (with subsequent withdrawals) in the beginning of June, 1976; however, Heinemann had not yet been able to find a withdrawal corresponding to the amount in question.

Mind you—it was admitted—it could well be a question of a gambling debt or a few fur coats for his wife or some mistress, or God only knows what. In any case, the inspector would be in touch again within the next few days.

"Good timing," said Reinhart for the second time that evening, but the chief inspector didn't even sigh.

"Say something sensible," he said instead, after a few minutes of silence in the darkness.

Reinhart struck a match and went to considerable lengths to light his pipe before answering.

"I think we're going to make a child," he said.

"A child?" said the chief inspector.

"Yes."

"Who?"

"Me," said Reinhart. "And a woman I know."

"How old are you?" asked the chief inspector.

"What the hell does that have to do with it?" said Reinhart. "But she'll soon be forty, so it's about time."

"Yes, I suppose it is," said the chief inspector.

Another minute passed.

"Well, I suppose I ought to congratulate you," said the chief inspector eventually. "I didn't even know you had a woman."

"Thank you," said Reinhart.

The other call was from Munckel, who reported the result of the preliminary medical examination. Werner Biedersen had been killed by a Berenger-75; three bullets in the chest, fired from a distance of about one meter. Two further bullets below the belt from about ten centimeters. Death had been more or less instantaneous, and had taken place at about ten minutes past nine.

Van Veeteren thanked the caller and hung up.

"There was something about that scene," he said after a while.

Reinhart's chair creaked in the darkness.

"I know," he said. "I've been thinking about it."

The chief inspector sat in silence for some time, searching for words. The clock on the wall between the two rectangular windows seemed to make an effort, but didn't have the strength to strike. He looked at his watch.

Half past one. The ferry must have been moored in Arnholt for at least half an hour by now. They ought to hear from there any minute now.

"That scene," he said again.

Reinhart lit his pipe for the twentieth time.

"All the women in there . . . International Women's Day . . . ," Van Veeteren went on. "A man shot below the belt in the toilets . . . by his daughter, dressed as a man . . . a thirty-year-old rape . . . International Women's Day . . ."

"That's enough," interrupted Reinhart. "Let's talk about something else."

"All right," said Van Veeteren. "Probably just as well. But it was stage-managed, that's obvious."

Reinhart inhaled deeply several times.

"It always is," he said.

"Eh?" said the chief inspector. "What do you mean?"

"I don't know," said Reinhart.

Van Veeteren suddenly seemed to be annoyed.

"Of course you do, stop pretending! What the hell do you know, in fact? You and I are sitting here in this godforsaken ramshackle house out in the sticks, in the middle of the night, God only knows where, waiting for . . . well, would you kindly tell me what exactly we are waiting for!"

"For dotting the i's and crossing the t's," said Reinhart.

The telephone rang and Van Veeteren answered. Reinhart listened in on earphones.

"Yes?"

"Chief Inspector Van Veeteren?"

"Yes."

"Schmidt. Harbor police in Arnholt. We've been through the ship now and . . ."

"And?"

". . . and what you say seems to be right. There is a passenger missing."

"Are you sure?"

"As sure as it's possible to be. Obviously, she might have managed to hide away somewhere on board, but we don't think so. We've been pretty thorough. In any case, we'll continue searching when the ferry sets sail again: if she is on board, we'll find her before we get to the next port of call."

He paused, but the chief inspector didn't say anything.

"Anyway, it's a woman," said Schmidt. "She had a first-class ticket, single cabin. She embarked, collected her key from Information, and evidently spent an hour in her cabin."

"Do you have her name?"

"Yes, of course. The ticket and the cabin were booked in the name of Biedersen."

"Biedersen?"

"Yes. But they never ask for ID proof when the passenger pays cash, which she did, so it could be a false name."

Van Veeteren sighed deeply.

"Hello? Are you still there?"

"Yes."

"Is there anything else, or can we allow them to set sail? They are over an hour late now."

"Of course," said Van Veeteren. "Cast off and get under way."

The call was terminated. Reinhart took off the earphones. Crossed his hands behind his head and leaned back, making the chair creak.

Van Veeteren put his hands on his knees and got to his feet with difficulty. Walked back and forth over the creaking floorboards before pausing in front of one of the windows. Rubbed the pane with the sleeve of his jacket and peered out into the darkness. Dug his hands down into his trouser pockets.

"What do you think she was called?" asked Reinhart.

"It's started raining again," said Van Veeteren.

A NOTE ABOUT THE AUTHOR

Håkan Nesser was awarded the 1993 Swedish Crime Writers' Academy Prize for new authors for his novel *Mind's Eye* (published in Sweden as *Det Grovmaskiga Nätet*). He received the best novel award in 1994 for *Borkmann's Point* and in 1996 for *Woman with Birthmark*. In 1999 he was awarded the Crime Writers of Scandinavia's Glass Key Award for the best crime novel of the year for *Carambole*. Nesser lives in Sweden and New York City.

A NOTE ABOUT THE TRANSLATOR

Laurie Thompson taught Swedish at the University of Wales and was editor of *Swedish Book Review* from its launch in 1983 until 2002. He has been a full-time literary translator for several years and has translated more than forty books from the Swedish. He was born in York, but now lives in rural West Wales with his Swedish wife and several cats.

A NOTE ON THE TYPE

This book was set in Monotype Dante, a typeface designed by
Giovanni Mardersteig (1892–1977). Conceived as a private type for
the Officina Bodoni in Verona, Italy, Dante was originally cut only
for hand composition by Charles Malin, the famous Parisian
punch cutter, between 1946 and 1952. Its first use was in an edition
of Boccaccio's *Trattatello in laude di Dante* that appeared in 1954.
The Monotype Corporation's version of Dante followed in 1957.
Although modeled on the Aldine type used for Pietro Cardinal
Bembo's treatise De Aetna in 1495, Dante is a thoroughly modern
interpretation of the venerable face.

Composed by Creative Graphics,
Allentown, Pennsylvania
Printed and bound by R. R. Donnelley,
Harrisonburg, Virginia
Designed by Virginia Tan